This is the information you will find for the 2,593 companies

Company Name

Address: verified & up-to-date

Cross-Streets for easy location

Telephone Number(s) with area codes

AAA THEATRICAL WIDGET CO. 800-555-9999
100 Shady Lane 4th Fl. (Grand-Spring) NYC 10000 212-555-1234
Hours: 8:15-6 Mon-Fri/ 10-3 Sat/ or by appt.

Overwhelming selection of theatrical widgets and gadgets. We carry complete line of Bosco, Mee, Graussmann and Aeon-Strand gadgets. Stock widgets in many colors and sizes- or we fabricate to your specs. We accept mail, credit card and purchase orders. (See display ad page 999.)

"Formerly 'Ace Theatrical Gadgets'. Best selection in town and fast custom work, ask for free product brochures." ed.

Business Hours

Suite, Floor, Building indication if necessary

Informative Advertising

Helpful tips and comments by the Editors.

in the
NEW YORK THEATRICAL SOURCEBOOK

THE NEW YORK THEATRICAL SOURCEBOOK

1985-86 Edition

Compiled and Edited
by
The Association of Theatrical
Artists and Craftspeople

BROADWAY PRESS
350 WEST 85 ST. NYC 10024-3832
212-724-6556

THE NEW YORK THEATRICAL SOURCEBOOK
1985-86 Edition

ISBN 0-911747-04-4

TABLE OF CONTENTS

Co-Editors:
Karen McDuffee, Josie Caruso

Contributing Editors:
Chris Gardyasz: props
Joanne Green: puppetry
Jerry Gum: puppetry
Larry Jameson: special effects
Jan Kastendieck: costumes
T. C. LaBiche: display houses
Marleen Marta: design resource
Jamie Seguin: costumes
C. J. Simpson: prop & scenic materials & services
Daphne Stevens-Pascucci: design resource

Verification:
Judy Boruta
Michael Denney
Chris Gardyasz
Larry Jameson
Deborah Alix Martin
Zoë Morsette
Joan Olssen
J. Matthew Reeves
Lisa Shaftel

Legal Counsel:
Carl Felsenfeld

Special thanks to:
Annette Zygarowicz, ATAC Board of Directors.

The Association of Theatrical Artists and Craftspeople
1742 Second Ave. #102
New York, NY 10128
718-596-0501
Referral Service 212-586-1925

FROM THE EDITORS...

Dear Colleagues,

You have before you the second edition of the New York Theatrical Sourcebook. This edition has been verified and updated to the best of our ability. We have added 421 new companies and 136 companies have been deleted or gone out of business. A total of 2497 companies are contained in this edition.

Those of you familiar with the first edition of the Sourcebook will find the overall organization has remained essentially the same. New categories have been created and some old ones reorganized to keep pace with the expanded content of the book. We hope you will discover the many new appendixes and find they are the valuable resource we believe them to be. The improved system of indexing should facilitate your search for those many items we are all asked to find at a moment's notice.

As editors of this project, we would wholeheartedly like to thank the Sourcebook Committee and ATAC members, whose unselfish contributions of time and sources have made the content of the book what it is. We would like to encourage feedback from the users of the Sourcebook. There is a tear-out postage paid form in the back of the book for you to send us your additions and/or corrections.

In closing, we would like to personally thank David Rodger and Cathy Blaser of Broadway Press for not only their belief in this project, but their hard work and dedication which has made the Sourcebook the successful book that it is.

Regards,

Karen McDuffee
Josie Caruso

August, 1985

A BRIEF HISTORY OF THE NEW YORK THEATRICAL SOURCEBOOK

The Association of Theatrical Artists and Craftspeople (ATAC) was formed in 1980 as a support organization for craftspeople working in the performance and display industries. The membership includes individuals and businesses who create puppets, props, costumes, masks, displays and special effects. The experience level of the members ranges from seasoned professionals to young craftspeople who are just beginning their careers. The Association is based in New York and is entirely member-run.

In 1981, the decision was made to compile a Sourcebook as a service to ATAC members. The book was to include sources for materials and services available to the New York area craftsperson, sources volunteered by the membership. A committee was formed to organize the material, which eventually included over 1200 sources ranging from lumber yards to button manufacturers to personal protective equipment. A year later, the ATAC Sourcebook was presented to the membership. In spite of its faults, having been prepared by a small group of people who had never "done a book" before, and whose free time was limited to evenings and weekends, the Sourcebook was enthusiastically received.

Due to the attention the book attracted from people outside the organization, and the fact that it would need to be updated periodically, ATAC decided to pursue the possibility of commercial publication for the next edition. One of our greatest concerns was the question of financing. Books of this type are generally paid for by advertising, the result being that the only merchants listed are those who are willing to pay. While the Sourcebook Committee realized that advertising revenues would play an important role in a project of this magnitude, it felt very strongly that the listings should not be limited by this criterion. Many of the most valuable sources for materials are not even aware of their importance to the theatrical market.

In August 1983, ATAC made contact with Broadway Press, a small publishing company whose partners have extensive theatrical backgrounds; and who, we felt, understood the goals of the project. Shortly thereafter, the new expanded Sourcebook Committee went back to work collecting and organizing sources and Broadway Press began to contact potential advertisers.

The book you have before you is the result of nearly a year's labor. It is the hope of the Association of Theatrical Artists and Craftspeople that you find the new NEW YORK THEATRICAL SOURCEBOOK the valuable resource that we believe it to be.

June, 1984

PRODUCTS AND SERVICES

All companies grouped by categories—similar to the "Yellow Pages" including advertising information supplied by the companies and descriptive annotations.

Information between quotes was provided by the editors, the Association of Theatrical Artists and Craftspeople.

ADHESIVES & GLUES

For millinery glues, see MILLINERY SUPPLIES
For leather glues, see LEATHERCRAFTERS & FURRIERS SUPPLIES

Adhesive Products Corp. 718-542-4600
1660 Boone Ave. (173rd) Bronx 10460
Hours: 9-4 Mon-Fri
"Double-grip contact cement, molding and casting materials, mold releases." ed.

BAER FABRICS 502-583-5521
515 East Market St., Louisville, KY 40202
Hours: 9-5:30 Mon-Sat
Glues for craft, costuming, leather and upholstery. (See display ad page 127.)
"Shipment within 24 hours for in-stock items." ed.

Bay Fastening Systems Inc. 212-259-0801
7204 20th Ave. (72nd) Bklyn 11204
Hours: 9-5 Mon-Fri
"Hot melts: adhesives, tools and repairs." ed.

Commercial Plastics 718-849-8100
98-31 Jamaica Ave. (101st) Richmond Hill, NY 11418
Hours: 8:30-4:30 Mon-Fri
"Comstik cement, mylar, acetate and lexan." ed.

Duo-Fast Corp. 718-726-2400
31-07 20th Rd. (31st St-20th Av) L.I.C. 11105
Hours: 8:30-5 Mon-Fri (closed for lunch 12-1)
"Complete line of Jet-Melt adhesives, Polygun applicators, and 3M aerosols." ed.

Eschem Specialty Chemical Corp. 212-966-2318
139 Allings Crossing Rd., West Haven, CT 06516 203-934-8661
Hours: 8-5 Mon-Fri
"Flexible glue, $100 minimum (two 5-gal. pails)." ed.

Gothic Color Co. 212-929-7493
727 Washington St. (Bank-11th) NYC 10014
Hours: 8:30-5 Mon-Th/ 8-4:30 Fri
"Gelatin, flexible, and polyvinyl glues; scenic pigments, brushes." ed.

Industrial Plastics 212-226-2010
309 Canal St. (B'way-Mercer) NYC 10013
Hours: 8:30-5 Mon-Fri/ 8:30-4 Sat
"Solvent cements for plastics; see Deena." ed.

Loctite Corp. 203-278-1280
705 N. Mountain Rd., Newington, CT 06111
Hours: 9-5 Mon-Fri
Salespeople and technical questions... 800-323-5106
Hours: 8am-8:30pm Mon-Fri
"Catalog available; customer and technical assistance." ed.

Modern Miltex Corp. 212-585-6000
280 East 134th St. (Lincoln-Alexander) Bronx 10454
Hours: 7:30-4:30 Mon-Fri
"Manufactures a clear glue for styrofoam; very good, cheap." ed.

H. G. PASTERNACK INC. 212-460-5233
151 West 19th St. (7th) NYC 10011
Hours: 9-5:30 Mon-Fri
Authorized distributor: 3M adhesives. Full line of spray adhesives, hot melts, cyanoacrylates, general adhesives. Call for free demonstration or catalog.
"Also authorized distributor of complete line of 3M tapes." ed.

REJOICE LTD./GARY ZELLER, JOYCE SPECTOR 212-869-8636
40 West 39 St. (5-6th) NYC 10018
Hours: By appt. or leave message
Non-toxic specialties. EZ Plastic, flexible glues.
(See display ad page 333.)
"Molding and casting supplies; special effects consultation and services." ed.

Slomon's Labs Inc. 201-623-0909
9-11 Linden St. Newark, NJ 07102
Hours: 8:30-5 Mon-Fri
"Sobo, Velverette, Quik Glue in quantity; phone orders delivered." ed.

Smooth-On-Corp. 201-647-5800
1000 Valley Rd., Gillette, NJ 07933
Hours: 8:50-4:30 Mon-Fri
"Epoxy resin formulations, polyurethane, flexible mold compounds." ed.

Spectra Dynamics Products 505-843-7202
415 Marble Ave. NW, Albuquerque, NM 87102
Hours: 9-5 Mon-Fri
"Phlexglu; see Ford Davis, terrific guy, very helpful; descriptive brochure.

Sprotzer Tools and Hardware Co. Inc 212-966-2220
7 Harrison St. (Greenwich St.-Hudson) NYC 10013
Hours: 8-5 Mon-Fri
"Hot glue guns and medium quantity cartons of pellets." ed.

Super Glue Corp. 718-454-4747
184-08 Jamaica, Hollis, NY 11423
Hours: 9-5:30 Mon-Fri
"Cyanoacrylates; catalog available." ed.

Swift Adhesives 212-966-2318
Allings Crossing Rd., West Haven, CT 06516 203-934-8661
Hours: 8-5 Mon-Fri
"Industrial adhesives: hot melt, resin, animal; phone orders only." ed.

Technical Library Services Inc. 212-736-7744
213 West 35th St. (7-8th) NYC 10001
Hours: 9-4:30 Mon-Fri (closed for lunch 11:30-1)
"Acid-free adhesives and glues, conservation supplies and bookbinding supplies." ed.

3M Adhesives 212-285-9600
15 Henderson Dr., West Caldwell, NJ 07006
Hours: 7:45-4:45 Mon-Fri
"3M adhesives and glues." ed.

United Resin Products Inc. 212-384-3000
100 Sutton St. Bklyn 11222
Hours: 8-5 Mon-Fri
"Resins, hot melt, pastes, animal glue." ed.

Van-Man Adhesives Corp. 718-384-6110
100 S. 4th St. (Berry-Bedford) Bklyn 11211
Hours: 8:30-4:30 Mon-Fri
"Resin and hot melt glue, lacquers." ed.

Viking-Criterion Paper Co. 718-392-7400
55-30 46th St. (near Maurice Ave) Maspeth, NY 11378
Hours: 9-5 Mon-Fri
"Hot glue by 25 lb. carton or more; phone orders delivered." ed.

AIRCRAFT

Beck's Photography Studio 718-424-8751
37-44 82nd St. (Roosevelt-37th Ave) Jackson Heights, NY 11372
Hours: 10-6:30 Mon-Sat
"Theatrical portraits; photoplane, their cameraman or yours." ed.

AMUSEMENTS

See also GAMES
See also TOYS

Antique Amusements 718-837-0405
1420 80th St. Bklyn 11228
Hours: By appt.
"New and old jukeboxes and pinball machines; leave a message on their machine." ed.

Back Pages Antiques 212-460-5998
125 Greene St. (Prince-Houston) NYC 10012
Hours: 11-6 Tues-Sat/ (12-6 Sun, Spring only)
"Jukeboxes, purchase or rental." ed.

Coin Machine Distributors Inc. 914-347-3777
425 Fairview Park Dr., Elmsford, NY 10523
Hours: By appt.
"Jukeboxes, pinball, vending machines; rentals; see Chris Hudson." ed.

NOVEL PINBALL & JUKEBOX CO. 212-736-3868
595 Tenth Ave. (43rd) NYC 10036
Hours: 9-5 Mon-Fri/ 10-4 Sat
We buy, sell, and rent jukeboxes, pool tables, pinball machines and all arcade games and vending machines.
"Large stock including video arcade games." ed.

ANIMAL RENTAL

For stuffed animal rental, see
TAXIDERMISTS & TAXIDERMY SUPPLIES

All-Tame Animals 212-752-5885
37 West 57th St. (5th) NYC 10019
Hours: 9-5 Mon-Fri
"Large variety of animals." ed.

Animal Actors International 201-689-7539
RD 3 Box 221 (Musconetcong River Rd.) Washington, NJ 07882
Hours: Call 9-5 Mon-Fri for appt.
"Large variety of animals." ed.

William Berloni Theatrical Animals 212-974-0922
314 West 52nd St., Box 37 (mail only), NYC 10019
Hours: By appt.
"Limited selection of animals." ed.

Captain Haggerty's Theatrical Dogs 212-410-7400
1748 1st Ave. (90th) NYC 10128
Hours: 9-5 Mon-Fri
"Dogs only, all types." ed.

Chateau Theatrical Animals 212-246-0520
608 West 48th St. (11-12th) NYC 10036
Hours: 7-7 every day
"Also carriages, wagons, carts." ed.

Claremont Riding Academy 212-724-5100
175 West 89th St. (Columbus-Amsterdam) NYC 10024
Hours: 6:30-10 Mon-Fri/6-5 Sat, Sun
"Horse and riding equipment rental, hay." ed.

Dawn Animal Agency 212-575-9396
160 West 46th St. (6-7th) NYC 10036
Hours: 10-5:30 Mon-Fri/ or by appt.
"Rental of exotic, domestic and tropical animals, with handlers; also carriages, wagons." ed.

Mr. Lucky Dog Training School 718-827-2792
27 Crescent St. Bklyn 11208
Hours: By appt.
"Dog stunts; brochure available." ed.

Tigers Only 201-928-4440
PO Box 1025, Freehold, NJ 07728
Hours: By appt.
"Tiger rental." ed.

ANIMAL & BIRD SKINS, FRESH

Delancey Live Poultry 212-475-9875
205 Delancey St. (Ridge St.) NYC 10002
Hours: 8-5 Mon-Fri/ 8-4 Sat/ 7-3 Sun
"Fresh killed poultry." ed.

L.I. Beef 212-243-8967
565 West St. (Gansevoort-W. 12th) NYC 10014
Hours: 5am-2pm Mon-Fri
"Pheasant, quail, game with feathers; also beef." ed.

Lobel's Prime Meats 212-737-1372
1096 Madison Ave. (82nd) NYC 10028
Hours: 9-6 Mon-Sat (closed Sat: June, July)
"Game with feathers; other meats." ed.

Nevada Meat Market 212-362-0443
2012 Broadway (68th) NYC 10023
Hours: 8-6 Mon-Sat
"Game with feathers, other meats; will deliver." ed.

Ottomanelli Bros. 212-772-7900
1549 York Ave. (82nd) NYC 10028
Hours: 8-6:30 Tues-Sat
"Game with feathers, other meats." ed.

Ottomanelli's Meat Market 212-675-4217
281 Bleecker St. (7th Ave. S.) NYC 10014
Hours: 7:30-6:30 Mon-Fri/ 6:30-6 Sat
"Game with feathers, other meats." ed.

Phoenix Poultry Market 212-226-5455
159 Grand St. (Lafayette) NYC 10013
Hours: 9:30-4 Mon-Fri
"Fresh killed poultry." ed.

St. James Gourmet Importers 212-243-1120
565 West St. (Gansevoort) NYC 10014
Hours: 4am-3pm Mon-Fri
"Restaurant supplier of game w/ feathers; nice guy, very helpful." ed.

ANTIQUES

For specific antique items, refer to INDEX
See also MEMORABILIA

Ace Galleries 212-260-2720
91 University (11-12th) NYC 10003
Hours: 9:30-5 Mon-Fri/ 10-3 Sat
"Whole estate buyers; Large selection furniture, lamps, paintings, china, silver, knick-knacks; see Lucille." ed.

Added Treasures 212-889-1776
577 Second Ave. (31-32nd) NYC 10016
Hours: By appt.
"Antique clothing, magazines, jewelry, glassware." ed.

William Albino Antiques 212-677-8820
56 East 11th St. (B'way-Univ.Pl.) NYC 10003
Hours: 9-5 Mon-Fri
"Exotica, unusual pieces." ed.

Alice's Antiques 212-874-3400
552 Columbus Ave. (86th) NYC 10025
Hours: 12-7:30 Mon-Sat/ 1-6 Sun
"Oak, Deco; pricey, nice pieces; will rent." ed.

America Hurrah Antiques 212-535-1930
766 Madison Ave. (66th) NYC 10021
Hours: 11-6 Tues-Sat
"Noted for quilts; some Americana decorative items; will rent." ed.

Ann-Morris Antiques 212-755-3308
239 East 60th St. (2-3rd) NYC 10022
Hours: 9-5:30 Mon-Fri
"Eclectic selection, mostly French & Americana country; expensive; will rent." ed.

Antiques Plus 718-941-8805
744 Coney Island Ave. (Ave. C) Bklyn 11218
Hours: 11-6 Mon-Sat
"Rugs, tapestries, glassware, china, silver, furniture." ed.

Architectural Antique Exchange 215-922-3669
715 N. 2nd St. (Brown-Fairmont Ave.) Philadelphia, PA 19123
Hours: 10-6 Mon-Fri/ 10-5 Sat
"Architectural artifacts: 1700's-1940's, mostly Victorian; will rent."

Jean Paul Beaujard 212-249-3790
209 East 76th St. (2-3rd) NYC 10021
Hours: 9-5 Mon-Fri (closed for lunch 11:30-12)/ sometimes 9-5 Sat
"Deco." ed.

Berkley Furniture Gallery of London 212-355-4050
899 First Ave. (50-51st) NYC 10022
Hours: 9-5 Mon-Fri
"English; will rent." ed.

Better Times Antiques 212-496-9001
500 Amsterdam Ave. (84th) NYC 10024 212-724-2286
Hours: 12-6:30 Sun-Tues,Thurs,Fri/11-6:30 Sat
"Americana pine and country items; nice stuff, nice people." ed.

Bijan Royal Inc. 212-228-3757
60 East 11th St. (B'way-University) NYC 10003 212-533-6390
Hours: 9-5 Mon-Fri
"French and English antique furniture and bronzes; rental or purchase; see Debbie." ed.

Michael Capo Antiques 212-982-3356
831 Broadway (11-12th) NYC 10003
Hours: 10-5 Mon-Sat
"18th and 19th century furniture, paintings; rentals available." ed.

Caswell-Massey Co. Ltd. 212-755-2254
518 Lexington Ave. (48th) NYC 10017
Hours: 9-6 Mon-Fri/ 10-6 Sat
"Antique apothecary bottles." ed.

Circa 1890 212-734-7388
265 East 78th St. (2-3rd) NYC 10021
Hours: 12-7:30 Tues-Thurs /12-5 Fri, Sat
"Oak; will rent." ed.

Chick Darrow's Fun Antiques 212-838-0730
1174 Second Ave. (61-62nd) NYC 10021
Hours: 11-6 Mon-Fri/ 11-4 Sat/ or by appt.
"Large selection antique toys and games; will rent." ed.

Depression Modern 212-982-5699
137 Sullivan St. (Prince-Houston) NYC 10012
Hours: 12-7 Wed-Sun
"Authentic furniture and fixtures; expensive." ed.

William Doyle Galleries 212-427-2730
175 East 87th St. (Lexington-3rd) NYC 10128
Hours: 9-5 Mon-Fri
"Primarily an auction house, sometimes will sell directly to theatres"

Eagles Antiques 212-772-3266
1097 Madison Ave. (82-83rd) NYC 10028
Hours: 10-5:30 Tues-Sat
"18th Century American and English furniture; will rent." ed.

East Side Antiques 212-677-8820
55 East 11th St. (B'way-Univ. Pl.) NYC 10003
Hours: 9-5 Mon-Fri
"Mostly French and Victorian." ed.

Echo Antiques 212-689-4241
451 Third Ave. (29th) NYC 10016
Hours: 12-7 Mon-Fri/ 12-6 Sat/ call for hours, Sun
"Deco and Victorian; will rent." ed.

Eclectic Properties 212-799-8963
204 West 84th St. (B'way-Amsterdam) NYC 10024
Hours: 9-5 Mon-Fri or by appt.
"Furniture, hand props and dressing; for rental only." ed.

Edith's Nostalgia 212-362-8713
469 Amsterdam Ave. (82-83rd) NYC 10024
Hours: 12-6 every day
"Large selection Art Deco lamps, small Deco furniture pieces." ed.

Ellington Galleries Ltd. 212-982-1522
93 University Place (11-12th) NYC 10003 212-982-1523
Hours: 9-5 Mon-Sat
"Lamps, clocks, porcelain, bronzes, furniture; antiques & repros." ed.

Garnett Brown Prop Rentals 212-691-5250
119 West 23rd St. #509 (6-7th) NYC 10011
Hours: 9-6 Mon-Fri or by appt.
"Rentals of American primitive and country furniture, paintings, rugs, kitchen and decorative accessories." ed.

Gotham Galleries 212-677-3303
80 Fourth Ave. (10-11th) NYC 10003
Hours: 10-6 Mon-Sat/ 1-6 Sun
"Furniture, oriental rugs, bronzes; rental or purchase; custom refinishing." ed.

Horseman V Antiques 212-683-2041
348 Third Ave. (25th) NYC 10010
Hours: 1-7 Mon-Fri/ 11-6 Sat/ 12-6 Sun
"Oak, repro and antique brass beds/items; rents by the day." ed.

Horseman VI Antiques 212-751-6222
995 Second Ave. (53rd) NYC 10022
Hours: 11-7 Mon-Fri/ 11-6 Sat/ 12-6 Sun
"Oak, repro and antique brass beds/items; rents by the day." ed.

Evan G. Hughes Inc. 212-683-2441
522 Third Ave. (35th) NYC 10016
Hours: 9-6 Mon-Sat
"Early American country, primitives, furniture." ed.

Johnny Jupiter 212-744-0818
884 Madison Ave. (71-72nd) NYC 10021
Hours: 10:15-6 Mon-Sat
"Antique dishes, linens, postcards; repro and antique toys, dolls, wind-up toys." ed.

Joia Interiors Inc. 212-759-1224
149 East 60th St. (Lexington-3rd) NYC 10022
Hours: 10-6 Mon-Fri
"Deco furniture, rental and purchase." ed.

Howard Kaplan French Country Store 212-674-1000
35 East 10th St. (University-B'way) NYC 10003
Hours: 10-6 Mon-Fri
"Oak, French country antiques, expensive." ed.

Kentshire Galleries 212-673-6644
37 East 12th St. (B'way-Univ. Pl.) NYC 10003
Hours: 9-5 Mon-Fri/ 9:30-1 Sat
"5 floors of English furniture; will rent." ed.

KUTTNER ANTIQUES 212-242-7969
56 West 22nd St. 5th Fl. (5-6th) NYC 10010
Hours: 10-5:30 Mon-Fri
American & English furniture, paintings, accessories, china, glassware, silver, linens, kitchenware. Rental only.
"Prefer short-term rentals for film and print work." ed.

Leo's Antiques 212-799-6080
2190 Broadway (77-78th) NYC 10024
Hours: 10-6:30 Mon-Fri/ 12:30-5:30 Sun
"Small objects: dishes, silverware, boxes, vases; some furniture." ed.

Mark's Antiques 718-284-4591
595 Coney Island Ave. (Beverly Rd.-Ave C) Bklyn 11218
Hours: 11-5 every day
"Bronzes, pottery, jewelry." ed.

Midtown Antique Shop 212-759-5450
814 Broadway NYC (11-12th) 10003 212-982-2150
Hours: 9-5 Mon-Fri
"French, English; will rent." ed.

Milton's Store 212-741-9684
255 West 17th St. (7-8th) NYC 10011
Hours: Call first
"Check for frequent auctions, good prices." ed.

Nedra Antiques Oak Furniture Co. 212-737-8747
1566 Second Ave. (81st) NYC 10028
Hours: 11-8 every day
"Oak, will rent; see Jerry." ed.

Newel Art Gallery 212-758-1970
425 East 53rd St. (Sutton-1st) NYC 10022
Hours: 9-5 Mon-Fri
"Extraordinary selection of antique furniture, art, architectural pieces, lamps, etc; all periods; rental or purchase; expensive." ed.

NICCOLINI ANTIQUES-PROP RENTALS 212-254-2900
114 East 25th St. (Park-Lexington) NYC 10010
Hours: 10-5 Mon-Fri/ 12-3 Sat/ or by appt.
Desks Files Clocks Tables Chairs Vanities Beds Lamps Mirrors Jukeboxes Baskets Accessories Globes Memorabilia.
"See Ronnie or Rita." ed.

Nostalgia Alley 212-695-6578
547 West 27th St. 3rd floor (10-11th) NYC 10001
Hours: 10-6 Mon-Fri
"Americana, quilts; rental only." ed.

Oaksmith Antiques 212-535-1451
1321 Second Ave (69-70th) NYC 10021
Hours: 11-8 Mon/ 12-9 Tues-Sat/ 1-8 Sun
"Carries pine and oak furniture, will rent; see Jerry." ed.

Oldies, Goldies & Moldies Ltd. 212-737-3935
1609 Second Ave. (83-84th) NYC 10028
Hours: 12-8 Mon-Fri/ 11-7 Sat/ 11-6 Sun
"Oak; will rent." ed.

Pierre Deux 212-243-7740
369 Bleecker St. (W. 11th) NYC 10014
Hours: 10-6 Mon-Sat (closed Sat: July, August)
"French country antiques." ed.

Place Off Second Avenue For Antiques 212-308-4066
993 Second Ave. (52-53rd) NYC 10022
Hours: 10:30-7 Mon-Fri/ 11-5 Sat
"Some unusual items; pricey." ed.

Platters & Props Inc. 212-473-4299
160 First Ave. (9-10th) NYC 10009
Hours: 1-9 Tues-Sat
"Bric-a-brac, some furnishings; no rentals." ed.

Pony Circus Antiques Ltd. 212-679-9637
381 Second Ave. (22nd) NYC 10010
Hours: 11-6 Mon-Sat/ 12-5 Sun
"Oak furnishings; will rent." ed.

Prophecies Antiques 718-855-4285
483 Atlantic Ave. (Nevins-3rd) Bklyn 11217
Hours: 10-6 every day
"Oak; see Lenny." ed.

Royal Oaksmith Ltd. 212-751-3376
982 Second Ave. (52nd) NYC 10022
Hours: 11-8 every day
"All oak; will rent." ed.

Salvage Barn Antiques 212-929-5787
525 Hudson St. (Charles-10th) NYC 10014
Hours: 12-7 Mon,Tues/ 11-6 Wed-Sat/ 12-6 Sun
"See Peter Lombard; good prices." ed.

Maya Schaper Cheese & Antiques 212-734-9427
152 East 70th St. (Lexington) NYC 10021
Hours: 10:30-6 Mon-Sat
"Small American country kitchen antiques and cheese." ed.

Scottie's Gallery & Antiques 718-851-8325
624 Coney Island Ave. Bklyn 11218
Hours: 11-7 Mon-Fri/ 12-3 Sat
"Oak and Victorian furniture; Tiffany lamps." ed.

Secondhand Rose 212-989-9776
573 Hudson St. (11th) NYC 10014
Hours: 10-6 Mon-Fri/ 12-6 Sat
"20th Century furniture and accessories; rentals for a price; many one-of-a-kind items." ed.

Sideshow 212-675-2212
184 Ninth Ave. (21-22nd) NYC 10011
Hours: 11-6:30 Tues-Sat
"Collection of a theme; ie. kitchen stuff, doctor's things, etc." ed.

Paul Siegel Antiques 212-533-5566
808 Broadway (11th) NYC 10003
Hours: 8:30-5 Mon-Fri
"French, Chinese, English; will rent." ed.

Smith & Watson Inc. 212-355-5615
305 East 63rd St. (1-2nd) NYC 10021
Hours: 9-5 Mon-Fri
"Traditional American, mostly repro; will rent." ed.

Speakeasy Antiques 212-533-2440
799 Broadway (11th) NYC 10003
Hours: 10:30-6 Tues-Sat (Thurs til 7)
"Period Americana knick-knacks and small items." ed.

Things Antique 212-873-4655
483 Amsterdam Ave. (83rd) NYC 10024
Hours: 10-6 every day
"Oak, large trunks; will rent." ed.

Village Oak 212-924-7651
456 Hudson St. (Barrow-Morton) NYC 10014
Hours: 11-7 every day
"Oak; will rent." ed.

Village Oaksmith Antiques 212-535-1451
1321 Second Ave. (69-70th) NYC 10021
Hours: 12-8 every day
"Oak; will rent; see Jerry or Stuart." ed.

WAVES 212-989-9284
32 East 13th St. (5th-University Pl) NYC 10003
Hours: 12-6 Tues-Fri/ 12-4 Sat
Vintage radios, phonographs, TV's & microphones rented.
"Selection of unique items also includes Victrolas, 78's." ed.

Welcome Home Antiques 212-362-4293
556 Columbus Ave. (87th) NYC 10024
Hours: 11-7 every day
"Deco, 40's furniture." ed.

Yankee Peddler 212-243-2005
639 Hudson St. (12th) NYC 10003
Hours: 11-6 Mon/ 11-7 Tues-Fri/ 12-6 Sat, Sun
"Victorian." ed.

APPLIANCES, ELECTRICAL & GAS

See also KITCHEN EQUIPMENT, HOUSEHOLD
See also KITCHEN EQUIPMENT, INDUSTRIAL

Berg & Brown Inc. 212-369-5800
1368 Lexington Ave. (90-91st) NYC 10128
Hours: 8:30-4:30 Mon-Fri
"Large appliances: electric and gas." ed.

Bernie's Discount Center 212-564-8582
821 Sixth Ave. (28-29th) NYC 10001
Hours: 9-5:30 Mon-Fri/ 11-3:30 Sat
"Small electrical appliances; good prices." ed.

Bloom & Krup 212-673-2760
206 First Ave. (12-13th) NYC 10009
Hours: 8:30-6 Mon-Sat
"Kitchen and bathroom appliances and fixtures, small electrical appliances." ed.

Bridge Refrigeration Inc. 212-674-0840
65 Second Ave. (E. 4th) NYC 10003
Hours: 10-6:30 Mon-Sat
"Used refrigerators, gas ranges, air conditioners; see Abe Bridge." ed.

J. Eis & Sons Appliances 212-475-2325
105 First Ave. (6-7th) NYC 10003
Hours: 9-5:30 Mon-Thurs/ 9-4 Fri/ 10-4 Sun
"Ranges, refrigerators, washers, dryers, televisions, air conditioners." ed.

Electric Appliance Rental & Sales 212-686-8884
40 West 29th St. 2nd Fl. (B'way-6th) NYC 10001
Hours: 8:30-5:30 Mon-Fri
"Megaphones, antique appliances(perhaps); call first." ed.

Gringer & Sons 212-475-0600
29 First Ave. (1-2nd) NYC 10003
Hours: 8:30-5 Mon-Fri/ 8:30-4:30 Sat
"Large electrical appliances." ed.

Hampton Sales 718-895-1335
750 Stewart Ave. Garden City, NY 11530
Hours: 9-9 Mon, Tues, Thurs, Fri/ 9-6 Wed, Sat
"Large and small electrical and gas appliances." ed.

Isabella 718-278-7272
24-24 Steinway St. (Astoria Blvd.) Astoria, NY 11103
Hours: 9-7 M,T,Th,Fri/9-6 W/9-5 Sat (closed Sat July-Aug)
"Large electrical/gas appliances, new and used." ed.

ARCHITECTURAL PIECES

See also FIREPLACES & EQUIPMENT
See also VACUUMFORMING & VACUUMFORMED PANELS
See also DISPLAY HOUSES

AA Abbingdon Ceiling Co. 718-236-3251
2149 Utica Ave. (Avs. M-N) Bklyn 11234 718-258-8333
Hours: 9-5 Mon-Fri (by appt only)
"Tin ceilings." ed.

American Wood Column Corp. 718-782-3163
913 Grand St. (Bushwick-Morgan) Bklyn 11211
Hours: 8-4:30 Mon-Fri
"Columns and pedestals." ed.

Amerlite Aluminum Co. 212-986-9559
211 West 28th St. (7-8th) NYC 10001 (showroom)
Hours: 9-5 Mon-Fri
"Anodized aluminum storefront doors and facades; will rent doors."

Architectural Antique Exchange 215-922-3669
715 N. Second St. (Brown-Fairmont St.) Philadelphia, PA 19123
Hours: 10-6 Mon-Fri/ 10-5 Sat
"Architectural artifacts: 1700's-1940's mostly Victorian; will rent."

L. Biagiotti 212-924-5088
259 Seventh Ave. (24-25th) NYC 10011
Hours: 9-4 Mon-Fri
"Custom work, columns, molding, sculptures, breakaways, etc." ed.

Chelsea Decorative Metal Co. 713-721-9200
6115 Cheena, Houston, TX 77096
Hours: 9-5 Mon-Fri
"Tin ceilings." ed.

GREAT AMERICAN SALVAGE CO./Architectural Antiques 212-505-0070
34 Cooper Square (3rd Ave.-6th) NYC 10003
Hours: 9:30-6 Mon-Sat (closed Sat in Summer)
16,000 sq. ft. showroom brimming with columns-doors-beveled glass-mantles-sinks-bars- etc. For sale or rental.
"Many hard-to-find items." ed.

Irreplaceable Artifacts

14 Second Ave. (Houston) NYC 10003 (warehouse) 212-777-2900
1046 Third Ave. (61st) NYC 10021 212-223-4411

Hours: 10-5 Mon-Fri/ by appt. Sat
"Architectural ornamentation from demolished buildings; will rent only in 'as is' condition." ed.

Kenneth Lynch and Sons 203-762-8363
78 Danbury Rd., Wilton, CT 06897
Hours: 8-4:30 Mon-Fri
"Molded zinc architectural detail; statuary in metal." ed.

Newel Art Gallery 212-758-1970
425 East 53rd St. (Sutton-1st) NYC 10022
Hours: 9-5 Mon-Fri
"Antique rental: columns, doors, and mantels; also furniture and lamps, etc." ed.

Stamford Housewrecking 203-324-9537
1 Barry Place, Stamford, CT 06902
Hours: 8:30-4:30 Mon-Fri/ 8:30-3:30 Sat
"Doors, toilets, sinks, windows, many architectural odds & ends." ed.

Urban Archeology 212-431-6969
135 Spring St. (Wooster-Greene) NYC 10012
Hours: 10-6 Mon-Fri/ 12-6 Sat, Sun
"Nice interior and exterior architectural pieces; expensive." ed.

United House Wrecking 203-348-5371
328 Selleck St. (exit 6, CT Thruwy) Stamford, CT 06902
Hours: 9-5 Tues-Sat
"Mantels, wrought iron, doors, windows, and much, much more." ed.

Vintage Wood Works 512-997-9513
513 S. Adams, Fredericksburg, TX 78624
Hours: 8-5 Mon-Fri
"Victorian gingerbread, large finials, newel posts, balusters; catalog." ed.

ARMS & ARMOR

See also FENCING EQUIPMENT
See also POLICE EQUIPMENT

Robert L. Brooks 212-486-9829
235 East 53rd St. (2-3rd) NYC 10022
Hours: 11-5 Mon-Fri
"Antique arms and armor." ed.

Centre Firearms 212-244-4040
10 West 37th St. (5-6th) NYC 10018
Hours: 10-4 Mon-Fri
"Rentals; call to verify specific need for permits." ed.

Collector's Armoury Inc. 703-684-6111
800 Slaters Lane, PO Box 1061, Alexandria, VA 22313 800-336-4572
Hours: 9-5 Mon-Fri
"Great prop and costume prop weapons." ed.

Colt Firearms 203-236-6311
545 New Park Ave., West Hartford, CT 06110
PO Box 1868 Hartford, CT 06102 (mail)
Hours: 8-4:30 Mon-Fri
"Custom orders only; gunsmith." ed.

Continental Arms Corp. 212-753-8331
697 Fifth Ave. 4th Fl. (54-55th) NYC 10022
Hours: 9-4:45 Mon-Fri
"Firearms, blank ammunition." ed.

COSTUME ARMOUR INC. 212-585-1199
PO Box 325, Shore Road, Cornwall-on-Hudson, NY 12520 914-534-9120
Hours: 9-4 Mon-Fri

20 years of theatrical service. Sales-Rentals: catalog & custom work. Armor, swords, guns. Credits: Met, NYC Opera, 'Camelot', 'Pippin', 'Othello', 'The Wiz', 'La Mancha', TV, film, display & promotion. (See display ad page 299.)

"Theatrical weapons of all periods; crowns, masks." ed.

Dixie Gun Works 901-885-0561
Highway 51 Bypass, Union City, TN 38261
Hours: 8-5 Mon-Fri
"Non-firing guns, gun parts, armor, weapons, etc." ed.

Gateway Hobbies Inc. 212-221-0855
60 West 38th St. 3rd Fl. (5-6th) NYC 10018
Hours: 10-5:45 Mon-Fri/ 10-4:45 Sat
"Replica guns." ed.

Harmony Hobby 718-224-6666
196-30 Northern Blvd. Bayside, NY 11358
Hours: 10-7 Mon-Thur/ 10-8 Fri/ 10-6 Sat/ 12-5 Sun
"Complete line plastic gun and rifle kits; very realistic looking and inexpensive, mostly military models." ed.

Princely Co. Inc. 212-685-5295
1201 Broadway (28-29th) NYC 10001
Hours: 9-5:30 Mon-Fri
"Replica non-firing pistols, muskets, powder horns." ed.

REJOICE LTD./GARY ZELLER, JOYCE SPECTOR 212-869-8636
40 West 39 St. (5-6th) NYC 10018
Hours: By appt. or leave message
Complete line of weapons for rental; blanks, etc. (See display ad page 333.)
"Special effects consultation and services." ed.

GEORGE SANTELLI INC. 201-871-3105
465 S. Dean St., Englewood, NJ 07631
Hours: 9-5 Mon-Fri/ 11-3 Sat (closed Sat June-Aug)
A complete line of modern fencing equipment & historical weaponry: accurate replicas of swords of all periods. Full color catalogues available. Visa & Mastercard accepted. Orders by mail, phone or over the counter.
"Very helpful." ed.

THEATRE MAGIC 614-459-3222
6099 Godown Rd., Columbus, OH 43220
Hours: 7:30-4:30 Mon-Fri
(See display ad page 334.)
"Swords designed to meet Soc. of American Fight Directors specs." ed.

World of Guns 516-249-1832
33 Gazza, Farmingdale, NY 11735
Hours: 9:30-9:30 Mon-Fri/ 9:30-6:30 Sat/ 11-5 Sun
"Firearms, reproduction guns." ed.

ART RENTAL

See also ANTIQUES
See also STATUARY

Art For Industry 212-757-3638
521 Fifth Ave. 17th Fl. (43rd) NYC 10036
Hours: 9-4:30 Mon-Fri
"Purchase, rental and installations of art pieces." ed.

Andrew Kolb & Son Ltd. 212-684-2980
112 Madison Ave. (30th) NYC 10016
Hours: 8-4:30 Mon-Fri
"Framed posters and prints, old and new." ed.

Phyllis Lucas Gallery 212-755-1516
981 Second Ave. (52nd) NYC 10022 212-753-1441
Hours: 9-5:30 Tues-Sat
"Rental of framed and unframed prints." ed.

J. Pocker and Son Inc. 212-838-5488
824 Lexington Ave. (63rd) NYC 10021
Hours: 9-5:30 Mon-Sat
"Posters, prints, framed pictures for purchase or rental." ed.

Raydon Gallery 212-288-3555
1091 Madison Ave. (82nd) NYC 10028
Hours: 10-6 Mon-Sat
"Rental of framed pictures." ed.

Showroom Outlet 212-581-0470
625-35 West 55th St. (11-12th) NYC 10019
Hours: 9-4:30 Mon-Thurs/ 9-4 Fri
"Modern; specializes in short term rentals." ed.

ARTIFICIAL EYES see DOLL PARTS
see TAXIDERMISTS & TAXIDERMY SUPPLIES

ARTIFICIAL FLOWERS, PLANTS & FOOD

See also TRIMMINGS: FEATHERS & FLOWERS
See also DISPLAY HOUSES

Corham 914-946-7373
300 Central Ave., White Plains, NY 10606
Hours: 9-5 Mon-Sat
"Artificial flowers." ed.

Cultured Design Ltd. 212-594-8690
548 West 28th St. (10-11th) NYC 10001
Hours: 8:30-5 Mon-Fri
"All types artificial flowers and foliage; also snow, fountains, rocks, statuary; see Gus." ed.

Florenco Foliage Systems Worldwide 212-402-0500
920 East 149th St. (Bruckner Blvd.) Bronx 10455
Hours: 8-5 Mon-Fri
"Artificial flowers, trees, grass; catalog available; sales, rental, installations; seasonal decor." ed.

William Fuss 212-688-0350
218 East 53rd St. (2-3rd) NYC 10022
Hours: 8-5 Mon-Fri
"Silk flowers, artificial plants and trees." ed.

Hub Floral 212-255-2447
155 West 23rd St. (6-7th) NYC 10011
Hours: 9-5 Mon-Fri
"Wholesale artificical flowers and foliage; also wicker items." ed.

K & D Export-Import 212-736-0556
101 West 28th St. (6th) NYC 10001
Hours: 8:30-5 Mon-Fri
"Silk flowers." ed.

Kervar Inc. 212-564-2525
119 West 28th St. (6-7th) NYC 10001
Hours: 6:30-3 Mon-Fri
"Silk, plastic foliage and flowers, fruits, vegetables, floral supplies; wholesale only." ed.

Diane Love Inc. 212-879-6997
851 Madison Ave. (70-71st) NYC 10021
Hours: 10-5:30 Mon-Sat
"Silk flowers and plants; modern arrangements; expensive." ed.

Charles Lubin Co. 914-968-5700
131 Saw Mill River Rd., Yonkers, NY 10701
Hours: 7:30-4 Mon-Fri
"Silk flowers, floral supplies." ed.

McHUGH/ROLLINS ASSOCIATES INC. 718-643-0990
79 Bridge St. (York-Front) Bklyn 11201
Hours: 9-6 Mon-Fri

Food creations in foam, plastic, rubber, latex. Some stock items available. Complete flower arranging. See Leslie. (See display ad page 300.)

"Full service prop shop." ed.

Modern Artificial Flowers & Display 212-265-0414
517 West 46th St. (10-11th) NYC 10036
Hours: 9-5 Mon-Fri
"Artificial flowers and foliage (flameproofed), fruits and vegetables, statuary; stock & custom; see Don or Sam." ed.

Nasco Life Form Models 414-563-2446
901 Janesville Ave., Fort Atkinson, WI 53538
Hours: 8-5 Mon-Fri
"Artificial food and scientific models; catalog available." ed.

People's Flowers Corp. 212-686-6291
786 Sixth Ave. (26-27th) NYC 10001
Hours: 8:30-6 every day
"Artificial flowers, foliage, fruits, fish, vegetables; floral supplies, good selection." ed.

Perma Plant Inc. 215-482-2100
123 Leverington Ave., Philadelphia, PA 19127
Hours: 8:30-5 Mon-Fri/ 10-3 Sat
"Silk and cloth flowers, foliage; floral accessories." ed.

RAINTREE ASSOCIATES 516-643-3835
8 Woodsend Rd. South, Dix Hills, NY 11746
Hours: 8-6 Mon-Fri

Also live plants, trees & flowers. Rentals.
We Are Known For Our Quality Work & Excellent Service.

"Highly recommended." ed.

Scafati & Co. 212-686-8784
225 Fifth Ave. Rm. 812 NYC 10010
Hours: 9-5 Mon-Fri
"Realistic looking artificial food; catalog; see Virginia or Tom." ed.

THE SET SHOP 212-929-4845
3 West 20th St. (5th) NYC 10011
Hours: 9-6 Mon-Fri/ 10-4 Sat
Artificial snow, grass, rocks, all set materials. (See display ad page 316.)
"Also full scene shop; non-union." ed.

Superior Specialties Inc. 212-543-1767
5925 Broadway (Van Cortland Park) Bronx 10463
Hours: 7-4:30 Mon-Fri
"Artificial fruit, vegetables other foods; brochure; orders by phone/mail." ed.

York Floral 212-686-2070
804 Sixth Ave. (27-28th) NYC 10001
Hours: 8:30-6 Mon-Fri (artificial dept. closed Thurs.)
"See Raymond or Kevin; floral supplies." ed.

ARTIFICIAL SNOW see DISPLAY HOUSES & MATERIALS

ARTISTS MATERIALS

See also PAINTS & DYES
See also SILKSCREENING SUPPLIES

Arthur Brown and Brothers Inc. 212-575-5555
2 West 46th St. (5th) NYC 10036
Hours: 8:45-5:45 Mon-Fri
"Artists, drafting, photo, framing supplies; Versatex, balsa, some casting supplies." ed.

Charrette Drafting Supply Corp.

215 Lexington Ave. (33rd) NYC 10016 212-683-8822
Hours: 8:30-8:30 M-F/ 8:30-6 Sat/ 12-5 Sun (except Jul, Aug)
"Artists, drafting, graphics, model building supplies; large stock of basswood; catalog." ed.

David Davis 212-982-7100
346 Lafayette (Bleecker) NYC 10002
Hours: 9:30-6 Mon-Fri/ 11-6 Sat (closed Sat July, August)
"Easels, custom brushes, fabric dye, lecturer's chalk, paints." ed.

DelSemme's Artists' Materials Inc. 212-675-2742
27 West 14th St. (5-6th) NYC 10011
Hours: 9-6 Mon-Fri/ 9-5 Sat
"Artists and graphics materials." ed.

Dieu Donne Press & Paper 212-226-0573
3 Crosby St. (Howard) NYC 10013
Hours: 10-6 Mon-Fri
"Paper making supplies." ed.

Eagle Supply Co. 212-246-6180
327 West 42nd St. (8-9th) NYC 10036
Hours: 9-4:30 Mon-Fri
"Artists, sign painters, and silk screening supplies; large stock of poster board." ed.

Eastern Artists & Drafting Materials 212-725-5555
352 Park Ave. South 11th Fl. (25-26th) NYC 10010
Hours: 8:30-6 Mon-Fri/ 11-5:30 Sat
"Small store, good selection, not crowded." ed.

80 Papers 212-966-1491
80 Thompson St. (Spring) NYC 10012
Hours: 1-7 Mon-Sat
"Fine art papers." ed.

Empire Artists Materials 212-737-5002
851 Lexington Ave. (64-65th) NYC 10021
Hours: 8:30-6 Mon-Fri/ 9-5 Sat
"Artists, drafting supplies, picture framing; will deliver." ed.

Sam Flax Art Supplies

15 Park Row (Ann-Nassau) NYC 10038 212-620-3030
Hours: 8:30-5:30 Mon-Fri/ 10-5 Sat

111 Eighth Ave. (15-16th) NYC 10011 212-620-3000
Hours: 9-6 Mon-Fri 212-620-3010

12 West 20th St. (5-6th) NYC 10011 212-620-3038
Hours: 8:30-5:30 Mon-Fri/ 10-5 Sat

25 East 28th St. (Madison-Park) NYC 10016 212-620-3040
Hours: 9-7 Mon-Fri/ 9-5 Sat

(continues next page)

747 Third Ave. (45-46th) NYC 10017 212-620-3050
Hours: 9-6 Mon-Fri/ 10-5 Sat/ 12-5 Sun

55 East 55th St. (Madison-Park) NYC 10022 212-620-3060
Hours: 9-6 Mon-Fri/ 10-5 Sat

"Artists, drafting, graphics, and photo materials; casting rubber and moulage." ed.

A. I. Friedman Inc. 212-575-0200
25 West 45th St. (5th) NYC 10036
Hours: 8:45-6 Mon-Fri/ 10-4 Sat (except summer)
"20% discount card for professionals; monthly sales with low prices."

Golden Typewriter & Stationery Corp. 212-749-3100
2525 Broadway (94th) NYC 10025
Hours: 9:30-6:45 Mon-Sat
"Artists supplies, office supplies, stationery." ed.

M. Grumbacher Inc. 212-279-6400
460 West 34th St. (9-10th) NYC 10001
Hours: 8:25-4:25 Mon-Fri
"Artists brushes and paint; wholesale only." ed.

Jamie Canvas Co. 212-505-1256
496 La Guardia Pl. (Bleecker-Houston) 10012
Hours: 10-6:30 Mon-Wed/ 10-8 Thur, Fri/ 10-6 Sat/ 12-6 Sun
"Artists, graphics supplies, toys." ed.

Lee Art Shop 212-247-0110
220 West 57th St. (7th-B'way) NYC 10019
Hours: 9-7 Mon-Fri/ 9:30-6 Sat
"Large stock artists materials; catalog." ed.

Joseph Mayer Co. Inc. 212-674-8100
22 West 8th St. (MacDougal) NYC 10011
Hours: 10-6:45 Mon-Fri/ 10-5:30 Sat/ 12-5:45 Sun
"Artists, drafting, graphics, photo, airbrush; limited inventory." ed.

Menash Inc.

2305 Broadway (83-84th) NYC 10024 212-877-2060
Hours: 9-6:30 Mon-Sat

462 7th Ave. (35th) NYC 10018 212-695-4900
Hours: 8:30-5:30 Mon-Fri

"Artists, drafting, graphics, office supplies, stationery; professional discount." ed.

NY Central Supply Co. 212-473-7705
62 Third Ave. (11th) NYC 10003
Hours: 8:30-6:30 Mon-Sat
"Artists materials." ed.

P. K. Supply Co. Inc. 718-377-6444
2291 Nostrand Ave. (Aves I-J) Bklyn 11210
Hours: 9:15-5:30 Mon-Fri (Thurs til 6:30)/ 9-5 Sat
"Art supplies, picture frame molding, silkscreen supplies." ed.

Parsons Art Supply 212-675-6406
70 Fifth Ave. (13th) NYC 10011
Hours: 9-6 Mon-Fri/ 9-5:30 Sat
"Artists materials." ed.

Pearl Art & Craft Supply Inc. 201-634-9400
Rt.1 & Gills Ln. (opp-Woodbridge Center) Woodbridge, NJ 07095
Hours: 10:30-9 Mon-Sat/ 12-5 Sun
"Easily accessible from central Jersey and Staten Island; large crafts section." ed.

Pearl Paint Co. Inc.

308 Canal St. (Mercer) NYC 10013 212-431-7932
Hours: 9-5:30 Mon-Sat/ 11-4:30 Sun

2411 Hempstead Turnpike, East Meadow, NY 11554 516-731-3700
Hours: 9:30-5:45 Mon-Sat (Wed, Fri til 8:45)

"Large art supply stores, well stocked; competitive prices." ed.

Pearl Showroom 212-431-7932
42 Lispenard St. (Church-B'way) NYC 10013 (showroom)
Hours: 9-5:30 Mon-Sat
"Easels, drafting machines, flat files, airbrushes, light boxes, office furniture." ed.

Tay Art Supplies Co. 212-475-7365
27 Third Ave. (8-9th) NYC 10003
Hours: 10-6:15 Mon-Fri/ 10-5:30 Sat
"Small art supply store." ed.

Utrecht Art & Drafting Supplies 212-777-5353
111 Fourth Ave. (11-12th) NYC 10003
Hours: 9:30-6 Mon-Sat
"Specializes in own brand paints and canvas; as well as other art supplies." ed.

Winsor and Newton Inc. 201-864-9100
555 Winsor Dr. Secaucus, NJ 07094
Hours: 9-4:30 Mon-Fri
"Wholesale artists paint, brushes, canvas." ed.

ASBESTOS SUBSTITUTES

Anchor Tool & Supply Co. 201-635-2094
PO Box 265, Chatham, NJ 07928
Hours: 1-5 Tues-Fri/ 10-3 Sat
"Non-asbestos cloth." ed.

Carborundum Corp./ Insulation Div. 716-278-6221
PO Box 808, Niagara Falls, NY 14302 716-278-2000
Hours: 9-5 Mon-Fri
"Non-asbestos yarn, rope, boards, heat shields, drapes." ed.

Eagle Ceramics 301-881-2253
12266 Wilkins Ave., Rockville, MD 20852
Hours: 9-5 Mon-Fri
"Gloves of Dupont Kevlar 29 Aramid fiber; catalog." ed.

W. H. Silver's Hardware 212-247-4406
832 Eighth Ave. (50-51st) NYC 10019 212-247-4425
Hours: 8-6 Mon-Fri/ 8-1 Sat
"Carries silicon cloth." ed.

Southern Manufacturing Corp. 704-372-2880
PO Box 32427, Charlotte, NC 28232
Hours: 8-5 Mon-Fri
"Non-asbestos mineral fiber textiles; also, fiberglas fabrics." ed.

AUDIO & VIDEO EQUIPMENT

See also LIGHTING & PROJECTION EQUIPMENT
See also RECORDS, PHONOGRAPH

Ace Audio Visual 212-683-2850
118 East 28th St. #508 (Park Ave. S.) NYC 10016
Hours: 8:30-5:30 Mon-Fri/ 9-12 Sat
"Televisions and stereo equipment." ed.

Audio Exchange

57 Park Place (W. B'way) NYC 10007 212-964-4570
Hours: 10-6 Mon-Fri/ 10-5 Sat

28 West 8th St. (5-6th) NYC 10011 212-982-7191
Hours: 11:30-6:45 Mon-Fri/ 10:30-6 Sat/ 12-5 Sun

"New and used stereo equipment." ed.

Crazy Eddie

405 Sixth Ave. (8th St) NYC 10011 212-242-1126
Hours: 10-10 Mon-Sat/ 12-5 Sun

212 East 57th St. (2-3rd) NYC 10022 — 212-980-5134
Hours: 10-10 Mon-Sat/ 12-5 Sun

"Will beat any price." ed.

Granada TV Rentals

416 Third Ave. (29th) NYC 10016 — 212-679-9600
Hours: 9-5 Mon-Sat

1410 Sixth Ave. (57th) NYC 10019 — 212-308-0900
Hours: 9-7 Mon-Fri/ 9-6 Sat

1069 Third Ave. (63rd) NYC 10021 — 212-935-4410
Hours: 9-7 Mon-Fri/ 9-5:30 Sat

"TV, VCR rental; minimum 3 months rental." ed.

Hampton Sales — 718-895-1335
750 Stewart Ave., Garden City, NY 11530
Hours: 9-9 M, T, TH, F/ 9-6 W, Sat
"Rental/purchase good quality TV's, washers, dryers, stoves, refrigerators, small electrical appliances." ed.

Harvey Electronics — 212-575-5000
2 West 45th St. (5th) NYC 10036
Hours: 9:30-6 Mon-Sat
"See Bonnie Levy for rentals of stereo equipment, very helpful." ed.

J & R Music World

23 Park Row (Beekman-Ann) NYC 10038 — 212-732-8600
Hours: 9:30-6:30 Mon-Sat
"Main store; popular records, tapes; stereo, TV, VCR equip." ed.

27 Park Row (Beekman-Ann) NYC 10038 — 212-227-4777
Hours: 9:30-6:30 Mon-Sat
"Portable and car stereos." ed.

33 Park Row (Beekman-Ann) NYC 10038 — (jazz) 212-349-8400
Hours: 9:30-6:30 Mon-Sat — (classical) 212-349-0062
"Classical and jazz records, tapes; good selection, prices." ed.

Jems Sound Ltd. — 212-838-4716
785 Lexington Ave. (61st) NYC 10021
Hours: 9:30-7 Mon-Sat
"TV's, radios, stereos, cameras; best prices; no rentals." ed.

R. C. I. Radio Clinic Inc.

2290 Broadway (82-83rd) NYC 10024 — 212-877-5151
2599 Broadway (98th) NYC 10025 — 212-864-6000
(service) 212-663-7700
Hours: 9-7 Mon-Fri/ 9-6 Sat
"Televisions, stereo equipment, electronics; will rent." ed.

Sound of Music 201-383-7267
PO Box 221, Stillwater, NJ 07875
Hours: By appt.
"Vintage 1950's radios; will help you locate almost anything; rental or sales; see Howard." ed.

Television Rental Co. 212-685-3344
118 East 28th St. #508 (Park Av. So.) NYC 10016
Hours: 8:30-5:30 Mon-Fri/ 9-12 Sat
"Televisions, rental only." ed.

Uncle Steve's 212-226-4010
343 Canal St. (Wooster-Greene) NYC 10013
Hours: 9:30-6 Mon-Sat/ 12-5 Sun
"Large selection, cash only; a real NYC experience." ed.

Waves 212-989-9284
32 East 13th St. (5th-Univ Pl.) NYC 10003
Hours: 12-6 Tues-Fri/ 12-4 Sat
"78's, Victrolas, radios; will rent." ed.

AUTOMOBILES

Antique Auto Props 201-933-0542
307 Patterson Ave., East Rutherford, NJ 07073
Hours: 8-5 Mon-Fri/ by appt.
"Antique cars." ed.

Cars of Yesterday Rentals 201-784-0030
State Hwy No. 9W, Alpine, NJ 07620
Hours: 9-5 Mon-Fri/ by appt.
"Antique autos." ed.

Cooper Classics 212-929-0094
132 Perry St. (Washington-Greenwich St.) NYC 10014
Hours: 9-5 Mon-Fri
"Classic cars, nice people." ed.

Donna Motor Sales 201-759-7838
15 Roosevelt Ave., Belleville, NJ 07109
Hours: 9-5 Mon-Fri
"Antique and modern cars, trucks, taxis, ambulances; rentals only; see Sonny." ed.

East Coast Film Cars 718-624-6050
749-57 Hicks St. (9th St-Huntington) Bklyn 11231 718-624-6881
Hours: By appt.
"Prop cars, wagons, cabs, rigging for stunts; Gino & Ralph Lucci." ed.

Film Fleet 212-245-8396
218 West 61st St. (Amsterdam-West End Ave.) NYC 10023
Hours: By appt.
"Antique and modern trucks, cars, taxis, ambulances, stock cars." ed.

Obsolete Fleet 212-255-6068
45 Christopher St. (7th Ave. S.) NYC 10014
Hours: By appt.
"Antique and classic vehicles; see Daniel List." ed.

AUTOMOTIVE SUPPLIES

See also TAXICAB ACCESSORIES

Aid Auto Stores

45 Avenue A (E.3rd) NYC 10009 212-777-0030
Hours: 8:30-6:30 Mon-Sat/ 10-4 Sun

645 11th Ave. (47th) NYC 10036 212-757-6969
Hours: 8:30-6 Mon-Fri/ 9-3 Sat

1365 First Ave. (73-74th) NYC 10021 212-535-3470
Hours: 9-7 Mon-Fri/ 9-6 Sat/ 10-4 Sun

1740 First Ave. (90th) NYC 10028 212-722-2688
Hours: 9-6:30 Mon-Fri/ 9-6 Sat/ 10-3 Sun

"Complete inventory of parts, accessories, chemicals, tools." ed.

Worth Auto Supply 212-777-5920
31 Cooper Square (E. 5th & 3rd Ave) NYC 10003
Hours: 9-6 Mon-Fri/ 9-3 Sat
"Older period parts and supplies; very helpful." ed.

BACKDROPS

See also SCENE SHOPS
For soft goods, see CURTAINS & DRAPERIES, THEATRICAL

Charles Broderson Inc. 212-925-9392
873 Broadway, Studio 612 (18-19th) NYC 10003
Hours: 9-5 Mon-Fri/ by appt.
"Backdrop rental." ed.

INTERNATIONAL PAPER COMPANY 704-872-8974
Taylorsville Road Highway 90, Statesville, NC 28677 800-438-1701
Hours: 8-5 Mon-Fri
GATORFOAM® Laminated Foam Panel. Call 800# for local dealer.
"Available in 4'x8' sheets; 5 thicknesses from 3/16" to 1½"." ed.

Lincoln Scenic Studios 212-244-2700
560 West 34th St. (11-12th) NYC 10001
Hours: 9-5 Mon-Fri
"Union shop; custom and rental." ed.

Oliphant Studio 212-741-1233
38 Cooper Sq. (3rd & 6th Ave.) NYC 10003
Hours: 8:30-5 Mon-Fri
"Non-union scenic; custom or rental." ed.

THE SET SHOP 212-929-4845
3 West 20th St. (5th) NYC 10011
Hours: 9-6 Mon-Fri/ 10-4 Sat
Backdrops: custom & rental; full scene shop; non-union. (See display ad page 316.)
"Also stocks theatrical paints and painters' supplies." ed.

Variety Scenic Studios 718-392-4747
25-19 Borden Ave. (25th) L.I.C. 11101
Hours: 7-5 Mon-Fri
"Backdrops: custom and rental; catalog." ed.

BAKERIES

Cake Masters

120 West 72nd St. (Columbus-B'way) NYC 10023 (main store) 212-787-1414
23 University Place (8th) NYC 10003 212-477-3370
236 Ninth Ave. (24th) NYC 10011 212-924-1818
1394 Sixth Ave. (57th) NYC 10019 212-581-3090
1111 Third Ave. (65th) NYC 10021 212-759-7212
1353A Third Ave. (77th) NYC 10021 212-879-1414
2345 Broadway (85th) NYC 10024 212-787-0998
2631 Broadway (99th) NYC 10025 212-749-3340

Hours: 8-8 every day
"Will make special prop cakes to order." ed.

Creative Cakes 212-794-9811
400 East 74th St. (1st) NYC 10021
Hours: 8-5 Tues-Fri/9-11 Sat
"Cakes made to order; very helpful." ed.

La Delice Bakery 212-532-4409
372 Third Ave. (27th) NYC 10016
Hours: 7:30-10 every day
"Will make cakes to order in one day; very helpful." ed.

Poseidon Bakery 212-757-6173
629 Ninth Ave. (44-45th) NYC 10036
Hours: 9-7 Tues-Sat/ 10-4 Sun
"Greek pastries." ed.

BALLOONS & HELIUM

Balloon Creations 212-719-5083
12 West 37th St. Suite 904 (5th) NYC 10018
Hours: By appt.
"Balloons, custom work." ed.

Balooms Ltd. 212-473-3523
147 Sullivan St. (Prince-Houston) NYC 10012 212-673-4007
Hours: 10-6 Mon-Fri/ 12-6 Sat
"Custom balloons, see Raymond." ed.

Kaysam Co. 201-684-5700
27 Kentucky Ave., Paterson, NJ 07503
Hours: 8:30-5 Mon-Fri
"Weather balloons." ed.

T.W. Smith Welding Supply 212-247-6323
545 West 59th St. (10-11th) NYC 10019
Hours: 7:30-4:45 Mon-Fri
"Helium, balloon attachments; deposit required." ed.

Toy Balloon Corp. 212-682-3803
204 East 38th St. (2-3rd) NYC 10016
Hours: 9-5 Mon-Fri
"Novelty, plain or printed balloons to order; helium." ed.

U.S. Balloon Mfg. Co. 718-646-1110
1613 Oriental Blvd. (Emmons Ave.) Bklyn 11235
Hours: 9-6 Mon-Fri
"Large selection of mylar and latex balloons; wholesale." ed.

BARRELS

Adelphia Container Corp. 718-388-5202
206 North 10th St., Bklyn 11211
Hours: 7-3:30 Mon-Fri
"Cardboard barrels and nail kegs; small and large orders." ed.

City Barrel 718-388-9227
421 Meeker Ave. (Manhattan-Graham) Bklyn 11222
Hours: 8-3:30 Mon-Fri
"Steel barrels." ed.

Greif Brothers 212-285-9844
24 West Lake Ave., Rahway, NJ 07065
Hours: 9-5 Mon-Fri
"Good source for cardboard, barrels." ed.

Tunnel Barrel & Drum Co. 212-925-8190
85 Triangle Blvd. (Veterans), Carlstadt, NJ 07072
Hours: 7-4 Mon-Fri
"Barrels and nail kegs." ed.

BASKETS

See also ETHNIC GOODS
See also WICKER ITEMS

Azuma

387 Sixth Ave. (Waverly) NYC 10012 212-989-8690
Hours: 10-9 Mon-Sat/ 11-7:30 Sun

25 East 8th St. (Univ. Pl.-5th) NYC 10003 212-673-2900
Hours: 10-9 Mon-Sat/ 11-7:30 Sun

666 Lexington Ave. (55th) NYC 10022 212-752-0599
Hours: 10-7:30 Mon-Fri/10-6:30 Sat/12-5:45 Sun

251 East 86th St. (2nd) NYC 10028 212-369-4928
Hours: 10-8 Mon-Sat/ 11-7 Sun

"Importers of baskets, wicker items, bamboo, housewares, clothing, gift items." ed.

Folklorica Imports Inc. 212-255-2525
89 Fifth Ave. (16-17th) NYC 10003
Hours: 10-7 Mon-Fri/ 11-6 Sat/ (Call for Sun hours)
"Primitive baskets, drums, masks, rugs, sweaters, etc.; expensive." ed.

Fran's Basket House 201-584-2230
295 Route 10, Succasunna, NJ 07876
Hours: 9:30-6 Mon-Sat/ 9:30-9 Thurs
"Large selection wicker baskets." ed.

Adele Lewis Inc. 212-594-5075
101 West 28th St. (6th) NYC 10001
Hours: 8-5 Mon-Fri
"Primitive baskets, pottery, musical instruments, stick furniture; wholesale or retail (formerly Potcovers)." ed.

Natural Furniture Warehouse 718-857-5967
604 Pacific St. (Flatbush) Bklyn 11217 718-857-5959
Hours: 10-7:30 Mon-Sat
"Baskets, importer of wicker furniture and wicker items; cheap." ed.

Pottery Barn

231 Tenth Ave. (24th) NYC 10011 (main store) 212-741-9120
Hours: 10-6:30 Mon-Sat/ 11-6 Sun
"Large selection, sometimes discounted at this location." ed.

49 Greenwich Ave. (6-7th Ave) NYC 10014 212-741-9140
Hours: 11-8 Mon-Sat/ 12-6 Sun

250 West 57th St. (8th) NYC 10107 212-741-9145
Hours: 10-7 Mon-Sat/ 12-6 Sun

117 East 59th St. (Lexington-Park) NYC 10022 212-741-9132
Hours: 10-6:30 Tues,Wed,Fri,Sat/10-8:30 Mon,Thurs/12-5 Sun

2109 Broadway (73-74th) NYC 10023 212-741-9123
Hours: 11-8 Mon-Sat/ 12-5 Sun

1451 Second Ave. (76th) NYC 10021 212-741-9142
Hours: 10:30-7:30 Mon-Fri/ 10-6:30 Sat/ 12-6 Sun

1292 Lexington Ave. (87-88th) NYC 10128 212-741-9134
Hours: 10-6:30 Mon-Sat/ 12-6 Sun

"Baskets, ironstone, glassware, housewares." ed.

Pottery World 212-242-2903
807 Sixth Ave. (27-28th) NYC 10001
Hours: 7-4:30 Mon-Fri/ 10-5:30 Sat
"Baskets, clay pots and planters." ed.

Al Saffer 212-675-2249
106 West 28th St. (6-7th) NYC 10001
Hours: 7-3 Mon-Fri
"Imports baskets and bamboo; floral supplies." ed.

The Wickery 212-889-3669
342 Third Ave. (25th) NYC 10010
Hours: 10:30-6:30 Mon-Fri/10:30-6 Sat
"Large selection wicker baskets and furniture." ed.

Wolfman-Gold & Good 212-431-1888
484 Broome St. (Wooster) NYC 10016
Hours: 11-6 Mon-Sat/ 12-5 Sun
"Beautiful antique and new linens; also baskets, cookie cutters, tureens, etc; will rent." ed.

BATHROOM ACCESSORIES

See also HARDWARE, DECORATIVE
See also LINENS
For fixtures, see KITCHEN & BATHROOM FIXTURES

Elegant John of Lex 212-935-5800
812 Lexington Ave. (62-63rd) NYC 10021
Hours: 10-6 Mon-Fri (Thurs til 7)
"Bathroom hardware and accessories, towels, shower curtains, toilet seats, etc; expensive." ed.

Gracious Home 212-535-2033
1220 Third Ave. (70-71st) NYC 10021
Hours: 9-7 Mon-Sat/ 10:30-5:30 Sun
"Large selection of housewares, hardware and small appliances." ed.

Janovic Plaza 212-772-1400
1150 Third Ave (67-68th) NYC 10021
Hours: 9:30-6:30 Mon-Fri/ 9:30-5:30 Sat
"Toilet seats, shower curtains, wallpaper, towels, towel bars, and other accessories." ed.

Howard Kaplan French Country Store 212-674-1000
35 East 10th St. (University-B'way) NYC 10003
Hours: 10-6 Mon-Fri
"Antique bathroom accessories and fixtures; french country furniture; expensive." ed.

BEAMS & TIMBERS

Murry M. Fine Lumber 718-381-5200
175 Varick Ave. (off Metropolitan & Grand) Bklyn 11237
Hours: 8-5 Mon-Fri
"Used large beams and timber." ed.

NYC Dept. of Parks - Forestry Div. no phone
Henry Hudson Pkwy & 148th St. Playground, NYC 10031
Hours: 24 hours everyday
"Pickup logs and branches from NYC parks; no charge." ed.

BEAUTY SALON EQUIPMENT

For beauty supplies, see HAIR SUPPLIES AND WIGS
see MAKE-UP SUPPLIES

Takara Belmont 212-541-6660
17 West 56th St. (5-6th) NYC 10019
Hours: 9-5 Mon-Fri/ by appt.
"Manufacturer of salon equipment." ed.

Charles Costello 212-391-8355
31 West 38th St. (5-6th) NYC 10018
Hours: 8:30-5:30 Mon-Fri
"Rents salon equipment; good selection beauty supplies." ed.

Lexington Equipment Co. 212-533-7840
35 East 19th St. (B'way-Park) NYC 10003
Hours: 8:30-5 Mon-Fri
"Rents beauty salon equipment." ed.

William Pahl Equipment Corp. 212-265-6083
232 West 58th St. (B'way-7th) NYC 10019
Hours: 9-5 Mon-Fri
"Beauty salon supply house, some equipment." ed.

Paramount Beauty 212-757-6996
251 West 50th St. (B'way-8th) NYC 10019
Hours: 7:30-5:30 Mon-Fri
"Beauty supplies." ed.

Ray Beauty Supply Co. Inc. 212-757-0175
721 Eighth Ave. (45-46th) NYC 10036
Hours: 9-5:30 Mon-Fri
"Rentals: see Bobby; also scissors, T-pins, hair dyes, etc." ed.

United Beauty Supply 212-719-2324
49 West 46th St. (5-6th) NYC 10036
Hours: 9-6 Mon-Fri/ 10-2 Sat
"Beauty salon supplies." ed.

BICYCLES & ACCESSORIES

Angelo's Bicycle Service 212-362-1122
140 West 83rd St. (Columbus-Amsterdam) NYC 10024
Hours: 10-7 Mon-Fri/ 9-7 Sat, Sun
"Rents." ed.

ANTIQUE BICYCLE PROP SERVICE 201-391-8780
113 Woodland, Mont Vale, NJ 07645 914-735-9769
Hours: By appt.

Established 1937. Unusual & antique bicycles rented for theatrical, tv commercials, photo studios, publicity/-product promotions, window displays. 1840 Boneshaker, 1878 highwheelers, tricycles, unicycles, bicycle with side-car, horse bicycle and bicycles built for 6-5-4-3-2. All in stock. We pickup and deliver.

"Very helpful." ed.

Dixon's Bicycle Shop 718-636-0067
792 Union St. (7th Ave.) Bklyn 11215
Hours: 10-7:30 Mon-Sat/ 10-6 Sun
"Sales and rental of new and used bikes." ed.

Gene's 79th St. Discount Bicycles 212-288-0739
242 East 79th St. (2-3rd) NYC 10021 212-249-9218
Hours: 9-7 every day
"Will rent all types of modern bikes." ed.

Larry & Jeff's 85th St. Bicycles 212-794-2201
204 East 85th St. (2-3rd) NYC 10028
Hours: 10-8 every day
"Rents; very nice people." ed.

Metro Bicycle Store

332 East 14th St. (1st) NYC 10003 212-228-4344
Hours: 9:30-6:30 every day

546 Sixth Ave. (15th) NYC 10011 212-255-5100
Hours: 9:30-6 every day

1311 Lexington Ave. (88th) NYC 10028 212-427-4450
Hours: 9:30-6:30 every day

"Rents; very helpful with bike accessories." ed.

Midtown Bicycles 212-581-4500
360 West 47th St. (9th) NYC 10036
Hours: 9:30-6:30 every day
"Very helpful with bike accessories; rents." ed.

Stuyvesant Bicycle 212-254-5200
349 West 14th St. (8-9th) NYC 10014
Hours: 9:30-6 Mon-Sat/ 12-5 Sun
"Rents; nice guy." ed.

Stuyvesant Bicycle East 212-254-9200
326 Second Ave. (19th) NYC 10003
Hours: 10-6 Tues-Sat/ 10-5 Sun
"Rental or purchase." ed.

West Side Bicycle 212-663-7531
231 West 96th St. (B'way-Amsterdam) NYC 10025
Hours: 9:30-6:30 every day
"Rents; very helpful with bike accessories." ed.

BLACKSMITHING

Ralph Causarano 718-728-2116
31-57 Vernon Blvd. L.I.C. 11106
Hours: 8-6 Mon, Tues, Wed/ 8-3 Thurs, Fri
"Good blacksmith; will fabricate to your designs; allow time." ed.

BLADE SHARPENING

Dayton Tool Grinding 212-675-1071
59 Carmine St. (7th-Varick) NYC 10014
Hours: 10-5:30 Mon-Fri/ 10-3 Sat
"See Lionel Held." ed.

Edge Grinding Shop 201-943-4109
388 Fairview Ave. Fairview, NJ 07022
Hours: 6-5 Mon, Thurs/ 7-2 Tues, Fri
"Scissors; call on Mon., Wed. pickup, return Thurs.; see Lenny." ed.

Kochendorfer 212-925-1435
413 West Broadway (Prince-Spring) NYC 10013
Hours: 7-5 Mon-Fri
"All types of sharpening, both scissors and blades." ed.

Ross Sales Co. 212-475-8470
58 Third Ave. (7th) NYC 10003
Hours: 8-5:30 Mon-Fri
"Barbers and beauticians scissors and sharpening." ed.

BLUEPRINTING MACHINERY & SUPPLIES

For blueprinters, see PRINTING & COPYING

Charrette Drafting Supply Corp.

215 Lexington Ave. (33rd) NYC 10016 — 212-683-8822
Hours: 8:30-8:30 Mon-Fri/ 8:30-6 Sat (12-5 Sun: Sept-June)

5 West 45th St. (5th) NYC 10036 — 212-921-1122
Hours: 8:30-7 Mon-Fri/ 10:30-7 Sat

"Sell print machines and supplies; artists materials; catalog." ed.

General Reproduction Products — 201-261-6666
401 Kinderkamack Rd., Oradell, NJ 07649
Hours: 9-5 Mon-Fri
"Lease and sell Diazo Darts; sell and deliver all supplies." ed.

BOOKBINDING SERVICES & SUPPLIES

Alpha-Pavia Bookbinding Co. Inc. — 212-929-5430
55 West 21st St. (5-6th) NYC 10010
Hours: 8:30-5:30 Mon-Fri
"Bookbinders; also sell and rent fake bookbacks." ed.

John Gailor — 212-243-5662
137 Varick St. 7th Fl. (Spring) NYC 10014
Hours: 8-5 Mon-Fri
"Gold-leaf stamping of books, portfolios; special orders." ed.

Angela Scott — 212-535-1839
341 East 78th St. (1-2nd) NYC 10021
Hours: By appt.
"Custom bookbinding, portfolios, restorations, new bindings, cases, will design for customers." ed.

Technical Library Services Inc. — 212-736-7744
213 West 35th St. (7-8th) NYC 10001
Hours: 9-4:30 Mon-Fri (closed for lunch 11:30-1)
"Bookbinding and conservation supplies; acid-free papers and adhesives." ed.

BOOKS, FAKE

Alpha-Pavia Bookbinding Co. Inc. 212-929-5430
55 West 21st St. (5-6th) NYC 10010
Hours: 8:30-5:30 Mon-Fri
"Fake bookbacks by the foot; sale or rental." ed.

THE GREAT AMERICAN MARKET 213-461-0200
826 N. Cole Ave., Hollywood, CA 90038
Hours: 8-5 Mon-Fri (Sat by appt. only)
(See display ad on divider page.)
"Fake bookbacks, vacuumformed panels of all kinds." ed.

BOOKSTORES

See also MAGAZINES & COMIC BOOKS
See also NEWSPAPERS

APPLAUSE THEATRE BOOKS 212-496-7511
100 West 67th St. (B'way-Columbus) NYC 10023 (sale & used books)
211 West 71st St. (B'way) NYC 10023 (main store)
Hours: 10-7 Mon-Sat/ 12-6 Sun
Over 5,000 titles from all publishers on every aspect of theatre and cinema. First rate professional service. We ship worldwide. (See display ad page 38.)
"Wide selection of plays, with emphasis on British drama." ed.

Argosy Book Stores Inc. 212-753-4455
116 East 59th St. (Park-Lexington) NYC 10022
Hours: 9-6 Mon-Fri/ 10-5 Sat
"Out-of-print books, maps, prints." ed.

Arte Primitivo Inc. 212-570-0393
3 East 65th St. (5th-Madison) NYC 10021
Hours: 11-5 Mon-Fri/ 11-3 Sat
"Books and papers on Pre-Columbian cultures; new, rare, and out-of-print." ed.

Astrology Bookshop 212-832-8958
789 Lexington Ave. 2nd Fl. (61-62nd) NYC 10021
Hours: 10-6 Mon-Fri/ 12-6 Sat
"Books on the subject of astrology." ed.

Barnes & Noble Bookstore Inc. 212-608-1023
199 Chambers St. (West Side Hwy) NYC 10007
Hours: 9-4 Mon-Fri
"Bargain priced hardcover and paperbacks, art books, classical records and tapes. (located inside Manhattan Comm. College)" ed.

DRAMA BOOK SHOP, INC.

Initially founded in 1921 by the New York Drama League the book shop has:

- **World's most complete stock of in print theatre literature**
- **Plays of all publishers**
- **Theatre books published abroad**
- **Many categories**

Film
Television
Biography
Directing
Anthologies
Restoration
Bibliographies
World Theatre
Playwrighting
Musicals
Dance
Costume
American Theatre
Happenings

Ancient Drama
Puppetry
Encyclopedias
Religious
Speech
Acting
Stage Design
Architecture
Teaching
Shakespeariana
Histories
Annuals
Lighting

Children's Theatre
Furniture
Armour
Mass Media
Scenarios
Magic
Creative Dramatics
Pantomime
Make-up
Producing
Records
Periodicals
Vocal Scores
Opera

Efficient and knowledgeable mail order department

723 Seventh Avenue

New York, New York 10019

212-944-0595

Barnes & Noble Bookstore Inc. (continued)

105 Fifth Ave. (18th) NYC 10003 212-807-0099
Hours: 9:45-6:45 Mon-Fri/ 9:45-6 Sat/ 10-5 Sun
"Great prices on remainders, used textbooks, games, and auction catalogs (check sale annex across the street)." ed.

600 Fifth Ave. (48th) NYC 10020 212-765-0590
Hours: 9:45-6:45 Mon-Fri/ 9:45-6 Sat/ 12-6 Sun
"Bargain priced hardcover and paperbacks, art books, classical records and tapes (located in Rockefeller Center)." ed.

Books of Wonder 212-989-3270
464 Hudson St. (Barrow) NYC 10014
Hours: 11-7 Mon-Thurs/ 12-9 Fri, Sat/ 12-6 Sun
"Wonderful collection of new and antique children's books; no rental."

China Books & Periodicals 212-677-2650
125 Fifth Ave. (19-20th) NYC 10003
Hours: 10-6 Mon-Sat
"Chinese books, newspapers, magazines, posters, kites, gift items." ed.

CINEMABILIA 212-989-8519
10 West 13th St. (5-6th) NYC 10011
Hours: 11-6:30 Mon, Wed, Sat/ 11-7 Tues, Thurs, Fri

Wide selection of current & out-of-print film books & related materials.

"The best source for books on film." ed.

Coliseum Books Inc. 212-757-8381
1771 Broadway (57th) NYC 10019
Hours: 8-10 Mon/ 8-11 Tues-Fri/ 10-11:30pm Sat/ 12-8 Sun
"Current books, large selection remainders and sale books, cheap picture books." ed.

B. Dalton, Booksellers

170 Broadway (Maiden Lane) NYC 10038 212-349-3560
Hours: 8-6:30 Mon-Fri/ 10-3 Sun
"Current books, some magazines." ed.

396 Sixth Ave. (8th St.) NYC 10012 212-674-8780
Hours: 10am-midnight every day
"Current books, some magazines." ed.

666 Fifth Ave. (52nd) NYC 10103 212-247-1740
Hours: 8:30-8 Mon-Fri/ 10-6:30 Sat/ 12:30-6:30 Sun
"Current books, some magazines; computer will help locate books." ed.

Doubleday Book Shop

673 Fifth Ave. (53rd) NYC 10022 212-953-4805
Hours: 9:30-midnight Mon-Sat/ 12-5 Sun

(continues next page)

724 Fifth Ave. (56th) NYC 10019 212-397-0550
Hours: 9:30-midnight Mon-Sat/ 12-5 Sun
"Good selection; very helpful locating books." ed.

Dover Publications Inc.

180 Varick St. (King-Carlton) NYC 10014 212-255-3755
Hours: 9-4 Mon-Fri
"Retail store; catalogs; also has selection of damaged books for half-price." ed.

31 East 2nd St. Mineola, NY 11501 516-294-7000
Hours: 9-4 Mon-Fri
"Mail order for Dover Books; catalogs available." ed.

DRAMA BOOKSHOP 212-944-0595
723 Seventh Ave. 2nd Fl. (48-49th) NYC 10036
Hours: 9:30-6 Mon-Fri (Wed til 8)/ 10:30-5 Sat
(See display ad page 39.)
"Huge selection of books on every aspect of the performing arts." ed.

Encyclopedia & Reference Book Center 212-677-2160
175 Fifth Ave. (23rd) NYC 10010
Hours: 10-4:30 Mon-Fri
"Very helpful; good drama selection; catalog available." ed.

Facsimile Book Shop Inc. 212-581-2672
16 West 55th St. (5-6th) NYC 10019
Hours: 10-6:30 Mon-Fri/ 11-6 Sat
"Irish books and records." ed.

Forbidden Planet 212-473-1576
821 Broadway (12th) NYC 10003
Hours: 10-7 Mon-Sat/ 11-6 Sun
"Science fiction, fantasy, comic books, magazines on special effects."

Samuel French Inc. 212-206-8990
45 West 25th St. (5-6th) NYC 10010
Hours: 9-5 Mon-Fri
"Scripts; catalog available." ed.

The French & Spanish Book Corp.

115 Fifth Ave. (19th) NYC 10003 212-673-7400
Hours: 10-6 Mon-Sat

610 Fifth Ave. (49-50th) NYC 10020 212-581-8810
Hours: 9:30-6:15 Mon-Fri/ 10-6:15 Sat

"French and Spanish books, magazines, newspapers." ed.

Gordon Books 212-759-7443
12 East 55th St. (5th-Madison) NYC 10022
Hours: 9-7 Mon-Fri/ 10-6 Sat
"Automotive, airplane, military books." ed.

Hacker Art Books 212-757-1450
54 West 57th St. (5-6th) NYC 10019
Hours: 9-6 Mon-Fri/ 9-5 Sat
"Current and out-of-print books; old prints." ed.

J. N. Herlin Inc. 212-431-8732
68 Thompson St. (Spring-Broome) NYC 10012
Hours: 11-6:30 Mon-Sat
"Out-of-print 20th Century art and film books, periodicals, posters, pre-1970's stills." ed.

Leslie Hodges Costume & Fashion Books 01-352-1176
Old Church St., London, England
"Current and out-of-print magazines, fashion plates, and clothes patterns." ed.

Victor Kamkin Inc. 212-673-0776
149 Fifth Ave. (21st) NYC 10010
Hours: 9:30-5:30 Mon-Fri/ 10-5 Sat
"Russian magazines and newspapers." ed.

Daphne Lucas 01-455-3110
28 Addison Way, London, NW, England 116AP
"New and out-of-print books on costumes, accessories, textiles." ed.

McGraw-Hill Bookstore 212-512-2000
1221 Sixth Ave. (48-49th) NYC 10036
Hours: 10-5:45 Mon-Sat
"Mostly technical, legal, science books." ed.

Morton Interior Design Bookshop 212-421-9025
989 Third Ave. (59th) NYC 10022
Hours: 11-7 Mon-Sat
"Books on interior design, architecture; current issues of design magazines." ed.

Museum Books Inc. 212-563-2770
6 West 37th St. 4th Fl. (5-6th) NYC 10018
Hours: 9-5 Mon-Fri
"Books and magazines (domestic and foreign) on decorative arts." ed.

New York Bound Bookshop/ Urban Graphics 212-245-8503
43 West 54th St. 4th Fl.(5-6th) NYC 10019
Hours: Tues-Fri 10-5:30 (Mon, Sat by appt.)
"Old maps of NYC; contact Linda Borsanger." ed.

Pageant Book & Print Shop 212-674-5296
109 East 9th St. (3-4th) NYC 10003
Hours: 10-6:30 Mon-Sat
"Mr. Soloman; rents books by subject area by the foot." ed.

Paperback Booksmith 212-889-7707
393 Fifth Ave. (36-37th) NYC 10016
Hours: 8:30-6:30 Mon-Fri/ 10:30-6:30 Sat/ 12-4:30 Sun
"Fashion and design books." ed.

Paragon Book Gallery Ltd. 212-496-2378
2130 Broadway (74-75th) NYC 10023
Hours: 10-5:45 Mon-Fri/ 11-5 Sat
"Books on Asia and the Orient." ed.

Rizzoli International Bookstore 212-759-2424
31 West 57th St. (5-6th) NYC 10019
Hours: 9-midnight Mon-Sat/12-8 Sun
"Art books, mostly foreign publications, magazines; expensive." ed.

Ruby's Book Sale 212-732-8676
119 Chambers St. (Church-W B'way) NYC 10007
Hours: 10-6 Mon-Fri/ 10-5:30 Sat
"Secondhand magazines, paperbacks, discounted coffee table books."

Shakespeare and Co. Booksellers 212-580-7800
2259 Broadway (81st) NYC 10024
Hours: 10-midnight Mon-Fri/ 10-1am Sat,Sun
"Well-stocked "general" bookstore; carries books for all the performing arts." ed.

R. L. Shep 206-468-2023
PO Box C-20, Lopez Island, WA 98261
"Books on costumes, clothing, textiles; out-of-print, used, antiquarian; catalog with subscription." ed.

Star Magic 212-228-7770
743 Broadway (8th-Waverly) NYC 10003
Hours: 12-9 Mon-Sat/ 12-7 Sun
"Spaceflight books; star maps and finders, space related posters and materials." ed.

Richard Stoddard Performing Arts 212-982-0440
90 East 10th St. (Lafayette-3rd) NYC 10003
Hours: 11-6 Wed-Sat/ 1-6 Sun
"Playbills; specializes in rare theatre books, with emphasis on scenic and costume design." ed.

Strand Book Store Inc.

828 Broadway (12th) NYC 10003 (main store) 212-473-1452
Hours: 9:30-6:30 Mon-Sat
"Used books and remainders; cheap; Richard Lilly will help find out-of-print art books." ed.

(continues next page)

159 John St. (Front St.) NYC 10038 212-809-0875
Hours: 10-10 every day
"Used books and remainders; cheap; at the South Street Seaport." ed.

THEATRE ARTS BOOKSHOP 212-564-0402
405 West 42nd St. (9-10th) NYC 10036 212-564-0403
Hours: 10-8 Mon-Sat/ 12-7 Sun
New & used theatre books, scripts, posters, records, custom framing.
"Also theatre-related gift items." ed.

Theatrebooks Inc. 212-757-2834
1576 Broadway 3rd Fl. (47-48th) NYC 10036
Hours: 10:30-6 Mon-Fri/ 12-5 Sat
"New, used, out-of-print theatre books." ed.

Three Lives & Company Ltd. 212-741-2069
154 West 10th St. (Waverly) NYC 10014
Hours: 11-10 Mon-Sat/ 1-7 Sun
"Good art, architecture, photography sections; will special order."

Tokyo Bookstore

521 Fifth Ave. (43-44th) NYC 10175 212-697-0840
Hours: 10-7 Mon-Sat/ 11:30-6:30 Sun

115 West 57th St. (6-7th) NYC 10019 212-582-4622
Hours: 10-8 Mon-Sat/ 12-7 Sun

"Japanese and Oriental books, gifts; calligraphy, painting supplies."

Samuel Weiser Inc. 212-777-6363
132 East 24th St. (Park Ave. S.-Lexington) NYC 10010
Hours: 9-5:50 M,T,W,F/ 10-6:50 Thurs/ 9:30-4:50 Sat
"Huge selection of books on religion and the occult." ed.

BRASS ITEMS

See also ANTIQUES
For brass hardware, see HARDWARE, DECORATIVE

Alyn Trading Corp. 212-689-7060
1141 Broadway (26th) NYC 10001
Hours: 9-5 Mon-Fri
"Hammered tinware in pewter, washed copper or brass finish." ed.

The Brass Loft 212-226-5467
20 Greene St. (Canal-Grand) NYC 10013
Hours: 10:30-5:30 Tues-Thurs, Sat, Sun
(Summer/ 10:30-5:30 Mon-Fri)
"Large stock of all types of brass items, samovars; reasonable." ed.

Horseman V Antiques 212-683-2041
348 Third Ave. (25th) NYC 10010
Hours: 1-7 Mon-Fri/ 11-6 Sat/ 12-6 Sun
"Oak, repro and antique brass beds/items; rents by the day." ed.

Horseman VI Antiques 212-751-6222
995 Second Ave. (53rd) NYC 10022
Hours: 11-7 Mon-Fri/ 11-6 Sat/ 12-6 Sun
"Oak, repro and antique brass beds/items; rents by the day." ed.

Ben Karpen Brass Corp. 212-755-3450
212 East 51st St. (2-3rd) NYC 10022
Hours: 9:30-5:30 Mon-Fri/ 10-4 Sat
"Repro brass items, brass beds, large selection; will rent." ed.

Majestic Reproductions Co. Inc. 212-753-1883
979 Third Ave. (58-59th) NYC 10022 212-753-1850
Hours: 9-5 Mon-Fri
"Repro brass items." ed.

Old Brassware 718-469-5644
797 Coney Island Ave. (Dorchester-Cortelyou) Bklyn 11218 718-646-6847
Hours: 11-5:30 Mon-Sat
"Brass doorknobs, candlesticks, andirons, samovars, etc." ed.

Hyman E. Piston Antiques 212-753-8322
1050 Second Ave. (55-56th) NYC 10022
Hours: 10-4 Mon-Fri/ 10-2:30 Sat
"Tie backs, andirons; antique copper, brass, pewter items." ed.

Charles P. Rogers 212-807-1989
149 West 24th St. (6-7th) NYC 10011
Hours: 10-6 Mon-Fri/ 12-5 Sun
"Mostly repro brass beds." ed.

BREAKAWAYS

See also SPECIAL EFFECTS SERVICES

L. Biagiotti 212-924-5088
259 Seventh Ave. (24-25th) NYC 10011
Hours: 9-4 Mon-Fri
"Breakaways, custom work, sculptures, etc. in plaster." ed.

Brooklyn Model Works 718-834-1944
61 Washington Ave. (Park-Flushing) Bklyn 11205
Hours: 9-5 Mon-Fri
"Breakaways, casting and reproduction; vacuumforming, machining, controls." ed.

McHUGH/ROLLINS ASSOCIATES INC. 718-643-0990
79 Bridge St. (York-Front) Bklyn 11201
Hours: 9-6 Mon-Fri
Stock bottles and glasses. Custom work available. Sheet and stained glass work. See Jim.(See display ad page 300.)
"Full service prop shop." ed.

REJOICE LTD./GARY ZELLER, JOYCE SPECTOR 212-869-8636
40 West 39 St. (5-6th) NYC 10018
Hours: By appt. or leave message
Bottles, glasses, windows, special crystal clear & giant panes. (See display ad page 333.)
"Also casting materials; special effects consultation, services." ed.

ROSCO LABORATORIES INC. 914-937-1300
36 Bush Ave., Port Chester, NY 10573 800-431-2338
Hours: 9-5 Mon-Fri
Bottles/glasses that shatter realistically, without danger. (See display ad inside back cover.)
"Five styles in stock; minimum order 1 dozen." ed.

Special Effects Unlimited 914-965-5625
18 Euclid Ave., Yonkers, NY 10705
Hours: By appt.
"See Mrs. Drohan; custom orders." ed.

THEATRE MAGIC 614-459-3222
6099 Godown Rd., Columbus, OH 43220
Hours: 7:30-4:30 Mon-Fri
(See display ad page 334.)
"Breakaway bottles, glass and panes; Pyccolastic resin." ed.

BURLAP BAGS

American National Bag & Burlap 718-857-8050
528 Bergen St. Bklyn 11217
Hours: 8-5 Mon-Fri
"Large or small orders." ed.

Rachman Bag Co. 718-625-1511
126 Front St. Bklyn 11201
Hours: 9-4 Mon-Fri
"Large or small orders." ed.

BUSINESS MACHINES & TYPEWRITERS

See also COMPUTERS

A & B Beacon Business Machines — 212-736-1440
36 West 33rd St. (5-6th) NYC 10001 — 212-564-7855
Hours: 8:30-5:30 Mon-Fri
"New and used, rental or purchase." ed.

Ajax Typewriter Corp. — 212-832-9650
230 East 59th St. (2-3rd) NYC 10022
Hours: 9-5 Mon-Fri (Thurs til 9)/ 10-3:30 Sat
"New and used typewriters, rental or purchase." ed.

Alpha Business Machines — 212-682-6666
300 Fifth Ave. (31st) NYC 10001
Hours: 9-5:30 Mon-Fri
"Typewriters, cash registers, copiers, for rental or purchase." ed.

Midtown Typewriter — 212-255-4752
124 West 23rd St. (6-7th) NYC 10011
Hours: 9-7 Mon-Thurs/ 9-5 Fri,Sat
"New and used typewriters." ed.

BUTCHER BLOCK

See also FURNITURE RENTAL & PURCHASE, RESTAURANT
See also KITCHEN EQUIPMENT, HOUSEHOLD
See also KITCHEN EQUIPMENT, INDUSTRIAL

Alexander Butcher Blocks & Supply — 212-226-4021
176 Bowery (Delancey) NYC 10013
Hours: 10-5 Mon-Fri/ 10-4 Sat, Sun
"Butcher block, tables, chairs, bentwoods." ed.

J & D Brauner — 212-477-2830
298 Bowery (Houston-Bleecker) NYC 10012
Hours: 8:30-5:30 Mon-Fri
"Good stock butcher block, tables, chairs." ed.

Building Block — 212-929-3347
33 West 21st. St. (5-6th) NYC 10010
Hours: By appt.
"Butcher block, tables, chairs." ed.

CAMERA RENTAL & SUPPLIES see PHOTOGRAPHIC EQUIPMENT

CANDLES

Candle Shop 212-989-0148
118 Christopher St. (Bleecker-Hudson) NYC 10014
Hours: 12-10 Mon-Sat/ 12-8 Sun
"Small store, good selection; very helpful." ed.

Faroy Inc. 212-679-5193
225 Fifth Ave. (26-27th) NYC 10010
Hours: 9-5 Mon-Fri
"See Virginia." ed.

CARDBOARD PRODUCTS see PAPER, CARDBOARD & FOAMCORE PRODUCTS

CARPETS see FLOORCOVERINGS

CASKETS

R. Conte 212-534-1416
1841 Park Ave. (126th) NYC 10035
Hours: 8-4:30 Mon-Sat
"Pine boxes to the most elaborate; will rent; very helpful." ed.

Ocean Caskets 718-497-0770
17 Thames St. (Bogart-Morgan) Bklyn 11206
Hours: 8-4 Mon-Fri
"See Frank Libraro." ed.

CASTING, CUSTOM

See also PROP & SCENIC CRAFTSPEOPLE
See also SPECIAL EFFECTS SERVICES

A-1 Astoria Foundry 718-392-2340
51-25 35th St. (Queens Blvd) L.I.C. 11101
Hours: 7-3 Mon-Fri
"Casting in metal." ed.

Allied Insulation Corp. 201-324-0040
319 Oak St., Perth Amboy, NJ 08861
Hours: 8-4:30 Mon-Fri
"Portable spray foam equip. for on-site work; see George Reha." ed.

Amtec International 516-751-8282
PO Box 527, E. Setauket, NY 11733
Hours: 9-5 Mon-Fri
"Professional polyurethane foam spraying; uniform carveable foam; contact Al." ed.

L. Biagiotti 212-924-5088
259 Seventh Ave. (24-25th) NYC 10011
Hours: 9-4 Mon-Fri
"Plaster statuary, vases, columns; stock and custom work; breakaways; will rent." ed.

Cast of Thousands 212-425-1631
50 West St. (Rector-Battery Tunnel) NYC 10006
Hours: By appt.
"Molds, lifecasts, architectural and art objects reproduced; contact Judi or Christopher." ed.

Gabriel Petrella 718-852-1656
196 Fourth Ave. (Sacket-DeGraw) Bklyn 11217
Hours: 8-4:30 Mon-Fri
"Casting, mold making, fiberglas and plaster." ed.

Seal Reinforced Fiberglass 516-842-2230
23 Bethpage Rd., Copiague, NY 11726
Hours: 8-5 Mon-Fri
"Custom fiberglas casting; speak to Tom Kaler; expensive." ed.

Norman Tempia 212-348-8944
409 East 90th St. #1B (1st-York) NYC 10128
Hours: By appt.
"Sculpture, special props, masks and puppets for film and tape." ed.

Westchester Fiberglass 914-939-5543
55 Purdy Ave., Port Chester, NY 10573
Hours: 9-6 Mon-Sat
"Fiberglas ornament, custom casting; ask for Don." ed.

Lawrence Whittman Co. 516-842-4770
1395 Morkoni Blvd., Copiague, NY 11726
Hours: 9-5 Mon-Fri
"Custom fiberglas molds, prototypes, props; see Charles Whittman." ed.

NOTES

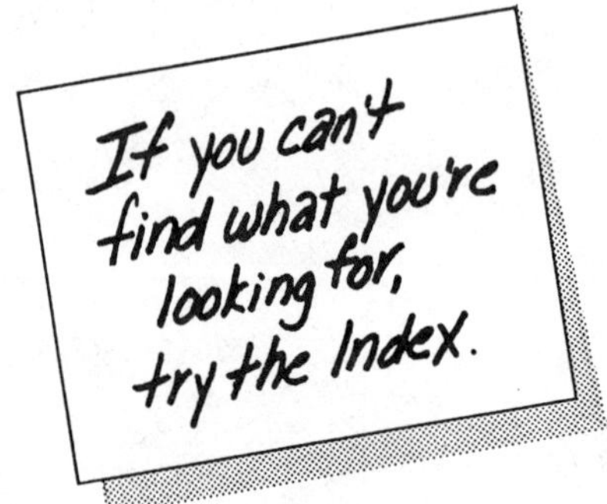
If you can't
find what you're
looking for,
try the Index.

CASTING SUPPLIES

See also CELASTIC
See also MAKE-UP SUPPLIES
For alginate, see DENTAL SUPPLY HOUSES
For plaster bandages, see SURGICAL SUPPLY HOUSES

Adhesive Products Corp. 718-542-4600
1660 Boone Ave. Bronx 10460
Hours: 8:30-4:30 Mon-Fri
"Adhesives, polyester resin, RTV rubber, latex, fillers, and mold releases." ed.

Alcone Co. Inc./Paramount Theatrical 718-361-8373
5-49 49th Ave. (49th-Vernon) L.I.C. 11101
Hours: 9:30-4 Mon-Fri
"Celastic, foam latex (subway #7 to L.I.C., Vernon/Jackson stop)." ed.

Berton Plastics Inc. 201-488-6700
170 Wesley St., So. Hackensack, NJ 07606 212-695-8135
Hours: 9-5 Mon-Fri
"Fiberglas mat, and cloth, polyester resin, gel cotes, dyes, releases, and catalyst." ed.

Arthur Brown and Brothers Inc. 212-575-5555
2 West 46th St. (5-6th) NYC 10036
Hours: 8:45-5:45 Mon-Fri
"Flexmold, casting resin, Celluclay, Shreddi-Mix; main business is art supplies." ed.

Cementex Co. Inc. 212-226-5832
480 Canal St. (Hudson) NYC 10013
Hours: 8:30-5 Mon-Fri
"Latex molding and casting compounds; custom mixes and coloring available; catalog." ed.

Chemco (Resin Crafts) 415-829-5000
6475 Sierra Lane, Dublin, CA 94568
Hours: 9-5 Mon-Fri
"Fiberglas, resin, dyes; wholesale or retail; reasonable prices." ed.

Chicago Latex Products 312-893-2880
1030 Morse Ave., Shaumburg, IL 60193
Hours: 9-5 Mon-Fri
"Rigid casting latex #501." ed.

City Chemical 212-929-2723
132 West 22nd St. (6-7th) NYC 10011
Hours: 9-4:30 Mon-Fri (closed for lunch 12-1)
"Stearic acid." ed.

Defender Industries 914-632-3001
255 Main St., New Rochelle, NY 10801
Hours: 9-5:45 Mon-Fri/ 9-2:45 Sat
"Fiberglas cloth, mat, polyester & epoxy resins; marine supplies." ed.

Douglas & Sturges 415-421-4456
730 Bryant St., San Francisco, CA 94107
Hours: 8:30-4 Mon-Fri
"Large selection of pigments, colorants, resin, glass products, mold materials; contact Arty." ed.

Dura-Foam Products Inc. 718-894-2488
63-02 59th Ave., Maspeth, NY 11378
Hours: 8-4:30 Mon-Fri
"Flexible and rigid urethane foam, also foam rubber and Scotfoam." ed.

Sam Flax Art Supplies

15 Park Row (Ann-Nassau) NYC 10018 212-620-3030
Hours: 8:30-5:30 Mon-Fri

111 Eighth Ave. (15-16th) NYC 10011 212-620-3000
Hours: 8:30-5:30 Mon-Fri 212-620-3010

12 West 20th St. (5-6th) NYC 10011 212-620-3038
Hours: 8:30-5:30 Mon-Fri/ 10-50 Sat

25 East 28th St. (Madison -Park) NYC 10016 212-620-3040
Hours: 9-7 Mon-Fri/ 9-5 Sat

747 Third Ave. (45-46th) NYC 10017 212-620-3050
Hours: 9-6 Mon-Fri/ 10-5 Sat/ 12-5 Sun

55 East 55th St. (Madison-Park) NYC 10022 212-620-3060
Hours: 9-6 Mon-Fri/ 10-5 Sat

"Casting rubber, moulage, art supplies." ed.

Flex Products 414-367-3331
West 34540 Rd. Q, Okauchee, WI 53069
Hours: By appt.
"Sells flexwax for making life casts; contact Robert Memmel." ed.

A. HAUSSMANN INTERNATIONAL CORP. 212-255-5661
118 West 22nd St. 9th Fl. (6-7th) NYC 10011
Hours: 10-6 Mon-Fri (sometimes later/call first)

Hatomold® single component flexible latex casting material. Hatoplast® three dimensional textured effects, good adherence to most surfaces, can be stenciled or molded. Armor Putty® protective coating for foam plastics and rigid styrofoam. All products are flame retardant. Call for free brochure. (See display ads pages 50, 260.)

"Also manufactures high quality scenic paints and brushes." ed.

Heveatex 617-675-0181
106 Ferry St., PO Box 2573, Fall River, MA 02722
Hours: 9-5 Mon-Fri
"Latex for molds, masks, balloons; shipping takes a week; flier." ed.

Industrial Plastics 212-226-2010
309 Canal St. (B'way-Mercer) NYC 10013
Hours: 8:30-5 Mon-Fri/ 8:30-4 Sat
"Two-part rigid urethane, RTV, resins, dyes, fiberglas; see Deena."

Monsanto, Plastics and Resins Div. 800-325-4330
Hours: 7:30-5:15 Mon-Fri
"Call for product information." ed.

Northwest Fibre-Glass Inc. 612-781-3494
3055 Columbia Ave. NE, Minneapolis, MN 55418
Hours: 9-5 Mon-Fri
"Flexible and rigid urethane foam, fiberglas, casting resins, color pastes; catalog." ed.

Polycoat Systems Inc. 518-747-0654
5 Depot St., Hudson Falls, NY 12839
Hours: 8-5 Mon-Fri
"Rigid polyurethane spray foam systems." ed.

Polytek Development Corp. 201-236-2990
PO Box 384, Lebanon, NJ 08833
Hours: 8-5 Mon-Fri
"Rubber mold products, plastic tooling compounds; contact Robert LeCompte." ed.

R & D Latex Corp. 213-724-6161
5901 Telegraph Rd., Commerce, CA 90040
Hours: 8-4:30 Mon-Fri
"Foam latex, some coloring for latex; RDL (foam)." ed.

REJOICE LTD./GARY ZELLER, JOYCE SPECTOR 212-869-8636
40 West 39 St. (5-6th) NYC 10018
Hours: By appt. or leave message
Non-toxic specialties. EZ Plastic, EZ Foam, Aqua Form. (See display ad page 333.)
"Also adhesives; special effects consultation and services." ed.

ROSCO LABORATORIES INC. 914-937-1300
36 Bush Ave., Port Chester, NY 10573 800-431-2338
Hours: 9-5 Mon-Fri
Puff Tex- useful for creating 3 dimensional effects. (See display ad inside back cover.)
"Also wide variety of scenic and fabric paints and dyes." ed.

Sculptor's Supplies Ltd. 212-673-3500
99 East 19th St. (Park-Irving Pl) NYC 10003
Hours: 9-6 Mon-Fri/ 12-4 Sat, Sun
"Tools, materials, bases; will mount sculpture." ed.

Sculpture Associates Ltd. 212-777-2400
40 East 19th St. (B'way-Park) NYC 10003
Hours: 9-6 Mon-Fri/ 9-3 Sat
"Tools, clay, moulage, plaster, molding and casting materials." ed.

Sculpture House Inc. 212-679-7474
38 East 30th St. (Madison-Park) NYC 10016
Hours: 8-5:30 Mon-Fri/ 10-3:30 Sat
"Sculpture tools, clay, moulage, plaster, molding and casting supplies."

Smooth-On-Corp 201-647-5800
1000 Valley Rd., Gillette, NJ 07933
Hours: 8:50-4:30 Mon-Fri
"Component foam, flexible mold compounds, epoxy resins." ed.

Stepan Chemical Co. (Urethane Dept.) 312-446-7500
22 West Frontage Rd., Northfield, IL 60093
Hours: 8:30-5 Mon-Fri
"Rigid and flexible urethane foam; 55 gal drums." ed.

THEATRE MAGIC 614-459-3222
6099 Godown Rd., Columbus, OH 43220
Hours: 7:30-4:30 Mon-Fri
(See display ad page 334.)
"Rubber casting resin, Pyccolastic breakaway resin, molds for architectural elements." ed.

United States Gypsum 609-933-2171
Kor Center East A/Interstate Industrial Park, Bellmawr, NJ 08031
Hours: By appt.
"Hydrocal with fibreglas mat reinforcement; on site demo, contact Thomas Soares." ed.

Urethane Products Co. Inc. 718-343-3400
Plaza Ave., New Hyde Park, NY 11040 516-488-3600
Hours: 8:30-5 Mon-Fri
"Rigid and flexible urethane foam; minimum order $80; see Harry Sloane." ed.

CELASTIC

Alcone Company Inc./Paramount Theatrical 718-361-8373
5-49 49th Ave. (49th-Vernon) L.I.C. 11101
Hours: 9:30-4 Mon-Fri
"Theatrical supply house. (subway #7 to L.I.C., Vernon/Jackson stop)"

David Hamberger

410 Hicks St. Bklyn 11201 718-852-7101
Hours: 9-5:30 Mon-Fri
"Celastic, papier mache, display materials." ed.

120 East 23rd St. #509 (Park-Lex) NYC 10010 (showroom) 212-852-7101
Hours: 9-5 Mon-Fri
"Celastic, styro shapes, displays in wood." ed.

REJOICE LTD./GARY ZELLER, JOYCE SPECTOR 212-869-8636
40 West 39 St. (5-6th) NYC 10018
Hours: By appt. or leave message
Aqua-Form, non-toxic, water based alternative material. (See display ad page 333.)
"Special effects consultation and services." ed.

Mutual Hardware 718-361-2480
5-45 49th Ave. L.I.C. 11101
Hours: 8:30-5 Mon-Fri
"Celastic, also scenic supplies." ed.

CHINA, CRYSTAL & GLASSWARE

See also ANTIQUES
See also KITCHEN EQUIPMENT, HOUSEHOLD
See also KITCHEN EQUIPMENT, INDUSTRIAL

Baccarat Inc. 212-826-4100
55 East 57th St. (Madison-Park) NYC 10022
Hours: 9:30-5:30 Mon-Sat
"Crystal, china." ed.

Balter Sales 212-674-2960
209 Bowery (Rivington) NYC 10002
Hours: 8-4:30 Mon-Fri
"Name brand glassware by the dozen." ed.

Cardel Ltd. 212-753-8880
615 Madison Ave. (58-59th) NYC 10022
Hours: 9:45-5:45 Mon-Sat
"Large selection of crystal, china, porcelain collectibles; will rent."

Ceramica Gift Gallery 212-354-9216
1009 Sixth Ave. (37-38th) NYC 10018
Hours: 9:30-6:15 Mon-Fri/ 11-5 Sat
"Fine china, crystal, porcelain, collectibles; see Shlomo; will ship anywhere." ed.

Chef Restaurant Supplies 212-254-6644
294-296 Bowery (Houston) NYC 10012
Hours: 9-5:30 Mon-Sat/ 11-5 Sun
"Inexpensive glassware and other restaurant supplies." ed.

Crystal Factory Outlet 212-925-8783
55 Delancey St. (Allen-Eldridge) NYC 10002
Hours: 10-5 Sun-Thurs
"Wholesale and retail crystal and china." ed.

Housewares & Gifts 212-473-8011
184 Orchard St. (Hudson-Stanton) NYC 10002
Hours: 9:30-5 Thurs-Tues
"China sets, figurines, glassware, chandeliers, clocks, pictures." ed.

Mayhew 212-759-8120
509 Park Ave. (59th) NYC 10022
Hours: 9-5 Mon-Fri
"China, crystal, ceramic and porcelain statues; also outdoor furniture; will rent." ed.

Mixing Times Ltd. 212-595-1505
2403 Broadway (88-89th) NYC 10024
Hours: 11-7 Tues-Sat/ 12-7 Sun
"Good selection old glassware and silverware; sets and singles; reasonable." ed.

Mixon, Aris & Co. 212-724-6904
381 Amsterdam Ave. (78-79th) NYC 10024
Hours: 12-7 Mon-Fri/ 11-6 Sat/ 2-6 Sun
"Excellent, expensive antique glassware and silverware; sets and singles." ed.

Pottery Barn

231 Tenth Ave. (24th) NYC 10011 (Main Store) 212-741-9120
Hours: 10-6:30 Mon-Sat/ 11-6 Sun

250 West 57th St. (8th) NYC 10107 212-741-9145
Hours: 10-7 Mon-Sat/ 12-6 Sun

117 East 59th St. (Lexington-Park) NYC 10022 212-741-9132
Hours: 10-6:30 Mon-Sat (Mon, Thurs til 8:30)/ 12-5 Sun

2109 Broadway (73-74th) NYC 10023 212-741-9123
Hours: 11-8 Mon-Sat/ 12-5 Sun

1451 2nd Ave. (76th) NYC 10021 212-741-9142
Hours: 10:30-7:30 Mon-Fri/ 10:30-6:30 Sat/ 12-6 Sun

1292 Lexington Ave. (87-88th) NYC 10128 212-741-9134
Hours: 10-6:30 Mon-Sat/ 12-6 Sun
"Good selection glassware; also ironstone, housewares, baskets." ed.

D. F. Sanders & Co.
386 W. Broadway (Spring-Broome) NYC 10012 212-925-9040
Hours: 11:30-7 Mon-Sat/ 12-5:30 Sun
952 Madison Ave. (75th) NYC 10021 212-879-6161
Hours: 10:30-6 Mon-Fri/ 11-6 Sat, Sun
"High tech supermarket: china, housewares, kitchenware, furniture."

Carole Stupell Ltd. 212-260-3100
61 East 57th St. (Madison-Park) NYC 10022
Hours: 9:30-6 Mon-Sat
"Fine china and crystal; will rent." ed.

Tiffany & Co. 212-755-8000
727 Fifth Ave. (57th) NYC 10022
Hours: 10-5:30 Mon-Sat
"Fine china, crystal, silver, clocks, watches, jewelry; the very best."

Wooden Indian Antiques 212-243-8590
60 West 15th St. (5-6th) NYC 10011
Hours: 11-7 Mon-Sat/ 12-6 Sun
"Used glassware, fountain/restaurant dishware; sets and singles." ed.

CLEANERS: CARPET, DRAPERY & UPHOLSTERY

Acme Carpet Cleaning 212-279-1448
241 West 17th St. (7-8th) NYC 10011
Hours: 9-5 Mon-Fri
"Expert repair of special rugs." ed.

Adler Rug Cleaning 718-328-4433
644 Whittier St. (off Randel) Bronx 10474
Hours: 9-5 Mon-Fri
"Carpet cleaners." ed.

Central Carpet Cleaning 212-567-9200
301 Norman Ave. (Morgan-Sutton) Bklyn 11222
Hours: 9-5 Mon-Fri
"Cleaners of carpet." ed.

General Drapery Services 212-924-7200
635 West 23rd St. (11-12th) NYC 10011
Hours: 9-4 Mon-Fri
"Cleaners, fireproofing service." ed.

Nemati Parviz 212-861-6700
790 Madison Ave. 2nd Fl. (67th) NYC 10021
Hours: 9-6 Mon-Fri/ 11-5 Sat
"All weaving and cleaning done by hand." ed.

REYNOLDS DRAPERY SERVICE INC. 315-845-8632
7440 Main St., Newport, NY 13416
Hours: 8-4 Mon-Fri

We manufacture and service theatrical draperies. Our service includes flameproofing, drycleaning and custom repair. (5 year flameproof guarantee in writing)

"Also curtain tracks and rigging." ed.

Helene Von Rosentiel Inc. 718-788-7909
382 11th St. (5-6th) Bklyn 11215
Hours: By appt.
"Cleaning & repairing of antique fabrics, drapery, rugs, clothing." ed.

CLEANERS: CLOTHING see DRYCLEANERS

CLEANERS: LEATHER & FUR

Leathercraft Process Corp. 212-586-3737
62 West 37th St. (5-6th) NYC 10018 212-564-8980
Hours: 9-5:30 Mon-Fri/ 9:30-1:45 Sat
"Costume services-dry cleaners, leather cleaners; free pick-up." ed.

R & S Cleaners Inc. 212-475-9412
188 Second Ave. (12th) NYC 10003
Hours: 7:30-6:30 Mon-Fri/ 7:30-5 Sat
"Costume, leather." ed.

US Fur Cleaners Inc. 212-736-4777
208 West 29th St. (7-8th) NYC 10001
Hours: 8-4 Mon-Fri
"Fur cleaners; pick-up and delivery." ed.

CLOCKS

Clock Hutt 212-759-2395
1050 Second Ave. (55-56th) NYC 10022
Hours: 10:30-5:30 Mon-Sat/ 1-5:30 Sun
"Antique clocks; will rent." ed.

Cuckoo Clock Mfg. Co. 212-255-5133
32 West 25th St. (5th) NYC 10010
Hours: 9-5 Mon-Fri
"Low cost cuckoo clocks to the trade; repairs." ed.

Niccolini Antiques - Prop Rentals 212-254-2900
114 East 25th St. (Park-Lexington) NYC 10010
Hours: 10-5 Mon-Fri/ 12-3 Sat/ or by appt.
"Antique clocks, furniture; rent or sell; see Ronnie or Rita." ed.

Sutton Clock Shop 212-758-2260
139 East 61st St. (Lexington) NYC 10021
Hours: 11-5 Mon-Fri
"Antique clock rental and purchase." ed.

Tic Tock Clock Co. 212-247-1470
763 Ninth Ave. (51-52nd) NYC 10019
Hours: 10-6 Tues-Fri/ 10-4 Sat
"New and used, antique and modern clocks; will rent." ed.

CLOTHING ACCESSORIES: BELTS & SUSPENDERS

Bond Street Suspender & Belt Corp. 718-361-8070
34-01 38th Ave. L.I.C. 11101
Hours: 9-5 Mon-Fri
"Suspenders by the dozen." ed.

Abraham Boxer 212-689-3210
34 West 27th St. 6th Fl. (6th-B'way) NYC 10001
Hours: 8:30-5 Mon-Fri
"Suspenders made to order; stock of clip and button suspenders." ed.

Reiter Brothers 212-226-4062
473 Broadway (Broome-Grand) NYC 10013
Hours: 8-4 Mon-Fri
"Suspenders wholesale by the dozen." ed.

Triumph Belt Inc. 212-564-5700
555 Eighth Ave. 24th Fl. (37-38th) NYC 10018
Hours: 9-5 Mon-Fri
"Manufacturer of ladies belts and novelties; covered belts while-you-wait." ed.

CLOTHING ACCESSORIES: BOOTS & SHOES

Anello & Davide Ltd. Theatrical Footwear 01-836-6744
30-35 Drury Lane, WC2, London, England
"Custom theatrical footwear; all period styles for men and women; can order by mail; catalog." ed.

Antique Shoes & Things Inc. 212-673-4532
18 First Ave. (Houston) NYC 10009
Hours: 12-7 Mon-Sat/ 12-6 Sun
"Never-worn antique shoes, 20's through 60's; also clocked socks and some clothing." ed.

G. Banks Theatrical & Custom Footwear 212-586-6476
320 West 48th St. (8-9th) NYC 10036
Hours: 9-5 Mon-Fri
"Excellent work, especially on one-of-a-kind items (moving Fall '85, check for new address)." ed.

Bloom Shoe Store 212-243-8749
311 Sixth Ave. (3rd St.) NYC 10014
Hours: 10-7:30 Mon-Thurs/ 10am-11pm Fri-Sat/ 2-6 Sun
"Men's and women's leather shoes, sandals, and cowboy boots; traditional." ed.

Der-Dav Custom Riding Boots & Shoes 718-856-6913
783 Coney Island Ave. Bklyn 11218
Hours: 9-5 Mon-Fri/ 9-2 Sat
"Boots to order; they make boots for Miller's and Kaufman's; can order direct for about 50% less." ed.

Freed of London Ltd. 212-489-1055
108 West 57th St. (6-7th) NYC 10019
Hours: 10-5:45 Mon-Sat (Mon, Thurs til 7)
"Specializes in dance shoes, also makes custom period shoes." ed.

Gold Seal Rubber Co. 212-564-3128
47 West 34th St. Rm. 725 (7th) NYC 10001
Hours: 9-5 Mon-Fri
"Call first; sneakers and boots." ed.

Joel Associates - On Stage 201-377-6466
PO Box 434, Madison, NJ 07940
Hours: By appt.
"Gamba shoes, custom period and dance shoes; catalog, good prices; will come to you for fittings." ed.

Kulyk Theatrical Footwear 212-674-0414
72 East 7th St. (1-2nd) NYC 10003
Hours: By appt.
"Ethnic and period shoes made to order; speak to Andre Kulyk." ed.

Lee's Mardi Gras Enterprises Inc. 212-947-7773
565 Tenth Ave. 2nd Fl. (41-42nd) NYC 10036
Hours: 12-6 Mon-Sat
"Ladies shoes for men; complete line of ladies apparel for men." ed.

Lord John Bootery 212-532-2579
428 Third Ave. (29-30th) NYC 10016
Hours: 9:30-6:30 Mon-Fri/ 9:30-5 Sat
"Cowboy boots, men's dress boots(high), period-looking men's and women's boots." ed.

McCreedy & Schreiber Boots & Shoes

37 West 46th St. (5-6th) NYC 10036 212-719-1552
Hours: 9-7 Mon-Sat (Thurs til 9)

213 East 59th St. (2-3rd) NYC 10022 212-759-9241
Hours: 9-7 Mon-Sat (Thurs til 9)/ 12-6 Sun

"High quality men's shoes and boots; good ankle lace-ups for period shoes; 19th-20th C." ed.

MONTANA LEATHERWORKS LTD. 212-431-4015
47 Greene St. (Grand-Broome) NYC 10013
Hours: 10-6 Mon-Fri
Theatrical footwear and leather accessories. Period boots and shoes for theatre, dance, opera, film. Custom work from your designs and measurements.
"See Sharlot Battin." ed.

Paradise Bootery 212-974-9855
1586 Broadway (47-48th) NYC 10036
Hours: 10:30-8 Mon-Sat
"Unique selection; character, specialty shoes; some custom work." ed.

Tall Size Shoes 212-736-2060
3 West 35th St. (5-6th) NYC 10001
Hours: 9:30-6 Mon-Sat (Thurs til 7)
"Women's large sizes." ed.

Tree Mark Shoe Co. Inc. 212-594-0720
27 West 35th St. (5-6th) NYC 10001
Hours: 9:30-7 Mon, Thurs/ 9:30-6 Tues, Wed, Fri, Sat
"Wide calf boots, all sizes, comfortable shoes for men (sizes 5-15) and women (sizes 3-12)." ed.

Van Doren Rubber Co. Inc. 714-772-8270
2220 Orangewood, Anaheim, CA 92806
Hours: 9-5 Mon-Fri
"Clown shoes." ed.

CLOTHING ACCESSORIES: COLLARS & CUFFS

Chandler Collar Replacement 212-962-7570
87 Nassau St. (Fulton-John) NYC 10038
Hours: 8-5 Mon-Fri
"Collar bands and collars." ed.

F. R. Tripler & Co. 212-922-1090
366 Madison Ave. (46th) NYC 10017
Hours: 9-5:45 Mon-Sat
"Excellent quality menswear, collarless 100% cotton shirts, and separate collars." ed.

CLOTHING ACCESSORIES: COSTUME JEWELRY

See also CLOTHING RENTAL & PURCHASE: ANTIQUE & VINTAGE
See also ETHNIC GOODS
For custom work, see COSTUME CRAFTSPEOPLE

American Costume Jewelry Novelty Co. 212-239-1222
104 West 29th St. (6-7th) NYC 10001
Hours: 9-5 Mon-Fri
"Costume jewelry." ed.

Dworkin & Daughter 212-988-3584
1214 Lexington Ave. (82nd) NYC 10028
Hours: 12:30-6 Mon-Sat
"Antique 19th-20th century jewelry, baby paraphernalia for rental; see Leslie." ed.

Louis Kipnis & Sons Inc. 212-674-7210
252 Broome St. (Ludlow-Orchard) NYC 10002 212-674-0397
Hours: 9:30-5 Sun-Fri
"Costume jewelry." ed.

La Belle Epoch 212-319-7870
211 East 60th St. (2-3rd) NYC 10022
Hours: 11:30-7 Mon-Fri/ 12-6 Sat
"Antique jewelry; will rent." ed.

Ellen O'Neill's 212-879-7330
242 East 77th St. (2-3rd) NYC 10021
Hours: 11-7 Mon-Sat/ 12-5 Sun
"Victorian trinkets, buttons, findings, trims." ed.

CLOTHING ACCESSORIES: EYEGLASSES

Economy Optical Co./Optical City 212-243-4884
135 West 14th St. (6-7th) NYC 10011
Hours: 10-6 Mon-Sat
"Modern frames and a few period frames." ed.

M. Eising & Co. 212-744-1270
1036 Lexington Ave. (74th) NYC 10021
Hours: 9:30-6 Mon-Sat (Wed til 7)
"Good selection period eyeglasses and pince-nez." ed.

The Eye Shop 212-673-9450
50 West 8th St. (6th Ave) NYC 10011
Hours: 9:30-7 Mon-Sat/ 11-6 Sun
"Good selection of styles; very friendly and helpful." ed.

E. B. Meyrowitz Inc.

40 Broad St. (Exchange Place) NYC 10038 212-267-3221
Hours: 8-5:45 Mon-Fri

520 Fifth Ave. (43-44th) NYC 10036 212-840-3880
Hours: 8:30-6 Mon-Fri/ 9:30-5 Sat

520 Madison Ave. (53-54th) NYC 10022 212-753-7536
Hours: 9-5:30 Mon-Fri/ 9-5 Sat

839 Madison Ave. (70th) NYC 10021 212-628-9202
Hours: 9-5:30 Mon-Fri/ 9-5 Sat

1171 Madison Ave. (86th) NYC 10028 212-744-6565
Hours: 9-5:30 Mon-Fri/ 9-5 Sat

"Modern eyeglasses and lorgnettes." ed.

Dr. M. Zimmet, Optometrist 212-246-5556
805 Eighth Ave. (48-49th) NYC 10019
Hours: 8:30-6 Mon-Fri/ 11-4 Sat
"Modern frames." ed.

CLOTHING ACCESSORIES: GLOVES

Colonial Gloves and Garments 516-968-8888
54 Penataquet Ave., Bayshore, NY 11706
Hours: 9-5 Mon-Fri
"See Victor and Vigdor." ed.

Finale Inc. 212-840-6255
15 West 37 St. (5-6th) NYC 10018
Hours: 9-4 Mon-Fri
"Vinyl, leather men's gloves; ladies gloves, including long lace." ed.

Glamour Glove Corp. 212-777-4633
902 Broadway (20-21st) NYC 10010
Hours: 9-5 Mon-Fri
"Wholesale gloves in volume, custom work, full fashion nylon gloves."

K & W Fashions 212-947-9380
40 West 37th St. 10th Fl. (5-6th) NYC 10018
Hours: 9-5 Mon-Fri
"Wholesale." ed.

Paul's Veil & Net Corp. 212-391-3822
66 West 38th St. (6-7th) NYC 10018 212-221-9083
Hours: 8:30-4:30 Mon-Fri
"Lace gloves." ed.

Sand & Siman Inc. 212-564-4484
34 West 32nd St. (B'way-5th) NYC 10001
Hours: 9-4:30 Mon-Fri
"Manufacturer white cotton gloves." ed.

CLOTHING ACCESSORIES: HANDBAGS

Ber-Sel Handbags 212-966-5517
79 Orchard St. (Grand-Broome) NYC 10002
Hours: 9:30-5:30 Sun-Fri
"Large selection ladies handbags." ed.

CLOTHING ACCESSORIES: HATS

See also COSTUME CRAFTSPEOPLE

Aegean Imports 415-593-8300
PO Box 1061, Belmont, CA 94002
"Greek fisherman's hats; quantity mail order only." ed.

American Uniform Headwear 201-943-0143
36 Anderson Ave., Fairview, NJ 07022
Hours: 9-4:30 Mon-Fri
"Large stock, made to order." ed.

Arden's 212-391-6968
1014 Sixth Ave. (37-38th) NYC 10018
Hours: 9:30-6 Mon-Fri/ 10-5 Sat
"Bridal crowns and veils, custom hats, bridal accessories." ed.

Bland's 303-573-6255
1554 California, Denver, CO 80202
Hours: By appt.
"Derbies, western hats." ed.

George Bollman & Co.

350 Fifth Ave. (34th) NYC 10118 — 212-564-6480
Hours: 9-5 Mon-Fri
"Wholesale." ed.

110 East Main, Adamstown, PA 19501 — 215-484-4361
Hours: 8-5 Mon-Fri
"Manufacturer of period hats." ed.

Gerry Cosby & Co. Inc. — 212-563-6464
3 Penn Plaza (32nd) NYC 10001
Hours: 9:30-8 Tues-Fri/ 9:30-6 Mon,Sat
"Sports hats." ed.

Dobbs Hats — 212-582-8650
1290 Sixth Ave. #1449 (51-52nd) NYC 10019
Hours: 9-5 Mon-Fri
"Wholesale, contemporary men's hats." ed.

Fibre-Metal Products Co. — 215-459-5300
Baltimore Pike, Concordville, PA 19331
Hours: 8-5 Mon-Fri
"Hard hats." ed.

Grey Owl Indian Crafts — 718-464-9300
113-15 Springfield Blvd., Queens Village, NY 11429
Hours: 9-5 Mon-Fri
"Kits for American Indian headdresses and crafts; catalog." ed.

Hat/Cap Exchange — 301-348-2244
Fourth & Main Sts., PO Box 266, Betterton, MD 21610
Hours: 10-6 Mon-Fri
"Wholesale hats, good prices; extra charge for split cartons." ed.

HATCRAFTERS — 215-623-2620
20 North Springfield Rd., Clifton Heights, PA 19018
Hours: 8-4:30 Mon-Fri
Theatrical hats. Military reproductions. In-stock service. Custom design to specifications. Professional discounts.
"Formerly Haentze Hatcrafters; good service." ed.

James & Sons Costumiers — 215-922-7409
1230 Arch, Philadelphia, PA 19107
"Period military headgear (especially Civil War); will rent." ed.

J. J. Hat Center — 212-244-8860
1276 Broadway (32-33rd) NYC 10001
Hours: 8:45-5:30 Mon-Sat
"Stetson hats." ed.

Keystone Uniform Cap 215-922-5493
428 North 13th St., Philadelphia, PA 19123
Hours: 8-4 Mon-Fri
"Uniform hats." ed.

Krieger Top Hats 516-599-3188
410 Sunrise Highway, Lynbrook, NY 11563
Hours: 9-5 Mon-Fri/ or by appt.
"Top hats, collapsible top hats, custom work; inexpensive." ed.

Langenberg Hat 314-422-3377
Box 38, Vienna, MO 65582
Hours: 7:30-4:15 Mon-Fri
"Period hats." ed.

Liberty Cap & Hat Mfg. Co. Inc. 718-456-6644
56 Bogart Bklyn 11206
Hours: 8-4:15 Mon-Fri
"Manufacturer of basic caps; men's and boy's." ed.

Jay Lord Hatters 212-221-8941
30 West 39th St. (5-6th) NYC 10018
Hours: 9:30-6 Mon-Fri/ 10-5 Sat
"Stock and custom men's hats; good quality, difficult to deal with." ed.

Max Millinery Center 212-221-8896
13 West 38th St. (5-6th) NYC 10018
Hours: 9:30-5:30 Mon-Fri/ 10-4:30 Sat
"Trim, artificial flowers, jewels, millinery supplies; custom bridal and evening hats; see Tara." ed.

Ernie Meckley's New Hat Shop 215-678-0160
Mountain Home Road, Sinking Spring, PA 19608
Hours: 11-6 Mon-Thurs/ 11-8 Fri
"A wide variety of men's hats at great prices; western, Amish, top hats, bowlers, caps, etc." ed.

Plume Trading Co. 914-782-8594
PO Box 585, Rt. 208, Monroe, NY 10950
Hours: 9-5 Mon-Fri
"Kits for American Indian headgear, crafts; great catalog." ed.

Rochelle Millinery 212-593-3232
700 Madison Ave. (62-63rd) NYC 10021
Hours: 10-5 Mon-Fri
"Chic ladies' streetwear." ed.

Roth Import Co. 212-840-1945
13 West 38th St. (5-6th) NYC 10018
Hours: 9-5:30 Mon-Fri
"Millinery for theatre, streetwear, bridal; costume trimmings." ed.

Sacred Feather — 608-255-2071
417 State, Madison, WI 53703
Hours: 10-6 Mon-Sat
"Derbies, toppers; no catalog." ed.

Scott Hatters Inc.

620 Eighth Ave. (40-41st) NYC 10018 (main store) — 212-840-2130
Hours: 9-7:15 Mon-Sat

201 West 42nd St. (7-8th) NYC 10036 — 212-947-3455
Hours: 9-9 Mon-Sat/ 10:30-6:30 Sun

"Wide range of men's hats, including bowlers; seasonal." ed.

Stetson Hat Co. — 816-483-8889
1775 Universal, Kansas City, MO 64120
Hours: By appt.
"Derbies, toppers, western hats." ed.

Stokes Cap & Regalia — 416-444-1188
475 Ellsmere, Scarborough, Ontario, Canada M1R4E5
Hours: 8:30-4:15 Mon-Fri
"Uniform headgear." ed.

VanDyke Hatters — 212-929-5696
90 Greenwich Ave. (12th) NYC 10011
Hours: 7:30-6 Mon-Sat
"Stetson, Borsalino, western, and house brand hats; also clean and block hats." ed.

CLOTHING ACCESSORIES: UMBRELLAS & CANES

Essex Umbrella Corp. — 212-674-3394
101 Essex St. (near Delancey) NYC 10002
Hours: 9-5:30 Mon-Fri/ 9-4:30 Sun
"Inexpensive." ed.

Peerless Umbrella — 212-239-0021
6 West 32nd St. (5-6th) NYC 10001
Hours: 9-5 Mon-Fri
"Made to order; see Mrs. Moskowitz." ed.

Uncle Sam Umbrella Shop

7 East 46th St. (5th) NYC 10017 — 212-687-4780
Hours: 9-5:45 Mon-Fri/ 10-5 Sat

161 West 57th St. (6-7th) NYC 10019 — 212-247-7163
Hours: 9-5:45 Mon-Fri/ 9-5 Sat — 212-582-1976

"Wide selection every type imaginable: custom umbrellas, walking sticks." ed.

CLOTHING RENTAL & PURCHASE: ANTIQUE & VINTAGE

See also THRIFT SHOPS
For military surplus, see CLOTHING RENTAL & PURCHASE: UNIFORMS

Added Treasures 212-889-1776
577 Second Ave. (31-32nd) NYC 10016
Hours: By appt.
"Antique clothing, jewelry, magazines, glassware." ed.

Alice's Underground 212-724-6682
380 Columbus Ave. (78th) NYC 10024
Hours: 12-8 every day.
"Vintage clothing, accessories and linens; retail, reasonably priced, good condition." ed.

Andy's Chee-Pees

14 St. Marks Place (2-3rd) NYC 10003 212-674-9248
Hours: 11-8 Mon-Sat/ 12-7 Sun

16 West 8th St. (5-6th) NYC 10011 212-460-8488
Hours: 11-8 Mon-Sat/ 12-7 Sun

"Wholesale, retail antique clothing and jeans, army surplus." ed.

Anichini Gallery 212-982-7274
7 East 20th St. (B'way) NYC 10003
Hours: By appt.
"Excellent period clothing, accessories, linens and lace; see Patrizia or Susan." ed.

Antique Shoes & Things Inc. 212-673-4532
18 First Ave. (Houston) NYC 10009
Hours: 12-7 Mon-Sat/ 12-6 Sun
"1930's through 60's, never worn shoes for men and women." ed.

The Best of Everything Ltd. 212-734-2492
307 East 77th St. (1-2nd) NYC 10021
Hours: 11-8 Mon-Fri/ 11-6:30 Sat, Sun
"Mostly ladies 20th century clothing, some jewelry." ed.

Bogies Antique Furs & Clothing 212-260-1199
201 East 10th St. (1-2nd) NYC 10003
Hours: 12:30-5:30 Mon-Sat
"30's-60's men's & women's vintage clothing; reasonably priced." ed.

Brascomb & Schwab

148 Second Ave. (9-10th) NYC 10003 212-777-5363
Hours: 12-7 Mon-Sat/ 1-6 Sun
"20's&30's dresses, bags, belts; 40's&50's men's shirts, pants." ed.

247 East 10th St. (1st Ave.) NYC 10003 212-254-3168
Hours: 2-7 Mon-Sat/ 1-6 Sun
"40's & 50's clothing." ed.

D/L Cerney 212-673-7033
13 East 7th St. (2-3rd) NYC 10003
Hours: 12-8 Tues-Sun
"Never-worn vintage clothing." ed.

CHEAP JACK'S VINTAGE CLOTHING

167 First Ave. (10-11th) NYC 10003 212-473-9599
Hours: 11-8 Mon-Sat/ 12-6 Sun

841 Broadway (13-14th) NYC 10003 212-777-9564
Hours: 11-8 Mon-Sat/ 12-6 Sun
Cheap! Cheap! Retail - Wholesale - Rentals
(See display ad page 69.)
"Really good prices." ed.

EARLY HALLOWEEN 212-691-2933
10 West 19th St. (5-6th) NYC 10011 212-243-1499
Hours: 12-6 Mon-Fri
Men's, women's & children's clothing, shoes, hats, accessories.
"Also vintage luggage, kitchenware, memorabilia." ed.

Fonda Boutique 212-759-3260
209 East 60th St. (2-3rd) NYC 10022
Hours: 11-7 Mon-Sat/ call for Sun hours
"Victorian and 20th Century clothing, also makes new clothes from antique fabric." ed.

Ian's Boutique Inc.

5 St. Marks Place (2-3rd) NYC 10003 212-420-1857
1151 Second Ave. (60-61st) NYC 10021 212-838-3969

Hours: 12-7 Mon-Sat
"Punk clothing." ed.

Gene London 212-533-4105
106 East 19th St. 9th Fl. (Irving-Park) NYC 10003
Hours: By appt.
"Rents men's and women's clothing from 1800's to 50's & 60's." ed.

Harriet Love 212-966-2280
412 West Broadway (Spring-Prince) NYC 10012
Hours: 12-7 Tues-Sat/ 1-6 Sun
"Antique clothing, lingerie, linens and accessories." ed.

Love Saves the Day 212-228-3802
119 Second Ave. (7th) NYC 10003
Hours: 12-11 Mon-Thurs/ 12-midnight Fri,Sat/ 1-8 Sun
"Affordable vintage clothing." ed.

110 West Antiques 212-505-0508
110 West Houston St. (Sullivan & Thompson) NYC 10012
Hours: 12-7 Wed-Sun
"A collection of kimonos, furs and other antique clothing." ed.

Ellen O'Neill's 212-879-7330
242 East 77th St. NYC 10021
Hours: 11-7 Mon-Sat/ 12-5 Sun
"Victorian trims, jewelry and lingerie." ed.

Panache Antique Clothing 212-242-5115
525 Hudson St. (10th-Charles) NYC 10014
Hours: 12-7 every day.
"Good quality men's and ladies wear, 30's to 50's; see Annie." ed.

Pentimenti 212-226-4354
126 Prince St. (Wooster-Greene) NYC 10012
Hours: 2:30-6 Tues-Sat
"Formerly East Bank." ed.

Edward Preston 212-989-7945
26 Cornelia St. (W. 4th) NYC 10014
Hours: Call for hours.
"Victorian and 20th Century clothing." ed.

Robert Pusilo Studio 212-675-2179
255 West 18th St. (7-8th) NYC 10011
Hours: By appt.
"Rental; 1880-1950 clothing for film and commercials only." ed.

Reminiscence Inc. 212-243-2292
74 Fifth Ave. (13th) NYC 10011
Hours: 12:30-8 Mon-Sat
"50's and later clothing and jewelry." ed.

Screaming Mimi 212-362-3158
100 West 83rd St. (Columbus-Amsterdam) NYC 10024
Hours: 11-7 Mon-Sat/ 12-6 Sun
"50's and punk." ed.

The Second Coming Ltd. 212-431-4424
72 Greene St. (Spring-Broome) NYC 10012
Hours: 12-7 Mon-Sat/ 1-6 Sun
"Good quality men's and women's clothing and never-worn shoes; 30's, 40's, & 50's." ed.

JACK SILVER 212-582-3298
1780 Broadway Rm. 303 (57-58th) NYC 10019 212-582-3389
Hours: 9-6 Mon-Fri/ 11-3 Sat
(See display ad page 75.)
"Extensive selection of period attire." ed.

Jana Starr 212-861-8256
236 East 80th St. (2-3rd) NYC 10021
Hours: 12-6:30 Mon-Sat
"Clothing, lace jewelry, collectibles." ed.

Trash & Vaudeville Inc. 212-982-3590
4 Saint Marks Place (2-3rd) NYC 10003
Hours: 12-8 Mon-Thurs/ 11:30-8 Fri/ 11-8 Sat/ 1-7 Sun
"Punk and 50's; wholesale or retail." ed.

Richard Utilla

112 Christopher St. (Bleecker) NYC 10014 212-929-7059
Hours: 11-6:30 Mon-Thurs/ 11-10:30 Fri,Sat/ 12-5:30 Sun
"Men's and women's clothing and accessories; 30's and onwards." ed.

244 East 60th St. (2-3rd) NYC 10022 212-737-6673
Hours: 11-6:30 Mon-Sat
"Mostly jewelry." ed.

Victoria Falls 212-254-2433
451 W. Broadway (Houston-Prince) NYC 10012
Hours: 12-7 Mon-Sat/ 1-6:30 Sun
"New clothes and lingerie from antique fabrics." ed.

CLOTHING RENTAL & PURCHASE: DANCEWEAR

See also CLOTHING ACCESSORIES: BOOTS & SHOES
See also COSTUME SHOPS

Bal-Toggery Knits Inc. 718-937-2400
43-10 23rd St. (43-44th Ave) L.I.C. 11101
Hours: 9-4:30 Mon-Fri/ 9-12:30 Sat
"Leotards, unitards, tights, Lycra, cotton Lycra; manufacturer." ed.

Capezio Dance-Theatre Shop 212-245-2130
755 Seventh Ave. (50th) NYC 10019
Hours: 9:30-5:45 Mon-Sat (Thurs til 7:30)
"Dancewear, shoes, large selection; call ahead for large orders." ed.

Capezio East 212-758-8833
136 East 61st St. (Lexington) NYC 10021
Hours: 10:30-6 Mon-Sat
"Dancewear." ed.

Capezio in the Village 212-477-5634
177 MacDougal St. (8th) NYC 10011
Hours: 12-8 Mon-Sat
"Dancewear, shoes, casual streetwear; buyer is Bob Welter." ed.

Capezio Wholesale Shoes 212-751-2828
717 Fifth Ave. (56th) NYC 10022
Hours: By appt.
"Showroom; street shoes, fashion shoes; salesperson on Wed's only."

Danskin Inc. 212-736-1006
350 Fifth Ave. (34th) NYC 10118
Hours: 9-5 Mon-Thurs/ 9-12 Fri/ by appt.
"Showroom for buyers; new styles of dancewear." ed.

Herbert Dancewear Co. 212-677-7606
902 Broadway 18th Fl. (20-21st) NYC 10010
Hours: 9-5 Mon-Fri/ 9-1 Sat
"Leotards, tights, Lycra." ed.

S & S Hosiery 212-586-3288
156 West 50th St. (6-7th) NYC 10019
Hours: 8:30-6:30 Mon-Fri/ 10:30-5:30 Sat
"Stockings, black and white tights, leotards, ladies' undergarments."

Taffy's Dancewear 212-586-5140
1776 Broadway 2nd Fl. (57th) NYC 10019
Hours: 10-5:45 Mon-Fri (Thurs til 8)/ 10-5 Sat
"Leotards, tights, unitards, cotton lycra." ed.

CLOTHING RENTAL & PURCHASE: ECCLESIASTICAL

See also COSTUME SHOPS

C. M. Almy & Son Inc. 914-967-6040
37 Purchase St. (near Rye train station) Rye, NY 10580
Hours: 9-5 Mon-Fri/ by appt.
"Vestments, sacred vessels; catalog; 2 week delivery." ed.

Bentley & Simon 212-695-0554
450 Seventh Ave. (34-35th) NYC 10123
Hours: 8:30-4:30 Mon, Wed, Fri
"Custom ecclesiastical clothing and choir robes." ed.

Craft Clerical Clothes 212-764-6122
247 West 37th St. 17th Fl. (7-8th) NYC 10018
Hours: 9:30-6 Mon-Fri/ 9:30-3 Sat
"Clothing; clerical." ed.

Duffy & Quinn Inc. 212-688-2885
366 Fifth Ave. (34th) NYC 10001
Hours: 9-5:30 Mon-Fri/ 9:30-2 Sat
"Clerical garb; not cheap; call first." ed.

Holy Land Art Co. Inc. 212-962-2130
160 Chambers (Greenwich St.) NYC 10007
Hours: 9-4:30 Mon-Thurs/ 9-4 Fri/ 9-2 Sat (Thanksgiving-Xmas)
"Clothing; clerical, etc; vestment materials; helpful." ed.

J. Levine Co. 212-966-4460
58 Eldridge St. (Hester-Canal) NYC 10002
Hours: 9-5:30 Mon-Thurs/ 9-1:30 Fri/ 9-5 Sun
"Prayer shawls, yarmulkas, lots of books." ed.

CLOTHING RENTAL & PURCHASE: FORMAL WEAR

See also COSTUME SHOPS

David's Outfitters Inc. 212-691-7388
36 West 20th St. (5-6th) NYC 10011
Hours: 9-5 Mon-Fri
"Formal wear and all types of uniforms for rent only" ed.

First Nighter Formals 212-675-5550
5 West 22nd St. (5th) NYC 10010
Hours: 8-4:30 Mon-Thurs/ 8-3 Fri
"New tailcoats in black and white, gloves" ed.

Herman's Formal Wear 212-245-2277
1190 Sixth Ave. (46-47th) NYC 10036
Hours: 9-6 Mon-Fri/ 9-4:30 Sat
"See Sid Tishman" ed.

Jack & Co. 212-722-4455
128 East 86th St. (Lexington-Park) NYC 10028 212-722-4609
Hours: 10-7 Mon-Fri/ 10-4 Sat
"Complete line of formal wear and accessories; rental and sales" ed.

Kasbah 212-982-8077
85 Second Ave. (5th St.) NYC 10003
Hours: 12:30-6:30 Mon-Sat
"Tailcoats, uniforms, inexpensive" ed.

Mel's Lexington Formal Wear 212-867-4420
129 East 45th St. (Lexington) NYC 10017
Hours: 8:30-7 Mon-Fri/ 9-3:30 Sat
"Formal clothing and accessories, men's & boy's; rental & sales" ed.

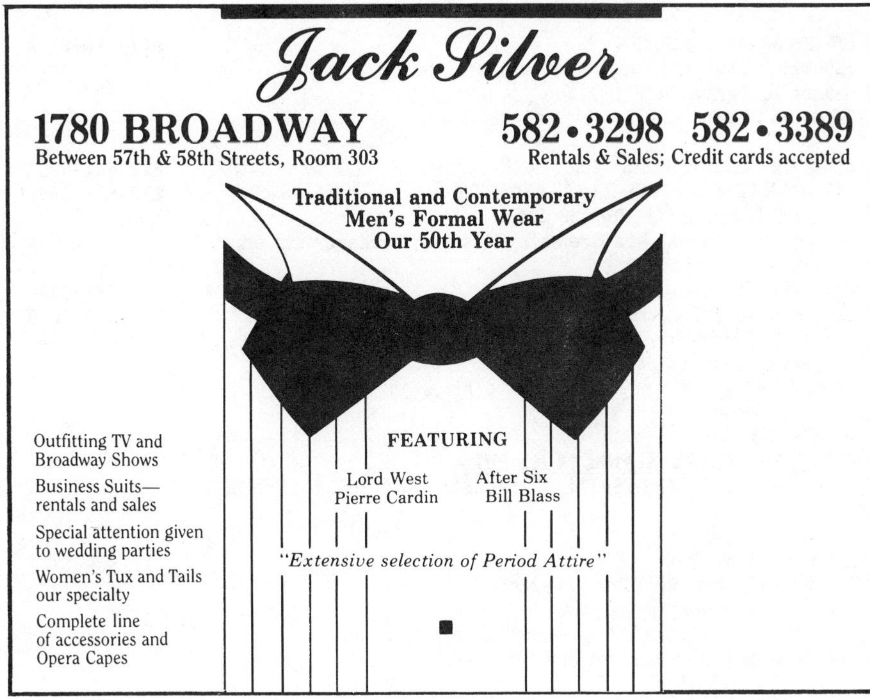
Jack Silver
1780 BROADWAY
Between 57th & 58th Streets, Room 303
582•3298 582•3389
Rentals & Sales; Credit cards accepted
Traditional and Contemporary
Men's Formal Wear
Our 50th Year
Outfitting TV and Broadway Shows
Business Suits—rentals and sales
Special attention given to wedding parties
Women's Tux and Tails our specialty
Complete line of accessories and Opera Capes
FEATURING
Lord West
Pierre Cardin
After Six
Bill Blass
"Extensive selection of Period Attire"

NOTES

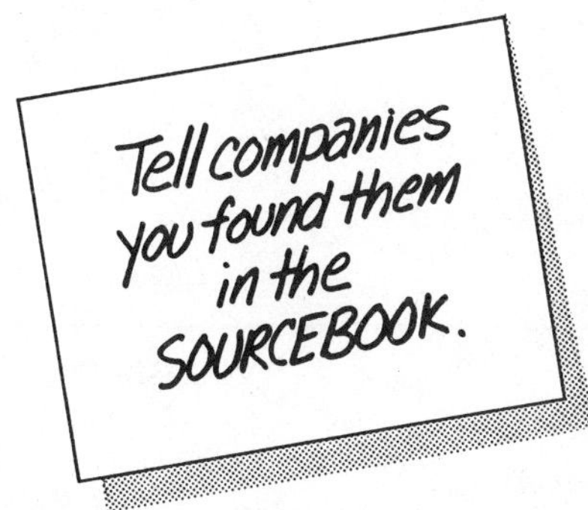
Tell companies you found them in the SOURCEBOOK.

Off-Broadway Boutique 212-724-6713
139 West 72nd St. (B'way-Columbus) NYC 10023
Hours: 10-8 Mon-Sat/ 1-7 Sun
"Women's tuxedos, collapsible top hats" ed.

S & L Dress Suit Rental Co. 212-582-4983
145 West 42nd St. (6th-B'way) NYC 10036 212-582-3858
Hours: 9-6 Mon-Fri/ 10-4:30 Sat
"Inexpensive formal wear rental; all sizes; accessories" ed.

JACK SILVER 212-582-3298
1780 Broadway Rm. 303 (57-58th) NYC 10019 212-582-3389
Hours: 9-6 Mon-Fri/ 11-3 Sat
(See display ad page 75.)
"Rental and sales; men's and women's tuxes and tails" ed.

CLOTHING RENTAL & PURCHASE: FURS

See also: CLOTHING RENTAL & PURCHASE: ANTIQUE & VINTAGE

ABET RENT-A-FUR 212-989-5757
307 Seventh Ave. Rm. 1203 (27-28th) NYC 10001
Hours: 9-4 Mon-Fri/ 9-1 Sat
Full stock of fine fur garments always on hand.
"Men's vintage raccoon, modern furs" ed.

Joseph Corn & Son Inc. 212-695-1635
141 West 28th St. (6-7th) NYC 10001
Hours: 10-6 Mon-Fri/ 10-5 Sat, Sun
"Secondhand furs; sales" ed.

CLOTHING RENTAL & PURCHASE: LADIES

See also COSTUME SHOPS
See also DEPARTMENT STORES
For specific types of clothing, see other headings in CLOTHING RENTAL & PURCHASE

Arthur Richards Ltd. 212-247-2300
91 Fifth Ave. 2nd Fl. (17-18th) NYC 10003
Hours: 10-5 every day
"Discount men's and women's suits; their own label" ed.

Forman's 212-228-2500
82 Orchard St. (Grand-Broome) NYC 10002
Hours: 9-6 Sun-Thurs/ 9-2 Fri
"Jones NY and classic styles at discounts" ed.

Gotham Wardrobe Rental (Bob Giraldi Prod.) 212-691-9200
581 Sixth Ave. (16-17th) NYC 10011
Hours: By appt.
"Wardrobe rental for contemporary clothes and accessories, men's or women's; see Connie Pavlounis." ed.

Lady Madonna Maternity Boutique 212-988-7173
793 Madison Ave. (67th) NYC 10021
Hours: 10:30-6 Mon-Sat (Thurs til 6:30)
"Fashionable maternity clothes." ed.

Rubicon Boutique Inc. 212-861-3000
849 Madison Ave. (70-71st) NYC 10021
Hours: 10-5:30 Mon-Sat
"New clothes with antique trim, bridal fittings and alteration." ed.

Saint Laurie Ltd. 212-473-0100
897 Broadway (20th) NYC 10003
Hours: 9-6 Mon-Sat (Thurs til 7:30)/ 12-5 Sun
"Discount prices; no rentals." ed.

The Scarlet Leather 212-255-1155
96 Christopher St. (Bleecker-Hudson) NYC 10014
Hours: 12-7 Tues-Sat
"Fast custom made leather goods; have leather fabric in stock." ed.

CLOTHING RENTAL & PURCHASE: LINGERIE

Alberts Hosiery

2113A Broadway (74th) NYC 10023 (main store) 212-595-5860
Hours: 9:30-6:30 Mon-Sat/ 12-5 Sun
"Complete line of lingerie, bras, corsets, leotards, unitards." ed.

20 West 43rd St. (5-6th) NYC 10036 212-719-5729
Hours: 8-6 Mon-Fri

600 Madison Ave. (57-58th) NYC 10022 212-755-6483
Hours: 8:30-6 Mon-Fri/ 10-5:30 Sat

611 Madison Ave. (58th) NYC 10022 212-753-7141
Hours: 9-6 Mon-Fri/ 10-5 Sat

925 Lexington Ave. (68th) NYC 10021 212-988-1195
Hours: 9-6:30 Mon-Fri/ 10-6 Sat

658 West 181 St. (B'way) NYC 10033 212-568-8600
Hours: 10-6:30 Mon-Sat

"Leotards, tights, seam stockings, pantyhose." ed.

Aileen Anderson Corset Shops Inc. 212-736-2338
977 Sixth Ave. (36th) NYC 10018
Hours: 9:30-5:30 Mon-Fri/ 9-4:30 Sat
"Corsets, bras, girdles." ed.

Brief Essentials 212-921-8344
1407 Broadway (38-39th) NYC 10018
Hours: 8:30-5:30 Mon-Fri
"All types of ladies lingerie." ed.

Cosmo Hosiery Shops 212-532-3111
425 Fifth Ave. (38th) NYC 10016
Hours: 9:30-6 Mon-Sat
"All types of ladies lingerie." ed.

Looking Too 212-874-0400
211 West 72nd St. (B'way-West End Ave.) NYC 10023
Hours: 11-7 Mon-Sat/ 1-6 Sun (Sun hours April, May, June)
"Elegant women's lingerie." ed.

Morris Trenk 212-674-3498
90 Orchard St. (Broome) NYC 10002
Hours: 9-5 Sun-Thurs/ 9-1 Fri
"Cotton lisle stockings, hosiery, underwear." ed.

The Village Corset Shop 212-473-1820
49 East 8th St. (University-B'way) NYC 10003
Hours: 10-6 Mon-Fri/ 11-7 Sat
"Women's lingerie; merry widows." ed.

Wifemistress 212-570-9529
1044 Lexington Ave. (74-75th) NYC 10021
Hours: 11-6:45 Mon-Fri/ 11-5:45 Sat
"Ladies lingerie." ed.

CLOTHING RENTAL & PURCHASE: MEN'S

See also COSTUME SHOPS
See also DEPARTMENT STORES
For specific types of clothing, see other headings in CLOTHING RENTAL & PURCHASE

Austin Ltd. 212-752-7903
140 East 55th St. (Lexington-3rd) NYC 10022
Hours: 10-6 Mon-Sat
"Men's clothing; rental to stylists for commercials; see Richard." ed.

Barney's New York 212-929-9000
106 Seventh Ave. (16-17th) NYC 10011
Hours: 10-9 Mon-Fri/ 10-8 Sat
"Quality contemporary men's clothing and accessories; pricey." ed.

BFO Plus Inc. 212-673-9026
149 Fifth Ave. 2nd Fl. (21st) NYC 10010
Hours: 9-5 every day
"Two floors of reasonably priced contemporary menswear." ed.

Blue & White Men's Shop Inc. 212-421-8424
50 East 58th St. (Park-Madison) NYC 10022
Hours: 10-6 Mon-Sat
"Wide selection of men's clothing." ed.

Bond Clothes 212-564-8310
1290 Broadway (33-34th) NYC 10001
Hours: 9:30-7 Mon-Fri (Mon, Thurs til 8)/ 9-6 Sat/ 12-5 Sun
"Big men's department on 2nd floor." ed.

Brooks Brothers 212-682-8800
346 Madison (44th) NYC 10017
Hours: 9:15-6 Mon-Sat
"The best in Ivy League menswear." ed.

Chips Men's Store 212-687-0850
14 East 44th St. (5th) NYC 10017
Hours: 9-5:45 Mon-Sat
"Men's suits, ties, pants, shirts, jackets; see Paul." ed.

Moe Ginsburg 212-242-3482
162 Fifth Ave. (21st) NYC 10010
Hours: 9:30-5:30 Mon-Sat (Thurs til 7:30)
"Discount men's clothing." ed.

Gotham Wardrobe Rental (Bob Giraldi Prod.) 212-691-9200
581 Sixth Ave. (16-17th) NYC 10011
Hours: By appt.
"Wardrobe rental for contemporary clothes and accessories, men's and women's; see Connie Pavlounis." ed.

Haar & Knobel Uniform Corp. 212-226-1812
49 Orchard St. (Grand-Hester) NYC 10002
Hours: 9-5 Sun-Thurs/ 9-2 Fri
"All sizes, 28"-56" waist sportswear; uniforms/industrial clothing."

Halstan II 212-496-8571
2056 Broadway (71st) NYC 10023
Hours: 10-9 Mon-Fri/ 10-7 Sat/ 12:30-6:30 Sun
"Men's designer clothing; excellent prices, good service." ed.

Imperial Wear Men's Clothing 212-719-2590
48 West 48th St. (5-6th) NYC 10036
Hours: 9-6 Mon-Sat (Thurs til 8)
"Tall sizes." ed.

Joseph M. Klein Tall Men's Stores 212-228-1166
118 Stanton St. (Essex) NYC 10002
Hours: 9-6 Mon-Fri/ 9-5 Sun
"Wide selection designer labels." ed.

Lee's Mardi Gras Enterprises Inc. 212-947-7773
565 Tenth Ave. 2nd Fl. (41-42nd) NYC 10036
Hours: 12-6 Mon-Sat
"Complete line ladies clothes for men, including shoes and wigs." ed.

London Majesty Inc. 212-221-1860
1211 Sixth Ave. (48th) NYC 10036
Hours: 9-6 Mon-Sat (Thurs til 8)
"Large sizes, variety of suits, pants and jackets." ed.

Mernsmart

75 Church St. (Vesey) NYC 10007 212-227-5471
Hours: 9:30-6:30 Mon-Fri/ 9:30-6 Sat
"Designer men's clothing, cut-rate." ed.

525 Madison Ave. (53-54th) NYC 10022 212-371-9175
Hours: 9:30-6:30 Mon-Fri (Thurs til 8)/ 9:30-6 Sat
"Also some women's clothes." ed.

David Rayne Ltd. 718-852-7866
130 Montague St. (Clinton-Henry) Bklyn 11201
Hours: 10-6:30 Mon-Fri (Thurs til 7)/ 10-6 Sat
"Outlet for Cardin, YSL, etc." ed.

Saint Laurie Ltd. 212-473-0100
897 Broadway (20th) NYC 10003
Hours: 9-6 Mon-Sat (Thurs til 7:30)/ 12-5 Sun
"Discount prices; no rentals." ed.

The Scarlet Leather 212-255-1155
96 Christopher St. (Bleecker-Hudson) NYC 10014
Hours: 12-7 Tues-Sat
"Custom made leather goods; fast." ed.

JACK SILVER 212-582-3298
1780 Broadway Rm. 303 (57-58th) NYC 10019 212-582-3389
Hours: 9-6 Mon-Fri/ 11-3 Sat
(See display ad page 75.)
"Business suits, formal wear and accessories; rental and sales." ed.

Sir George Ltd. 212-866-2700
2884 Broadway (112-113th) NYC 10025
Hours: 10-6:45 Mon-Sat
"Men's clothing; tailor at shop." ed.

Paul Stuart 212-682-0320
Madison Ave. at 45th (45th) NYC 10017
Hours: 8-6 Mon-Fri/ 9-6 Sat
"Beautiful, fashionable menswear." ed.

Superior Fashion Menswear 212-431-8505
85 Orchard St. (Grand-Broome) NYC 10002
Hours: 10-6 Mon-Thurs/ 10-4 Fri/ 9-6 Sun
"Shirts, accessories; designer shirts at reasonable prices." ed.

Syms Clothing 212-791-1199
45 Park Place (Church-W. B'way) NYC 10007
Hours: 9-7 Mon-Wed/ 9-8 Thurs, Fri/ 9-6 Sat
"Good selection men's, women's name-brand clothing; great prices."

F. R. Tripler & Co. 212-922-1090
366 Madison Ave. (46th) NYC 10017
Hours: 9-5:45 Mon-Sat
"Excellent quality menswear, 100% cotton collarless shirts with separate collars available." ed.

CLOTHING RENTAL & PURCHASE: SPORTS APPAREL

See also FENCING EQUIPMENT
See also RIDING EQUIPMENT
See also SPORTING GOODS

Arbee Men's Wear Inc. 212-737-4661
1598 Second Ave. (83rd) NYC 10028
Hours: 9-7 Mon-Fri/ 9-6 Sat
"Men's and boy's sport clothes and equipment." ed.

Eisner Brothers 212-475-6868
76 Orchard St. (Broome-Grand) NYC 10002
Hours: 9-6 Mon-Thurs/ 9-3:30 Fri/ 9-5 Sun
"Caps, t-shirts, sweatshirts, baseball, football, etc." ed.

H Bar C Ranchwear 212-924-5180
101 West 21st St. (6-7th) NYC 10011
Hours: 9-5 Mon-Fri
"Western clothing, sports clothes, manufacturer." ed.

Tepee Town Inc. 212-563-6430
Port Authority Bus Terminal (40-41st on 8th) NYC 10036
Hours: 8:30-6:30 Mon-Fri/ 9:30-6:30 Sat
"Indian goods and western wear." ed.

The Unique Clothing Warehouse 212-674-1767
718 Broadway (Washington-Waverly) NYC 10003
Hours: 10-9 Mon-Sat/ 12-8 Sun
"Modern casual dress, sportswear and parachute fabric clothes and accessories." ed.

CLOTHING RENTAL & PURCHASE: UNIFORMS

See also COSTUME SHOPS
See also POLICE EQUIPMENT

Academy Clothes Inc. 212-765-1440
1703 Broadway (54th) NYC 10019
Hours: 9-6 Mon-Fri
"Half-price tuxedoes, waiters, police, chauffer, hotel uniforms." ed.

Allan Uniform Rental 212-242-3338
738 Broadway (8th) NYC 10003
Hours: 10-7 Mon-Sat
"Army/Navy surplus clothing." ed.

Army & Navy Supply Stores 212-534-1600
1938 Third Ave. (107th) NYC 10029
Hours: 9:30-7 Mon-Fri
"Military clothing and surplus." ed.

Canal Army & Navy 212-334-9680
334 Canal St. (B'way-Church) NYC 10013
Hours: 10-6 every day
"Military clothing and surplus." ed.

Canal Jean Co. Inc.

304 Canal St. (B'way-Mercer) NYC 10013 212-431-8439
Hours: 10:30-8 every day

504 Broadway (Broome-Spring) NYC 10013 212-226-1130
Hours: 10-8 every day

"Some 50's and 60's clothing; also sportswear and military." ed.

The Cockpit 212-420-1600
627 Broadway 7th Fl. (Bleecker-Houston) NYC 10012
Hours: 11-4 Mon-Fri
"Great selection WW II-to-current aviation gear; great catalog." ed.

David's Outfitters Inc. 212-691-7388
36 West 20th St. (5-6th) NYC 10011
Hours: 9-5 Mon-Fri
"Formal wear and all types of uniforms; rental only." ed.

Haar & Knobel Uniform Corp. 212-226-1812
49 Orchard St. (Grand-Hester) NYC 10002
Hours: 9-5 Sun-Thurs/ 9-2 Fri
"Industrial uniforms, white ducks, large sizes." ed.

Hudson's 212-473-7320
105 Third Ave. (12-13th) NYC 10003 212-473-0981
Hours: 9:30-6:30 Mon-Sat/ 12-5 Sun
"New and used army clothing, painter's pants, camping outfits." ed.

KAUFMAN SURPLUS INC. ARMY & NAVY 212-757-5670
319 West 42nd St. (8-9th) NYC 10036
Hours: 9:30-6 Mon-Sat (open later some nights-call first)
Genuine military clothing, work clothes, jeans & boots.
"Hard-to-find military items. Helpful & reliable. Ask for Jim." ed.

Leitner Uniforms Inc. 212-267-8740
26 Bowery (1 blk below Canal) NYC 10013 212-267-8765
Hours: 9:30-6:30 Mon-Fri/ 10-6 Sat
"Contemporary Air Force and Navy officers uniforms, policemen, firemen, letter carriers, etc." ed.

Madison Men's Shop 212-741-9777
26 Eleventh Ave. (W. 15th) NYC 10011
Hours: 8-5:30 Mon-Fri/ 9-3:30 Sat
"Everything for the blue collar working person to wear; hard hats, work clothes, work boots, etc." ed.

Medicraft Shops Inc. 212-288-7128
1313 York Ave. (70th) NYC 10021
Hours: 9:30-6:30 Mon-Fri/ 10-6 Sat
"Medical clothing." ed.

Louis Nathin Inc. 212-962-4851
47 Bayard St. (Elizabeth-Bowery) NYC 10013
Hours: 9-5 Sun-Fri
"Secondhand clothing and uniforms, wholesale." ed.

O.K. Uniform Co. Inc. 212-966-1984
512 Broadway (Spring-Broome) NYC 10012 212-966-4733
Hours: 9:15-5:30 Mon-Thurs/ 9:30-4 Fri/ 11-4 Sun
"Service and industrial uniforms; purchase orders accepted on large orders." ed.

RELIABLE & FRANK'S NAVAL UNIFORMS 718-858-6033
106 Flushing Ave. (Adelphi St.-Carlton Ave.) Bklyn 11205
Hours: 9-5 Mon-Fri/ 9-4 Sat (closed Sat July-Aug)
New & used military clothing, insignias, equipment, etc.
"Good selection of real uniforms; good prices." ed.

Russell Uniform Co. 212-674-1400
44 East 20th St. (B'way-Park) NYC 10003
Hours: 9-4:30 Mon-Fri
"Police and firemen's uniforms." ed.

B. Schlesinger & Sons Inc. 212-206-8022
249 West 18th St. (7-8th) NYC 10011
Hours: 9-6 Mon-Fri/ 10-5 Sat
"Police and security guard uniforms." ed.

Supply Store NYFD 718-403-1635
250 Livingston (near Fulton) Bklyn 11201
Hours: 9-3 Mon-Fri
"Firemen's uniforms." ed.

The Trader 212-925-6610
385 Canal St. (Thompson-W. B'way) NYC 10013 212-925-6634
Hours: 10-7 every day
"Used uniforms and military clothing." ed.

Uniform World 718-981-4000
Oswald Place, Staten Island, NY 10309
Hours: 8-4:30 Mon-Fri
"Band uniforms, flight attendant uniforms, and career apparel; order ahead." ed.

Weiss & Mahoney 212-675-1915
142 Fifth Ave. (19-20th) NYC 10011 212-675-1367
Hours: 9-6 Mon-Fri/ 9-5 Sat
"Inexpensive military clothing and surplus goods; shoes, medals, camping attire and equipment." ed.

COINS & CURRENCY

Brigandi Coin Co. 212-869-5350
60 West 44th St. (5-6th) NYC 10036
Hours: 9:30-5:30 Mon-Fri
"Coin and paper money, including foreign.." ed.

Dory Duplicates 518-854-7613
PO Box W, Salem, NY 12865
"Mail order coin reproductions, many finishes available.." ed.

Eclectic Properties Inc. 212-799-8963
204 West 84th St. (B'way-Amsterdam) NYC 10024
Hours: 9-5 Mon-Fri/ or by appt.
"Coins and currency rental for motion pictures; see Suri.." ed.

Jules J. Karp 212-279-1024
372 Seventh Ave. (30-31st) NYC 10001
Hours: 9-5 Mon-Fri/ 10-3 Sat
"Rare coins and currency.." ed.

Lee Lee Coins 212-586-7782
32 West 47th St. (5-6th) NYC 10036
Hours: 9-3 Mon-Fri
"Coin and paper money, including foreign." ed.

Harmer Rooke 212-751-1900
3 East 57th St. (5th-Madison) NYC 10022
Hours: 10-5 Mon-Fri/ 10-2:30 Sat
"Rare coins, stamps, currency." ed.

COMPUTERS

Datel Stores of NY 212-921-0110
1211 Sixth Ave. (48th) NYC 10036
Hours: 8:30-5:30 Mon-Fri/ 10-4:30 Sat
"Rentals when available." ed.

P C Computer Rental 212-532-2555
1 Penn Plaza #4532 (7-8th) NYC 10001
Hours: 8-6 Mon-Fri
"Rents IBM PC's; will pick up and deliver." ed.

Personal Computer Service 212-206-1480
322 Eighth Ave. (26th) NYC 10001
Hours: 9-5:30 Mon-Fri
"Rents; needs 2-3 days notice; see Suzanne." ed.

Wolff Computer 212-307-6545
1841 Broadway (60th) NYC 10023
Hours: 8:30-5 Mon-Fri/ 10-3 Sat (1st & 3rd Sat of month)
"Rentals when available." ed.

CORK

For corks, see WINEMAKING SUPPLIES

Abetter Cork Co. 212-925-7755
262 Mott St. (Houston-Prince) NYC 10012
Hours: 8:30-5 Mon-Fri
"Large stock, various sizes, shapes, colors; inexpensive." ed.

American Star Cork Co. Inc. 718-388-7126
175 N. 9th St. (Driggs-Bedford) Bklyn 11211
Hours: 9-6 Mon-Fri
"Cork and tin pans." ed.

CONSOLIDATED DISPLAY CO. INC. 312-486-3040
4501 W. Cortez St., Chicago, IL 60651
Hours: 8-4:30 Mon-Fri

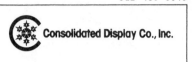

Snow blankets, glitters, foils, mylar, foliage, fabrics, Scatter Flakes® Snow.

"28 colors and styles of cork display flooring." ed.

Cork Products Co. Inc. 212-691-0960
19 West 21st St. (5th) NYC 10011
Hours: 9-5 Mon-Fri
"Cork and wallcoverings; wholesale." ed.

Wolf-Gordon Wallcovering Inc. 212-255-3300
132 West 21st St. (6-7th) NYC 10011
Hours: 9-4 Mon-Fri
"Wallcoverings: vinyl, cork; showroom." ed.

CORKS see WINEMAKING SUPPLIES

COSTUME CRAFTSPEOPLE

See also MASK MAKERS

Ronald E. Ames 212-242-4956
712 Washington St. #GA (11th-Perry) NYC 10014
Hours: By appt.
"Body puppets, jewelry, and millinery for stage, TV and promotion." ed.

Reggie Augustine 212-787-4176
100 West 72nd St. #4C (Columbus) NYC 10023
Hours: By appt.
"Freelance milliner; fashion, period hats, novelty items." ed.

Joseph Bigelow 914-477-3864
RR 4, PO Box 291A, Greenwood Lake, NY 10925 212-586-0260
Hours: By appt.
"Manages Grace Costumes." ed.

GARY BROUWER 212-645-1615
100 West 23rd St. 2nd Fl. (6th) NYC 10011
Hours: By appt.

Fashion and theatrical millinery.

"Experienced milliner; everything from 7th Ave. to the circus." ed.

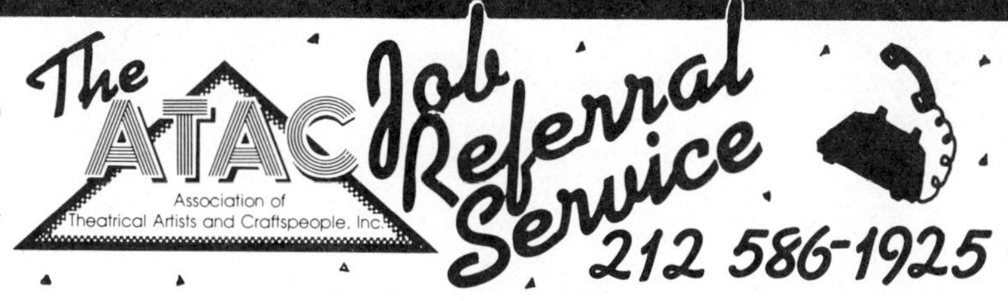

The ATAC Job Referral Service is a valuable resource that puts the prospective employer in contact with the right artists and craftspeople to meet their needs. Names and telephone numbers are provided. Not only does the Job Referral Service benefit the freelance artist but it offers the employer access to a diversified pool of creative talent.

Call the ATAC Job Referral Service (212) 586-1925

Hours: 10 a.m.-6 p.m. Mon.-Fri.

ATAC, The Association of Theatrical Artists and Craftspeople, is a professional trade association for craftspeople working in the production fields of entertainment, performance, and presentational media industries. Its membership represents many areas of expertise – props, special effects, puppets, display, shop management, design, etc. For more information on ATAC – Call (718) 596-0501.

** The Job Referral Service is administered by TAP — Technical Assistance Project — a professional service of the American Dance Festival.*

Production Design
Scenic Design
Art Direction
Costume Design
Stylists
Lighting Design
Scenic Artists
Mural Artists
Modelmakers
Specialty Prop
Specialty Costume
Special Effects
Crafts

for film, stage and television in the United States, Canada, and Britain

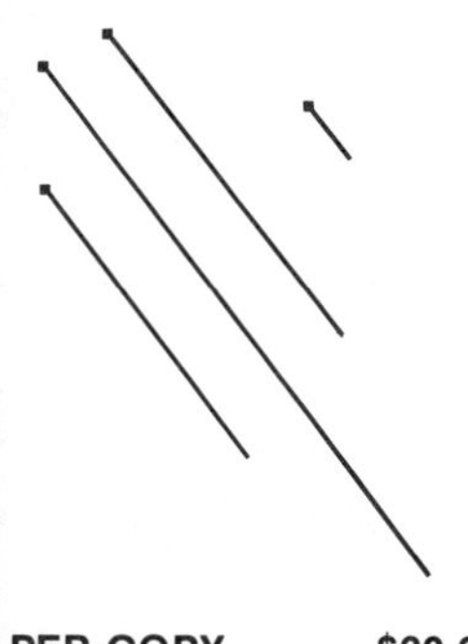

PER COPY	**$30.00**
POSTAGE & HANDLING	**$ 3.50**

NEW YORK RESIDENTS ADD SALES TAX

SEND FULL PAYMENT ALONG WITH NAME AND ADDRESS TO:

Lymelite Group Inc.
G.P.O. Box 1260
New York, N.Y. 10116

Register 85

ORDER YOUR COPY TODAY

Diane Chapman 212-719-5604
117 West 69th St. #1B (Columbus-B'way) NYC 10023 212-246-8484
Hours: By appt.
"Costume designer, specializing in special effects, period and fantasy costumes." ed.

Brenda Colling 718-383-3839
592 Manhattan Ave. #3L, Bklyn 11222
Hours: By appt.
"Costume designer: costumes for theatre, film, dance, video." ed.

Eileen Connor 212-246-6346
PO Box 154 Radio City Sta. NYC 10101
Hours: By appt.
"Scenic painting, fabric painting, prop and costume crafts, millinery/ headdresses." ed.

June DeCamp 212-568-9331
120 Haven Ave. #22 (172nd) NYC 10032
Hours: By appt.
"Scenic painting, trompe l'oeil, costume crafts." ed.

Janet Delvoye 201-985-7381
7 Suydam Ave. #2, Edison, NJ 08817
Hours: By appt.
"Jewelry, millinery, costume crafts." ed.

James Feng 212-499-1601
425 14th St. #A2 (8th) Bklyn 11215
Hours: By appt.
"Scenery, props, costumes, models designed, built and painted." ed.

Bruce E. Flesch, Artisan in Leather 212-673-7129
72 East 7th St. (1-2nd) NYC 10003
Hours: By appt.
"Leather accessories for theatrical purposes; repairs and alterations." ed.

FLYING ROBERT THEATRICAL CRAFTS 212-334-9130
101 Wooster St. (Spring) NYC 10012
Hours: By appt.
Specialty costumes & masks: foam rubber, celastic, latex rubber, etc. Duplication and multiples.
"Speak to Charles Kulziski." ed.

K. L. Fredericks 212-255-4539
203 West 20th St. (7th) NYC 10011
Hours: 10-6 Mon-Sat
"Designer, cutter, draper, upholsterer, dyer; wardrobe, dancewear, soft sculpture; own shop." ed.

Frank Frisbee 212-242-4956
712 Washington St. #GA (11th-Perry) NYC 10014
Hours: By appt.
"Body puppets and costume crafts for stage, TV and promotion." ed.

GIRARD DESIGNS/JANET GIRARD 212-782-6430
300 Morgan Ave. (Grand) Bklyn 11211
Hours: By appt.
Design and/or execution of custom designs on fabric & leather using airbrushing, handpainting, and quilting.
"Excellent quality." ed.

Elizabeth Goodall 212-477-6437
175 Bleecker St. #4 (MacDougal) NYC 10012
Hours: By appt.
"Prop making, scenic painting, sculpting, moldmaking, costume painting." ed.

Rodney Gordon 212-620-9018
39 West 14th St. Rm. 501 (5-6th) NYC 10001 718-522-7081
Hours: 10-6 Mon-Fri
"Costume crafts: specializing in millinery and masks." ed.

Joanne Green 212-989-1664
39 Charles St. #3 (7th Ave. S.) NYC 10014 212-794-2400
Hours: By appt.
"Costume props, especially millinery; puppet designer and builder."

Jerry Gum 718-788-2599
399 4th St. (6th) Bklyn 11215
Hours: By appt.
"Construction for foam and other full-body characters, costume draping." ed.

JANET HARPER STUDIO 212-966-1886
279 Church St. (White St.) NYC 10013
Hours: 10-6 Mon-Fri
Costume props. Masks. Specialty costumes including body puppets & animal costumes. Millinery. Jewelry.
"Theatre, film and promotional work." ed.

MARTIN IZQUIERDO STUDIO LTD. 212-807-9757
118 West 22nd St. 9th floor (6-7th) NYC 10011
Hours: By appt.
Costume painting, props, masks, silkscreening, creatures and graphic design. Rosco and Haussmann Distributor.
"Also sells English tutu net and tubular horsehair." ed.

Johns-Cronk Inc. 212-741-8161
39 West 19th St. 11th Fl. (5-6th) NYC 10011 212-741-8162
Hours: 9-5 Mon-Fri or by appt.
"Fabric painting, costume props, animal and novelty costumes; see Joni or Wes." ed.

Jan Kastendieck 212-962-1042
40 Harrison St. #14B (West St.) NYC 10013
Hours: By appt.
"Draper, patternmaker, cutter, dyer, upholstery, shop foreman." ed.

Janet Knechtel 01-431-1835
41 Florence St., London, England N1
Hours: By appt.
"Crafts: oversize cast shoes, specialty costumes, puppets, props." ed.

Bryan Kollman 212-505-1524
30 East 20th St. (B'way-Park Ave. S.) NYC 10003
Hours: By appt.
"Fine theatrical textile painting." ed.

Robin S. Kusten 718-789-1737
246 Vanderbilt Ave. (DeKalb) Bklyn 11205
Hours: 9-5 Mon-Fri
"Soft sculpture, 3-D illustration, props, sets, costumes." ed.

Larue 212-620-9018
14 West 39th St. Rm. 501 (5-6th) NYC 10001 212-477-3529
Hours: 10-6 Mon-Fri
"Costume design/production; promotional, theatrical; craftwork." ed.

Cathy Lazar Inc. 212-473-0363
155 East 23rd St. (Lexington-3rd) NYC 10010
Hours: By appt.
"Specialty costumes, soft props for TV, film, print, performance, promotion." ed.

Herbert Leith Design 201-871-9532
250 Walnut St. (Brayton St.) Englewood, NJ 07631
Hours: By appt.
"Specialty costumes, puppets, soft props, special effects for stage and film." ed.

Celeste Livingston 212-226-4182
57 Thompson St. #2C (Broome) NYC 10012
Hours: By appt.
"Draper." ed.

Marleen Marta 212-989-4684
25 Grove St. (Bedford-Bleecker) NYC 10014
Hours: By appt.
"Masks, props, scenic and costume painting, set decoration." ed.

KAREN McDUFFEE 718-643-1655
72A Fourth Ave. (Bergen) Bklyn 11217
Hours: By appt.
"Costume crafts, soft goods, shopping; prop co-ordination; prompt, reliable." ed.

Perry McLamb 212-265-1378
461 West 49th St. #2A (9-10th) NYC 10019
Hours: By appt.
"Humorous mechanical and wearable props, including special rigging."

Sherry McMorran 416-465-9752
31 Hampton Ave., Toronto, Ontario, Canada M4K2Y5
Hours: By appt.
"Costume supervisor, draper and design assistant." ed.

Maria R. McNamara 612-224-7267
677 Oakdale Ave., St. Paul, MN 55107
Hours: By appt.
"Puppets, props, masks, costume crafts." ed.

Stacey Morse 718-783-4375
42 Berkley Place (5-6th) Bklyn 11217
Hours: By appt.
"Animal/specialty costumes in foam, celastic, fabric; portraiture, character heads." ed.

Zoe Morsette 718-784-8894
11-14 46th Ave. #2-I (11th) L.I.C. 11101
Hours: By appt.
"Costume props, props, millinery, display, miniature work, soft sculpture." ed.

MULDER/GOODWIN INC. 212-689-9037
1200 Broadway #2C (29th) NYC 10001
Hours: 9-6 Mon-Fri
Custom made character and animal costumes for television, theatre and film.
(See display ad page 302.)
"See Mary Mulder or Rick Goodwin." ed.

FREDERICK NIHDA STUDIO 212-966-1886
279 Church St. (White St.) NYC 10013
Hours: 10-6 Mon-Fri
Custom Props & Costumes for Theatre, Film, Promotions, TV.
"Body puppets, masks, jewelry, armor, mechanisms and hand props." ed.

Randall Ouzts 212-288-1637
1390 Second Ave. #5B (72nd) NYC 10021
Hours: 11-7 Mon-Fri
"Costume designer for film, theatre, ballet." ed.

Dennis Paver 212-924-9411
41 Union Sq. West #206 (B'way-17th) NYC 10003
Hours: 10-6 Mon-Fri
"Costume design, construction, illustration; costumes, props for theatre, display." ed.

Enrique Plested 212-799-2950
126 Riverside Dr. #6A (85th) NYC 10024
Hours: By appt.
"Sculpting, moldmaking, casting, portraiture, model building, hand finishing of costumes." ed.

Rosemary Ponzo 718-932-1161
14-21 30th Dr. (21st) Astoria, NY 11102
Hours: By appt.
"Costume designer, fashion co-ordinator, fashion designer." ed.

J. Matthew Reeves 718-596-4293
105 Bergen St. (Smith-Hoyt) Bklyn 11201
Hours: By appt.
"Millinery and theatrical headdresses." ed.

Jody Schoffner 718-726-1476
20-59 36th St. (20th) Astoria, NY 11105
Hours: 9-6 Mon-Fri
"Draper for stage or specialty costumes, puppet maker." ed.

Linda C. Schultz 212-222-0477
125 West 96th St. #6J (Columbus-Amsterdam) NYC 10025
Hours: By appt.
"Costumer, stylist, wardrobe, cutter, draper, soft goods (props)." ed.

Jamie Paul Seguin 212-580-8275
355 West 85th St. #8 (Riverside Dr.) NYC 10024
Hours: By appt.
"Costume design: dance, theatre; shopper, wardrobe, make-up teacher."

Katherine Silverii 212-924-9411
41 Union Square W. (B'way-17th) NYC 10003
Hours: 10-6 Mon-Fri
"Designer and constructor of custom display and costume pieces." ed.

Daphne Stevens-Pascucci 212-724-9898
146 West 73rd St. #2B (Columbus) NYC 10023
Hours: By appt.
"Costume and scenic artist, fabric designing, painting, distressing, dyeing." ed.

RICHARD TAUTKUS 212-691-8253
100 West 23rd St. (6th) NYC 10011
Hours: By appt.
Theatrical Craftsman.
"Masks, millinery, etc.; specialty props." ed.

Jeffrey Ullman 212-929-5614
145 West 27th St. #4E (6-7th) NYC 10001
Hours: By appt.
"Costume designer and stylist; cutter, draper; home workshop." ed.

Jill Van Dyke 212-533-4192
154 East 7th St. #RW (Ave. A-B) NYC 10009
Hours: By appt.
"Fabric and costume painting, millinery." ed.

Linda Vigdor 212-289-1218
53 East 97th St. #1B (Madison) NYC 10029
Hours: By appt.
"Costume and fabric designer/ painter; specialty costumes." ed.

THE WINTER CO. INC. 718-499-2206
323 6th St. Top Fl. (5th Ave.) Bklyn 11215
Hours: By appt.
"Fine arts, costume crafts, props, custom exhibitry, electronics." ed.

Vernon Yates 212-666-4191
782 West End Ave. (96th) NYC 10025
Hours: By appt.
"Costume painter and dyer; small yardage orders." ed.

Louise Gartlemann Young 212-675-7497
243 West 21st St. #1D (21st) NYC 10011
Hours: 9-6 Mon-Fri
"Puppets, costume props, lifesized creatures, soft sculpture construction." ed.

Donna E. Zanki 303-364-5299
1923 Oswego St., Aurora, CO 80010
Hours: By appt.
"Costume crafts: leatherwork, footwear, masks, jewelry, armor." ed.

COSTUME SHOP & WARDROBE SUPPLIES, MISCELLANEOUS

See also DRESS FORMS
See also LABELS, WOVEN
See also SEWING MACHINE: SALES, SERVICE & PARTS
See also IRONS & STEAMERS
For garment racks and shelving, see SHELVING, METAL

AMERICAN HANGER & FIXTURE INC. 212-279-5280
520 West 27th St. (10-11th) NYC 10001
Hours: 9-5 Mon-Fri
Garment hangers, racks (rental & purchase), steamers, mannequins, plastic covers. Immediate delivery! Free catalog!
"THE place for coathangers; formerly 'Wally Hanger Co'." ed.

BAER FABRICS 502-583-5521
515 East Market, Louisville, KY 40202
Hours: 9-5:30 Mon-Sat
All workroom and dry cleaning supplies and equipment. (See display ad page 127.)
"Shipment within 24 hours for in-stock items." ed.

Bacig Mfg. Co. 718-871-6106
3611 14th Ave. Bklyn 11218
Hours: 9-5 Mon-Thurs/ 9-1 Fri
"Garment bags." ed.

C-Thru Ruler Co. 203-243-0303
6 Britton Drive, PO Box 356, Bloomfield, CT 06002
Hours: 9-4:30 Mon-Fri
"C-Thru plastic rulers." ed.

Costumer Service Co. 415-931-7349
1695 North Pointe #301, San Francisco, CA 94123
Hours: By appt.
"Iron Keepers- keep iron from falling off board." ed.

Housner Co. 212-244-1655
240 West 35th St. (7-8th) NYC 10001
Hours: 9-5 Mon-Fri
"Cardboard tags, stationers, printers; good prices." ed.

JAF Industries 212-868-2350
248 West 35th St. (7-8th) NYC 10001 212-563-3831
Hours: 9-5 Mon-Fri
"Plastic drycleaning bags by the roll." ed.

Mutual Hardware 718-361-2480
5-45 49th Ave. (Vernon Blvd.-East River) L.I.C. 11101
Hours: 8:30-5 Mon-Fri
"Canvas hampers on casters; main business is theatrical hardware; catalog." ed.

Pincover Industrial Supply Co. Inc. 212-926-1019
4730 Broadway (near G.W. Bridge) NYC 10040
Hours: 9:30-4:30 Mon-Fri
"Razorblades." ed.

Louis Price Paper Co. Inc. 212-564-3810
350 West 31st St. (8-9th) NYC 10001
Hours: 8-4:30 Mon-Fri
"Pattern and grading paper." ed.

Showroom Display Hangers 212-695-5167
155 West 29th St. (6-7th) NYC 10001
Hours: 9-5 Mon-Fri
"All types of garment hangers in various finishes; fast and helpful service." ed.

COSTUME SHOPS

ACCU-COSTUMES 212-260-1496
84 East 7th St. (1-2nd) NYC 10003 212-228-4389
Hours: 10-6 Mon-Fri
Formerly Shnoz & Shnoz, now including rental service.
"Construction for Off-B'way, commercials, regional, educational theatre; non-union; see Sally Lesser." ed.

Animal Outfits for People Co. 212-840-6219
252 West 46th St. (8th-B'way) NYC 10036
Hours: 10-3 Mon-Fri
"Animal costumes made to order." ed.

BROADWAY CLOTHING 212-675-6019
39 West 14th St. #502 (5-6th) NYC 10011
Hours: 9-6 Mon-Fri
Construction only. B'way, film, opera, dance, commercials, regional theatre. See Marc Happel.
"Excellent new shop." ed.

Carelli Costumes 212-765-6166
594 Ninth Ave. 2nd Fl. (42-43rd) NYC 10036
Hours: 9-5 Mon-Fri
"Construction shop; modern dance and ballet; see Carolyn." ed.

Chenko Studio 212-944-0215
167 West 46th St. (6-7th) NYC 10036
Hours: 9-7 Mon-Fri
"Animal costumes; some rental." ed.

The Costume Collection (adm) 212-221-0885
601 West 26th St. (11-12th) NYC 10001 212-989-5855
Hours: 10-6 Mon-Fri
"Rental for non-profit organizations only; some construction; see Whitney Blausen." ed.

Eaves-Brooks Costume Co. 718-729-1010
21-07 41st Ave. L.I.C. 11101
Hours: 10-4 Mon-Fri
"Largest construction and rental shop on the East Coast; see Bert Stillman." ed.

ECCENTRICITIES 212-924-9411
41 Union Square West (B'way-17th) NYC 10003
Hours: 10-6 Mon-Fri
Custom design and fabrication of costumes, millinery, masks, soft props; styling and shopping service.
"See Dennis Paver or Kathy Silverii." ed.

Grace Costumes 212-586-0260
250 West 54th St. #502 (B'way-8th) NYC 10019
Hours: 9-5 Mon-Fri
"Construction only: Broadway, opera, dance, and commercials; see Joe Bigelow." ed.

Hooker Howe Costume Company 617-373-3731
46-52 South Main, Haverhill, MA 01830
Hours: 9-5 Mon-Fri
"Rent waiters, busboys, bell-hops, doormen uniforms, etc.; see Paul Hefernen." ed.

Johns-Cronk Inc. 212-741-8161
39 West 19th St. 11th Fl. (5-6th) NYC 10011 212-741-8162
Hours: 9-5 Mon-Fri or by appt.
"Hand painted fabrics, costume props, animal and novelty costumes; see Joni or Wes." ed.

Malabar Ltd. 416-598-2581
14 McCaul St., Toronto, Ontario, CAN M5T-1V6
Hours: 9-5 Mon-Fri/ 9-2 Sat (closed Sat July-Aug)
"Large costume rental house." ed.

Barbara Matera 212-475-5006
890 Broadway 5th Fl. (19-20th) NYC 10003
Hours: 9-5:30 Mon-Fri
"Construction, all areas: Broadway, film, opera, ballet, and dance; see Barbara Matera." ed.

Michael-Jon Costumes Inc. 212-741-3440
39 West 19th St. (5-6th) NYC 10011
Hours: 9:30-5 Mon-Fri
"Construction only: B'way, film, TV, variety; see Michael or Jon." ed.

MULDER/GOODWIN INC. 212-689-9037
1200 Broadway #2C (29th) NYC 10001
Hours: 9-6 Mon-Fri
Custom made character and animal costumes for television, theatre and film. (See display ad page 302.)
"See Mary Mulder or Rick Goodwin." ed.

Jimmy Myers 212-947-8115
250 West 35th St. (7-8th) NYC 10001
Hours: 9-5 Mon-Fri
"Construction for Broadway, commercials, fashion, print, and TV; see Jimmy." ed.

PARSONS-MEARES LTD. 212-242-3378
142 West 14th St. 5th Fl. (6-7th) NYC 10011
Hours: By appt.
Costumes for theatre, dance, film and video.
"Construction only; see Barbara." ed.

John Reid Costumes Inc. 212-242-6059
49 West 24th St. 7th Fl. (5-6th) NYC 10010
Hours: 9-5:30 Mon-Fri
"Costume construction." ed.

STUDIO 212-924-4736
250 West 14th St. (7-8th) NYC 10011
Hours: 9-5 Mon-Fri/ or by appt.
Costumes built for full-scale productions and individual projects. Animal, circus, other unusual requirements.
"Construction for B'way, Off-B'way, dance, commercials, industrials and more." ed.

Terilyn Costumes 212-496-1639
210 West 70th St. #311 (Amsterdam) NYC 10023
Hours: By appt.
"Builds period costumes for dance, opera, theatre." ed.

Vincent's 212-741-3423
136 West 21st St. 6th Fl. (6-7th) NYC 10011
Hours: 8:30-5:30 Mon-Fri
"Men's tailoring for NY costume shops and free-lance designers; construction and tailoring." ed.

Western Costume Co. 213-469-1451
5335 Melrose Ave., Hollywood, CA 90038
Hours: 9-5:30 Mon-Fri
"Largest costume rental house on West Coast; film stock." ed.

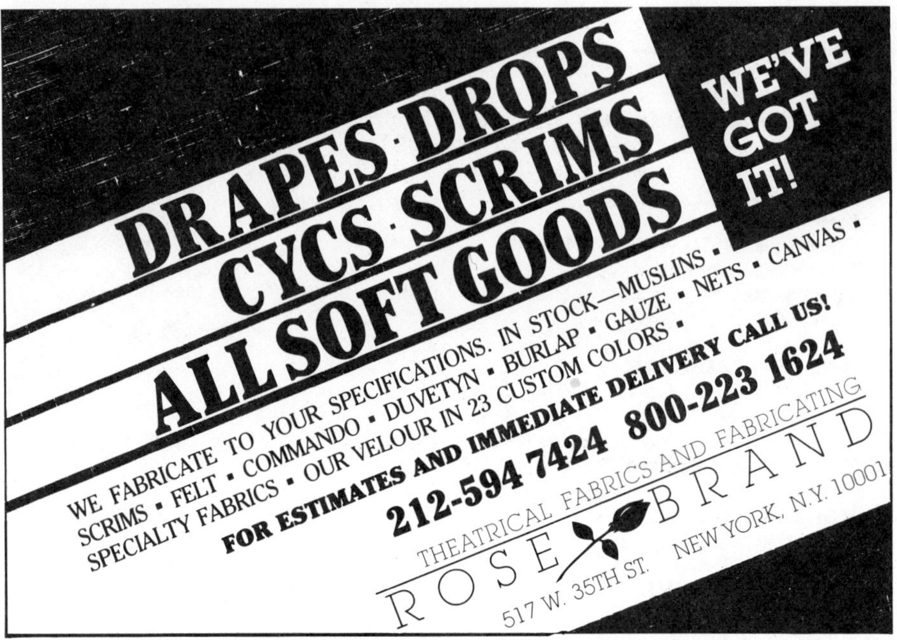
DRAPES·DROPS
CYCS·SCRIMS
ALL SOFT GOODS
WE'VE GOT IT!
WE FABRICATE TO YOUR SPECIFICATIONS. IN STOCK—MUSLINS •
SCRIMS • FELT • COMMANDO • DUVETYN • BURLAP • GAUZE • NETS • CANVAS •
SPECIALTY FABRICS • OUR VELOUR IN 23 CUSTOM COLORS •
FOR ESTIMATES AND IMMEDIATE DELIVERY CALL US!
212-594 7424 800-223 1624
THEATRICAL FABRICS AND FABRICATING
ROSE BRAND
517 W. 35TH ST. NEW YORK, N.Y. 10001

If it isn't a GERRIETS R.P. screen~ ~you probably paid too much!
Gerriets international
RR 1 Box 950 Allentown, NJ 08501
Telephone: (609) 758-9121

CURTAINS & DRAPERIES, THEATRICAL

For rigging, see also THEATRICAL HARDWARE & RIGGING EQUIPMENT

Alcone Company Inc./Paramount Theatrical — 718-361-8373
5-49 49th Ave. L.I.C. 11101
Hours: 9:30-4 Mon-Fri
"Fabrics, draperies, track; theatrical supply house; catalog." ed.

ASSOCIATED DRAPERY & EQUIPMENT CO. — 718-895-8668, 516-671-5245
40 Sea Cliff Ave., Glen Cove, NY 11542
Hours: 8:30-5 Mon-Fri
Custom made Curtains & Drops shipped anywhere. Scenic fabrics. Flameproof fabrics. Catalog available. RUSH ORDERS.
"Helpful; contact Howard Kessler." ed.

COMMERCIAL DRAPES CO. INC. — 718-649-8080
9209 Flatlands Ave. (E. 92nd- E. 93rd) Bklyn 11236
Hours: 8-4:30 Mon-Fri
Fabricator of Stage Curtains, Scrims, Drops, Cycloramas. We install or sell Travelers Tracks, Hardware, Movie Screens, Manila Ropes.
Stage maintenance. Rentals. Flameproofing. Fire retardant fabric by the yard. 35 Years in the Trade.
"Good prices; see Joseph Shuster." ed.

CONSOLIDATED DISPLAY CO. INC. — 312-486-3040
4501 W. Cortez St., Chicago, IL 60651
Hours: 8-4:30 Mon-Fri

Snow blankets, glitters, foils, mylar, foliage, fabrics, Scatter Flakes® Snow.

"Custom mylar fringe drapes at stock prices." ed.

GERRIETS INTERNATIONAL — 609-758-9121
RR #1, 950 Hutchinson Rd., Allentown, NJ 08501
Hours: 8:30-5 Mon-Fri
*MANUFACTURER: 10', 14', 20', and 33' wide seamless muslin; natural, flameproofed, dyed or bleached white.
*Stage draperies, velours, scrims and cycloramas manufactured to your specifications.
*Front/Rear projection screens; maximum 100' high.
*Reversible, double-sided portable dance floor.
*Stage draperies: Opera dimensions.
*Inherently non-flammable, wide width fabrics.
*Large inventory. (See display ads pages 98, 204.)
"Their "Scenographers Sourcebook" contains samples and specifications; a valuable resource." ed.

Joseph C. Hansen 212-246-8055
423 West 43rd St. (9-10th) NYC 10036
Hours: 8:30-5 Mon-Fri
"Theatrical curtain rental: cycs, scrims, velours, etc." ed.

QUARTET THEATRICAL DRAPERIES CORP. 718-857-2841
1163 Atlantic Ave., Bklyn, 11216
Hours: 7:30-3 Mon-Fri
Complete custom service for all your theatrical needs. A full range of domestic and imported fabrics. Technical advice and consultation. "The Union Shop".
"Rentals available." ed.

REYNOLDS DRAPERY SERVICE INC. 315-845-8632
7440 Main St., Newport, NY 13416
Hours: 8-4 Mon-Fri
We manufacture and service theatrical draperies. Our service includes flameproofing, drycleaning and custom repair. (5 year flameproof guarantee in writing)
"Also curtain tracks and rigging." ed.

ROSCO LABORATORIES INC. 914-937-1300
36 Bush Ave., Port Chester, NY 10573 800-431-2338
Hours: 9-5 Mon-Fri
Wide range of specialized fabrics for theatre, film & television applications. (See display ad inside back cover.)
"Samples available on request." ed.

ROSE BRAND TEXTILE FABRICS 212-594-7424
517 West 35th St. (10-11th) NYC 10001 800-223-1624
Hours: 8:30-4:45 Mon-Fri
We sew to your specifications: cycs, drops, scrims, drapes, borders, legs, rain curtains. Our staff is available to offer you technical assistance. We stock 23 colors of flame retardant velour and a full line of theatrical fabrics.
CALL ON US. (See display ads pages 98, 142.)
"Wide selection flame retardant fabrics, by the yard or bolt." ed.

Variety Scenic Studios 718-392-4747
25-19 Borden Ave. (25th) L.I.C. 11101
Hours: 7-5 Mon-Fri
"Custom and rental; catalog." ed.

I. WEISS & SONS INC. 212-246-8444
2-07 Borden Ave., (Vernon-Jackson) L.I.C. 11101
Hours: 8:30-4:30 Mon-Fri

90 Years of Serving the Broadway Theatre and all types of Touring Companies. Internationally Known for Our Quality and Service.

MANUFACTURERS & DESIGNERS OF: Custom Drapery
*Scrims, Muslins and Ground Cloths
*Applique, Rain, Sky and Chase Light Drops
*Projection Screens, Travel Bags, Hampers
*Hardware, Motorized Systems & Installation
*Hard Legs that Travel Soft

OUR EXPERIENCE IS AT YOUR SERVICE- PLEASE CALL

"Complete flameproofing and drycleaning service." ed.

CURTAINS, SHADES & BLINDS

JOYCE AMES 212-535-3047
335 East 65th St. (1-2nd) NYC 10021
Hours: By appt.

Specializing in antique & period laces, linens & floral print drapery. Restoration and on-the-spot construction available. Rentals and sales. Consultation to TV and film.

"Also tablecloths, bedspreads, antimacassars, etc." ed.

S. Beckenstein 212-475-4525
130 Orchard St. (Delancey) NYC 10002
Hours: 9-5:30 Sun-Fri/ closed Sat
"Large selection ready-made curtains and shades; will make to order; fabrics." ed.

BZI Distributors 212-966-6690
105 Eldridge St. (Grand-Broome) NYC 10002
Hours: 9-5:30 Mon-Fri/ 9-5 Sun
"Vertical and mini blinds, many styles of curtain rods and hardware."

Decorator's Walk (Showroom) 212-355-5300
979 Third Ave. 18th Fl. (56th) NYC 10022 212-688-4300
Hours: 9-5 Mon-Fri
"Curtains to the trade; Irish point, lace, embroidered, net; expensive."

Eclectic Properties Inc. 212-799-8963
204 West 84th St. (B'way-Amsterdam) NYC 10024
Hours: 9-5 Mon-Fri/ or by appt.
"Original oil cloth shades made to size without rollers." ed.

Eisner Shade 718-389-5850
29 Norman Ave. (Banker) Bklyn 11222
Hours: 9-4:30 Mon-Fri
"Venetian, Levolor blinds; will rent." ed.

M. Epstein and Sons 212-265-3960
809 Ninth Ave. (53-54th) NYC 10019
Hours: 8-5:15 Mon-Fri/ 8:30-3 Sat (except summer months)
"Window shades, Levolor and vertical blinds for sale." ed.

General Drapery Services 212-924-7200
635 West 23rd St. (11-12th) NYC 10011
Hours: 9-4 Mon-Fri
"Custom work only; curtains, draperies." ed.

Janovic Plaza

159 West 72nd St. (Columbus-Amsterdam) NYC 10023 212-595-2500
Hours: 7:30-6:30 Mon-Fri (Thurs til 8)/ 9-6 Sat/ 11-5 Sun

213 Seventh Ave. (23rd) NYC 10011 212-243-2186
Hours: 7:30-6:30 Mon-Fri/ 9-6 Sat

1150 Third Ave. (67-68th) NYC 10021 212-772-1400
Hours: 9:30-6:30 Mon-Fri/ 9:30-5:30 Sat

"Window shades, vertical blinds in stock or custom work." ed.

Paterson Silks 212-929-7861
36 East 14th St. (University Pl) NYC 10003
Hours: 9-7 Mon-Sat
"Remnants, discount fabrics, draperies; foam for cushions." ed.

Pintchik Paints 212-982-6600
278 Third Ave. (22nd) NYC 10010 212-777-3030
Hours: 8:30-7 Mon-Fri (Mon, Thurs til 8)/9-6:30 Sat/ 11-5 Sun
"Shades and blinds of all types." ed.

Harold Rudin Decorators Inc. 212-265-4716
753 Ninth Ave. (50-51st) NYC 10019 212-757-5639
Hours: 9-5 Mon-Fri
"Custom work; see Harold." ed.

Twentieth Century Draperies Inc. 212-925-7707
70 Wooster St. (Spring-Broome) NYC 10012
Hours: 9-5 Mon-Fri
"Custom draperies, curtains, bedspreads, tablecloths, upholstery; see Ken Sandberg; your fabric or theirs." ed.

Harry Zarin Co. 212-226-3492
72 Allen St. 2nd Fl. (Grand) NYC 10002
Hours: 9-5:30 Sun-Fri
"Vertical and mini blinds, draperies, bedspreads, drapery rods and fabric." ed.

DANCE & STAGE FLOORING

Byrke Decks — 201-249-3863, 609-924-7446
22 Freeman St., New Brunswick, NJ 08901
Hours: 9-5 Mon-Fri
"Dance flooring; rental available." ed.

Thomas A. Deming Co. Inc. — 201-333-8609, 212-732-2659
470 Westside Ave., Jersey City, NJ 07304
Hours: 9-5 Mon-Fri
"Interlocking wooden dance floor sections: 3'x7'-6"x3"; speak to Mr. Jackson." ed.

GERRIETS INTERNATIONAL — 609-758-9121
RR #1, 950 Hutchinson Rd., Allentown, NJ 08501
Hours: 8:30-5 Mon-Fri

Manufacturer of VARIO PORTABLE DANCE FLOOR. Nonflammable, non-skid, reversible, matte, 63" wide and available in 8 colors, two bolt lengths, 98' & 131'. (See display ads pages 98, 204.)

"Speak to Nick Bryson." ed.

Oasis/ Stage Werks — 801-363-0364
263 Rio Grande, Salt Lake City, UT 84101
Hours: 9-5 Mon-Fri
"D'anser floor, resilient sub-floor; 30'x40' rentable dance floor." ed.

ROSCO LABORATORIES INC. — 914-937-1300, 800-431-2338
36 Bush Ave., Port Chester, NY 10573
Hours: 9-5 Mon-Fri

Roscofloor: durable, non-skid, non-reflective, matte vinyl for ballet or modern dance. (See display ad inside back cover.)

"Also portable 4'x8' interlocking dance flooring." ed.

Stage Step — 212-567-6662, 800-523-0961
PO Box 328, Philadelphia, PA 19105
Hours: 9-5 Mon-Fri
"Sale/rental of stage and dance floors; sales of used floors." ed.

DENTAL SUPPLY HOUSES

Arista Surgical Supply Co. — 212-679-3694
67 Lexington Ave. (25th) NYC 10010
Hours: 8:30-5 Mon-Fri/ 9-12 Sat
"Surgical and dental supplies; will rent." ed.

B. L. Dental Co. Inc. 718-658-5440
135-24 Hillside Ave., Richmond Hills, NY 11418
Hours: 8:30-4:30 Mon-Fri
"Bio-fast in clear, white and pink; dental supplies." ed.

Ethical Dental Supplies 718-376-2025
3217 Quenten Rd. (Nostrand Ave.) Bklyn 11234
Hours: 8:45-4:45 Mon-Fri
"Equipment, supplies, and teeth." ed.

Gemco Dental Lab Inc. 718-438-3270
1010 McDonald Ave. Bklyn 11230 718-871-3900
Hours: 6:30-6 Mon-Fri
"Dental tools, teeth, lab equipment; see Leo Weiss." ed.

Hudson Dental Supplies 212-362-5488
153 Amsterdam Ave. (66-67th) NYC 10023
Hours: 9-4:30 Mon-Fri
"Importers of Optima Swiss Diamond Precision Instruments." ed.

Huntington Dental Supply 212-563-0818
29 West 35th St. (5-6th) NYC 10001
Hours: 9-5 Mon-Fri
"Dental tools and supplies, alginate." ed.

REJOICE LTD./GARY ZELLER, JOYCE SPECTOR 212-869-8636
40 West 39 St. (5-6th) NYC 10018
Hours: By appt. or leave message
Kopy Kat alginate. Works directly with EZ Plastic. (See display ad page 333.)
"Special effects consultation and services." ed.

University Dental Supply Co. 212-889-0232
220 East 23rd St. (2-3rd) NYC 10010
Hours: 8:30-4:30 Mon-Fri
"Dental tools and supplies, alginate." ed.

DEPARTMENT STORES

See also VARIETY STORES

Alexander's Department Store

731 Lexington Ave. (58th) NYC 10022 212-593-0880
Hours: 10-9 Mon-Sat/ 12-5 Sun

4 World Trade Center (Liberty) NYC 10048 212-466-1414
Hours: 8-5:45 Mon-Fri/ 10-5 Sat
"Basic department store; reasonable prices." ed.

B. Altman's 212-679-7800
361 Fifth Ave. (34th) NYC 10016
Hours: 10-6 Mon-Sat (Thurs til 8)
"Clothing to furniture; good china, kitchenware, upholstery and drapery fabrics." ed.

Bergdorf Goodman 212-753-7300
754 Fifth Ave. (57-58th) NYC 10019
Hours: 10-6 Mon-Sat (Thurs til 8)
"High fashion clothing department store." ed.

Bloomingdales 212-355-5900
1000 Third Ave. (Lexington) NYC 10022
Hours: 10-6:30 Mon-Sat (Mon,Thurs til 9)/ 12-5 Sun
"Designer clothing, housewares, linens, draperies; pricey." ed.

Bonwit Teller 212-593-3333
4 East 57th St. (5th-Madison) NYC 10022
Hours: 10-7 Mon-Fri (Thurs til 8)/ 10-6 Sat/ 12-5 Sun
"Mostly clothing." ed.

Gimbels Department Store

1275 Broadway (32-33rd) NYC 10001 212-736-5100
Hours: 10-8:30 M,Th,F/ 10-7 T,W,Sat/ 12-6 Sun

125 East 86th St. (Lexington) NYC 10028 212-348-2300
Hours: 10-9 Mon-Sat/ 12-6 Sun

"An alternative to Macy's; sometimes less expensive." ed.

Hammacher-Schlemmer 212-421-9000
147 East 57th St. (Lexington-3rd) NYC 10022
Hours: 10-6 Mon-Sat
"Unusual gift items and gadgets; no cookware anymore." ed.

Lord & Taylor 212-391-3344
424 Fifth Ave. (38-39th) NYC 10018
Hours: 10-6 Mon-Sat (Thurs til 8)
"Stylish women's clothing; good kitchenware department." ed.

Macy's Department Store 212-971-6000
151 West 34th St. (B'way) NYC 10001
Hours: 9:45-8:45 M,Th,F/9:45-6:45 T,W/9:45-7 Sat/12-6 Sun
"The world's largest department store; great kitchenware, housewares, gifts." ed.

May's Department Store 212-677-4000
44 East 14th St. (B'way-Univ. Pl.) NYC 10003
Hours: 10-7 M-W/ 10-8 Th,F/ 10-7 Sat/ 12-5 Sun
"Everything; really cheap." ed.

Ohrbach's 212-695-4000
5 West 34th St. (5th) NYC 10001
Hours: 10-6:45 Mon-Fri (Thurs til 8:30)/ 10-6 Sat/12-6 Sun
"Clothing and accessories; some bargains." ed.

Saks Fifth Ave. 212-753-4000
611 Fifth Ave. (49-50th) NYC 10022
Hours: 10-6 Mon-Sat (Thurs til 8)
"Fashionable clothing and accessories; great memo service for stylists and designers." ed.

DISPLAY HOUSES & MATERIALS

See also MANNEQUINS
For specific materials, see INDEX

Kurt S. Adler 212-924-0900
1107 Broadway (24-25th) NYC 10010
Hours: 9-5:30 Mon-Fri
"Christmas: lights, decorations, ornaments, nativity scenes, 'Santa's World'; wholesale, $250 minimum." ed.

AD-MART INC. 212-777-4141
200 Park Ave. South (17th) NYC 10003 800-354-2102
Hours: 8:30-5 Mon-Fri

Ad-Lite® flexible plastic tubing, 13 colors / 4 diameters. Realistic inexpensive neon effect. Also 3-dimensional signs, logos, letters.

ad-mart

"Custom displays, prop fabrication, graphics and letters; consultation services." ed.

Austen Display Corp. 212-924-6261
139 West 19th St. (6-7th) NYC 10011
Hours: 9-5 Mon-Fri
"Manufacturer of and importer of displays and fixtures, cardboard props, photo-blowups; contact Art Fruchter." ed.

Barrett Hill Inc. 212-242-4745
133 West 25th St. 3rd Fl. (6-7th) NYC 10010
Hours: 9-5 Mon-Fri
"Decorative props, furniture, lamps, fabrics, photo reproductions." ed.

Bond Parade Float Co. 201-778-3333
551 Main Ave. (Paulison Av-Highland) Wallington, NJ 07057
Hours: 8:30-4:30 Mon-Fri
"Poly-petal, plastic fringe; floats and float ornaments, sales or rental." ed.

L. J. Charrot Co. Inc. 212-242-1933
149 West 24th St. (6-7th) NYC 10011
Hours: 9-5 Mon-Fri
"Contemporary/classical columns, busts, urns; silk and paper flowers, sculpture." ed.

Colonial Decorative Displays 212-255-9620
160 11th Ave. (23rd) NYC 10011
Hours: 10-4 Mon-Fri
"Primarily a floral house; Christmas decor, display props; see Irving." ed.

Susan Crane Inc. 214-631-6490
8107 Cancellor Row, Dallas, TX 75247 212-260-0580
"Seasonal display items, furniture, sculpture, vases, giftwrap; highly recommended." ed.

CONSOLIDATED DISPLAY CO. INC. 312-486-3040
4501 W. Cortez St., Chicago, IL 60651
Hours: 8-4:30 Mon-Fri

Snow blankets, glitters, foils, mylar, foliage, fabrics, Scatter Flakes® Snow.

Consolidated Display Co., Inc.

"Custom mylar fringe drapes at stock prices." ed.

Crown River 718-706-0420
50-25 34th St. L.I.C. 11101
Hours: 8:30-4:30 Mon-Fri
"Designers and builders of exhibits and displays." ed.

Cultured Design Ltd. 212-594-8690
548 West 28th St. (10-11th) NYC 10001
Hours: 8:30-5 Mon-Fri
"Snow, fountains, rocks, statuary, artificial flowers and foliage. Will rent; see Gus." ed.

DAZIAN INC. 212-307-7800
423 West 55th St. (9-10th) NYC 10019
Hours: 9-5 Mon-Fri

Theatrical and display fabrics. Mostly Flame Resistant. (See display ad page 143.)

"Rain curtains, decorator felt, novelty fabrics and more; catalog, color cards." ed.

DESIGN ETC. INC. 212-874-3814
155 West 68th St. #825 (Broadway) NYC 10023
Hours: By appt.

Showroom design, environmental displays, ego free!

"Design and display service; contact Don Campbell." ed.

Discoveries Inc. 212-254-8591
120 East 23rd St. Rm. 305 (Lexington-Park) NYC 10010
Hours: 9-5 Mon-Fri
"Seasonal display props." ed.

ECCENTRICITIES 212-924-9411
41 Union Square West (B'way-17th) NYC 10003
Hours: 10-6 Mon-Fri
Custom design and fabrication of soft props, mechanical animations, window and showcase decorations.
"See Kathy Silverii or Dennis Paver." ed.

Electra Displays 212-420-1327
90 Remington Blvd., Ronkonkoma, NY 11779 516-585-5659
"Electric signs, letters, efx., architectural and vacuumformed pieces, props; see Art Ruderman." ed.

emptybirdcage studios 718-272-5281
9235 Foster Ave. Bklyn 11236
Hours: By appt.
Mail order mfrs of 2-dimensional graphics & silhouettes. Complete catalog of unique designs, colors & sizes. Custom & special orders. For visual merchandising, theatrical sets, promotion, film/video/TV.
"Contact Annette or T.J.; graphics and silhouette catalog, $2." ed.

Feartek Productions/ Canthus Inc. 212-741-5190
15 West 20th St. (5-6th) NYC 10011
Hours: 9-5 Mon-Fri
"Animated monsters for amusement parks, large scale sculptures; contact Earle." ed.

Florenco Foliage Systems Worldwide 212-402-0500
920 East 149th St. (Bruckner Blvd.) Bronx 10455
Hours: 9-5 Mon-Fri
"Rental, sales, and instalation of all types artificial turf; Christmas; catalog." ed.

David Hamberger

410 Hicks St. Bklyn 11201 718-582-7101
Hours: 9-5:30 Mon-Fri

120 East 23rd St. #509 (Park-Lexington) NYC 10010 212-852-7101
Hours: 9-5 Mon-Fri
"Mechanicals, props and fabrication, sculptures in fiberglas, plaster, acrylic, or soft; celastic, sonotube." ed.

INTERNATIONAL PAPER COMPANY 704-872-8974
Taylorsville Road Highway 90, Statesville, NC 28677 800-438-1701
Hours: 8-5 Mon-Fri
GATORFOAM® Laminated Foam Panel. Call 800# for local dealer.
"Available in 4'x8' sheets; 5 thicknesses from 3/16" to 1½"." ed.

Irving's Food Center Inc. 212-220-0800
48-01 Metropolitan Ave., Ridgewood, NY 11385
Hours: 9-5 Mon-Fri
"Supermarket fixtures; rental, by appointment, from warehouse in Queens." ed.

Lupari Displays Ltd. 718-727-4986
225 Port Richmond Ave., Staten Island, NY 10302
Hours: 10-6 Mon-Fri
"Custom display work; sells 13" Sonotube." ed.

Modern Artificial Flowers & Display 212-265-0414
517 West 46th St. (10-11th) NYC 10036
Hours: 8:30-4:30 Mon-Fri
"Flowers, plants, statuary, snow; stock and custom pieces and environments; see Don or Sam." ed.

Nasti Displays Inc. 718-835-2271
93-13 Liberty Ave., Ozone Park, NY 11417
Hours: 8-4:30 Mon-Fri
"Custom mechanicals/animation, talking puppets." ed.

Niedermaier 212-675-1106
435 Hudson (Morton) NYC 10014
Hours: 9-5 Mon-Fri
"Chic display items; pottery, columns, sculpture, oversized items."

Provost Displays 212-279-5770
618 West 28th St. (11-12th) NYC 10001
Hours: 9-4:30 Mon-Fri
"Vacuumform shapes and simulated surfaces." ed.

Robelan Displays Inc. 516-747-5300
150 Fulton Ave., Garden City, NJ 11040
Hours: 9-5 Mon-Fri
"Animation, display props and fabrication, foliage, artificial snow, snow blankets." ed.

Screamers 212-245-3237
423 West 55th St. (9-10th) NYC 10019
Hours: 9-5 Mon-Fri
"Sales of stock and custom dark ride gimmicks." ed.

Seven Continents Enterprises Inc. 212-691-1195
133 West 25th St. 9th Fl. (6-7th) NYC 10001
Hours: 9:30-5:30 Mon-Thurs (call first)
"Good quality silk, display props, sculpture, foliage, artificial food; expensive." ed.

Spaeth Design Inc. 212-489-0770
423 West 55th St. (9-10th) NYC 10019
Hours: 9-5 Mon-Fri
"Mechanicals and animation, display props and fabrication, fiberglas props, specialty props; helpful." ed.

Trim Corporation of America 212-989-1616
459 West 15th St. (10th) NYC 10011
Hours: 9-5 Mon-Fri
"Display materials, mannequins, floral; ask for Ken Marsak." ed.

Harriet Witkin Assoc. 212-691-1286
210 Eleventh Ave. 4th Fl. (24-25th) NYC 10001
Hours: 9-5 Mon-Fri
"Full service commercial interiors and trade show exhibit firm." ed.

DOLL PARTS

American Optical Co. 617-765-9711
14 Mechanic St., South Bridge, MA 01550
Hours: 8-5 Mon-Fri
"Doll and mannequin eyes." ed.

S. Axelrod Co. Inc. 212-594-3022
7 West 30th St. (5th-B'way) NYC 10001
Hours: 9-5:30 Mon-Fri
"Moving eyes." ed.

Dollspart Supply Co. Inc. 718-361-0888
5-15 49th Ave. L.I.C. 11101
Hours: 1:30-3 Tues, Thurs
"All parts for dolls; collector dolls; catalog." ed.

Eastern Doll Corp. 212-226-1535
37 Greene St. (Broome) NYC 10013
Hours: 9-5 Mon-Fri
"Doll parts; catalog." ed.

Gampel Supply Corp. 212-398-9222
39 West 37th St. (5-6th) NYC 10018
Hours: 8:45-4:30 Mon-Fri
"Wood doll heads in 3 sizes; plastic and wood beads." ed.

Margon Corp. 212-943-2797
2195 Elizabeth Ave., Rahway, NJ 07065 201-382-7700
Hours: 8:30-5 Mon-Fri
"Doll eyes." ed.

Premier Doll Accessories Inc. 718-788-8051
168 7th St. (off 3rd Ave) Bklyn 11215
Hours: 9-4 Mon-Fri
"Eyes." ed.

Sol Spitz Co. 516-231-0010
50 Commerce Dr., Hauppaugue, NY 11788
Hours: 8:30-4:30 Mon-Fri
"Doll parts, wholesale; also artificial flowers." ed.

Walbead Inc. 718-392-7616
29-76 Northam Blvd. L.I.C. 11101
Hours: 8-4 Mon-Fri
"Doll heads and eyes; catalog." ed.

DOLLS & DOLLHOUSES

See also TOYS
For additional basswood moldings, see HOBBY SHOPS & SUPPLIERS

Iris Brown 212-593-2882
253 East 57th St. (2nd) NYC 10022
Hours: 11-6 Mon-Fri/ 12:30-5:30 Sat
"Antique dolls and dollhouses; will rent." ed.

Dollsandreams 212-876-2434
1421 Lexington Ave. (92-93rd) NYC 100128
Hours: 10-6 Mon-Sat
"Dolls and dollhouses." ed.

Dollspart Supply Co. Inc. 718-361-0888
5-15 49th Ave. L.I.C. 11101
Hours: 9-5 Mon-Fri
"Collector's dolls; doll eyes, parts and stringing hooks; catalog available." ed.

Eugene Doll & Novelty Co.

4012 Second Ave. (41st) Bklyn 11232 718-788-1313
Hours: 9-5 Mon-Fri 718-965-2958
"Doll factory; catalog." ed.

200 Fifth Ave. (23rd) NYC 10010 212-675-8020
Hours: 9-5 Mon-Fri
"Doll showroom; catalog." ed.

Manhattan Doll Hospital 212-989-5220
176 Ninth Ave. (21st) NYC 10011
Hours: 10-4:30 Sun-Fri/ closed Sat
"Will rent." ed.

NY Doll Hospital 212-838-7527
787 Lexington Ave. (61-62nd) NYC 10021
Hours: 10-6 Mon-Sat
"Dollhouse lumber, turnings, props." ed.

Palo Imports 203-792-2411
184 Greenwood Ave., Bethel, CT 06801
Hours: 9:30-6 Mon-Fri
"Dollhouse supplies; catalog available, mail order." ed.

B. Shackman & Co. Inc. 212-989-5162
85 Fifth Ave. (16th) NYC 10003
Hours: 9-5 Mon-Fri
"Dollhouse furniture, props; mostly 1" scale; toy and doll antique reproductions." ed.

Tiny Doll House 212-752-3082
231 East 53rd St. (2-3rd) NYC 10022
Hours: 11-5:30 Mon-Fri/ 11-5 Sat
"Dollhouse molding, turnings, decorative castings, lighting systems and parts; catalog." ed.

DOWN, BATTING & FIBERFILL

See also UPHOLSTERY TOOLS & SUPPLIES

BAER FABRICS 502-583-5521
515 East Market, Louisville, KY 40202
Hours: 9-5:30 Mon-Sat
Upholstery, craft, quilting, pillow forms, etc. (See display ad page 127.)
"Shipment within 24 hours for in-stock items." ed.

Buffalo Batt and Felt Corp. 716-683-4100
3307 Walden Ave., Depew, NY 14043
Hours: 8:30-4:45 Mon-Fri
"Polyester batting by the roll; mail order." ed.

Canal Rubber Supply Co. 212-226-7339
329 Canal St. (Greene) NYC 10013
Hours: 9-5 Mon-Fri/ 9-4:30 Sat
"Fluffy dacron batting by the yard or roll." ed.

Comet Fibers Inc. 718-388-1887
845 Meeker Ave. (Varick-Van Dam) Bklyn 11222
Hours: 7:30-4 Mon-Fri
"Dacron fluff." ed.

Comfort Industries 718-392-5300
39-35 21st St. (near 59th St. Bridge) L.I.C. 11101
Hours: 8:30-4:30 Mon-Fri
"Dacron fluff, down feathers." ed.

Down East Enterprises Inc. 212-925-2632
240 Lafayette St. (Spring) NYC 10012
Hours: 12-6 Mon-Fri (Thurs til 7)/ 11-2 Sat
"Do-it-yourself down products; down, nylon fabric, Fastex buckles, zippers, snaps." ed.

Paterson Silks 212-929-7861
36 East 14th St. (University) NYC 10003
Hours: 9-7 Mon-Sat
"Fiberfill by the bag; also foam cushions, fabrics." ed.

York Feather & Down Corp. 718-497-4120
10 Evergreen Ave. (Flushing Ave) Bklyn 11206
Hours: 9-5 Mon-Fri
"Feather, down, goose and duck; comforters, custom pillows." ed.

DRESS FORMS

BAER FABRICS 502-583-5521
515 East Market, Louisville, KY 40202
Hours: 9-5:30 Mon-Sat
Adjustable 'Athena', 'Uniquely You' & 'My Double' forms. (See display ad page 127.)
"Shipment within 24 hours for in-stock items." ed.

Fox Sewing Machines Inc. 212-594-2438
307 West 38th St. (8-9th) NYC 10018
Hours: 8-5 Mon-Fri
"Sewing machine sales, rental, repair; new and used dress and coat forms; steam irons, cutting machines, factory supplies." ed.

Garment Center Sewing Machine Inc. 212-279-8774
555 Eighth Ave. (37-38th) NYC 10018
Hours: 8-5:30 Mon-Fri
"Used machines and dress forms, factory supplies." ed.

Willie Roland 718-854-3325
4017 15th Ave. Bklyn 11218
Hours: Call for hours.
"Sales and repair on domestic, industrial machines, Sussmans, merrows; parts, used dress forms." ed.

Superior Model Forms Co. 212-947-3633
545 Eighth Ave. (37-38th) NYC 10018
Hours: 8:30-4:45 Mon-Fri
"Sewing machines, dress forms; see Mr. Shuster." ed.

Wolf Forms 212-255-4508
39 West 19th St. 8th Fl. (5-6th) NYC 10011
Hours: 8-4 Mon-Fri (closed for lunch 12-12:30)
"Custom dress forms only; no stock." ed.

DRYCLEANERS

Lincoln Terrace Cleaners 212-874-3066
149 Amsterdam Ave. (66th) NYC 10023
Hours: 7:30-7 Mon-Fri/ 8-5 Sat
"Bulk and special theatrical drycleaning." ed.

Neighborhood Cleaners Association 212-684-0945
116 East 27th St. (Park Ave.) NYC 10016
Hours: 9-5 Mon-Fri
"Theatrical drycleaning; very cooperative; very good." ed.

Norton Drapery Services 212-575-8266
151 West 19th St. (6-7th) NYC 10011
Hours: 7:30-6 Mon-Fri
"Drycleaning." ed.

Ernest Winzer 212-294-2400
1828 Cedar Ave. (179-Major Deegan) Bronx 10453
Hours: 6-5 Mon-Fri
"Drycleaning; pickup and delivery service." ed.

DYERS

See also COSTUME CRAFTSPEOPLE

Master Dyeing Co. 718-726-1001
24-47 44th St. L.I.C. 11103
Hours: 8:30-4:30 Mon-Fri
"Fabric dyers." ed.

Petcar Textile Dyers 718-782-0424
34 South 1st (near Williamsburg Bridge) Bklyn 11211
Hours: 7-5 Mon-Fri
"Steam setting for silkscreen printers." ed.

20-20 Colorists 212-255-6579
20 West 20th St. (5-6th) NYC 10011
Hours: 9-5 Mon-Fri or by appt.
"Fabric dyers and painters, distressing, etc.; ask for Marie." ed.

ELECTRICAL & ELECTRONICS SUPPLIES

See also MOTORS AND MECHANICAL COMPONENTS

American Surplus Trading 201-939-2710
62 Joseph St., Moonachie, NJ 07074
Hours: 9-5 Mon-Sat
"Miscellaneous electric supplies; chassis fans." ed.

Barbizon Electrical Co. 212-586-1620
426 West 55th St. (9-10th) NYC 10019
Hours: 8-5 Mon-Fri
"Theatrical electrics; distribute Rosco products (including fabric paints)." ed.

Blan Electronics 212-233-6288
56 Warren St. (B'way-Church) NYC 10007
Hours: 9-5 Mon-Fri
"Electronics: special relays, switches, solenoids, etc." ed.

Brite Electric Sales Corp. 212-687-1313
221 East 38th St. (3rd) NYC 10016
Hours: 8-4:30 Mon-Fri
"Electrical supply house." ed.

Broadway Electric 212-673-3906
862 Broadway NYC (17th) 10003
Hours: 9-5 Mon-Fri (closed for lunch 12-1)
"Electrical and electronics supplies." ed.

City Electric Supply Co. 212-564-5454
510 West 34th St. (10th) NYC 10001
Hours: 8-4:30 Mon-Thurs/ 8-4 Fri
"Large supplier of electrical parts, conduit, florescent fixtures, etc."

Jensen Tools Inc. 602-968-6231
7815 S. 46th St., Phoenix, AZ 85040
Hours: 9-5 Mon-Fri
"Electronic test tools, cases, dental tools." ed.

Magnet Wire Inc. 718-651-0900
112-01 Northern Blvd., Corona, NY 11368
Hours: 9-5 Mon-Fri
"Carries tungsten wire, piano wire, as well as a large selection of other wire." ed.

Newark Electronics 212-349-7087
25 Rte. 22 E., Springfield, NJ 07081 201-376-9500
Hours: 9-5 Mon-Fri
"Electronic components and equipment; voluminous catalog available to serious users." ed.

Rosetta Electrical Co. Inc.

73 Murray St. (Greenwich St.-W.B'way) NYC 10007 212-233-9088
Hours: 9-5:30 Mon-Fri/ 9:30-5 Sat
"Large selection lamps, fixtures." ed.

21 West 46th St. (5-6th) NYC 10036 212-719-4381
Hours: 9-5:45 Mon-Fri
"Good selection fixtures, conduit, misc. supplies." ed.

S & L Jack Electronics 718-545-8843
28-14 Steinway St., Astoria, NY 11103
Hours: 9:30-5:45 Mon-Sat
"Miniature lamps, other electronic supplies." ed.

Henry Sticht Co. 212-732-8163
27 Park Place (Church-B'way) NYC 10007
Hours: 9-5 Mon-Fri
"Meters; friendly service." ed.

Switches Unlimited 718-478-5000
34-11 56th St., Woodside, NY 11377
Hours: 8-4:30 Mon-Fri
"Switches and indicator, panel lights." ed.

Techni-Tool 215-825-4990
Apollo Road, Plymouth Meeting, PA 19462
Hours: 8:30-5 Mon-Fri
"Specializes in electronic tools & testing tools; catalog." ed.

Tudor Electrical Supply Co. Inc. 212-867-7550
226 East 46th St. (2-3rd) NYC 10017
Hours: 8:30-5 Mon-Thurs/ 8:30-4:30 Fri
"Electrical supplies." ed.

ELEVATORS

Able Elevator & Door Repair Co. Inc. 212-674-7607
37 Cooper Square (3rd Ave.) NYC 10003
Hours: 8-4:30 Mon-Fri
"Very helpful; has elevator door track; come before noon." ed.

Century Elevator 718-937-6200
4 Court Sq. L.I.C. 11101
Hours: 8:30-4:30 Mon-Fri
"Installations and repair." ed.

Circle Elevator 212-431-1319
272 Lafayette St. (Houston-Prince) NYC 10012 (service) 212-254-4086
Hours: 8-4:30 Mon-Fri
"Installations and repair; very helpful." ed.

EMBROIDERY, PLEATING & BUTTONHOLES

Acme Emblem 212-255-7880
122 West 26th St. (6-7th) NYC 10001
Hours: 9-4 Mon-Fri
"Custom work, 100 pc. min., 3-4 wk. delivery; see Mr. Mark." ed.

Buttonhole Fashions Inc. 212-354-1420
580 Eighth Ave. 5th Fl. (38-39th) NYC 10018
Hours: 8-5 Mon-Fri
"Leather buttonholes, piped and keyhole buttonholes, pockets." ed.

City Emblem Mfg. Co. 718-366-2040
6031 Myrtle Ave. (Sommerfield) Bklyn 11385
Hours: 10-8 Mon,Thurs,Fri/ 10-6 Tues,Wed,Sat
"Chenille, embroidered, felt lettering; one week service." ed.

D & R Embroidery Co. 212-686-6920
29 East 31st St. (5th-Madison) NYC 10010
Hours: 9-5 Mon-Fri
"Embroidery in bulk; not one of a kind." ed.

De'Cor Embroideries Co. Inc. 212-354-8668
250 West 40th St. (7-8th) NYC 10018
Hours: 8-4 Mon-Fri
"Applique, rhinestones, nailheads, bonnaz, crochet beading, hand embroidery." ed.

Jack Goldman Embroidery 212-391-0816
250 West 40th St. (8th) NYC 10018
Hours: 9-5 Mon-Fri
"Dresses in bulk, crochet beading; mostly to dress manufacturers." ed.

Joel & Aronoff Inc. 212-695-0855
425 Victoria Terrace, Ridgefield, NJ 07657 201-945-8686
Hours: 9-5 Mon-Fri
"Embroidered and screen printed bullion crests and emblems for fire, police, security; stock and custom; catalog." ed.

Koppel Pleating Inc. 212-736-9494
240 West 37th St. 10th Fl. (7-8th) NYC 10018
Hours: 7-5 Mon-Fri
"Custom pleating service." ed.

Kraus & Sons Inc. 212-620-0408
245 Seventh Ave. (24th) NYC 10001
Hours: 9-5 Mon-Fri
"Embroidered emblems, emblematic jewelry, flags, trophies." ed.

Majestic Embroideries & Stitching 212-244-5450
325 West 38th St. 6th Fl. (8-9th) NYC 10018
Hours: 8:30-4 Mon-Fri
"Beading, pearls, applique stitching; large orders only." ed.

Metropolitan Keller Embroidery 212-391-0990
270 West 38th St. (7-8th) NYC 10018 212-563-2591
Hours: 8-5 Mon-Fri
"Beading in bulk for shows and films." ed.

Raymond Miligi Pleating Co. 516-783-1713
660 Newbridge Rd., East Meadow, NY 11554
Hours: call for hours
"See Mr. Gaspare." ed.

Paramount Buttonhole & Eyelet Co. 212-279-3908
580 Eighth Ave. 5th Fl. (38-39th) NYC 10018
Hours: 8-5 Mon-Fri
"Piped, bound, stitched buttonholes and pockets." ed.

REYNOLDS DRAPERY SERVICE INC. 315-845-8632
7440 Main St., Newport, NY 13416
Hours: 8-4 Mon-Fri
"Complete drapery service, manufacture, repair, cleaning, pleating."

Singer Buttonhole & Eyeleting Co. 212-736-1943
302 West 37th St. (8th) NYC 10018
Hours: 8-4 Mon-Fri
"Piped and bound, machine buttonholes and eyelets; work must be in by 3:30." ed.

Star Buttonhole & Button Works Co. 212-736-4960
242 West 36th St. (7-8th) NYC 10018
Hours: 8-4:30 Mon-Fri (closed Mon Jul-Aug)
"Buttonholes, eyelets, covered buttons." ed.

Tremont Pleating Ltd. 212-279-2232
306 West 37th St. (8-9th) NYC 10018 212-279-4266
Hours: 7:30-5:30 Mon-Fri
"Immediate service, good prices." ed.

ENGRAVERS

Baskin Engravers 212-869-5048
21 West 47th St. (5-6th) NYC 10036
Hours: 10-6 Mon-Sat
"Engraving while-you-wait, jewelry, crests, nameplates; silverware, pewter, etc." ed.

Marvin Tischler 212-719-1647
74 West 47th St. (5-6th) NYC 10036
Hours: 9:30-5 Mon-Fri
"While-you-wait." ed.

EROTIC GOODS

Pink Pussycat Boutique 212-243-0077
161 West 4th St. (6th) NYC 10012
Hours: 11am-2am Sun-Thurs/ 11am-3am Fri, Sat
"Leather, studs, lingerie, inflatable dolls, handcuffs, drug paraphernalia, sex toys." ed.

Pleasure Chest

156 Seventh Ave. South (Charles-Perry) NYC 10014 212-242-2158
Hours: 12-12 Mon-Sat/ 2-8 Sun

302 East 52nd St. (1st-2nd) NYC 10022 212-371-4465
Hours: 12-12 Mon-Sat/ 2-8 Sun

"Erotic postcards, leather goods, lingerie, S & M items, sex toys." ed.

ETHNIC GOODS: AFRICAN & WEST INDIAN

AFRICAN FABRIC PRINTS 212-725-1199
303 Fifth Ave. Rm. 813 (corner 31st) NYC 10016
Hours: Call 9-5 Mon-Fri to make an appt.
African Fabric Prints: Bulk fabrics & finished garments.
"Leave name and phone number with answering service." ed.

African Trader 212-724-3114
138 West 72nd St. (B'way-Columbus) NYC 10023
Hours: 11-7 Tues-Sat
"African goods." ed.

Cool Runnin' 212-473-6311
73 Second Ave. (4-5th) NYC 10003
Hours: 12-8 Mon-Sat
"Rastafarian items, reggae records, t-shirts, buttons." ed.

Craft Caravan Inc. 212-966-1338
127 Spring St. (Greene) NYC 10012
Hours: 10-6 Sun-Fri
"African imports; clothing, hats, jewelry." ed.

Folklorica Imports Inc. 212-255-2525
89 Fifth Ave. (16-17th) NYC 10003
Hours: 10-7 Mon-Fri/ 10-6 Sat/ call on Sundays
"African and primitive baskets, masks, drums, instruments, jewelry."

ETHNIC GOODS: EAST INDIAN

Anand India Shop 212-247-2054
30 Rockefeller Plaza, Shop 11 NYC 10112
Hours: 9-6 Mon-Fri/ 11-5 Sat
"Indian jewelry, gifts, brass, hammered tinware." ed.

BAER FABRICS 502-583-5521
515 East Market, Louisville, KY 40202
Hours: 9-5:30 Mon-Sat
Madras, palace, Indian silks and much more. (See display ad page 127.)
"Shipment within 24 hours for in-stock items." ed.

Goel India Co. 212-683-0290
17 West 29th St. (B'way) NYC 10001
Hours: 10-6 Mon-Fri/ 12-4 Sat
"Indian brass items and clothing." ed.

Pan American Textiles Inc. 718-478-4636
37-12 74th St., Jackson Hts., NY 11372
Hours: 10:30-7:30 every day
"Specializes in saris; also silks, woolens, etc." ed.

ETHNIC GOODS: MEXICAN, SOUTH AMERICAN, AMERICAN INDIAN

Arte Primitivo Inc. 212-570-0393
3 East 65th St. (5th-Madison) NYC 10021
Hours: 11-5 Mon-Fri/ 11-3 Sat
"Books and papers on Pre-Columbian cultures; new, rare, out-of-print." ed.

Casa Moneo Imports 212-929-1644
210 West 14th St. (7-8th) NYC 10011
Hours: 9-7 Mon-Sat/ 11-5 Sun
"Spanish and Mexican groceries, clothing, gifts; also mail order, $25 minimum." ed.

Grey Owl Indian Crafts 718-464-9300
113-15 Springfield Blvd., Queens Village, NY 11429
Hours: 9-5 Mon-Fri
"Kits for American Indian headdresses and crafts; catalog." ed.

Mexican Folk Art 212-673-1910
108 West Houston (Thompson) NYC 10012
Hours: 12:30-7 Tues-Fri (closed 2:30-3:30)
"Mexican clothes and artifacts, sportswear." ed.

Plume Trading Co. 914-782-8594
PO Box 585, Rt. 208, Monroe, NY 10950
"Kits for American Indian headgear, crafts; great catalog; mail order." ed.

Tianguis Folk Art 212-799-7343
284 Columbus Ave. (74th) NYC 10023
Hours: 11-8 Mon-Sat/ 12-6 Sun
"Mexican and South American goods: masks, dolls, baskets." ed.

ETHNIC GOODS: MIDDLE EASTERN

Aegean Imports 415-593-8300
PO Box 1061, Belmont, CA 94002
"Greek fishermen's hats; quantity mail order only." ed.

Jacques Carcanagues Inc. 212-431-3116
119 Spring St. (Greene) NYC 10012
Hours: 10:30-5 Tues-Sun
"Middle to Far Eastern clothing, jewelry, rugs, textiles, furniture, baskets; rental, purchase or loan for credit." ed.

Poseidon Bakery 212-757-6173
629 Ninth Ave. (44-45th) NYC 10036
Hours: 9-7 Tues-Sat/ 10-4 Sun/ (Closed Mon)
"Greek pastries." ed.

ETHNIC GOODS: ORIENTAL

Asian House 212-581-2294
888 Seventh Ave. (56th) NYC 10019
Hours: 10-6 Mon-Sat
"Oriental goods; furniture, lamps, prints, jewelry, etc." ed.

Azuma

387 Sixth Ave. (Waverly) NYC 10012 212-989-8690
Hours: 10-9 Mon-Sat/ 11-7:30 Sun

25 East 8th St. (Univ. Pl. & 5th) NYC 10003 212-673-2900
Hours: 10-9 Mon-Sat/ 11-7:30 Sun

666 Lexington Ave. (55th) NYC 10022 212-752-0599
Hours: 10-7:30 Mon-Fri/ 10-6:30 Sat/ 12-5:45 Sun

251 East 86th St. (2nd) NYC 10028 212-369-4928
Hours: 10-8 Mon-Sat/ 11-7 Sun

"Importers of baskets, wicker items, bamboo, housewares, clothing, gift items." ed.

Bok Lei Tat Inc. 212-226-1703
213 Canal St. (Mulberry-Mott) NYC 10013
Hours: 9:30-7:30 every day
"Samauri swords, karate equipment and clothing." ed.

Cheung Fat Co. 212-349-0727
61 Mott St. (Canal-White) NYC 10013
Hours: Call for hours
"Limited selection of Chinese goods; sparklers, lanterns, fans, umbrellas." ed.

China Books & Periodicals 212-677-2650
125 Fifth Ave. (19-20th) NYC 10003
Hours: 10-6 Mon-Sat/ 12-5 Sun
"Chinese books, newspapers, magazines, posters, kites, gift items." ed.

China Seas 212-752-5555
979 Third Ave. (58-59th) NYC 10022
Hours: 9-5 Mon-Fri
"Chinese fabrics; some silks, mostly cottons; also some clothing." ed.

Chinatown 10 Cent Store 212-966-4778
25 Elizabeth St. (Bayard) NYC 10013
Hours: Call for hours
"Small Chinese department store." ed.

East-East 212-861-3692
230 East 80th St. (2-3rd) NYC 10021
Hours: 12:30-6:15 Mon-Fri/ 12-6 Sat
"Chinese and Japanese clothing; rental and sales; see Ligra Varoon."

Five Eggs 212-226-1606
436 W. Broadway (Prince-Spring) NYC 10012
Hours: 12:30-7 Tues-Sun
"Japanese handicrafts, housewares, books, clothing." ed.

Katagiri & Co. Inc. 212-755-3566
224 East 59th St. (2-3rd) NYC 10022
Hours: 9:30-6:30 Mon-Fri/ 10-6 Sat
"Japanese groceries, cooking utensils, giftware; good selection Japanese lanterns." ed.

Northsouth Trading Inc. 212-964-4459
28 Elizabeth St. (Near Canal) NYC 10013
Hours: 11-7 Mon-Fri
"Oriental fabrics and dresses, brocades, silks." ed.

Orienhouse Enterprises Inc. 212-431-8060
424-426 Broadway (Grand-Canal) NYC 10013
Hours: 9:30-6 Mon-Sat
"Tablecloths, oriental gifts and handicrafts, Chinese embroidered blouses, kung-fu and karate equipment." ed.

The Oriental Dress Co. 212-349-0818
38 Mott St. (Bayard) NYC 10013
Hours: 10-7 everyday
"Chinese brocade." ed.

Paragon Book Gallery Ltd. 212-496-2378
2130 Broadway (74-75th) NYC 10023
Hours: 10-5:45 Mon-Fri/ 11-5 Sat
"Books on Asia and the Orient." ed.

Pearl River Chinese Products Emporium 212-966-1010
13-15 Elizabeth St. (Canal-Bayard) NYC 10013
Hours: 10-8 every day
"Chinese groceries, cookware, dishware, clothing, fans, lanterns, tablecloths; great selection." ed.

Shui Hing Inc. 212-964-0548
46-48 Bowery, Arcade 26 (Elizabeth) NYC 10013
Hours: 11-7 every day
"Oriental silks and brocades; dressmaker." ed.

Sino-American Commodities Center Inc. 212-741-8833
27-33 West 23rd St. (5-6th) NYC 10010
Hours: 9:30-6 Mon-Sat/ 12-5 Sun
"Chinese department store; furniture, rugs, apparel, shoes, housewares." ed.

Tokyo Bookstore

521 Fifth Ave. (43-44th) NYC 10175 212-697-0840
Hours: 10-7 Mon-Sat/ 11:30-6:30 Sun

115 West 57th St. (6-7th) NYC 10019 212-582-4622
Hours: 10-8 Mon-Sat/ 12-7 Sun

"Japanese and Oriental books, gift section, calligraphy and painting supplies." ed.

Vee's Fashions 212-962-3063
5 Pell St. (Bowery-Mott) NYC 10013
Hours: 10-5 every day
"Oriental fabrics." ed.

Yomiuri Press/ Yomiuri Shimbun 212-661-5977
41 East 42nd St. (Park Ave.) NYC 10017
Hours: 9-5 Mon-Fri
"Current Japanese newspapers." ed.

ETHNIC GOODS: SCOTTISH & IRISH

Facsimile Book Shop Inc. 212-581-2672
16 West 55th St. (5-6th) NYC 10019
Hours: 10:30-6:30 Mon-Fri/ 11-6 Sat
"Irish books and records." ed.

Haskins Shamrock Irish Store 212-288-3918
205 East 75th St. (2-3rd) NYC 10021
Hours: 11-6 Mon-Sat
"Irish goods, clothing." ed.

Scottish Products Inc. 212-755-9656
133 East 55th St. (Lexington) NYC 10022
Hours: 10:30-6 Mon-Fri/ 10:30-5 Sat
"Scottish clothing, fabrics, clan plaids." ed.

ETHNIC GOODS: SPANISH

Casa Moneo Imports 212-929-1644
210 West 14th St. (7-8th) NYC 10011
Hours: 9-7 Mon-Sat/ 11-5 Sun
"Spanish and Mexican groceries, clothing, gifts; also mail order, $25 minimum." ed.

The French & Spanish Book Corp.

115 Fifth Ave. (19th) NYC 10003 212-673-7400
Hours: 10-6 Mon-Sat

610 Fifth Ave. (49-50th) NYC 10020 212-581-8810
Hours: 9:30-6:15 Mon-Fri/ 10-6:15 Sat

"French and Spanish books, magazines, newspapers." ed.

ETHNIC GOODS: RUSSIAN

Victor Kamkin Inc. 212-673-0776
149 Fifth Ave. (21st) NYC 10010
Hours: 9:30-5:30 Mon-Fri/ 10-5 Sat
"Current Russian newspapers, periodicals, books." ed.

FABRICS, GENERAL

For specific types of fabrics, see other FABRICS headings

A & N Fabrics 212-719-1773
268 West 39th St. (7-8th) NYC 10018
Hours: 8:30-6 Mon-Fri/ 9-5 Sat
"Dress goods and interior fabrics; retail, wholesale." ed.

Andros Imported Shirting Inc. 212-279-7313
39 West 32nd St. (5th-B'way) NYC 10001
Hours: 9-5 Mon-Fri
"Shirting fabrics; see Angelo." ed.

Art-Max Fabrics 212-398-0755
250 West 40th St. (7-8th) NYC 10018 212-398-0756
Hours: 8:30-5:45 Mon-Fri/ 9-4:45 Sat
"Silks, jerseys, woolens, organza, dress goods; see Allan or Herman."

Ashil Fabrics 212-560-9049
101 West 34th St./1313 Broadway NYC 10006
Hours: 9-6 Mon-Wed,Sat/ 9-6:30 Thurs,Fri
"Mill ends, some pile fabrics." ed.

B & J Fabrics 212-354-8150
263 West 40th St. (7-8th) NYC 10018 212-354-8212
Hours: 8-5:45 Mon-Fri/ 9-4:45 Sat
"Designer fabrics and linings, crepes, tricot, polyknits; see Mel." ed.

BAER FABRICS 502-583-5521
515 East Market, Louisville, KY 40202
Hours: 9-5:30 Mon-Sat

Over 1/2 million yards, imported, domestic, all fibers. (See display ad page 127.)

"Shipment within 24 hours for in-stock items." ed.

S. Beckenstein 212-475-4525
130 Orchard St. (Delancey) NYC 10002
Hours: 9-5:30 Sun-Fri
"Silks, cottons, woolens, sparkle sheer, upholstery and casements, some trims." ed.

Dear
Fellow Designers,
Please let us try to
help you with any or
all of your fabric needs.
Please send for our samples
or send us swatches of
items you are seeking.
We hope to see you soon.
Best Regards, Phil Lawrence
LAWRENCE TEXTILES, INC.
1412 Broadway
New York, New York 10018
212-730-7750

Jerry Brown Imported Fabrics 212-753-3626
37 West 57th St. (5-6th) NYC 10019
Hours: 9-6 Mon-Sat
"Expensive; silks, woolens, cottons." ed.

C & F Liberty Fabrics 212-354-9360
250 West 39th St. (7-8th) NYC 10018
Hours: 9-6 Mon-Fri/ 9-6 Sat
"General fabrics, muslin; reasonable prices, good stock." ed.

D & C Textile Corp. 212-564-6200
124 West 36th St. (7-8th) NYC 10018
Hours: 9-5 Mon-Fri
"Cottons, poplins, jacquards, broadcloth; will order; one week delivery." ed.

Diamond Discount Fabric Center 212-228-8189
165 First Ave. (Stanton) NYC 10009 212-674-9612
Hours: 11-8 Mon-Sat/ 11-7 Sun
"Batiste, poly, slipcover goods." ed.

Discount Fabrics of Burlington NJ 212-354-9275
202 West 40th St. (7th) NYC 10018
Hours: 8-6 Mon-Fri/ 9-5 Sat
"Mostly poly blends; fashion sample remnants, cut pieces only; inexpensive." ed.

Empress Gala 212-719-1315
260 West 39th St. 14th Fl. (7-8th) NYC 10018
Hours: 9-5 Mon-Fri
"Glitter lames, sponge lames, eyelash; primarily wholesale; great prices." ed.

N. Erlanger, Blumgart & Co. 212-221-7100
1450 Broadway (40-41st) NYC 10018
Hours: 9-5 Mon-Fri
"Manufacturer linings, silks, poly/cottons, poly/linens; large quantities only." ed.

F & R Fabric Shop Inc. 212-391-9083
239 West 39th St. (7-8th) NYC 10018 212-391-9084
Hours: 8:30-5:45 Mon-Fri/ 10-4:30 Sat
"Wools, silks, cottons, tapestries, bridal velvets." ed.

Fabric Warehouse 212-431-9510
406 Broadway (Canal) NYC 10013
Hours: 9-6 Mon-Fri (Thurs til 7:30)/ 10-5 Sat, Sun
"Inexpensive, remnants, five floors; notions and trims in the basement." ed.

Fabrications 617-661-6276
1740 Massachusetts Ave., Cambridge, MA 02138
Hours: 10-6 Mon-Fri (Thurs til 8)/ 10-5 Sat/ 12-5 Sun
"Widest selection of batiks, Merrimeko, Haitian cottons." ed.

Fe-Ro Fabrics 212-581-0240
147 West 57th St. (6-7th) NYC 10019
Hours: 9-6:30 Mon-Sat
"Cottons, woolens, silks, velvets, organza, peau-de-soie, designer fabrics, trimmings." ed.

Felsen Fabric Corp. 212-398-9010
264 West 40th St. (7-8th) NYC 10018
Hours: 8-5:45 Mon-Fri/ 9-4:30 Sat
"Selection of laces, embroideries and bridal fabrics, silks, wools and cut velvets." ed.

Fisher & Gentile, Ltd. 212-221-1800
1412 Broadway (39th) NYC 10018
Hours: 9-5 Mon-Fri
"Prints, 30's fabrics, crepes; cash only." ed.

Herbert Gladson 212-730-0602
45 West 45th St. (5-6th) NYC 10036
Hours: 9-6 Mon-Fri/ 10-4 Sat
"Imported and domestic, dress goods, woolens, drapery fabrics, trims, notions, patterns." ed.

GLADSTONE FABRICS 212-765-0760
16 West 56th St. 2nd Fl. (5-6th) NYC 10019
Hours: 9-5 Mon-Fri
(See display ad inside front cover.)
"Wide selection of theatrical fabrics: sequin cloth, lames, milliskin, spandex, gold mesh, etc." ed.

Henry Glass and Co. 212-840-8200
1071 Sixth Ave. (40-41st) NYC 10018
Hours: 9-5 Mon-Fri
"Cottons." ed.

Jasco Fabrics Inc. 212-563-2960
450 Seventh Ave. (34-35th) NYC 10123
Hours: By appt.
"Knits." ed.

Kabat Textile Corp. 212-398-0011
215 West 40th St. (7-8th) NYC 10018
Hours: 8:30-5:30 Mon-Fri
"Light crepe, silk and poly chiffon." ed.

Kalmo Textiles Inc. 212-221-1033
125 West 45th St. (6-7th) NYC 10036
Hours: 9-4:30 Mon-Fri
"Good for tulle, glitzy, day-glo fabrics; very cooperative." ed.

Kordol Fabrics 212-254-8319
194 Orchard St. (Houston-Stanton) NYC 10002
Hours: 8:30-5 Sun-Fri
"Knits, woolens, big selection crepe-de-chine; no swatches, no checks." ed.

Laura Ashley Inc. 212-371-0606
714 Madison Ave. (63-64th) NYC 10021
Hours: 10-6 Mon-Sat (Thurs til 8)
"Calico, Laura Ashley prints, dress and upholstery fabrics, matching wallpaper." ed.

LAWRENCE TEXTILES INC. 212-730-7750
1412 Broadway (39th) NYC 10018
Hours: 9-5 Mon-Fri
(See display ad page 126.)
"Costume fabrics; see Phil Lawrence." ed.

Listokin & Sons Fabrics Inc. 212-226-6111
87 Hester St. (Orchard-Allen) NYC 10002
Hours: 9:30-5:30 Sun-Thurs/ 9:30-4 Fri
"Bridal and formal fabrics; polyester heaven." ed.

Maxine Fabrics Co. 212-391-2282
62 West 39th St. (5-6th) NYC 10018
Hours: 9-5 Mon-Fri
"Milliskin, vyella, cotton batiste, dress goods, unitard patterns; call first." ed.

Mid-Century Textile Corp. 212-239-4411
212 West 35th St. (8-9th) NYC 10018
Hours: 9-5 Mon-Fri
"Silks, polyesters, general dress goods; also glitzy fabrics, lurex; jobber." ed.

Millions of Fabrics Inc. 212-719-2113
584 Eighth Ave. (38-39th) NYC 10018
Hours: 8-5:30 Mon-Fri/ 9:30-4:30 Sat
"Woolens, cotton silks, linens." ed.

Modlin Fabrics 212-391-4130
240 West 40th St. (7-8th) NYC 10018
Hours: 8:30-6 Mon-Fri/ 9-5 Sat
"Lots of poly chiffons, knits, sheers; excellent prices." ed.

A. E. Nathan Co. 212-354-8160
11 East 36th St. (5th) NYC 10018
Hours: 9-5 Mon-Fri
"Piece goods, shirting; see Andy." ed.

Paron Fabrics

60 West 57th St. (6th) NYC 10019 212-247-6451
37 West 57th St. (6th) NYC 10019 212-980-0052

Hours: 9-6 Mon-Sat
"Cottons, silks, woolens, velvets, novelties; quality dress goods, reasonable prices." ed.

Paterson Silks 212-929-7861
36 East 14th St. (University) NYC 10003
Hours: 9-7 Mon-Sat
"Remnants, discount fabrics, draperies, foam cushions." ed.

Pierre Deux Fabrics 212-675-4054
381 Bleecker St. (Charles-Perry) NYC 10014
Hours: 10-6 Mon-Sat
"Country french prints." ed.

Picheny & Konner 212-944-8877
270 West 39th St. (8-9th) NYC 10018
Hours: 9-5 Mon-Fri
"Jobber; double-knits, cottons, brocades." ed.

Plitt, Segall & Sons Inc. 212-921-4040
137 West 37th St. (B'way-7th) NYC 10018
Hours: 9-5 Mon-Fri
"Rayon, velvet, velveteen." ed.

Poli Fabrics 212-245-7589
132 West 57th St. (6-7th) NYC 10019
Hours: 9-6 Mon-Sat
"Silk taffeta and satin, woolens, brocades, cottons, imports; good quality, reasonable." ed.

Rosen & Chadick 212-869-0136
246 West 40th St. (7-8th) NYC 10018
Hours: 8:45-6 Mon-Fri/ 9-5 Sat
"Quality dress goods, difficult to swatch." ed.

Scher Fabrics Inc. 212-736-0240
5 Penn Plaza (34th) NYC 10001
Hours: 9-5 Mon-Fri
"Crepes, crepe backed satin, bengaline moire." ed.

Segal Fabric Center Inc. 212-673-3430
159 Orchard St. (Stanton) NYC 10002
Hours: 8-5:30 Mon-Thurs/ 8-5 Fri/ 8:30-5:45 Sun
"Wholesale, retail; cotton, silk, wool, rayon, novelties." ed.

D. Singer Textile Co. 212-925-4818
55 Delancey St. (Eldridge) NYC 10002
Hours: 10-5 Sun-Thurs/ 10-1 Fri
"Wool suiting, imported linens, cottons, some silks." ed.

Harry Snyder 212-925-0855
70 Hester St. (Allen-Orchard) NYC 10002
Hours: 9-5:30 Sun-Thurs/ 9-12 Fri
"Good selection imported cottons, silks, wools." ed.

Stylecrest Fabrics, Ltd. 212-354-0123
214 West 39th St. (7-8th) NYC 10018
Hours: 8:30-6 Mon-Fri/ Sat by appt. only
"Three floors of cotton voile, silks; wholesale, good prices." ed.

Sutter Textile Co. 212-398-0248
257 West 39th St. (7-8th) NYC 10018
Hours: 9-6 Mon-Fri/ 10-5 Sat
"Dress goods, remnants, upholstery and drapery fabrics; inexpensive."

Testfabrics Inc. 201-469-6446
200 Blackford Ave., Middlesex, NJ 08846
Hours: 8-5 Mon-Fri
"Undyed cottons, rayons, silks; order from swatchbook; one week delivery." ed.

Trebor Textiles Inc. 212-221-1818
275 West 39th St. (7-8th) NYC 10018
Hours: 9-5:30 Mon-Fri/ 10-3 Sat
"Good assortment, inexpensive." ed.

Velvets Inc. 201-379-4272
PO Box 165, Short Hills, NJ 07078
Hours: Leave message anytime
"Wholesale by the yard or piece; order from color card; will custom dye." ed.

Weiss & Katz 212-477-1130
187 Orchard St. (Houston) NYC 10002
Hours: 9-5 Sun-Fri
"Acrylic challis." ed.

Weller Fabrics Inc. 212-247-3790
54 West 57th St. (5-6th) NYC 10019
Hours: 9-6:30 Mon-Sat
"Lots of silk chiffon, brocades." ed.

The Yardstick Fabric Store 212-924-7131
54 West 14th St. (5-6th) NYC 10011
Hours: 9:30-7 Mon-Sat/ 10:30-5 Sun
"Cottons, velvets, rayon jersey." ed.

FABRICS: BURLAP, CANVAS, GAUZE, MUSLIN

See also FABRICS: SCENIC

ATLAS CLEANING CLOTH CORP. 212-226-1042
10 Greene St. (Canal-Grand) NYC 10013 212-925-6661
Hours: 9-4 Mon-Fri (with appt. to 6:30)
All grades bleached and unbleached cheesecloth and muslin.
"Gauze by yd. or box. Very helpful. See Enid or Happy." ed.

BAER FABRICS 502-583-5521
515 East Market, Louisville, KY 40202
Hours: 9-5:30 Mon-Sat
All widths, weights and colors; well stocked. (See display ad page 127.)
"Shipment within 24 hours for in-stock items." ed.

John Boyle & Co. 914-347-3170
3 Westchester Plaza, Elmsford, NY 10523
Hours: 8:30-5 Mon-Fri
"Cotton duck." ed.

Canvas Specialty Co. 718-326-1900
8000 Cooper Ave., Glendale, NY 11385
Hours: 9-5 Mon-Fri
"Packing blankets, webbing, burlap, canvas, cheesecloth, muslin." ed.

Consolidated Canvas Co. 212-929-4880
89 Seventh Ave. (15th) NYC 10011
Hours: 9-5 Mon-Fri
"Canvas." ed.

DAZIAN INC. 212-307-7800
423 West 55th St. (9-10th) NYC 10019
Hours: 9-5 Mon-Fri
Theatrical and display fabrics. Mostly Flame Resistant. (See display ad page 143.)
"Canvas, burlap, gauze, muslin, and more; samples on request." ed.

GLADSTONE FABRICS 212-765-0760
16 West 56th St. 2nd Fl. (5-6th) NYC 10019
Hours: 9-5 Mon-Fri
(See display ad inside front cover.)
"Muslin, chincha; great selection theatrical fabrics." ed.

Jensen-Lewis Co. Inc. 212-929-4880
89 Seventh Ave. (15th) NYC 10011
Hours: 10-7 Mon-Sat (Thurs til 8)/ 12-5 Sun
"Heavyweight canvas by the yard, all colors; also furniture." ed.

LAWRENCE TEXTILES INC. 212-730-7750
1412 Broadway (39th) New York, NY 10018
Hours: 9-5 Mon-Fri
(See display ad page 126.)
"Costume fabrics; speak to Phil Lawrence." ed.

Matera Canvas Products 212-966-9783
5 Lispenard St. (B'way-Church) NYC 10013
Hours: 9:30-5:30 Mon-Fri
"Canvas." ed.

Phylmor Furrier Supply Inc. 212-563-5410
149 West 28th St. (6-7th) NYC 10001
Hours: 8-5 Mon-Fri
"Muslin, drill, canvas and skins." ed.

QUARTET THEATRICAL DRAPERIES CORP. 718-857-2841
1163 Atlantic Ave., Bklyn, 11216
Hours: 7:30-3 Mon-Fri
Complete custom service for all your theatrical needs. A full range of domestic and imported fabrics. Technical advice and consultation. "The Union Shop".
"Curtain rentals available." ed.

Robbie Robinson Textile Corp. 212-921-1164
270 West 39th St. (7-8th) NYC 10018
Hours: 9-5:15 Mon-Fri
"Muslin, burlap, percale, monkscloth; by the bolt only." ed.

ROSE BRAND TEXTILE FABRICS 212-594-7424
517 West 35th St. (10-11th) NYC 10001 800-223-1624
Hours: 8:30-4:45 Mon-Fri
Flame retardant and non flame retardant canvas and muslins in many weights and widths, burlap, scrims, bobinette, gauzes, felt, duvetyn, commando, velour, many hard-to-find fabrics. Sewing to your specifications. (See display ads pages 98, 142.)
"By the yard or by the bolt; nice people." ed.

Saxon Textile Corp. 212-677-3680
744 Broadway (Astor Place) NYC 10003
Hours: 8:30-5:30 Mon-Fri
"Twill, duck, pre-shrunk white gabardine." ed.

Zanfini Canvas/ Zanfini Brothers 718-625-6630
57 Front St. (York) Bklyn 11201
Hours: 5am-3pm Mon-Fri/ or by appt.
"Canvas specialties, custom bags, tarps; see Tony." ed.

FABRICS: DRAPERY, SLIP COVER, UPHOLSTERY

BAER FABRICS 502-583-5521
515 East Market, Louisville, KY 40202
Hours: 9-5:30 Mon-Sat
Huge selection of all major lines. (See display ad page 127.)
"Shipment within 24 hours for in-stock items." ed.

S. Beckenstein 212-475-4525
130 Orchard St. (Delancey) NYC 10002
Hours: 9-5:30 Sun-Fri
"Upholstery and drapery fabrics, some trims, good casements, (upstairs)." ed.

Calico Corners 914-698-9141
1040 Mamaroneck Ave., Mamaroneck, NY 10543
Hours: 9:30-5:30 Mon-Sat (Thurs til 7:30)
"Large selection of discounted drapery and upholstery fabrics." ed.

Decorator's Walk 212-355-5300
979 Third Ave. 18th Fl. (56th) NYC 10022 (Showroom) 212-688-4300
Hours: 9-5 Mon-Fri
"To the trade; upholstery, taffetas, drapery fabrics; expensive." ed.

Esro Products Inc. 212-777-6010
900 Broadway (19-20th) NYC 10011
Hours: 9-4:30 Mon-Fri
"Wholesale; flame retardant drapery lining, muslin." ed.

Frontier Fabrics 212-925-3000
144 Chambers (W. B'way-Greenwich St.) NYC 10007
Hours: 10-6 Mon-Fri
"Very inexpensive upholstery, drapery and cottons." ed.

Gurian's 212-689-9696
276 Fifth Ave. (30th) NYC 10001
Hours: 9-5 Mon-Fri
"Embroidered crewel fabric by the yard; drapery and upholstery fabrics." ed.

Inter-Coastal Textile Corp. 212-925-9235
480 Broadway (Broome-Grand) NYC 10013 212-925-9236
Hours: 9-6 Mon-Thurs/ 9-5 Fri
"Upholstery, slip cover and drapery fabrics; inexpensive, nice about swatching." ed.

Laura Ashley Inc. 212-371-0606
714 Madison Ave. (63rd) NYC 10021
Hours: 10-6 Mon-Sat (Thurs til 7)
"Fabrics and wallcoverings in coordinating patterns." ed.

Liberty of London Shops Inc. 212-888-1057
229 East 60th St. (2-3rd) NYC 10022
Hours: 11-7 Mon-Fri/ 10-6 Sat
"Fine cotton prints and paisleys; English fabrics; special order." ed.

Marimekko Store 212-581-9616
7 West 56th St. (Fifth Ave.) NYC 10019
Hours: 10-6:30 Mon-Fri/ 10-6 Sat
"Fabrics, sheets, bedding, toys, clothes." ed.

Paterson Silks 212-929-7861
36 East 14th St. (University) NYC 10003
Hours: 9-7 Mon-Sat
"Discount drapery and upholstery fabric; custom work available, foam and batting." ed.

Scalamandre Silks Inc. 212-980-3888
950 Third Ave. (57th) NYC 10022 (Showroom)
Hours: 9-5 Mon-Fri
"Wide selection of drapery, upholstery, decorator fabrics; very expensive." ed.

Schumacher 212-644-5900
939 Third Ave. (56th) NYC 10022 (Showroom)
Hours: 9-5 Mon-Fri
"To the trade; collection of Victorian wallpaper and matching fabrics." ed.

Silk Surplus

223 East 58th St. (2-3rd) NYC 10022 212-753-6511
1147 Madison Ave. (85-86th) NYC 10028 212-794-9373

Hours: 10-5:15 Mon-Fri/ 11-4 Sat
"Outlet for Scalamandre fabrics; trims & casements; good about swatching." ed.

Stroheim & Romann Inc. 212-691-0700
155 East 56th St. (3rd-Lexington) NYC 10022 (Showroom)
Hours: 9-5 Mon-Fri
"Expensive, beautiful, upholstery and drapery fabrics; order 24 hrs. before pickup." ed.

Harry Zarin Co. 212-226-3492
72 Allen St. 2nd Fl. (Grand) NYC 10002
Hours: 9-5:30 Sun-Fri
"Large selection of drapery and upholstery fabrics; good prices, helpful." ed.

FABRICS: FELT, VINYL, VELCRO, FOAMBACKED

For millinery felt, see MILLINERY SUPPLIES

Aetna Felt Corp. 201-688-0760
1075 Lousons Rd., Union, NJ 07083
Hours: 8:30-4:30 Mon-Fri
"Industrial felt; catalog." ed.

American Felt & Filter Co. 914-561-3560
34 John St., Newburg, NY 12550
Hours: 9-5 Mon-Fri
"Industrial felt, hat felt, light-weight felt; color cards, will send information." ed.

BAER FABRICS 502-583-5521
515 East Market, Louisville, KY 40202
Hours: 9-5:30 Mon-Sat
Large selection for craft, costume and industrial use. (See display ad page 127.)
"Shipment within 24 hours for in-stock items." ed.

Barr Specialty Corp. 212-243-4562
236 West 26th St. (7-8th) NYC 10001
Hours: 9:30-4:30 Mon-Thurs/ 9:30-2:30 Fri
"Vinyl, web straps, chains, leashes." ed.

Beckmann Felt Co. 212-226-8400
120 Baxter St. (Canal) NYC 10013
Hours: 9-5 Mon-Fri (closed for lunch 12-1)
"All types of felt by the yard." ed.

Bella & Co. 516-921-6868
200 Michael Dr., Syosset, NY 11791
Hours: 8:30-4:30 Mon-Fri/ 8:30-12 Sat
"Distributor of U.S. Naugahyde." ed.

Central Shippee 201-838-1100
46 Star Lake Rd., Bloomingdale, NJ 07403
Hours: 9-5 Mon-Fri
"Catalog; industrial and decorator felt." ed.

Circle Fabrics 212-247-2260
263 West 38th St. (7-8th) NYC 10018 212-719-5153
Hours: 9-5 Mon-Fri
"Felt, vinyl, glitzy, novelty fabrics." ed.

Commonwealth Felt 212-243-7779
160 Fifth Ave. Rm. 714 (22nd) NYC 10010
Hours: Call for hours
"Manufacturer and die cutter of wool and synthetic felts and non-woven fabrics." ed.

Continental Felt 212-929-5262
22 West 15th St. (5-6th) NYC 10011
Hours: 9-4:30 Mon-Fri
"Catalog; industrial and decorator felt by the yard or piece." ed.

DAZIAN INC. 212-307-7800
423 West 55th St. (9-10th) NYC 10019
Hours: 9-5 Mon-Fri
Theatrical and display fabrics. Mostly Flame Resistant. (See display ad page 143.)
"Swatch cards for theatrical and display fabrics; decorator felt; see Norman Paine." ed.

Design Craft Fabric Corp. 312-647-0888
7227 Oak Park, Niles, IL 60648
Hours: 8:30-5 Mon-Fri
"Foam-backed fabric, loop weave fabric for velcro applications; 'attaches like magic'." ed.

Economy Foam Center (AAA Foam Center) 212-473-4462
173 East Houston (Allen) NYC 10002
Hours: 9:30-5:45 Sun-Fri
"Vinyl fabrics, foam rubber sheets, shapes, batting." ed.

LAWRENCE TEXTILES INC. 212-730-7750
1412 Broadway (39th) New York, NY 10018
Hours: 9-5 Mon-Fri
(See display ad page 126.)
"Costume fabrics; speak to Phil Lawrence." ed.

Mechanical Felt & Textiles Co. 201-688-0690
1075 Lousons Rd., Union, NJ 07083
Hours: 9-5 Mon-Fri
"Industrial felt, novelty felt, light felt; swatch catalog." ed.

Standard Felt Co.

13636 S. Western Ave., Blue Island, IL 60406 312-597-9870
Hours: 8-4:30 Mon-Fri

Box 871 (115 S. Palm Ave.) Alhambra, CA 91802 818-282-3165
Hours: 7:30-4:30 Mon-Fri

"Manufacturer of industrial and decorator felt; stock in LA and Chicago." ed.

Superior Specialties Inc. 212-543-1767
5925 Broadway (Van Cortland Pk.) Bronx 10463
Hours: 7-4:30 Mon-Fri
"Patent vinyl fabrics; including pearlized, metallic, crinkle; samples and price list available." ed.

Supreme Felt & Abrasives Co. 312-344-0134
4425 T-James Place, Melrose Park, IL 60160
Hours: 8-4:30 Mon-Fri
"Industrial felt." ed.

FABRICS: FUR & PILE

BAER FABRICS 502-583-5521
515 East Market, Louisville, KY 40202
Hours: 9-5:30 Mon-Sat
Huge selection of plush, shag and craft furs. (See display ad page 127.)
"Shipment within 24 hours for in-stock items." ed.

Beu-Tex 212-398-1681
25 West 39th St. #700 (5-6th) NYC 10018
Hours: 9-5 Mon-Fri
"Wholesale, call first." ed.

Big Four Pile Fabrics 212-966-2466
452 Broadway (Grand-Canal) NYC 10013
Hours: 9-4:30 Mon-Thurs/ 9-2 Fri
"Outlet for fur fabrics." ed.

Borg Textiles 212-221-0570
1450 Broadway (41st) NYC 10018
Hours: 9-5 Mon-Fri
"Wholesale fur and pile fabrics; color card and samples; 500 yard minimum." ed.

DuKane Fabrics 212-964-1554
453 Broadway (Grand) NYC 10013 212-925-8400
Hours: 9-5 Mon-Fri
"Jobber." ed.

Dyersburg & Morgan Inc. 212-679-7733
240 Madison Ave. (37-38th) NYC 10016
Hours: 9-5 Mon-Fri
"Wholesale fur and pile fabrics, also sweatshirt, terry velour; large quantities only." ed.

GLADSTONE FABRICS 212-765-0760
16 West 56th St. 2nd Fl. (5-6th) NYC 10019
Hours: 9-5 Mon-Fri
(See display ad inside front cover.)
"Great selection of theatrical fabrics." ed.

House of Pile Fabric Inc. 212-226-1568
27 Mercer St. (Grand-Canal) NYC 10013
Hours: 8:30-5 Mon-Thurs/ 8:30-2 Fri
"Fake furs, all colors; wholesale." ed.

LAWRENCE TEXTILES INC. 212-730-7750
1412 Broadway (39th) New York, NY 10018
Hours: 9-5 Mon-Fri
(See display ad page 126.)
"Costume fabrics; speak to Phil Lawrence." ed.

FABRICS: LINING, INTERFACING, FUSIBLE

See also NOTIONS: GENERAL & TAILOR'S

Armo Co., Div. of Crown Textiles 212-391-5880
1412 Broadway (39th) NYC 10018
Hours: 9-5 Mon-Fri
"Interfacing; woven, non-woven, fusible, non-fusible; polycrepe lining, poly underlining." ed.

BAER FABRICS 502-583-5521
515 East Market, Louisville, KY 40202
Hours: 9-5:30 Mon-Sat
All weights, every branded type plus manufacturing. (See display ad page 127.)
"Shipment within 24 hours for in-stock items." ed.

GLADSTONE FABRICS 212-765-0760
16 West 56th St. 2nd Fl. (5-6th) NYC 10019
Hours: 9-5 Mon-Fri
(See display ad inside front cover.)
"Lining fabrics; great selection of theatrical fabrics." ed.

Gold Rose Fabrics 212-869-2590
209 West 37th St. (7-8th) NYC 10018
Hours: 9-5 Mon-Fri
"Swatch card; lining, underlining, rayon, siri." ed.

Hymo Textile Corp. 212-226-3583
444 Broadway (Grand-Howard) NYC 10013
Hours: 9-5 Mon-Fri
"Jobber for Hymo." ed.

LAWRENCE TEXTILES INC. 212-730-7750
1412 Broadway (39th) New York, NY 10018
Hours: 9-5 Mon-Fri
(See display ad page 126.)
"Costume fabrics; speak to Phil Lawrence." ed.

Pellon Corp. 212-391-6300
119 West 40th St. (6th) NYC 10018
Hours: 9-5 Mon-Fri
"Wholesale interfacing; non-woven fusible and non-fusible; catalog."

Robbie Robinson Textile Corp. 212-921-1164
270 West 39th St. 4th Fl. (7-8th) NYC 10018
Hours: 9-5:15 Mon-Fri
"Interfacing; woven, non-woven, fusible, non-fusible Stitch Witchery; other basic fabrics." ed.

Staflex Co. 212-279-3000
7 West 36th St. (5-6th) NYC 10018
Hours: 9-5 Mon-Fri
"Wholesale interfacing; non-woven, woven, fusible; catalog." ed.

FABRICS: SCENIC

See also FABRICS: BURLAP, CANVAS, MUSLIN & GAUZE

Alcone Company Inc./Paramount Theatrical 718-361-8373
5-49 49th Ave. L.I.C. 11101
Hours: 9:30-4 Mon-Fri
"Muslin, scrim, velour, repp; theatrical supply house; catalog." ed.

ASSOCIATED DRAPERY & EQUIPMENT CO. 718-895-8668
40 Sea Cliff Ave., Glen Cove, NY 11542 516-671-5245
Hours: 8:30-5 Mon-Fri
Flameproof fabrics: canvas, duvetyne, repp, velour, scrim, mylar, muslin (33"-69"), Ultralure, blackout and many more. Catalog. RUSH ORDERS.
"Helpful; contact Howard Kessler." ed.

BAER FABRICS 502-583-5521
515 East Market, Louisville, KY 40202
Hours: 9-5:30 Mon-Sat
108" muslin, artist canvas, etc. (See display ad page 127.)
"Shipment within 24 hours for in-stock items." ed.

DAZIAN INC. 212-307-7800
423 West 55th St. (9-10th) NYC 10019
Hours: 9-5 Mon-Fri
Theatrical and display fabrics. Mostly Flame Resistant. (See display ad page 143.)
"Wide selection; samples on request; catalog, color cards." ed.

DRAPES·DROPS
CYCS·SCRIMS
ALL SOFT GOODS
WE'VE GOT IT!
WE FABRICATE TO YOUR SPECIFICATIONS. IN STOCK—MUSLINS ·
SCRIMS · FELT · COMMANDO · DUVETYN · BURLAP · GAUZE · NETS · CANVAS ·
SPECIALTY FABRICS · OUR VELOUR IN 23 CUSTOM COLORS ·
FOR ESTIMATES AND IMMEDIATE DELIVERY CALL US!
212-594 7424 800-223 1624
THEATRICAL FABRICS AND FABRICATING
ROSE BRAND
517 W. 35TH ST. NEW YORK, N.Y. 10001

NOTES

F.Y.I.
Order cards for add'l SOURCEBOOK's are in the back.

Esro Products Inc. 212-777-6010
900 Broadway (19-20th) NYC 10011
Hours: 9-4:30 Mon-Fri
"Wholesaler of flame retardant drapery lining and muslin." ed.

GERRIETS INTERNATIONAL 609-758-9121
RR #1, 950 Hutchinson Rd., Allentown, NJ 08501
Hours: 8:30-5 Mon-Fri
*MANUFACTURER: 10', 14', 20', and 33' wide seamless muslin; natural, flameproofed, dyed or bleached white.
*Stage draperies, velours, scrims and cycloramas manufactured to your specifications.
*Front/Rear projection screens; maximum 100' high.
*Reversible, double-sided portable dance floor.
*Stage draperies: Opera dimensions.
*Inherently non-flammable, wide width fabrics.
*Large inventory. (See display ads pages 98, 204.)
"Their "Scenographers Sourcebook" contains samples and specifications; a valuable resource." ed.

GLADSTONE FABRICS 212-765-0760
16 West 56th St. 2nd Fl. (5-6th) NYC 10019
Hours: 9-5 Mon-Fri
(See display ad inside front cover.)
"Monkscloth, muslin, two-way stretch fabrics." ed.

QUARTET THEATRICAL DRAPERIES CORP. 718-857-2841
1163 Atlantic Ave., Bklyn, 11216
Hours: 7:30-3 Mon-Fri
Complete custom service for all your theatrical needs. A full range of domestic and imported fabrics. Technical advice and consultation. "The Union Shop".
"Curtain rentals available." ed.

Reeves Brothers 212-315-2323
1271 Sixth Ave. (50-51st) NYC 10020
Hours: 9-5 Mon-Fri
"Fire retardant fabric." ed.

ROSCO LABORATORIES INC. 914-937-1300
36 Bush Ave., Port Chester, NY 10573 800-431-2338
Hours: 9-5 Mon-Fri
Call for complete line of theatrical fabrics and screens. (See display ad inside back cover.)
"Samples of fabrics and r.p. screen available." ed.

ROSE BRAND TEXTILE FABRICS 212-594-7424
517 West 35th St. (10-11th) NYC 10001 800-223-1624
Hours: 8:30-4:45 Mon-Fri

Flame retardant and non-flame retardant canvas & muslin in many weights and widths. Scrim, bobbinette, burlap, felt, duvetyn, commando, jute webbing, tapes. We stock 23 colors of velour, many hard-to-find fabrics. Sewing to your specifications. CALL ON US. (See display ads pages 98, 142.)

"By the yard or by the bolt; nice people." ed.

Sterling Net & Twine Co. Inc. 201-783-9800
18 Label St., Montclair, NJ 07042
Hours: 9-5 Mon-Fri
"Theatrical, decorative, agricultural, fishing, cargo nets; bulk and custom." ed.

Vadar Industries Ltd. 212-307-6556
750 Tenth Ave. (51st) NYC 10019 800-221-9511
Hours: 8:30-5 Mon-Fri
"Muslin, canvas, blackout cloths, scrim; catalog." ed.

I. WEISS & SONS INC. 212-246-8444
2-07 Borden Ave. (Vernon-Jackson) L.I.C. 11101
Hours: 8:30-4:30 Mon-Fri

90 Years of Serving the Broadway Theatre and all types of Touring Companies.

- *Complete theatrical hardware and rigging
- *Velour, Muslin, Scrim, Commando,
- *Flame Retardant fabrics,
- *Front & rear projection screens
- *Custom fringe, braid and tassles

OUR EXPERIENCE IS AT YOUR SERVICE- PLEASE CALL

"Also manufactures draperies to your specifications." ed.

FABRICS: SHEERS, NETS, LACES, TAFFETA

See also MILLINERY SUPPLIES

BAER FABRICS 502-583-5521
515 East Market, Louisville, KY 40202
Hours: 9-5:30 Mon-Sat

Sheers/taffeta all colors, fibers; laces import/domestic. (See display ad page 127.)

"Shipment within 24 hours for in-stock items." ed.

Max Drucker Fabrics Inc. 212-244-5015
469 Seventh Ave. (36th) NYC 10018
Hours: 12-4:30 Mon-Fri/ or by appt.
"Specializes in taffeta and faille." ed.

Friedman & Distillator 212-233-6394
88 W. Broadway 5th Fl. (Chambers-Warren) NYC 10007
Hours: 9-5 Mon-Fri
"Silk organza, speak to Toni." ed.

GLADSTONE FABRICS 212-765-0760
16 West 56th St. 2nd Fl. (5-6th) NYC 10019
Hours: 9-5 Mon-Fri
(See display ad inside front cover.)
"Great selection of theatrical fabrics; carry nude souffle."

MARTIN IZQUIERDO STUDIO LTD. 212-807-9757
118 West 22nd St. 9th Fl. (6-7th) NYC 10011
Hours: By appt.
English tutu net- soft & stiff in black, white and natural. Also tubular horsehair.
"Costume and prop crafts; Rosco and Haussmann distributor." ed.

LAWRENCE TEXTILES INC. 212-730-7750
1412 Broadway (39th) New York, NY 10018
Hours: 9-5 Mon-Fri
(See display ad page 126.)
"Costume fabrics; speak to Phil Lawrence." ed.

Lew Novik Inc. 212-221-8960
45 West 38th St. (5-6th) NYC 10018 212-354-5046
Hours: 9-5:15 Mon-Fri/ 9:30-2:30 Sat
"Lace motifs and yardage; net, tulle, maline, marquisette." ed.

Ben Raymond Co. 212-777-7350
623 Broadway (Bleecker-Houston) NYC 10012
Hours: 8-5:30 Mon-Fri/ 9-3 Sat
"Jobber; laces, embroidered batistes." ed.

Robbie Robinson Textile Corp. 212-921-1164
270 West 39th St. (7-8th) NYC 10018
Hours: 9-5:15 Mon-Fri
"Jobber; by the piece; net, tulle; also basic fabrics and interfacing."

Stern & Stern Textiles Inc. 212-460-1980
315 Park Ave. South (23-24th) NYC 10022
Hours: 8-6 Mon-Fri
"Nylon net." ed.

Dora Tamary 212-944-0272
264 West 40th St. (7-8th) NYC 10018 212-992-9031
Hours: By appt. only
"Polyester chiffon." ed.

Tinsel Trading 212-730-1030
47 West 38th St. (5-6th) NYC 10018
Hours: 10:30-5 Mon-Fri/ 12-5 Sat
"Gold mesh fabrics; also metallic and antique trims." ed.

FABRICS: SILKS

See also ETHNIC GOODS: AFRICAN & WEST INDIAN
See also ETHNIC GOODS: EAST INDIAN
See also ETHNIC GOODS: ORIENTAL

BAER FABRICS 502-583-5521
515 East Market, Louisville, KY 40202
Hours: 9-5:30 Mon-Sat
Hundreds, all types; prints/solids/jacquards/designer. (See display ad page 127.)
"Shipment within 24 hours for in-stock items." ed.

Far Eastern Fabrics, Ltd. 212-683-2623
171 Madison Ave. (33-34th) NYC 10016
Hours: 9-5 Mon-Fri
"Silks, mummy cloth, ikat, ethnic fabrics." ed.

GLADSTONE FABRICS 212-765-0760
16 West 56th St. 2nd Fl. (5-6th) NYC 10019
Hours: 9-5 Mon-Fri
(See display ad inside front cover.)
"China silk; great selection of theatrical fabrics." ed.

Grand Silk House 212-475-0114
357 Grand St. (Essex) NYC 10002
Hours: 9-5:30 Sun-Thurs/ 9-5 Fri
"Silk, woolens, cottons, velvets, gauze." ed.

Horikoshi Inc. 212-354-0133
55 West 39th St. (5-6th) NYC 10018
Hours: 9-5 Mon-Fri
"Real china silk (color card), crepe-de-chine, charmeuse, silk/rayon china silk, $25 minimum." ed.

Joong WHA Industrial of NY Inc. 212-840-1570
55 West 39th St. (5-6th) NYC 10018
Hours: 9-5 Mon-Fri
"Silks at good prices." ed.

LAWRENCE TEXTILES INC. 212-730-7750
1412 Broadway (39th) New York, NY 10018
Hours: 9-5 Mon-Fri
(See display ad page 126.)
"Costume fabrics; speak to Phil Lawrence." ed.

Shamash & Sons Inc. 212-840-3111
42 West 39th St. (5-6th) NYC 10018
Hours: 9-5 Mon-Fri
"Silks: raw, jacquard, taffeta, fashion; printed wool challis; wholesale." ed.

Silk Surplus

223 East 58th St. (2-3rd) NYC 10022 212-753-6511
1147 Madison Ave. (85-86th) NYC 10028 212-794-9373

Hours: 10-5:15 Mon-Fri/ 11-4 Sat
"Outlet for Scalamandre fabrics at greatly reduced prices; good about swatching." ed.

Super Textile Co. Inc. 212-354-5725
108 West 39th St. 5th Fl. (B'way-6th) NYC 10018
Hours: 9-4:30 Mon-Fri
"Silks, 15 yard minimum." ed.

FABRICS: STRETCH & CORSET

BAER FABRICS 502-583-5521
515 East Market, Louisville, KY 40202
Hours: 9-5:30 Mon-Sat
Lycra spandex, 2 weights, all colors; girdle fabric; tricot.
(See display ad page 127.)
"Shipment within 24 hours for in-stock items." ed.

Charbert Fabrics Corp. 212-986-8081
90 Park Ave. (40th) NYC 10016
Hours: 9:30-5:30 Mon-Fri
"Cotton knits and stretch similar to milliskin; wholesale; nice people." ed.

GLADSTONE FABRICS 212-765-0760
16 West 56th St. 2nd Fl. (5-6th) NYC 10019
Hours: 9-5 Mon-Fri
(See display ad inside front cover.)
"Spandex, milliskin, stretch lames, two way stretch fabrics; wide selection of theatrical fabrics." ed.

E. de Grandmont Inc. 212-943-2740
43 Broadway #1941 (Morris) NYC 10004
Hours: 8:30-4 Mon-Fri
"Stretch fabrics, corset supplies, bras, swim form pads." ed.

L. Laufer & Co. 212-685-2181
39 West 28th St. (B'way-6th) NYC 10001
Hours: 9-4 Mon-Fri
"All corset supplies, Scotch-mate; call first." ed.

LAWRENCE TEXTILES INC. 212-730-7750
1412 Broadway (39th) New York, NY 10018
Hours: 9-5 Mon-Fri
(See display ad page 126.)
"Costume fabrics; speak to Phil Lawrence." ed.

Maxine Fabrics Co. 212-391-2282
62 West 39th St. (5-6th) NYC 10018
Hours: 9-5 Mon-Fri
"Black and white milliskin; also quality dress goods." ed.

Milliken & Co. 212-819-4200
1045 Sixth Ave. (39-40th) NYC 10018
Hours: 9-5 Mon-Fri
"Milliskin." ed.

Herbert L. Toffler & Sons Inc. 212-982-5700
902 Broadway (20-21st) NYC 10010
Hours: 8-5 Mon-Fri
"Spandex, milliskin, etc. by the piece; jobber, good prices." ed.

FABRICS: WOOLENS & UNIFORM FABRICS

BAER FABRICS 502-583-5521
515 East Market, Louisville, KY 40202
Hours: 9-5:30 Mon-Sat
Woolens/worsteds, all wts, solids/stripes/plaids/prints. (See display ad page 127.)
"Shipment within 24 hours for in-stock items." ed.

M. J. Cahn Co. Inc. 212-477-3570
15 East 22nd St. (B'way-Park) NYC 10010
Hours: 9-5 Mon-Fri
"Woolens for uniforms and menswear; period fabrics." ed.

European Woolens Inc. 212-254-1520
177 Orchard St. (Stanton) NYC 10002
Hours: 10-5 Mon-Thurs/ 10-4 Fri/ 9-5 Sun
"Also silks, cottons." ed.

GLADSTONE FABRICS 212-765-0760
16 West 56th St. 2nd Fl. (5-6th) NYC 10019
Hours: 9-5 Mon-Fri
(See display ad inside front cover.)
"Wide selection of theatrical fabrics." ed.

Hamburger Woolen Co. Inc. 212-505-7500
440 Lafayette St. (Astor-8th) NYC 10011
Hours: 9-5 Mon-Fri
"Uniform, tropical weight, gabardines, solid colors." ed.

La Lame, Inc. 212-921-9770
250 West 39th St. 5th Fl. (7-8th) NYC 10018
Hours: 9-5 Mon-Fri
"Great for ecclesiastical costumes: metallic and non-metallic brocades and tapestries." ed.

Lafitte Inc. 212-354-6780
151 West 40th St. 19th Fl. (7th-B'way) NYC 10018
Hours: 9-5:30 Mon-Fri/ by appt.
"Fine wools, wool crepe; expensive." ed.

LAWRENCE TEXTILES INC. 212-730-7750
1412 Broadway (39th) New York, NY 10018
Hours: 9-5 Mon-Fri
(See display ad page 126.)
"Costume fabrics; speak to Phil Lawrence." ed.

Modern Woolens 212-473-6780
129 Orchard St. (Delancey-Rivington) NYC 10002
Hours: 9-6 Sun-Fri
"Complete line English worsteds, mohairs, blends for men and women; major credit cards." ed.

Padob Fabrics Inc. 212-221-7808
251 West 39th St. 3rd Fl. (7-8th) NYC 10018
Hours: 9-5 Mon-Fri
"Uniform woolens, gabardine, solids, plaids; tropical weights." ed.

Scottish Products Inc. 212-755-9656
133 East 55th St. (Lexington) NYC 10022
Hours: 10:30-6 Mon-Fri/ 10:30-5 Sat
"Authentic clan plaids." ed.

Edward Stein Woolen Co. 718-454-7475
184-08 Jamaica Ave., Hollis, NY 11423
Hours: 9-5 Mon-Fri
"Gabardine, fabrics for uniforms." ed.

FENCING EQUIPMENT

American Fencer's Supply Co. 415-863-7911
1180 Folsom St., San Francisco, CA 94103
Hours: 9-5 Mon-Fri (Wed til 7:30)/ 10-2 Sat
"Epees, foils, rapiers, hilts, blades, mats, clothing; catalog is $3." ed.

Blade 212-620-0114
212 West 15th St. (6-7th) NYC 10011
Hours: 10-6 Mon-Fri/ 11-5 Sat
"Fencing equipment and clothing; catalog." ed.

GEORGE SANTELLI INC. 201-871-3105
465 S. Dean St., Englewood, NJ 07631
Hours: 9-5 Mon-Fri/ 11-3 Sat (closed Sat June-Aug)
A complete line of modern fencing equipment & historical weaponry- accurate replicas of swords of all periods. Full color catalogues available. Visa & Mastercard accepted. Orders by mail, phone or over the counter.
"Very helpful." ed.

Santelli Salle D'Armes 212-683-2823
40 West 27th St. (B'way-6th) NYC 10001
Hours: 12-10:30 Mon-Fri/ 12-6 Sat
"Fencing school; small stock of Santelli equipment; will order; evenings best time to call." ed.

FIBRE CASES

Fibre Case and Novelty Co. Inc. 212-254-6060
708 Broadway 7th Fl. (4th-Waverly) NYC 10003
Hours: 9-5 Mon-Fri
"Custom fibre cases; ask for Elliot." ed.

Ikelheiner-Ernst Inc. 212-675-5820
601 West 26th (11th) NYC 10001
Hours: 8-4:30 Mon-Fri
"Fibre storage and shipping cases; will do custom work." ed.

Lee Fordin Sales 212-840-7799
19 West 44th St. (5-6th) NYC 10036
Hours: 9-5:45 Mon-Fri
"Fibre (polypropylene) board and fibre cases." ed.

Oxford Fibre Cases 718-858-0009
762 Wythe Ave. (10th) Bklyn 11211 212-226-6561
Hours: 8-6 Mon-Fri
"Good fibre cases; see Wilber." ed.

Progressive Fibre Products Inc. 212-777-0487
826 Broadway (12th) NYC 10003
Hours: 8:30-5 Mon-Fri
"Inexpensive." ed.

FIREPLACES & EQUIPMENT

See also ARCHITECTURAL PIECES
See also BRASS ITEMS

Danny Alessandro Ltd. 212-421-1928
1156 Second Ave. (61st) NYC 10021 212-759-8210
Hours: 10-6 Mon-Fri
"Period reproduction mantels and fireplace accessories." ed.

Irreplaceable Artifacts
14 Second Ave. (Houston) NYC 10003 212-777-2900
1046 Third Ave. (61st) NYC 10021 212-223-4411
Hours: 10-5 Mon-Fri/ by appt. Sat
"Architectural ornamentation from demolished buildings; antique fireplaces; will rent only in 'as is' condition." ed.

William H. Jackson Co. 212-753-9400
3 East 47th St. (5th-Madison) NYC 10017
Hours: 9-4:30 Mon-Fri
"Antique and reproduction mantels and fireplace accessories; will rent." ed.

Ben Karpen Brass Corp. 212-755-3450
212 East 51st St. (2-3rd) NYC 10022
Hours: 9:30-5:30 Mon-Fri/ 10-4 Sat
"Repro brass items; andirons, fireplace screens, brass beds, etc." ed.

REJOICE LTD./GARY ZELLER, JOYCE SPECTOR 212-869-8636
40 West 39 St. (5-6th) NYC 10018
Hours: By appt. or leave message
Rentals of gas controlled systems with logs. (See display ad page 333.)
"Special effects consultation and services." ed.

FIREWOOD see ICE & DRY ICE

FISHING TACKLE

See also MARINE EQUIPMENT
See also SPORTING GOODS

Capitol Fishing Tackle 212-929-6132
218 West 23rd St. (7-8th) NYC 10011
Hours: 8-5:30 Mon-Fri/ 9-4 Sat
"Tackle, monofilament, black nylon fishline, high test squid line; small or large orders." ed.

Gudebrod Inc. 215-327-4050
262 King St., PO Box 357, Pottstown, PA 19464
Hours: 9-5 Mon-Fri
"Braided fishline, variety of tests on spools; $150 minimum." ed.

PA-KO Cutlery & Scales 212-962-8641
104 South St. (Beekman) NYC 10038
Hours: 2am-10am Mon-Fri
"Scales, knives, gloves, hooks, scalers, brushes; see Jimmy." ed.

FLAGS & BANNERS

AAA American Flag Decorating Co. Inc. 212-279-4644
40 West 37th St. 3rd Fl. (5-6th) NYC 10018
Hours: 8:30-4:30 Mon-Thurs/ 8:30-4 Fri
"Custom flags, banners, bunting." ed.

Abacrome Inc. 212-989-1190
151 West 26th St. 6th Fl. (6-7th) NYC 10001
Hours: 9-5 Mon-Fri
"Custom flags and banners; heavy-duty nylon fabric by the yard; catalog." ed.

ACE BANNER & FLAG CO. 212-620-9111
107 West 27th St. (6th) NYC 10001
Hours: 8:30-5 Mon-Fri

> **Large stock foreign and U.S. flags. Custom mfg. banners, flags, bunting, pennants, etc. Sewing and screen printing capabilities, T-shirts, emblems, armbands, posters, etc. Serving production companies, ad agencies, stylists, movie companies and theatres since 1916.**

"Also gavels, advertising buttons." ed.

Arista Flag Corp. 212-947-8887
575 Eighth Ave. 4th Fl. (38th) NYC 10018
Hours: 8:30-5 Mon-Fri
"Custom orders; heavy duty nylon by the yard; $25 min." ed.

Art Flag Co. Inc. 212-473-8282
6 West 18th St. (5th) NYC 10011 212-929-3035
Hours: 8:30-5 Mon-Fri
"Custom and stock, flags and banners." ed.

Kraus & Sons Inc. 212-620-0408
245 Seventh Ave. (24th) NYC 10001
Hours: 9-5 Mon-Fri
"Flags, banners, trophies, embroidered emblems." ed.

National Flag & Display 212-675-5230
43 West 21st St. (5-6th) NYC 10011
Hours: 9-5 Mon-Fri
"Stock flags; custom work." ed.

FLAMEPROOFING SERVICES & SUPPLIES

For flameproof/flame retardant fabrics, see also FABRICS: SCENIC

ASSOCIATED DRAPERY & EQUIPMENT CO. 718-895-8668
40 Sea Cliff Ave., Glen Cove, NY 11542 516-671-5245
Hours: 8:30-5 Mon-Fri
Flameproofing compound. Flameproof fabrics. RUSH ORDERS!
"Helpful, see Howard Kessler." ed.

Atlantic Research Labs Corp. 718-784-8825
29-05 40th Rd. (29th) L.I.C. 11101
Hours: 8-5 Mon-Fri
"Equipment and supplies." ed.

Bayridge Flameproofing 718-748-5216
8321 Third Ave. Bklyn 11209
Hours: 8-6 Mon-Sat
"Anything, anywhere!, free estimates; also do carpet cleaning." ed.

Flameproof Chemical Co. 212-242-2265
635 West 23rd St. (11-12th) NYC 10011
Hours: 9-5 Mon-Fri
"Distributors of DuPont fire retardants." ed.

General Drapery Services 212-924-7200
635 West 23rd St. (11-12th) NYC 10011
Hours: 9-4 Mon-Fri
"Flameproofing service and supplies." ed.

Gothic Color Co. 212-929-7493
727 Washington St. (Bank-11th) NYC 10014
Hours: 8:30-5 Mon-Thurs/ 8-4:30 Fri
"Sells flameproofing compounds." ed.

Kiesling-Hess Finishing Co. 212-206-7177
525 West 24th St. (10-11th) NYC 10011 215-457-0906
Hours: 9-4:30 Mon-Fri (closed for lunch 11:45-1)
"Contact NY office; materials to be flameproofed are sent to Philadelphia plant." ed.

NEW YORK FLAMEPROOFING CO. INC. 212-924-7200
635 West 23rd St. (12th) NYC 10011
Hours: 9-5 Mon-Fri

We flameproof fabrics, finished draperies, bamboo, moss and many other specialty items used for stage craft. We have in-house drapery sewing and stage rigging operation which is the only shop of its kind in the Big Apple or elsewhere! We sell flameproof confetti, snow and flameproofing compounds with instructions and affidavits of flameproofing are supplied. Expert answers to all flameproofing questions.

"Will take small and large jobs." ed.

QUARTET THEATRICAL DRAPERIES CORP. 718-857-2841
1163 Atlantic Ave., Bklyn, 11216
Hours: 7:30-3 Mon-Fri

Complete custom service for all your theatrical needs. A full range of domestic and imported fabrics. Technical advice and consultation. "The Union Shop".

"Curtain rentals available." ed.

REJOICE LTD./GARY ZELLER, JOYCE SPECTOR 212-869-8636
40 West 39 St. (5-6th) NYC 10018
Hours: By appt. or leave message

Flameaway fire retardant. Zel-Jel for fire stunts. (See display ad page 333.)

"Special effects consultations and services." ed.

REYNOLDS DRAPERY SERVICE INC. 315-845-8632
7440 Main St., Newport, NY 13416
Hours: 8-4 Mon-Fri

We manufacture and service theatrical draperies. Our service includes flameproofing, drycleaning and custom repair. (5 year flameproof guarantee in writing.)

"Also curtain tracks and rigging." ed.

I. WEISS & SONS INC. 212-246-8444
2-07 Borden Ave., L.I.C. 11101
Hours: 8:30-4:30 Mon-Fri

90 Years of Serving the Theatre Community
*Complete Flameproofing and Drycleaning Services
OUR EXPERIENCE IS AT YOUR SERVICE- PLEASE CALL

"Also carry flame retardant scenic fabrics." ed.

FLOCKING SERVICES & SUPPLIES

American Finish and Chemical Co. 617-884-6060
1012 Broadway, Chelsea, MA 02150
Hours: 8:30-4:30 Mon-Fri
"Flock glue." ed.

Dekor Flocking 914-342-1432
183 Wisner Ave., Middleton, NY 10940
Hours: call for hours.
"Flock and flocking equipment; wholesalers, importers." ed.

Donjer Products Co. 516-293-5822
55 Alder St., West Babylon, NY 11704
Hours: 9-4:30 Mon-Fri/ by appt.
"Flocking, flocking equipment and tools." ed.

Vertipile Co. 212-679-6390
261 Fifth Ave. Rm. 503 (29th) NYC 10016 800-225-6315
Hours: 9-5 Mon-Fri
"Ask for Ralph Grasso at New York number." ed.

FLOORCOVERINGS

See also ANTIQUES
See also DANCE & STAGE FLOORING
See also TILE, BRICKS & COBBLESTONES

ABC Carpet Co. Inc. 212-677-6970
881 Broadway (19th) NYC 10003
Hours: 9-6 Mon-Sat (till 8 Thurs)/ 11-5 Sun
"Carpet remnants and runners, large stock downstairs; also linoleum."

Alexander Oriental Rug & Carpet Co. 914-634-3070
8 Crambrook Rd., New City, NY 10956
Hours: By appt.
"Oriental carpets." ed.

Samuel Aronson & Son 212-243-4993
135 West 17th St. (6-7th) NYC 10011
Hours: 8-5 Mon-Fri (Thurs til 6)/ 10-4:30 Sat
"Moderate to good selection of linoleum; also ceramic tile and carpeting." ed.

Canick's Floor Coverings 212-582-4759
611 Ninth Ave. (43rd) NYC 10036
Hours: 8:30-5:30 Mon-Fri/ 8:30-4:30 Sat
"Large selection in stock linoleum and carpeting; remnants." ed.

Carpet Loft

161 Sixth Ave (Spring) NYC 10013 — 212-924-2400
Hours: 9-6 Mon-Sat (Thurs til 8)

903 Broadway (20th) NYC 10010 — 212-505-0770
Hours: 9-6 Mon-Sat (Thurs til 8)/ 12-5 Sun

"Carpet and linoleum; will rent." ed.

Central Carpet — 212-787-8813
426 Columbus Ave. (80-81st) NYC 10024
Hours: 9-6 M,T,W,F/ 10-7:30 Th/ 9-5 Sat/ 11-5 Sun
"Oriental carpets." ed.

Daniels Carpet Service — 718-377-2387
3322 Ave. K Bklyn 11210
Hours: By appt.
"Large selection of floorcoverings, to the trade; see Lou Fanelli." ed.

M. Epstein and Sons — 212-265-3960
809 Ninth Ave. (53-54th) NYC 10019
Hours: 8-5:15 Mon-Fri/ 8-3 Sat
"Linoleum, tile; paint of all types; shades, wallpaper, etc." ed.

Fifth Ave. Rug Exchange — 212-688-2088
665 Fifth Ave. (52-53rd) NYC 10022
Hours: 10-7 Every day
"Persian and Oriental carpets only." ed.

A. J. Heller — 718-729-5210
21-21 51st Ave. (21st) L.I.C. 11101
Hours: Call first
"Industrial tile, carpet, rubber treading in red and black; good prices." ed.

Victor Henschel — 212-688-1732
1061 Second Ave. (56th) NYC 10022
Hours: 9-5:30 Mon-Fri
"Carpeting for sale or rent; good source for linoleum, will order." ed.

D. Kalfarans & Sons Inc. — 718-875-2222
475 Atlantic Ave. (Nevins-3rd) Bklyn 11217
Hours: 9-5 every day
"See George Kalfarans; also do carpet cleaning; remnants at 321 Dean St., Bklyn." ed.

Rug Warehouse — 212-787-6665
2222 Broadway (79th) NYC 10024
Hours: 10-6 Mon-Sat/ 11-5 Sun
"Will rent Oriental carpets." ed.

FLORAL SUPPLIES

See also ARTIFICIAL FLOWERS, PLANTS & FOOD
For containers, see BASKETS
see POTTERY & GREENWARE

A & S Ribbon Supply Co. 212-255-0280
108 West 27th St. (6-7th) NYC 10001
Hours: 5am-2pm Mon-Fri
"Wholesale satin and grosgrain ribbon." ed.

Asty (Div. of A & T Importers) 718-383-8100
150 Green St. Bklyn 11222
Hours: 9-5 Mon-Fri
"Flowers, plants, Christmas decorations for display." ed.

Chingos & Sons Inc. 212-689-0476
818 Sixth Ave. (28-29th) NYC 10001 212-684-6938
Hours: 4am-3pm Mon-Fri
"Wholesale floral supplies and flowers." ed.

Joel Harvey Distributors Inc. 718-859-9103
783 East 42nd St. Bklyn 11210
Hours: 9-5 Mon-Fri
"Floral supplies; art flowers, wire, paint, tape, etc." ed.

Kervar Inc. 212-564-2525
119 West 28th St. (6-7th) NYC 10001
Hours: 6:30-3 Mon-Fri
"Floral supplies, silk flowers, artificial greenery, fruits, vegetables; wholesale only." ed.

Charles Lubin Co. 914-968-5700
131 Saw Mill River Rd., Yonkers, NY 10701
Hours: 7:30-4 Mon-Fri
"Floral supplies, silk flowers." ed.

New York Florists Supply Co. 212-564-6086
103 West 28th St. (6th) NYC 10001
Hours: 5-2:30 Mon-Fri/ 5-12 Sat
"Floral supplies; wholesale only; open Saturday!." ed.

N K Industries Inc. 212-725-5546
43 West 28th St. (B'way-6th) NYC 10001
Hours: 8am-10am Mon-Fri (all other time by appt.)
"Vases, wrapping papers, wax papers, cellophane papers; speak to Nick Campus." ed.

P & S Trading Co. 212-924-7040
159 Varick St. (Vandam) NYC 10013
Hours: 9-5 Mon-Fri
"Plastic and lace ribbon, tulle, net." ed.

Paramount Wire Inc. 718-256-2112
1523 63rd St. (15-16 Ave) Bklyn 11219
Hours: 9-5 Mon-Fri
"Cotton and rayon covered wire; paper stakes." ed.

People's Flowers Corp. 212-686-6291
786 Sixth Ave. (26-27th) NYC 10001
Hours: 8:30-6 every day
"Floral supplies, silk flowers, greenery, artificial food; retail or wholesale." ed.

Al Saffer 212-675-2249
106 West 28th St. (6-7th) NYC 10001
Hours: 7-3 Mon-Fri
"Floral supplies, imported baskets and bamboo." ed.

FLOWERS & PLANTS, ARTIFICIAL
see ARTIFICIAL FLOWERS, PLANTS & FOOD
see TRIMMINGS: FEATHERS & FLOWERS

FLOWERS & PLANTS, LIVE

For containers, see BASKETS
see POTTERY & GREENWARE

Bonsai Dynasty Co. 212-695-2973
851 Sixth Ave. (30th) NYC 10001
Hours: 8:30-6 Mon-Fri/ 9:30-5 Sat/ 11-5 Sun
"Everything for Bonsai." ed.

Farm & Garden Nursery 212-431-3577
2 Sixth Ave. (White-Walker) NYC 10013
Hours: 9-6 every day
"Best nursery in Manhattan; good selection trees, plants, seeds, gardening tools." ed.

Greenhouse Garden Center 718-636-0020
115 Flatbush Ave. (4th) Bklyn 11217
Hours: 9-7:30 Mon-Sat/9-5 Sun
"Gardening supplies, flowers, plants, pots; very helpful; will deliver."

Greenwich Nursery 212-947-1170
506 Ninth Ave. (38th) NYC 10018
Hours: 8-6 Mon-Sat/ 9-5 Sun
"Basic nursery supplies; good midtown location." ed.

New York Gardener Ltd. 212-929-2477
501 West 23rd St. (10th) NYC 10011
Hours: 9-5 every day
"Plants, flowers, landscaping; see David." ed.

Noble Plants 212-206-1164
106 West 28th St. (6th) NYC 10001
Hours: 9:30-6 Mon-Fri/ 10-6 Sat
"Plants; rental available." ed.

Paradise Design 212-684-3397
800 Sixth Ave. (27-28th) NYC 10001
Hours: 9-7 every day (opens at 7:30 W,Th,F)
"See Larry or Jim." ed.

Paradise Palms Inc. 212-689-4968
810 Sixth Ave. (27-28th) NYC 10001
Hours: 9-7 every day (opens at 7:30 W,Th,F)
"Sales and rentals." ed.

People's Flowers Corp. 212-686-6291
786 Sixth Ave. (26-27th) NYC 10001
Hours: 8:30-6 every day
"Live plants of all types; artificial plants, food, floral supplies." ed.

RAINTREE ASSOCIATES 516-643-3835
8 Woodsend Rd. South, Dix Hills, NY 11746
Hours: 8-6 Mon-Fri
Sales-Rentals-Installations.
Horticultural Maintenance Services.
"Highly recommended." ed.

Rialto Florist 212-688-3234
707 Lexington Ave. (57th) NYC 10022
Hours: 24 hrs. every day
"Good stock fresh flowers, plants; they never close." ed.

Twigs Inc. 212-620-8188
399 Bleecker (11th St.) NYC 10014
Hours: 10-6 Mon-Fri/ 12-5 Sat
"Special stuff." ed.

York Floral 212-686-2070
804 Sixth Ave. (27-28th) NYC 10001
Hours: 8:30-6 Mon-Fri
"Live and artificial plants, flowers; rental or purchase; artificial department is closed on Thursdays." ed.

FLYING

FOY INVENTERPRISES INC. 702-732-3396
PO Box 60141, Las Vegas, NV 89160 702-732-4077
Hours: 8-4 Mon-Fri
FLYING BY FOY "The Standard of the Industry".
"Contact Peter Foy or Garry Foy." ed.

David Hale 215-848-2448
6762 Elmen St., Philadelphia, PA 19119
Hours: By appt.
"Flys people." ed.

Pook, Diemont, & Ohl 212-982-7583
135 Fifth Ave. (20th) NYC 10010
Hours: 9-6 Mon-Fri
"Consultation and contracting of all types of rigging; flys people." ed.

FOAM, COMPONENT see CASTING SUPPLIES

FOAMCORE see PAPER, CARDBOARD & FOAMCORE PRODUCTS

FOAM SHEETING & SHAPES

See also UPHOLSTERY SUPPLIES

ABC Foam Rubber Center Inc. 212-431-9485
77 Allen St. (Delancey-Grant) NYC 10002
Hours: 9-5:30 Mon-Fri (Sat til 3)
"Flexible foam sheets and shapes; pillow forms." ed.

A & S Novelty Packaging & Display Corp 201-861-4226
2179 83rd St., North Bergen, NJ 07047
Hours: 8-5:30 Mon-Fri
"Ethafoam rod and sheet, styrofoam; will die cut foam." ed.

Acme Foam 718-622-5600
900 Dean St. Bklyn 11238
Hours: 9-5 Mon-Fri
"Ethafoam plank and roll." ed.

BAER FABRICS 502-583-5521
515 East Market, Louisville, KY 40202
Hours: 9-5:30 Mon-Sat
All sizes and shapes cut to order. (See display ad page 127.)
"Shipment within 24 hours for in-stock items." ed.

Canal Rubber Supply Co. 212-226-7339
329 Canal St. (Greene) NYC 10013
Hours: 9-5 Mon-Fri/ 9-4:30 Sat
"Good stock of foam rubber, variety of type, size, thickness, and density; also latex and rubber tubing." ed.

Comfort Industries 718-392-5300
39-35 21st St. L.I.C. 11101
Hours: 8:30-4:30 Mon-Fri
"Aerated foam; cushions: foam, fiber, feather, down." ed.

Dixie Foam Co. 212-777-3626
20 East 20th St. (Park S.-B'way) NYC 10003
Hours: 10-6 Mon-Sat (Thurs til 8)
"Foam rubber, mattress sizes; pricey." ed.

Dura-Foam Products Inc. 718-894-2488
63-02 59th Ave., Maspeth, NY 11378
Hours: 8-4:30 Mon-Fri
"Rigid and flexible urethane foam, foam rubber and Scotfoam." ed.

Economy Foam Center/AAA Foam Center 212-473-4462
173 East Houston (Allen) NYC 10002
Hours: 9:30-5:45 Sun-Fri
"Foam rubber sheets, shapes, batting by bag or roll, pillow shapes, vinyl fabrics." ed.

Foam Tex 212-674-8440
51 East 21st St. (Park Av.S.-B'way) NYC 10010
Hours: 9-5 Mon-Fri/ 11-4 Sat
"Ethafoam rod, small or large orders." ed.

Industrial Plastics 212-226-2010
309 Canal St. (B'way-Mercer) NYC 10013
Hours: 8:30-5 Mon-Fri/ 8:30-4 Sat
"Styrofoam sheets and shapes; component foams and resins." ed.

Inner Space Foam & Upholstery Center 212-533-9590
34 Avenue A (2nd St.) NYC 10009 212-982-5382
Hours: 10:30-6 Mon-Sat.
"Foam rubber in all thicknesses from 1/16 and up." ed.

Modern Miltex Corp. 212-585-6000
280 East 134th St. (Alexander Ave.) Bronx 10454
Hours: 8-4 Mon-Fri
"Styrofoam, styro shapes, adhesives." ed.

Rempac Foam Corp. 201-773-8880
84-182 Dayton Ave. (Bldg. 1F), Passaic, NJ 07055
Hours: 9-5 Mon-Fri
"Ethafoam rod and sheet, beadboard, estafoam; will die cut foam." ed.

Rogers Foam Corp. 203-246-7234
3580 Main St., Hartford, CT 06120
Hours: 8-4 Mon-Fri
"Scotfoam." ed.

Snow Craft Co. Inc. 718-347-4473
112 South 6th St., New Hyde Park, NY 11040
Hours: 9-5 Mon-Fri
"Styrofoam, will cut to size; delivery is extra." ed.

Styro Sales Co. Inc. 718-786-1791
25-34 50th Ave. L.I.C. 11101
Hours: 7-5 Mon-Fri
"Sheet styrofoam; good stock, reasonable prices; pickups til 3:30." ed.

FOG MACHINES & FOG JUICE

See also SPECIAL EFFECTS SERVICES

Mutual Hardware 718-361-2480
5-45 49th Ave. (Vernon Blvd.) L.I.C. 11101
Hours: 8:30-5 Mon-Fri
"Fog powder, fog juice in stock; theatrical hardware." ed.

Production Arts Lighting Inc. 212-489-0312
636 Eleventh Ave. (46th) NYC 10036
Hours: 9-5:30 Mon-Fri
"Fog machines and fog juice, lighting equipment rental." ed.

REJOICE LTD./GARY ZELLER, JOYCE SPECTOR 212-869-8636
40 West 39 St. (5-6th) NYC 10018
Hours: By appt. or leave message
Non-toxic Bio-Fog, Navy Fog. No smell! No residue! (See display ad page 333.)
"Also atmospheric effects; special effects consultation and services." ed.

ROSCO LABORATORIES INC. 914-937-1300
36 Bush Ave., Port Chester, NY 10573 800-431-2338
Hours: 9-5 Mon-Fri
Safe, realistic smoke: non-toxic, non-irritating. (See display ad inside back cover.)
"Fog machines and chemicals; for specialized applications, call Rosco." ed.

THE SET SHOP 212-929-4845
3 West 20th St. (5th) NYC 10011
Hours: 9-6 Mon-Fri/ 10-4 Sat
Dry ice style, juice style. (Electric, butane, Ram Jet). Fog Juice. (See display ad page 316.)
"Full scene shop; non-union." ed.

Stage Lighting Distributors

346 West 44th St. (8-9th) NYC 10036 — 212-489-1370
Hours: 9-5 Mon-Fri

1653 N. Argyle Ave., Hollywood, CA 90028 — 213-466-8324
Hours: 9-5 Mon-Fri — 800-228-0222

"Opti-Mist fog and smoke." ed.

THEATRE MAGIC — 614-459-3222
6099 Godown Rd., Columbus, OH 43220
Hours: 8:30-5:30 Mon-Fri
(See display ad page 334.)
"Fog-master machines and Aquafog component; also cobweb system." ed.

Times Square Stage Lighting — 212-245-4155
318 West 47th St. (8-9th) NYC 10036
Hours: 8:30-5:30 Mon-Fri/ 10-2 Sat (Sat hours: Sept-May only)
"Mainly stage electrics; stocks fog materials." ed.

FORMICA

See also LUMBER

LeNoble Lumber Co. Inc. — 212-246-0150
500 West 52nd St. (10-11th) NYC 10019
Hours: 8-3 Mon-Fri (closed for lunch 12-1)
"Doors, plywood, formica, moldings, masonite, millwork, windows, sonotube." ed.

Manhattan Laminates Ltd. — 212-239-8588
520 West 36th St. (10-11th) NYC 10018
Hours: 7:30-4 Mon-Fri
"See Paul." ed.

THE SET SHOP — 212-929-4845
3 West 20th St. (5th) NYC 10011
Hours: 9-6 Mon-Fri/ 10-4 Sat
We stock 50 colors in many finishes. Custom formica fabrication. (See display ad page 316.)
"Full scene shop; non-union." ed.

FRAMES & FRAMING

See also ARTISTS MATERIALS
For picture glass, see also GLASS & MIRRORS

APF Inc. — 212-988-1090
783 Madison Ave. (66-67th) NYC 10021
Hours: 9:30-5:30 Mon-Fri/ 10-5 Sat
"Custom framing." ed.

Art Outlet Inc. 212-751-5443
200 East 59th St. (2-3rd) NYC 10022
Hours: 11-7 Mon-Sat
"Picture framing at discount prices; custom work." ed.

Arthur Brown and Brothers Inc. 212-575-5555
2 West 46th St. (5-6th) NYC 10036
Hours: 8:45-5:45 Mon-Fri
"Framing supplies, custom framing available; art supplies." ed.

G. Elter 212-734-4680
740 Madison Ave. (64-65th) NYC 10021
Hours: Call for hours
"Victorian brass and porcelain picture frames, small lampshades." ed.

Fleischer Frames 212-840-2248
32 West 39th St. (5-6th) NYC 10018
Hours: 8-5 Mon-Fri
"Inexpensive frames and framing." ed.

Frames By You Inc. 212-874-2337
136 West 72nd St. (Columbus-B'way) NYC 10023
Hours: 11-9 Mon-Thurs/ 11-6 Fri/ 10-5 Sat/ 12-5 Sun
"Helpful for making your own frames; custom frames; see owner, Bernard." ed.

INTERNATIONAL PAPER COMPANY 704-872-8974
Taylorsville Road Highway 90, Statesville, NC 28677 800-438-1701
Hours: 8-5 Mon-Fri
GATORFOAM® Laminated Foam Panel. Call 800# for local dealer.
"Available in 4'x8' sheets; 5 thicknesses from 3/16" to 1½"." ed.

Lee Art Shop 212-247-0110
220 West 57th St. (7th-B'way) NYC 10019
Hours: 9-7 Mon-Fri/ 9:30-6 Sat
"Framing supplies, custom framing; art supplies." ed.

New York Frame and Picture Co. 212-233-3205
29 John St. 2nd Fl. (Nassau) NYC 10038
Hours: 8:30-4:30 Mon-Fri
"Framing, lamination; mats cut and glass replaced while-you-wait." ed.

One Hour Framing Shop 212-944-9429
1169 Sixth Ave. (45-46th) NYC 10036
Hours: 9-7 Mon-Fri/ 10-6 Sat
"Metal, wood frames, custom framing, dry mounting." ed.

Pearl Paint Co. Inc.

308 Canal St. (Mercer) NYC 10013 212-431-7932
Hours: 9-5:30 Mon-Sat/ 11-4:30 Sat

2411 Hempstead Turnpike, East Meadow, NY 11554 516-731-3700
Hours: 9:30-5:45 Mon-Sat (Wed, Fri til 8:45)

"Large selection of section frames and stock sizes; art supplies." ed.

J. Pocker & Son Inc. 212-838-5488
824 Lexington Ave. (63rd) NYC 10021
Hours: 9-5:30 Mon-Sat
"Frames, custom framing, dry mounting; posters and prints; very helpful." ed.

Charles Ree Co. Inc. 212-685-9077
381 Fifth Ave. (35-36th) NYC 10016 212-532-3552
Hours: 9-6:30 Mon-Fri/ 9-5:30 Sat
"Framing while-you-wait on stock sizes; mats and glass cut." ed.

FURNITURE PARTS

See also HARDWARE, DECORATIVE

Alexanders Hardware 212-267-0336
60 Reade St. (B'way-Church) NYC 10007
Hours: 8:30-5:45 Mon-Fri/ 8:30-5 Sat
"Decorative furniture hardware, turnings, odds and ends." ed.

American Wood Column Corp. 718-782-3163
913 Grand St. (Bushwick-Morgan) Bklyn 11211
Hours: 8-4:30 Mon-Fri
"Columns, pedestals, architectural and furniture pieces." ed.

Arnold Wood Turning Co. 914-235-0822
38 Nardozzi Pl., New Rochelle, NY 10801
Hours: 8:30-4:30 Mon-Fri
"Finials." ed.

Decorators Hardware Co. 212-755-2168
155 East 52nd St. (3rd-Lexington) NYC 10022 212-755-0895
Hours: 8:30-6 Mon-Fri/ 9-4 Sat
"Furniture legs, many shapes and sizes, decorative hardware." ed.

FURNITURE RENTAL & PURCHASE: GENERAL

See also ANTIQUES
See also DEPARTMENT STORES
See also PROP RENTAL HOUSES
See also THRIFT SHOPS

Adirondack Rents — 212-972-1700
219 East 42nd St. 5th Fl. (2-3rd) NYC 10017
Hours: 9-5 Mon-Fri
"Contemporary furniture rental; chairs, tables, desks." ed.

E. J. Audi — 212-679-7580
317 East 34th St. (1-2nd) NYC 10016
Hours: 9:30-5:30 Mon-Fri (Thurs til 8)/ 9:30-5:30 Sat
"American traditional furniture, rental or purchase." ed.

Broadway Bazaar — 212-873-9153
2025 Broadway (69th) NYC 10023

Columbus Avenue Bazaar — 212-362-7335
540 Columbus Ave. (86th) NYC 10024

First Avenue Bazaar — 212-737-2003
1453 First Ave. (75th) NYC 10021

Lexington Avenue Bazaar — 212-734-8119
1037 Lexington Ave. (74th) NYC 10021

Madison Avenue Bazaar — 212-348-3786
1186 Madison Ave. (86th) NYC 10028

Second Avenue Bazaar — 212-683-2293
501 Second Ave. (28th) NYC 10016

Third Avenue Bazaar — 212-988-7600
1145 Third Ave. (66th) NYC 10021

Third Avenue Bazaar — 212-861-5999
1362 Third Ave. (77th) NYC 10021

West Third Street Bazaar — 212-673-4138
125 West 3rd St. (6th) NYC 10012

Hours: 10-6:30 Mon-Sat/ 11-5:30 Sun
"Modern kitchenware, furniture, lamps, picture frames, accessories."

Bon-Marche

55 West 13th St. (5-6th) NYC 10011 (main store/warehouse) — 212-620-5550
Hours: 10:30-6:30 Mon-Sat
"Contemporary chairs, tables, marble table tops, sofas, desks, bookcases, lamps and accessories." ed.

(continues next page)

1060 Third Ave. (62-63rd) NYC 10021 212-620-5592
Hours: 10:30-6:30 Mon-Sat (Thurs til 9)
"Contemporary chairs, tables, marble table tops, sofas, desks, bookcases." ed.

Brancusi of N.Y. City Inc. 212-688-7980
938 First Ave. (51-52nd) NYC 10022
Hours: 9:30-6 Mon-Sat (Mon, Thurs til 8)
"Glass tables, coffee tables; rental or purchase." ed.

Conran's

160 East 54th St. (Lexington) NYC 10022 212-371-2225
2-8 Astor Place (8th-B'way) NYC 10003 212-505-1515

Hours: 10-9 Mon-Fri/ 10-7 Sat/ 12-6 Sun
"Contemporary/high-tech furniture and accessories for the home." ed.

Decorator's Warehouse 212-489-7575
665 Eleventh Ave. (48-49th) NYC 10019
Hours: 10-6 Mon-Sat/ 12-5 Sun
"Contemporary furniture, rental or purchase." ed.

Thomas A. Deming Co. Inc. 201-333-8609
470 Westside Ave., Jersey City, NJ 07304 212-732-2659
Hours: 9-5 Mon-Fri
"Chairs, tables, bleachers, tents; rental only; see Mr. Jackson; very helpful." ed.

Design Furniture Warehouse 212-673-8900
902 Broadway (20th) NYC 10011
Hours: 10-6 Mon-Fri/ 10-5 Sat/ 12-5 Sun
"Contemporary furniture, rental or purchase." ed.

The Door Store

1 Park Ave. (33rd) NYC 10022 212-679-9700
210 East 51st St. (2-3rd) NYC 10022 212-753-2280

Hours: 10-6 Mon-Sat (Thurs til 8)
"Contemporary furniture." ed.

Eclectic Furniture Center 516-283-8850
35 Main St., Southampton, NY 11968
Hours: 10-6 Mon-Sat/ 12-5 Sun
"Modern, contemporary furniture; purchase only." ed.

Fairfield County Estate Liquidators Inc. 203-838-6541
66 Fort Point Rd., E. Norwalk, CT 06855
(off Exit 16, CT Thruway; turn right, follow signs)
Hours: 9-5 Mon-Sat/ 10-5 Sun
"Wide selection of furniture and housewares from estates; Victorian to modern; great prices." ed.

Gotham Galleries 212-677-3303
80 Fourth Ave. (10-11th) NYC 10003
Hours: 10-6 Mon-Sat/ 1-6 Sun
"Furniture, oriental rugs, bronzes; rental or purchase; custom refinishing." ed.

International Home 212-684-4414
440 Park Ave. South (30th) NYC 10016
Hours: 10-5:30 Mon-Sat/ 11-5 Sun
"Modern furniture, modular and formica units; rental or purchase." ed.

George J. Kempler Co. Inc. 212-989-1180
160 Fifth Ave. 3rd Fl. (21st) NYC 10010
Hours: 9-5 Mon-Fri (Thurs til 8)/ 10-4 Sat
"Early American to modern furniture; large store, good looking stuff; pricey; see Jerry for rentals." ed.

J. J. Peoples Ethan Allen Galleries 212-989-1700
71 Fifth Ave. (15th) NYC 10003
Hours: 10-6 Mon-Sat (Thurs til 8:30)
"American traditional; rental or purchase." ed.

Seminole Furniture Shops Inc. 212-505-7211
115 East 23rd St. (Park-Lexington) NYC 10010
Hours: 9:30-5 Mon-Fri/ 9:30-2:30 Sat
"Contemporary furniture, limited stock; rental, purchase." ed.

William Spencer 609-235-3764
Creek Road, Mount Laurel, NJ 08060
Hours: 10-5 Mon-Thurs/ 10-5, 7-9 Fri
"Antique repro furniture, toys, lamps, and lighting fixtures." ed.

Workbench

470 Park Ave. South (32nd) NYC 10016 212-481-5454
2091 Broadway (72-73rd) NYC 10023 212-724-3670
1320 Third Ave. (76th) NYC 10021 212-753-1173

Hours: 10-6 Mon-Sat (Thurs til 8)/ 12-5 Sun
"Contemporary furniture." ed.

FURNITURE RENTAL & PURCHASE: CHILDREN'S

Ben's Babyland 212-674-1353
87 Avenue A (5-6th) NYC 10009
Hours: 9-5:30 Mon-Sat (Tues til 8)/ 10-5 Sun
"Children's furniture, rental or purchase." ed.

Childcraft Center

155 East 23rd St. (3rd-Lexington) NYC 10010 212-674-4754
150 East 58th St. (3rd-Lexington) NYC 10155 212-753-3196

Hours: 10-5:45 Mon-Fri/ 10-4:45 Sat
"Children's furniture, rental or purchase." ed.

Lewis of London NYC Inc. 212-688-3669
215 East 51st St. (2-3rd) NYC 10022
Hours: 10-6 Mon-Sat (Thurs til 8)
"Well designed children's furniture; expensive." ed.

Schachters Babyland 212-777-1660
81 Avenue A (6th St.) NYC 10009
Hours: 9-5:30 every day
"Children's furniture, rental or purchase." ed.

Schneider's 212-228-3540
20 Avenue A (2nd St.) NYC 10009
Hours: 10-6 Mon-Sat (Mon, Thurs til 8)/ 10-5 Sun
"Children's furniture, rental or purchase; see Roy." ed.

FURNITURE RENTAL & PURCHASE: FRAMES

Artistic Frame Co. 212-289-2100
390 McGuinness Blvd. (Dupont) Bklyn 11222
Hours: 9-5 Mon-Fri/ by appt. Sat
"Period reproduction furniture frames, raw or finished; see Lois; catalog; reasonable." ed.

Devon Shops 212-686-1760
111 East 27th St. (Lexington-Park) NYC 10016
Hours: 10-6 Mon-Fri/ 11-5 Sat, Sun
"Period reproduction furniture; raw frame or finished with upholstery; expensive." ed.

IPF International 201-345-7440
11-13 Maryland Ave., Paterson, NJ 07503
"Period reproduction furniture, raw frame or finished with upholstery; catalog." ed.

Ressler Importers Inc. 212-674-4477
80 West 3rd St. (Sullivan) NYC 10012 212-533-5750
Hours: 8-4:30 Mon-Fri (call for appointment)
"Period reproductions, raw furniture frames; catalog." ed.

FURNITURE RENTAL & PURCHASE: GARDEN

A-Flushing Woodworking — 718-357-4373
196-15 Northern Blvd., Flushing, NY 11358 — 718-357-4244
Hours: 9-5 Mon-Fri
"Oak and pine outdoor furniture, including Adirondack and cedar log styles; benches and swings; brochure." ed.

Florentine Craftsmen Inc. — 718-937-7632
46-24 28th St. L.I.C. 11101 — 212-532-3926
Hours: 8:30-4:30 Mon-Fri
"Fountains, statues, columns, tables, chairs, benches for outdoor use; expensive." ed.

Jensen-Lewis Co. Inc. — 212-929-4880
89 Seventh Ave. (15th) NYC 10011
Hours: 10-7 Mon-Sat (Thurs til 8)/ 12-5 Sun
"Lawn and home furniture; many colors of heavy weight canvas by the yard." ed.

Mayhew — 212-759-8120
509 Park Ave. (59th) NYC 10022
Hours: 9-5 Mon-Fri
"Garden furniture; also china, crystal, ceramic and porcelain; will rent." ed.

FURNITURE RENTAL & PURCHASE: OFFICE

Abie's Baby Inc. — 212-741-1920
524 West 23rd St. (10-11th) NYC 10011
Hours: 9-5 Mon-Fri/ 10:30-4 Sat
"Office furniture; rental or purchase." ed.

Allen Office Furniture — 212-929-8228
165 West 23rd St. (6-7th) NYC 10011
Hours: 9-5 Mon-Fri
"Office furniture; see Sol." ed.

Chelsea Desk Co. — 212-682-6050
360 Lexington Ave. (40-41st) NYC 10017
Hours: 9-5 Mon-Fri
"New and used desks." ed.

Dallek — 212-684-4848
269 Madison Ave. (39-40th) NYC 10017
Hours: 9-5 Mon-Fri
"Office furniture; rental or purchase; expensive." ed.

Charles S. Nathan Clearance Center 212-683-8990
711 Third Ave. (44th) NYC 10017
Hours: 9-4:30 Mon-Fri
"Rental or purchase." ed.

Pearl Showroom 212-431-7932
42 Lispenard (Church-B'way) NYC 10013
Hours: 9-5:30 Mon-Sat
"Drafting tables, chairs, lamps, easels, flat files, blueprint racks, etc." ed.

Regan Furniture Corp. 212-683-8990
711 Third Ave. (44th) NYC 10017
Hours: 9-5 Mon-Fri
"Office furniture; rental or purchase; expensive." ed.

Security Office Furniture Co. Inc. 212-924-1485
140 West 23rd St. (6-7th) NYC 10011
Hours: 8:30-5 Mon-Fri
"See Gail for rentals." ed.

Wolff Office Equipment 212-246-7890
1860 Broadway (61-62nd) NYC 10023
Hours: 8:30-5 Mon-Fri
"Office equipment; rental or purchase." ed.

FURNITURE RENTAL & PURCHASE: RESTAURANT

See also BUTCHER BLOCK
See also KITCHEN EQUIPMENT, INDUSTRIAL

AAA Restaurant Equipment 212-966-1891
284 Bowery (Houston) NYC 10012
Hours: 9-5 Mon-Fri/ 9-2 Sat
"New and used restaurant furniture, kitchen appliances and equipment; very reasonable." ed.

Alexander Butcher Block & Supply 212-226-4021
176 Bowery (Delancey) NYC 10013
Hours: 10-5 Mon-Fri/ 10-4 Sat, Sun
"Tables, chairs, bentwoods, butcher block." ed.

Empire State Chair Co. Inc. 212-421-9470
305 East 63rd St. (1st-2nd) NYC 10021
Hours: 9-5 Mon-Fri
"Bentwood chairs, raw or finished; must order 6-8 weeks in advance; 12 piece minimum ." ed.

William Koniak Inc. 212-475-9877
191 Bowery (Spring-Delancey) NYC 10002
Hours: 8-5 Mon-Fri/ 9-4 Sat
"Used tables, chairs, stools." ed.

Tip Top/Lebensfeld Top Equipment Corp. 212-925-1998
222 Bowery (Prince-Spring) NYC 10012 212-925-1999
Hours: 8:30-4:30 Mon-Fri/ 9-2:30 Sat
"Restaurant and office chairs, tables, stools, cast iron table bases; see Chris." ed.

Thonet Industries 212-421-3520
305 East 63rd St. 14th Fl. (1st-2nd) NYC 10021
Hours: 9-5 Mon-Fri
"Quality bentwood chairs, raw or finished; catalog." ed.

FURNITURE RENTAL & PURCHASE: UNFINISHED

For antique repro frames, see FURNITURE: FRAMES

Beta Custom Furniture

18 West 23rd St. (5-6th) NYC 10011 212-243-3695
Hours: 10-7 Mon-Fri/ 10-5 Sat

228 East 51st St. (2-3rd) NYC 10022 212-355-1029
Hours: 10-7 Mon-Fri/ 10-5 Sat

1519 Third Ave. (85-86th) NYC 10028 212-794-9222
Hours: 10-7 Mon-Fri/ 10-5 Sat/ 12-5 Sun

"Unfinished custom and stock furniture; will do formica work." ed.

Castile Unpainted Furniture 212-662-1474
2737 Broadway (104-105th) NYC 10025
Hours: 10-6:30 Mon-Fri/ 10-5 Sat,Sun
"Custom and ready-made unfinished furniture." ed.

Gothic Cabinet Craft

168 Fifth Ave. (21-22) NYC 10010 212-242-1897
Hours: 10-7 Mon-Fri/ 10-6 Sat/ 11-5 Sun

1655 Second Ave. (86th) NYC 10028 212-288-2999
Hours: 10-7 Mon-Fri/ 10-6 Sat/ 11-5 Sun

2543 Broadway (95-96th) NYC 10025 212-749-2020
Hours: 10-7 Mon-Fri/ 10-6 Sat/ 12-5 Sun

"Custom and ready-made unfinished furniture; formica work; cheap."

Olympic Unpainted Furniture 212-982-8504
141 Fifth Ave. (21st) NYC 10010 212-533-0843
Hours: 9:30-6:30 Mon-Fri/ 10-5 Sat, Sun
"Custom and ready-made unfinished furniture." ed.

Unpainted Furniture by Knosos 212-242-0966
538 Sixth Ave. (14-15th) NYC 10011
Hours: 9-7 Mon-Fri/ 9-5:30 Sat, Sun
"Custom and ready-made unfinished furniture." ed.

FURNITURE REPAIR & REFINISHING

See also UPHOLSTERERS
For supplies,see FURNITURE PARTS
see UPHOLSTERY TOOLS & SUPPLIES

Artbench 212-427-3770
254 East 89th St. (2-3rd) NYC 10128
Hours: 10-3 Mon-Fri
"Refinishing and repair." ed.

Barewood Furniture Stripping

106 Ferris St. Bklyn 11231 718-875-9037
Hours: 8-6 Mon-Fri/ 8-12 Sat

141 Atlantic Ave. Bklyn 11201 718-875-3833
Hours: By appt. Mon-Fri/ 10-4 Sat

"Will strip any piece." ed.

Chairs Caned 212-724-4408
133 West 72nd St. 7th Fl. (Columbus-B'way) NYC 10023
Hours: 1-5 Thurs-Sat
"Caner; lovely work, reasonable prices." ed.

Gotham Galleries 212-677-3303
80 Fourth Ave. (10-11th) NYC 10003
Hours: 10-6 Mon-Sat/ 1-6 Sun
"Custom refinishing; furniture, oriental rugs, bronzes; rental or purchase." ed.

Fine Art Finishing 212-831-6128
315 East 91st St. 6th Fl. (1-2nd) NYC 10028
Hours: 8-4:30 Mon-Fri
"Stripping." ed.

Veteran Caning Shop 212-868-3244
550 West 35th St. (10-11th) NYC 10001
Hours: 8-4:30
"Fast and friendly service; also sells supplies." ed.

York End Antiques 212-534-0777
1388 Lexington Ave. (91-92nd) NYC 10128
Hours: 10-6:45 Mon-Fri/ 11-6 Sat (closed Sat. during Summer)
"Caning and rushwork; furniture repair." ed.

GAMES

See also TOYS
For pinball machines, see AMUSEMENTS

Chess Shop — 212-475-9580
230 Thompson St. (Bleecker-3rd) NYC 10012
Hours: 12-12 every day
"Chess sets, books, boards." ed.

The Compleat Strategist — 212-685-3880
11 East 33rd St. (Madison-5th) NYC 10016
Hours: 10:30-6 Mon-Sat
"Games and miniature figures; soldiers and tanks, military model kits."

Global Imports — 212-741-0700
160 Fifth Ave. (21st) NYC 10010
Hours: 8-5:30 Mon-Fri
"Dice, cards, backgammon, dominoes." ed.

Marion & Co. — 212-868-9155
315 West 39th St. 16th Fl. (8-9th) NYC 10018
Hours: 8-5:30 Mon-Fri/ 8-1 Sat
"Playing cards." ed.

U.S. Games Systems Inc. — 212-685-4300
38 East 32 St. (Park-Madison) NYC 10016
Hours: 9-5 Mon-Fri
"Some tarot cards, fortune telling cards, and occult books; see George Bennett." ed.

GLASS & MIRRORS

S. A. Bendheim Co. Inc. — 212-226-6370
122 Hudson St. (North Moore) NYC 10013
Hours: 9-5 Mon-Fri/ 9-1 Sat
"Stained glass tools and supplies." ed.

Collyer-Sparks Construction Corp. — 212-684-0900
30 East 33rd St. (Park-Madison) NYC 10016
Hours: 8-5 Mon-Fri
"Large glass company, many types of glass; installation; see Donna."

Gem Glass Co. — 212-247-7145
790 Eleventh Ave (54-55th) NYC 10019
Hours: 8:45-4:30 Mon-Fri
"Picture glass and framing; glass is cut in late afternoon." ed.

NOTES

Morris Glasser & Son Inc.Glasser Morris & Son Inc. 212-831-8750
234 East 128th St. (2nd-3rd) NYC 10035
Hours: 7:30-5 Mon-Fri
"Glass, mirror; very fast and helpful; worth the trip." ed.

Glassmasters Guild 212-929-7978
27 West 23rd St. 4th floor (5-6th) NYC 10010
Hours: 11-5:30 Mon-Fri (Thurs til 6:30)/ 10-5 Sat
"Stained glass supplies and tools." ed.

KAMAR PRODUCTS INC. 914-591-8700
PO Box 227, Irvington-on-Hudson, NY 10533
Hours: 9-4:30 Mon-Fri
Large size unbreakable mirrors. (See display ad page 176.)
"Manufacturers of Mirrolite®; lightweight, shatterproof mirror; will do custom work." ed.

A. Laub Glass 212-734-4270
1873 Second Ave. (96-97th) NYC 10029
Hours: 8-5 Mon-Fri/ 9-4 Sat
"Stained and leaded glass." ed.

Manhattan Shade & Glass Co. 212-288-5616
1297 Third Ave. (74-75th) NYC 10021
Hours: 8:30-5:30 Mon-Fri/ 10-4 Sat
"Glass and mirror." ed.

Mirrex Corp. 201-353-3370
7 Evans Terminal, Hillside, NJ 07205
Hours: 9-5 Mon-Fri
"Heat shrink mirror and two-way mirror, built to order on metal frames." ed.

Rambusch 212-675-0400
40 West 13th St. (5-6th) NYC 10011
Hours: By appt.
"Manufacturer of stained glass." ed.

Rosen-Paramount Glass 212-532-0820
45 East 20th St. (Park Av.S.-B'way) NYC 10003
Hours: 9-4 Mon-Fri
"Glass and mirror." ed.

Saraco Glass Corp. 718-438-7757
3710 13th Ave. (Utica-Schnectady) Bklyn 11218
Hours: 7:30-4 Mon-Fri/ by appt. Sat,Sun
"All types of glass and mirrors." ed.

Seguin Mirror & Brass Inc. 212-628-1460
202 East 70th St. (3rd) NYC 10021
Hours: 8:30-5 Mon-Fri
"Rental and purchase of mirror, glass, glass table tops." ed.

Shadovitz Brothers Dist. Inc. 718-774-9100
1565 Bergen St. Bklyn 11213
Hours: 7:30-3:30 Mon-Fri
"Colored and patterned glass, mirror, wire, supplies." ed.

Thompson Art Mirror Co. Inc. 212-929-3085
50 Dey St., Jersey City, NJ 07306
Hours: 8:30-4:30 Mon-Fri
"Mirrors in all shapes and sizes; catalog." ed.

GLASSWORKERS

Art Cut Glass Studio 201-583-7648
RD# 1, Box 10, Fawn Drive, Matawan, NJ 07747
Hours: 9-5 Tues-Fri/ or by appt.
"Cutting, engraving, monogramming; design and repair." ed.

B. Gilsoul & Partners 212-868-8414
247 West 29th St. (7-8th) NYC 10001
Hours: 8-5 Mon-Fri or by appt.
"Artistic and architectural stained glass, carved and etched glass, sculpture; beautiful work." ed.

HAIR SUPPLIES & WIGS

See also BEAUTY SALON EQUIPMENT

Animal Hair Mfg. 718-852-3592
175 Beard St. (Van Brunt) Bklyn 11231
Hours: 8-5 Mon-Fri
"Real horses tails, etc; mfg. brushes, not wigs." ed.

Chicago Hair Goods Co. 312-427-8600
428 S. Wabash Ave, Chicago, IL 60605
Hours: 9-7 Mon, Thurs/ 9-5 Tues, Wed, Fri
"Inexpensive wigs; catalog." ed.

Jaques Darcel Inc. 212-753-7576
50 West 57th St. (5-6th) NYC 10019
Hours: 10-6 Mon-Sat
"Wigs and hairpieces." ed.

Empire Hair Processing Corp. 718-438-5777
4514 Eleventh Ave., Bklyn 11219
Hours: 8-5 Mon-Fri
"Synthetic hair by the pound; see Bob." ed.

Goldsmith Mannequins 718-937-8476
10-09 43rd Ave. L.I.C. 11101
Hours: 9-4:30 Mon-Fri
"Wig heads, pins, picks, brushes, combs." ed.

Herzberg-Robbins Inc. 212-354-6030
209 West 38th St. (7-8th) NYC 10018
Hours: 9-4:30 Mon-Fri
"Horsehair wigs, new and secondhand mannequins." ed.

Paul Huntley Productions Inc. 212-243-4475
10 West 19th St. (5-6th) NYC 10011
Hours: 10-5 Mon-Fri
"Custom made, excellent quality wigs; expensive." ed.

Ideal Wig Co. 718-361-8601
37-11 35th Ave. (37-38th) Astoria, NY 11101
Hours: 9-5 Mon-Fri
"Character wigs; catalog." ed.

Bob Kelly Wig Creations Inc. 212-819-0030
151 West 46th St. (6-7th) NYC 10036
Hours: 9-4:30 Mon-Thurs/ 9-3 Fri
"Wigs, hairpieces, artificial hair, straight or styled; theatrical make-up; catalog." ed.

Lee's Mardi Gras Enterprises Inc. 212-947-7773
565 Tenth Ave. 2nd Fl. (41-42nd) NYC 10036
Hours: 12-6 Mon-Sat
"Ladies wigs for men; complete line of ladies apparel for men." ed.

Charles Lopresto 212-947-7281
330 West 38th St. (8-9th) NYC 10018
Hours: By appt.
"Custom made wigs." ed.

Pucci Manikins 212-219-0142
578 Broadway (Houston-Prince) NYC 10012
Hours: 9-4:30 Mon-Fri
"Mannequin wigs." ed.

Ray Beauty Supply Co. Inc. 212-757-0175
721 Eighth Ave. (45-46th) NYC 10036
Hours: 9-6 Mon-Fri/ 10:30-5 Sat
"Wide variety hair supplies and make-up; beauty salon equipment rental; see Bobby." ed.

Ross Sales Co. 212-475-8470
58 Third Ave. (7th) NYC 10003
Hours: 8-5:30 Mon-Fri
"Barbers and beauticians scissors and sharpeners; beauty supplies, barber supplies." ed.

Ira Senz 212-752-6800
13 East 47th St. (5th-Madison) NYC 10017
Hours: 8-5 Mon-Fri
"Wigs." ed.

Wig City 212-585-3300
2895 Third Ave. (150-151st) Bronx 10455
Hours: 10-7 Mon-Sat/ 12-5 Sun
"Wigs." ed.

Zauder Brothers 516-379-2600
10 Henry St., Freeport, NY 11520
Hours: 9:30-5 Mon-Thurs/ 9:30-3 Fri
"Yak hair: fringe and loose, wigs, hairpieces, facial hair; also make-up." ed.

HAMPERS

Mutual Hardware 718-361-2480
5-45 49th Ave. (Vernon Blvd.) L.I.C. 11101
Hours: 8:30-5 Mon-Fri
"Canvas storage hampers; theatrical hardware." ed.

W. H. Silver's Hardware 212-247-4406
832 Eighth Ave. (50-51st) NYC 10019 212-247-4425
Hours: 8-6 Mon-Fri/ 8-1 Sat
"Specialty hampers, hand trucks, handling equipment." ed.

State Supply Equipment Co. Inc. 212-645-1431
210 Eleventh Ave. (25th) NYC 10001
Hours: 8:30-5 Mon-Fri
"Canvas hampers; sales and rental; also prop rental." ed.

HANDBAG & LUGGAGE REPAIR

Canal Luggage Inc. 212-925-9750
378 Canal St. (W. B'way-Church) NYC 10013
Hours: 9:30-5:30 every day
"Luggage and repairs." ed.

John R. Gerardo Inc. 212-695-6955
30 West 31st St. (B'way-5th) NYC 10001
Hours: 9-5 Mon-Fri/ 10-2 Sat
"Good work done on repairs; also sells luggage." ed.

Kay Leather Goods Repair Service 212-564-1769
10 West 32nd St. (5-6th) NYC 10001
Hours: 8-6 Mon-Fri
"Luggage and handbag repair; leather handles." ed.

Lexington Luggage Ltd. 212-223-0698
793 Lexington Ave. (61-62nd) NYC 10021
Hours: 9-6 Mon-Sat
"Repairs done on premises; luggage, trunks, leather gifts for sale; pricey." ed.

Zipper Service 212-947-7770
11 West 32nd St. (5-6th) NYC 10001
Hours: 8:30-5:30 Mon-Thurs/ 8:30-5 Fri/ 8:30-1 Sat
"Handbag and luggage zippers repaired and replaced." ed.

HANDBAGS see CLOTHING ACCESSORIES: HANDBAGS

HANDICRAFTS

See also ETHNIC GOODS
for specific craft materials, refer to INDEX

The Elder Craftsmen 212-861-5260
846 Lexington Ave. (64th) NYC 10021
Hours: 11-5:30 Mon/ 10:30-5:30 Tues-Sat (closed Sat. in Summer)
"Handmade toys, gift items." ed.

NY Exchange for Women's Work 212-753-2330
660 Madison Ave. (60th-61st) NYC 10021
Hours: 9:30-5:15 Mon-Fri/ 10-5 Sat
"Handmade toys, dolls, stuffed animals, linens, afghans." ed.

HARDWARE, DECORATIVE

See also LUMBER

Alexanders Hardware 212-267-0336
60 Reade St. (B'way-Church) NYC 10007
Hours: 8:30-5:45 Mon-Fri/ 8:30-5 Sat
"Decorative furniture hardware and turnings, odds and ends." ed.

Charlotte Ford Trunk Ltd. 806-659-3027
PO Box 536, Spearman, TX 79081
Hours: 9-4:30 Mon-Fri
"Trunk supplies and parts; locks, draw-bolts, corners, hinges; catalog." ed.

Decorator's Hardware Co. 212-755-2168
155 East 52nd St. (3rd-Lexington) NYC 10022 212-755-0895
Hours: 8:30-6 Mon-Fri/ 9-4 Sat
"Large assortment of hardware; also metal and wood furniture legs and pedestals." ed.

Gracious Home 212-535-2033
1220 Third Ave. (70-71st) NYC 10021
Hours: 9-7 Mon-Sat/ 10:30-5:30 Sun
"General and decorative hardware, housewares, household supplies; large store, a bit of everything." ed.

P. E. Guerin 212-243-5270
23 Jane St. (12-13th) NYC 10014
Hours: 9-4:30 Mon-Fri
"Excellent selection all types of hardware for the home; catalog; expensive." ed.

William Hunrath 212-758-0780
153 East 57th St. (3rd-Lexington) NYC 10022
Hours: 9-5 Mon-Fri/ 9-3 Sat
"Decorative brass hardware." ed.

Kraft Hardware Inc. 212-838-2214
306 East 61st St. (1-2nd) NYC 10021
Hours: 9-5 Mon-Fri
"Door, cabinet and bathroom hardware." ed.

Dave Sanders and Co. 212-334-9898
111 Bowery (Grand-Hester) NYC 10002
107 Bowery, NYC 10002 (mailing address)
Hours: 8-4:45 Mon-Fri
"Catalog available; large assortment decorative hardware." ed.

Selby Furniture Hardware Co. 212-673-4097
17 East 22nd St. (B'way-5th) NYC 10010
Hours: 9-4:30 Mon-Fri
"Furniture hardware wholesalers; $15 cash minimum, $25 check minimum." ed.

Simon's Hardware 212-532-9220
421 Third Ave. (29-30th) NYC 10016
Hours: 8-4:30 Mon-Fri
"Enormous selection decorative hardware; go early in the day; expensive." ed.

Tremont Nail Co. 617-295-0038
PO Box 111, Wareham, MA 02517
Hours: 9-5 Mon-Sat
"20 varieties of old-fashioned and special patterned cut nails; catalog." ed.

HARDWARE, GENERAL

See also: LUMBER

Barry Supply Co. 212-242-5200
36 West 17th St. (5-6th) NYC 10011
Hours: 10-5 Mon-Fri
"Replacement parts for all windows and patio doors." ed.

Brown & Silver Inc. 212-589-7200
813 Westchester Ave. (E. 158th) Bronx 10455
Hours: 8-5 Mon-Fri
"General hardware, very helpful." ed.

Canal Hardware 212-226-0825
305 Canal St. (B'way-Mercer) NYC 10013
Hours: 10-5 every day
"Hardware, tools." ed.

Decorator's Hardware Co. 212-755-0895
155 East 52nd St. (3rd-Lexington) NYC 10022 212-755-2168
Hours: 8:30-6 Mon-Fri/9-4 Sat
"Large assortment of hardware; also metal and wood furniture legs; wholesale and retail." ed.

B. Dulchin Inc. 212-243-6741
170 Seventh Ave. (20-21st) NYC 10011
Hours: 8-4:30 Mon-Fri
"Very good prices, selection, service on hardware, tools." ed.

Eastern Chain Works Inc. 212-242-2500
144 West 18th St. (6-7th) NYC 10011
Hours: 9-4:30 Mon-Fri
"Chain: all types, all metals." ed.

Glazier Hardware Supply 718-361-0556
25-07 36th Ave., (36th) L.I.C. 11106
Hours: 8:30-5 Mon-Fri
"See Paul." ed.

Gracious Home 212-535-2033
1220 Third Ave. (70-71st) NYC 10021
Hours: 9-7 Mon-Sat/ 10:30-5:30 Sun
"General and decorative hardware, housewares, household supplies; large store, a bit of everything." ed.

Hippodrome Hardware 212-840-2791
23 West 45th St. (5-6th) NYC 10036
Hours: 8-5:45 Mon-Fri/ 9-3 Sat
"General hardware, near theatre district." ed.

Kaminstein Brothers 212-777-7170
29 Third Ave. (9th) NYC 10003
Hours: 9-6 Mon-Fri/ 8:30-5:30 Sat
"Good selection general and household hardware and tools." ed.

New Era Hardware & Supply 212-265-4183
832 Ninth Ave. (54-55th) NYC 10019
Hours: 8:30-5 Mon-Fri
"Hardware, rigging supplies, casters, piano wire, tools, hand trucks."

Screw and Supply 718-383-8710
71 Box St., Bklyn 11222
Hours: 9-5 Mon-Fri
"Any size or type of threaded hardware." ed.

Sid's Hardware 718-875-2259
345 Jay St. (Myrtle-Willoughby) Bklyn 11201
Hours: 7:30-6:30 Mon-Fri/ 8:30-6:30 Sat/ 10-4:45 Sun
"Large selection of general and household hardware, power tools, household supplies." ed.

Weinstock Brothers Inc. 212-532-8057
384 Third Ave. (28th) NYC 10016
Hours: 7:30-4 Mon-Fri
"Nuts, bolts, washers; industrial supplier." ed.

HARDWARE, THEATRICAL see THEATRICAL HARDWARE & RIGGING EQUIPMENT

HARDWOODS & VENEERS

See also LUMBER

Albert Constantine & Sons 212-792-1600
2050 Eastchester Rd. (Seminole) Bronx 10461
Hours: 8-6 Mon-Fri (Thurs til 8)/ 8-3 Sat
(May-Aug: close at 5pm M-F, at 1pm Sat)
"Hardwoods, veneers, exotic woods, molding, woodworking tools." ed.

Rosenzweig Lumber Corp. 212-585-8050
801 East 135th St. (near Bruckner) Bronx 10454
Hours: 8-5 Mon-Fri
"Good selection hardwoods, veneers, lumber; good prices, prompt next day delivery." ed.

H. L. Wild 212-228-2345
510 East 11th St. (near Ave. A) NYC 10009
Hours: 8:30-12:30 M,Tu/ 8-12:30 Th-Sat/ closed Wed, Sun
"Hardwoods and veneers." ed.

HAY

Claremont Riding Academy 212-724-5100
175 West 89th St. (Columbus-Amsterdam) NYC 10024
Hours: 6:30am-10pm Mon-Fri/ 6-5 Sat,Sun
"Hay, riding equipment rental." ed.

HOBBY SHOPS & SUPPLIERS

See also DOLLS & DOLLHOUSES

America's Hobby Center (Modad's) 212-675-8922
146 West 22nd St. (6-7th) NYC 10011
Hours: 8:45-5:30 Mon-Fri (Thurs til 6:30)/ 8:45-3:30 Sat
"Train and airplane kits, model hardware; slow service; catalogs." ed.

Brooklyn Model Masters 718-339-9250
1307 Gravesend Neck Rd. Bklyn 11229
Hours: 12-7 Mon-Fri (Mon, Thurs til 9)/10-6 Sat
"Radio parts; Kraft, Futaba; see Bob." ed.

Charles Miniatures 212-966-1580
246 Lafayette St. (Prince-Spring) NYC 10012
Hours: 9-5 Mon-Fri
"Tools, lumber, moldings, lighting fixtures, etc; limited selection." ed.

Charrette Drafting Supply Corp. 212-683-8822
215 Lexington Ave. (33rd) NYC 10016
Hours: 8:30-8:30 Mon-Fri/ 8:30-6 Sat (12-5 Sun Sept-June)
"Basswood molding; drafting supplies and equipment." ed.

The Compleat Stragetist 212-685-3880
11 East 33rd St. (Madison-5th) NYC 10016
Hours: 10:30-6 Mon-Sat
"Games and miniature figures, soldiers and tanks, military model kits."

Detail Associates 805-934-1868
PO Box 197, Santa Monica, CA 93454
Hours: 9-5 Mon-Fri
"Cast metal props for model railroads, 1/4" scale." ed.

Dremel Service Center 414-554-1390
PO Box 1468, Racine, WI 53401
Hours: 9-5 Mon-Fri
"Cleaning and repair of Dremel tools." ed.

Eastern Model Aircraft 718-768-7960
365 40th St. (3rd-4th Ave.) Bklyn 11232
Hours: 9-5 Mon-Fri
"Balsa wood, wholesale; flier available." ed.

Engineering Model Associates

570 Grove Rd., Thorofare, NJ 08086 609-848-7700
Hours: 8:45-4:45 Mon-Fri

PO Box 63258, Los Angeles, CA 90063 213-261-8171
Hours: 9-4:30 Mon-Fri

"Wide selection of plastic industrial model parts for architectural and engineering models." ed.

Harmony Hobby 718-224-6666
196-30 Northern Blvd., Bayside, NY 11358
Hours: 10-7 Mon-Thurs/ 10-8 Fri/ 10-6 Sat/ 12-5 Sun
"Military models, realistic looking plastic gun and rifle kits; inexpensive." ed.

Holgate & Reynolds 312-251-2455
1000 Central Ave., Wilmette, IL 60091
Hours: 10-5 Mon-Fri
"Embossed brick, field stone, cement block in plastic sheets; HO to 1/2" scale." ed.

Life-Like Products Inc. 301-889-1023
1600 Union Ave., Baltimore, MD 21211
Hours: 8:30-5 Mon-Fri
"Lychen, surface texturing materials, trees; various local distributors; catalog." ed.

M. H. Industries 717-774-7096
PO Box 322, New Cumberland, PA 17070
"Basswood, stripwood, moldings, dollhouse lumber; small minimum order; flier." ed.

Model Masterpieces 303-789-4898
PO Box 1634, Englewood, CO 80150
"Cast metal props for model railroads for 1/4" models." ed.

Model Shipways Co. Inc. 201-342-7920
39 W. Ft. Lee Rd., PO Box 85, Bogota, NJ 07603
Hours: 9-5 Mon-Fri
"Hardware, fittings, props for model ships; variety of scales; catalog; fast delivery." ed.

Northeastern Scale Models Inc. 617-688-6019
Box 425, Methuen, MA 01844
Hours: 9-5 Mon-Fri
"Precision scale modeling shapes in basswood & other hardwoods; samples available." ed.

Pearl Paint Co. Inc.

308 Canal St. (Mercer) NYC 10013 212-431-7932
Hours: 9-5:30 Mon-Sat/ 11-4:30 Sun

2411 Hempstead Turnpike, East Meadow, NY 11554 516-731-3700
Hours: 9:30-5:45 Mon-Sat (Wed, Fri til 8:45)

"Basswood, balsa, Sculpey, Dremel tools, brass; art supplies." ed.

Polk's Model Craft Hobbies Inc. 212-279-9034
314 Fifth Ave. (31-32nd) NYC 10001
Hours: 9:30-5:45 Mon-Fri/ 9:30-5 Sat
"Models: trains, planes, cars, ships, dollhouses; texturing materials, hardware, tools." ed.

Polyform Products 312-678-4836
9420 W. Byron St., Schiller Park, IL 60176
Hours: 9-4:30 Mon-Fri
"Sculpey manufacturer." ed.

The Red Caboose 212-575-0155
16 West 45th St. 4th Fl. (5-6th) NYC 10036
Hours: 10-7 Mon-Sat
"Brass, simulated surfaces, Choppers; train and ship models and accessories." ed.

Special Shapes Co. Inc. 312-586-8517
1354 Napierville, PO Box 487R, Romeoville, IL 60441
"Brass rod & shapes in 3' lengths; 2-3 week delivery; flier." ed.

The Train Shop 212-730-0409
23 West 45th St. (5-6th) NYC 10036
Hours: 10-6 Mon-Fri/ 10-5 Sat
"Model train supplies; brass rod & shapes (12" shapes); cast metal props 1/4" scale." ed.

Westchester Hobby 914-949-7943
102 East Post Rd., White Plains, NY 10601
Hours: 9-5 Mon-Sat (Thurs til 6:45)
"Model trains, cars, ships, airplanes; miniature molding, wallpaper, food, lighting." ed.

X-Acto Corp. 718-392-3333
45-35 Van Dam St. L.I.C. 11101
Hours: 8:45-5 Mon-Fri
"Knives, blades, files, tool sets; catalog; wholesale." ed.

HOME DECORATING & IMPROVEMENT CENTERS

Channel Home Center

101 Terhune Ave. (Circle Dr.) Lodi, NJ 07644 201-473-4950
Hours: 9:30-9 Mon-Fri/ 9-9 Sat/ 9:30-5 Sun

(continues next page)

23 West Glen Ave., Paramus, NJ 07652 201-447-0444
Hours: 9:30-9:30 Mon-Sat

"Flooring, wallcoverings, paint, wood, and more." ed.

Kay's Home Decorating 201-843-4400
Rt. 17 North, Lodi, NJ 07644
Hours: 9-9:30 Mon-Sat/ 9:30-6 Sun
"One-of-a-kind; shutters, carpet, tile, paint, cinderblocks." ed.

Martin Paint

73 Christopher St. (7th Ave. S.) NYC 10014 212-929-8223
Hours: 10-9 Mon,Thurs,Fri/ 10-7 Tues,Wed,Sat/ 10-5 Sun

387 Park Ave. South (27-28th) NYC 10016 212-684-8119
Hours: 10-7 Mon-Fri/ 9-6 Sat

588 Ninth Ave. (42nd) NYC 10036 212-664-9875
Hours: 10-7 Mon,Thurs,Fri/ 10-6 Tues,Wed,Sat/ 10-5 Sun

1489 Third Ave. (84th) NYC 10028 212-650-9563
Hours: 10-8:45 Mon-Sat

308 West 125th St. (7th) NYC 10027 212-864-9712
Hours: 10-6:45 Mon-Sat/ 10-4:45 Sun

"Wallcoverings, paint, vinyl and fabric spray paint, and more." ed.

Pintchik Paints

478 Bergen St. (Flatbush) Bklyn 11217 718-783-3333
Hours: 8:30-8 M,Th/ 8:30-7 T,W,F/ 8:30-6:30 Sat/ 10-5 Sun
"This is the "Mothership", the largest store." ed.

278 Third Ave. (22nd) NYC 10010 212-982-6600
Hours: 8:30-8 M,Th/ 8:30-7 T,W,F/ 9-6:30 Sat/ 11-5 Sun

1555 Third Ave. (87th) NYC 10028 212-289-6300
Hours: 8:30-8 M,Th/ 8:30-7 T,W,F/ 9-6:30 Sat/ 11-5 Sun

8419 5th Ave. (85th) Bklyn 11209 718-238-5333
Hours: 9-8 Mon, Thurs/ 9-6 Tues, Wed, Fri, Sat

4209 Avenue U (Flatbush) Bklyn 11234 718-951-9300
Hours: 9-7 Mon-Wed/ 9-8:30 Thurs,Fri/ 9-6:30 Sat/ 10-5 Sun

31-48 Steinway St. (B'way) Astoria, NY 11103 718-721-5321
Hours: 9-8 Mon, Thurs, Fri/ 9-7 Tues, Wed

"Flooring, window treatments, housewares, paints, wallcoverings, and more." ed.

Rickels 718-448-3434
1520 Forest Ave., Staten Island, NY 10302
Hours: 9:30-9:30 Mon-Sat/ 9-5:30 Sun
"Shingles, tile, blinds, paint, floor and wallcoverings, and more." ed.

HOSPITAL EQUIPMENT see MEDICAL EQUIPMENT

HYDRAULICS & PNEUMATICS
See also SCENIC SHOPS

Paul Hardman Machinery Co. 914-664-6220
621 South Columbus Ave., Mt. Vernon, NY 10553
Hours: 8-5 Mon-Fri
"Suppliers of pneumatic equipment." ed.

HYDRO/AIR INC. 718-338-5068
PO Box 131 Ryder Station, Bklyn 11234 212-267-4524
Hours: 9-5 Mon-Fri
Air and Hydraulic equipment, local stock. Friendly technical assistance and application advice.
"Wide selection of brand name components and systems." ed.

Northern Hydraulics Inc. 612-894-8310
801 East Cliff Rd., Burnsville, MN 55337
Hours: 8-6 Mon-Fri/ 9-2 Sat
"Pumps, valves, accessories; catalog available." ed.

ICE & DRY ICE

AA Armato & Son 212-737-1742
1701 Second Ave. (88th) NYC 10028
Hours: 9-7 every day
"Ice, dry ice, firewood." ed.

Brusca Ice & Wood 212-744-6986
2148 2nd Ave. (110th) NYC 10029
Hours: 9-8 every day
"Ice, dry ice, firewood." ed.

Casamassima & Sons 212-355-3734
407 East 50th St. (Beekman-1st) NYC 10022
Hours: 8-6 Mon-Sat/ 8-1 Sun
"Ice; block, cube; call day before for dry ice; firewood." ed.

Circle Ice & Cube Co. 212-535-8864
491 Tenth Ave. (37-38th) NYC 10018 212-873-7469
Hours: 7:30-9 Mon-Thurs/ 7:30-midnight Fri, Sat/ 9-8 Sun
"Dry ice, ice sculpture." ed.

Diamond Ice Cube Co. Inc. 212-675-4115
216 West 23rd St. (7-8th) NYC 10011
Hours: 7-7 Mon-Sat/ 8-5 Sun
"Ice, dry ice." ed.

Stuyvesant Town Ice & Cube 212-473-6784
325 East 21st St. (1-2nd) NYC 10010
Hours: 7-7 Mon-Fri/ 9-8 Sat/ 9-5 Sun
"Free delivery after midnight with $25 order or more; ice: dry, block, crushed, cubes." ed.

United City Ice Cube Co. 212-563-0819
44th & Tenth Ave. NYC 10019
Hours: 24 hours, every day
"24 hour delivery service; block, cube, dry ice; purchases may be made at truck on 44th and Tenth Ave." ed.

IRONS & STEAMERS

Automatic Steam Products Corp. 718-937-4500
43-20 34th St. L.I.C. 11101
Hours: 9-5 Mon-Fri
"Manufacturer of Sussman irons and steamers." ed.

BAER FABRICS 502-583-5521
515 East Market, Louisville, KY 40202
Hours: 9-5:30 Mon-Sat
Portable, commercial steam irons and steamers. (See display ad page 127.)
"Shipment within 24 hours for in-stock items." ed.

Superior Steam Iron Co. Inc. 718-699-6464
111-31 44th Ave., Corona, NY 11368
Hours: 8-4:30 Mon-Fri
"Sussman products, new and used; some repair work done." ed.

Supreme Steam Appliance Corp. 212-929-7349
157 West 26th St. (6-7th) NYC 10001
Hours: 7-4 Mon-Fri
"Sussman products, new and used, vacuum cleaners." ed.

JEWELERS TOOLS & SUPPLIES

See also METALS & FOILS
See also TRIMMINGS: BEADS, SEQUINS, RHINESTONES, PEARLS

Abbey Materials Corp. 212-772-0380
575 Underhill Blvd., Syosset, NY 11791
"Mail order; call for catalog, prices." ed.

Allcraft Tool & Supply Co. 212-246-4740
64 West 48th St. (5-6th) NYC 10036
Hours: 9-4:30 Mon-Fri
"Casting, enameling, soldering supplies; sheet, wire, tube metal; Dremel; catalogs." ed.

Helen Behar World of Bargains 212-924-3588
195 Seventh Ave. (21-22nd) NYC 10011
Hours: 12-5 Mon-Sat (closed Sat., May-Labor Day)
"Huge selection findings, trinkets, chain, beads; small orders ok." ed.

Eastern Findings Corp. 212-695-6640
19 West 34 St. 12th Fl. (5-6th) NYC 10001
Hours: 9-4:30 Mon-Fri (closed for lunch 12:30-1)
"Jewelry findings, bracelet and necklace chain; check for minimum orders." ed.

Edwin Freed Inc. 212-391-2170
151 West 46th St. (6-7th) NYC 10036
Hours: 9-4 Mon-Fri
"Jewelers tools and cleaners; jewelry display cases." ed.

C. R. Hill, Co. 313-543-1555
2734 West 11 Mile Rd., Berkley, MI 48072
Hours: 9-5 Mon-Fri
"Jewelers tools, casting supplies, metal sheet and tubing; catalog."

Sam Levin Metal Products Corp. 718-782-6885
1002 Grand St., Bklyn 11211
Hours: 8-4:30 Mon-Thurs/ 8-2 Fri
"Wholesale; metal findings, buckles; catalog." ed.

C. S. Osborne Tools 201-483-3232
125 Jersey St., Harrison, NJ 07029
Hours: 8:30-5 Mon-Fri
"Tools for metalwork; catalog." ed.

T. W. Smith Welding Supply 212-247-6323
545 West 59th St. (10-11th) NYC 10019
Hours: 7:30-4 Mon-Fri
"Soldering and welding supplies, propane." ed.

Weller Soldering Equipment (Div/Cooper Group) 919-362-7510
Box 728, Apex, NC 27502
Hours: 8-4:30 Mon-Fri
"Soldering tools; catalog." ed.

KEYS

Abbey Locksmiths 212-535-2289
1617 Second Ave. (81st) NYC 10028
Hours: 7:30-6 Mon-Fri/ 8-5 Sat
"Antique keys, locksmiths." ed.

Bonded Locksmiths 212-586-6886
2414 Broadway (88-89th) NYC 10024
Hours: 8:30-6 Mon-Sat
"Antique keys for rent; locksmith." ed.

KITCHEN & BATHROOM FIXTURES

See also BATHROOM ACCESSORIES
See also PLUMBING SUPPLIES

Alter Bath & Kitchen 212-683-1682
317 Lexington Ave. (29th) NYC 10016 212-683-6012
Hours: 9-5 Mon-Fri
"Kitchen and bathroom sinks and fixtures." ed.

Aqua Baths Inc. 212-431-4840
351 West Broadway (Broome) NYC 10013
Hours: 9:30-5:30 Mon-Fri/ 12-5 Sat
"Bathroom fixtures, whirlpool equipment, sinks; very helpful." ed.

Bakit Bath & Construction Corp. 212-683-6093
32 East 30th St. (Madison-Park) NYC 10016
Hours: 8-5 Mon-Fri
"Bathroom fixtures." ed.

P. E. Guerin 212-243-5270
23 Jane St. (12-13th) NYC 10014
Hours: 9-4:30 Mon-Fri
"Wonderful hardware and bathroom fixtures; catalog; expensive." ed.

Isabella 718-278-7272
24-24 Steinway St., (Astoria Blvd.) Astoria, NY 11103
Hours: 9-7 M,T,Th,F/ 9-6 W/ 9-5 Sat (closed Sat., July-Aug)
"See Nick or Aldona." ed.

Leesam Plumbing 212-243-6482
124 Seventh Ave. (17-18th) NYC 10011
Hours: 9:30-6 Mon-Fri
"New and salvage sinks, toilets, bathtubs, radiators, plumbing parts; formica to order; reasonable." ed.

P & G New and Used Plumbing Supply 718-384-6310
155 Harrison Ave. Bklyn 11206
Hours: 8:30-4:30 Mon-Fri/ 8:30-1:30 Sat
"Good selection period and contemporary fixtures and parts, salvage; reasonable; very helpful." ed.

Simon Hardware 212-532-9220
421 Third Ave. (29-30th) NYC 10016
Hours: 8-4:30 Mon-Fri
"Bathroom fixtures, accessories, decorative hardware, faucets; expensive." ed.

Smolka Co. Inc. 212-679-2700
182 Madison Ave. (34th) NYC 10016
Hours: 9-6 Mon-Fri/ 10-5 Sat
"Bathroom fixtures and accessories; expensive." ed.

Sherle Wagner International Inc. 212-758-3300
60 East 57th St. (Park) NYC 10022
Hours: 9:30-5 Mon-Fri
"Bathroom fixtures, expensive." ed.

KITCHEN EQUIPMENT, HOUSEHOLD

See also APPLIANCES, ELECTRICAL & GAS
For ethnic cooking supplies,
see ETHNIC GOODS: MEXICAN, SOUTH AMERICAN, AMERICAN INDIAN
see ETHNIC GOODS: ORIENTAL
see ETHNIC GOODS: SPANISH

Broadway Bazaar 212-873-9153
2025 Broadway (69th) NYC 10023

Columbus Avenue Bazaar 212-362-7335
540 Columbus Ave. (86th) NYC 10024

First Avenue Bazaar 212-737-2003
1453 First Ave. (75th) NYC 10021

Lexington Avenue Bazaar 212-734-8119
1037 Lexington Ave. (74th) NYC 10021

Madison Avenue Bazaar 212-348-3786
1186 Madison Ave. (86th) NYC 10028

Second Avenue Bazaar 212-683-2293
501 Second Ave. (28th) NYC 10016

Third Avenue Bazaar 212-988-7600
1145 Third Ave. (66th) NYC 10021

Third Avenue Bazaar 212-861-5999
1362 Third Ave. (77th) NYC 10021

(continues next page)

West Third Street Bazaar 212-673-4138
125 West 3rd St. (6th) NYC 10012
Hours: 10-6:30 Mon-Sat/ 11-5:30 Sun
"Modern kitchenware, furniture, lamps, picture frames, accessories."

Bowl & Board 212-673-1724
9 Saint Marks Place (2nd-3rd) NYC 10003
Hours: 10-7 Mon-Sat/ 2-6 Sun
"Wooden items: bowls, plates, trays, cups, boards, furniture, etc." ed.

Bridge Kitchenware 212-688-4220
214 East 52nd St. (2-3rd) NYC 10022
Hours: 9-5:30 Mon-Fri/ 10-5 Sat
"Large selection of industrial and household kitchenware and glassware." ed.

Broadway Panhandler 212-966-3434
520 Broadway (Spring) NYC 10012
Hours: 10:30-6 Mon-Fri/ 11-5:30 Sat
"Kitchen equipment and utensils, cake decorating supplies, ironstone, mugs, etc." ed.

Dean & Deluca 212-254-7774
121 Prince St. (Wooster) NYC 10012
Hours: 10-7 every day
"Small electrical appliances, baking and cooking equipment, groceries, herbs; expensive." ed.

First Stop Housewares 212-838-0007
1025 Second Ave. (54th) NYC 10022
Hours: 10-6 Mon-Sat
"Nice selection kitchenware; very helpful; will order." ed.

La Cuisiniere 212-861-4475
968 Lexington Ave. (70-71st) NYC 10021
Hours: 10-6 Mon-Fri/ 10-5:30 Sat
"French antique and modern kitchen accessories; very expensive." ed.

Gracious Home 212-535-2033
1220 Third Ave. (70-71st) NYC 10021
Hours: 9-7 Mon-Sat/ 10:30-5:30 Sun
"Large selection of housewares, hardware, and small appliances." ed.

Manhattan Ad Hoc Housewares 212-752-5488
842 Lexington Ave. (64th) NYC 10021
Hours: 10-7 Mon,Thurs/ 10-6:30 Tues,Wed,Fri/ 10-6 Sat
"High tech kitchenware." ed.

D. F. Sanders

386 West Broadway (Spring-Broome) NYC 10012 212-925-9040
Hours: 11:30-7 Mon-Sat/ 12-5:30 Sun

952 Madison Ave. (75th) NYC 10021 212-879-6161
Hours: 10:30-6 Mon-Fri/ 11-6 Sat,Sun

"High tech supermarket: china, housewares, kitchenware, furniture."

Winston's Contemporaneous Hardware 212-242-1681
91 Greenwich Ave. (Bank-12th) NYC 10014
Hours: 11-7 Mon-Fri/ 10-7 Sat/ 1-6 Sun
"Good selection of housewares, some general hardware." ed.

Wolfman-Gold & Good 212-431-1888
484 Broome St. (Wooster) NYC 10016
Hours: 11-6 Mon-Sat/ 12-5 Sun
"Beautiful antique and new linens; also baskets, cookie cutters, tureens, etc.; will rent." ed.

Zabar's Mezzanine 212-787-2000
2245 Broadway (80th) NYC 10024
Hours: 9-6 every day
"Large selection kitchen equipment, pots, pans, small electrical appliances; very reasonable." ed.

KITCHEN EQUIPMENT, INDUSTRIAL

See also BUTCHER BLOCK
See also FURNITURE RENTAL & PURCHASE: RESTAURANT

AAA Restaurant Equipment 212-966-1891
284 Bowery (Houston) NYC 10012
Hours: 9-5 Mon-Fri/ 9-2 Sat
"New and used kitchen appliances, very reasonable." ed.

Bari Restaurant Equipment 212-925-3786
240 Bowery (Houston-Prince) NYC 10012
Hours: 9-5 Mon-Fri/ 9-3 Sat
"Big selection used and new appliances, furnishings." ed.

Bass & Bass 212-228-5120
265 Park Ave. South (20-21st) NYC 10010
Hours: 9-5 Mon-Fri
"Restaurant supplies; by the case." ed.

Bridge Kitchenware 212-688-4220
214 East 52nd St. (2-3rd) NYC 10022
Hours: 9-5:30 Mon-Fri/ 10-5 Sat
"Large selection of industrial and household kitchenware and glassware." ed.

Chef Restaurant Supplies 212-254-6644
294-296 Bowery (Houston) NYC 10012
Hours: 9-5:30 Mon-Sat/ 11-5 Sun
"Restaurant supplies, inexpensive glassware." ed.

Daroma Restaurant Equipment Corp. 212-226-6774
196 Bowery (Spring) NYC 10012
Hours: 9-5 Mon-Fri
"Stocks metro shelving." ed.

H. Friedman & Sons 201-348-3555
225 Secaucus Rd., Secaucus, NJ 07094
Hours: 8:30-5 Mon-Fri
"Wholesale restaurant supplies." ed.

Kabram & Sons Inc. 212-477-1480
257 Bowery (Prince-Houston) NYC 10002
Hours: 8-4:30 Mon-Fri
"Good selection standard items; will rent." ed.

Paragon Restaurant World 212-226-0954
250 Bowery (Prince-Houston) NYC 10012
Hours: 8-5 Mon-Fri/ 9-4 Sat (closed Sat in Summer)
"Small restaurant accessories: salt shakers, melamine plates, large jars of condiments." ed.

LAB & SCIENTIFIC EQUIPMENT

See also DENTAL SUPPLY HOUSES
See also MEDICAL EQUIPMENT

Anatomical Chart Co. 312-764-7171
7124 N. Clark St., Chicago, IL 60626 800-621-7500
Hours: By appt.
"Biological and scientific products; skeletons, skulls, anatomical charts; catalog." ed.

Carolina Biological Supply 919-584-0381
2700 York Rd., Burlington, NC 27215
Hours: 8-5 Mon-Fri (closed for lunch, 12-1)/ 8-12 Sat
"Human anatomical parts, charts, skulls, bones, skeletons; catalog; good prices." ed.

Eck & Krebs Scientific Lab Glass Apparatus Inc. 718-786-6077
27-09 40th Ave. (27-28th) L.I.C. 11101
Hours: 9-5 Mon-Fri
"Laboratory glass and scientific equipment; will custom build glass apparatus." ed.

Edmund Scientific Co. 609-547-3488
101 East Gloucester Pike, Barrington, NJ 08007 800-257-6173
Hours: 9-5 Mon-Fri
"Lab equipment, optics, microscopes, pumps, scientific toys." ed.

Maxilla Mandidle Ltd. 212-724-6173
78 West 82nd St. (Columbus) NYC 10024
Hours: 12-7 every day
"Human and animal skulls, bones, skins, horns; rental and purchase."

Mercer Glassworks Inc. 718-625-4555
55 Washington St. Bklyn 11201
Hours: 8:30-4 Mon-Fri
"Lab equipment; prefer large orders." ed.

Nasco Life Form Models 414-563-2446
901 Janesville Ave., Fort Atkinson, WI 53538
Hours: 8-5 Mon-Fri
"Scientific models, artificial food; catalog available." ed.

LABELS, WOVEN

American Silk Label 516-829-8300
1 Linden Place, (near Middle Neck Rd.) Great Neck, NY 11022
Hours: 9-5:30 Mon-Fri
"Woven and printed labels." ed.

Anchor Label & Tag Co. 212-244-4363
10 West 33rd St. Rm. 1222 (5th-B'way) NYC 10001
Hours: 9-5 Mon-Fri
"1000 woven labels per roll, 5000 label minimum." ed.

Supreme Label Corp. 212-255-2090
109 West 27th St. (6-7th) NYC 10001
Hours: 8-4:30 Mon-Fri
"Labels." ed.

Treo Label Co. Inc. 212-243-6561
16 West 22nd St. (5-6th) NYC 10010
Hours: 8:30-6 Mon-Fri
"Woven labels." ed.

LADDERS

Ace High Ladder 212-665-9700
611 Jackson Ave. (151st) Bronx 10455
Hours: 9-5 Mon-Fri
"Sales and rental of wood and aluminum ladders." ed.

Manhattan Ladder Co. Inc. 718-721-3352
31-24 14th St. (31st Rd.) L.I.C. 11106
Hours: 7-4 Mon-Fri
"Sales and rental of wood and aluminum ladders; delivery." ed.

Putnam Rolling Ladder Co. Inc. 212-226-5147
32 Howard St. (B'way-Lafayette) NYC 10013
Hours: 8-4:15 Mon-Fri
"Sells rolling ladders." ed.

LAMINATION

Idesco Corp. 212-889-2530
25 West 26th St. (5-6th) NYC 10010
Hours: 8:30-4:30 Mon-Fri
"All kinds of laminating, fast service." ed.

Laminex-Craft 212-751-6143
892 Second Ave. (47-48th) NYC 10017
Hours: 9-6 Mon-Fri
"Laminating specialists, signs." ed.

Malcolm & Hayes Silversmiths 212-682-1316
694 Third Ave. (43rd) NYC 10017
Hours: 8:30-6 Mon-Fri
"Silver cups, awards, trophies, ribbons, certificates; engraving, printing and lamination." ed.

LATEX see CASTING SUPPLIES
see MAKE-UP SUPPLIES

LATEX TUBING see PIPE & TUBING
see SURGICAL SUPPLY HOUSES

LEATHER & FUR

Art Handicrafts Leather Co. 718-252-6622
3512 Flatlands Ave. (E 35-36th) Bklyn 11234
Hours: 9-4:30 Mon-Fri/ 9:30-2 Sat/ call for appt.
"Leathercraft supply; tools, glovers, lacing needles, thread, dyes, paints; catalog." ed.

Atlas Leather Co. 212-736-7044
155 West 29th St. (6-7th) NYC 10001
Hours: 9-5:30 Mon-Fri
"Leather; surplus and job lots." ed.

Blumenthal Leather Corp. 212-242-3650
1123 Broadway (25-26th) NYC 10010
Hours: 9-5 Mon-Fri
"Reptile skins and exotic leathers." ed.

Garden State Tanning — 212-679-8910
215 Lexington Ave. (32-33rd) NYC 10016
Hours: 9-5 Mon-Fri (by appt.)
"Suede splits, auto, furniture, belt leather." ed.

Joseph Jacobs Leather Corp. — 212-683-7460
10 East 33rd St. 9th Fl. (5th-Madison) NYC 10001 — 212-683-7985
Hours: By appt.
"Suede, cabretta, cowhide, pigskin; dyed; catalog." ed.

Diamond Kamvakis — 212-736-1924
165 West 29th St. (6-7th) NYC 10001
Hours: 8-5 Mon-Fri
"Furs and skins." ed.

Leathersales (aka Minerva Leather) — 212-925-6270
78 Spring St. (Lafayette-B'way) NYC 10012
Hours: 8:30-4:30 Mon-Fri
"Leather garment, upholstery, suede, cowhide." ed.

Mac Leather Co. Inc. — 212-964-0850
428 Broome St. (B'way-Lafayette) NYC 10013 — 212-431-9440
Hours: 8-4 Mon-Fri/ 8-1 Sat
"Leather, sheepskin, lacing, tools, hardware; catalog." ed.

Phylmor Furrier Supply Inc. — 212-563-5410
149 West 28th St. (6-7th) NYC 10001
Hours: 8-5 Mon-Fri
"Muslin, drill, canvas, skins." ed.

Renar Leather Co. — 212-349-2075
68 Spring St. (Lafayette) NYC 10012
Hours: 9-5 Mon-Fri
"Leather, chamois, shoe, garment, novelty." ed.

Sigma Leather Inc. — 212-679-8000
68 Spring St. (Lafayette) NYC 10013
Hours: 8:30-5:30 Mon-Fri
"Leather; wholesale only." ed.

Tandy Leather Co. — 212-947-2533
330 Fifth Ave. (32-33rd) NYC 10001
Hours: 9:15-5:45 Mon-Fri/ 10-3:45 Sat
"Leather, leathercraft supplies; hobby oriented; catalog (ask to be on their mailing list)." ed.

Seymour Winik Inc. — 212-563-3622
245 West 29th St. (7-8th) NYC 10001
Hours: 9-4 Mon-Fri
"Good furs, Icelandic sheepskins, beaver skins." ed.

LEATHERCRAFTERS & FURRIERS TOOLS & SUPPLIES

See also NOTIONS: BUTTONS, BUCKLES, GROMMETS, etc.

A & B Leather and Findings Co. 212-265-8124
500 West 52nd St. (10-11th) NYC 10019
Hours: 6-3 Mon-Fri
"Barge, Magix, Fiebings, rawhide lacing, glovers and lacing needles."

Samuel Bauer & Sons Inc. 212-868-4190
145 West 29th St. (6-7th) NYC 10001
Hours: 8-5:30 Mon-Fri
"Furriers' supplies; dyes for leather and fur." ed.

Gewirtz-Egert (aka World Associates) 212-563-2420
160 West 28th St. (6-7th) NYC 10001
Hours: 8-5 Mon-Fri
"Furriers' supplies, fur dyes." ed.

Joseph M. Hart & Sons 516-567-7722
365 Central Ave., Bohemia, NY 11716
Hours: 9-5 Mon-Fri
"Grommets, studs, boot hooks." ed.

Sam Levin Metal Products Corp. 718-782-6885
1002 Grand St. Bklyn 11211
Hours: 8-4:30 Mon-Thurs/ 8-2 Fri
"Wholesale metal buckles, hardware for leather work; catalog." ed.

Magid Corp. (Magix) 516-234-1660
4 Allwood Ave., Central Islip, NY 11722
Hours: 8:30-5 Mon-Fri
"Manufacturer of Magix spray." ed.

National Leather & Shoe Findings Co 212-982-6227
313 Bowery (1-2nd) NYC 10003
Hours: 8:30-4:30 Mon-Fri
"Good stock Magix, leather dyes, lacing; phone in orders and pick up."

Northern Leather 718-875-7720
166 Flatbush Ave. Bklyn 11217 718-783-7755
Hours: 7-4 Mon-Fri
"Shoe findings, Magix, Fiebings dye, needles, thread." ed.

Ohio Traveling Bag 216-621-5963
811 Prospect Ave., Cleveland, OH 44115
Hours: 9-5 Mon-Fri
"Wholesale and retail; buckles, hardware for leatherwork; catalog."

C. S. Osborne Tools 201-483-3232
125 Jersey St., Harrison, NJ 07029
Hours: 8:30-5 Mon-Fri
"Tools for leatherwork, saddlery; catalog." ed.

Shoe Repair Supply Corp. 202-842-0505
1250 4th St. NE, Washington, DC 20002
Hours: 8-5 Mon-Fri
"Magix shoe spray." ed.

Veteran Leather Co. 718-768-0300
204 25th St. (4th Ave) Bklyn 11232
Hours: 8-4:30 Mon-Fri
"Leather dyes, leather needles, etc." ed.

LIGHTING & PROJECTION EQUIPMENT

Altman Stage Lighting 914-476-7987
57 Alexander, Yonkers, NY 10701
Hours: 8:30-5 Mon-Fri
"Sales and rental, also other theatrical supplies." ed.

American Stage Lighting 914-636-5538
1331 North Ave., New Rochelle, NY 10804 212-584-5600
Hours: 9-5 Mon-Fri
"Equipment rental and sales." ed.

Audio-Visual Promotion Aids Inc. 212-477-5540
611 Broadway (Houston) NYC 10012
Hours: 10-6 Mon-Fri
"Rent and sell carousels, screens, video and lighting equipment and controls." ed.

AUDIO VISUAL RENTALS INC. 212-807-1563
75 Ninth Ave. (15-16th) NYC 10011
Hours: 9-5 Mon-Fri or by appt.
Technical direction & staging services for theatrical, industrial & multi-media presentations. Equipment rentals for long term or daily use. Sound systems for up to 1500 people. Slide & film systems for AV applications. Staging personnel for local and out of town events.
"Large or small projects; very professional, very cooperative." ed.

BARBIZON ELECTRIC CO. INC. 212-586-1620
426 West 55th St. (9-10th) NYC 10019
Hours: 8:30-4:30 Mon-Fri
Mole-Richardson Dist. and allied equipment and supplies.
"Theatrical lighting supplier." ed.

BASH
BIGGER, BRIGHTER
For quite some time now, we've been keeping America's Entertainment Industry shining. Supplying quality products and systems to get the show lit right the first time and every performance after. Offering 24 hour service to guarantee the show will go on. Service and efficiency at very competitive rates are what you're entitled to, and what you should expect from us. We deliver.
Suppliers to the 1984 TONY AWARDS, 1984 REPUBLICAN NATIONAL CONVENTION.
With Bold Insights in Light!
BASH
THEATRICAL LIGHTING, INC.
3401 Dell Ave. • No. Bergen, N.J. 07047
201-863-3300 • 212-279-9265

BASH THEATRICAL LIGHTING INC. 212-279-9265
3401 Dell Ave., North Bergen, NJ 07047 201-863-3300
Hours: 9-5 Mon-Fri/ 10-1 Sat (closed Sat June, July, Aug)

Rental-Sales-Service of Lighting Equipment, Controls and Dimming Systems. Very large inventory color and bulbs. Master supplier of packages for Broadway, TV, Ballet, Opera and Industrial Tours. (See display ad facing page.)

"Large selection of lighting equipment; union shop." ed.

BESTEK THEATRICAL PRODUCTIONS LTD.
386 East Meadow Ave., East Meadow, NY 11554 (rental shop) 516-794-3953
218 W. Hoffman Ave., Lindenhurst, NY 11757 (prod'n shop) 516-225-0707
Hours: 10-6 Mon-Fri

Equipment sales & rentals. Installation available. (See display ad page 315.)

"Lighting, platforms, searchlights, scenery construction." ed.

Big Apple Lights 212-226-0925
533 Canal St. (Washington-Greenwich St.) NYC 10013
Hours: 10-5 Mon-Fri
"Sales, rental, consulting; non-union; good prices." ed.

Bradford Consultants 609-854-1404
16 East Homestead Ave., Collingswood, NJ 08108
Hours: 9-5 Mon-Fri
"Reproduction period light bulbs; brochure available." ed.

Cine 60 212-586-8782
630 Ninth Ave. (44-45th) NYC 10036
Hours: 8:30-5 Mon-Fri
"Cine and video equipment for sale and rent; specialty; source for battery belts and packs." ed.

D.H.A. Lighting Ltd. 212-219-2218
533 Canal St. (Washington-Greenwich St.) NYC 10013
Hours: 9:30-5 Mon-Fri
"'David Hersey Associates'; stock and custom lighting templates." ed.

Electra Displays 516-585-5659
90 Remington Blvd. Ronkonkoma, NY 11779 212-240-1327
Hours: 9-5 Mon-Fri
"Mirror balls, sheets and projecting kaleidoscopes." ed.

FISCHER DISPLAY LIGHTING INC. 212-597-7576
PO Box 140 Westchester Station, Bronx 10461
Hours: 8:30-5 Mon-Fri

Manufacturer of lighting specials. Custom fabrication-miniature and "Special" lamp assemblies and strings for scenery- star drops- costume lighting. Single and multi circuit pre-wired assemblies- parallel wired strings.

"Miniature incandescent specialty lamps, strings, assemblies; contact Howard Neff." ed.

NOTES

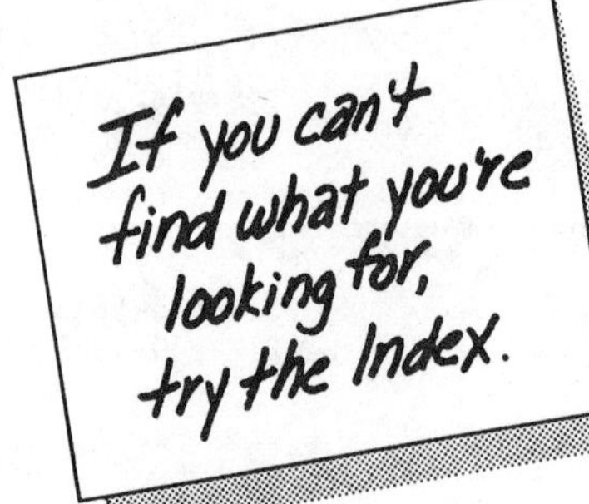
If you can't
find what you're
looking for,
try the Index.

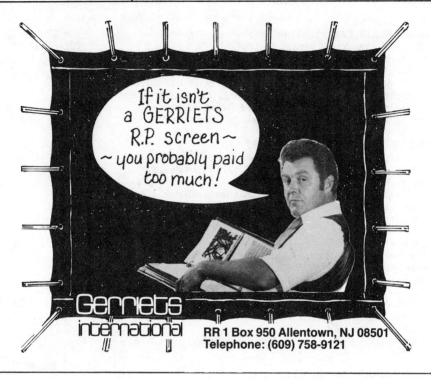

Fischer Display Lighting Inc. 718-498-5236
836 Logan St. (Linden Blvd.-Stanley Ave.) Bklyn 11208
Hours: 7-5 Mon-Fri
"Factory." ed.

Four Star Stage Lighting 212-993-0471
585 Girard Ave. (149-150th) Bronx 10451
Hours: 9-5 Mon-Fri
"Lighting equipment: boards, cable, instruments; major supplier of packages for B'way, etc." ed.

GERRIETS INTERNATIONAL 609-758-9121
RR #1, 950 Hutchinson Rd., Allentown, NJ 08501
Hours: 8:30-5 Mon-Fri

Manufacturer of six different front/rear projection screen materials which can be heat welded to your specifications. Up to 100 feet high by any width. (See display ads pages 98, 204.)

"Speak to Nick Bryson." ed.

Harry Gitlin Inc. 212-243-1080
121 West 19th St. (6-7th) NYC 10011
Hours: 8:30-4:30 Mon-Fri
"Track lighting, museum and gallery lighting installations; very expensive, but good." ed.

THE GREAT AMERICAN MARKET 213-461-0200
826 N. Cole Ave., Hollywood, CA 90038
Hours: 8-5 Mon-Fri/ Sat by appt. only

Steel projection Patterns, scenic projectors; still & moving effects, supplies, paint, accessories; Special effects, lighting & control, incl. low voltage. Design service, custom work, questions answered, free binder. (See display ad on divider page.)

"Also vacuumformed scenery, tin ceilings, architectural elements, bookbacks." ed.

Kliegl Brothers 718-786-7474
32-32 48th Ave. L.I.C. 11101
Hours: 8:30-5 Mon-Thurs/ 8:30-2 Fri
"Equipment sales and consultation." ed.

Martin Audio 212-541-5900
423 West 55th St. (9-10th) NYC 10019
Hours: 9-5:30 Mon-Fri
"Cine and video; lamps, umbrellas, etc." ed.

Precision Projection Systems Inc. 213-865-2534
11563 Radley St., Artesia, CA 90701
Hours: 9-6 Mon-Fri
"Lasers for stage and film, laser repair; see Carl Hannigan." ed.

Production Arts Lighting Inc. 212-489-0312
636 Eleventh Ave. (46th) NYC 10036
Hours: 9-5:30 Mon-Fri
"Lighting equipment rental: boards, cable, instruments; does lots of Off-B'way; good prices." ed.

Raven Screen 212-534-8408
124 East 124th St. (Park-Lexington) NYC 10035
Hours: 9-5 Mon-Fri
"Rear projection equipment." ed.

Staging Techniques 212-736-5727
342 West 40th St. (8-9th) NYC 10018
Hours: 9-5 Mon-Fri
"Audio visual house; programming facilities, screening room; equipment rental and sales." ed.

THEATRE MAGIC 614-459-3222
6099 Godown Rd., Columbus, OH 43220
Hours: 7:30-4:30 Mon-Fri
(See display ad page 334.)
"Stock and custom gobos." ed.

Times Square Stage Lighting 212-245-4155
318 West 47th St. (8-9th) NYC 10036
Hours: 8:30-5:30 Mon-Fri/ 10-2 Sat (open Sat: Sept-May only)
"Strobes, mirror balls, chaser lights; catalog." ed.

VANCO STAGE LIGHTING INC. 914-942-0075
RR1 Box 477A Rt. 210, Stony Point, NY 10980 800-55VANCO
Hours: 8-5 Mon-Fri

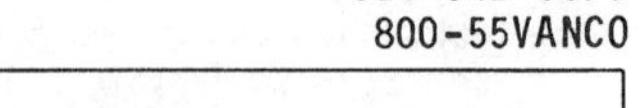

'Our job is mot merely to provide you with a lamp, a clamp, and a cable. From concept to realization, our approach to your project is both professional and personal. We feel that advice and counsel are an integral part of our service. We strive not to be the biggest, simply the best.' T.V.B.

"Large union shop; rental, sales; B'way, tours, TV; specialize in custom packages." ed.

LIGHTING FIXTURES & LAMP PARTS

See also ANTIQUES

Bon-Marche (Main Store/Warehouse) 212-620-5550
55 West 13th St. (5-6th) NYC 10011
Hours: 10:30-6:30 Mon-Sat
"Contemporary lighting fixtures & accessories." ed.

Bowery Lighting Corp.

132 Bowery (Grand) NYC 10013 212-966-4034
Hours: 9-5:30 every day

1144 Second Ave. (60th) NYC 10022 212-832-0990
Hours: 10:30-5:30 every day (Mon, Wed til 8)

275 Columbus Ave. (73rd) NYC 10023 212-877-7014
Hours: 10-9 Mon-Fri/ 10-7 Sat/ 12-5 Sun

"General range of lighting fixtures at good prices." ed.

Cibu Lighting 212-535-9529
1482 Third Ave. (83-84th) NYC 10028
Hours: 9-6 Mon-Fri/ 10-5 Sat
"Modern fixtures, rental or purchase." ed.

City Knickerbocker Inc. 212-586-3939
781 Eighth Ave. (47-48th) NYC 10036
Hours: 8-4:30 Mon-Fri
"Good selection period lamps, chandeliers, sconces; rental or purchase; see Ken." ed.

Conran's

160 East 54th St. (Lexington) NYC 10022 212-371-2225
2-8 Astor Place (8th-B'way) NYC 10003 212-505-1515

Hours: 10-9 Mon-Fri/ 10-7 Sat/ 12-6 Sun
"Furnishings for the home, housewares, lighting fixtures." ed.

Edith's Nostalgia 212-362-8713
469 Amsterdam Ave. (82-83rd) NYC 10024
Hours: 12-6 every day
"Gas and electric chandeliers, sconces, lamps; Deco." ed.

Gem Monogram & Cut Glass Corp. 212-674-8960
623 Broadway (Houston-Bleecker) NYC 10012
Hours: 9-5 Mon-Fri
"Cut glass chandeliers for days." ed.

Grand Brass Lamp Parts 212-226-2567
221 Grand St. (Elizabeth) NYC 10013
Hours: 8-5 Mon-Sat/ 10-4 Sun
"Lamp bases, globes, chimneys, metal shades, lamp hardware; very helpful." ed.

Just Shades 212-966-2757
21 Spring St. (Elizabeth) NYC 10012
Hours: 9:30-4 Thurs-Tues (closed Wed)
"Fabric lampshades in silk, velvet, parchment; stock & custom." ed.

Kawahara Lighting

1288 Third Ave. (73-74th) NYC 10021 212-249-0007
1461 Third Ave. (82-83rd) NYC 10028 212-772-9777

Hours: 10-7 Mon-Sat
"Good selection fabric lampshades and lamps." ed.

George Kovacs Lighting Inc. (retail) 212-861-9500
831 Madison Ave. (69th) NYC 10021 (wholesale) 212-861-9848
Hours: 10-6 Mon-Sat/ 12-5 Sun
"High tech lamps and lighting fixtures." ed.

Lee's Studio Gallery 212-265-5670
211 West 57th St. (B'way-7th) NYC 10019
Hours: 10-7 Mon-Fri/ 10-6 Sat
"Contemporary and avant garde lighting for the home or studio; pricey; rental available." ed.

Light Inc. 212-838-1130
1162 Second Ave. (61st) NYC 10021
Hours: 10-6 Mon-Fri
"Great modern fixtures; will rent." ed.

Lincoln Lite 212-581-7610
761 Tenth Ave. (51-52nd) NYC 10019
Hours: 9-6 Mon-Fri/ 10-4 Sat
"Lamps, track lighting, globes, shades, recessed fixtures; rental or purchase." ed.

Harry Loutzker & Sons 212-473-1880
312 East 22nd St. (1-2nd) NYC 10010
Hours: 7:30-4 Mon-Fri
"Wood turnings for lamps." ed.

Louis Mattia 212-753-2176
980 Second Ave. (52nd) NYC 10022
Hours: 9-6 Mon-Fri
"Antique lamps and lighting fixtures; some custom work." ed.

Miller Tube Corp. of America 718-939-3000
133-05 32nd Ave., Flushing, NY 11354
Hours: 9-5 Mon-Fri
"Lamp pipe, arms and poles." ed.

Paris Lighting Fixture Co. Inc. 212-226-7420
136 Bowery (Grand) NYC 10013
Hours: 9-5 Mon-Fri/ 9-4:30 Sat
"Good prices and selection of fixtures." ed.

Practicals Catalog 805-544-3650
PO Box 3118, San Luis Obispo, CA 93403
Hours: 1-4 Mon-Fri
"Catalog of practical lights, candelabras, candles, etc." ed.

Rosetta Electrical Co. Inc.

73 Murray St. (Greenwich St.-W B'Way) NYC 10007 212-233-9088
Hours: 9-5:30 Mon-Fri/ 9:30-5 Sat

21 West 46th St. (5-6th) NYC 10036 212-719-4381
Hours: 9-5:45 Mon-Fri

"Contemporary fixtures, lamps, electrical supplies, some lamp parts."

Sanelle Wood Products Corp. 212-348-1500
315 East 86th St. (1-2nd) NYC 10028
Hours: By appt.
"Lamp bases and parts; wholesale only; salesman will visit you." ed.

Sarsaparilla - Deco Designs 201-863-8002
5711 Washington St., West New York, NJ 07093
Hours: 8:30-4:30 Mon-Fri
"Art Deco reproduction lamps, tin signs; wholesale; catalog $5." ed.

Shadey Business 212-255-1480
163 West 10th St. (7th) NYC 10014
Hours: 11:30-6 Mon-Sat/ 1-5 Sun
"Custom covering of lampshade frames, also limited stock of lampshades." ed.

William Spencer 609-235-235-3764
Creek Road, Mount Laurel, NJ 08060
Hours: 10-5 Mon-Fri
"Antique repro lighting fixtures, toys and furniture." ed.

Superior Lamp & Electrical Supply Co. Inc. 212-677-9191
394 Broadway (22nd) NYC 10010
Hours: 8-5 Mon-Fri
"Track lighting, industrial and institutional flourescent fixtures; discounts on large purchases." ed.

Teddy's Lamp & Lighting Fixture Parts 212-925-5067
182 Grand St. (Mulberry-Baxter) NYC 10013
Hours: 8-4:30 Mon-Fri
"Great selection glass shades and globes; price is right." ed.

Thunder and Light 212-219-0180
171 Bowery (Delancey) NYC 10002
Hours: 9:30-5:30 Tues-Sun
"High tech, some repro styles, Italian designs; catalogs." ed.

U.S. Balloon Mfg. Co. 718-646-1110
1613 Oriental Blvd. (Emmons Ave.) Bklyn 11235
Hours: 9-6 Mon-Fri
"Lighted balloon fixtures, 3 sizes; rental or purchase." ed.

Randy Wicker's Uplift Inc. 212-929-3632
506 Hudson St. (Christopher-10th) NYC 10014
Hours: 1-8 every day
"Great selection of art deco sconces, lamps and floor lamps." ed.

LINENS

JOYCE AMES 212-535-3047
335 East 65th St. (1-2nd) NYC 10021
Hours: By appt.
Specializing in antique & period laces, linens & floral print drapery. Restoration and on-the-spot construction available. Rentals and sales. Consultation to TV and film.
"Also tablecloths, bedspreads, antimacassars, etc." ed.

Anichini Gallery 212-982-7274
7 East 20th St. (B'way) NYC 10003
Hours: By appt.
"Period linens, textiles, clothing accessories, quilts; Patrizia Anichini or Susan Dollemaier." ed.

Boutross Imports 212-685-5860
260 Fifth Ave. 7th Fl. (28-29th) NYC 10001
Hours: 9-5 Mon-Fri
"Damask linen tablecloths; see Eddy." ed.

Ezra Cohen Corp. 212-925-7800
307 Grand St. (Allen) NYC 10002
Hours: 9-5 Mon-Thurs/ 9-4 Fri/ 9-5 Sun
"Good selection of sheets, towels, bathroom accessories." ed.

Eldridge Textile Co. 212-925-1523
277 Grand St. (Eldridge) NYC 10002
Hours: 9-5:30 Sun-Fri
"Sheets, bedding, towels, tablecloths." ed.

James G. Hardy 212-689-6680
11 East 26th St. (5th-Madison) NYC 10010
Hours: 9-5 Mon-Fri
"Institutional and household tablecloths and napkins." ed.

K. Katen & Co. Inc. 212-683-5257
244 Fifth Ave. 4th Floor (27-28th) NYC 10001
Hours: 8:45-4:45 Mon-Fri
"Table linens, beautiful damask and cut work; see Alfred Katen." ed.

Marimekko Store 212-581-9616
7 West 56th St. (5th) NYC 10019
Hours: 10-6:30 Mon-Fri/ 10-6 Sat
"Fabrics, sheets, bedding, toys, clothes." ed.

Orienhouse Enterprises Inc. 212-431-8060
424-426 Broadway (Grand-Canal) NYC 10013
Hours: 9:30-6 Mon-Sat
"Tablecloths, oriental gifts and handicrafts, Chinese embroidered blouses, kung-fu and karate equipment." ed.

J. Schacter Corp. 212-533-1150
115 Allen St. (Delancey) NYC 10002
Hours: 9-5 Sun-Thurs/ 9-2:30 Fri
"Sheets, pillows, quilts; some custom work." ed.

Wolfman-Gold & Good 212-431-1888
484 Broome St. (Wooster) NYC 10016
Hours: 11-6 Mon-Sat/ 12-5 Sun
"Beautiful antique and new linens; also baskets, cookie cutters, tureens, etc." ed.

LINOLEUM see FLOORCOVERINGS

LUGGAGE

See also HANDBAG & LUGGAGE REPAIR

ALTMAN LUGGAGE 212-254-7275
135 Orchard St. (Delancey-Rivington) NYC 10002
Hours: 9:30-6 Sun-Fri
New, used & antique trunks & luggage. Rentals/Repairs.
"See Dan Bettinger." ed.

Bettinger's Luggage 212-674-9411
80 Rivington St. (Orchard-Allen) NYC 10002
Hours: 10-6 Sun-Fri
"Rental and sales of luggage and trunks." ed.

Crouch & Fitzgerald 212-753-1808
400 Madison Ave. (48th) NYC 10017 212-755-5888
Hours: 9-6 Mon-Sat
"Luggage, expensive." ed.

Eton's Luggage Shop 212-921-1212
1124 Sixth Ave. (43-44th) NYC 10036
Hours: 9-6 Mon-Fri/ 10:30-5:30 Sat
"Modern, good looking luggage; will rent." ed.

Jad Luggage Shop 212-752-8251
1420 Sixth Ave. (58th) NYC 10019
Hours: 9-7 Mon-Fri/ 9-6 Sat
"Diverse selection luggage, small leather goods." ed.

Moormends Luggage Shop 212-289-3978
1228 Madison Ave. (88-89th) NYC 10128
Hours: 9-6 Mon-Fri/ 9-5 Sat
"Luggage, expensive." ed.

LUMBER

See also HARDWOODS & VENEERS
See also HOME DECORATING & IMPROVEMENT CENTERS

Aasbo Lumber & Cabinet Makers 212-222-6200
1834 Second Ave. (95th) NYC 10128
Hours: 9-7 Mon-Sat
"Will deliver, small orders ok; pleasant; expensive but good quality."

Bay Ridge Lumber

6303 5th Ave. (63-64th) Bklyn 11220 212-492-3300
Hours: 8-3:30 Mon-Fri

East Second and Hobart Ave., Bayonne, NJ 07002 212-745-7311
Hours: 8:30-5 Mon-Fri

"Fire retardant and pressure treated plywood, Homopol, Nevamar laminates, moldings; good prices, will deliver." ed.

Blue Bell Lumber & Moulding Co. Inc.

501 East 164th St. (Washington-3rd) Bronx 10456 212-923-0200
2360 Amsterdam Ave. (177-178th) NYC 10033 212-923-0200

Hours: 8-5 Mon-Fri/ 8-12 Sat
"Treated fir plywood, hardwoods, millwork, doors." ed.

Butler Lumber

220 West 14th St. (7-8th) NYC 10011 212-243-2612
Hours: 8-4:15 Mon-Sat (Sat til 5:15)
"Formicas, wall paneling, molding, millwork, hardware." ed.

2311 Third Ave. (125-126th) NYC 10035 212-369-9012
Hours: 8-4:30 Mon-Sat/ 8-3:30 Sun
"Formicas, wall paneling, molding, millwork, hardware." ed.

Canal Lumber 212-226-5987
18 Wooster St. (Canal-Grand) NYC 10013
Hours: 8-5 Mon-Fri/ 8-1 Sat
"Power tools, formica, millwork; fireproof lumber, plywood." ed.

Dykes Lumber

348 West 44th St. (8-9th) NYC 10036 212-246-6480
Hours: 8-5 Mon-Fri/ 8-3:30 Sat
"Excellent, for Midtown; moldings, millwork." ed.

26-16 Jackson Ave. (near Queens Plaza) L.I.C. 11101 718-534-1640
Hours: 8-4:30 Mon-Fri
"Lumber, plywood, moldings, millwork." ed.

Feldman Lumber

2 Woodward Ave., (Metropolitan Ave) Ridgewood, NY 11385 718-495-5000
Hours: 8-5 Mon-Fri (pick up by 2pm)
"Large orders at good prices; see Walter or Brian; will deliver." ed.

63 Third Ave. (Union) Bayshore, NY 11706 516-665-3800
Hours: 8-5 Mon-Fri/ 7-2 Sat

692 Hopkinson Ave. (Dumont Ave) Bklyn 11212 718-498-8200
Hours: 8-5 Mon-Fri (pick up by 2pm)

"Lumber." ed.

Murry M. Fine Lumber 718-381-5200
175 Varick Ave. (Metropolitan-Grand) Bklyn 11237
Hours: 8-5 Mon-Fri (pick up by 4pm)
"Used large beams and timber." ed.

Foremost Lumber 718-388-7777
60 North 1st St. (Kent-Wythe) Bklyn 11211
Hours: 8-4:30 Mon-Fri
"Lumber, molding, some cabinet plywood, micas, special millwork; good prices." ed.

Grillion Corp. 718-875-8545
191 First St. (3-4th Ave) Bklyn 11215
Hours: 8-4:30 Mon-Fri/ call for Sat hours
"Decorative wooden panels and grillwork." ed.

Lenoble Lumber Co. Inc. 212-246-0150
500 West 52nd St. (10-11th) NYC 10019
Hours: 8-3:30 Mon-Fri (closed for lunch 12-1)
"Doors, plywood, formica, moldings, masonite, millwork, windows, sonotube." ed.

Lumberland 212-696-0022
409 Third Ave. (29th) NYC 10016
Hours: 9-6 Mon-Sat
"Wooden spindles, hardwood, some decorative hardware, power tools."

Maxwell Lumber

211 West 18th St. (7-8th) NYC 10011 212-929-6088
Hours: 8-5 Mon-Fri

25-30 Borden Ave. L.I.C. 212-929-6088
Hours: 8-5 Mon-Fri

"Lumber, large molding catalog, doors, spindles, newel posts." ed.

Metropolitan Lumber & Hardware

175 Spring St. (W. B'way-Thompson) NYC 10012 212-246-9090
Hours: 8-6 Mon-Fri/ 8-5:30 Sat/ 10-4 Sun

617 11th Ave. (46-47th) NYC 10036 212-246-9090
Hours: 7-7 Mon-Fri/ 8-5:30 Sat/ 10-4 Sun

"Hardwoods, plywood, hand and power tools, doors, windows, formica, molding; free delivery over $100." ed.

Mike's Carpenter Shop 212-595-8884
254 West 88th St. (B'way-Amsterdam) NYC 10024
Hours: 9-6 Mon-Fri/ 9-4:30 Sat
"Formicas, some hardware, unfinished furniture, doors, stain, moldings." ed.

Miron Lumber Co. 718-497-1111
268 Johnson Ave. (near Bushwick) Bklyn 11206
Hours: 7:30-2:30 Mon-Fri (closed for lunch 11:30-1)
"Hardwood, molding, good prices, will deliver to Manhattan." ed.

Prince Lumber Co. Inc. 212-777-1150
406 West 15th St. (9-10th) NYC 10011
Hours: 7-3:30 Mon-Fri
"Pleasant, good service; formica, plywood, molding, doors, windows."

Rosenzweig Lumber Co. 212-585-8050
801 East 135th St. (near Bruckner) Bronx 10454
Hours: 8-5 Mon-Fri
"Hardwoods, veneers, lumber; good prices, prompt next day delivery."

System Lumber Co. 212-695-0380
517 West 42nd St. (10-11th) NYC 10036
Hours: 7-4:30 Mon-Fri/ 8-2:30 Sat
"Fireproof and treated lumber." ed.

Walter E. Umla Inc. 718-624-3350
180 6th St. (2-3rd Ave) Bklyn 11215
Hours: 8-3:30 Mon-Fri
"Plywood, treated lumber, millwork, beams." ed.

MACHINISTS & MACHINISTS TOOLS

Peter Johnke 212-868-7567
400 West 43rd St. (9-10th) NYC 10036
Hours: By appt.
"Electrical-mechanical product rigs; stocks motion devices, linear, turntables, etc. for rent." ed.

Manhattan Supply Co. 718-895-1474
151 Sunnyside Blvd., Plainview, NY 11803
Hours: 8-6 Mon-Fri
"Mail order machine tools; drills, reamers, cutters, etc; great catalog." ed.

Bernard Manhertz 212-925-8586
44 Greene St. (Grand-Broome) NYC 10013
Hours: 9-5 Mon-Sat
"Free lance machinist." ed.

Mathieson 212-675-5081
153 West 27th St. Rm. 803 (6-7th) NYC 10001
Hours: 8-4:30 Mon-Fri
"Complete machine shop; friendly, reliable service." ed.

S. Pomponio 212-925-9453
6 Varick St. (W B'way-Franklin) NYC 10013
Hours: 9-6 Mon-Fri
"Cuts stencils, models, jigs, lighting templates, trophy bases." ed.

Sherov Machine Corp. 516-454-8899
149 Allen Blvd., East Farmingdale, NY 11735
Hours: 9-5:30 Mon-Fri
"Reliable machinists; can be available for small orders; ask for Joe."

Sol Tool Co. 212-925-0923
164 Lafayette (Grand) NYC 10013
Hours: 8-4:30 Mon-Fri
"Good stock of machine tools; catalogs sometimes." ed.

Victor Machinery Exchange 212-226-3494
251 Centre St. (Grand-Broome) NYC 10013
Hours: 8:30-4 Mon-Fri
"Tool room equipment, vises, micrometers, etc." ed.

MAGAZINES & COMIC BOOKS

See also BOOKSTORES

A & S Book Co. 212-695-4897
274 West 43rd St. (B'way-8th) NYC 10036
Hours: 10-6 Mon-Fri/ 10-4 Sat
"Back date magazines and comic books." ed.

Abraham's Magazine Service 212-777-4700
56 East 13th St. (B'way-University) NYC 10003
Hours: 9-5 Mon-Fri
"Back issues." ed.

Back Date Magazines 212-243-9349
228 West 23rd St. (7-8th) NYC 10011
Hours: 9:30-6:30 Mon-Sat/ 11-5 Sun
"Back date magazines and comic books." ed.

Forbidden Planet 212-473-1576
821 Broadway (12th) NYC 10003
Hours: 10-7 Mon-Sat/ 11-6 Sun
"Current and back issue special effects magazines, fantasy comic books." ed.

Funny Business Comics 212-799-9477
666 Amsterdam (92-93rd) NYC 10025
Hours: 1-5 Mon-Thurs/ 1-6 Fri/ 12-5 Sat, Sun
"Great selection current and back date comic books." ed.

Hotaling News Agency 212-840-1868
142 West 42nd St. (B'way-6th) NYC 10036
Hours: 7:30-9:25 Mon-Sat/ 7:30-7:30 Sun
"Good selection current foreign out-of-town magazines and newspapers." ed.

International University Booksellers 212-254-4100
30 Irving Place (16th) NYC 10003
Hours: By appt.
"Back date medical, scientific and scholarly magazines." ed.

Jay Bee Magazine Stores Inc. 212-675-1600
134 West 26th St. Basement (6-7) NYC 10001
Hours: 9:30-5 Mon-Fri/ 10-3 Sat
"Large stock back date magazines; list of titles carried available."

Supersnipe Comic Book Art Emporium 212-879-9628
PO Box 1102, Gracie Station, NYC 10028
Hours: 10-2:30 Tues,Thurs phone manned, other times: machine
"Current and back issues of science fiction, fantasy, special effects, comics and movie magazines; mail order only; catalog." ed.

West Side Comics 212-724-0432
107 West 86th St. (Amsterdam-Columbus) NYC 10024
Hours: 12-6 Mon-Thurs/ 12-5 Fri/ 12-6 Sat/ 1-5 Sun
"Current and back date comic books." ed.

MAGIC SUPPLIES & NOVELTIES

Funny Store Inc. 212-730-9582
1481 Broadway (42nd) NYC 10036
Hours: 9-9 every day
"Gags, magic tricks." ed.

GORDON NOVELTY CO. INC. 212-254-8616
933 Broadway (21-22nd) NYC 10010
Hours: 9-4:30 Mon-Fri

The Premiere Novelty Shop. 4,000 items in stock. Masks, disguise novelties, seasonal items, novelty & theatrical hats, party favors, convention items, dance accessories, carnival items, flags, parasols, canes, fans, glitter, ostrich plumes, costumes, weapons, makeup, hair goods, rubber chickens & ducks, artificial food, wigs, mustaches, beards, police & military badges & medals, Santa Claus costumes, etc.etc. Phone and mail accepted. Established sixty years.

"Wholesale and retail; great prices; extensive catalog." ed.

D. Robbins & Co. Inc. 718-625-1804
70 Washington St. Bklyn 11201
Hours: 8-4:30 Mon-Fri
"Wholesale magic supplies; quantity sales only." ed.

Louis Tannen Inc. 212-239-8383
6 West 32nd St. 4th Fl. (5-B'way) NYC 10001
Hours: 9-5:30 Mon-Fri (Thurs til 7)/ 9-3 Sat
"Flash powder, flash paper; will assist with complicated tricks; consulting service available." ed.

THEATRE MAGIC 614-459-3222
6099 Godown Rd., Columbus, OH 43220
Hours: 7:30-4:30 Mon-Fri

(See display ad page 334.)

"Stocks light-up canes, flash powder and paper; consultation on magic tricks." ed.

Think Big 212-925-7300
390 Broadway (Spring-Broome) NYC 10012
Hours: 9-6 Mon-Thurs/ 9-7 Fri/ 11-7 Sat/ 11-6 Sun
"5' crayons, pencils, toothbrushes, paint brushes, tennis balls, etc; catalog available." ed.

Times Square Shoppers World Ltd. 212-765-8342
201 West 49th St. (B'way-7th) NYC 10019
Hours: 10-6:30 Mon-Sat
"Gags, magic tricks, stage props; halloween masks and costumes, exotic lingerie." ed.

MAKE-UP SUPPLIES

See also HAIR SUPPLIES & WIGS
For artificial eyes, see TAXIDERMISTS AND TAXIDERMY SUPPLIES
For additional latex suppliers, see CASTING SUPPLIES

A. D. M. Tronics Inc. 201-767-6040
153 Ludlow Ave., North Vale, NJ 07647
Hours: 9-5 Mon-Fri
"Pros-Aide adhesive, a prosthesis glue (can be used on latex as painting ground)." ed.

Alcone Company Inc./ Paramount Theatrical 718-361-8373
5-49 49th Ave. L.I.C. 11101
Hours: 9:30-4 Mon-Fri
"Theatrical make-up, stage blood, latex, foam latex; catalog." ed.

Hosmer Dorrance Corp. 408-379-5151
PO Box 37, Campbell, CA 95009
Hours: 7-4:30 Mon-Fri
"Prosthetic making supplies; latex and pigments; catalog." ed.

Bob Kelly Wig Creations Inc. 212-819-0030
151 West 46th St. (6-7th) NYC 10036
Hours: 9-4:30 Mon-Thurs/ 9-3 Fri
"Theatrical make-up; also wigs, hairpieces, artificial hair; catalog."

Lillian Costumes 516-746-6060
226 Jericho Turnpike, Mineola, NY 11501
Hours: 9-5:30 Tues-Sat
"Large supplier of Mehron products." ed.

The Make-Up Center Ltd. 212-977-9494
150 West 55th St. (6-7th) NYC 10019
Hours: 10-6 Mon-Fri (Thurs til 8)/ 10-5 Sat
"Make-up and supplies, many brands, stage blood." ed.

Mehron Inc. 212-997-1011
45E Route 303, Valley Cottage, NY 10989 914-268-4106
Hours: 9-5 Mon-Fri
"Theatrical make-up, kits; catalog, new color chart." ed.

Ben Nye Makeup Inc. 213-477-0443
11571 Santa Monica Blvd., W. Los Angeles, CA 90025
Hours: 9-5 Mon-Fri
"Theatrical make-up kits; catalog." ed.

REJOICE LTD./GARY ZELLER, JOYCE SPECTOR 212-869-8636
40 West 39 St. (5-6th) NYC 10018
Hours: By appt. or leave message
Non-toxic moldmaking, casting supplies for prosthetics. (See display ad page 333.)
"Special effects consultation and services." ed.

Research Council of Make-Up Artists 617-459-9864
52 New Spaulding St., Lowell, MA 01851
Hours: 9-5 Mon-Fri
"Prosthetic latex, mold materials, adhesives, make-up; catalog." ed.

Sperling Beauty Supplies 818-781-6300
13639 Vanowen, Van Nuys, CA 91405
Hours: 8:30-6 Mon-Fri/ 8:30-3 Sat
"Non-staining blood." ed.

Stagelight Cosmetics Ltd. 212-757-4851
630 Ninth Ave. (44-45th) NYC 10036
Hours: 11:30-7 Mon-Fri
"Theatrical make-up supplies." ed.

STEIN'S COSMETIC CO. 212-226-2430
430 Broome St. (Crosby) NYC 10013
Hours: 9-4:30 Mon-Fri

Write for our Free 32 page booklet "Makeup for the Professional".
"Full line of cream, cake and greasepaint; wholesale at this location."

Zauder Brothers 516-379-2600
10 Henry St., Freeport, NY 11520
Hours: 9:30-5 Mon-Thurs/ 9:30-3 Fri
"Make-up; also hair goods." ed.

MANNEQUINS

Ace Display Fixture 212-279-5927
2 West 31st St. (5th) NYC 10001
Hours: 9-5 Mon-Fri
"Mannequins; will rent." ed.

American Hanger & Fixture Inc. 212-279-5280
520 West 27th St. (10-11th) NYC 10001
Hours: 9-5 Mon-Fri
"Men's, women's, infants' and children's mannequins; formerly Wally Hanger Co." ed.

Bernstein & Sons 212-683-2260
30 West 29th St. (B'way) NYC 10001
Hours: 9-5:30 Mon-Fri
"Mannequins, all types display fixtures, hangers, 3-fold mirrors, clothes steamers; will rent." ed.

Herzberg-Robbins Inc. 212-354-6030
209 West 38th St. (7-8th) NYC 10018
Hours: 9-4:30 Mon-Fri
"New and secondhand mannequins; also, horsehair wigs, display fixtures and racks." ed.

Pucci Mannequins 212-219-0142
578 Broadway (Houston-Prince) NYC 10012
Hours: 10-5 Mon-Fri
"Mannequins and mannequin wigs." ed.

Jerry Roe Enterprises Inc. 212-993-7766
432 Austin Place, Bronx 10455
Hours: 8:30-4 Mon-Fri
"Mannequins; fliers available." ed.

MAPS

Argosy Book Stores Inc. 212-753-4455
116 East 59th St. (Lexington-Park) NYC 10022
Hours: 9-6 Mon-Fri/ 10-5 Sat
"Out of print books, maps, prints." ed.

Hammond Map Store Inc. 212-398-1222
57 West 43rd St. (5-6th) NYC 10036
Hours: 8:45-5:45 Mon-Fri
"Wide selection national and foreign maps; globes." ed.

New York Nautical 212-962-4522
140 West Broadway (Thomas-Duane) NYC 10013
Hours: 9-5 Mon-Fri/ 9-12 Sat
"Star and nautical maps of the world; nautical instruments." ed.

Rand McNally & Co. 212-751-6300
10 East 53rd St. (Madison-5th) NYC 10022
Hours: 9:15-5:15 Mon-Fri
"Up-to-date Rand McNally maps and guide books." ed.

South Street Seaport Museum: Store 212-669-9400
207 Front St. (Fulton) NYC 10038
Hours: 10-9 Mon-Sat/ 11-6 Sun
"Maritime maps and books." ed.

MARBLE

Acme Marble Works Inc. 718-788-0527
160 17th St. (3-4th) Bklyn 11215 718-965-3560
Hours: 8-4 Mon-Fri
"Large selection of marble, custom work and cutting; nice people." ed.

Marble Textures Ltd. 212-755-5891
140 East 59th St. (Lexington) NYC 10022
Hours: 9:30-5 Mon-Fri
"Samples on display, will rent; next day pickup." ed.

New York Marble Works Inc. 212-534-2242
1399 Park Ave. (104th) NYC 10029
Hours: 8-4:30 Mon-Fri
"Rentals, cut to size." ed.

MARINE EQUIPMENT

See also FISHING TACKLE

Capt. Hook Marine Antiques & Shells 212-344-2262
South Street Seaport (Fulton) NYC 10038
Hours: 10-10 every day
"Marine antiques and seashells." ed.

J. Cowhey & Sons Inc. 718-625-5587
440 Van Brunt St. Bklyn 11231
Hours: 9-4:30 Mon-Fri
"Good prices marine equipment, aircraft cable, etc." ed.

Defender Industries 914-632-3001
255 Main St., New Rochelle, NY 10801
Hours: 9-5:45 Mon-Fri/ 9-2:45 Sat
"Extensive stock marine supplies: boat hardware to sailcloth to fiberglas supplies." ed.

Goldberg's Marine 212-840-8280
12 West 37th St. (5-6th) NYC 10018
Hours: 9:30-5:45 Mon-Fri (Thurs til 6:45)/ 9:30-2:45 Sat
"Everything for the sail and power boat, scuba and marine equipment."

Manhattan Marine & Electric Co. Inc. 212-267-8756
116 Chambers St. (Church-W. B'way) NYC 10007
Hours: 8:30-5 Mon-Fri
"Good stock boating hardware, rain gear, nylon rope." ed.

Nelson's Folly Antiques 212-755-0485
152 East 79th St. (Lexington-3rd) NYC 10021
Hours: 11-6 Mon-Sat
"Antique marine items; will rent." ed.

MASK MAKERS

Robert Flanagan 718-636-6280
124 Hall St. (Myrtle Ave.) Bklyn 11205
Hours: By appt.
"Puppets, masks, props, special effects." ed.

Jane Gootnick 212-724-2056
204 West 88th St. (B'way) NYC 10024
Hours: By appt.
"Props, masks, creatures." ed.

Rodney Gordon 212-620-9018
39 West 14th St. Rm. 501 (5-6th) NYC 10001 718-522-7081
Hours: 10-6 Mon-Fri
"Costume crafts: specializing in millinery and masks." ed.

JANET HARPER STUDIO 212-966-1886
279 Church St. (White) NYC 10013
Hours: 10-6 Mon-Fri
Costume props. Masks. Specialty costumes including body puppets & animal costumes. Millinery. Jewelry.
"Theatre, film and promotional work." ed.

MARTIN IZQUIERDO STUDIO LTD. 212-807-9757
118 West 22nd St. 9th Fl. (7-8th) NYC 10011
Hours: By appt.
Costume painting, props, masks, silkscreening, creatures & graphic design. Rosco and Haussmann Distributor.
"Also sells English tutu net and tubular horsehair." ed.

Robert W. Jones 212-410-4341
329 East 92nd St. #3B (1st-2nd) NYC 10128
Hours: By appt.
"Props for theatre and commercials; masks, celastic fabricator." ed.

Ralph Lee 212-929-4777
463 West St. #D405 (W. 12th) NYC 10014
Hours: By appt.
"Masks, larger-than-life puppets and costumes; wide range of materials." ed.

Marleen Marta 212-989-4684
25 Grove St. (Bedford-Bleecker) NYC 10014
Hours: By appt.
"Masks, props, scenic and costume painting, set decoration." ed.

Susan McClain-Moore/ MCL Designs Inc. 212-206-7500
31 West 21st St. 7th Fl. (5-6th) NYC 10010
Hours: 9-5 Mon-Fri
"Customized full-figure body puppets, hand puppets, props and masks."

Maria R. McNamara 612-224-7267
677 Oakdale Ave., St. Paul, MN 55107
Hours: By appt.
"Puppets, props, masks, costume crafts." ed.

FREDERICK NIHDA STUDIO 212-966-1886
279 Church St. (White) NYC 10013
Hours: 10-6 Mon-Fri
Custom Props & Costumes for Theatre, Film, Promotions, TV.
"Body puppets, masks, jewelry, armor, mechanisms, and hand props." ed.

Lisa Shaftel 212-249-2581
332 East 74th St. #4B (1-2nd) NYC 10021
Hours: By appt.
"Scenic/lighting design, scene painting, carpentry, puppets, animal figures, masks." ed.

Willa Shalit 212-316-3470
340 Riverside Dr. (106th) NYC 10025
Hours: By appt.
"Expert life-casting, mask making, marbelizing; quality, reliability, promptness, cheer." ed.

Julie Taymor 212-475-4829
718 Broadway #10C (Waverly) NYC 10003
Hours: By appt.
"Writer/director; designer: puppetry and masks for film, TV and theatre." ed.

Norman Tempia 212-348-8944
409 East 90th St. #1-B (1st-York) NYC 10128
Hours: By appt.
"Sculpture, special props, masks and puppets for film and tape." ed.

Brad Williams 212-865-0088
214 Riverside Dr. #109 (94th) NYC 10025
Hours: 9-9 Mon-Fri
"Puppets designed, built, performed for stage, film, video; masks, props, graphics." ed.

Donna E. Zanki 303-364-5299
1923 Oswego St., Aurora, CO 80010
Hours: By appt.
"Costume crafts; leatherwork, footwear, masks, jewelry, armor." ed.

MEDICAL EQUIPMENT

See also DENTAL SUPPLY HOUSES
See also LAB & SCIENTIFIC EQUIPMENT

American International Medical Equipment Sales 718-993-4400
780 East 138th St. (Willow Ave.) Bronx 10454
Hours: 8-5 Mon-Fri
"Lab and hospital equipment, wheelchairs; rental or purchase; very helpful." ed.

Archer Surgical Supplies Inc. 212-695-5553
544 West 27th St. (10-11th) NYC 10001
Hours: 9:30-4:30 Mon-Thurs/ 9:30-4 Fri
"Surgical supplies, medical equipment; see Kenny for rentals." ed.

Arista Surgical Supply Co. 212-679-3694
67 Lexington Ave. (25th) NYC 10010
Hours: 8:30-5 Mon-Fri/ 9-12 Sat
"Surgical and dental supplies; will rent." ed.

Bell Medical Supply 212-744-4059
40 East 65th St. (Madison-Park) NYC 10021
Hours: 9-5 Mon-Fri
"Phone orders only, no showroom; wheelchairs, sickroom supplies."ed.

Falk Surgical Corp. 212-744-8082
259 East 72nd St. (2nd) NYC 10021
Hours: 9-7:30 Mon-Fri/ 9:30-6 Sat/ 10-6 Sun
"Orthopedic and sickroom equipment." ed.

Holmes Medical & Ambulance 718-287-5858
510 Flatbush Ave. Bklyn 11225
Hours: 9-5 Mon-Sat
"Will rent or sell; new and used equipment." ed.

Keefe & Keefe Ambulance 212-988-8800
429 East 75th St. (York-1st) NYC 10021
Hours: 9-5 Mon-Sat
"Motorized wheelchairs, canes, crutches, walking accessories." ed.

N. S. Low & Co. Inc. 212-532-4120
220 East 23rd St. 3rd Fl. (2-3rd) NYC 10010
Hours: 9-5 Mon-Fri
"Plaster and elastic bandages by the box, scalpels." ed.

Marburger Surgical 212-420-1166
34 Irving Place (16th St. between 3rd & 4th) NYC 10003
Hours: 8:30-5 Mon-Thurs/ 8:30-3 Fri
"Surgical equipment; some rentals." ed.

Tower Chemist Inc. 212-838-1490
1257 Second Ave. (66th) NYC 10021
Hours: 9am-10pm Mon-Fri/ 10-8 Sat, Sun
"Plaster bandages; drugstore with some surgical and orthopedic supplies." ed.

A. Wittenberg Surgical Appliance 212-876-7023
1400 Madison Ave. (97th) NYC 10029
Hours: 9-5:30 Mon-Fri
"Minimum rental 1 month; new and used equipment." ed.

MEMORABILIA

Added Treasures 212-889-1776
577 Second Ave. (31-32nd) NYC 10016
Hours: By appt.
"Antique signs, period magazines, clothing, jewelry, etc." ed.

Coca-Cola Bottling Co. 212-292-2424
977 East 149th St. (Bruckner Blvd.) Bronx 10455
Hours: 9-5 Mon-Fri
"Helpful with hard to find items; see Tom Mulrooney." ed.

Coca-Cola Co./Public Relations 213-877-0607
11969 Ventura Blvd. Suite 107, Studio City, CA 91604
Hours: 8:30-5:30 Mon-Fri
"Mostly film work; submit script; speak to Ken Mason." ed.

The Coco-Nut 404-564-0244
4529 Woodhaven Ave., Marietta, GA 30067
Hours: 10-6 Mon-Fri
"Coca-Cola collectibles, old and new; see June Tindall." ed.

CULVER PICTURES 212-645-1672
150 West 22nd St. #300 (6-7th) NYC 10011
Hours: 9-5 Mon-Fri (call first)
9,000,000 choice old photos, engravings, prints, movie stills, trade cards, sheet music covers, old greeting cards, tintypes & glass plate negatives. Leased for reproduction.
"Everything from Stone Age to Space Age." ed.

Kover King 212-575-7744
120 West 44th St. (6th-B'way) NYC 10036
Hours: 9-5 Mon-Fri
"Antique valentines, postcards, letters, envelopes w/stamps; postage stamps for collectors. (moving Fall '85, check for new location)." ed.

Nostalgia Decorating Co. 717-288-1795
PO Box 1312, Kingston, PA 18704
Hours: 9-5 Mon-Fri
"Repro prints, turn of the century ads and magazine covers; also enameled metal ad signs; $50-$100 minimum; brochure." ed.

Sarsaparilla-Deco Designs 201-863-8002
5711 Washington St., West New York, NJ 07093
Hours: 8:30-4:30 Mon-Fri
"Tin signs, art deco reproduction lamps; wholesale; catalog." ed.

Speakeasy Antiques 212-533-2440
799 Broadway (11th) NYC 10003
Hours: 10:30-6 Tues-Sat (Thurs til 7)
"Decals, luggage stickers, tin signs, ephemera; will rent." ed.

Statue of Liberty Gallery Shop 212-929-4180
519 Hudson St. (10th) NYC 10014
Hours: 1-6 Tues-Sun
"Articles dealing with the Statue of Liberty; see Merv Venderwald."

MEMORABILIA: THEATRE AND FILM

Actor's Heritage 212-944-7490
262 West 44th St. (B'way-8th) NYC 10036
Hours: 10-8 Mon/ 10am-11:30pm Tues-Sat/ 12-7 Sun
"B'way t-shirts, sweatshirts, records, cassettes, posters; scripts, books, programs, film stills." ed.

Cinemabilia 212-989-8519
10 West 13th St. (5-6th) NYC 10011
Hours: 11-6:30 Mon, Wed, Sat/ 11-7 Tues, Thurs, Fri
"Current and out-of-print books and memorabilia related to film." ed.

CULVER PICTURES 212-645-1672
150 West 22nd St. Rm.300 (6-7th) NYC 10011
Hours: 9-5 Mon-Fri (call first)
9,000,000 choice old photos, engravings, prints, movie stills, trade cards, sheet music covers, old greeting cards, tintypes & glass plate negatives. Leased for reproduction.
"Everything from Stone Age to Space Age." ed.

Memory Shop 212-431-8732
68 Thompson St. (Spring-Broome) NYC 10012
Hours: 11-6:30 Mon-Sat
"Out-of-print 20th Century art and film books, periodicals, posters, pre-1970's stills." ed.

Movie Star News 212-620-8160
134 West 18th St. (6-7th) NYC 10011
Hours: 10-6 Mon-Sat
"Movie posters and stills." ed.

Jerry Ohlinger's Movie Material Store Inc. 212-674-8474
120 West 3rd St. (6th-MacDougal) NYC 10012
Hours: 1-8 every day
"8x10's, film stills, movie posters." ed.

PACKAGE PUBLICITY SERVICE 212-255-2872
27 West 24th St. Rm.402 (5-6th) NYC 10010
Hours: 10-5 Mon-Fri
"Show posters, logos, iron-on t-shirt transfers; press kits for hundreds of shows." ed.

Silver Screen 212-679-8130
35 East 28th St. (Park-Madison) NYC 10016
Hours: 11-7 Mon-Sat
"Color, black and white photos of film stars, 1930 to present; posters, memorabilia." ed.

MERCHANDISING & PROMOTION

Omicron Production Service/Don Marks 212-245-2570
333 West 52nd St. Suite 410 (8-9th) NYC 10019
Hours: 8:30-6 Mon-Fri or by appt.
"Prop promotion for plays." ed.

Omicron Production Service/George Fenmore 212-977-4140
254 West 54th St. (B'way-8th) NYC 10019
Hours: 9-5:30 Mon-Fri
"Prop promotion for plays." ed.

Ruth Sussman 212-757-8968
340 West 57th St. (8th-Columbus) NYC 10019
Hours: By appt.
"Prop promotion for plays." ed.

METALS & FOILS

See also JEWELERS TOOLS & SUPPLIES
For model brass, see HOBBY SHOPS & SUPPLIERS

Alufoil Products Co. Inc. 718-789-3069
135 Oser Ave., Hauppauge, NY 11787
Hours: 7:30-4 Mon-Fri
"Large manufacturer of foils." ed.

Bob Michael's Surplus Metals 212-226-6467
321 Canal St. (B'way-Greene) NYC 10013
Hours: 8:30-5:25 Mon-Fri/ 9-4:25 Sat
"Brass, copper, tin, aluminum, etc. in sheets, wire, rod, tubing." ed.

Canal Surplus 212-966-3275
363 Canal St. (Wooster) NYC 10013
Hours: 8-4:30 every day
"Good source sheet metal, pierced metal, wire, chain, 'junk'." ed.

T. E. Conklin Brass & Copper Inc. 212-691-5100
345 Hudson (Varick-King) NYC 10014
Hours: 9-5 Mon-Fri
"Brass and copper sheets, rods; minimum requirements, will cut; catalog." ed.

Hadco Aluminum and Metal Corp. 718-291-8060
104-20 Merrick Blvd., Jamaica, NY 11433
Hours: 8:30-5:30 Mon-Fri
"Aluminum plate, rod, tubes, sheets, etc." ed.

Small Parts Inc. 305-751-0856
6901 NE 3rd Ave., PO Box 381736, Miami, FL 33238
Hours: 8:30-4:30 Mon-Fri
"Fusible metals." ed.

Space Surplus Metals Inc. 212-966-4358
325 Church St. (Canal-Lispenard) NYC 10013
Hours: 8:30-5:30 Mon-Fri/ 8:30-4:30 Sat
"Inexpensive; reasonably complete stock." ed.

Tunnel Machinery Exchange 212-226-0727
353 Canal St. (Greene/Wooster) NYC 10013
Hours: 9-5 Mon-Fri/ 9-1 Sat
"Steel straps and bars; see Ronnie." ed.

Whiting and Davis — 212-736-5810
10 West 33rd St. (5th) NYC 10001
Hours: 9-4:45 Mon-Fri
"Metal purse mesh, chain mail; see Kenneth Davis." ed.

MILLINERS & HATTERS see CLOTHING ACCESSORIES: HATS
see COSTUME CRAFTSPEOPLE

MILLINERY SUPPLIES

See also FABRICS
See also SPRINGS, SPRING STEEL & WIRE
See also TRIMMINGS

Beacon Chemical — 914-699-3400
125 MacQuesten Parkway South, Mt. Vernon, NY 10550
Hours: 8:30-4:30 Mon-Fri
"Millinery adhesives and lacquers." ed.

Beatty-Page Inc. — 718-522-6400
360 Furman St. Bklyn 11201
Hours: 8:30-4:30 Mon-Fri
"Manufacturer of hatbands; very helpful." ed.

Paul Craig Ltd. — 01-437-5467
14-15 D'Arblay St., London, England W1V3SP
"Willow." ed.

Eagle Buckram Co. Inc. — 212-477-5529
8 Washington Place (Mercer) NYC 10003
Hours: 9-5 Mon-Fri
"Buckram." ed.

Friedman & Distillator — 212-233-6394
88 W. Broadway (Chambers-Warren) NYC 10007
Hours: 9-5 Mon-Fri
"French belting, ribbon, wire, custom bindings; will ship; see Toni."

Frielich Bros./Deutsch Bros. — 212-777-3051
670 Broadway (Great Jones) NYC 10012
Hours: 8:30-4:30 Mon-Fri
"Buckram, custom cap bills (large orders), visors, straps, trimmings."

Gampel Supply Corp. — 212-398-9222
39 West 37th St. (5-6th) NYC 10018
Hours: 8:45-4:30 Mon-Fri
"Wire, buckram, sizing, styro shapes, trims, stiff rayon net." ed.

GLADSTONE FABRICS 212-765-0760
16 West 56th St. 2nd Fl. (5-6th) NYC 10019
Hours: 9-5 Mon-Fri
(See display ad inside front cover.)
"Double buckram, miracle cloth, theatrical fabrics." ed.

I. J. Herman 212-221-8981
15 West 38th St. (5-6th) NYC 10018
Hours: 9-5 Mon-Fri/ 9:30-3:30 Sat
"Felt and velour bodies, accessories." ed.

J & L Mfg. Co. 203-368-1609
21 Castle Ave., Fairfield, CT 06430
Hours: 8:30-4:30 Mon-Fri
"Hat stretchers; see Jim Haversat." ed.

La Mode Hat Block Co. 212-947-0638
64 West 36th St. (5-6th) NYC 10018
Hours: 9-3 Mon-Fri
"See Frank; very nice and helpful." ed.

Manny's Millinery Supply Co. 212-840-2235
63 West 38th St. (5-6th) NYC 10018
Hours: 9-5:30 Mon-Fri/ 9-3 Sat
"Buckram, sizing, Sobo, millinery wire, felt bodies, hatblocks, trimmings; catalog." ed.

Max Millinery Center 212-221-8896
13 West 38th St. (5-6th) NYC 10018
Hours: 9:30-5:30 Mon-Fri/ 10-4:30 Sat
"Trim, artificial flowers, jewels, millinery supplies, and custom hats; see Tara." ed.

National Hatters Supply Co. Inc. 212-777-0232
670 Broadway (3rd-Bond) NYC 10012
Hours: 9-4:30 Mon-Fri
"Hatters supplies and machinery; stock hat blocks; catalog; call first." ed.

Portuguese Fur Felt Hat Co.

84 Pryor St. SW, Atlanta, GA 30303 404-688-6719
Hours: 9-4 Mon-Fri

PO Box 517, Adamstown, PA 19501 215-484-4361
Hours: 9-4 Mon-Fri

"Felt bodies." ed.

Vogue Hat Block & Die Corp. 212-243-6400
129 West 20th St. (6-7th) NYC 10011
Hours: By appt.
"Hat blocks." ed.

Washington Millinery Supply 301-963-4444
8501 Atlas Dr., Gathersburg, MD 20760
Hours: 8-4 Mon-Fri
"Millinery supplies, cape net." ed.

Zeeman Corp. 212-947-3558
575 Eighth Ave. (38th) NYC 10018
Hours: 9-5 Mon-Fri
"Buckram, adhesives, sizing, ribbons, cape net." ed.

MOLDINGS

See also LUMBER

Bendix Moldings 212-597-6666
235 Pegasus Ave., Northvale, NJ 07647
Hours: 9-5 Mon-Fri
"Moldings and ornaments; catalog available." ed.

Albert Constantine & Sons 212-792-1600
2050 Eastchester Road (off Pelham Pkwy) Bronx 10461
Hours: 8-6 Mon-Fri (Thurs til 8)/ 8-3 Sat
(May-Aug: closes at 5pm M-F, at 1pm Sat)
"Wood molding; woodworking tools; exotic woods." ed.

Dykes Lumber 212-246-6480
348 West 44th St. (8-9th) NYC 10036
Hours: 8-5 Mon-Fri/ 8-3:30 Sat
"Lumber, large molding catalog; friendly service." ed.

Flex Molding 201-487-8080
16 East Lafayette St., Hackensack, NJ 07601
Hours: 8:30-4:30 Mon-Fri
"Flexible and rigid moldings; large selection of decorative ornaments; catalog." ed.

Kenneth Lynch and Sons 203-762-8363
78 Danbury Rd., Wilton, CT 06897
Hours: 9-5 Mon-Fri
"Molded zinc architectural detail." ed.

Maxwell Lumber

211 West 18th St. (7-8th) NYC 10011 212-929-6088
25-30 Borden Ave. L.I.C. 11101 212-929-6088

Hours: 8-5 Mon-Fri
"Lumber, large molding; catalog." ed.

Yale Picture Frame and Molding Co. 718-788-6200
770 Fifth Ave. Bklyn 11232
Hours: 8-4 Mon-Thurs/ 8-3 Fri/ 9-2 Sun
"As in the name." ed.

MOTORS & MECHANICAL COMPONENTS

American Design Components 201-939-2710
62 Joseph St., Moonachie, NJ 07074
Hours: 9-5 Mon-Fri
"Stock synchros, gear motors, transducers, etc.; good prices; catalog." ed.

B & B Electric Motor & Control Corp 718-784-1313
39-40 Crescent (39th Ave) L.I.C. 11101
Hours: 9-5 Mon-Fri
"Speed controls, servo systems, clutches, brakes, design and modification." ed.

Beardslee Transmission Equip. Co.

27-22 Jackson Ave. L.I.C. 11101 718-784-4100
Hours: 8-5:30 Mon-Fri
"American stock gears; chains, sprockets, v-belts, pulleys, bushings, bars." ed.

290 East Jericho Turnpike, Mineola, NY 11501 516-747-5557
Hours: 8-5:30 Mon-Fri/ 8-1 Sat
"Gear boxes, belts, ball bearings, maintenance items." ed.

Winfred Berg 516-599-5010
499 Ocean Ave., East Rockaway, NY 11518
Hours: 8:30-5 Mon-Fri
"Suppliers of precision mechanical components from stock; catalog."

Edmund Scientific Co. 609-547-3488
101 East Gloucester Pike, Barrington, NJ 08007 800-257-6173
"Fine catalog, hobby motors, magnets, lasers, kaleidoscopes, mirrors, strobes, etc." ed.

Grainger

58-45 Grand Ave., Maspeth, NY 11378 718-326-1598
1 Park Dr., Melville, NY 11747 516-391-3030

Hours: 8-5 Mon-Fri
"Dayton motors, bearings; catalog." ed.

H & R Corporation 215-426-1708
401 East Erie Ave., Philadelphia, PA 19134
Hours: 8:30-4:45 Mon-Fri/ 9:30-2 Sat
"Surplus motors, fans, electrics, lenses, etc." ed.

Jerryco Co. Inc. 312-475-8440
601 Linden Place, Evanston, IL 60202
"'Sail On' surplus catalog of gadgets and weird items from industrial and military surplus." ed.

Micro-Mo Electronics Inc. 813-822-2529
742 Second Ave. S., St. Petersburg, FL 33701
Hours: 9-5 Mon-Fri
"Services PM motors and gearheads, encoders, tachs at list prices."

Northern Hydraulics Inc. 612-894-8310
801 East Cliff Rd., Burnsville, MN 55337
Hours: 8-6 Mon-Fri/ 9-2 Sat
"Generators, compressors, air tools, winches, accessories; catalog."

Pic Designs 203-758-8272
PO Box 1004, Benson Rd., Middlebury, CT 06762
Hours: 8-5 Mon-Fri
"Stock mail order mechanical components; ask for catalog #37." ed.

Patron Transmission Co. Inc. 212-226-1140
129 Grand St. (Crosby) NYC 10013
Hours: 8-5 Mon-Fri
"Power transmission equipment, conveyers, gears, chains, sprockets, etc; catalog." ed.

Polk's Model Craft Hobbies Inc. 212-279-9034
314 Fifth Ave. (31-32nd) NYC 10001
Hours: 9:30-5:45 Mon-Fri/ 9:30-5 Sat
"Distributors of Aristocraft miniature AC/DC motors." ed.

Sava Industries Inc. 201-835-0882
70 Riverdale Ave., Riverdale, NJ 07454
"Aircraft cable, fittings, small ball bearing pulleys; minimum order applies; catalog #10-R3 is good." ed.

Segal Brothers 718-383-2995
205 Nassau St. (Russell) Bklyn 11201
Hours: 8-5 Mon-Fri
"Large selection of motors." ed.

Small Parts Inc. 305-751-0856
6901 NE 3rd Av, PO Box 381736, Miami, FL 33138
Hours: 9-5 Mon-Fri
"Catalog; mechanical parts and gears." ed.

Stock Drive Products 516-328-0200
55 South Denton Ave., New Hyde Park, NY 11040 (sales) 516-328-3300
Hours: 8:30-5 Mon-Fri
"Invaluable catalog of mechanical components, gears, rack and pinions, timing belts, etc." ed.

Frank Tracy (Bearing Industry Corp.) 212-226-3500
14 Wooster St. (Grand-Canal) NYC 10013
Hours: 8-5 Mon-Fri
"Gears, bearings, transmissions, small mechanicals." ed.

Tunnel Machinery Exchange 212-226-0727
353 Canal St. (Greene-Wooster) NYC 10013
Hours: 9-5 Mon-Fri/ 9-1 Sat
"Electric motors, pulleys." ed.

MOVING, TRANSPORT & STORAGE

See also SHIPPING
For packing materials and containers,
See FIBRE CASES
See PACKING MATERIALS

Anthony Augliera 203-933-3994
34 Hamilton St., West Haven, CT 06516
Hours: 9-4:30 Mon-Fri
"Interstate theatrical haulers." ed.

Baron Art and Antique Movers 212-475-3791
143 First Ave. (9th) NYC 10003
Hours: 9-5 Mon-Fri
"What their name says." ed.

Bell Moving 718-461-8870
43-47 162nd St., Flushing, NY 11358
Hours: 9-5 Mon-Fri/ 9-3 Sat
"Expert piano movers." ed.

Central Movers 718-622-2660
358 Classon Ave. (Clifton Pl-Lafayette) Bklyn 11238
Hours: 9-5 Mon-Fri
"Interstate and local." ed.

Clark Transfer 212-580-4075
121 New York Ave., Trenton, NJ 08638 609-396-1100
Hours: 8:45-5 Mon-Thurs/ 8:45-4:30 Fri
"Interstate theatrical hauling." ed.

Consolidated Productions 213-469-5000
PO Box 277, Duarte, CA 91010
"Theatrical hauling throughout US; ask for Richard Schneider." ed.

Valentin Cotto 212-663-0334
117 West 96th St. (Columbus-Amsterdam) NYC 10025
Hours: By appt.
"Van with driver." ed.

Crozier Fine Arts 212-741-2024
630 West 26th St. (11-12th) NYC 10003
Hours: 10:30-6:30 Mon-Fri
"Fine art movers; custom crates." ed.

Michael Davis Shipping Corp. 212-832-3655
29 East 61st St. (Park-Madison) NYC 10021
Hours: 9-5 Mon-Fri
"Packing and shipping of fine art work; expensive." ed.

Hahn Brothers 212-926-1505
571 Riverside Dr. (134th) NYC 10031
Hours: 8-5 Mon-Fri
"Art movers." ed.

Happy Hoosier Trucking Co. 212-765-7868
342 West 56th St. (B'way) NYC 10019
Hours: leave message on machine
"Local moving man w/van, reliable." ed.

M. A. Hittner & Sons Inc. 212-477-6500
39 East 4th St. (3rd Ave) NYC 10003
Hours: 8-6:30 Mon-Fri/ 8-5 Sat/ 8-3 Sun
"Cheap; a real NYC experience; late drop off." ed.

Midtown Truckers 212-683-5838
3rd Ave. & 32nd St. NYC
Hours: 8-6 every day
"Messenger service; local moving." ed.

Overseas Moving Specialists Inc. 718-963-4200
112 North 12th St. Bklyn 11211 718-388-1000
Hours: 8-5:30 Mon-Fri
"Steel containerized service." ed.

The Padded Wagon 212-222-4880
120 West 107th St. (Amsterdam-Columbus) NYC 10025
Hours: 9-5 Mon-Sat
"Furniture and art movers." ed.

U-Haul Moving & Storage 212-562-3800
562 West 23rd St. (10-11th) NYC 10011
Hours: 24 hour rental arrangements
"Truck rental; packing blankets, dollies, boxes." ed.

Van Gogh Movers 212-226-0500
126 Wooster St. (Prince) NYC 10012 212-431-5450
Hours: 9-6 Mon-Fri
"Pack, store and/or ship." ed.

Walton Hauling & Warehouse Corp. 212-246-8685
609 West 46th St. (11-12th) NYC 10036
Hours: 7-5:30 Mon-Fri
"106 year old theatrical hauling company; local, some storage; nice people." ed.

MUSIC & MUSICAL INSTRUMENTS

Sam Ash Music Stores 212-245-4778
160 West 48th St. (6-7th) NYC 10036
Hours: 9-6 Mon-Sat
"Guitars, amps, wind and string instruments, sheet music; rental, repair, purchase." ed.

Ayers Percussion 212-582-8410
415 West 48th St. (9-10th) NYC 10036
Hours: 10-6 Mon-Fri
"Rental, sales and repair of accoustic percussion; will custom build; very helpful." ed.

Bargain Spot 212-674-1188
64 Third Ave. (11th) NYC 10003
Hours: 8:30-5 Mon-Sat
"Rental or purchase, old and new musical instruments, cameras, binoculars, power tools, etc." ed.

Beethoven Pianos 212-288-2099
1645 First Ave. (85-86th) NYC 10028
Hours: 7:30-7 Mon-Sat
"Piano rentals." ed.

Carroll Musical Instrument Service Corp. 212-868-4120
351 West 41st St. (8-9th) NYC 10036
Hours: 8-7 Mon-Fri/ 9-12 Sat
"Large stock instruments, stands, etc; rental only; see Dennis." ed.

Carroll Sound Inc. 212-533-6230
88 Executive Ave., Edison, NJ 08817
Hours: 9-4 Mon-Fri
"Wholesale purchase of musical instruments; catalog; see Joseph Gulas." ed.

Center for Musical Antiquities 212-744-8168
544 East 86th St. (York-East End) NYC 10028
Hours: By appt.
"Antique and foreign musical instruments; see Lillian or Stuart Kaplan." ed.

Colony Records 212-265-2050
1619 Broadway (49th) NYC 10019
Hours: 9:30am-2:30am Mon-Fri/ 10am-3am Sat
"Large selection of sheet music, records; will ship anywhere." ed.

Giardinelli Band Instrument Co. 212-575-5959
151 West 46th St. (6-7th) NYC 10036
Hours: 8:30-5:30 Mon-Fri/ 9-2 Sat
"Brass and woodwind instruments." ed.

Lincoln Piano Service 212-734-6385
1459 Third Ave. (82-83rd) NYC 10028
Hours: 11-6 Mon-Fri/ 11-5 Sat
"Rental or purchase; some older period-type upright pianos." ed.

Music Exchange 212-354-5858
151 West 46th St. 10th Fl. (6-7th) NYC 10036
Hours: 9:30-5 Mon-Fri
"Sheet music; for a fee, will track down anything." ed.

Music Inn 212-243-5715
169 West 4th St. (7th Ave) NYC 10011
Hours: 12-7 Mon-Sat
"Antique, ethnic, standard musical instruments." ed.

Music Store at Carl Fisher 212-677-0821
62 Cooper Square (4th) NYC 10003
Hours: 10-5:45 Mon-Sat
"Good source for sheet music." ed.

Night Owl Musical Supply 212-563-6410
251 West 30th St. (7-8th) NYC 10001
Hours: 10:45-midnight Mon-Sat/ 12-midnight Sun
"Mostly rock 'n roll, guitars, drums, amps." ed.

Joseph Patelson Music House 212-582-5840
160 West 56th St. (6-7th) NYC 10019
Hours: 9-6 Mon-Sat
"Large selection of sheet music, scores, opera libretti; books and records." ed.

Pioneer Piano Corp. 212-586-3718
934 Eighth Ave. (55th) NYC 10019
Hours: 9:30-5 Mon-Fri/ 10:30-4 Sat
"Pianos, rental or purchase." ed.

Pro Piano 212-206-8794
85 Jane St. (Washington) NYC 10014
Hours: 8:30-6 Mon-Fri
"Pianos, rental or purchase." ed.

Schirmer Music 212-541-6236
40 West 62nd St. (B'way-Columbus) NYC 10023
Hours: 10-8 Mon-Sat
"Sheet music, libretti." ed.

Steinway & Sons 212-246-1100
109 West 57th St. (5-6th) NYC 10019 (factory)718-721-2600
Hours: 9-6 Mon-Fri (Thurs til 9)/ 9-5 Sat
"Will promote pianos." ed.

Studio Instrument Rentals 212-975-0920
310 West 52nd St. (8-9th) NYC 10019
Hours: 8-midnight every day
"Large selection of instruments for rent." ed.

Terminal Music 212-869-5270
166 West 48th St. (6-7th) NYC 10036
Hours: 9-6 Mon-Sat
"Recorders, drums, keyboards, amps, woodwinds, sheet music, accessories." ed.

Matt Umanov Guitars 212-675-2157
273 Bleecker St. (near 7th Ave) NYC 10014
Hours: 11-7 Mon-Sat
"New and used guitars, repairs." ed.

Universal Musical Instrument Co. 212-254-6917
732 Broadway (8th-Waverly) NYC 10003
Hours: 9:30-6 Mon-Fri
"Finger cymbals, castenets, guitars, sheet music." ed.

Village Flute & Sax Shop 212-243-1276
35 Carmine St. (Bleecker-6th) NYC 10014
Hours: 12-5 Mon-Fri
"See Rick; some relics and parts make great props." ed.

NEWSPAPERS

Dependable Delivery Inc. 212-586-5552
360 West 52nd St. (8-9th) NYC 10019
Hours: 8-1pm Mon-Fri
"Back date NYC newspapers, previous 2 years only." ed.

Eclectic Properties, Inc. 212-799-8963
204 West 84th St. (B'way-Amsterdam) NYC 10024
Hours: 9-5 Mon-Fri or by appt.
"Reproduction newspapers and custom orders for motion picture or theatrical use." ed.

Harvest Printing 212-246-8635
250 West 54th St. (8th) NYC 10019
Hours: 8:15-4:45 Mon-Fri
"Newspaper reprints; also typesetting, press work, binding, business stationery." ed.

Earl Hays Press 818-765-0700
10707 Sherman Way, Sun Valley, CA 91352
Hours: 9-5 Mon-Fri
"Period repro newspapers and books; also license plates, labels, etc."

Headlines 212-246-5762
200 West 48th St. (B'way-7th) NYC 10036
Hours: 12-11 Mon-Sat
"Cheap printing of custom newspaper headlines." ed.

Historic Newspaper Archives 201-381-2332
1582 Hart St., Rahway, NJ 07065 800-526-7843
Hours: orders taken 24 hrs a day
"Back date newspapers, originals, 1880-1974, of major US cities; catalog available." ed.

Hotaling News Agency 212-840-1868
142 West 42nd St. (B'way-6th) NYC 10036
Hours: 7:30-9:25 Mon-Sat/ 7:30-7:30 Sun
"Large selection current foreign and out-of-town newspapers and magazines." ed.

Victor Kamkin Inc. 212-673-0776
149 Fifth Ave. (21st) NYC 10010
Hours: 9:30-5:30 Mon-Fri/ 10-5 Sat
"Current Russian newspapers, periodicals, books." ed.

Yomiuri Press/ Yomiuri Shimbun 212-661-5977
41 East 42nd St. (5th) NYC 10017
Hours: 9:30-5:30 Mon-Fri
"Current Japanese newspapers." ed.

NOTIONS: GENERAL & TAILORS

AGH Distributors Inc. 212-221-3440
225 West 39th St. (7th) NYC 10018
Hours: 9-5 Mon-Fri
General sewing notions and hand tools." ed.

American Notion Co. Inc. 212-563-0480
336 West 37th St. (8-9th) NYC 10018
Hours: 8:15-5:15 Mon-Fri
"Notions, horsehair, zippers, elastic." ed.

NOTES

Amity Notions 212-279-3129
315 West 36th St. (8-9th) NYC 10018
Hours: 8-5 Mon-Fri
"Notions, Dorcas pins." ed.

BAER FABRICS 502-583-5521
515 East Market, Louisville, KY 40202
Hours: 9-5:30 Mon-Sat

Every kind of wholesale tailors' supplies. (See display ad page 127.)

"Shipment within 24 hours for in-stock items." ed.

Abe Bloom & Sons Inc. 212-924-2560
144 West 19th St. (6-7th) NYC 10011
Hours: 7-4 Mon-Fri
"Tailors' notions." ed.

Dritz-Scovill 803-576-5050
PO Box 5028, Spartanburg, SC 29304
Hours: 8-4:30 Mon-Fri
"Manufacturer of sewing notions; catalog." ed.

40th St. Trimmings Inc. 212-354-4729
252 West 40th St. (7-8th) NYC 10018
Hours: 9-5:45 Mon-Fri/ 10-5 Sat
"Notions, trimmings, novelties; wholesale and retail." ed.

GREENBERG & HAMMER INC. 212-246-2835
24 West 57th St. (5-6th) NYC 10019
Hours: 9-6 Mon-Fri/ 9-4 Sat (except July, Aug)

Over 65 years of experience supplying notions to costume shops, theatres, colleges & the apparel industry. Costume hooks & eyes, snaps, threads, elastic, tapes, corset boning, interfacings, muslin, safety & straight pins, needles, carbon paper, sewing aids, dress shields, velcro, Tintex, zippers, belting, professional steam irons & garment steamers, etc. Write for free catalogue.

"Enormous selections of sewing notions; phone and mail orders; see Dottie or Frank." ed.

Joseph Hersh 212-391-6615
1000 Sixth Ave. (37th) NYC 10018
Hours: 9:30-5:30 Mon-Fri/ 11-4 Sat
"Notions and tailors' supplies." ed.

Howard Notion and Trimming Co. 212-674-4550
149 Essex St. (Grand) NYC 10002 212-674-1321
Hours: 9-6 Mon-Fri/ 9-1 Sun
"General notions." ed.

A. Meyers & Sons Corp. 212-279-6632
325 West 38th St. (8-9th) NYC 10018
Hours: 9-5 Mon-Fri
"Notions, Dorcas pins." ed.

Primrose Trimming Co. 212-736-8214
333 West 39th St. (8-9th) NYC 10018
Hours: 9-4:30 Mon-Fri
"All tailors' notions." ed.

William Prym Inc. 203-774-9671
Main St., Dayville, CT 06241 800-243-1832
Hours: 8-4:30 Mon-Fri
"Wholesale and retail notions; catalog." ed.

S. Reisman Sons Inc. 212-947-3121
244 West 39th St. (7-8th) NYC 10018 212-947-3122
Hours: Call first.
"Jobber." ed.

RICHARD THE THREAD/ROY COOPER 213-874-1116
1433 N. Orange Grove, Hollywood, CA 90046 800-621-0849x226
Hours: By appt.
#6 Hooks-n-Bars, Nylon Bobbinette, Whopper Poppers, Soufel, Prussian Tape. We find the Impossible.
"Catalog, mail and phone orders; specializes in hard-to-find items."

STEINLAUF & STOLLER INC. 212-869-0321
239 West 39th St. (7-8th) NYC 10018 800-637-1637
Hours: 8-5:30 Mon-Fri
A complete sewing notions jobber. Wholesale & Retail. (See display ad page 240.)
"One of the most complete suppliers of sewing notions." ed.

NOTIONS: BIAS & STRAIGHT BINDINGS

A & S Bias Binding Co. Inc. 212-924-7040
159 Varick St. (Vandam) NYC 10013
Hours: 8:30-5 Mon-Fri
"Manufacturer of bias, straight, folded cord-edge; samples." ed.

Arnold Bias Products & Trimming Co. 212-966-3017
591 Broadway (Houston-Prince) NYC 10012
Hours: 7-4 Mon-Fri
"Bias, straight, ruffles, elastic shirring and smocking, etc.; samples; rush orders." ed.

Associated Manufacturers Tubular Pipings Inc. 212-736-3458
252 West 37th St. (7-8th) NYC 10018
Hours: 8:30-4:30 Mon-Fri
"Tubular pipings." ed.

BAER FABRICS 502-583-5521
515 East Market, Louisville, KY 40202
Hours: 9-5:30 Mon-Sat
Bias- natural/synthetic, full selection; twill- all widths, black/white. (See display ad page 127.)
"Shipment within 24 hours for in-stock items." ed.

Friedman & Distillator 212-233-6394
88 W. Broadway (Chambers-Warren) NYC 10007
Hours: 9-5 Mon-Fri
"Ribbons, braids, cords, french belting, millinery supplies; speak to Toni." ed.

NY Bias Binding Corp. 212-564-0680
370 West 35th St. (8-9th) NYC 10001
Hours: 8:30-5:30 Mon-Fri
"Bias bindings." ed.

Success Binding Corp. 212-226-6161
636 Broadway (Bleecker-Houston) NYC 10012
Hours: 8:30-4:30 Mon-Fri
"Bias, straight, spaghetti, cord-edge, peco edge, folded, etc." ed.

NOTIONS: BONES, BONING, HOOPWIRE

BAER FABRICS 502-583-5521
515 East Market, Louisville, KY 40202
Hours: 9-5:30 Mon-Sat
Feather boning, metal hooping, stays, spiralflex stays. (See display ad page 127.)
"Shipment within 24 hours for in-stock items." ed.

GREENBERG & HAMMER INC. 212-246-2835
24 West 57th St. (5-6th) NYC 10019
Hours: 9-6 Mon-Fri/ 9-4 Sat (except July, Aug)
See listing in "Notions: General & Tailors'".
"Feather boning, corset boning, spring steel; Dottie can help with difficult items." ed.

L. Laufer & Co. 212-685-2181
39 West 28th St. (B'way-6th) NYC 10001
Hours: 9-4 Mon-Fri (call first)
"All corset supplies, Scotch-mate (like velcro)." ed.

NOTIONS: BONES, BONING, HOOPWIRE

Nathan's Boning Co. 212-244-4781
302 West 37th St. 4th Fl. (8-9th) NYC 10018
Hours: 8:30-5:30 Mon-Thurs/ 8:30-5 Fri
"Feather and spring steel boning, tutu wire in buckram." ed.

Patriarche & Bell Inc. 201-824-8297
94 Parkhurst, Newark, NJ 07114 212-242-4400
Hours: 8:30-4 Mon-Fri
"Hoop steel." ed.

NOTIONS: BUTTONS, BUCKLES, GROMMETS, SNAPS, ETC.

A & S Button Co. 212-674-0669
131 Essex St. (Grand) NYC 10002
Hours: 10-4:30 Mon-Fri/ 10:30-3 Sun (except summer months)
"Jobber: buttons, buckles, novelties." ed.

Arlene Novelty Corp. 212-921-5711
263 West 38th St. (7-8th) NYC 10018
Hours: 9-5 Mon-Fri
"Plastic covered buttons." ed.

BAER FABRICS 502-583-5521
515 East Market, Louisville, KY 40202
Hours: 9-5:30 Mon-Sat
Incredible selection and depth of stock- plus tools. (See display ad page 127.)
"Shipment within 24 hours for in-stock items." ed.

Bond Button Co. 212-719-2100
203 West 38th St. 3rd Fl. (7-8th) NYC 10018
Hours: 8-5 Mon-Fri
"Buttons, buckles, ornaments." ed.

Bonnie Enterprises Inc. 201-272-9300
22 Jackson Dr., Cranford, NJ 07016
Hours: 9-5 Mon-Fri
"Plastic buckles for bras, swimwear, marine gear; samples." ed.

Broadway Button & Buckle Co. 212-575-0520
35-37 West 38th St. (5-6th) NYC 10018
Hours: 8:30-4:30 Mon-Fri
"Covered buttons, buckles, nailheads." ed.

C & C Metal Products 212-695-1679
48 West 37th St. (5-6th) NYC 10018
Hours: 8-9:30 and 4-5 Mon-Fri for salesperson, or by appt.
"Metal buttons, buckles, nailheads, eyelets, etc; rhinestones, settings; catalog." ed.

Corset Accessories 212-677-0223
611 Broadway Rm. 626 (Houston) NYC 10012
Hours: 8-4:30 Mon-Fri
"Boning, hook and snap tape, bust pads." ed.

Defiance Button Machine 212-594-0330
456 Nordhoff Pl., Engelwood, NJ 07631
Hours: 9-5 Mon-Fri
"Metal buttons and studs. Place order by phone two days ahead. $50 minimum order." ed.

Diane Button Co. 212-921-8383
225 West 37th St. (7-8th) NYC 10018
Hours: 8:30-5 Mon-Fri
"Wood, metal, plastic, casein buttons." ed.

Duplex Novelty 212-564-1352
575 8th Ave. (38-39th) NYC 10018
Hours: 8:15-5 Mon-Fri
"Wooden buttons, buckles, beads; wholesale; catalog." ed.

Eisen Brothers Inc. 212-398-0263
239 West 39th St. 3rd Fl. (7-8th) NYC 10018
Hours: 9-5 Mon-Fri
"Studs." ed.

Fastex, Div. of Illinois Tool Works 312-299-2222
195 Algonquin Rd., Des Plaines, IL 60016
"Plastic buckles, grommets, rivets, fasteners of all kinds in plastic; wholesale large orders; catalog." ed.

Friedman & Distillator 212-233-6394
88 W. Broadway (Chambers-Warren) NYC 10007
Hours: 9-5 Mon-Fri
"Hook and eye tape, snap tape; millinery supplies; speak to Toni." ed.

Guardian Rivet & Fastener 516-585-4400
70 Air Park Dr., Ronkonkoma, NY 11779
Hours: 9-5 Mon-Fri
"Wholesale rivets." ed.

Glick & Blitz 212-594-2267
246 West 37th St. (7-8th) NYC 10018
Hours: 9-5 Mon-Fri
"Buttons, buckles, frogs, chains, belts." ed.

Gordon Button Co. Inc. 212-921-1684
142 West 38th St. (B'way-7th) NYC 10018
Hours: 9-5:30 Mon-Fri
"Buckles, buttons, belt chain, some necklace chain." ed.

Joseph M. Hart & Sons 516-567-7722
365 Central Ave., Bohemia, NY 11716
"Studs, boot hooks, grommets." ed.

La Bern Novelty Co. Inc. 212-719-2131
1011 Sixth Ave. (37-38th) NYC 10018
Hours: 7:45-4:30 Mon-Fri
"Buttons and covered buttons; large variety; cheap." ed.

Sam Levin Metal Products Corp. 718-782-6885
1002 Grand St., Brooklyn 11211
Hours: 8-4:30 Mon-Thurs/ 8-2 Fri
"Metal buckles, leather hardware, etc.; wholesale; catalog." ed.

Liberty Die and Button Mold Corp. 212-564-3860
264 West 35th St. Rm. 1200 (8th) NYC 10001
Hours: 9-5 Mon-Fri
"Manufacturer of button molds; fabrication in metal, buckles." ed.

M. E. Yarn & Trimmings 212-260-2060
177 East Houston St. (1st) NYC 10002
Hours: 8:30-5 Mon-Fri
"Good prices on lace in quantity; can deal; also trims, buttons, yarn."

M & J Trimmings 212-391-9072
1008 Sixth Ave. (37-38th) NYC 10018
Hours: 9-6 Mon-Fri/ 10-5 Sat
"Buttons, buckles, frogs; general trimmings." ed.

Metropolitan-Keller Co. 212-563-2591
270 West 38th St. (7-8th) NYC 10018
Hours: 9-4:30 Mon-Fri
"Buttons, belts." ed.

Pollyanna Corp. 212-563-5340
535 Eighth Ave. 19th Fl. (36-37th) NYC 10018
Hours: 8:30-2 Mon-Fri (call first)
"Snap fasteners by the gross." ed.

Richard the Thread/ Roy Cooper 213-874-1116
1433 N. Orange Grove, Hollywood, CA 90046 800-621-0846 (x226)
"Whopper Poppers, #6 hooks and bars; catalog, mail and phone orders."

Service Trimmings 212-921-1680
142 West 38th St. (B'way-7th) NYC 10018
Hours: 8:30-5:30 Mon-Fri
"Buttons, buckles, zippers." ed.

Shantz Associates Inc. 212-889-1770
15 East 40th St. (6th) NYC 10016
Hours: 8-6 Mon-Fri
"Buttons; see Ira." ed.

Sher Plastics 212-760-9660
450 Seventh Ave. (34th) NYC 10123
Hours: 9-5 Mon-Fri
"Studs, buttons, gold-coin studs." ed.

Siff Brothers 212-730-1045
251 West 39th St. (7-8th) NYC 10018
Hours: 8-5:30 Mon-Fri (by appt.)
"Buttons, collar studs." ed.

George C. Siska 201-794-1124
8 Rosol Lane, Saddlebrook, NJ 07662
Hours: 8-5 Mon-Fri
"Eyelets, grommets; 1000 minimum order." ed.

Edwin B. Stimpson & Co. Inc. 516-472-2000
900 Sylvan Ave., Bayport, NY 11705
Hours: 8:30-4:45 Mon-Fri
"Grommets, snaps, rivets." ed.

Sure-Snap Corp. 212-921-5515
241 West 37th St. (7-8th) NYC 10018
Hours: 8:30-5 Mon-Fri
"Buckles, snaps, rivets, grommets, eyelets; snap tape made-to-order; machines and dies." ed.

Tender Buttons 212-758-7004
143 East 62nd St. (Lexington-3rd) NYC 10021
Hours: 11-6 Mon-Fri/ 11-5:30 Sat
"Beautiful antique and modern buttons, buckles; antique cufflinks." ed.

L. P. Thur 212-243-4913
126 West 23rd St. (6-7th) NYC 10011
Hours: 9-6 Mon-Fri
"Trims, antique buttons." ed.

NOTIONS: ELASTIC

American Cord & Webbing Co. Inc. 212-695-7340
505 Eighth Ave. (35th) NYC 10018
Hours: 9-5:30 Mon-Fri
"Elastic cord; also webbing tape, binding; $75 minimum." ed.

BAER FABRICS 502-583-5521
515 East Market, Louisville, KY 40202
Hours: 9-5:30 Mon-Sat

Knit/woven, ALL widths, full rolls, white/black, round, lace.
(See display ad page 127.)

"Shipment within 24 hours for in-stock items." ed.

Falcon Safety Products 201-233-5000
1065 Bristol Rd., Mountainside, NJ 07092
Hours: 8:30-4:30 Mon-Fri
"All sizes elastic cord." ed.

Lafayette Button Co. 212-354-3020
237 West 37th St. (7-8th) NYC 10018
Hours: 9-5 Mon-Fri
"Elastic in colors and fleshtones by the roll; large orders only." ed.

Staylastic-Smith Inc. 617-999-6431
90 Hatch St., PO Box C-903, New Bedford, MA 02741
Hours: 8-4:30 Mon-Fri
"Stay elastic; $20 minimum order." ed.

Stribbons Ltd. 212-532-3000
11 East 26th St. 12th Fl. (5th-Madison) NYC 10010
Hours: 9-5 Mon-Fri
"Sparkle cord." ed.

NOTIONS: NEEDLES & PINS

BAER FABRICS 502-583-5521
515 East Market, Louisville, KY 40202
Hours: 9-5:30 Mon-Sat
Dressmaker, satin, T, safety, bulk; all hand/machine needles.
(See display ad page 127.)
"Shipment within 24 hours for in-stock items." ed.

Diamond Needle 212-929-2277
159 West 25th St. (6-7th) NYC 10001
Hours: 8:30-5 Mon-Fri
"Industrial or domestic: pkg. of 100 for $2; machine feet." ed.

Needle-Needle Co. 212-684-0226
11 East 31st St. (Madison-5th) NYC 10016
Hours: 9-3:30 Mon-Fri
"Hand sewing, glover's lacing needles; wholesale." ed.

Prym Newey Canada Inc. 514-336-5874
1854 Beaulac, St. Laurent, Quebec, H4R 2E7
Hours: 9-5 Mon-Fri
"Many types of pins, notions." ed.

Union Pin Co. 203-379-3397
Box 427, New Hartford, CT 06057
"Pins." ed.

NOTIONS: THREAD

Atwater Inc. 717-779-9568
627 West Main St., PO Box 247, Plymouth, PA 18651
Hours: 8:30-5 Mon-Fri
"Nylon fuzzy thread." ed.

BAER FABRICS 502-583-5521
515 East Market, Louisville, KY 40202
Hours: 9-5:30 Mon-Sat
200+ colors, all fibers, all weights, all size spools. (See display ad page 127.)
"Shipment within 24 hours for in-stock items." ed.

Ideal Thread Co. 212-677-0118
915 Broadway (21st) NYC 10010
Hours: 9-4:30 Mon-Fri
"Silk, cotton, synthetic, sewing and embroidery threads; also notions."

La Lame Inc. 212-921-9770
250 West 39th St. 5th Fl. (7-8th) NYC 10018
Hours: 9-5 Mon-Fri
"Lumi thread - metallic for Merrow machines." ed.

Paramount Thread 212-255-0470
151 West 26th St. 4th Fl. (6-7th) NYC 10001
Hours: 9-5 Mon-Fri
"Manufacturer of nylon thread, industrial threads." ed.

Sebro Thread Corp. 516-872-6125
145 Ave. & Hook Creek Blvd., Valley Stream, NY 11581 212-525-1004
Hours: 9-5 Mon-Fri
"Stretch thread; wholesale only." ed.

Soltex Thread and Yarn Co. 212-243-2000
30 West 24th St. (5-6th) NYC 10001
Hours: 9-5:30 Mon-Fri
"Cotton and synthetic thread for industrial use, embroidery supplies for machine embroidery." ed.

NOTIONS: VELCRO

BAER FABRICS 502-583-5521
515 East Market, Louisville, KY 40202
Hours: 9-5:30 Mon-Sat
5/8" to 2" regular or self adhesive, available in colors. (See display ad page 127.)
"Shipment within 24 hours for in-stock items." ed.

Design Craft Fabric Corp. 312-527-2580
7227 Oak Park, Niles, IL 60648
Hours: 9-5 Mon-Fri
"Foam-backed fabrics, loop weave fabric for Velcro." ed.

GLADSTONE FABRICS 212-765-0760
16 West 56th St. 2nd Fl. (5-6th) NYC 10019
Hours: 9-5 Mon-Fri
(See display ad inside front cover.)
"Also wide selection of theatrical fabrics." ed.

J. M. Lynne 516-582-4300
59 Gilpin Ave., Haupaug, NY 11788
Hours: 9-5 Mon-Fri
"Velcro distributors; by the roll; also Velcro fabrics." ed.

Velcro USA

406 Browne Ave., PO Box 4806, Manchester, NH 03108 603-669-4892
Hours: 9-5 Mon-Fri
"Manufacturer and wholesaler." ed.

220 Little Falls Rd., Cedargrove, NJ 07009 201-661-0714
Hours: 9-5 Mon-Fri
"Sample card available; small stock; order large quantities direct from Manchester (see above)." ed.

NOTIONS: ZIPPERS

BAER FABRICS 502-583-5521
515 East Market, Lousiville, KY 40202
Hours: 9-5:30 Mon-Sat
All weights/lengths, jacket, dress, upholstery, continuous chain. (See display ad page 127.)
"Shipment within 24 hours for in-stock items." ed.

Nat Geffman Co. 212-947-3864
237 West 35th St. (7-8th) NYC 10001 212-947-3865
Hours: 7:45-6 Mon-Fri
"Industrial zippers, cut to size; also cotton goods, poly thread." ed.

Talon Zippers 212-564-6300
1350 Broadway Rm. 1815 (36th) NYC 10018
Hours: 9-5 Mon-Fri
"Industrial zippers, cut to length." ed.

NOVELTIES see MAGIC SUPPLIES & NOVELTIES

OCCULT PARAPHERNALIA

Enchantments Inc. 212-228-4394
341 East 9th St. (1st) NYC 10003
Hours: 12-9 Mon-Sat/ 1-8 Sun
"Books, herbs, oils, incense, crystal balls, robes, jewelry, and occult paraphernalia." ed.

Warlock Shop/ Magical Childe 212-242-7182
35 West 19th St. (5-6th) NYC 10011
Hours: 11-8 Mon-Sat/ 12-6 Sun
"Human skulls, weapons, incense, crystal balls, occult paraphernalia; odd assortment." ed.

Samuel Weiser Inc. 212-777-6363
132 East 24th St. (Park Ave. S.-Lexington) NYC 10010
Hours: 9-5:50 M,T,W,F/ 10-6:50 Thurs/ 9:30-4:50 Sat
"40-50 kinds of Tarot cards, crystal balls, yarrow stalks in season; primarily books." ed.

PACKING MATERIALS

See also TAPE, ADHESIVE
See also TWINES & CORDAGE
See also PAPER, CARDBOARD & FOAMCORE PRODUCTS

Alps Paper Parnes Co. 212-279-3219
225 Division Ave. #10-F, Bklyn 11211
Hours: 9-5 Mon-Fri
"Packing twines, tapes, boxes." ed.

Baehm Paper Co. 212-267-1892
53 Murray St. (Church-W B'way) NYC 10007
Hours: 8-2 Mon-Fri
"Kraft and corrugated paper, will deliver." ed.

Better-Pak Container Co. 212-675-7330
555 West 25th St. (10-11th) NYC 10001
Hours: 8-4 Mon-Fri
"Boxes." ed.

Falcon Supply Co. 201-225-5050
468 Newfield Ave. Raritan Ctr., Edison, NJ 08837
Hours: 9-5 Mon-Fri
"Tapes, staples and staplers, packing lists." ed.

Hildan Crown Containers 212-947-0130
15th & Bloomfield, PO Box 371, Hoboken, NJ 07030
Hours: 9-4 Mon-Fri
"Retail & wholesale boxes." ed.

Robert Karp Container Corp. 212-586-4474
618 West 52nd St. (11-12th) NYC 10019
Hours: 8-4 Mon-Fri
"Boxes, twine, tape, tissue, kraft paper, jiffy bags, bubble-pak." ed.

George Millar and Co. 212-741-6100
161 Sixth Ave. (Spring St) NYC 10013
Hours: 9-5 Mon-Fri
"General packaging." ed.

Movers Supply House Inc. 212-671-1200
1476 East 122nd St., Bronx, NY 10469
Hours: 8-5 Mon-Fri
"Packing blankets, loading straps, hampers, j-bars; good prices; will ship COD." ed.

Lawrence Piller 718-633-3555
1930 47th St. (McDonald Ave) Bklyn 11204
Hours: 9-4:45 Mon-Fri
"Packing blankets, costume boxes." ed.

United Corrugated Shipping Supplies 718-855-7755
84 Ferris (off Van Brunt) Bklyn 11231
Hours: 8-4:30 Mon-Fri
"Boxes, likes large orders, but will cooperate." ed.

Wolf Paper and Twine Co. 212-675-4870
680 Sixth Ave. (21-22nd) NYC 10010
Hours: 9-4:30 Mon-Fri
"Boxes, corrugated paper, padded envelopes; will take small orders."

PAINTS & DYES: BRONZING POWDERS & LEAFING SUPPLIES

Atlantic Powdered Metals Inc. 212-267-4900
225 Broadway (Barclay) NYC 10007
Hours: 9-5 Mon-Fri
"Bronzing powders, gold leaf, dutch metal; minimum orders." ed.

M. Epstein and Sons 212-265-3960
809 Ninth Ave. (53-54th) NYC 10019
Hours: 8-5:15 Mon-Fri/ 8:30-3 Sat (except summer months).
"Bronzing powders, theatrical paint supplies; nice people."

Gold Leaf & Metallic Powders Inc. 212-267-4900
2 Barclay St. (Church) NYC 10007
Hours: 9-5 Mon-Fri
"Genuine and composition gold, silver, aluminum leaf, bronzing powder; good prices; call ahead to check stock." ed.

Gothic Color Co. 212-929-7493
727 Washington St. (Bank) NYC 10014
Hours: 8:30-5 Mon-Thurs/ 8-4:30 Fri
"Bronzing powders; also aniline dye, powered pigments, animal glue, scenic brushes." ed.

A. HAUSSMANN INTERNATIONAL CORP. 212-255-5661
118 West 22nd St. 9th Fl. (6-7th) NYC 10011
Hours: 10-6 Mon-Fri (sometimes later/call first)

An extraordinary group of metallic powders with high reflective qualities. Extensive color range. Call for free brochure. (See display ads pages 50, 260.)

"Also manufacture high quality scenic paints and brushes." ed.

Lee Art Shop 212-247-0110
220 West 57th St. (7th-B'way) NYC 10019
Hours: 9:30-7 Mon-Fri/ 9:30-6 Sat
"Leafing supplies; drafting, framing, drawing, painting supplies." ed.

NY Central Supply Co. 212-473-7705
62 Third Ave. (11th) NYC 10003
Hours: 8:30-6:30 Mon-Sat
"Gold leaf, bronzing powders, art supplies." ed.

Pearl Paint Co. Inc.

308 Canal St. (Mercer) NYC 10013 212-431-7932
Hours: 9-5:30 Mon-Sat/ 11-4:30 Sun

2411 Hempstead Turnpike, East Meadow, NY 11554 516-731-3700
Hours: 9:30-5:45 Mon-Sat (Wed, Fri til 8:45)

"Dutch metal, silver, copper and gold leaf; bronzing powders and liquids." ed.

ROSCO LABORATORIES INC. 914-937-1300
36 Bush Ave., Port Chester, NY 10573 800-431-2338
Hours: 9-5 Mon-Fri

Powders with high reflective qualities. (See display ad inside back cover.)

"Gold and silver bronzing powders by the pound." ed.

United States Bronze Powders 201-782-5454
PO Box 31, Route 202, Flemington, NJ 08822
Hours: 9-5 Mon-Fri
"Wholesale; minimum order $75." ed.

Wolf Paints 212-245-7777
771 Ninth Ave. (51-52nd) NYC 10019
Hours: 7:30-5:30 Mon-Fri/ 8-5 Sat
"Bronzing powders, dyes, brushes; house and theatrical paints." ed.

PAINTS & DYES: FABRIC

See also ARTISTS MATERIALS
See also SILKSCREENING SUPPLIES
For Fiebings and Magix see LEATHERCRAFTERS & FURRIERS TOOLS & SUPPLIES

ALJO MFG. CO. INC. 212-966-4046
450 Greenwich St. (2 blks below Canal) NYC 10013
Hours: 9-5 Mon-Fri
Specializing in Aniline Dyes for costume dyeing/painting and scenic work since 1917. All ALJO dyes are sold in dry powder form with instructions for correct use and application. PROMPT SHIPMENT DAILY VIA UPS. Pick-up at store Mon-Fri 9-5.
"Direct, disperse, fiber-reactive, acid, basic dyes; very helpful." ed.

The American Crayon Co. 419-625-9121
1706 Hayes Ave., PO Box 2358, Sandusky, OH 44870
Hours: 8:30-5 Mon-Fri
"Accolite colors, binders, Prang textile paints." ed.

Bachmeier & Co. Inc. 201-997-0606
31 Rizzolo Rd., PO Box 400, Kearny, NJ 07032
Hours: 9-5 Mon-Fri
"Direct, disperse, acid dyes; 24 hours to pick-up." ed.

Barbizon Electrical Co. 212-586-1620
426 West 55th St. (9-10th) NYC 10019
Hours: 8-5 Mon-Fri
"Distributor for Rosco (incl. paints); also lighting and electrical supplies." ed.

Cerulean Blue Ltd. 206-625-9647
119 Blanchard, PO Box 21168, Seattle, WA 98111
Hours: 10:30-5:30 Thurs,Fri,Sat or by appt.
"Textile art supplies; dyes, fabrics, resists, tools, chemicals; catalog." ed.

Colorcraft Ltd. 800-243-2712
PO Box 936, Avon, CT 06001 203-282-0020
Hours: 9-5 Mon-Fri
"Manufacturer of Createx, an inexpensive heat-set fabric paint; catalog." ed.

W. Cushing & Co. 207-967-3711
PO Box 351, Kennebunkport, ME 04046
Hours: 10-4 Mon-Sat (Sat hours in Summer only)
"Manufacturer of dyes and disperse agents." ed.

Dharma Trading Co. 415-456-1211
PO Box 916, San Rafael, CA 94915
Hours: 8:30-4:30 Mon-Fri (mail order)
"Textile art supplies; dyes, fabrics, tools, books; catalog." ed.

Empire Dyestuffs Corp. 212-925-8737
206 Spring St. (6th) NYC 10012
Hours: 9-4:30 Mon-Fri
"Disperse dyes." ed.

Fabdec 915-944-1031
3553 Old Post Road, San Angelo, TX 76904
Hours: 9-5 Mon-Fri
"Procion dyes, tools, fabric." ed.

Fine Arts Materials Inc. 212-982-7100
346 Lafayette St. (B'way-Bleecker) NYC 10012
Hours: 9:30-6 Mon-Fri/ 11-6 Sat
"Tinfix in quarts, stretchers for silk; art materials; catalog." ed.

A. HAUSSMANN INTERNATIONAL CORP. 212-255-5661
118 West 22nd St. 9th Fl. (6-7th) NYC 10011
Hours: 10-6 Mon-Fri (sometimes later/call first)

Sprila® glazing colors & Hatotex B2® colors; washable, dry cleanable, compatible with each other, Haussmann weave fillers and Armor Putty®. Call for free brochure. (See display ads pages 50, 260.)

"All products are flame retardant." ed.

Ivy Crafts Import Co. 301-779-7079
5410 Annapolis Rd., Bladensburg, MD 20710
Hours: 10-5 Mon-Fri
"Tinfix in quarts; color card." ed.

Knomark Corp. 718-276-3400
132-20 Merrick Blvd., Jamaica, NY 11434
Hours: 9-5 Mon-Fri
"Manufacturer of Tintex, Esquire shoe products, fabric softeners; $95 minimum order, pre-paid." ed.

PRO CHEMICAL & DYE INC. 617-676-3838
PO Box 14, Somerset, MA 02726
Hours: 24 hour phone service.

Fabric Dyes, Textile Pigment Inks and associated supplies for coloration of costumes, backdrops and scenery. Dyes are washfast and may be flameproofed. Free catalogue and technical assistance.

"Cold water dyes, wide variety of colors." ed.

Rivoli Merchandise Co. 212-966-5035
54 Howard St. (Canal & Grand) NYC 10013
Hours: 8-6 Sun-Fri
"Rit and Tintex by the dozen." ed.

ROSCO LABORATORIES INC. 914-937-1300
36 Bush Ave., Port Chester, NY 10573 800-431-2338
Hours: 9-5 Mon-Fri
Polydyes- for coloring most polyester fabric. (See display ad inside back cover.)
"Non-toxic, totally colorfast, re-useable." ed.

Rosco Research Center 212-929-1300
118 West 22nd St. 9th Fl. (6-7th) NYC 10011
Hours: 10-6 Mon-Fri
"Fabric dyes, paints, texturizers; very helpful; catalog." ed.

Royal Wear Hosiery 212-226-2450
23 Orchard St. (Hester) NYC 10002
Hours: 8:30-5 every day
"Tintex by the doz." ed.

RUPERT, GIBBON & SPIDER INC. 707-433-9577
718 College St., Healdsburg, CA 95448
Hours: 9-5 Mon-Fri
Silk & cotton fabrics. Paints & dyes. SPEEDY SERVICE.
"Also glass and slide paints." ed.

Special Products 317-632-5321
1437 W. Morris St., Indianapolis, IN 46221
Hours: 8-4 Mon-Fri
"Rit wholesale; minimum: 10 doz. retail size packages." ed.

Straw Into Gold 415-548-5241
3006 San Pablo Ave., (Ashby) Berkeley, CA 94702
Hours: 9:30-5:30 Mon-Sat
"Procion M." ed.

Stroblite Co. Inc. 212-929-3778
430 West 14th St. Rm. 507 (8-9th) NYC 10014
Hours: 9-5 Mon-Fri
"Ultraviolet fabric paints, feather dip; flier." ed.

Textile Resources 213-431-9611
PO Box 90245, Long Beach, CA 90809
Hours: 9:30-5 Mon-Fri
"Textile arts supplies; dyes, fabrics, tools, resists, chemicals; catalog." ed.

Tricon Colors Inc. 201-794-3800
16 Leliarts Lane, Elmwood Park, NJ 07407
Hours: 8:30-5 Mon-Fri
"Dyes; soluble in water, alcohol, oil; small minimum orders; flier." ed.

PAINTS & DYES: FOAM & RESIN see CASTING SUPPLIES

PAINTS & DYES: GLASS & SLIDE

Barbizon Electrical Co. 212-586-1620
426 West 55th St. (9-10th) NYC 10019
Hours: 8-5 Mon-Fri
"Theatrical lighting supplies; Rosco glass paints." ed.

Glassmasters Guild 212-929-7978
27 West 23rd St. 4th Fl. (5-6th) NYC 10010
Hours: 11-5:30 Mon-Fri (Thurs til 6:30)/ 10-5 Sat
"Dyes and paints for glass, stained glass and supplies." ed.

A. HAUSSMANN INTERNATIONAL CORP. 212-255-5661
118 West 22nd St. 9th Fl. (6-7th) NYC 10011
Hours: 10-6 Mon-Fri (sometimes later/call first)
Reprolux® slide paints. Brilliant, transparent lacquer colors for hand painting on glass, plastic and special effect loops. Call for free brochure. (See display ads pages 50, 260.)
"Also manufacture high quality scenic paints and brushes." ed.

Pearl Paint Co. Inc.

308 Canal St. (Mercer) NYC 10013 212-431-7932
Hours: 9-5:30 Mon-Sat/ 11-4:30 Sun

2411 Hempstead Turnpike, East Meadow, NY 11554 516-731-3700
Hours: 9:30-5:45 Mon-Sat (Wed, Fri til 8:45)

"Stained glass paints; also complete art/craft supplies." ed.

ROSCO LABORATORIES INC. 914-937-1300
36 Bush Ave., Port Chester, NY 10573 800-431-2338
Hours: 9-5 Mon-Fri
Transparent lacquer colors for glass projection slides. Colorine Lamp Dip. (See display ad inside back cover.)
"Test kits available with nine colors, opaque black, thinner and extender." ed.

PAINTS & DYES: HOUSEHOLD

See also HOME DECORATING & IMPROVEMENT CENTERS

Brooklyn Paint Fair 718-434-8000
1010 Coney Island Ave., Bklyn 11230
Hours: 7-6 Mon-Fri/ 7-4 Sat
"Scenic and painting materials, casein, deep colors, aniline, wallcoverings." ed.

M. Epstein and Sons 212-265-3960
809 Ninth Ave. (53-54th) NYC 10019
Hours: 8-5:15 Mon-Fri/ 8:30-3 Sat (except summer months)
"Rollers, brushes, household and theatrical paints; roller patterns."

Janovic Plaza

213 Seventh Ave. (21-22nd) NYC 10011 212-243-2186
Hours: 7:30-6:30 Mon-Fri/ 9-6 Sat

1150 Third Ave. (67th) NYC 10021 212-772-1400
Hours: 7:30-6:30 Mon-Fri/ 8-5:45 Sat

159 West 72nd St. (B'way-Columbus) NYC 10023 212-595-2500
Hours: 7:30-6:30 Mon-Fri (Tues til 8)/ 9-6 Sat/ 11-5 Sun

"Household paints and paint supplies; tile, home decorating center."

Pearl Paint Co. Inc.

308 Canal St. (Mercer) NYC 10013 212-431-7932
Hours: 9-5:30 Mon-Sat/ 11-4:30 Sun

2411 Hempstead Turnpike, East Meadow, NY 11554 516-731-3700
Hours: 9:30-5:45 Mon-Sat (Wed, Fri til 8:45)

"Large selection household paints; flourescent and wrinkle spray paint; also art/craft supplies." ed.

Pintchik Paints 212-982-6600
278 Third Ave. (22nd) NYC 10010 212-777-3030
Hours: 8:30-8 M,Th / 8:30-7 T,W,F/ 9-6:30 Sat/ 11-5 Sun
"Household and theatrical paints and wallcoverings." ed.

THE SET SHOP 212-929-4845
3 West 20th St. (5th) NYC 10011
Hours: 9-6 Mon-Fri/ 10-4 Sat
Household & theatrical paints & all painters' supplies. Texturing supplies. (See display ad page 316.)
"Also wallboards and canvas." ed.

Wolf Paints 212-245-7777
771 Ninth Ave. (51-52nd) NYC 10019
Hours: 7:30-5:30 Mon-Fri/ 8-5 Sat
"Household and theatrical paints; roller patterns." ed.

PAINTS & DYES: LEATHER see LEATHERCRAFTERS & FURRIERS TOOLS & SUPPLIES

PAINTS & DYES: SCENIC

Alcone Company Inc./Paramount Theatrical 718-361-8373
5-49 49th Ave. L.I.C. 11101
Hours: 9:30-4 Mon-Fri
"Convenient to subway; theatrical supply house; catalog." ed.

Brooklyn Paint Fair 718-434-8000
1010 Coney Island Ave., Bklyn 11230
Hours: 7-6 Mon-Fri/ 7-4 Sat
"Scenic and painting materials, casein, deep colors, aniline, wallcoverings." ed.

M. Epstein and Sons 212-265-3960
809 Ninth Ave. (53-54th) NYC 10019
Hours: 8-5:15 Mon-Fri/ 8:30-3 Sat (except in summer months)
"Theatrical scenic supplies; paints, dyes, brushes." ed.

Gothic Color Co. 212-929-7493
727 Washington St. (Bank-11th) NYC 10014
Hours: 8:30-5 Mon-Thurs/ 8-4:30 Fri
"Powdered pigments, gelatin and flexible glue, brushes and dyes." ed.

A. HAUSSMANN INTERNATIONAL CORP. 212-255-5661
118 West 22nd St. 9th Fl. (6-7th) NYC 10011
Hours: 10-6 Mon-Fri (sometimes later/call first)

Unique system of weave fillers, Armor Putty® and Hatoplast® for coating and 3D relief. Compatible with Hatotex® color system and Sprila® glazing colors. Exceptionally fine European scenic brushes, full range of styles and sizes. Call for free brochure. (See display ads pages 50, 260.)

"Full line of high quality scenic brushes." ed.

Mutual Hardware 718-361-2480
5-45 49th Ave. (Vernon Blvd) L.I.C. 11101
Hours: 8:30-5 Mon-Fri
"Scenic supplies and Flo-paint; catalog." ed.

ROSCO LABORATORIES INC. 914-937-1300
36 Bush Ave., Port Chester, NY 10573 800-431-2338
Hours: 9-5 Mon-Fri

Manufacturers of Iddings Deep Colors and Iddings Dry Pigments, Supersaturated Paint and Off Broadway Scenic Paint. (See display ad inside back cover.)

"Wide variety of scenic paints to meet diverse needs." ed.

NOTES

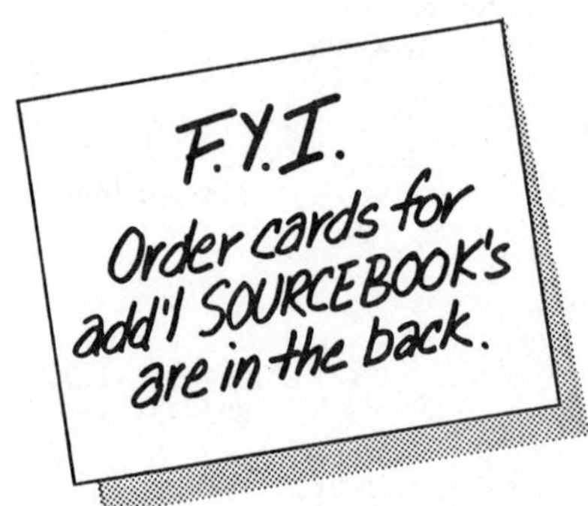
F.Y.I.
Order cards for add'l SOURCEBOOK's are in the back.

THE SET SHOP 212-929-4845
3 West 20th St. (5th) NYC 10011
Hours: 9-6 Mon-Fri/ 10-4 Sat
Rosco scenic supplies. (See display ad page 316.)
"Full scene shop, non-union." ed.

Tricon Colors Inc. 201-794-3800
16 Leliarts Lane, Elmwood Park, NJ 07407
Hours: 8:30-5 Mon-Fri
"Colors and dyes soluble in water, alcohol, oil; anilines." ed.

Wolf Paints 212-245-7777
771 Ninth Ave. (51-52nd) NYC 10019
Hours: 7:30-5:30Mon-Fri/ 8-5 Sat
"Theatrical paint and dyes, clear latex, brushes; delivery." ed.

PAINTS & DYES: SIGN & POSTER

Eagle Supply Co. 212-246-6180
327 West 42nd St. (8-9th) NYC 10036
Hours: 9-4:30 Mon-Fri
"Artists, sign, and silkscreening supplies; large stock poster board."

M. Epstein and Sons 212-265-3960
809 Ninth Ave. (53-54th) NYC 10019
Hours: 8-5:15 Mon-Fri/ 8:30-3 Sat (except summer months)
"Sign and poster paints; theatrical paints; nice people." ed.

N. Glantz & Son 718-439-7707
218 57th St. (2-3rd) Bklyn 11220
Hours: 9-5 Mon-Fri
"Paints, boards, neon; everything for signmaking; wholesale Cutawl sales." ed.

Pearl Paint Co. Inc.

308 Canal St. (Mercer) NYC 10013 212-431-7932
Hours: 9-5:30 Mon-Sat/ 11-4:30 Sun

2411 Hempstead Turnpike, East Meadow, NY 11554 516-731-3700
Hours: 9:30-5:45 Mon-Sat (Wed, Fri til 8:45)

"Poster paint, board, brushes; complete art/craft supplies." ed.

ROSCO LABORATORIES INC. 914-937-1300
36 Bush Ave., Port Chester, NY 10573 800-431-2338
Hours: 9-5 Mon-Fri
Crown Tempera- designer colors for artists and students. (See display ad inside back cover.)
"18 color palette available in 4 oz.-1 gallon units." ed.

PAINTS & DYES: SPECIALIZED, MISC.

See also CASTING SUPPLIES
See also FLORAL SUPPLIES
See also LEATHERCRAFTERS & FURRIERS TOOLS & SUPPLIES
See also SILKSCREENING SUPPLIES

Day-Glo Color Corp. 212-986-1120
303 Wilson Ave., Newark, NJ 07105
Hours: 8:30-4:30 Mon-Fri
"Flourescent and UV paints; wholesale; call first." ed.

Mearl Corp. 212-573-8500
41 East 42nd St. Rm. 708 (Madison) NYC 10017
Hours: 9-5 Mon-Fri
"Pearlizer pigment for make-up and paint." ed.

Old-Fashioned Milk Paint Co. 617-448-6336
PO Box 222, Groton, MA 01450
Hours: 9-5 Mon-Fri
"Dry powder milk base paint; natural earth colors." ed.

Prince Lacquer & Chemical Corp. 718-387-8313
413 Kent Ave. (B'way-S 8th) Bklyn 11211
Hours: 9-5 Mon-Fri
"Lacquers." ed.

ROSCO LABORATORIES INC. 914-937-1300
36 Bush Ave., Port Chester, NY 10573 800-431-2338
Hours: 9-5 Mon-Fri
Iddings Ice Colors, flourescent paints & pigments, Colorine Lamp Dip. (See display ad inside back cover.)
"Also bronzing powders, irridescent paint, puff tex and polydyes." ed.

Stroblite Co. Inc. 212-929-3778
430 West 14th St. Rm. 507 (8-9th) NYC 10014
Hours: 9-4:30 Mon-Fri
"Flourescent and UV paints; black lights and such." ed.

PAPER, CARDBOARD & FOAMCORE PRODUCTS

See also: ARTIST MATERIAL & SUPPLIES
See also: PACKING MATERIALS

APPLE FOAM & PLASTIC INC. 516-433-2151
180 Miller Place, Hicksville, NY 11801 718-529-5991
Hours: 8:30-6 Mon-Fri

Distributors of Fome-Cor®, Foam-X®, Cellulite®, Sintra®, and all Foam Boards. Reflective foils on all of our foam boards are available. Also Colors! Free metro area delivery on orders of $150.

"Good prices; speak to Joe Knapp." ed.

Baehm Paper Co. 212-267-1892
53 Murray St. (Church-W. B'way) NYC 10007
Hours: 8-2 Mon-Fri
"Kraft and corrugated paper; will deliver." ed.

Blake-Harrison Paper Corp. 201-868-4200
2179 83rd St., N. Bergen, NJ 07047 212-868-2360
Hours: 8:30-4:30 Mon-Fri
"Butcher paper, kraft paper; formerly Sidel Paper Co." ed.

GILSHIRE CORP. SCENERY STUDIO PROD. DIV. 718-786-1381
11-20 46th Rd., L.I.C. 11101
Hours: 8:30-4:30 Mon-Fri
(See display ad page 264.)
"Wax, Kraft, and grey bogus scenery papers." ed.

David Hamberger

410 Hicks St., Bklyn 11201 718-852-7101
Hours: 9-5:30 Mon-Fri

120 East 23rd St. Rm. 509 (Park-Lexington) NYC 10010 (Showroom) 212-852-7101
Hours: 9-5 Mon-Fri

"Sonotube cut to order, 3"-16" diameter." ed.

International Honeycomb Corp. 203-288-7722
456 Sacket Point Rd., North Haven, CT 06473
Hours: 8:30-5 Mon-Fri
"Air-Lite panels, white or Kraft finish, ½"-2" thick; contact Dian." ed.

INTERNATIONAL PAPER COMPANY 704-872-8974
Taylorsville Road Highway 90, Statesville, NC 28677 800-438-1701
Hours: 8-5 Mon-Fri
GATORFOAM® Laminated Foam Panel. Call 800# for local dealer.
"Available in 4'x8' sheets; 5 thicknesses from 3/16" to 1½"." ed.

Kern & Son 212-431-6273
250 West Broadway (6th-Beech) NYC 10013
Hours: 8:30-4:30 Mon-Fri
"Paper tubing ½"-6" diameter, various thicknesses; custom work, stock." ed.

Lenoble Lumber Co. Inc. 212-246-0150
500 West 52nd St. (10-11th) NYC 10019
Hours: 8-3 Mon-Fri (closed for lunch 12-1)
"Sonotube; also masonite, Formica, plywood, etc." ed.

Lupari Displays Ltd. 718-727-4986
225 Port Richmond Ave., Staten Island, NY 10302
Hours: 10-6 Mon-Fri
"13" Sonotube; custom display work." ed.

Party Bazaar 212-695-6820
390 Fifth Ave. (36th) NYC 10018
Hours: 8-6 Mon-Wed/ 8-8 Thurs/8-7 Fri/9:30-6 Sat
"Colored corrugated cardboard in two widths; party supplies." ed.

Salwen Paper Co. 201-225-4000
PO Box 4008, Edison, NJ 08816
Hours: 9-5 Mon-Fri
"Gatorfoam board by the carton; contact Tom Lagowski." ed.

THE SET SHOP 212-929-4845
3 West 20th St. (5th) NYC 10011
Hours: 9-6 Mon-Fri/ 10-4 Sat
Sonotubes, convolutely wound cardboard shapes, curved Finnish plywood, PVC tubing. All set materials & fabrication--we cut Sonotubes to length. (See display ad page 316.)
"Full scene shop, non-union." ed.

Sonoco Products Co. (Tubes & Cores) 201-263-1400
PO Box 582, Montville, NJ 07045
Hours: 8-4:45 Mon-Fri
"Sonotube and cores." ed.

U.S. Egg 212-925-1713
1 Worth St. (Hudson) NYC 10013
Hours: 6-2:30 Mon-Fri
"Egg cartons and flats." ed.

PARTY GOODS

See also MAGIC SUPPLIES & NOVELTIES

Broadway Party Service 718-783-2700
868 Kent Ave. Bklyn 11205
Hours: 7-5 Mon-Fri/ 7:30-11 Sat
"Party rental items: A-Z." ed.

Paper East 212-249-0129
866 Lexington Ave. (65th) NYC 10021
Hours: 10-6 Mon-Sat
"Giftwrap, cards, paper plates & napkins." ed.

Paper House

18 Greenwich Ave. (10th) NYC 10011 212-741-1569
Hours: 10-10 M,T/10-10:30 W,Th/10-11 F/9:30-11:30 Sat/11-10 Sun

300 Columbus Ave. (74th) NYC 10023 212-799-2076
Hours: 10-10 M,T/ 10-10:30 W/ 10-11 Th,F/
9:30-11:30 Sat/ 10:30-10 Sun

1370 Third Ave. (78th) NYC 10021 212-879-2937
Hours: 9:30-10 Mon-Fri/ 9-10:30 Sat/ 10:30-6:30 Sun

2235 Broadway (79-80th) NYC 10024 212-595-5656
Hours: 9:30-10 M-W/9:30-10:30 Th/9:30-11 F/9-11:30 Sat/10-10 Sun

"Giftwrap, cards, paper plates & napkins." ed.

Party Bazaar 212-695-6820
390 Fifth Ave. (36th) NYC 10018
Hours: 8-6 Mon-Wed/ 8-8 Thurs/ 8-7 Fri/ 9:30-6 Sat
"Good selection party favors, giftwrap, streamers, glitter, cards, paper plates, etc." ed.

Service Party-Rental Co. 212-288-7384
521 East 72nd St. (York) NYC 10021 212-288-7361
Hours: 8:30-4:30 Mon-Fri
"Chairs, tables, bars, coat racks, silverware, china, linens, etc. for party rental." ed.

PATTERNS, PERIOD

RICHARD THE THREAD/ROY COOPER 800-621-0849(x226)
1433 N. Orange Grove, Hollywood, CA 90046 213-874-1116
Hours: By appt.
Gothic, Renaissance, Elizabethan, Victorian and Edwardian.
Men's & Women's. Free catalogue. 800-621-0849 x 226.
"Complete line of sewing notions; mail and phone orders." ed.

PET SUPPLIES

See also TROPICAL FISH

American Kennels

55 West 8th St. (5-6th) NYC 10011 212-260-6230
Hours: 12-7 every day

786 Lexington Ave. (61st) NYC 10021 212-838-8460
Hours: 10-7 Mon-Sat/ 12-6 Sun

"Basic neighborhood pet supply store." ed.

Animal World 212-685-0027
219 East 26th St. (2-3rd) NYC 10010
Hours: 10-7 Mon-Fri/ 10-6 Sat
"Pet toys, food, accessories; good dog bowls." ed.

Bird Jungle 212-242-1757
401 Bleecker St. (11th St.) NYC 10014
Hours: 12:30-6:45 Mon-Sat/ 12:30-5:45 Sun
"Good selection of large birdcages and birds; will order." ed.

Fish & Pet Town 212-752-9508
241 East 59th St. (2-3rd) NYC 10022
Hours: 11-7:30 Mon-Fri/ 10:30-6 Sat/ 12-5 Sun
"Large selection fish, dog and cat supplies." ed.

JBJ Discount Pet Shop 212-982-5310
151 East Houston St. (1-2nd) NYC 10002
Hours: 10-6 Mon-Sat
"Good selection small aminals, rabbits, mice, etc; very helpful." ed.

Petland Discounts

132 Nassau St. (Ann-Beekman) NYC 10038 212-964-1821
Hours: 9-7 Mon-Fri/ 10-6 Sat/ 11-5 Sun

7 East 14th St. (5th) NYC 10003 212-675-4102
Hours: 9-8 Mon-Fri/ 10-6:30 Sat/ 11-5 Sun

304 East 86th St. (2nd) NYC 10028 212-472-1655
Hours: 10-9 Mon-Fri/ 10-6 Sat/ 11-5 Sun

"Good selection of pet supplies; birds, fish, small animals." ed.

Ben Richter Co. 212-255-5373
85 Fifth Ave. (16th) NYC 10003
Hours: By appt. only
"Wholesaler of dog furnishings: leashes, coats, etc.; also carries food bowls." ed.

PEWTER ITEMS
See also ANTIQUES

Alyn Trading Corp. 212-689-7060
1141 Broadway (26th) NYC 10001
Hours: 9-5 Mon-Fri
"Hammered tinware in pewter washed copper & brass finish; flyer available." ed.

Lovelia Enterprises Inc. 212-490-0930
356 East 41st St. (in Tudor City Place) NYC 10017
Hours: By appt.
"Antique pewter; prefers short-term rentals." ed.

Macy's Department Store 212-971-6000
151 West 34th St. (B'way) NYC 10001
Hours: 9:45-8:45 M,Th,F/9:45-6:45 T,W/ 9:45-7 Sat/12-6 Sun
"Pewter in Colonial Shop, 8th floor." ed.

Hyman E. Piston Antiques 212-753-8322
1050 Second Ave. (55-56th) NYC 10022
Hours: 10-4 Mon-Fri/ 10-2:30 Sat
"Antique copper, brass & pewter items." ed.

Wilton Co. 717-684-9000
18th & Franklin St., Columbia, PA 17512
Hours: 8-5 Mon-Fri, mail order only
"Wholesale pewter dinnerware, goblets, pitchers, mugs, candleholders; catalog; quick delivery." ed.

PHOTOGRAPHIC BLOW-UPS & MURALS

Duggal Color Projects 212-242-7000
9 West 20th St. (5-6th) NYC 10011
Hours: 7:30-10 Mon-Fri/ 9-5 Sat, Sun
"In-house work, cibachromes, color murals, light boxes; highly recommended." ed.

Giant Photo Inc. 212-982-3840
200 Park Ave. South 5th Fl. (17th) NYC 10003
Hours: 9-5 Mon-Fri
"Photostats, large blow-ups, dry mounting." ed.

H-Y Photo Service 212-986-0390
16 East 52nd St. (5th-Madison) NYC 10022
Hours: 9-5:30 Mon-Fri
"Photo blow-ups, will mount work." ed.

INTERNATIONAL PAPER COMPANY 704-872-8974
Taylorsville Road Highway 90, Statesville, NC 28677 800-438-1701
Hours: 8-5 Mon-Fri
GATORFOAM® Laminated Foam Panel. Call 800# for local dealer.
"Available in 4'x8' sheets; 5 thicknesses from 3/16" to 1½"." ed.

Metro Giant Photo 212-477-1792
200 Park Ave. South Rm. 501 (17th) NYC 10003
Hours: 9-5 Mon-Fri
"Very large blow-ups." ed.

ROSCO LABORATORIES INC. 914-937-1300
36 Bush Ave., Port Chester, NY 10573 800-431-2338
Hours: 9-5 Mon-Fri
Process converts transparencies or opaque art to large textile drops. (See display ad inside back cover.)
"Beautiful results; contact Rosco for details." ed.

S M P Graphic Service Center 212-254-2282
26 East 22nd St. (B'way-Park Ave. S.) NYC 10010
Hours: 24 hours Mon-Fri/ 11-6 Sat, Sun
"Dry mounting, blow-ups to 4'x8', many other services." ed.

Stewart Color Labs Inc. 212-868-1440
563 Eleventh Ave. (42-43rd) NYC 10036
Hours: 8:30-6 Mon-Fri
"Expert color lab; displays, mounting, retouching; builds crates for shipping murals; see Jimmy Walker." ed.

PHOTOGRAPHIC EQUIPMENT

B & H Foto & Electronics Corp. 212-206-1010
119 West 17th St. (6-7th) NYC 10011 212-807-7474
Hours: 9-6 Mon-Thurs/ 9-1 Fri/ 10-4 Sun
"Good prices on film, photographic equipment & accessories." ed.

Bargain Spot 212-674-1188
64 Third Ave. (11th) NYC 10032
Hours: 8:30-5 Mon-Sat
"New and used camera equipment; rental or purchase; also musical instruments, binoculars, etc." ed.

Bi-Rite Photo Electric Inc. 212-685-2130
15 East 30th St. (5th-Madison) NYC 10016
Hours: 9-6 Mon-Thurs/ 9-1 Fri/ 10:30-3:30 Sun
"Very low prices on cameras and electronic equipment." ed.

The Camera Barn Inc. 212-947-3510
1272 Broadway (32nd) NYC 10001
Hours: 8:30-6 Mon-Fri/ 9-6 Sat
"Good selection camera equipment and accessories, darkroom supplies; new and used." ed.

Dumont Camera Corp. 212-475-1700
893 Broadway (19-20th) NYC 10003
Hours: 8:30-5:45 Mon-Fri/ 9-5:45 Sat
"Film and darkroom supplies, processing." ed.

Executive Photo & Supply Corp. 212-947-5290
120 West 31st St. (6-7th) NYC 10001
Hours: 9-6 Mon-Thurs/ 9-2 Fri/ 10-5 Sun
"Stock all leading brands cameras and equipment." ed.

47th St. Photo Inc.

35 East 18th St. (Park Ave S-B'way) NYC 10003 212-260-4410
Hours: 9-5 Mon-Thurs/ 9-1:45 Fri/ 10-4 Sun (mail order) 800-221-7774
"Cameras & photo equipment; darkroom store." ed.

116 Nassau St. (Ann-Beekman) NYC 10038 212-608-6934
Hours: 9-6 Mon-Thurs/ 9-2 Fri/ 10-4 Sun

115 West 45th St. (6-B'way) NYC 10036 212-260-4410
Hours: 9-6 Mon-Thurs/ 9-2 Fri/ 10-4 Sun

67 West 47th St. (5-6th) NYC 10036 212-260-4410
Hours: 9-6 Mon-Thurs/ 9-2 Fri/ 10-4 Sun

"Cameras and photo equipment, computers, typewriters, etc.; watch for frequent sales." ed.

Ken Hansen Photographic Co. 212-777-5900
920 Broadway (21st) NYC 10010
Hours: 9:30-5:30 Mon-Fri
"Stock many leading brands camera and equipment." ed.

Jay Bee Photo Suppliers 212-420-9797
133 Fifth Ave. (20th) NYC 10003
Hours: 8-6 Mon-Fri
"Equipment rentals available." ed.

Olden Camera 212-725-1234
1265 Broadway (32nd) NYC 10001
Hours: 9-7 Mon-Fri (Thurs til 8)/9-6 Sat/ 10-5 Sun
"Old and new camera equipment; rental, purchase, repairs; see Carl Thompson." ed.

Photo Exchange 212-675-6582
1 West 20th St. (5th) NYC 10011
Hours: 9-6 Mon-Fri/ 11-4 Sat
"Film, video tapes; sales and rental of studio and video equipment."

Twentieth Century Plastics — 213-731-0900
3628 Crenshaw Blvd., Los Angeles, CA 90016
"Plastic sleeves for slides and photos; quick mail order service." ed.

Wall St. Camera Exchange Inc. — 212-344-0011
82 Wall St. (Pearl-Water) NYC 10005
Hours: 9-6 Mon-Thurs/ 9-3 Fri/ 10-3 Sun
"New and used cameras, camera equipment, repairs; calculators, computers, watches." ed.

Willoughby-Peerless Camera Store — 212-564-1600
110 West 32nd St. (6-7th) NYC 10001
Hours: 9-7 Mon-Fri (Thurs til 8)/ 9-6:30 Sat/ 10:30-5:30 Sun
"Excellent selection camera equipment and accessories; while-you-wait print processing." ed.

PHOTOGRAPHIC SERVICES

For photostats, see PRINTING & COPYING

ASAP Photo Lab — 212-832-1223
40 East 49th St. (Madison-Park) NYC 10017
Hours: 8-5:45 Mon-Fri
"Color lab; rush service." ed.

Berkey K & L Custom Services — 212-661-5600
222 East 44th St. (2-3rd) NYC 10017
Hours: 8-6:30 Mon-Fri
"Regular and rush service; prints from stats." ed.

Color Wheel Inc. — 212-697-2434
227 East 45th St. (2-3rd) NYC 10017
Hours: 9-5 Mon-Fri
"Custom printing; not cheap but best quality." ed.

Duggal Color Projects Inc. — 212-242-7000
9 West 20th St. (5-6th) NYC 10011
Hours: 7:30-10 Mon-Fri/ 9-5 Sat,Sun
"Fast service on slides; photo murals, cibachromes, studio rental." ed.

Dumont Camera Corp. — 212-475-1700
893 Broadway (19-20th) NYC 10003
Hours: 8:30-5:45 Mon-Fri/ 9-5:45 Sat
"Film processing, darkroom supplies, film." ed.

Four Colors Photo Lab — 212-889-3399
10 East 39th St. (5th-Madison) NYC 10016
Hours: 9-5 Mon-Fri/ 10-4 Sat
"Contact prints, transparencies, c-prints, B & W, retouching." ed.

Jamie Canvas Co. 212-505-1256
496 La Guardia Pl. (Bleecker-Houston) NYC 10022
Hours: 10-6:30 Mon-Wed/ 10-8 Thurs,Fri/ 10-6 Sat/ 12-6 Sun
"Will make cibachrome prints from slides on premises." ed.

Jellybean Photographics 212-679-4888
99 Madison Ave. (29-30th) NYC 10016
Hours: 8-6 Mon-Fri
"Complete photo lab; reasonable prices; very helpful." ed.

Larson Color Corp. 212-674-0610
123 Fifth Ave. (19-20th) NYC 10003
Hours: 8-9 Mon-Fri
"Color processing for professional work; slides and prints." ed.

Slide Shop Inc. 212-725-5200
220 East 23rd St. 4th Fl. (2-3rd) NYC 10010
Hours: 9-10pm Mon-Fri
"Full service on slides." ed.

Thru the Lens Foto Co. 212-734-0245
1296 First Ave. (69-70th) NYC 10021
Hours: 9:30-7 Mon-Fri/ 10-6 Sat
"Arthur Laszlo, owner; friendly, quick Kodak processing." ed.

Vidachrome Inc. 212-391-8124
1260 West 35th St. Rm. 503 (7-8th) NYC 10018
Hours: 9-5:45 Mon-Fri
"Custom B & W, color prints." ed.

Jack Ward Color 212-725-5200
220 East 23rd St. 4th Fl. (2-3rd) NYC 10010
Hours: 8-10pm Mon-Fri
"B & W and color lab; high contrast copy, reverse image negative slides." ed.

PIPE & TUBING

See also ELECTRICAL & ELECTRONICS SUPPLIES
See also PLASTICS: SHEETS, TUBES, RODS, SHAPES
See also PLUMBING SUPPLIES
See also SURGICAL SUPPLY HOUSES

For Sonotube see PAPER, CARDBOARD & FOAMCORE PRODUCTS

Canal Rubber Supply Co. 212-226-7339
329 Canal St. (Greene) NYC 10013
Hours: 9-5 Mon-Fri (Sat til 4:30)
"Latex and rubber tubing." ed.

Carlyle Rubber Co. Inc. 212-349-3810
40 Worth St. Rm. 700 NYC 10006
Hours: 9-5 Mon-Fri
"Latex and rubber tubing." ed.

Fisher Scientific Co. 201-379-1400
52 Fadem Rd., Springfield, NJ 07081
Hours: 9-5 Mon-Fri
"All sorts of tubing and lab equipment." ed.

Fleischer Tube Distributing Corp. 516-968-8822
71 Saxon Ave., Bayshore, NY 11706
Hours: 9-6 Mon-Fri
"Any kind of metal tube, including thin wall; will deliver." ed.

PVC Supply Co. 212-741-0900
304 Spring St. (Hudson-Greenwich St.) NYC 10013
Hours: 8-4:30 Mon-Fri
"Complete stock of PVC and CPVC." ed.

PLASTIC FOAMS see FOAM SHEETING & SHAPES

PLASTIC FOAMS: COMPONENT see CASTING SUPPLIES

PLASTIC ITEMS

Ain Plastics 212-473-2100
300 Park Ave. South (22-23rd) NYC 10010 (warehouse) 212-823-4200
Hours: 9-5:30 Mon-Fri
"Plastic items, sheets, rods, tubes, film." ed.

Industrial Plastics 212-226-2010
309 Canal St. (B'way-Mercer) NYC 10013
Hours: 8:30-5 Mon-Fri/ 8:30-4 Sat
"Plastic items, shapes, sheets, film, rods, tubes; fiberglas statuary and supplies." ed.

Lucidity Inc. 212-861-7000
775 Madison Ave. (66-67th) NYC 10021
Hours: 10:30-6:30 Mon-Fri/ 11-6 Sat
"Large selection of Lucite items: trays, bowls, serving utensils, etc."

Outwater Plastics 201-340-1040
PO Drawer 403, Wood Ridge, NJ 07075 800-631-8375
Hours: 8:30-5 Mon-Fri
"Decorative trim, tubing, frames, boxes in plastic." ed.

Plastic Fabricators 718-468-2233
1804 Plaza Ave., New Hyde Park, NY 11040
Hours: 9-3:45 Mon-Fri
"Plastic display items, bath fixtures in plexiglass; catalog." ed.

Plastic Works

2107 Broadway (74th) NYC 10023 212-362-1000
Hours: 10-7 Mon-Sat/ 11:30-6 Sun

1407 Third Ave. (80th) NYC 10021 212-535-6486
Hours: 10-7 Mon-Sat/ 12:30-5:30 Sun

"Ready made acrylic and other plastic household goods; bath accessories, picture frames." ed.

PLASTIC RESINS see CASTING SUPPLIES

PLASTICS FABRICATION

See also VACUUMFORMING & VACUUMFORMED PANELS

Accurate Plastics 914-476-0700
18 Morris Place, Yonkers, NY 10705
Hours: 9-5:15 Mon-Fri
"Plexiglass fabrication." ed.

Ain Plastics Inc. 212-473-2100
300 Park Ave. South (22-23rd) NYC 10010 (warehouse) 212-823-4200
Hours: 9-5:30 Mon-Fri
"Fabrication and manufacturing of sheets, rods, tubes, film." ed.

S. Pomponio 212-925-9453
6 Varick St. (W. B'way-Franklin) NYC 10013
Hours: 9-6 Mon-Fri
"Will cut plastic or any other material." ed.

RB Studios 212-505-7474
235 Park Ave. South (19th) NYC 10003
Hours: 8:30-4:30 Mon-Fri
"Design specialty house; large or small acrylic fabrication; see Robert Brussel." ed.

THE SET SHOP 212-929-4845
3 West 20th St. (5th) NYC 10011
Hours: 9-6 Mon-Fri/ 10-4 Sat
Large selection of acrylic sheets. Custom fabrication. Acrylic ice cubes. (See display ad page 316.)
"Full scene shop; non-union." ed.

Starbuck Studios 212-807-7299
162 West 21st St. (6-7th) NYC 10011
Hours: 10-6 Mon-Fri
"Acrylic props made to order; fake ice cubes." ed.

PLASTIC FOAM see CASTING SUPPLIES
see FOAM SHEETING & SHAPES

PLASTIC RESIN see CASTING SUPPLIES

PLASTICS: SHEETS, TUBES, RODS, SHAPES

Accurate Plastics 914-476-0700
18 Morris Place, Yonkers, NY 10705
Hours: 9-5:15 Mon-Fri
"Plexi sheets, tubes, rods." ed.

Ain Plastics Inc. 212-473-2100
300 Park Ave. South (22-23rd) NYC 10010 (warehouse) 212-823-4200
Hours: 9-5 Mon-Fri
"Plexi sheets, rods, tubes, shapes; rather pricey." ed.

Almac Plastics Inc. 718-937-1300
47-42 37th St. L.I.C. 11101
Hours: 9-5 Mon-Fri
"Latex tubing, Teflon, nylon, plexi, Lexan, acetate." ed.

Bloomfield Plastic Co. 201-743-6900
28 Montgomery (exit 41 off Pkway) Bloomfield, NJ 07003
Hours: 8-5 Mon-Fri/ 8-2 Sat
"All types of plastics: colors, mirrors, cloth; catalog; fabricators."

Cadillac Plastic & Chemical Co. 718-721-8484
35-21 Vernon Blvd. (35-36th) L.I.C. 11106
Hours: 8:30-5 Mon-Fri
"Plexiglass, nylon, Lexan, Teflon." ed.

Canal Plastic Center 212-925-1032
345 Canal St. (Wooster-Greene) NYC 10013 212-925-1164
Hours: 9-5:30 Mon-Fri/ 11-4 Sun
"Wholesale and retail Lexan, acetate, vinyl, rods, tubes, mirror." ed.

Clifton Plastics Inc. 215-622-3900
557 E. Baltimore Ave., Clifton Heights, PA 19018
Hours: 9-5 Mon-Fri
"Precision plastic balls in PVC, phenolic, polyethelene, nylon." ed.

Commercial Plastics 718-849-8100
98-31 Jamaica Ave. (101st) Richmond Hill, NY 11418
Hours: 8:30-4:30 Mon-Fri
"Plexi, Lexan, nylon, Teflon, mylar, acetate, Comstik cements." ed.

E & T Plastic Mfg. Co. Inc 718-729-6226
45-33 37th St. (off Queens Blvd) L.I.C. 11101
Hours: 9-5 Mon-Fri
"Plexi, acrylic, acetate, Lexan, Teflon, mylar, polystyrene, vacuumforming; call Elliot." ed.

Franklin Fibre-Lamitex Corp. 718-347-2120
2040 Jericho Turnpike, PO Box 1146, New Hyde Park, NY 11040 516-437-7791
Hours: 9-5 Mon-Fri
"Nylon stocks, coils, sheets, tubes; acetate, Lexan, Teflon, mylar." ed.

Industrial Plastics 212-226-2010
309 Canal St. (B'way-Mercer) NYC 10013
Hours: 8:30-5 Mon-Fri/ 8:30-4 Sat
"Plexiglass, fiberglas supplies, Lexan, mylar, acetate, component foams and resins; see Deena." ed.

Premier Plastics-Premier Plexiglass 212-288-9300
220 East 60th St. (2-3rd) NYC 10022
Hours: 10-6 Mon-Sat
"See Tony or Frank: very helpful on special orders." ed.

PLATING & METAL FINISHES

ARTHUR FRISCH CO. INC. 212-589-4100
1816 Boston Rd. (175th) Bronx 10460
Hours: 9-4:30 Mon-Fri
Vacuum plating on plastic, glass, metal, other surfaces.
"Good with plastics." ed.

Black Ox Metal Finishing 718-274-2104
34-11 10th St. (35th Ave) L.I.C. 11106
Hours: 8:30-5 Mon-Fri
"Special finishes, anodizing, by the batch; $25 min. order." ed.

Columbia Lighting and Silversmiths 212-725-5250
499 Third Ave. (33-34th) NYC 10016
Hours: 9:30-6 Mon-Fri (Thurs til 8)/ 10-6 Sat
"Brass plating." ed.

Hudson Chromium Co. Inc. 718-226-7046
20-20 Steinway St. (near 20th Ave) L.I.C. 84119
Hours: 8:30-5:30 Mon-Fri
"Chrome, silver plating, sword blade sharpening; see Mr. Galfont." ed.

Regal Plating Co. Inc. 401-421-2704
85 South St., Providence, RI 02903
Hours: 9-5 Mon-Fri
"Chrome plating." ed.

Standard Plating Corp. 212-925-5313
71 Spring St. (B'way-Lafayette) NYC 10012
Hours: 8-4 Mon-Fri
"Plating; polishing service available." ed.

PLUMBING SUPPLIES

For additional fixtures, see KITCHEN & BATH FIXTURES

Eigen Supply Co.

236 West 17th St. (7-8th) NYC 10011 212-255-1200
Hours: 7:30-4:30 Mon-Fri

1751 First Ave. (90-91st) NYC 10128 212-255-1200
Hours: 7:30-4:30 Mon-Fri

317 Atlantic Ave. (Smith-Hoyt) Bklyn 11201 212-255-1200
Hours: 7:30-4:30 Mon-Fri

"Basic plumbing supplies, wholesale and retail." ed.

Greenwich Village Plumbers Supply 212-254-9450
35 Bond St. (Bowery-Lafayette) NYC 10012
Hours: 8-4:30 Mon-Fri
"Basic plumbing supplies, wholesale and retail." ed.

Leesam Plumbing 212-243-6482
124 Seventh Ave. (17-18th) NYC 10011
Hours: 9:30-6 Mon-Fri
"New and salvage plumbing supplies, bathroom fixtures, radiators; reasonable." ed.

Metropolitan Lumber & Hardware

175 Spring St. (W. B'way-Thompson) NYC 10012 212-246-9090
Hours: 8-6 Mon-Fri/ 9-6 Sat/ 10-5 Sun

617 Eleventh Ave. (46th) NYC 10036 212-246-9090
Hours: 7-7 Mon-Fri/ 8-6 Sat/ 10-4 Sun

"Some retail plumbing supplies." ed.

NY Replacement Parts 212-534-0818
1464 Lexington Ave. (94th) NYC 10128
Hours: 7:30-4:30 Mon-Fri/ 9-1 Sat
"Repro faucet and plumbing parts: bring in sample for repro." ed.

P & G New and Used Plumbing Supply 718-384-6310
155 Harrison Ave. Bklyn 11206
Hours: 8:30-4:30 Mon-Fri/ 8:30-1:30 Sat
"New & salvage plumbing parts, fixtures, bathtubs, sinks, toilets, stoves; helpful." ed.

Solco Plumbing Supply Co. 212-243-2569
209 West 18th St. (7-8th) NYC 10011
Hours: 7:30-4:30 Mon-Fri
"Wholesale/retail plumbing supplies." ed.

POLICE EQUIPMENT

See also CLOTHING RENTAL & PURCHASE: UNIFORMS

Best Emblem & Insignia Co. 212-677-4332
636 Broadway (Houston-Bleecker) NYC 10012
Hours: 8:30-5 Mon-Fri
"Bobby badges, custom metal work." ed.

F & J Police Equipment 212-665-4535
904 Melrose Ave. (162nd) Bronx 10451
Hours: 9-6 Mon-Fri/ 9-5 Sat
"Uniforms, guns, shoes, bulletproof vests." ed.

Robert S. Frielich Inc.

396 Broome St. (Mulberry-Centre) NYC 10013 212-254-3045
Hours: 8-4 Mon-Fri

211 East 21st St. (2-3rd) NYC 10010 212-777-4477
Hours: 8-4 Mon-Fri

"Police equipment & accessories; handcuffs, billy clubs, flashlights, badges, holsters; nice people." ed.

Marco Co. 212-966-6025
187 Lafayette St. (Grand-Broome) NYC 10013
Hours: 9-4 Mon-Fri
"Holsters, belts." ed.

B. Schlesinger & Sons Inc. 212-206-8022
249 West 18th (7-8th) NYC 10011
Hours: 9-6 Mon-Fri/ 10-5 Sat
"Uniforms, handcuffs, nightsticks." ed.

Smith & Grey Corp. 212-674-1400
44 East 20th St. (B'way-Park) NYC 10003
Hours: 9-5 Mon-Fri
"Nightsticks, handcuffs, accessories." ed.

Smith & Warren Co. 212-966-1917
154 Grand St. (Centre-Lafayette) NYC 10013
Hours: 8-4:30 Mon-Fri
"Badges, insignia, handcuffs, leather goods." ed.

Some's Uniforms 201-843-1199
65 Rt. 17, Paramus, NJ 07652 212-564-6274
Hours: 9-6 Mon-Sat (Tues, Thurs til 9)
"Uniforms, nightsticks, handcuffs, holsters; wholesale; catalog." ed.

POSTERS & PRINTS

See also MEMORABILIA, THEATRE & FILM

Argosy Book Stores Inc. 212-753-4455
116 East 59th St. (Park-Lexington) NYC 10022
Hours: 9-6 Mon-Fri
"Prints, maps, out-of-print books." ed.

Margo Feiden Galleries 212-677-5330
51 East 10th St. (B'way-University) NYC 10003
Hours: 11-6 Mon-Fri/ 2-5 Sat
"Art and drama prints, lithographs, Hirschfield drawings." ed.

Andrew Kolb & Son Ltd. 212-684-2980
112 Madison Ave. (30th) NYC 10016
Hours: 8-4:30 Mon-Fri
"Framed posters and prints, old and new." ed.

Lee's Studio Gallery 212-265-5670
211 West 57th St. (B'way-7th) NYC 10019
Hours: 9:30-6:30 Mon-Fri/ 9:30-6 Sat
"Contemporary art posters and lighting fixtures." ed.

Phyllis Lucas Gallery 212-755-1516
981 Second Ave. (52nd) NYC 10022 212-753-1441
Hours: 9-5:30 Tues-Sat
"Rental of framed and unframed prints." ed.

Nostalgia Decorating Co. 717-288-1795
PO Box 1312, Kingston, PA 18704
Hours: 9-5 Mon-Fri
"Repro prints, ads, magazine covers; $50 minimum wholesale, any quantity retail; brochure." ed.

Oestreicher's Prints 212-719-1212
43 West 46th St. (5-6th) NYC 10036
Hours: 9-5 Mon-Fri
"Good stock, custom orders take 2 weeks; custom framing service available." ed.

Pageant Book & Print Shop 212-674-5296
109 East 9th St. (3-4th) NYC 10003
Hours: 10-6:30 Mon-Sat
"Older type prints and etchings, also book rental and purchase." ed.

Personality Posters 212-977-3210
653 Eleventh Ave. (47-48th) NYC 10036
Hours: 10-5 Mon-Fri
"Call first for in-stock personality posters." ed.

J. Pocker & Son Inc. 212-838-5488
824 Lexington Ave. (63rd) NYC 10021
Hours: 9-5:30 Mon-Sat
"Good stock posters, prints; custom orders within two weeks; framing service available." ed.

Poster America/Yesterday 212-206-0499
138 West 18th St. (6-7th) NYC 10011
Hours: 11-6 Tues-Sat
"Original American and European posters 1890-1950; original movie posters- silent to 1960; rental available." ed.

Poster Mat 212-228-4027
37 West 8th St. (5-6th) NYC 10011
Hours: 10-8 Mon-Sat
"Rock & Roll posters." ed.

Posters Originals Ltd. Art Posters 212-861-0422
924 Madison Ave. (73rd) NYC 10021
Hours: 10-6 Mon-Sat
"Contemporary American art posters." ed.

Star Magic 212-228-7770
743 Broadway (8th-Waverly) NYC 10003
Hours: 12-9 Mon-Sat/ 12-7 Sun
"Space related posters, books, star maps and finders." ed.

TRITON GALLERIES INC. 212-765-2472
323 West 45th St. (8-9th) NYC 10036
Hours: 10-6 Mon-Sat

Most complete collection of Broadway posters. Phone orders accepted with credit card. Picture and poster framing.

"Also some foreign theatre and film posters." ed.

POTTERY & GREENWARE

Ceramic Supply of NY & NJ Inc. 212-475-7236
534 La Guardia Pl. (Bleecker) NYC 10012
Hours: 9-6 Mon-Fri/ 10-5 Sat
"Ceramic materials and supplies." ed.

The Clay Pot 718-788-6564
162 Seventh Ave. (Carroll) Bklyn 11215
Hours: 10:30-6:30 Mon-Wed,Sat/ 10:30-7:30 Thurs,Fri/ 12-5 Sun
"A 'pottery gallery' featuring a number of quality potters; nice stuff."

Earthworks & Artisans 212-873-5220
251 West 85th St. (B'way) NYC 10024
Hours: 1-7 Mon-Fri/ 12-5 Sat, Sun
"Nice pottery pieces: bowls, vases, mugs, tea sets." ed.

Adele Lewis Inc. 212-594-5075
101 West 28th St. (6-7th) NYC 10001
Hours: 8-5 Mon-Fri
"Ethnic pottery small and large; also, baskets, primitive musical instruments; (formerly Potcovers)." ed.

Mad Monk 212-242-6678
500 Sixth Ave. (12-13th) NYC 10011
Hours: 11-7 Mon-Sat/ 12-7 Sun
"Basic pottery: mugs, tea sets, bowls, platters, gift items." ed.

Mud, Sweat & Tears 212-974-9121
654 Tenth Ave. (46th) NYC 10036
Hours: 12-6 every day
"Nice gift selection and classes." ed.

Perosi Ceramic Studio 718-981-9686
166 Morningstar Rd., Staten Island, NY 10303
Hours: 10-3 Mon-Wed/ also Tues eves. 7:30-10:30
"Greenware, ceramic supplies, classes, glazes, kilns, molds; call for directions." ed.

Pottery World 212-242-2903
807 Sixth Ave. (27-28th) NYC 10001
Hours: 7-4:30 Mon-Fri/ 10-5 Sat
"Wholesale terra cotta and glazed pottery, vases, planters; baskets."

Stefanie Ceramics 201-436-3161
973 Broadway, Bayonne, NJ 07002
Hours: 10-10 Mon-Thurs/ 10-2 Fri,Sat
"Greenware; see Mario." ed.

Supermud Pottery 212-865-9190
2875 Broadway (111-112th) NYC 10025
Hours: 10-9 M/ 12-10 T/ 12-6 W/ 12-9 Th/ 10-6 Fri/ 12-6 Sat,Sun
"Pottery, also classes available." ed.

PRINTING & COPYING

Allied Reproductions 212-943-9067
11 Stone St. 5th Fl. (B'way-Whitehall) NYC 10004
Hours: 9-5 Mon-Thurs/ 9-8 Fri
"Offset printing, good service, inexpensive." ed.

Ampex Copy World 212-889-1400
135 Madison Ave. (31-32nd) NYC 10016
Hours: 8:30-5:30 Mon-Fri
"Color, black and white photostats, great color xerox service." ed.

Atlantic Blue Print Co. Inc. 212-755-3388
575 Madison Ave. (57th) NYC 10022
Hours: 9-5 Mon-Fri
"Blueprinting, offset, xerox; pick-up and delivery." ed.

Boro Blue Print Co. Inc. 718-625-3227
52 Court St. (Joralemon-Livingston) Bklyn 11201
Hours: 9-5 Mon-Fri
"Blueprints, photostats." ed.

Circle Blue Print Co. 212-265-3674
225 West 57th St. (B'way) NYC 10019
Hours: 9-5 Mon-Fri
"Blueline, blackline, sepia; large size xerox, xerox reductions." ed.

Columbia Blue & Photoprint Co. Inc. 212-532-9425
14 East 39th St. (5-6th) NYC 10016
Hours: 9-5:30 Mon-Fri
"Blueprints, xerox, photostats, offset." ed.

Corinne Offset 212-777-8083
737 Broadway (8th-Waverly) NYC 10003
Hours: 8-6 Mon-Fri
"Very dependable, reasonable; specializes in resumes." ed.

East Side Copy Center 212-807-0465
15 East 13th St. (5th-B'way) NYC 10003
Hours: 9-10 Mon-Fri/ 10-6 Sat/ 12-6 Sun
"Color copying, Kodak Ektaprint." ed.

A. Esteban & Co. 212-989-7000
8-10 West 19th St. (5-6th) NYC 10011
Hours: 9-5 Mon-Fri
"Blueprints, sepias, giant xerox to 24": pickup and delivery service available." ed.

Ever Ready Blue Print 212-228-3131
200 Park Ave. South (17th) NYC 10003
Hours: 9-5:30 Mon-Sat/ 12-4 Sun
"Blueprints, sepias, mylar prints: giant xerox to 36" wide (variable enlargement & reduction) on bond, vellum and mylar film; flier." ed.

Exchange Photo Offset Corp. 212-962-4040
111 Broadway (Lower Lobby) NYC 10006
Hours: 9-5:30 Mon-Fri
"Offset; good rag paper; very nice work." ed.

57th St. Copy Center 212-581-8046
151 West 57th St. (6-7th) NYC 10019
Hours: 8:15-5:15 Mon-Thurs/ 8:15-2:30 Fri
"Full service xerox, color xerox from slides." ed.

Grass Roots Press 212-732-0557
6 Murray St. (Church-B'way) NYC 10007
Hours: 10-5 Mon-Fri
"Offset printing, binding; wonderful people and prices." ed.

Hamilton Copy Center

967 Lexington Ave. (70th) NYC 10021 212-535-2456
Hours: 8-7 Mon-Fri/ 9-5 Sat

2933 Broadway (114-115th) NYC 10025 212-666-3179
Hours: 8-11:30pm Mon-Fri/ 9-7 Sat/ 10-6 Sun

"Xerox, color xerox, labels." ed.

Hart Multi-Copy Inc. 212-730-0277
152 West 42nd St. (B'way-6th) NYC 10036
Hours: 9-5 Mon-Fri
"Xerox, offset, typesetting." ed.

Harvest Printing 212-246-8635
250 West 54th St. (B'way-8th) NYC 10019
Hours: 9-4:45 Mon-Fri
"Newspaper reprints, typesetting, presswork, binding, business stationery." ed.

HEUSTON COPY

11 Waverly Place (Greene-Waverly) NYC 10003 212-222-2180
2372 Broadway (86th) NYC 10024 212-222-2149

(continues next page)

HEUSTON COPY (continued)
2879 Broadway (112th) NYC 10025 212-222-2149
Hours: 8-11 Mon-Thurs/ 8-9 Fri/ 9-9 Sat/ 12-11 Sun

Open Late! Reductions, Enlargements, Color Xerox, Transparencies.

"Labels, card stock, binding, free collating." ed.

Image Bound 212-686-0773
220 East 23rd St. (2-3rd) NYC 10010
Hours: 9-6 Mon-Fri
"Photostats, Kodak photocopies." ed.

Images 212-889-8510
9 East 37th St. 8th Fl. (Madison-5th) NYC 10016
Hours: 24 hours
"Typesetting; expensive, very good and reliable; see Steve Mahler."

Independent Printing Co.

215 East 42nd St. (2-3rd) NYC 10017 (pickups) 212-661-3222
Hours: 8:30-5:30 Mon-Fri

141 East 25th St. (Lexington-3rd) NYC 10010 (plant) 212-689-5100
Hours: 8:30-5 Mon-Fri

"Blueprinting on a variety of stocks; photostats at 42nd St.; rush service may be available." ed.

Lettering Directions Inc. 212-869-3130
29 West 38th St. 6th Fl. (5-6th) NYC 10018
Hours: 8:30-8 Mon-Fri
"Typesetting; any kind you want." ed.

Millner Brothers 212-966-1810
472 Broome St. (Greene-Wooster) NYC 10013
Hours: 8-4 Mon-Fri
"Offset printing." ed.

National Reprographics Inc.

110 West 32nd St. (6-7th) NYC 10001 212-736-5674
Hours: 9-4:30 Mon-Fri

666 Third Ave. (42-43rd) NYC 10017 212-736-5674
Hours: 9-4:30 Mon-Fri

"Blueprinting, photostats, xerox, color xerox, B & W and color acetate xerox." ed.

Park Slope Typing & Copy Center 718-783-0268
90 Seventh Ave. (Berkley-Union) Bklyn 11217
Hours: 8:30-6:30 Mon-Fri/ 10-5 Sat/ 12-5 Sun
"Typing, word processing, Kodak copies, printing." ed.

Penny Copy Center 212-222-6047
2643 Broadway (100-101st) NYC 10025
Hours: 8-9 Mon-Fri/ 10-6 Sat/ 12-6 Sun
"Xerox: reductions, acetate; self-service machine; offset printing."

Perfection Blue Print Co. Inc. 212-541-9060
6 West 48th St.(#1 Rockefeller Pl. Concourse, Shop #6) NYC 10020
Hours: 9-5 Mon-Fri
"Blueprinting, blueprint reduction on bond or vellum; call ahead for while-you-wait service." ed.

Preferred Typographics 718-339-3800
2209 Coney Island Ave. (Ave. R-S) Bklyn 11223
Hours: 9-5:30 Mon-Thurs/ 9-5 Fri
"Typesetting, photostats, paste-ups: reliable.

Pro Print Copy Center

134 Fifth Ave. (18th) NYC 10011 212-807-1900
Hours: 8:30-6 Mon-Fri/ 10-4 Sat

236 Park Ave. South (19th) NYC 10003 212-677-7691
Hours: 8:30-6 Mon-Fri/ 10-4 Sat

51 East 19th St. (5-6th) NYC 10003 212-473-3200
Hours: 8:30-6 Mon-Fri/ 10-4 Sat

41 East 28th St. (Park-Madison) NYC 10016 212-685-4990
Hours: 8:30-6 Mon-Fri/ 10-4 Sat

51 West 43rd St. (5-6th) NYC 10036 212-302-0446
Hours: 8:30-6 Mon-Fri/ 10-4 Sat

"Printing, Xerox, stats, veloxes, color stats, color Xerox, typesetting, layout/design." ed.

Remco Press Inc. 212-242-4647
54 West 21st St. (5-6th) NYC 10010
Hours: 9-5 Mon-Fri
"Good offset printing; see Tony or Paul; very nice, helpful, good prices." ed.

S M P Graphic Service Center (Stat Shop) 212-254-2282
26 East 22nd St. (B'way-Park Ave. S.) NYC 10010
Hours: 24 hours Mon-Fri/ 11-6 Sat, Sun
"Color and B & W photostats, dry mounting, blow-ups, many other services." ed.

Speed-Graphics 212-486-0209
150 East 58th St. (Lexington-3rd) NYC 10155
Hours: 10-6 Mon-Fri
"See Chuck for photostats; very good, prompt service; print mounting."

Stat Store 212-929-0566
148 Fifth Ave. (19-20th) NYC 10011
Hours: 9-6:30 Mon-Fri/ 12-4 Sat, Sun
"B & W and color xerox, B & W and color photostats, cibachromes." ed.

Studio 305 Inc. 212-724-8758
305 Amsterdam Ave. (74-75th) NYC 10023
Hours: 9-6:30 Mon-Fri/ 10-6 Sat
"Xerox, color and B & W photostats, offset." ed.

380 Services 212-255-6652
380 Bleecker St. (Perry-Charles) NYC 10014
Hours: 8-8:30pm Mon-Fri/ 10-6 Sat/ 12-5 Sun
"Color xerox; excellent service." ed.

Unsloppy Copy Shop 212-254-7336
5 West 8th St. (5th Ave) NYC 10011
Hours: 8:30-10pm M-Th/ 8:30-8 F/ 10-7 Sat/ 12-6 Sun
"Color xerox, reduction, enlargement, offset, B & W and color photostats." ed.

PROP & SCENIC CRAFTSPEOPLE

Susan D. Andrews 301-685-3200
700 N. Calvert St., Center Stage, Baltimore, MD 21202
Hours: By appt.
"Props, set dressing, design ass't., illustration." ed.

Charley Beal 212-260-2912
203 Bleecker St. #7 (6th-MacDougal) NYC 10012
Hours: By appt.
"USA Local 829 set designer." ed.

Joanne Beckerich 201-963-8575
400 Madison St. (4th St.) Hoboken, NJ 07030
Hours: By appt.
"Displays, exhibits, showrooms, trade shows, graphics." ed.

Sharon Braunstein 404-898-1133
1280 Peachtree St. NE, Alliance Theatre, Atlanta, GA 30309
Hours: By appt.
"Sculptor, upholsterer, shopper, craftsperson, propmaster." ed.

Josie Caruso 212-876-8551
327 East 89th St. #4W (1-2nd) NYC 10128
Hours: By appt.
"Model construction." ed.

The ATAC Job Referral Service is a valuable resource that puts the prospective employer in contact with the right artists and craftspeople to meet their needs. Names and telephone numbers are provided. Not only does the Job Referral Service benefit the freelance artist but it offers the employer access to a diversified pool of creative talent.

Call the ATAC Job Referral Service (212) 586-1925.

Hours: 10 a.m.-6 p.m. Mon.-Fri.

ATAC, The Association of Theatrical Artists and Craftspeople, is a professional trade association for craftspeople working in the production fields of entertainment, performance, and presentational media industries. Its membership represents many areas of expertise – props, special effects, puppets, display, shop management, design, etc. For more information on ATAC – Call (718) 596-0501.

* *The Job Referral Service is administered by TAP — Technical Assistance Project — a professional service of the American Dance Festival.*

Production Design
Scenic Design
Art Direction
Costume Design
Stylists
Lighting Design
Scenic Artists
Mural Artists
Modelmakers
Specialty Prop
Specialty Costume
Special Effects
Crafts

for film, stage and television in the United States, Canada, and Britain

Register 85

ORDER YOUR COPY TODAY

PER COPY	**$30.00**
POSTAGE & HANDLING	**$ 3.50**

NEW YORK RESIDENTS ADD SALES TAX

SEND FULL PAYMENT ALONG WITH NAME AND ADDRESS TO:

Lymelite Group Inc.
G.P.O. Box 1260
New York, N.Y. 10116

Nadine Charlsen 718-625-0262
364 Union St. #2 (Smith-Hoyt) Bklyn 11231
Hours: By appt.
"Set and prop design and construction, lighting design, Equity S.M."

Eileen Connor 212-246-6346
PO Box 154 Radio City Sta. NYC 10101
Hours: By appt.
"Scenic painting, fabric painting, prop and costume crafts, millinery/headdresses." ed.

Kevin Daley 718-326-1130
59-42 57 Rd., Maspeth, NY 11378
Hours: By appt.
"Carpentry, properties building and buying, metalwork, furniture construction and repair." ed.

June DeCamp 212-568-9331
120 Haven Ave. #22 (172nd) NYC 10032
Hours: By appt.
"Scenic painting, trompe l'oeil, costume crafts." ed.

Sal Denaro 718-875-1711
174 Degraw St. (Bond-Nevins) Bklyn 11232
Hours: By appt.
"Character design puppets, props, stop-motion models, soft sculpture."

Michael Denney 212-861-7303
23 East 74th St. #14B (Madison-5th) NYC 10021
Hours: By appt.
"Set decorator, prop shopper." ed.

Stephen Edelstein 212-666-9198
771 West End Ave. #4C (97th) NYC 10025
Hours: By appt.
"Scenic/lighting designer, tech director; scenery, prop construction, painting, cars." ed.

Karen Beth Eliot 212-410-4106
1469 Lexington Ave. #71 (95th) NYC 10128
Hours: By appt.
"Upholstery, soft goods, shopper, shop manager, scenic artist, set decorator, crafts." ed.

David Ellertson 212-736-8730
400 West 43rd St. #23R (9th) NYC 10036
Hours: By appt.
"Woodworking, furniture, models, fiberglas, foams, weaponry." ed.

Robin Farbman 212-580-1291
225 West 80th St. (Broadway) NYC 10024
Hours: 'round the clock, every day.
"Sculptor/designer, props and prototypes for display and promotional purposes, product designer." ed.

Marjorie Fedyszyn 718-596-4655
360 Union St. #D1 (Smith-Hoyt) Bklyn 11231
Hours: By appt.
"Prop shopping, styling, modelmaking, set decoration." ed.

James Feng 718-499-1601
425 14th St. #A2 (8th) Bklyn 11215
Hours: By appt.
"Scenery, props, costumes, models; designed, built & painted." ed.

Joseph Fiore 516-867-1812
66 Hayes St., Freeport, NY 11520
Hours: By appt.
"Carpentry (rough and finishing), painting, drawing, metalwork, modelmaking." ed.

Elizabeth Fischer 718-643-3949
72A Fourth Ave. (Bergen) Bklyn 11217
Hours: By appt.
"Set design/dressing, scenic painting, sculpting, prop fabrication."

Robert Flanagan 718-636-6280
124 Hall St. (Myrtle Ave.) Bklyn 11205
Hours: By appt.
"Puppets, masks, props, special effects." ed.

Thom Flowers 718-389-8574
13A Newel St. (Nassau-Driggs) Bklyn 11222
Hours: By appt.
"Modelmaking, furniture construction, metalwork, moldmaking, fiberglassing, celastic, sculpture, drafting." ed.

FLYING ROBERT THEATRICAL CRAFTS 212-334-9130
101 Wooster St. (Spring) NYC 10012
Hours: By appt.
Specialty costumes and masks: foam rubber, celastic, latex rubber, etc. Duplication and multiples.
"Speak to Charles Kulziski." ed.

Dan Folkus 609-858-9736
465 Haddon Ave., Collingswood, NJ 08108 212-929-7988
Hours: By appt.
"Murals, sculpture, animatics and exhibit designs." ed.

Michael Foxworthy 212-397-1119
430 West 49th St. #14 (9-10th) NYC 10019
Hours: By appt.
"Set decorator, set design, model construction." ed.

Nomi Fredrick 212-348-8944
409 East 90th St. (1st-York) NYC 10128
Hours: By appt.
"Special effects, sculpture, puppets, props, creatures, models, prototypes, foam latex." ed.

Christine Fye 212-243-8703
147 West 22nd St. (6-7th) NYC 10011
Hours: By appt.
"Sculpting in plastine & clay, portraiture, decorative animals, figurine restoration." ed.

Elizabeth Goodall 212-477-6437
175 Bleecker #4 (MacDougal) NYC 10012
Hours: By appt.
"Prop making, scenic painting, sculpting, moldmaking, costume painting." ed.

Richard Hoover 212-662-5455
240 West 98th St. (Broadway) NYC 10025
Hours: 9-5 Mon-Sat
"Scenic carpentry, painting, modelbuilding, props, celastic, fiberglas, foam, welding." ed.

MARTIN IZQUIERDO STUDIO LTD. 212-807-9757
118 West 22nd St. 9th Fl. (6-7th) NYC 10011
Hours: By appt.
Costume painting, props, masks, silkscreening, creatures and graphic design. Rosco and Haussmann Distributor.
"Also sells English tutu net and tubular horsehair." ed.

Susan Johnson 212-369-9594
1469 Lexington Ave. #33 (95th) NYC 10128
Hours: By appt.
"Scenic artist, light carpentry and sewing, assorted craft skills, furniture restoration." ed.

Robert W. Jones 212-410-4341
329 East 92nd St. #3B (1-2nd) NYC 10128
Hours: By appt.
"Props for theatre and commercials; masks, celastic fabricator." ed.

Warren Jorgenson 212-369-1642
309 East 92nd St. #2A (1-2nd) NYC 10128
Hours: By appt.
"Set design, furniture and hand props; foams, resins, sculpting." ed.

CLAUDIA KAVENAGH 212-666-5682
220 West 98th St. (B'way) NYC 10025
Hours: By appt.
"Own shop: carpentry, furniture construction & repair; sculptural props, upholstery." ed.

Vikki Kite 718-852-7791
105 Bergen St. #4 (Smith-Hoyt) Bklyn 11201
Hours: By appt.
"Sculpting, celastic, latex, lettering, scene painting." ed.

Janet Knechtel 01-431-1835
41 Florence St., London, England N1
Hours: By appt.
"Crafts: oversized cast shoes, specialty costumes, puppets, props." ed.

Valerie Kuehn 201-798-0537
525 Monroe St., Hoboken, NJ 07030
Hours: By appt.
"Properties artist, scenic sculptor, moldmaking, fiberglas casting and fabrication." ed.

Beth Kushnick 212-924-0729
400 West 25th St. #1F (9th) NYC 10001
Hours: By appt.
"Art direction, propmaster, stylist." ed.

Robin S. Kusten 718-789-1737
246 Vanderbilt Ave. (Dekalb) Bklyn 11205
Hours: 9-5 Mon-Fri
"Soft sculpture, 3-D illustration, props, sets, costumes." ed.

T. C. LaBiche 718-802-9484
159 Carroll St. #1L (Clinton-Henry) Bklyn 11231
Hours: By appt.
"Prop, display and scenic construction and painting; model construction." ed.

Cathy Lazar Inc. 212-473-0363
155 East 23rd St. (Lexington-3rd) NYC 10010
Hours: By appt.
"Specialty costumes, soft props for TV, film, print, performance, promotion." ed.

Herbert Leith Design 201-871-9532
250 Walnut St. (Brayton St.) Englewood, NJ 07631
Hours: By appt.
"Specialty costumes, puppets, soft props, special effects for stage and film." ed.

Marleen Marta 212-989-4684
25 Grove St. (Bedford-Bleecker) NYC 10014
Hours: By appt.
"Masks, props, scenic and costume painting, set decoration." ed.

Deborah Alix Martin 718-499-4649
580 Tenth St. (7-8th) Bklyn 11215
Hours: By appt.
"Prop/scenic construction, all materials." ed.

Susan McClain-Moore/MCL Designs Inc. 212-206-7500
31 West 21st St. 7th Fl. (5-6th) NYC 10010
Hours: 9-5 Mon-Fri
"Customized full-figure body puppets, hand puppets, props and masks."

KAREN McDUFFEE 718-643-1655
72A Fourth Ave. (Bergen) Bklyn 11217
Hours: By appt.
"Propmaster: co-ordination, shopping, construction, soft goods; costume crafts; prompt, reliable." ed.

Francie Anne McGuire 201-332-6003
23 Old Bergen Rd., Jersey City, NJ 07305
Hours: By appt.
"Scenic artist, faux finishes, trompe l'oeil murals; stage, film, interiors." ed.

James P. McHugh 212-222-3509
110 West 94th St. #2A (Columbus) NYC 10025 718-643-0990
Hours: By appt.
"Lighting design, electrics, electrification of props." ed.

Betsy McKearnan 718-788-1942
616 Second St. (8th-Prospect) Bklyn 11215 212-902-2286
Hours: By appt.
"Craftsperson, prop builder, shopper, experienced prop master." ed.

Maria R. McNamara 612-224-7267
677 Oakdale Ave., St. Paul, MN 55107
Hours: By appt.
"Puppets, props, masks, costume crafts." ed.

Zoe Morsette 718-784-8894
11-46 46 Ave. #2-I (11th) L.I.C. 11101
Hours: By appt.
"Costume props, props, millinery, display, miniature work, soft sculpture." ed.

Lyndon Mosse 212-724-5413
160 West End Ave. (66th) NYC 10023
Hours: By appt.
"Store, window and interior design: visual merchandising." ed.

Christopher Murphy 212-543-5902
3605 Sedgwick Ave. #B12, Bronx, NY 10463
Hours: By appt.
"Model building, props, scenic art, display." ed.

Ronald Naversen
c/o Theatre Dept., Univ of Florida, Gainesville, FL 32611
Hours: By appt.
"Properties design." ed.

Andrew Ness 718-204-0287
23-17 38th St. #1R (23rd) Astoria, NY 11105
Hours: By appt.
"Drafting, modelmaking, set dressing, styrofoam carving, plastics, upholstery, shopping." ed.

FREDERICK NIHDA STUDIO 212-966-1886
279 Church St. (White St.) NYC 10013
Hours: 10-6 Mon-Fri
Custom Props & Costumes for Theatre, Film, Promotions, TV.
"Body puppets, masks, jewelry, armor, mechanisms, and hand props." ed.

V. A. (Tori) Nourafchan 212-673-0642
514 East 5th St. #8 (Ave. A) NYC 10009
Hours: By appt.
"Scenic designer, display work, scenic artist." ed.

NINO NOVELLINO/COSTUME ARMOUR INC. 914-534-9120
PO Box 325, Shore Road, Cornwall-on-Hudson, NY 12520 212-585-1199
Hours: 9-4 Mon-Fri
Sculpture, props, armor, vacuum forming, artificial food, masks, display. Credits: 'Cats', 'La Cage', 'Singin in the Rain'. (See display ad page 299.)
"20 years of theatrical service." ed.

Irvin K. (Abby) Okin 212-663-0483
244 West 102nd St. #1B (West End Ave-B'way) NYC 10025
Hours: By appt.
"Propmaster: co-ordination, construction, shopping, trick props; theatre and film." ed.

Dennis Paver 212-924-9411
41 Union Sq. W. #206 (B'way-17th) NYC 10003
Hours: 10-6 Mon-Fri
"Costume design, construction, illustration; costumes, props for theatre, display." ed.

Robin Lu Payne 718-383-5329
159 Milton St. #2W, Bklyn 11222
Hours: By appt.
"Scenic designer, prop crafts, scenic artist, sculpture, upholstery."

Enrique Plested 212-799-2950
126 Riverside Dr. #6A (85th) NYC 10024
Hours: By appt.
"Sculpting, moldmaking, casting, portraiture, model building, hand finishing of costumes." ed.

Derald G. Plumer Ltd. 212-243-2089
153 West 27th St. #502 (6-7th) NYC 10001
Hours: By appt.
"Repairs and custom furniture built to designer's specifications." ed.

John A. Ralbovsky 212-410-4106
1469 Lexington Ave. #71 (95th) NYC 10128
Hours: By appt.
"Scenic artist, props craftsman, foam sculpture, applique and painted finishes." ed.

Leslie Rollins 212-222-3509
110 West 94th St. #2A (Columbus) NYC 10025 718-643-0990
Hours: By appt.
"Flower arrangements." ed.

Jim Rule 305-586-7842
9 North C St. #D, Lake Worth, FL 33460
Hours: By appt.
"Production designer, art director; props for film and video." ed.

Catherine Schmitt 201-224-6272
744 Undercliff Ave., Edgewater, NJ 07020
Hours: By appt.
"All types of sculpture, especially prototypes; all media." ed.

Linda C. Schultz 212-222-0477
125 West 96th St. #6J (Columbus-Amsterdam) NYC 10025
Hours: By appt.
"Costumer, stylist, wardrobe cutter, draper, soft goods (props)." ed.

Lisa Shaftel 212-249-2581
332 East 74th St. #4B (1-2nd) NYC 10021
Hours: 10-6 Mon-Sat
"Scenic/lighting design, scene painting, carpentry, puppets, animal figures, masks." ed.

Nina A. Sheffy 212-662-0709
838 West End Ave. (101st) NYC 10025
Hours: By appt.
"Set decorator and still life stylist." ed.

Christopher Shriver 212-925-0933
144 Franklin St. (6th-Varick) NYC 10013
Hours: By appt.
"Scenic and lighting design, especially for industrials." ed.

C. J. Simpson 212-924-3272
401 West 24th St. #16 (9th) NYC 10011
Hours: By appt.
"Model construction." ed.

David Smith 212-595-8626
127 West 85th St. #3B (Amsterdam-Columbus) NYC 10024 212-730-1188
Hours: By appt.
"Set decorator, prop shopper, designer's asst; member NABET outside props." ed.

Daphne Stevens-Pascucci 212-724-9898
146 West 73rd St. #2B (Columbus) NYC 10023
Hours: By appt.
"Costume and scenic artist, fabric designing, painting, distressing, dyeing." ed.

Richard Tautkus 212-691-8253
100 West 23rd St. (6th) NYC 10011
Hours: By appt.
"Specialty props, masks, millinery, etc." ed.

Kathy Urmson 718-522-0368
252 Carlton Ave. (DeKalb-Willoughby) Bklyn 11205
Hours: By appt.
"Trompe l'oeil, faux finishes, glazing, stenciling and other decorative painted finishes." ed.

Mark Victor Venaglia 212-691-1141
244 West 21st St. (7-8th) NYC 10011
Hours: By appt.
"Scenic artist, set designer and assistant; theatre/mural restoration." ed.

Linda Vigdor 212-289-1218
53 East 97th St. #1B (Madison) NYC 10029
Hours: By appt.
"Painter/designer, murals, trompe l'oeil; scenic art." ed.

Brad Williams 212-865-0088
214 Riverside Dr. #109 (94th) NYC 10025
Hours: 9-9 Mon-Fri
"Puppets designed, built, performed for stage, film, video; masks, props, graphics." ed.

THE WINTER CO. INC. 718-499-2206
323 Sixth St. Top Fl. (5th) Bklyn 11215
Hours: By appt.
"Fine arts, costume crafts, props, custom exhibitry, electronics." ed.

Louise Gartlemann Young 212-675-7497
243 West 21st St. #1D (7-8th) NYC 10011
Hours: 9-6 Mon-Fri
"Puppets, costume props, lifesized creatures, soft sculpture construction." ed.

Scott Yuille 718-858-4161
59 Strong Place (Kane-DeGraw) Bklyn 11231
Hours: By appt.
"Experience in stage properties, lighting design, technical director."

ANNETTE ZYGAROWICZ 718-272-5281
9235 Foster Ave. (93rd) Bklyn 11236
Hours: By appt.
"Freelance: illustration, collage, set decorator, props, graphic design." ed.

PROP RENTAL HOUSES

Cinema Galleries Ltd. 212-244-2243
515 West 26th St. (10-11th) NYC 10001
Hours: 8-5 Mon-Fri (closed 12-1)
"Limited selection 20's, 30's, 40's furniture and prop rental." ed.

EARLY HALLOWEEN 212-691-2933
10 West 19th St. (5-6th) NYC 10011 212-243-1499
Hours: 12-6 Mon-Fri
Vintage luggage, kitchenware, linens, drapes. Diverse collection of memorabilia.
"Also carry vintage clothing." ed.

Eclectic Properties Inc. 212-799-8963
204 West 84th St. (B'way-Amsterdam) NYC 10024
Hours: 9-5 Mon-Fri/ or by appt.
"Furniture, hand props and dressing, ephemera and research service; see Suri." ed.

Encore Studio 212-246-5237
410 West 47th St. (9-10th) NYC 10036
Hours: 9-4:30 Mon-Fri
"Know what you want before you go: 6 floors, a million unusual items."

Kenmore Leasing Corp. 212-683-1888
352 Park Ave. South (25th) NYC 10010
Hours: 8-4:30 Mon-Fri
"Rental and purchase, modern and period furniture, dressings, props; see Ray Wolf." ed.

KUTTNER ANTIQUES 212-242-7969
56 West 22nd St. 5th Fl. (5-6th) NYC 10010
Hours: 10-5:30 Mon-Fri
American & English furniture, paintings, accessories, china, glassware, silver, linens, kitchenware. Rental only.
"Prefer short-term rentals for film and print work." ed.

New York Prop Rental 212-924-5111
Pier 62-North River (W.23/W. Side Hwy) NYC 10011
Hours: 9-5 Mon-Fri
"Period props, architectural pieces; see Shari for rentals." ed.

New York Shakespeare Festival 212-598-7100
425 Lafayette St. (8-Waverly) NYC 10003
Hours: 9:30-5 Mon-Fri (closed 1-2)
"Rentals from NYSF stock to not-for-profit theatres only." ed.

Newel Art Gallery 212-758-1970
425 East 53rd St. (Sutton-1st) NYC 10022
Hours: 9-5 Mon-Fri
"Extraordinary selection antique furniture, art, lamps, architectural pieces, all periods; rental or purchase." ed.

NICCOLINI ANTIQUES-PROP RENTALS 212-254-2900
114 East 25th St. (Park-Lexington) NYC 10010
Hours: 9:30-5 Mon-Fri
All Your Rental Needs! See our listing under 'Antiques'.
"See Ronnie or Rita." ed.

Nostalgia Alley 212-695-6578
547 West 27th St. 3rd Fl. (10-11th) NYC 10001
Hours: 10-6 Mon-Fri
"Americana, quilts, kitchenware, china; rental only; see Carol." ed.

The Prop House Inc. 212-713-0760
653 Eleventh Ave. 4th Fl. (48th) NYC 10036
Hours: 8-5 Mon-Fri
"Good source for period props." ed.

Props, Displays & Interiors Inc. 212-620-3840
132 West 18th St. (6-7th) NYC 10011
Hours: 9-5 Mon-Fri
"Rental or purchase of architectural elements; stock or custom work."

Props for Today 212-206-0330
15 West 20th St. 7/8th Fl. (5th) NYC 10011
Hours: 9-5 Mon-Fri
"Good selection contemporary furniture and decorative accessories; see Dyann Klein." ed.

Showroom Outlet 212-581-0470
625-35 West 55th St. (11-12th) NYC 10019
Hours: 9-4:30 Mon-Thurs/ 9-4 Fri
"Modern, specializes in short term rentals." ed.

State Supply Equipment Co. Inc. 212-645-1431
210 Eleventh Ave. (25th) NYC 10001
Hours: 8:30-5 Mon-Fri
"Good source for many items; large stock." ed.

PROP SHOPS

For display props see also DISPLAY HOUSES & MATERIALS

Arts and Crafters Inc. 718-875-8151
175 Johnson St. (Flatbush Ext.) Bklyn 11201
Hours: 9-5:30 Mon-Fri
"Sculpture, 3-D effect props in any material to your specifications."

Thomas Bramlett Assoc. Inc. 201-659-3565
219 Grand St. (2nd-3rd) Hoboken, NJ 07030 212-255-7018
Hours: 9-6 Mon-Fri
"Props, sculpture, painting, effects and scenery construction; space rental." ed.

Brooklyn Model Works 718-834-1944
60 Washington Ave. (Park-Flushing) Bklyn 11205
Hours: 9-5 Mon-Fri
"Casting and reproduction; machining, vacuumforming, breakaways, electrical-mechanical controls." ed.

COSTUME ARMOUR INC. 914-534-9120
PO Box 325, Shore Road, Cornwall-on-Hudson, NY 12520 212-585-1199
Hours: 9-4 Mon-Fri
Custom props, sculpture, vacuum forming, artificial food, masks, display figures. Credits: 'Cats', 'La Cage', 'Singin in the Rain'. (See display ad page 299.)
"Also theatrical weapons and armor of all periods." ed.

emptybirdcage studios 718-272-5281
9235 Foster Ave. Bklyn 11236
Hours: By appt.
"Props and graphics for theatre, display and film." ed.

McHUGH/ROLLINS ASSOCIATES INC. 718-643-0990
79 Bridge St. (York-Front) Bklyn 11201
Hours: 9-6 Mon-Fri
Complete service shop. Vacuumforming, Sculpting, Crafts, Soft Goods, Metal Fabrication, Painting, Upholstery, Breakaways. Individual items or complete productions. See Leslie or Jim. (See display ad page 300.)
"Props for theatre, film, commercials, interior displays." ed.

We are more than Just Armor Props, sculpture & vacuum forming

COSTUME ARMOUR, INC.
& CHRISTO-VAC

P.O. Box 325 Shore Road
Cornwall-on-Hudson, NY 12520
(914) 534-9120 (212) 585-1199
Nino Novellino, Sculptor

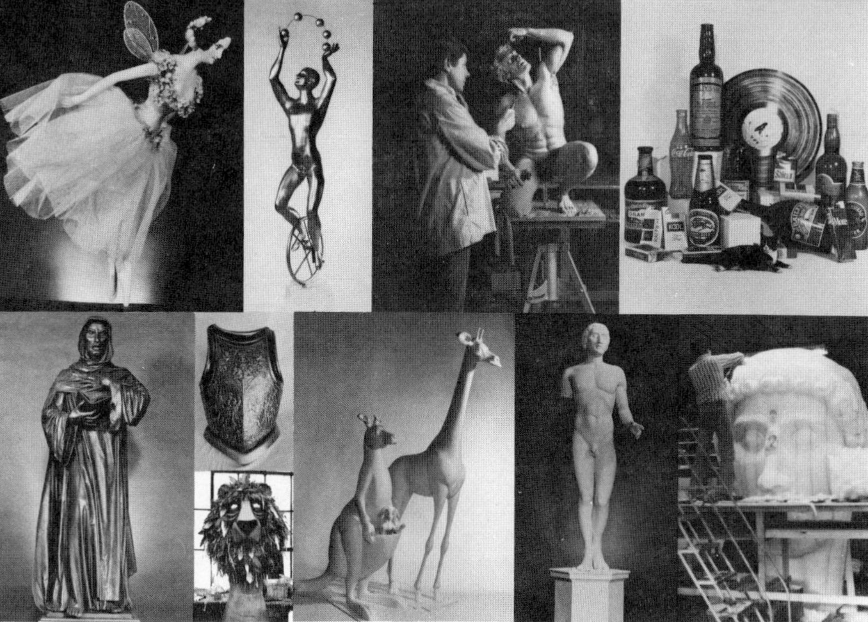

NOTES

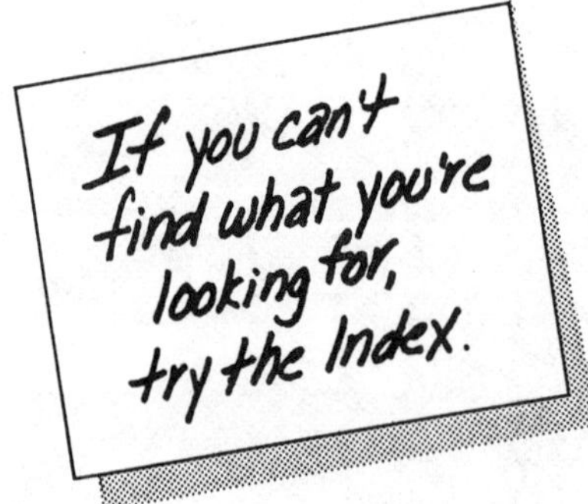
If you can't find what you're looking for, try the Index.

THE SET SHOP 212-929-4845
3 West 20th St. (5th) NYC 10011
Hours: 9-6 Mon-Fri/ 10-4 Sat
Custom props; mold making, from small to huge. All media. (See display ad page 316.)
"Full scene shop; non-union." ed.

Eoin Sprott Studio Ltd. 718-784-1407
Astoria Studio, 37-11 35th Ave., Astoria, NY 11106 718-784-1629
Hours: 8-5:30 Mon-Fri
"Custom props, model making, miniatures, sculpture/molds, mechanical animation rigs." ed.

PETER WEISS DESIGNS 212-477-2659
32 Union Square East (17th-Park Ave. S.) NYC 10003
Hours: 9-6 Mon-Fri
Props, models, miniature sets, castings, sculpture. (See display ad page 333.)
"Also special effects design and construction." ed.

PROPANE see WELDING SUPPLIES

PUPPETRY

Pam Arciero 203-429-0786
RFD #1, PO Box 210, Ashford, CT 06278 212-580-7257
Hours: By appt.
"Professional puppeteer; designs and builds puppets." ed.

Cheryl Blalock 212-799-5424
308 West 78th St. (West End Ave.-Riverside) NYC 10024 212-580-2800
Hours: By appt.
"Professional puppeteer for hand and rod puppets; commercials, TV, film." ed.

Edward G. Christie 212-799-0216
208 West 88th St. (B'way) NYC 10024
Hours: By appt.
"TV, stage, screen; puppet design and construction (no costume), puppeteer." ed.

Janet Delvoye 201-985-7381
7 Suydam Ave. #2, Edison, NJ 08817
Hours: By appt.
"Large-scale millinery, shoes, accessories for full-body characters."

Character costumes,
Puppets,
Props.
Mulder/Goodwin
1200 Broadway 2C, NYC, 10001
212-689-9037

NOTES

Call us.
212-724-6556
Discount coupons
given for new
sources
and corrections.

Sal Denaro 718-875-1711
174 Degraw St. (Bond-Nevins) Bklyn 11232
Hours: By appt.
"Puppet creator/designer; stop-motion models, foam latex and moldmaking." ed.

FANTASY FACTORY OF MANHATTAN INC. 201-656-3160
PO Box 1405, 1500 Hudson St., Hoboken, NJ 07030
Hours: By appt./ Answering Machine

Puppet Manufacturers, Costume Building, Animators. Several show packages including Christmas, Spectaculars, Theme Park Shows and Vegas Revues. Celebrity & Fantasy Puppets 6' to 25' tall! Industrial Shows, Commercial & TV Characters designed & created. Errol Manoff, director.

Robert Flanagan 718-636-6280
124 Hall St. (Myrtle Ave.) Bklyn 11205
Hours: By appt.
"Puppets, masks, props, special effects." ed.

Flexitoon Ltd. 212-877-2757
Craig and Olga Marin, creators
46 West 73rd St. Rm. 3A (Columbus-Central Park W.) NYC 10023
Hours: By appt.
"Designers, builders, and performers of flexible cartoon puppets." ed.

Nomi Fredrick 212-348-8944
409 East 90th St. (1st-York) NYC 10128
Hours: By appt.
"Special effects, sculpture, puppets, props, creatures, models, prototypes, foam latex." ed.

Fred Garbo 207-743-2860
PO Box 129, Norway, ME 04268
Hours: By appt.
"Puppeteer for full body puppets, hand and rod, puppet performance."

Jane Gootnick 212-724-2056
204 West 88th St. (B'way) NYC 10024
Hours: By appt.
"Puppets and special effects (radio-cable) creatures." ed.

Joanne Green 212-989-1664
39 Charles St. #3 (7th Ave. S.) NYC 10014 212-794-2400
Hours: By appt.
"Very high quality custom millinery for puppets." ed.

Lynn Hippen 212-757-2058
411 West 50th St. #2-B (Columbus-Amsterdam) NYC 10019
Hours: By appt.
"Professional puppeteer; designs/builds portrait puppets; celastic and puppet costumes." ed.

Jane Hirsh 203-974-2145
PO Box 204, Eastford, CT 06242
Hours: By appt.
"Design, sculpting, painting of puppets; puppeteer." ed.

Hudson Vagabond Puppets 914-359-1144
Lois Bohovesky, Director 914-735-5732
Van Wyck Ave., Blauvelt, NY 10913
Hours: By appt.
"Perform musicals with lifesized puppets; will build large-scale puppets." ed.

Larry Jameson 718-834-1714
390 Union St. (Smith-Hoyt) Bklyn 11231 212-794-2400
Hours: By appt.
"Electrical/mechanical, radio-control effects, puppets for TV and film." ed.

Janet Knechtel 01-431-1835
41 Florence St., London, England N1
Hours: By appt.
"Crafts: oversize cast shoes, specialty costumes, puppets, props." ed.

Kroupa's Kreatures (Jim Kroupa) 212-691-0699
429 West 24th St. #43 (9-10th) NYC 10011
Hours: By appt.
"Professional puppeteer; puppets for film, TV and stage." ed.

Herbert Leith Design 201-871-9532
250 Walnut St. (Brayton St.) Englewood, NJ 07631
Hours: By appt.
"Specialty costumes, puppets, soft props, special effects for stage and film." ed.

Susan McClain-Moore/MCL Designs Inc. 212-206-7500
31 West 21st St. 7th Fl. (5-6th) NYC 10010
Hours: 9-5 Mon-Fri
"Customized full-figure body puppets, hand puppets, props and masks."

Sherry McMorran 416-465-9752
31 Hampton Ave., Toronto, Ontario, Canada M4K2Y5
Hours: By appt.
"Puppet costumes." ed.

Maria R. McNamara 612-224-7267
677 Oakdale Ave., St. Paul, MN 55107
Hours: By appt.
"Hand and rod puppets; design and construction." ed.

Jim McPherson 201-795-0697
413 Washington St. #1, Hoboken, NJ 07030
Hours: By appt.
"Caricature puppets." ed.

MULDER/GOODWIN INC. 212-689-9037
1200 Broadway #2C (29th) NYC 10001
Hours: 9-6 Mon-Fri
Full body and hand puppets for television, theatre, and film.
(See display ad page 302.)
"See Mary Mulder or Rick Goodwin." ed.

National Theatre of Puppet Arts 516-487-3684
Carol Fijan, Director
58 Rose Ave., Great Neck, NY 11021
Hours: By appt.
"Performer oriented school for professionals, educators, others; available for commercials." ed.

John Orberg 212-741-2392
32 Leroy St. (Hudson) NYC 10014
Hours: By appt.
"Puppet characters for TV and film; soft toy prototypes." ed.

Pandemonium Puppet Co. 203-423-5882
Bart Roccoberton, Director
58 Spring St., Williamantic, CT 06226
Hours: By appt.
"Perform custom designed or package shows; video, commercials, live; workshops, residencies." ed.

Poko Puppets Inc. 718-522-0225
Larry Engler, Artistic Director.
12 Everit St., Bklyn 11201
Arthur Shafman Int'l Ltd, Business Manager 212-575-0488
Hours: By appt.
"Puppets/props: custom designed, created, performed for commercials, industrials, live shows." ed.

The Puppet Loft 212-431-7627
180 Duane St. (Greenwich St.-Hudson) NYC 10013
Hours: By appt.
"Exhibitions, rehearsal/performance space; available for performance engagements and workshops." ed.

The Puppet People 212-869-1600
c/o Mallory Factor Inc.
275 Seventh Ave. (26th) NYC 10001
Hours: By appt.
"Custom or package shows; commercials, industrials; body puppet, marionette construction." ed.

Puppet Works 718-638-5217
Nicholas Coppola, Director
287 3rd Ave. (Union) Bklyn 11215
Hours: By appt.
"Creates shows for touring schools; industrials, film, TV, workshops; primarily marionettes." ed.

Martin P. Robinson 212-406-9760
46 Gold St. (Fulton) NYC 10038
Hours: By appt.
"Professional puppeteer, puppet designer and builder." ed.

Jan Rosenthal 212-254-4991
126 St. Marks Place #18 (1st Ave.) NYC 10009
Hours: By appt.
"Character design, puppets, toy fabrication, soft and cast sculpture."

Jody Schoffner 718-726-1476
20-59 36th St. (20th) Astoria, NY 11105
Hours: 9-6 Mon-Fri
"Puppet maker; draper for stage or specialty costumes." ed.

Danny Segrin 212-227-5986
56 Warren St. (Church) NYC 10007
Hours: By appt.
"Professional puppeteer; puppets for film, TV and commercials." ed.

Lisa Shaftel 212-249-2581
332 East 74th St. #4B (1st-2nd) NYC 10021
Hours: By appt.
"Puppets, animal figures, masks; scenic/lighting design, scene painting, carpentry, puppets, animal figures, masks." ed.

Julie Taymor 212-475-4829
718 Broadway #10-C (Waverly) NYC 10003
Hours: By appt.
"Writer/director; designer: puppetry and masks for film, TV and theatre." ed.

Norman Tempia 212-348-8944
409 East 90th St. #1B (1st-York) NYC 10128
Hours: By appt.
"Sculpture, special props, masks and puppets for film and tape." ed.

Richard Termine 212-289-4057
434 East 89th St. #A (1st-York) NYC 10128
Hours: By appt.
"Puppet design and construction; puppeteer." ed.

David Velasquez 212-929-1724
523 Hudson St. #5RS (Charles) NYC 10014
Hours: By appt.
"Puppet clothes designed and built." ed.

Brad Williams 212-865-0088
214 Riverside Dr. #109 (94th) NYC 10025
Hours: 9-9 Mon-Fri
"Design, construction, puppeteer for theatre, film and video." ed.

Louise Gartlemann Young 212-675-7497
243 West 21st St. #1D (7-8th) NYC 10011
Hours: 9-6 Mon-Fri
"Puppets, costume props, lifesized creatures, soft sculpture construction." ed.

Steve Young 212-675-7497
243 West 21st St. #1D (7-8th) NYC 10011
Hours: By appt.
"Professional puppeteer (10 years experience) for film, video, industrials; major credits." ed.

QUILTS

America Hurrah Antiques 212-535-1930
766 Madison Ave. (66th) NYC 10021
Hours: 11-6 Tues-Sat
"Quilts, Americana decorative items; will rent." ed.

The Gazebo 212-832-7077
660 Madison Ave. (61st) NYC 10021
Hours: 9-6:30 Mon-Sat/ 1:30-6 Sun
"Quilts, wicker furniture; expensive." ed.

Kelter-Malce 212-989-6760
361 Bleecker St. (10th-Charles) NYC 10014
Hours: 11-7 Tues-Sat (also 11-7 Mon, except Winter)
"Quilts, American country & primitive antiques; will rent." ed.

Judith & James Milne Inc. 212-472-0107
524 East 73rd St. (York-E. River Dr.) NYC 10021
Hours: 9:30-5 Mon-Fri
"Quilts, country antiques." ed.

Spirit of America Antiques 212-255-3255
269 West 4th St. (Perry-11th) NYC 10014
Hours: 1-7 Tues-Sat
"Quilts." ed.

Thomas K. Woodard American Antiques/Quilts 212-988-2906
835 Madison Ave. (69-70th) NYC 10021
Hours: 11-6 Mon-Sat
"Antique quilts, antiques." ed.

RATTAN, REED, RAFFIA, WILLOW

For finished products see BASKETS
see WICKER ITEMS

Bamboo and Rattan Works 201-370-0220
470 Oberlin Ave. S., Lakewood, NJ 08701
Hours: 8:30-4:30 Mon-Fri
"Wholesale rattan, matting, bamboo, caning and tools; helpful." ed.

Charles Demarest Inc. 201-492-1414
PO Box 238, Bloomingdale, NJ 07043
Hours: 9-5 Mon-Fri
"Wholesale only: bamboo poles, decorative matting (bales only)." ed.

Inter-Mares Trading Co. Inc. 516-957-3467
1064 Rt. 109, Lindenhurst, NY 11757
Hours: 9-5 Mon-Fri
"Rattan, reed, willow, cane: full rolls, bales, eases and reels." ed.

Oriental Rattan Co. 718-386-8200
1154 Flushing Ave. (Wyckoff-Irving) Bklyn 11237
Hours: 9-5 Mon-Fri
"All raw materials: rattan, reed, willow." ed.

The Otto Gerdau Co. 212-709-9647
82 Wall St. (Pearl-Water) NYC 10005
Hours: 9-5 Mon-Fri
"Chair caning, webbing; wholesale only." ed.

Peerless Rattan and Reed Mfg. Co. 914-968-4046
222 Lake Ave., PO Box 636, Yonkers, NY 10701
Hours: 9-4 Mon-Fri (answering machine)
"Rattan, reed, cane." ed.

H. H. Perkins Inc. 203-389-9501
10 South Bradley Rd., Woodbridge, CT 06525
Hours: 9-5 Mon-Fri/ 9:30-12 Sat
"Reed, cane, craft supplies." ed.

Rainbow Trading Co. Inc. 718-784-3700
5-05 48th Ave. L.I.C. 11101
Hours: 9-5 Mon-Fri
"Rattan and reed." ed.

Veteran Caning Shop 212-868-3244
550 West 35th St. (10-11th) NYC 10001
Hours: 7:30-5:30 Mon-Fri
"Fast and friendly caning supplies." ed.

RECORDS, PHONOGRAPH
See also AUDIO & VIDEO EQUIPMENT

Colony Records 212-265-2050
1619 Broadway (49th) NYC 10019
Hours: 9:30-2:30am Mon-Fri/ 10-3am Sat
"Large selection records, sheet music; will ship anywhere." ed.

Disc-O-Mat

474 Seventh Ave. (36th) NYC 10001 212-736-1150
Hours: 9-7 Mon-Fri/ 10-7 Sat/ 12-5 Sun

1518 Broadway (44th) NYC 10036 212-575-0686
Hours: 10-9 Mon-Wed/ 10-11pm Thurs-Sat/ 12-7 Sun

716 Lexington Ave. (58th) NYC 10022 212-759-3777
Hours: 10:15-9:45 Mon-Sat/ 12-5 Sun

"Mostly popular records; top-40." ed.

Sam Goody

666 Third Ave. (43rd) NYC 10017 212-986-8480
Hours: 9:30-7 Mon-Fri/ 9:30-6:30 Sat/ 12-5 Sun

51 West 51st St. (6th) NYC 10019 212-246-8730
Hours: 9:30-6:45 Mon-Fri/ 9:30-6:15 Sat/ 12:30-5:30 Sun

"Pricey; top 40 and some of everything." ed.

House of Oldies 212-243-0500
35 Carmine St. (6th-Bleecker) NYC 10014
Hours: 11-7 Mon-Sat
"Old rock 'n roll, 45's, 78's, 33's; catalog available." ed.

J & R Music World

33 Park Row (Beekman-Ann) NYC 10038 (classical) 212-349-0062
Hours: 9:15-6:15 Mon-Sat (jazz) 212-349-8400
"Classical and jazz records and tapes; video; good selection and prices." ed.

23 Park Row (Beekman-Ann) NYC 10038 212-732-8600
Hours: 9:15-6:15 Mon-Sat
"Popular records and tapes; good selection and prices; also stereo equipment, TV, VCR." ed.

Tower Records

692 Broadway (4th) NYC 10012 212-505-1500
1961 Broadway (66th) NYC 10023 212-799-2500

Hours: 9am-midnight every day
"Good selection, extensive classical, jazz, soundtrack, original casts, electronic, popular, 45's, tape & video." ed.

RELIGIOUS GOODS

See also CLOTHING RENTAL & PURCHASE: ECCLESIASTICAL

Barclay Church Supply Inc. 212-267-9432
26 Warren St. 2nd Fl. (B'way-Church) NYC 10007
Hours: 10-5 Mon-Fri/ 10-3 Sat
"Crosses, rosaries, church supplies." ed.

Bendix Carvings Inc. 516-249-9191
17 Gazza Blvd., Farmingdale, NY 11735
Hours: 10-4:30 Mon-Fri
"Carved wooden crucifixes, creches, etc; flier available; nice people." ed.

Catholic Book Shop of New York 212-594-8431
150 West 32nd St. (6-7th) NYC 10001
Hours: 10-6 Mon-Fri/ 10-5 Sat
"Charcoal for incense burners, rosaries, crosses." ed.

Holy Land Art Co. Inc. 212-962-2130
160 Chambers St. (Greenwich St.) NYC 10007
Hours: 9-4:30 M-Th/ 9-4 F/(9-2 Sat: Thanksgving - X-mas only)
"Large stock; crosses, rosaries, battery-operated candles, vestments, etc.; helpful." ed.

RESTORATION

See also REWEAVERS

Margo Feiden Galleries 212-677-5330
51 East 10th St. (B'way-University) NYC 10003
Hours: 11-6 Mon-Fri/ 2-5 Sat
"Restoration of papers, drawings, watercolors, paintings." ed.

Hiream Hoelzer Inc. 212-288-3211
1411 Third Ave. 16th Fl. (80th) NYC 10021
Hours: By appt.
"Restoration of paintings and painted surfaces; nice person." ed.

David Immerman 914-632-6463
40 Calton Lane, New Rochelle, NY 10804
Hours: By appt.
"Restoration of oil paintings, re-stretching, portrait painting." ed.

A. Laub Glass 212-734-4270
1873 Second Ave. (96-97th) NYC 10029
Hours: 8-5 Mon-Fri/ 9-4 Sat
"Stained and leaded glass repair and restoration." ed.

Phillis Maginsen 212-534-1672
c/o Museum of the City of NY
Fifth Ave. & 103rd St. NYC 10029
Hours: 9-4:30 Mon-Fri
"Consultation, cleaning, repair of costumes and textiles." ed.

Rambusch 212-675-0400
40 West 13th St. (5-6th) NYC 10011
Hours: By appt.
"Painting and mural restoration." ed.

Helene Von Rosentiel Inc. 718-788-7909
382 11th St. (5-6th) Bklyn 11215
Hours: By appt.
"Cleaning and repair of antiques." ed.

REWEAVERS

Alice Zotta 212-840-7657
2 West 45th St. (5th) NYC 10036
Hours: 8-6 Mon-Fri/ 8-2 Sat
"Reweaving; personal service." ed.

RIDING EQUIPMENT

H. Kauffman & Sons Saddlery Co. Inc. 212-684-6060
139 East 24th St. (Lexington-3rd) NYC 10010
Hours: 9:30-6 Mon-Sat
"Riding equipment and western apparel: riding crops, whips, harnesses, saddle bags." ed.

M. J. Knoud 212-838-1434
716 Madison Ave. (63-64th) NYC 10021
Hours: 9-5 Mon-Sat
"Select riding equipment, expensive." ed.

Miller Harness Co. Inc. 212-673-1400
123 East 24th St. (Park-Lexington) NYC 10010
Hours: 9-5:30 Mon-Sat
"Riding equipment & western apparel." ed.

RIGGING EQUIPMENT
see THEATRICAL HARDWARE & RIGGING EQUIPMENT

ROCKS & MINERALS

See also MARBLE
For artificial rocks see DISPLAY HOUSES & MATERIALS

Astro Minerals 212-889-9000
155 East 34th St. (Lexington-3rd) NYC 10016
Hours: 10-6 Mon-Sat/ 12-6 Sun
"Rocks, gems, polished stones." ed.

Crystal Resources Inc. 212-744-1171
130¼ East 65th St. (Lexington-Park) NYC 10021
Hours: 12-7 Mon-Sat
"Decorative minerals and fossils." ed.

Star Magic 212-228-7770
743 Broadway (8th-Waverly) NYC 10003
Hours: 12-9 Mon-Sat/ 12-7 Sun
"Gem stones, space related books, posters, toys, star maps and finders." ed.

RUBBER STAMPS

Adequate Rubber Stamp Co. Inc. 212-840-1588
141 West 41st St. (6th-B'way) NYC 10036
Hours: 8:30-5:30 Mon-Fri
"Custom rubber stamps, silkscreening, signs, engraved signs." ed.

J. C. Casey 212-243-0357
55 Seventh Ave. South (Bleecker-Morton) NYC 10014
Hours: 10:30-6:30 Mon-Fri/ 12-6:30 Sat
"Stock and custom rubber stamps." ed.

Mythology Unlimited Inc. 212-874-0774
370 Columbus Ave. (77-78th) NYC 10024
Hours: 11-9 Mon-Fri/ 11-6 Sat, Sun
"Wide selection of novelty rubber stamps; toys." ed.

Rubber Stamps Inc. 212-675-1180
16 West 22nd St. (5th) NYC 10011
Hours: 7:30-4 Mon-Fri
"Some stock, mostly custom work." ed.

SCENIC SHOPS

See also BACKDROPS

ACADIA SCENIC INC. 201-332-1327
100 Newark Ave., Jersey City, NJ 07303
Hours: 8-5 Mon-Fri

Non-union scene shop for theater, industrial and commercial work. Contact Duane Sidden or David Lawson.

"Also produces special effects, rigging." ed.

ADIRONDACK SCENIC 518-798-8321
20 Elm, Glens Falls, NY 12801
Hours: 8-5 Mon-Fri

Fabrication, painting, lighting and transportation.

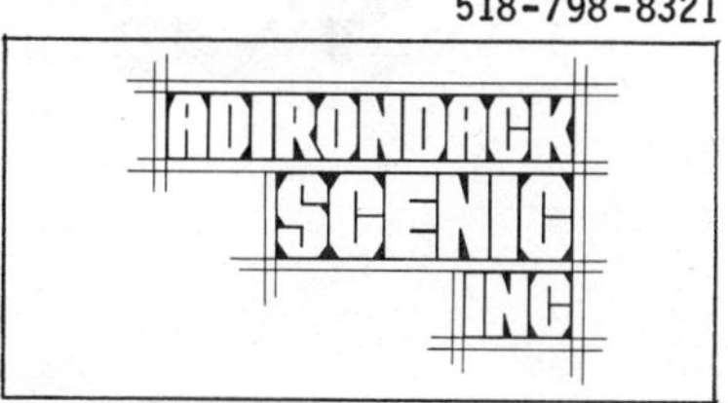

"Also rigging supplies and equipment below list price." ed.

Atlas Scenic Studios Ltd. 203-334-2130
46 Brookfield Ave., (Exit 30, CT Trnpk) Bridgeport, CT 06610
Hours: 8-4 Mon-Fri
"Union shop for scenery construction, painting, soft goods rental, rigging." ed.

BESTEK THEATRICAL PRODUCTIONS LTD.
386 East Meadow Ave., East Meadow, NY 11554 (rental shop) 516-794-3953
218 West Hoffman Ave., Lindenhurst, NY 11757 (prod'n shop) 516-225-0707
Hours: 10-6 Mon-Fri

Lighting, platforms, searchlights, scenery, confetti cannons. Custom construction & machinery. Equipment for sale & rent. (See display ad page 315.)

"Non-union shop; also lighting equipment rental, sales, installation; consultation." ed.

Thomas Bramlett Assoc. Inc.Bramlett Thomas Assoc. Inc. 201-659-3565
219 Grand St. (2nd-3rd) Hoboken, NJ 07030 212-255-7018
Hours: 9-6 Mon-Fri
"Props, sculpture, painting, effects and scenery construction; space rental." ed.

<u>ARTIFICIAL SNOW</u> Artificial snow, grass, rocks, all set materials.

<u>BACKDROPS</u> Backdrops: custom & rental; full scene shop; non-union.

<u>FOG MACHINES</u> Dry ice style, juice style. (Electric, butane, Ram Jet). Fog Juice.

<u>FORMICA</u> We stock 50 colors in many finishes. Custom formica fabrication.

<u>PAINTS & DYES-HOUSEHOLD</u> Household & theatrical paints & all painters supplies. Texturing supplies.

<u>PAINTS & DYES-THEATRICAL</u> Rosco scenic supplies.

<u>PLASTIC FABRICATION</u> Large selection of acrylic sheets. Custom fabrication. Acrylic ice cubes.

<u>PROP SHOPS</u> Custom props; mold making, from small to huge. All media.

<u>SCENIC SHOPS</u> Fabrication for still, video, film, theatre, exhibits. We work in all media. 10,000 square feet wood, metal, and scenic shop. Paint platform, spray booth.

<u>SONOTUBES</u> Sonotubes, convolutely wound cardboard shapes, curved Finnish plywood, PVC tubing. All set materials & fabrication--we cut sonotubes to length.

<u>SPECIAL EFFECTS</u> Special props, mold making. Artificial ice, rocks, columns, grass. Fog, wind, cobwebs. Rainbow generators. Custom & rental.

<u>TAPE</u> Over 30 kinds of tapes for theatre and photographic sets.

<u>SCENIC SHOPS</u>

Custom & Rental Backdrops
Custom & Rental Sets
Carpenters
Signage
Scenic Artist

We work in all media. Custom fabrication for the theatre, still, TV, video and exhibits. Paint platform and spraybooth.

Screen printing, lining, gradations, texturing, mottling, welding. From miniature molds to large sets.

<u>WE STOCK:</u>

Formica
Plexi
Cardboard
Gels (Lee & Rosco)
Tape (30 kinds)
Fine wood veneers
Plywood
Paints
Barnwood
Wallboards
Roll Surfaces
Columns
Pilasters
Balustrades
Diffusion materials
Reflective materials
Foamcore
Artificial rocks, grass, ice
Fog, wind, cobweb, rainbow machines
Generators
Canvas
Flocked material
Breakaways
Sonotubes, cardboard tubes, curved plywood moldings
Closed & open cell foam
Gator board

Set Shop 3 West 20 NYC 10011 (212) 929-4845 Accounts: 255-8875
Set Two 20 West 20 NYC 10011 (212) 924-1191
Hours: Monday-Friday 9AM-4PM Radio dispatched delivery

Brooklyn Model Works 718-834-1944
60 Washington Ave. (Park-Flushing) Bklyn 11205
Hours: 9-5 Mon-Fri
"Miniatures, sets, props and effects; machining, rigging, vacuumforming and controls." ed.

BRUCE & BRUCE SCENERY 212-460-5050
155 Attorney St. (Houston-Ave. B) NYC 10002
Hours: 8-5:30 Mon-Fri
(See display ad page 314.)
"Full service scene shop; non-union." ed.

CRAWFORD & FIELD INC. 718-855-4431
111 Water St. (btw. Bklyn & Manhattan bridges) Bklyn 11201
Hours: 8-4:30 Mon-Fri
Stage- Television- Films- Display- Conventions- Meetings.
"Scenery for all media; non-union shop." ed.

Design Associates 609-397-1588
76 S. Union St., Lambertville, NJ 08530
Hours: 8-5 Mon-Fri or by appt.
"Union: theatrical, industrial, set construction; painting, rigging, special effects." ed.

FELLER PRECISION INC. 212-589-9600
1290 Oak Point Ave. (Coster- Faille) Bronx 10474
Hours: 9-5 Mon-Fri
Theatrical Automation.
Standard and Custom Automation, Mechanical Devices and Structures including: Winches, Hoists, Rigging, Hydraulic and Pneumatic Equipment for Broadway, Industrials and Concerts.
Peter Feller, President.
"Handles mechanization for most Broadway shows." ed.

FOREPLAY STUDIOS 212-226-0188
33 Greene St. (Broome) NYC 10013
Hours: Call for hours.
Scenery for motion pictures. Local 52 IATSE.
"Contact Merle Eckert." ed.

The Fourth Wall 718-258-7953
3010 Ave. J (Nostrand-Flatbush) Bklyn 11210
Hours: 8-6 Mon-Fri
"Non-union: great with complex details, welcome small jobs; see Lenny." ed.

HORIZON SCENIC STUDIOS INC. 201-481-6070
161 Abington Ave., Newark, NJ 07107
Hours: 10-5 Mon-Fri
Custom Scenery, Props & Backdrops. Free Brochure.
Theatre- Film- Video- Photography- Displays- Exhibits.
"Speak to Charles Pye." ed.

HUDSON SCENIC STUDIO 212-585-6704
125 Bruckner Blvd. (Brook-St. Ann) Bronx 10454
Hours: 8:30-4:30 Mon-Fri and By appt.

Complete fabrication for all scenic needs for Broadway, Off-Broadway, TV and Industrial productions. On site supervision and labor also arranged.

"Speak to Neal Mazzella or Gene O'Donovan." ed.

Lincoln Scenic Studios 212-244-2700
560 West 34th St. (11-12th) NYC 10001
Hours: 9-5 Mon-Fri
"Union shop: film, TV, theatre; large stock of rental drops for film and theatre." ed.

Bernard Link Theatrical 212-929-6786
104 West 17th St. (6-7th) NYC 10011
Hours: 10-5 Mon-Fri
"Non-union: theatrical, fashion, industrial construction and scenic painting." ed.

Messmore & Damon 212-594-8070
530 West 28th St. (10-11th) NYC 10001
Hours: 8-5 Mon-Fri
"Union: theatrical, industrial, TV commercial construction; scenic painting." ed.

Metro Scenery Studios Inc. 718-464-6328
215-31 99th Ave. (Jamaica Ave.) Queens Village, NY 11429
Hours: 8-3:30 Mon-Fri
"Union shop offering complete theatrical service; also rental of tracks." ed.

Nolan Scenery Studio 718-783-6910
1163 Atlantic Ave. (Herkimer Pl.) Bklyn 11216
Hours: 8-3 Mon-Fri
"Union scenic painting studio." ed.

J. Patterson Scenic Studios 201-866-0316
4312 Liberty Ave., North Bergen, NJ 07047 212-864-5499
Hours: 9-5:30 Mon-Fri
"Non-union set shop; see John Reed." ed.

John Romeo Workshop Inc. 914-965-3994
44 Wells Ave., Yonkers, NY 10701
Hours: 9-5 Mon-Fri
"Union; theatrical, industrials, scenic painting; 15 minutes north of NYC." ed.

THE SET SHOP 212-929-4845
3 West 20th St. (5th) NYC 10011
Hours: 9-6 Mon-Fri/ 10-4 Sat
Fabrication for still, video, film, theatre, exhibits. We work in all media. 10,000 square feet wood, metal and scenic shop. Paint platform, spray booth. (See display ad page 316.)
"Backdrop rental, plastics fabrication, mold making." ed.

Show Tech 203-854-9336
15 Chapel St., Norwalk, CT 06850
Hours: 8-5 Mon-Fri
"Full service union scene shop: speak to Bill Mensching, Dennis Owens or Dan Hoffman." ed.

Stieglbauer Assoc. Inc. 718-624-0835
29 Front St. (under Bklyn Bridge) Bklyn 11201
Hours: 7-2:30 Mon-Fri
"Union: TV, theatrical and industrial set construction; see Mike or Cliff." ed.

THEATRE MACHINE 201-488-5270
20 River Road, Bogota, NJ 07603
Hours: 10-6 Mon-Fri
(See display ad page 314.)
"Non-union; theatrical, industrials, TV/video." ed.

Theatre Techniques Associates Inc. 212-585-1070
PO Box 335, Cornwall-on-Hudson, NY 12520
Hours: 8-5 Mon-Fri
"Union; scenery construction." ed.

Variety Scenic Studios 718-392-4747
25-19 Borden Ave. (near Midtown Tun.) L.I.C. 11101
Hours: 7-5 Mon-Fri (office)
"Union: full service including scenic painting, soft goods rental, stock scenery, hydraulics, pneumatics." ed.

Westchester Scenic 914-423-0407
578 Nepperhan Ave., Yonkers, NY 10701
Hours: call for hours.
"Scenery and platforms for TV, film; custom, rental, sales." ed.

SCISSORS

Cooper-Wiss 201-622-4670
33 Littleton Ave., Newark, NJ 07107
Hours: 8-4:30 Mon-Fri
"Scissors, sheers, snips." ed.

Delbon & Co. 212-244-2297
121 West 30th St. (6-7th) NYC 10001
Hours: 9-5:30 Mon-Fri/ 11-3 Sat
"Scissors and cutlery: Wiss, etc.; woodcarving tools." ed.

Hoffritz

515 West 24th St., Dept. K29, (10-11th) NYC 10011 (Main Office) 212-924-7300
Hours: 9-6 Mon-Sat

Penn Station Terminal (34th btw 7-8th) NYC 10001 212-736-2443
Hours: 8-6 Mon-Fri/ 9-6 Sat

Grand Central Terminal (42nd-Lexington) NYC 10017 212-682-7808
Hours: 8-6 Mon-Sat

331 Madison Ave. (43rd) NYC 10017 212-697-7344
Hours: 9-6 Mon-Sat

30 Rockefeller Plaza (50-51st) NYC 10112 212-757-3497
Hours: 9-6 Mon-Sat

203 West 57th St. (7th-B'way) NYC 10019 212-757-3431
Hours: 9-6 Mon-Sat

"Scissors, Swiss army knives, cutlery, bar supplies; catalog." ed.

Ross Sales Co. 212-475-8470
58 Third Ave. (7th) NYC 10003
Hours: 8:30-5 Mon-Fri/ 10-4 Sat
"Barbers and beauticians scissors and sharpening." ed.

SEASHELLS

Capt. Hook Marine Antiques & Shells 212-344-2262
South Street Seaport (Fulton) NYC 10038
Hours: 10-10 every day
"Seashells and marine antiques." ed.

Collector's Cabinet 212-355-2033
153 East 57th St. (Lexington-3rd) NYC 10022
Hours: 10-6 Mon-Sat
"Limited selection seashells, butterflies, minerals." ed.

Seashell Boutique 212-595-3024
208A Columbus Ave. (69th) NYC 10023
Hours: 12-9 every day
"Seashells, jewelry." ed.

Seashells Unlimited Inc. 212-532-8690
590 Third Ave. (38-39th) NYC 10016
Hours: 11-6 Mon-Sat
"Seashells." ed.

SEWING MACHINES: SALES, SERVICE & PARTS

AAB AMERICAN TRADING CORP. 212-691-3666
599 Sixth Ave. (17-18th) NYC 10011
Hours: 9-5 Mon-Fri

All types sewing machines, including portable overlock and hemming machines. Needles, bobbins, irons, steamers and all sewing supplies. Write or call for latest brochures and specials.

"Industrial machines. Rental, sales and repair." ed.

A-1 Advance Sewing Machine Co. Inc. 212-226-5621
521 Broadway (Spring-Broome) NYC 10012
Hours: 9-5 Mon-Fri/ 10-3 Sat
"Rents and sells industrial and home sewing machines." ed.

BAER FABRICS 502-583-5521
515 East Market, Louisville, KY 40202
Hours: 9-5:30 Mon-Sat

Bernina 'The Finest', most industrial, sales & service. (See display ad page 127.)

"Shipment within 24 hours for in-stock items." ed.

Henry Blader 212-327-8632
1020 N. Central Ave., Woodmere, NY 11598
Hours: 8-6 Mon-Fri
"Sewing machine sales, repair, service; Singer, Union, Merrow; makes house and shop calls." ed.

Continental Sewing Supply Co. 212-255-8837
104 West 25th St. (6-7th) NYC 10001
Hours: 9-4 Mon-Fri
"Industrial and home machine supplies." ed.

Crown Sewing Maching Service 212-663-8968
2792 Broadway (107-108th) NYC 10025
Hours: 9:30-6 Mon-Fri/ 9:30-5:30 Sat
"New and used sewing machines." ed.

Diamond Needle 212-929-2277
159 West 25th St. (6-7th) NYC 10001
Hours: 9-5 Mon-Fri
"Industrial and domestic machines, machine feet." ed.

E & J Repair Service 212-691-7171
245 Eighth Ave. (22-23rd) NYC 10011
Hours: 9:30-6 Mon-Fri/ 9:30-4 Sat
"Sewing machine and Merrow repair, supplies; scissor sharpening; new and used machine sales." ed.

Fox Sewing Machines Inc. 212-594-2438
307 West 38th St. (8-9th) NYC 10018
Hours: 8-5 Mon-Fri
"Sewing machine sales, rental, repair, new and used; dress forms, steam irons, cutting machines." ed.

Garment Center Sewing Machine Inc. 212-279-8774
555 Eighth Ave. (37-38th) NYC 10018
Hours: 8-5:30 Mon-Fri
"Used machine and dress forms, factory supplies." ed.

Hecht Sewing Machine & Motor Co. Inc. 212-563-5950
304 West 38th St. (8-9th) NYC 10018
Hours: 9-5 Mon-Fri
"Machine sales, service, rental; lamps, oil, belting." ed.

S. Hoffman Sewing Center 718-851-1776
5507 13th Ave. (55-56th) Bklyn 11219
Hours: 10-7 Mon-Fri
"Most types: Singer, industrial, Merrow; repairs." ed.

Merrow Sales Corp. 914-769-4909
364 Elwood Ave., PO Box 98, Hawthorne, NY 10532
Hours: 8-4:30 Mon-Fri
"Merrow machines: service, parts, needles." ed.

Metro Sewing Machines 212-725-4770
148 East 20th St. (Lexington) NYC 10016
Hours: 10-6 Mon-Fri/ 10-5 Sat
"Sales, service on domestic portables; needles, feet." ed.

Park East Sewing Center 212-737-1220
1358 Third Ave. (77th) NYC 10021 212-737-9189
Hours: 9:30-7 Mon-Thurs/ 9:30-6 Fri/ 10-6 Sat
"Sales, service, parts, supplies: domestic and industrial." ed.

Willie Roland 718-854-3325
4017 15th Ave. Bklyn 11218
Hours: Call for hours
"Sales and repair on domestic and industrial machines; used dress forms." ed.

St. Marks Place Sewing Machines 212-254-3480
78 East 1st St. (1st Ave.) NYC 10009
Hours: 10-6 Mon-Sat
"Sales and repairs, used industrial sewing machines; good scissors sharpening." ed.

SHELVING, METAL

AAAA Metropolitan Co. 212-741-3385
165 West 23rd St. (6-7th) NYC 10011
Hours: 9-5 Mon-Fri/ 9-4 Sat
"Steel shelving, new and used." ed.

Allracks Industry Inc. 212-244-1069
325 West 38th St. (8-9th) NYC 10018
Hours: 8:30-4:30 Mon-Fri
"Shelving, garment racks." ed.

B and Z Steel 212-966-5855
78 Greene St. (Spring-Broome) NYC 10012
Hours: 8:30-4:30 Mon-Fri
"Steel shelving." ed.

Evans-Friedland Steel Productions 212-532-1011
155 East 29th St. (3rd) NYC 10016
Hours: 9-5 Mon-Fri
"Steel shelves, lockers, cabinets, parts bins, flammable liquids containers; catalog available." ed.

SHIPPING

See also MOVING, TRANSPORT & STORAGE

Air Systems Courier 212-687-6240
122 East 42nd St. (Lexington) NYC 10017 800-223-6795
Hours: 9-5 Mon-Fri
"Domestic and international service; no size or weight limitation; reliable." ed.

DHL Worldwide Courier Express 718-917-8000
2 World Trade Center, NYC 10048
Hours: 9-7 Mon-Fri
"Overnight domestic delivery; 3-day service worldwide; max. weight = 70 lbs, max. size = 70" sum of height/width/length." ed.

Emery Worldwide 212-995-6400
184-54 149th Ave., Jamaica, NY 11413
Hours: 24 hours at airport office
"Fast service by air." ed.

Federal Express 212-777-6500
560 West 42nd St. (10-11th) NYC 10036
Hours: 9:15am-9:30pm Mon-Fri/ 8:30-5 Sat
"Will accept packages and hold for pick-up at over 30 locations in NYC; free catalog; 150 lb. limit." ed.

Greyhound Package Service (gen. info.) 212-971-6405
Port Authority Bus Terminal (priority svc.) 212-971-6331
9th Ave. & 41st NYC 10036 (arrival info.) 212-6311
Hours: 24 hours every day (pickup & delivery) 212-971-6407
(pickup & delivery) 212-971-0483
"Inexpensive shipping by bus. Check for size limitations." ed.

Radix Group Int'l/Friedman & Slater 718-656-5912
Cargo Bldg. 80 (near ASPCA) Room 215, Jamaica, NY 11430
Hours: 8:30-5 Mon-Fri
"International service; see Artie Schwartz." ed.

United Parcel Service 212-695-7500
601 West 43rd St. (11th) NYC 10036
Hours: 8-7 Mon-Fri
"Overnight, 2-day, or guaranteed 5 day service." ed.

SHOE ALTERATION, REPAIR & DRESSINGS

Anania Brothers 212-869-5336
46 West 46th St. (5-6th) NYC 10036
Hours: 9-6 Mon-Fri/ 10-4 Sat
"Shoe alteration, repair; also orthopedic shoes." ed.

Hollywood Shoe Service 212-239-8625
78 West 36th St. (6th) NYC 10018
Hours: 7:30-5:30 Mon-Fri
"Shoe repair and dressings.

Pete Ktenas 212-247-4850
166 West 50th St. (6-7th) NYC 10019
Hours: 9-5:45 Mon-Fri/ 9:30-4:30 Sat
"This is the Pete's who puts rubber on all the dance shoes." ed.

Westmore Shoe Repair 212-245-7487
331 West 57th St. (8-9th) NYC 10019
Hours: 8-6 Mon-Sat
"Shoe alteration and repair." ed.

SHOES see CLOTHING ACCESSORIES: BOOTS & SHOES

SHOP SPACE RENTAL

ACADIA SCENIC INC. 201-332-1327
100 Newark Ave., Jersey City, NJ 07303
Hours: 8-5 Mon-Fri
10,000 square feet. Reasonable rates. Contact Duane Sidden.
"For carpentry and painting. Easy to get to (across the street from the Grove St. PATH train stop)." ed.

Thomas Bramlett Assoc. Inc. 201-659-3565
219 Grand St. (2nd-3rd) Hoboken, NJ 07030 212-255-7018
Hours: 9-6 Mon-Fri
"Props, sculpture, painting, effects and scenery construction; space rental." ed.

The Costume Collection
1501 Broadway (44th) NYC 10036 (admin. off.) 212-221-0885
601 West 26th St. (11-12th) NYC 10001 (rentals) 212-989-5855
Hours: 9:30-5 Mon-Fri
"Speak with Whitney Blausen; workroom available for rent to not-for-profit groups." ed.

Eclectic Properties Inc. 212-799-8963
204 West 84th St. (B'way-Amsterdam) NYC 10024
Hours: 9-5 Mon-Fri or by appt.
"Speak with Suri." ed.

HORIZON SCENIC STUDIOS INC. 201-481-6070
161 Abington Ave., Newark, NJ 07107
Hours: 10-5 Mon-Fri
"Paint deck available." ed.

McHUGH/ROLLINS ASSOCIATES INC. 718-643-0990
79 Bridge St. (York-Front) Bklyn 11201
Hours: 9-6 Mon-Fri
A work table to a complete shop including tools and craftspeople. Daily or weekly rates. See Jim.
(See display ad page 300.)
"Paint booth (8'x16'x8') for prop and soft goods." ed.

THE SET SHOP 212-929-4845
3 West 20th St. (5th) NYC 10011
Hours: 9-6 Mon-Fri/ 10-4 Sat
Paint spray booth & paint platform available. (See display ad page 316.)
"Full scene shop; non-union; sells a wide variety of set materials."

THE WINTER CO. INC. /J. Milgram- E. Winter 718-499-2206
323 Sixth St. Top Fl. (5th) Bklyn 11215
Hours: By appt.
"2800 sq. ft.; flexible terms; painting, carpentry shop; open space, high-amp. electric." ed.

Women's Inter-Art Center 212-246-1050
549 West 52nd St. (10-11th) NYC 10019
Hours: 9:30-5 Mon-Fri
"Shop space rental." ed.

SIGNS & LETTERS

See also FLAGS & BANNERS
See also SILKSCREENING

ABCO Signs 212-496-8284
212 West 79th St. (B'way-Amsterdam) NYC 10024
Hours: By appt.
"Leave your name and phone # with service; Bill Space will return your call." ed.

Adco Signs 212-564-8773
122 West 29th St. (6-7th) NYC 10001
Hours: 10-6 Mon-Fri
"Signs; also large silkscreen printing." ed.

Alpha Engraving Co. 212-247-5266
888 Eighth Ave. (52-53rd) NYC 10019
Hours: 9-5:30 Mon-Fri
"Metal and plastic engraved signs, also name tags." ed.

ArtKraft Strauss Sign Corp. 212-265-5155
830 Twelfth Ave. (57th) NYC 10019
Hours: 9-5 Mon-Fri
"Custom signs: metal, wood, neon, computerized." ed.

Nick Cheffo Signs 718-769-0034
2317 East 21st St., Bklyn 11229
Hours: 9-5 Mon-Fri
"Wood and metal signs, wooden letters." ed.

De-Sign Letters 212-673-6211
15 East 18th St. (5th-B'way) NYC 10003
Hours: 9-5 Mon-Fri
"Cut letters and designs; see Howard Schwartz." ed.

NOTES

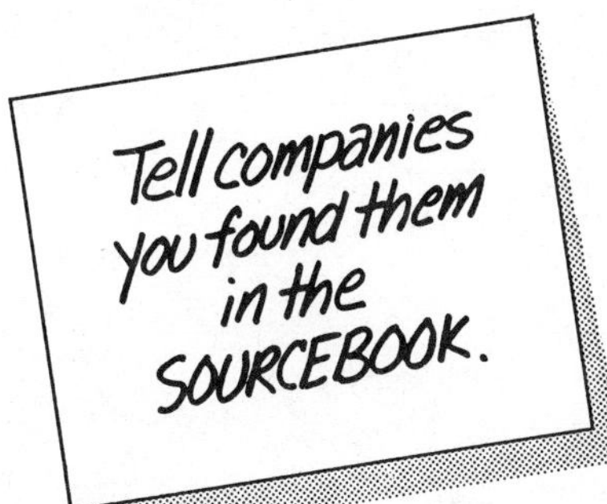

Electra Displays 516-585-5659
90 Remington Blvd., Ronkonkoma, NY 11779 212-420-1327
Hours: 9-5 Mon-Fri
"Electric signs and letters; mirror balls, projecting kaleidescopes."

INTERNATIONAL PAPER COMPANY 704-872-8974
Taylorsville Road Highway 90, Statesville, NC 28677 800-438-1701
Hours: 8-5 Mon-Fri
GATORFOAM® Laminated Foam Panel. Call 800# for local dealer.
"Available in 4'x8' sheets; 5 thicknesses from 3/16" to 1½"." ed.

Let There Be Neon 212-226-4883
38 White St. (Church-B'way) NYC 10013
Hours: By appt. only
"Neon signs." ed.

Letter Craft Inc. 212-582-7799
1128 Madison Ave., Patterson, NJ 07503 201-684-1130
Hours: 8-4 Mon-Fri
"Stock letters in plastic; also does custom work." ed.

Mail Order Plastics Inc. 212-226-7308
302 Canal St. (B'way-Church) NYC 10013
Hours: 8:30-5- Mon-Fri/ 9-4:30 Sat/ 10-4 Sun
"Plastic letters." ed.

Manhattan Neon Signs Corp. 212-714-0430
335 West 38th St. (8-9th) NYC 10018
Hours: 8-5 Mon-Fri
"Speak to Pat or Marilyn Tomasso." ed.

Mercury Neon Signs (Friedman Signs) 212-369-0220
69 East 116th St. (Madison-Park) NYC 10029
Hours: By appt.
"Neon signs: purchase or rental; for custom work see Mr. Friedman."

Midtown Neon Sign Corp. 212-736-3838
550 West 30th St. (10-11th) NYC 10001
Hours: By appt.
"Stock and custom neon, name brand and generic; will rent; nice people." ed.

Mitten Letters 212-741-1000
85 Fifth Ave. (16th) NYC 10003
Hours: 9-5 Mon-Fri
"Plaster letters." ed.

Neon Eddy 707-433-1400
PO Box 753, Healdsburg, CA 95448
Hours: 9-5 Mon-Fri
"Modular neon lighting units; specs available." ed.

Say It In Neon 212-691-7977
434 Hudson St. (St. Luke's Pl.) NYC 10014
Hours: 12-6 Mon-Fri
"Custom neon art and signs." ed.

SPECIALTY SIGNS CO. INC. 212-243-8521
6 West 18th St. (5th-6th) NYC 10011
Hours: 8-5 Mon-Fri
(See display ad page 327.)
"Stock signs: vacuumformed, plastic, magnetic, vinyl letters; rush service!" ed.

SILKSCREENING

Adco Signs 212-564-8773
122 West 29th St. (6-7th) NYC 10001
Hours: 10-6 Mon-Fri
"Signs, large silkscreen printing." ed.

Ambassador Arts 212-243-4290
122 West 27th St. 8th Fl. (6-7th) NYC 10001
Hours: 9-5 Mon-Fri
"Frank Agostino; does large screening art and signs on plexi, wood, etc."

THE FIFTH SEASON INC. 516-933-6250
180 Miller Pl., Hicksville, NY 11801
Hours: 9-5 Mon-Fri
Silk screened panels up to 48" x 96". Custom & stock items.
"Designs are screened on 3/16" foam board." ed.

SILKSCREENING SUPPLIES

See also ARTISTS MATERIALS
See also PAINTS & DYES: FABRIC

Eagle Supply Co. 212-246-6180
327 West 42nd St. (8-9th) NYC 10036
Hours: 9-4:30 Mon-Fri
"Silkscreen supplies; also artists' and poster paints." ed.

INTERNATIONAL PAPER COMPANY 704-872-8974
Taylorsville Road Highway 90, Statesville, NC 28677 800-438-1701
Hours: 8-5 Mon-Fri
GATORFOAM® Laminated Foam Panel. Call 800# for local dealer.
"Available in 4'x8' sheets; 5 thicknesses from 3/16" to 1½"." ed.

P. K. Supply Co. Inc. 718-377-6444
2291 Nostrand Ave. Bklyn 11210
Hours: 9:15-5:30 Mon-Fri (Thurs til 6:30)/ 9-5 Sat
"Silkscreen supplies; also art supplies, picture frame molding." ed.

SILVER ITEMS

See also ANTIQUES

Michael C. Fina Co. 212-869-5050
580 Fifth Ave. (47th) NYC 10036
Hours: 9-5:30 Mon-Fri
"Silver, silverware, china; good prices; catalog available." ed.

Fortunoff 212-758-6660
681 Fifth Ave. (53-54th) NYC 10022
Hours: 10-6 Mon-Sat (Thurs til 8)
"Reasonably priced silver items." ed.

Jean's Silversmiths 212-575-0723
16 West 45th St. (5th) NYC 10036
Hours: 9:30-5 Mon-Thurs/ 9:30-3:30 Fri
"Large selection tea sets, candelabras, etc.; expensive; will rent; go early in the day." ed.

Malcolm & Hayes Silversmiths 212-682-1316
694 Third Ave. (43rd-44th) NYC 10017
Hours: 8:30-6 Mon-Fri
"Silver cups; also awards, trophies, ribbons, certificates; engraving and printing done." ed.

Service Party-Rental Co. 212-288-7384
521 East 72nd St. (York) NYC 10021 212-288-7361
Hours: 8-5 Mon-Fri
"Silverware, candelabras, chafing dishes, coffee pots, etc., for rent."

SMOKING SUPPLIES

Arnold Tobacco Shop 212-697-1477
323 Madison Ave. (42-43rd) NYC 10017
Hours: 8:30-5:30 Mon-Fri/ 9:30-5 Sat
"Pipes, tobacco, cigars, lighters, repairs." ed.

Barclay-Rex Pipe Shop 212-962-3355
7 Maiden Lane (B'way) NYC 10038
Hours: 8-6 Mon-Fri
"Pipes, cigars, tobacco, humidors, repairs." ed.

Connoisseur Pipe Shop 212-247-6054
51 West 46th St. (5-6th) NYC 10036
Hours: 10-6 Mon-Fri/ 10-5 Sat
"Briar, Meerschaum, custom pipes and repairs, pouches, accessories."

De La Concha 212-757-3167
1390 Sixth Ave. (56-57th) NYC 10019
Hours: 8:30-8:30 Mon-Fri/ 10-8 Sat
"Cigars, cigarettes, pipes, tobacco; imported and domestic; nice people." ed.

Oliverio Diaz 212-475-7080
866 Broadway (17-18th) NYC 10003
Hours: 7:30-5:45 Mon-Fri
"Cigars, cigarettes, tobacco." ed.

Alfred Dunhill of London 212-481-6950
620 Fifth Ave. (50th) NYC 10020
Hours: 9:30-6 Mon-Fri/ 9:30-5:30 Sat
"Pipes, cigars, tobacco, humidors; expensive." ed.

Wally Frank Ltd. 212-687-9222
344 Madison Ave. (44th) NYC 10017
Hours: 8:30-6 Mon-Sat
"Good pipe selection, cigars, humidors, tobacco." ed.

Pipeworks 212-755-1118
400 Madison Ave. (47th) NYC 10019
Hours: 10-5:30 Mon-Fri/ 9-4 Sat
"Handmade briar, American pipes and repairs, tobacco." ed.

Nat Sherman 212-751-9100
711 Fifth Ave. (55th) NYC 10022
Hours: 9-6:15 Mon-Sat
"Large selection cigars, cigarettes, tobacco." ed.

Wilke Pipe Shop 212-755-1118
400 Madison Ave. (47-48th) NYC 10017
Hours: 8:30-5:30 Mon-Fri/ 10-5 Sat
"Foreign and domestic smoking supplies; briar root pipes, repairs."

SOFT GOODS see CURTAINS & DRAPERIES, THEATRICAL

SONOTUBE see PAPER, CARDBOARD & FOAMCORE PRODUCTS

SOUND EQUIPMENT RENTAL

ERSKINE-SHAPIRO THEATRE TECHNOLOGY INC. 212-929-5380
37 West 20th St. (6th) NYC 10011
Hours: 10-6 Mon-Fri
Rental of pro sound equipment. Studio facilities for sound effects, performance tapes and duplication. System design and running crews available.
"Contact Louis Shapiro or Peter Erskine." ed.

MASQUE SOUND & RECORDING CORP. 212-245-4623
331 West 51st St. (8-9th) NYC 10019
Hours: 9:30-5 Mon-Fri
Rentals and Sales; Mics, Tape Decks, Amps, Headsets, etc.
"Contact Bob Bender or Jack Shearing." ed.

PRO-MIX INC. 914-633-3233
50 Webster Ave., New Rochelle, NY 10801
Hours: 9-5 Mon-Fri
Rentals and Sales; Serving Broadway, Tours, Club Acts, Industrials, Permanent Installations, etc.
"Ask for Lew or Bob." ed.

Sound Associates Inc. 212-757-5679
424 West 45th St. (9-10th) NYC 10036
Hours: 10-5:30 Mon-Fri
"Full sound shop; rentals, sales, mail and phone orders." ed.

SPECIAL EFFECTS SERVICES

See also BREAKAWAYS

A.P.A. Studios 212-929-9436
230 West 10th St. (Bleecker-Hudson) NYC 10014 212-675-4894
Hours: 10-6 Mon-Fri
"Special effects for film and tape; custom casting and reproductions, flying/rigging." ed.

Arrow Graphics 212-807-0816
514 West 24th St. (10-11th) NYC 10011
Hours: 9-5 Mon-Fri
"Scenic effects, drops." ed.

Brooklyn Model Works 718-834-1944
60 Washington Ave. (Park-Flushing) Bklyn 11205
Hours: 9-5 Mon-Fri
"Casting, reproductions; machining, vacuumforming, breakaways, electrical/mechanical controls." ed.

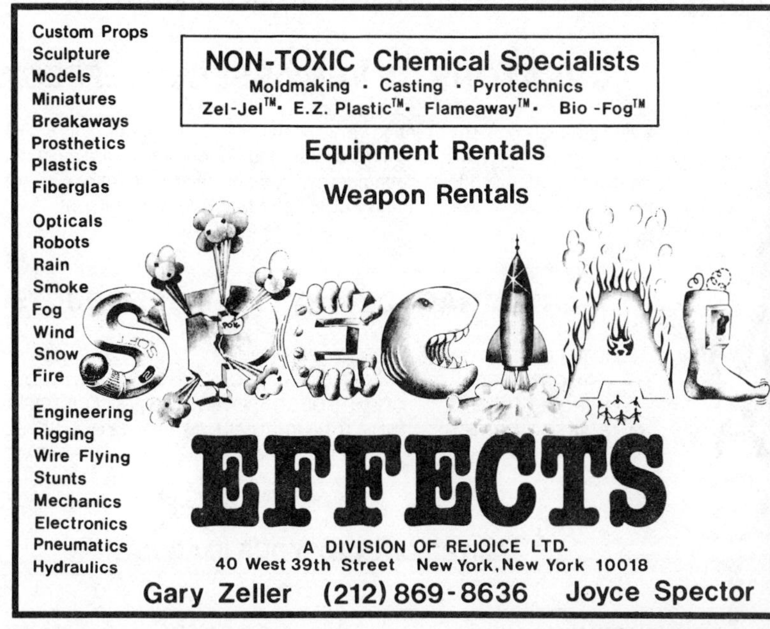

PETER WEISS DESIGNS

32 Union Square East • New York City 10003

(212) 477–2659

Special Effects Design and Construction

Custom Props • Models • Rigs

Electromechanical Effects • Atmospherics

Equipment Rentals: *Rain* • *Fog* • *Snow*

Motorized Rigs • *Turntables*

NOTES

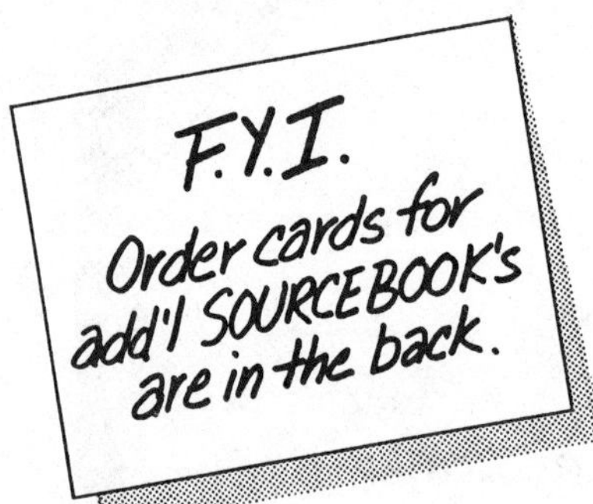
F.Y.I.
Order cards for add'l SOURCEBOOK's are in the back.

Fred Buchholz 212-874-7700
202 West 88th St. (B'way-Amsterdam) NYC 10024
Hours: By appt.
"Special effects, props, rigging and pyrotechnics for film, theatre, video; props incorporating light." ed.

Dancing Waters 212-247-1348
250 West 57th St. (B'way) NYC 10019
Hours: 9:30-5:30 Mon-Fri
"Rental of large musically choreographed theatrical fountains for stage and TV; contact Lynn." ed.

Dom DeFillipo Studio Inc. 212-986-5444
215 East 37th St. (2-3rd) NYC 10016 212-867-4220
Hours: 9-6 Mon-Fri
"Effects and special props for film and tape; some rentals." ed.

EFEX Specialists 718-937-2417
35-39 37th St., L.I.C. 11101
Hours: 8:30-5:30 Mon-Fri
"All types of special effects: water, smoke, fire; equipment rental."

Fireworks by Grucci 516-286-0088
Association Rd., Belleport, NY 11713 800-227-0088
Hours: 9-5 Mon-Fri
"Top name fireworks entertainment in the country." ed.

Larry Jameson 718-834-1714
390 Union St. (Smith-Hoyt) Bklyn 11231 212-794-2400
Hours: By appt.
"Electrical/mechanical, radio-control effects, puppets, for TV and film." ed.

Jauchem & Meeh (NY office) 718-875-0140
79 Bridge St. (York-Front) Bklyn 11201 (service) 212-382-3535
55 Rose Ave., Venice, CA 90291 (LA office) 213-396-2803
Hours: By appt.
"Special effects design, consultation, execution; xenon lighting, fog, butane torches, licensed pyro; sales and rentals." ed.

Peter Johnke 212-868-7567
400 West 43rd St. (9-10th) NYC 10036
Hours: By appt.
"Electrical/mechanical product rigs; will rent turntables, linear motion rigs, etc." ed.

Peter Kunz Co. Inc. 914-687-0400
RD 1 Creek Rd., PO Box 223, High Falls, NY 12440
Hours: 9-5:30 Mon-Fri
"Pyrotechnics, atmospherics, model making; rentals." ed.

Luna Tech Inc. 205-533-1487
PO Box 2495, Huntsville, AL 35804
Hours: 8:30-5 Mon-Fri
"Atmospheric, pyrotechnic devices; Pyropak brand." ed.

Dale Malli & Co. Inc. 718-706-1233
35-30 38th St. (Steinway St.) L.I.C. 11101
Hours: By appt.
"Designers and fabricators of custom props and effects for theatre, print, film." ed.

Michael Maniatis 212-620-0398
48 West 22nd St. (5-6th) NYC 10010
Hours: By appt.
"Special props, custom casting and reproduction, Vacuumforming, remote control, electrical/mechanical efx." ed.

McHUGH/ROLLINS ASSOCIATES INC. 718-643-0990
79 Bridge St. (York-Front) Bklyn 11201
Hours: 9-6 Mon-Fri
Mechanical and electrical effects designed and fabricated. See Jim. (See display ad page 300.)
"Also custom and stock breakaways." ed.

Ray Mendez - Props, Models, Creatures 212-864-4689
220 West 98th St. #12-B (Amsterdam) NYC 10025
Hours: 9:30-7 Mon-Fri
"Insect, reptile, amphibian wrangling." ed.

REJOICE LTD./GARY ZELLER, JOYCE SPECTOR 212-869-8636
40 West 39 St. (5-6th) NYC 10018
Hours: By appt. or leave message
You name it-we'll create it. Custom, sales, rentals. Also, fireworks- spectacular shows, effects; indoor miniature displays. (See display ad page 333.)
"Non-toxic chemical specialists." ed.

Deed Rossiter 914-358-7474
130 Sickletown Rd., West Nyack, NY 10994
Hours: By appt.
"Atmospherics, electrical/mechanical effects and models; licensed pyrotechnician." ed.

THE SET SHOP 212-929-4845
3 West 20th St. (5th) NYC 10011
Hours: 9-6 Mon-Fri/ 10-4 Sat
Special props, mold making. Artificial ice, rocks, columns, grass. Fog, wind, cob webs. Rainbow generators. Custom & rental. (See display ad page 316.)
"Full scene shop; non-union." ed.

Special Effects Unlimited 914-965-5625
18 Euclid Ave., Yonkers, NY 10705
Hours: By appt.
"See Mrs. Drohan; custom orders." ed.

Eoin Sprott Studio Ltd. 718-784-1407
Astoria Studio, 37-11 35th Ave., Astoria, NY 11106 718-784-1629
Hours: 8-5:30 Mon-Fri
"Custom props, model making, miniatures, sculpture, molds, mechanical animation rigs." ed.

Sussel Electronics, Howard Sussel 212-935-0632
411 East 53rd St. (1st) NYC 10022
Hours: 9-5 Mon-Fri
"Design and builds circuits for special effects projects." ed.

Norman Tempia 212-348-8944
409 East 90th St. #1-B (1st-York) NYC 10128
Hours: By appt.
"Sculpture, special props, masks and puppets for film and tape." ed.

THEATRE MAGIC 614-459-3222
6099 Godown Rd., Columbus, OH 43220
Hours: 7:30-4:30 Mon-Fri
(See display ad page 334.)
"Pyrotechnics and miniature pneumatics, blood effects, atmospherics."

Theatreffects, Lewis Gluck 212-242-6754
152 West 25th St. (6-7th) NYC 10001
Hours: By appt.
"Atmospherics, electrical/mechanical, radio controls, machinists, flying harness work." ed.

Tri-Ess Sciences Inc. 818-247-6910
622 West Colorado St., Glendale, CA 91204
Hours: 9-5 Mon-Fri/ 8-12 Sat
"Smoke pots, flash powder, etc." ed.

PETER WEISS DESIGNS 212-477-2659
32 Union Square East (17th & Park Ave. S.) NYC 10003
Hours: 9-6 Mon-Fri
Special effects, props, models, rigs, equipment rentals. (See display ad page 333.)
"Also electromechanical and atmospheric effects." ed.

Bill Schmeeler Wellington Enterprises 914-429-3377
55 Railroad Ave. Bldg 10, PO Box 315, Garnerville, NY 10923
Hours: 7-5:30 Mon-Thurs
"Special effects services; large shop." ed.

Mark Yurkiw Ltd. 212-226-6338
568 Broadway (Prince) NYC 10012
Hours: 9-6 Mon-Fri
"Special effects model making for advertising; problem solving for photographers." ed.

SPONGES

Beam Supply Inc. 212-475-5253
45-40 21st St. (near Jackson) L.I.C. 11101
Hours: 8-5 Mon-Fri
"Industrial maintenance supply house, paper goods, buckets, bulk cleaning supplies." ed.

National Sponge Corp. 718-383-5055
231 Norman Ave. (Russell) Bklyn 11222
Hours: 8:30-5 Mon-Fri/ 8-12 Sat
"Natural sponges." ed.

J. Racenstein Co. 212-477-3383
611 Broadway (Houston-Bleecker) NYC 10012 212-477-2353
Hours: 8-4:30 Mon-Fri
"Natural Mediterranean sponges and synthetic ones; nice people." ed.

Sculpture House Inc. 212-679-7474
38 East 30th St. (Madison-Park) NYC 10016
Hours: 8-6 Mon-Fri/ 10-4 Sat
"Natural sponges." ed.

Shell Sponge & Chamois Co. 212-966-3250
384 Broadway (Canal-Walker) NYC 10013
Hours: 9-5 Mon-Fri
"Natural and synthetic sponges, janitorial supplies." ed.

SPORTING GOODS

See also FENCING EQUIPMENT
See also RIDING EQUIPMENT

Atlantis 2 Total Scuba 212-924-7556
498 Sixth Ave. (12-13th) NYC 10011
Hours: 10-7 Mon,Thurs-Sat/ 12-7 Tues,Wed
"Water sports equipment, rental or sales." ed.

Blatt Bowling & Billiard Corp. 212-674-8855
809 Broadway (11-12th) NYC 10003
Hours: 9-6 Mon-Fri/ 9:30-4 Sat
"All types bowling and billiard supplies." ed.

Gerry Cosby & Co. Inc. 212-563-6464
3 Penn Plaza (7th Ave. & 32nd St.) NYC 10001
Hours: 9:30-8 Tues-Fri/ 9:30-6 Mon,Sat
"Sporting goods; large inventory of major league T-shirts and memorabilia." ed.

Cougar Sports Inc. 914-723-2266
590 Central Park Ave., Scarsdale, NY 10583
Hours: 10-6 Mon-Wed/ 10-7 Thurs/ 10-8 Fri/ 10-5 Sat
"Archery equipment, arrows made to size; also scuba diving gear." ed.

Dream Wheels 212-677-0005
295 Mercer St. (8th) NYC 10012
Hours: 12-8 Tues-Sat
"Roller skates; rentals in adult sizes." ed.

Eastern Mountain Sports

611 Broadway (Houston) NYC 10012 212-505-9860
Hours: 10-7 Mon-Fri/ 10-6 Sat/ 12-5 Sun

20 West 61st St. (B'way-Columbus) NYC 10023 212-397-4860
Hours: 10-7 Mon-Fri

"Equipment rental and sales." ed.

Gem Sporting Goods 212-255-5830
29 West 14th St. (5-6th) NYC 10011
Hours: 9-6:30 Mon-Fri/ 9-6 Sat/ 12-5 Sun
"Sporting goods." ed.

Herman's World of Sporting Goods

110 Nassau St. (Ann) NYC 10038 212-233-0733
Hours: 9-6 Mon-Fri/ 9-5 Sat

39 West 34th St. (5-6th) NYC 10001 212-279-8900
Hours: 9:30-7 Mon-Fri/ 9:30-6:30 Sat/ 12-5 Sun

135 West 42nd St. (6-7th) NYC 10036 212-730-7400
Hours: 9:30-7 Mon-Fri/ 9:30-6 Sat

845 Third Ave. (51st) NYC 10022 212-688-4603
Hours: 9:30-7 Mon-Fri/ 9:30-6 Sat

"Large selection sporting goods." ed.

Hudson's 212-473-7320
105 Third Ave. (12-13th) NYC 10003 212-473-0981
Hours: 9:30-6:30 Mon-Sat/ 12-5 Sun
"Camping equipment, work clothes, some military; tent rentals, May-Sept." ed.

Modell's

200 Broadway (Fulton) NYC 10038 212-962-6200
Hours: 8:30-6:15 Mon-Fri

111 East 42nd St. (Park-Lexington) NYC 10017 212-962-6200
Hours: 8:30-6:15 Mon-Fri 212-279-7143

243 West 42nd St. (7-8th) NYC 10036 212-962-6200
Hours: 8:30-6:15 Mon-Fri/ 9-7:30 Sat

"Discount sporting goods." ed.

Paragon Sporting Goods Co. 212-255-8036
867 Broadway (18th) NYC 10003
Hours: 9:30-6:30 Mon-Sat (Thurs til 7:30)/ 12-6 Sun
"Very large store; excellent selection of sporting goods, camping and hiking gear." ed.

Richards Aqua Lung & Sporting Goods 212-947-5018
233 West 42nd St. (7-8th) NYC 10036
Hours: 9:15-7:30 Mon-Sat
"Everything for the scuba diver and swimmer." ed.

Safari Archery 718-441-8883
86-15 Lefferts Blvd., Richmond Hill, NY 11418
Hours: 1-midnight Mon-Fri/ 1-9 Sat, Sun (Aug-Nov)
1-midnight Mon, Wed, Fri/ 1-9 Sat, Sun (Dec-Jul)
"Archery equipment; see Joe Durken." ed.

Scandinavian Ski Shop 212-757-8524
40 West 57th St. (5-6th) NYC 10019
Hours: 9-6 Mon-Sat (Thurs til 7)/ (open Sun for ski season)
"Large selection ski equipment." ed.

Soccer Sport Supply Co. 212-427-6050
1745 First Ave. (90-91st) NYC 10128
Hours: 10-6 Mon-Fri/ 10-3 Sat
"Good selection of anything related to soccer." ed.

Spiegels 212-227-8400
105 Nassau St. (Ann) NYC 10038
Hours: 9-6 Mon-Fri/ 10-5 Sat
"Sporting goods, team equipment and uniforms." ed.

Sportiva-Sporthaus Inc. 212-734-7677
1627 Second Ave. (84-85th) NYC 10028
Hours: 10-7 Mon-Fri (Thurs til 8)/ 10-6 Sat/ 11-5 Sun
"Ski equipment." ed.

Tent & Trails 212-227-1760
21 Park Place (Church-B'way) NYC 10007
Hours: 9:30-6 Mon-Fri (Thurs til 7)
"Large selection camping and climbing equipment, accessories, food; knowledgeable staff." ed.

Weiss & Mahoney 212-675-1915
142 Fifth Ave. (19-20th) NYC 10011 212-675-1367
Hours: 9-6 Mon-Fri/ 9-5 Sat
"Inexpensive camping attire and equipment; military clothes, shoes, medals, work clothes." ed.

SPRINGS, SPRING STEEL & WIRE

See also FLORAL SUPPLIES
See also MILLINERY SUPPLIES

ABC Spring Co. 212-675-1629
16 West 22nd St. (5-6th) NYC 10010
Hours: 9:30-5 Mon-Fri
"Stock and custom made springs, spring steel." ed.

D and R Auslander Hardware 212-267-3520
123 Chambers St. (W. B'way-Church) NYC 10007
Hours: 8-6 Mon-Fri/ 9-5 Sat
"Job lot springs; good source for unusual hardware." ed.

BZI Distributors 212-966-6690
105 Eldridge St. (Grand-Broome) NYC 10002
Hours: 9-5:30 Mon-Fri/ 9-5 Sun
"Springs for upholstery; large upholstery supply house." ed.

Ford Piano Supply Co. 212-569-9200
4898 Broadway (204-207th) NYC 10034
Hours: 8-5:30 Mon-Fri/ call for Sat hours
"Piano wire; nice people." ed.

Lee Spring Co. 718-236-2222
1462 62nd St. (near 15th) Bklyn 11219
Hours: 8-4 Mon-Fri
"Stock and custom order springs." ed.

Magnet Wire Inc. 718-651-0900
112-01 Northern Blvd., Corona, NY 11368
Hours: 9-5 Mon-Fri
"Carries piano wire, tungsten wire, as well as large selection of other wire." ed.

Modern International Wire 718-728-1475
35-11 9th St., PO Box 6072, L.I.C. 11106
Hours: 9-5:30 Mon-Fri
"All types of wire." ed.

New Era Hardware and Supply 212-265-4183
832 Ninth Ave. (54-55th) NYC 10019
Hours: 8-4:30 Mon-Fri
"Piano wire, rigging, casters, trucks, handling equipment, tools." ed.

Paramount Wire Inc. 718-256-2112
1523 63rd St. Bklyn 11219
Hours: 9-4:30 Mon-Fri
"Millinery, piano, ribbon wire, cotton and rayon covered wire, paper stakes." ed.

STATIONERY & OFFICE SUPPLIES

For OFFICE EQUIPMENT see BUSINESS MACHINES & TYPEWRITERS
see COMPUTERS
For OFFICE FURNITURE see FURNITURE RENTAL & PURCHASE: OFFICE

Arrow Stationers Inc. 212-986-5659
9 East 46th St. (5th) NYC 10017
Hours: 8:30-5:30 Mon-Fri/ 10-4:30 Sat
"Office supplies, pens, rubber stamps." ed.

Flynn Stationers 212-758-2080
46 East 59th St. (Madison-Park) NYC 10022
Hours: 8:30-5:30 Mon-Fri
"Stationery supplies; excellent pen repair department, specializing in older fountain pens." ed.

Golden Typewriter & Stationery Corp. 212-749-3100
2525 Broadway (94th) NYC 10025
Hours: 9:30-6:45 Mon-Sat
"Stationery, office supplies, artist supplies." ed.

Grolan Stationers Inc. 212-247-2676
1800 Broadway (58th) NYC 10019 212-247-1684
Hours: 8:45-5:45 Mon-Fri
"Stationery, office supplies, including legal forms." ed.

Holland Cut Rate Stationery 212-226-0118
325 Canal St. (Greene-Mercer) NYC 10013
Hours: 8:30-4:30 Mon-Fri
"Older type bound journals and ledgers; limited selection stationery supplies." ed.

Hudson Envelope Corp. 212-691-3333
West 17th St. (5-6th) NYC 10011
Hours: 9-5 Mon-Fri
"All sizes of envelopes, also makes rubber stamps; see Michael Jacobs." ed.

Kroll Stationers 212-541-5000
145 East 54th St. (Lexington-3rd) NYC 10022
Hours: 8:30-5:45 Mon-Fri
"Excellent stock of stationery supplies." ed.

Menash Inc.

462 Seventh Ave. (35th) NYC 10018 212-695-4900
Hours: 8:30-5:30 Mon-Fri

2305 Broadway (83-84th) NYC 10024 212-877-2060
Hours: 9-6:30 Mon-Sat

"Artists, drafting, graphics, office supplies; stationery: professional discount." ed.

Pineider Inc. 212-688-5554
725 Fifth Ave. (56th) NYC 10022 212-688-5613
Hours: 10-6 Mon-Sat
"Fine writing papers, Italian engraving; expensive." ed.

Rose Stationery 212-255-6340
79 Fifth Ave. (16th) NYC 10003
Hours: 8:30-5:30 Mon-Fri/ 11-4 Sat
"General stationery supplies, some file cabinets and desks." ed.

State Office Supply & Printing Co. Inc. 212-243-8025
150 Fifth Ave. (20th) NYC 10011
Hours: 8:30-5:30 Mon-Fri
"Good selection of office supplies and desk accessories." ed.

Stevdan Stationers 212-243-4222
474 Sixth Ave. (11-12th) NYC 10011
Hours: 8:30-6:20 Mon-Fri/ 10-5:40 Sat
"Stationery, rubber stamps." ed.

Tunnel Stationery 212-431-6330
301 Canal St. (B'way) NYC 10013
Hours: 8:30-4:45 Mon-Fri/ 10:15-4:30 Sat
"Discount priced stationery." ed.

STATUARY

See also CASTING CUSTOM
See also DISPLAY HOUSES
See also PROP & SCENIC CRAFTSPEOPLE

L. Biagiotti 212-924-5088
259 Seventh Ave. (24-25th) NYC 10001
Hours: 9-4 Mon-Fri
"Plaster statuary, sculpture, vases, columns, stock or custom work, breakaways; will rent." ed.

Florentine Craftsmen Inc. 212-532-3926
46-24 28th St. L.I.C. 11101 718-937-7632
Hours: 8:30-4:30 Mon-Fri
"Outdoor statuary, fountains, garden furniture; expensive; catalog."

Industrial Plastics 212-226-2010
309 Canal St. (B'way-Mercer) NYC 10013
Hours: 8:30-5 Mon-Fri/ 8:30-4 Sat
"Fiberglas statuary, urns, fountains, animals; rental or purchase; see Deena." ed.

Eugene Lucchesi Inc. 212-744-6773
859 Lexington Ave. (64th) NYC 10021
Hours: 8:30-3 Mon-Fri
"Plaster statuary." ed.

Kenneth Lynch and Sons 203-762-8363
78 Danbury Rd., Wilton, CT 06897
Hours: 8-4:30 Mon-Fri
"Statuary in metal, molded zinc architectural detail." ed.

Sculpture House Casting 212-684-3445
38 East 30th St. (5th-Madison) NYC 10016
Hours: 8-5:30 Mon-Fri/ 10-4 Sat
"Expensive plaster and metal statuary, busts, some casting materials."

STERNO

A. Sargenti Co. Inc. 212-989-5555
453 West 17th St. (9-10th) NYC 10011
Hours: 9-5 Mon-Fri
"Sterno by the case." ed.

SURGICAL SUPPLY HOUSES see MEDICAL EQUIPMENT

SURPLUS MERCHANDISE

For military surplus clothing and gear, see
CLOTHING RENTAL & PURCHASE: UNIFORMS

H & R Corporation 215-426-1708
401 East Erie Ave., Philadelphia, PA 19134
Hours: 8:30-4:45 Mon-Fri/ 9:30-2 Sat
"Surplus motors, fans, electrics, lenses, etc." ed.

Jerryco Co. Inc. 312-475-8440
601 Linden Place, Evanston, IL 60202
Hours: 9-5 Mon-Fri
"'Sail On' surplus catalog of gadgets and weird items from industrial and military surplus." ed.

NYC Dept. of General Services, Warehouse 718-643-4677
11 Water St. Bklyn 11201
Hours: 9-2:30 Mon-Fri
"Rotating stock of used items; typewriters, chairs, desks, etc; open to the public Wed. only." ed.

Romano Trading Inc. 212-581-4248
628 West 45th St. (12th) NYC 10036
Hours: 8-5 Mon-Fri/ 8-4:30 Sat
"Rotating stock; luggage, clothes, radios, answering machines, towels; good prices." ed.

Trieste Export Corp. 212-246-1548
568 Twelfth Ave. (44th) NYC 10036
Hours: 7-5:30 Mon-Fri/ 8-4 Sun
"Large selection, rotating stock at discount prices." ed.

TAPE, ADHESIVE

See also PACKING MATERIALS

Duo-Fast Corp. 718-726-2400
31-07 20th Rd. L.I.C. 11105
Hours: 8:30-5 Mon-Fri (closed for lunch 12-1)
"High and low tack tapes, hot melt glues." ed.

Great Atlantic Paper Packaging Corp. 718-858-3636
281-289 Butler St. Bklyn 11217
Hours: 9-5 Mon-Fri
"Gaffers, duct, many types of pressure sensitive tapes." ed.

H. G. PASTERNACK INC. 212-460-5233
151 West 19th St. (7th) NYC 10011
Hours: 9-5:30 Mon-Fri
Authorized distributor: 3M tapes. Full line of 3M Double-Coated Tapes, masking tapes, electrical tapes, cloth tapes. Call for free samples or catalog.
"Also authorized distributor: 3M adhesives." ed.

Pro-Tape and Supply Inc. 212-586-8873
832 Eighth Ave. (50-51st) NYC 10019
Hours: 8-5 Mon-Fri
"Excellent stock, any type of paper or adhesive tape; large orders only." ed.

ROSE BRAND TEXTILE FABRICS 212-594-7424
517 West 35th St. (10-11th) NYC 10001 800-223-1624
Hours: 8:30-4:45 Mon-Fri
Gaffers tape in grey or black, cloth duct tape, masking tape, luminous glow tape. Ask about case lot discounts. (See display ads pages 98, 142.)
"Wide selection of flame retardant fabrics by the yard or by the bolt."

THE SET SHOP 212-929-4845
3 West 20th St. (5th) NYC 10011
Hours: 9-6 Mon-Fri/ 10-4 Sat
Over 30 different kinds of tapes for theatre and photographic sets. (See display ad page 316.)
"Stocks wide variety of set materials." ed.

Stick-A-Seal Tape (United Mineral) 212-966-4330
129 Hudson St. (N. Moore) NYC 10013
Hours: 9-4:45 Mon-Fri (call first)
"Full line of common type gaffer, electrical, duct tapes; $50 minumum."

TAXICAB ACCESSORIES

For taxicabs, see AUTOMOBILES

Argo Taximeter Shop 718-937-4600
21-46 44th Dr. (Ely-21st St.) L.I.C. 11101
Hours: 8:30-4:30 Mon-Fri/ 8-12 Sat
"Taxi stickers, license holders, meters, taxi accessories." ed.

B & M Sales & Service 212-929-8170
29 Seventh Ave. South (Christopher) NYC 10014
Hours: 8-5 Mon-Fri
"Taxi stickers, meters, license holders, accessories." ed.

TAXIDERMISTS & TAXIDERMY SUPPLIES

See also ANIMAL & BIRD SKINS, FRESH

Jonas Brothers Taxidermy (supply dept.) 303-777-3377
1901 S. Bannock, Denver, CO 80223
Hours: 8-5:30 Mon-Fri/ 8-12:30 Sat
"Animal forms, taxidermy supplies." ed.

Schoepfer Studios 212-736-6939
138 West 31st St. (6-7th) NYC 10001
Hours: 9:30-3:30 Mon-Fri
"Glass animal eyes; rental or purchase of stuffed animals." ed.

Westchester Taxidermy Quality Mounts 914-245-1728
2814 Hickory St., Yorktown Heights, NY 10598
Hours: By appt.
"Rental and purchase; over 300 animals and birds; taxidermy supplies; very nice." ed.

TELEPHONES

Brins Telecommunications 212-807-6000
126 West 26th St. (6-7th) NYC 10001
Hours: 9-5 Mon-Fri
"Business telephones, sales and leasing." ed.

The Fone Booth 212-751-8310
12 East 53rd St. (5th-Madison) NYC 10022
Hours: 10-6 Mon-Sat (Thurs til 8)
"Telephones, telephone related items." ed.

47th St. Photo

116 Nassau St. (Ann-Beekman) NYC 10038 212-608-6934
115 West 45th St. (6th-B'way) NYC 10036 212-260-4410
67 West 47th St. (5-6th) NYC 10036 212-260-4410

Hours: Hours: 9-6 Mon-Thurs/ 9-2 Fri/ 10-4 Sun
"Cameras and photo equipment, computers, typewriters, telephones, etc.; watch for frequent sales." ed.

J & R Music World 212-513-1858
25 Park Row (Beekman-Ann) NYC 10038
Hours: 9:30-6:30 Mon-Sat
"Telephones." ed.

Phone Boutique 212-319-9650
828 Lexington Ave. (63-64th) NYC 10021
Hours: 10-6 Mon-Sat
"Telephones and answering machines." ed.

Phone City Inc.

1152 Sixth Ave. (44-45th) NYC 10036 212-869-9898
Hours: 9:30-6 Mon-Sat

126 East 57th St. (Lexington-Park) NYC 10022 212-644-6300
Hours: 9:30-7 Mon-Fri/ 10-6 Sat/ 1-6 Sun

"Sales; new and reproductions of older styles; pricey." ed.

Phoneco 608-582-4124
Route 2, Galesville, WI 54630
Hours: 9-5 Mon-Fri
"Will rent antique and repro telephones." ed.

State Supply Equipment Co. Inc. 212-645-1431
210 Eleventh Ave. (25th) NYC 10001
Hours: 8:30-5 Mon-Fri
"Rental of period and contemporary phone equipment, including switchboards." ed.

TELESCOPES

Bargain Spot 212-674-1188
64 Third Ave. (11th) NYC 10003
Hours: 8:30-5 Mon-Sat
"Telescopes, binoculars, cameras, musical instruments; rental or purchase." ed.

Clairmont-Nichols Inc. 212-758-2346
1016 First Ave. (56th) NYC 10022
Hours: 8:30-5:30 Mon-Fri/ 9-4 Sat
"Sales and repairs, also binoculars." ed.

Rensay Inc. 212-688-0195
49 East 58th St. (Madison) NYC 10022
Hours: 8:30-5:30 Mon-Fri/ 11-3 Sat
"Sales, rentals, repairs of telescopes and binoculars." ed.

Star Magic 212-228-7770
743 Broadway (8th-Waverly) NYC 10003
Hours: 12-9 Mon-Sat/ 12-7 Sun
"Telescopes, star maps and finders, space related books and posters."

Tower Optical 203-866-4535
PO Box 251, South Norwalk, CT 06856
Hours: 8-5 Mon-Fri
"Maintains and owns all coin operated binoculars in NYC area, will rent: extremely helpful." ed.

THEATRICAL HARDWARE & RIGGING EQUIPMENT

See also THEATRICAL SUPPLY HOUSES

BESTEK THEATRICAL PRODUCTIONS LTD.
386 East Meadow Ave., East Meadow, NY 11554 (rental shop) 516-794-3953
218 W. Hoffman Ave., Lindenhurst, NY 11757 (prod'n shop) 516-225-0707
Hours: 10-6 Mon-Fri
Dealers for major suppliers. Installation & rentals available. (See display ad page 315.)
"Scenic and lighting services." ed.

Colson Casters 516-354-1540
Meecham Ave.,(Hempstead Tpk) Elmont, NY 11003
Hours: 9-5 Mon-Fri
"Specialize in casters." ed.

COMMERCIAL DRAPES CO. INC. 718-649-8080
9209 Flatlands Ave. (E.92-93rd) Bklyn 11236
Hours: 8-4:30 Mon-Fri
Fabricator of Stage Curtains, Scrims, Drops, Cycloramas. We install or sell Travelers Tracks, Hardware, Movie Screens, Manila Ropes.
Stage maintenance. Rentals. Flameproofing. Fire retardant fabric by the yard. 35 Years in the Trade.
"Good prices. See Joseph Shuster." ed.

J. Cowhey & Sons Inc. Marine Equip. 718-625-5587
440 Van Brunt St. Bklyn 11231
Hours: 9-4:30 Mon-Fri
"Good prices on aircraft cable, Crosby clamps, etc." ed.

GERRIETS INTERNATIONAL 609-758-9121
RR #1, 950 Hutchinson Rd., Allentown, NJ 08501
Hours: 8:30-5 Mon-Fri
Exclusive distributor of the TRIPLE E loose pin and tight pin hinges. This LP hinge was the winner of the Best Product of the Year Gold Award in 1984 presented by the Assoc. of British Theater Technicians. Write or call for your free LP hinge sample. (See display ads pages 98, 204.)
"Speak to Nick Bryson." ed.

Hoboken Bolt & Screw 201-792-0450
1700 Willow Ave., Hoboken, NJ 07030
Hours: 9-5 Mon-Fri
"Aircraft cable, fittings, etc.; brochures available." ed.

Kee Klamps 716-685-1250
PO Box 207, Buffalo, NY 14225
Hours: 9-5 Mon-Fri
"Manufacturers of Kee Klamps, use with 1/2" to 2" pipe." ed.

Longacre Hardware Supply Co. 212-246-0855
801 Eighth Ave. (48-49th) NYC 10019
Hours: 8:30-6:45 Mon-Fri/ 8:30-6 Sat
"Complete line of theatrical hardware; barge and solvents in quantity." ed.

Magnet Wire Inc. 718-651-0900
112-01 Northern Blvd., Corona, NY 11368
Hours: 9-5 Mon-Fri
"Carries tungsten wire, piano wire, as well as a large selection of other wire." ed.

Mutual Hardware 718-361-2480
5-45 49th Ave. (Vernon) L.I.C. 11101
Hours: 8:30-5 Mon-Fri/ 8:30-6 Sat
"Complete stage hardware, casters, scenic paint, rigging, tracks, drapes." ed.

New Era Hardware and Supply 212-265-4183
832 Ninth Ave. (54-55th) NYC 10019
Hours: 8-4:30 Mon-Fri
"Rigging supplies, casters, hand trucks and handling equipment, piano wire, tools." ed.

NOVELTY SCENIC 516-671-5245
40 Sea Cliff Ave., Glen Cove, NY 11542 718-895-8668
Hours: 8:30-5 Mon-Fri
The complete theatrical equipment source: Curtains, tracks, rigging, motors, custom curtains & drops. Catalog available. RUSH ORDERS.
"Helpful, contact Howard Kessler." ed.

Frederich Pfeifer 212-964-5230
53 Warren St. (W. B'way-Church) NYC 10007
Hours: 9-4:45 Mon-Fri
"Theatrical hardware, casters, dollies." ed.

POOK DIEMONT & OHL INC. 212-982-7583
135 Fifth Ave. (20th) NYC 10010
Hours: By appt.
Rigging contractors & consultants: Stage & Studio. Safety analysis, equipment installation & maintenance.
"Speak to Barbara Pook, Tony Diemont or Ted Ohl." ed.

REYNOLDS DRAPERY SERVICE INC. 315-845-8632
7440 Main St., Newport, NY 13416
Hours: 8-4 Mon-Fri
We manufacture and service theatrical draperies. Our service includes flameproofing, drycleaning and custom repair. (5 year flameproof guarantee in writing)
"Curtain tracks and rigging equipment." ed.

Segal Brothers 718-383-2995
205 Nassau St. (Russell) Bklyn 11201
Hours: 8-5 Mon-Fri
"Crosby clamps, industrial hardware, tools, motors." ed.

SILVER & SONS HARDWARE 212-247-6969
711 Eighth Ave. (44-45th) NYC 10036
Hours: 9-6 Mon-Fri/ 9-5:30 Sat
Theatrical & General Hardware, Tools, All kinds of Tape.
Located in the Heart of the Theatrical District.
"Great selection; very helpful." ed.

W. H. Silver's Hardware 212-247-4406
832 Eighth Ave. (50-51st) NYC 10019 212-247-4425
Hours: 8-6 Mon-Fri/ 8-1 Sat
"Great selection of theatrical hardware, rigging equipment, tools, tape; very helpful." ed.

Simmons Fastener Corp. 518-463-4234
1750 Broadway, Albany, NY 12204
Hours: 8:30-5 Mon-Fri
"Case hardware, roto-locks, screw buttons." ed.

THEATRICAL SUPPLY HOUSES

ADIRONDACK SCENIC 518-798-8321
20 Elm, Glens Falls, NY 12801
Hours: 8-5 Mon-Fri

Supplies & equipment
* BELOW LIST PRICE *
Quantity Discounts.

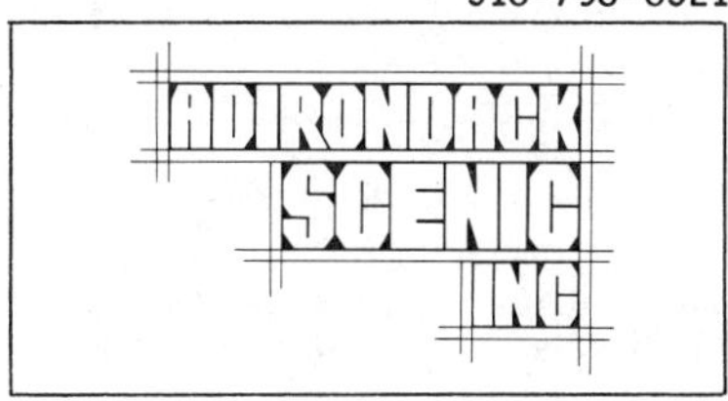

"Also scenery construction." ed.

Alcone Company Inc./Paramount Theatrical 718-361-8373
5-49 49th Ave. L.I.C. 11101
Hours: 9:30-4 Mon-Fri
"Lighting equipment, rigging equipment, fabrics, paint, etc." ed.

Theatre Production Services 212-206-7555
133 West 19th St. (6-7th) NYC 10011
Hours: 9-5 Mon-Fri
"Theatrical supply house; catalog available." ed.

Vadar Industries Ltd. 212-307-6556
750 Tenth Ave. (51st) NYC 10019 800-221-9511
Hours: 8:30-5 Mon-Fri
"Scenic supplies and lighting equipment, stage hardware; catalog available." ed.

THRIFT SHOPS

Cancer Care Thrift Shop 212-879-9868
1480 Third Ave. (84th) NYC 10028
Hours: 10-5 Mon-Sat
"Limited selection, mostly clothing, some jewelry, picture frames, knick-knacks." ed.

Everybody's Thrift Shop 212-355-9263
261 Park Ave. South (20-21st) NYC 10010
Hours: 10-4:45 Mon-Sat (Tues til 7)
"Limited selection." ed.

Godmother's League 212-988-2858
1457 Third Ave. (82-83rd) NYC 10028
Hours: 10-5 Mon-Sat
"Limited selection clothing, knick-knacks, furniture." ed.

Goodwill Industries of Greater NY 212-679-0786
402 Third Ave. (29th) NYC 10016
Hours: 9-4:30 Mon-Sat
"Limited selection, mostly clothing." ed.

Greenwich House Thrift Shop 212-473-3065
548 LaGuardia Place (Bleecker-3rd) NYC 10012
Hours: 11-6 Mon-Sat
"Some clothing; 60's and 70's." ed.

Irvington House Thrift Shop 212-879-4555
1534 Second Ave. (80th) NYC 10021
Hours: 9:30-5:50 Mon-Sat (Wed til 7:50)
"Good selection: furniture, clothing, dishes, knick-knacks; sometimes pricey." ed.

Memorial Sloan-Kettering Thrift Shop 212-535-1250
1410 Third Ave. (80th) NYC 10028
Hours: 10-4:45 Mon-Sat
"Limited selection, mostly clothing, books, knick-knacks." ed.

Planned Parenthood Thrift Shop 212-371-1580
324 East 59th St. (1-2nd) NYC 10022
Hours: 10-4:45 Mon-Sat
"Limited selection." ed.

Repeat Performance Thrift Shop 212-684-5344
220 East 23rd St. (2-3rd) NYC 10010
Hours: 10-5 Mon-Sat
"Clothing, furniture, carpets, silver items, knick-knacks." ed.

Salvation Army Store

536 West 46th St. (10-11th) NYC 10036 212-757-2311
Hours: 9-4:45 Mon-Sat
"Main store; large selection, good prices." ed.

40 Avenue B (3-4th) NYC 10009 212-473-9492
Hours: 9-4 Mon-Sat

180 First Ave. (11th) NYC 10009 212-475-9560
Hours: 8:30-4:15 Mon-Sat

208 Eighth Ave. (20-21st) NYC 10011 212-929-9719
Hours: 9-4:30 Mon-Sat

268 West 96th St. (B'way-West End) NYC 10025 212-864-8609
Hours: 9-4:30 Mon-Sat

26 East 125th St. (5th-Madison) NYC 10035 212-289-9617
Hours: 9-4:30 Mon-Sat

34-06 Steinway L.I.C. 11101 718-784-9880
Hours: 9-5:45 Mon-Wed/ 9-7:45 Thurs,Fri/ 9-4 Sat

"A bit of everything; good prices." ed.

Search N' Save Thrift Shop 212-988-1320
1465 Third Ave. (83rd) NYC 10028
Hours: 9:30-5 Mon-Sat
"Limited selection furniture, lamps, clothing, picture frames, knick-knicks." ed.

Second Time Around Thrift Shop 212-685-2170
220 East 23rd St. (2-3rd) NYC 10010
Hours: 10-5:45 Mon-Sat
"A bit of everything, limited selection." ed.

Spence-Chapin Thrift Shop 212-737-8448
1424 Third Ave. (80-81st) NYC 10028
Hours: 10-5 Mon-Sat
"Mostly clothing, some books, magazines, furniture, bric-a brac." ed.

Thrift Shop East 212-744-5429
1430 Third Ave. (81st) NYC 10028
Hours: 10-5:45 Mon-Sat
"Large selection; pricey." ed.

TILE, BRICKS & COBBLESTONES

Belden-Stark — 212-686-3939
386 Park Ave. South (27-28th) NYC 10016
Hours: 9-5 Mon-Fri
"Bricks, tilepaper, glazed tile; (Mfg., not distributor)." ed.

Ceramica Mia — 212-759-2339
405 East 51st St. (1st) NYC 10022
Hours: 10-6 Mon-Fri/ 10-5 Sat
"Italian ceramic tile importers." ed.

Country Floors — 212-758-7414
300 East 61st St. (2nd) NYC 10021
Hours: 9-6 Mon-Fri/ 9-5 Sat
"Handpainted tiles, large selection of terra cotta tiles." ed.

Giurdanella Brothers — 212-674-2097
4 Bond St. (B'way-Lafayette) NYC 10012 — 212-674-2176
Hours: 7:30-4:30 Mon-Fri
"American Olean dealer, very helpful, fast service, samples available."

Hastings Tile & Il Bagno Collection — 212-755-2710
201 East 57th St. (3rd) NYC 10022
Hours: 9:30-5 Mon-Fri
"Huge selection of ceramic tile; very helpful, samples available, quick service." ed.

A. J. Heller — 718-729-5210
21-21 51st Ave. (21st) L.I.C. 11101
Hours: Call first.
"Industrial tile, carpet, rubber treading in red & black; good prices."

Italian Tile Import Corp. — 201-796-0722
410 Market St., Elmwood Park, NJ 07407 — 212-736-0383
Hours: 8:30-5 Mon-Fri (Thurs til 8)/ 10-4 Sat
"Ceramic tile by the square foot; reasonably priced, good quality." ed.

NY Builders — 212-255-7752
99 Jane St. (Washington-West St) NYC 10013
Hours: 7-3:30 Mon-Fri
"Cobblestones, bricks, cinderblocks." ed.

The Quarry (Quarry Enterprises Inc.) — 212-679-2559
183 Lexington Ave. (31-32nd) NYC 10016
Hours: 9-6 Mon-Fri/ 10-4 Sat (except Jun-Aug)
"Ceramic tile only; excellent selection; very helpful; samples available." ed.

Standard Tile 718-465-8282
214-70 Jamaica Ave., Queens Village, NY 11428
Hours: 8-4:30 Mon-Fri/ 8-2 Sat
"Ceramic tile." ed.

Tile Distributors 914-633-7200
7 King's Highway, New Rochelle, NY 10801
Hours: 7:30-4:30 M-F (Th til 7)/ 9-4:30 Sat (Summer Sat's 9-1:30)
"If they don't carry it they'll help you find distributors." ed.

TOOLS, CARPENTRY

AAA Appliance Rentals & Sales Co. 212-686-8884
40 West 29th St. (B'way-6th) NYC 10001
Hours: 8:30-5:30 Mon-Fri
"Electric power tool rental and sales." ed.

Abbey Rent-All

203-16 Northern Blvd., Bayside, NY 11361 718-428-0400
Hours: 8-5:30 Mon-Fri

301 S. Broadway, Hicksville, NY 11801 516-681-1323
(on Rt. 107, 3 blks. south of Old Country Road)
Hours: 8-5:30 Mon-Fri/ 8-5 Sat

"Power tool rental." ed.

Allcraft Tool & Supply Co. 212-246-4740
64 West 48th St. (5-6th) NYC 10036
Hours: 9-4:45 Mon-Fri
"Sells and repairs Cutawls; hand and power tools; metalcraft supplies." ed.

American Machine & Motor Co. 212-226-4577
22 Howard St. (B'way-Lafayette) NYC 10013
Hours: 8:30-3 Mon-Thurs
"Woodworking power tools; ask for Barry." ed.

Ames Stapling and Nailing Systems 212-684-4667
1261 Broadway 9th Fl. (31-32nd) NYC 10001
Hours: 9-5 Mon-Fri/ call for weekend hours.
"Aerosmith and Hansen tools; see Steve Ames." ed.

Bargain Spot 212-674-1188
64 Third Ave. (11th) NYC 10003
Hours: 8:30-5 Mon-Sat
"Sales and rental of power tools, hand tools." ed.

Rudolph Bass 212-226-4000
175 Lafayette St. (near Broome) NYC 10013
Hours: 9-5 Mon-Fri/ 9-1 Sat
"Specialty is large power tools, including parts and maintenance." ed.

Best Hardware & Mill Supply Inc. 516-354-0529
1513 Jericho Turnpike, New Hyde Park, NY 11040
Hours: 8-5:30 Mon-Sat
"Cobalt drill bits, milling supplies, tools, case-hardened bolts, hardware." ed.

C K & L Surplus 212-966-1745
307 Canal St. (B'way-Mercer) NYC 10013
Hours: 9-4:45 every day
"Inexpensive, home-quality hand tools." ed.

Carter, Milchman & Frank 718-361-2300
28-10 37th Ave. (29th) L.I.C. 11101
Hours: 9-5 Mon-Fri
"Large power tools, repair parts for tools." ed.

Charrette Drafting Supply Corp.

5 West 45th St. (5th) NYC 10036 212-921-1122
Hours: 8:30-7 Mon-Fri/ 10-7 Sat

215 Lexington Ave. (33rd) NYC 10016 212-683-8822
Hours: 8:30-8:30 Mon-Fri/ 8:30-6 Sat/ (Sun 12-5 Sept.-June)

"Cutawl rental and purchase; Dremel tools, art supplies; 20% discount card available." ed.

Albert Constantine & Sons 212-792-1600
2050 Eastchester Road Bronx 10461
Hours: 8-6 Mon-Fri (Thurs til 8)/ 8-3 Sat
(May-August: 8-5 Mon-Fri/ 8-1 Sat)
"Fine woodworking tools; hardwoods, veneers." ed.

Cutawl Co. 203-792-8622
Route 6, Bethel, CT 06801
Hours: 9-5 Mon-Fri
"Cutawls; catalog available." ed.

Direct Fastening Service Corp. 212-533-4260
132 West Houston St. (MacDougal-Sullivan) NYC 10012
Hours: 8-4:30 Mon-Fri
"Mostly heavy equipment; Skil, Millwaukee power tools." ed.

B. Dulchin Inc. 212-243-6741
170 Seventh Ave. (20-21st) NYC 10011
Hours: 8-4:30 Mon-Fri
"Good prices on hand, power, bench tools; Porter-Cable power tools & Rockwell machinery; see Ed Dulchin." ed.

DUO-FAST CORP. 718-726-2400
31-07 20th Rd. (31st St.-20th Ave.) L.I.C. 11105
Hours: 8:30-5 Mon-Fri (closed for lunch 12-1)
Staplers, nailers, tackers (air and electric). Tapes and adhesives. Mobile service vans. Local salesman.
"Complete line of Jet-Melt and adhesives and Polygun applicators." ed.

Enkay Trading Co. Inc. 718-272-5570
600 Atkins Ave. (Linden) Bklyn 11208
Hours: 8:30-4:30 Mon-Fri
"Polishing equipment, drill bits, files, rotary files; imported and domestic tools; minimum order $100." ed.

Force Machinery Co. 201-688-8270
2271 US Hwy 22, Union, NJ 07083
Hours: 7:30-5:30 Mon-Thurs/ 7:30-8:20 Fri/ 8:30-4 Sat
"Excellent for shop equipment; all types of hand and power tools." ed.

The Garrett Wade Co. Inc. 212-807-1155
161 Sixth Ave. (Spring) NYC 10013
Hours: 9-5:30 Mon-Fri/ 10-3 Sat
"Fine woodworking tools from all countries." ed.

Grainger 718-326-1598
58-45 Grand Ave., (near 61st) Maspeth, NY 11378
Hours: 8-5 Mon-Fri
"Wide selection of hand and power tools, tool boxes, chests." ed.

H. T. Sales 212-265-0747
718 Tenth Ave. (49-50th) NYC 10019
Hours: 8-4 Mon-Fri
"Rental and sales of hand and power tools." ed.

Hippodrome Hardware 212-840-2791
23 West 45th St. (5-6th) NYC 10036
Hours: 8-5:45 Mon-Fri/ 9-3 Sat
"Dremel accessories, hardware." ed.

Industrial Supply Co. of Long Island 718-784-1291
47-30 Vernon Blvd. L.I.C. 11101
Hours: 8:30-5:30 Mon-Fri
"Industrial tools, carpentry tools." ed.

Kaminstein Brothers 212-777-7170
29 Third Ave. (9th) NYC 10003
Hours: 9-6 Mon-Fri/ 8:30-5:30 Sat
"Power, hand tools; general and decorative hardware, industrial hardware." ed.

Kochendorfer 212-925-1435
413 West Broadway (Prince-Spring) NYC 10013
Hours: 7-5 Mon-Fri
"Bandsaw blades, blade sharpening." ed.

McKilligan Supply 607-798-9335
435 Main St., Johnson City, NY 13790
Hours: 9-5 Mon-Fri
"Suppliers of foundry equipment, heavy equipment, tools, bench tools, hardwoods to schools; catalog." ed.

Microflame Inc. 612-935-3777
3724 Oregon Ave. South, Minneapolis, MN 55426
Hours: 8-5 Mon-Fri
"Electronically controlled styrofoam cutter; ask for Jim Boyer." ed.

Mutual Hardware 718-361-2480
5-45 49th Ave. (Vernon) L.I.C. 11101
Hours: 8:30-5 Mon-Fri/ 8:30-6 Sat
"Cutawls, Dremels, routers, drills, saws, sanders, hand tools; catalog available." ed.

New Era Hardware and Supply 212-265-4183
832 Ninth Ave. (54-55th) NYC 10019
Hours: 8-4:30 Mon-Fri
"Large selection of Greenlee & Brown and Sharpe tools." ed.

Dave Sanders and Co. 212-334-9898
111 Bowery (Grand-Hester) NYC 10002
Hours: 8-4:45 Mon-Fri
"One of NYC's largest selections of power tools; hardware." ed.

Segal Brothers 718-383-2995
205 Nassau St. (Russell) Bklyn 11201
Hours: 9-5 Mon-Fri
"Large selection of tools, Crosby clamps, motors." ed.

Seven Corners Ace Hardware 800-328-0457
216 West 7th St., St. Paul, MN 55102
Hours: 9-5 Mon-Fri
"Very good prices on power and hand tools; catalog." ed.

W. H. Silver's Hardware 212-247-4406
832 Eighth Ave. (50-51st) NYC 10019 212-247-4425
Hours: 8-6 Mon-Fri/ 8-1 Sat
"Bosch, Rockwell, Makita power tools; theatrical hardware, tape; very helpful." ed.

Skil Corp. 212-226-7630
75 Varick St. (Canal) NYC 10013
Hours: 8-5 Mon-Fri
"Tool rental and sales." ed.

Tool Warehouse 516-420-1420
9 Willow Park Center, Farmingdale, NY 11735
Hours: 8-6 Mon-Fri/ 9-5 Sat/ 11-5 Sun
"Good discounts on hand tools and power tools." ed.

Travers Tool Co. 718-932-9400
25-26 50th St., Woodside, NY 11377
Hours: 8:30-4:30 Mon-Fri
"Drill bits, chuck keys, clamps, sanding belts, etc." ed.

US General Hardware 516-433-2562
700 Mid-Island Shopping Plaza, Hicksville, NY 11801
Hours: 9:30-9:30 Mon-Sat/ 12-5 Sun
"Large selection of power, hand tools; catalog." ed.

Harold C. Wolff Inc. Hardware 212-227-2128
127 Fulton St. 3rd Fl. (Williams-Nassau) NYC 10038
Hours: 8-4 Mon-Fri
"Power and hand tools, casters." ed.

TOOLS, JEWELERS see JEWELERS TOOLS & SUPPLIES

TOOLS, LEATHERCRAFT
see LEATHERCRAFTERS & FURRIERS TOOLS & SUPPLIES

TOOLS, SCULPTORS see CASTING SUPPLIES

TOOLS, UPHOLSTERY see UPHOLSTERY TOOLS & SUPPLIES

TOOLS & PARTS, MACHINE see MACHINISTS & MACHINE TOOLS

TOYS

See also DOLLS & DOLLHOUSES

Childcraft Center

155 East 23rd St. (3rd-Lexington) NYC 10010 212-674-4754
150 East 58th St. (3rd-Lexington) NYC 10155 212-753-3196

Hours: 10-5:45 Mon-Fri/ 10-4:45 Sat
"Children's furniture and toys; rental or purchase." ed.

Chick Darrow's Fun Antiques 212-838-0730
1174 Second Ave. (61-62nd) NYC 10021
Hours: 11-6 Mon-Fri/ 11-4 Sat/ or by appt.
"Large selection antique toys and games; will rent." ed.

FAO Schwarz 212-644-9400
745 Fifth Ave. (58th) NYC 10151
Hours: 10-6 Mon-Sat (Thurs til 8)
"Large selection stuffed toys, dolls, dollhouses, games, trains, playground equipment." ed.

Go Fly A Kite

153 East 53rd St. (Citicorp Bldg., 3rd-Lexington) NYC 10022 212-308-1666
Hours: 10:30-7:30 Mon-Fri/ 10-6 Sat/ 10-5 Sun

1201 Lexington Ave. (81-82nd) NYC 10028 212-472-2623
Hours: 10-5:45 Mon-Sat/ 12-4:45 Sun

"Kites: all types and sizes." ed.

Johnny Jupiter 212-744-0818
884 Madison Ave. (71-72nd) NYC 10021
Hours: 10:15-6 Mon-Sat
"Repro and antique toys, dolls, wind-up toys; antique linens, postcards, dishes." ed.

The Last Wound-up 212-787-3388
290 Columbus Ave. (73-74th) NYC 10023
Hours: 10-8 Mon-Sat/ 12-7 Sun
"Fabulous selection of wind-up toys." ed.

Mythology Unlimited Inc. 212-874-0774
370 Columbus Ave. (77-78th) NYC 10024
Hours: 11-9 Mon-Fri/ 11-6 Sat, Sun
"Interesting selection antique repro to high tech toys, foreign film posters." ed.

B. Shackman & Co. Inc. 212-989-5162
85 Fifth Ave. (16th) NYC 10003
Hours: 9-5 Mon-Fri
"Antique repro toys, dolls, dollhouses and dollhouse furniture; wholesale." ed.

Star Magic 212-228-7770
743 Broadway (8th-Waverly) NYC 10003
Hours: 12-9 Mon-Sat/ 12-7 Sun
"Space-related toys, posters, books, star maps and finders; crystals."

Toy Park 212-427-6611
112 East 86th St. (Park-Lexington) NYC 10028
Hours: 10-6 Mon/ 10-7 Tues-Sat (Thurs til 8)/ 12-5 Sun
"Large selection toys, games, models, dolls, stuffed animals." ed.

TRIMMINGS: BEADS, SEQUINS, RHINESTONES, PEARLS

BAER FABRICS 502-583-5521
515 East Market, Louisville, KY 40202
Hours: 9-5:30 Mon-Sat
All colors, styles, sizes; loose, trim, applique. (See display ad page 127.)
"Shipment within 24 hours for in-stock items." ed.

Helen Behar World of Bargains 212-924-3588
195 Seventh Ave. (21-22nd) NYC 10011
Hours: 12-5 Mon-Sat (closed Sat., May-Labor Day)
"All types of beads, wide selection." ed.

C & C Metal Products 212-695-1679
48 West 37th St. (5-6th) NYC 10018
Hours: 8-9:30am and 4-5pm Mon-Fri for salesman, or by appt.
"Rhinestones, jewels, settings, metal buttons, buckles, nailheads; catalog." ed.

Sidney Coe Inc. 212-391-6960
65 West 37th St. (6th) NYC 10018
Hours: 9-5 Mon-Fri
"Beads, jewels, motifs, sew-on mirrors." ed.

Duplex Novelty 212-564-1352
575 Eighth Ave. (38th) NYC 10018
Hours: 9-5 Mon-Fri
"Wooden beads, buttons, buckles; wholesale; catalog." ed.

Ellis Import Co. Inc. 212-947-6666
44 West 37th St. (5-6th) NYC 10018
Hours: 8-2:30 Mon-Fri
"Rhinestones, jewels, spangles, pearls, beads chains, novelties."

Elvee Pearl Co. 212-947-3930
40 West 37th St. (5-6th) NYC 10018
Hours: 9-4 Mon-Fri
"Simulated pearls; wholesale; minimum: 1 gross, 1 doz. strings; catalog." ed.

Fred Frankel & Sons Inc. 212-840-0810
19 West 38th St. (5-6th) NYC 10018
Hours: 9-4:30 Mon-Fri
"Rhinestone, pearl, beaded, sequined trims and motifs; catalog." ed.

Glori Bead Shoppe 212-924-3587
172 West 4th St. (6-7th) NYC 10014
Hours: 12-8 Mon-Fri/ 12-10 Sat, Sun
"Beads and small packages of findings." ed.

Elliot Greene & Co. Inc. 212-391-9075
37 West 37th St. (5-6th) NYC 10018
Hours: 9:30-4:30 Mon-Fri
"Rhinestones, spangles, jewels, pearls, beaded trims." ed.

Grey Owl Indian Crafts 718-464-9300
113-15 Springfield Blvd., Queens Village, NY 11429
Hours: 9-5 Mon-Fri
"Indian beads, feathers, kits; catalog." ed.

Harman Importing Corp. 212-947-1440
16 West 37th St. (5-6th) NYC 10018
Hours: 9:30-3:30 Mon-Fri
"Jewels, findings, seashells." ed.

Kahaner Inc. 212-840-3030
228 West 38th St. (7-8th) NYC 10018
Hours: 8:30-5 Mon-Fri
"Trims, especially rhinestone, sequin and beaded; catalog." ed.

M & J Trimmings 212-391-9072
1008 Sixth Ave. (37-38th) NYC 10018
Hours: 9-6 Mon-Fri/ 10-5 Sat
"Sequins, beads, jeweled motifs; also wide selection general trimmings." ed.

Margola Import Corp. 212-695-1115
48 West 37th St. (5-6th) NYC 10018
Hours: 9-4:30 Mon-Fri
"Rhinestones, beads, rosemontees." ed.

Mayer Import Co. Inc. 212-391-3830
25 West 37th St. (5-6th) NYC 10018
Hours: 9-5 Mon-Fri
"Jewels, pearls, cameos, trade beads, faceted plastic domes, etc; catalog." ed.

Plume Trading Co. 914-782-8594
PO Box 585 Rt. 208, Monroe, NY 10950
Hours: 9-5 Mon-Fri
"Indian beads, feathers, kits for Indian crafts; catalog." ed.

Roth Import Co. 212-840-1945
13 West 38th St. (5-6th) NYC 10018
Hours: 9-5:30 Mon-Fri
"Sequin and beaded applique, sequins and rhinestones by the yard."

Ruben Bead Importing Co. Inc. 212-840-0500
45 West 37th St. (5-6th) NYC 10018
Hours: 8:30-4 Mon-Fri
"Manufacturer of sequin fabrics, stretch and non-stretch, 45", all colors." ed.

Sequins International Corp. 212-221-3121
110 West 40th St. (6-7th) NYC 10018
Hours: 9-5 Mon-Fri
"Sequins, beads, custom sequin cloth." ed.

Shellcraft, Div. of Cresthill Ind. 212-947-1960
519 Eighth Ave. (35-36th) NYC 10018
Hours: 9-5 Mon-Fri
"Beads, sequins." ed.

Sheru 212-730-0766
49 West 38th St. (5-6th) NYC 10018
Hours: 9-6 Mon-Fri/ 9:30-5 Sat
"Beads, shells, findings, sequins, jewelry, craft supplies; wholesale and retail." ed.

Walbead Inc. 718-392-7616
29-76 Northam Blvd. L.I.C. 11101
Hours: 8-4 Mon-Fri
"Beads, bugle beads, pearls, rhinestones, spangles, sequins, glitter; catalog." ed.

York Novelty Imports Inc. 212-594-7040
10 West 37th St. (5-6th) NYC 10018
Hours: 9-5 Mon-Fri
"Beads, jewels, pearls, spangles, rhinestones, trims, chain, novelties."

TRIMMINGS: CUSTOM

Ideal Cord and Trimming 201-656-2414
317 St. Paul's Ave., Jersey City, NJ 07306
Hours: 7-3:30 Mon-Fri
"Manufacturer of trim from cord; reasonable prices; 3 week delivery."

Lending Trimming Co. Inc. 212-242-7502
179 Christopher St. (West Side Hwy) NYC 10014
Hours: 9-5 Mon-Fri
"Chainette made to order." ed.

Standard Trimming Corp. 212-755-3034
1114 First Ave. 5th Fl. (61st) NYC 10021
Hours: 9-5 Mon-Fri
"Custom trims and tassels; stock of very old and elaborate trims; see Ed Goodman." ed.

TRIMMINGS: FEATHERS & FLOWERS

AA Feather Co./Gettinger Feather Corp. 212-695-9470
16 West 36th St. (5-6th) NYC 10018 212-695-9471
Hours: 9:30-5:30 Mon-Thurs/ 9:30-4 Fri
"Natural and dyed feathers." ed.

AMCAN Feather Co./Sil-Ko Mfg. 718-729-1552
26-32 Skillman Ave. (Hunter's Point) NYC 11101
Hours: 8:30-4 Mon-Thurs/ 8:30-3 Fri
"Natural and dyed feathers, boas, dyed turkey, etc; excellent prices, nice people." ed.

Associated Fabrics Corp. 212-689-7186
104 East 25th St. (Lexington-Park) NYC 10010
Hours: 8:30-4 Mon-Fri
"Nice ostrich plumes over 18"; ask for Armand." ed.

BAER FABRICS 502-583-5521
515 East Market, Louisville, KY 40202
Hours: 9-5:30 Mon-Sat
Maribou/ostrich/turkey boas; plumes; millinery/craft flowers.
(See display ad page 127.)
"Shipment within 24 hours for in-stock items." ed.

Cinderella Flower and Feather Co. 212-840-0644
57 West 38th St. (5-6th) NYC 10018
Hours: 9-4:30 Mon-Fri/ 11-2 Sat
"Good selection fancy feathers, boas, flowers, fruit." ed.

Dulken & Derrick Inc. 212-929-3614
12 West 21st St. 6th Fl. (5-6th) NYC 10010
Hours: 9-4 Mon-Fri
"Silk and fancy flowers; will custom-make." ed.

Grey Owl Indian Crafts 718-464-9300
113-15 Springfield Blvd., Queens Village, NY 11429
Hours: 9-5 Mon-Fri
"Feathers for American Indian headdresses; also beads, kits." ed.

Imperial Feather Co. 718-748-1700
6209 Fifth Ave. (62nd) Bklyn 11220
Hours: call for appt, 7-9am Mon-Fri
"Feathers for contemporary millinery; ask for Norman." ed.

Listokin & Sons Fabrics Inc. 212-226-6111
87 Hester St. (Orchard-Allen) NYC 10002
Hours: 9:30-5:30 Sun-Thurs/ 9:30-4 Fri
"Bridal fabric, boas, white cotton net." ed.

M & J Trimmings — 212-391-9072
1008 Sixth Ave. (37-38th) NYC 10018
Hours: 9-6 Mon-Fri/ 10-5 Sat
"Feather boas, bird skins; also general trimmings." ed.

Manny's Millinery Supply Co. — 212-840-2235
63 West 38th St. (5-6th) NYC 10018
Hours: 9-5:30 Mon-Fri/ 9-3 Sat
"Small of selection feathers and fruit; good selection of millinery supplies." ed.

Metropolitan Impex Inc. — 212-564-0398
966 Sixth Ave. (35-36th) NYC 10018 — 212-244-8558
Hours: 9-7 Mon-Sat
"Feathers, bridal trims." ed.

Paul's Veil & Net Corp. — 212-391-3822
66 West 38th St. (6-7th) NYC 10018 — 212-221-9083
Hours: 8:30-4:30 Mon-Fri
"Bridal laces, flowers." ed.

Plume Trading Co. — 914-782-8594
PO Box 585 Rt. 208, Monroe, NY 10950
Hours: 9-5 Mon-Fri
"Feathers for American Indian crafts and headdresses; kits, beads; catalog." ed.

Roth Import Co. — 212-840-1945
13 West 38th St. (5-6th) NYC 10018
Hours: 9-5:30 Mon-Fri
"Pure silk flowers, feathers, and good selection of trimmings." ed.

M. Schwartz & Sons Feathers Corp. — 516-234-7722
45 Hoffman Ave., Haupaug, NY 11787
Hours: 8:30-5 Mon-Fri
"Wholesale natural and dyed feathers and novelties." ed.

Sil-Ko Mfg. Co. Inc./AMCAN Feather — 212-729-1552
1385 Broadway Rm. 1006 (37-38th) NYC 10018
Hours: 9-4 Mon-Thurs/ 9-3 Fri
"Wholesale, dyed, wired, etc. made to order; feather jackets; see John Coles." ed.

SOUTH AFRICAN FEATHERS — 215-925-5219
325 N. 13th St., Philadelphia, PA 19107
Hours: 8:30-4:30 Mon-Fri

Natural and custom dyed feathers, boas and band plumes.
Mention this ad for 2% discount. Fast delivery.

"By the pound; special orders; catalog." ed.

Zucker Products Corp. 212-741-3400
236 West 18th St. (7-8th) NYC 10003
Hours: 9-5 Mon-Fri
"Boas, maribou, feather flowers; see Monte. (moving, check for new address)." ed.

TRIMMINGS: LACE & LACE MOTIFS

See also FABRICS: SHEERS, NETS, LACES, & TAFFETA

American Fabrics Co. 212-868-0100
29 West 36th St. (5-6th) NYC 10018
Hours: 9-5 Mon-Fri
"Lace, schiffle embroidery, embroidered collars, table linens, flame retardant lace." ed.

Astor Lace and Trimmings 212-736-0475
132 West 36th St. (B'way-7th) NYC 10018
Hours: 7-6 Mon-Fri
"Laces, schiffle embroideries, novelties, trims." ed.

BAER FABRICS 502-583-5521
515 East Market, Louisville, KY 40202
Hours: 9-5:30 Mon-Sat

Alencon, val, venise, cluney, embroidery, vintage/domestic. (See display ad page 127.)

"Shipment within 24 hours for in-stock items." ed.

40th St. Trimmings Inc. 212-354-4729
252 West 40th St. (7-8th) NYC 10018
Hours: 9-5:45 Mon-Fri/ 10-5 Sat
"Notions, trimmings, novelties; wholesale, retail." ed.

M. E. Yarn & Trimmings 212-260-2060
177 East Houston St. (1st) NYC 10002
Hours: 8:30-5 Mon-Fri
"Good prices on lace in quantity; also trims, buttons, yarn." ed.

Lew Novick Inc. 212-221-8960
45 West 38th St. (5-6th) NYC 10018 212-354-5046
Hours: 9-5:15 Mon-Fri/ 9:30-2:30 Sat
"Lace motifs and yardage; nets, maline, tulle, marquisette." ed.

Paul's Veil & Net Corp. 212-391-3822
66 West 38th St. (6-7th) NYC 10018 212-221-9083
Hours: 8:30-4:30 Mon-Fri
"Flowers, bridal laces, lace gloves." ed.

Smith & Yates — 212-666-4191
782 West End Ave. (98th) NYC 10025
Hours: By appt.
"High quality laces and trims; order from sample books." ed.

TRIMMINGS: RIBBONS, BRAIDS, CORD, & TASSELS

Alfred Mfg. Corp. — 201-332-9100
350 Warren, (near Holland Tun) Jersey City, NJ 07302
Hours: 9-4:30 Mon-Fri
"Manufacturer of rayon, cotton, chainette cord." ed.

Artistic Ribbon and Novelty Co. — 212-255-4224
22 West 21st St. (5-6th) NYC 10010
Hours: 9-5 Mon-Fri
"Satin, grosgrain, velvet, poly ribbon; washable, flame retardant." ed.

BAER FABRICS — 502-583-5521
515 East Market, Louisville, KY 40202
Hours: 9-5:30 Mon-Sat
All types, size, color- ribbon, cord, soutache, millinery braid.
(See display ad page 127.)
"Shipment within 24 hours for in-stock items." ed.

Beer-Stern Co. — 212-279-4380
50 West 34th St. (5th-B'way) NYC 10001
Hours: 9-5 Mon-Fri
"By the piece only; jacquard, fancy braid, fringe, novelty trimmings."

Circle Braid Co. — 212-730-8171
247 West 37th St. (9-10th) NYC 10018
Hours: 9-5 Mon-Fri
"Metallic trims, edging braid, fringe, soutache, embroidered motifs, hood cords." ed.

Daytona Trimmings Co. — 212-354-1713, 212-354-1716
251 West 39th St. (7-8th) NYC 10018
Hours: 7-5 Mon-Fri
"Ric-rac, laces, scarves, emblems." ed.

40th St. Trimmings Inc. — 212-354-4729
252 West 40th St. (7-8th) NYC 10018
Hours: 9-5:45 Mon-Fri/ 10-5 Sat
"Notions, trimmings, novelties; wholesale, retail." ed.

Friedman & Distillator (Owl Mills) — 212-233-6394
88 W. Broadway (Chambers-Warren) NYC 10007
Hours: 9-5 Mon-Fri
"Trimmings and fabrics; catalog; speak to Toni." ed.

Gampel Supply Corp. 212-398-9222
39 West 37th St. (5-6th) NYC 10018
Hours: 8:45-4:30 Mon-Fri
"Rattail, soutache, decorative and beaded cord." ed.

Gelberg Braid Co. Inc. 212-730-1121
243 West 39th St. (7-8th) NYC 10018
Hours: 9-5 Mon-Fri
"Manufacturer of dress trimmings, braids, tassels, cords, braided buttons; see Irwin." ed.

Harold Trimming Co. 212-695-4098
315 West 36th St. (8-9th) NYC 10018
Hours: 8-5 Mon-Fri
"See Mitchell." ed.

Hyman Hendler & Sons 212-840-8393
67 West 38th St. (5-6th) NYC 10018
Hours: 9-5:30 Mon-Fri
"Quality ribbons; grosgrain, satin, everything; some drapery, upholstery, antique trims." ed.

Jay Notions & Novelties Inc. 212-921-0440
22 West 38th St. (5-6th) NYC 10018
Hours: 9-5 Mon-Fri
"Wholesale ribbon, braid, trim." ed.

La Lame Inc. 212-921-9770
250 West 39th St. 5th Fl. (7th-8th) NYC 10018
Hours: 9-5 Mon-Fri
"Selection of metallic trims is excellent." ed.

M. E. Yarn & Trimmings 212-260-2060
177 East Houston St. (1st) NYC 10002
Hours: 8:30-5 Mon-Fri
"Trims, buttons, yarn; good prices on lace in quantity." ed.

M & J Trimmings 212-391-9072
1008 Sixth Ave. (37-38th) NYC 10018
Hours: 9-6 Mon-Fri/ 10-5 Sat
"Braids, cord, ribbon, tassels; also wide selection general trimmings."

C. M. OFFRAY & SONS INC. 201-879-4700
Route 24, PO Box 601, Chester, NJ 07930
Hours: 8:30-4:30 Mon-Fri

Offray Ribbons are available in many colors, widths and patterns: Satin, Grosgrain, Velvet, Plaids, Stripes, etc. Two collections are offered: quality Woven-Edge Ribbons (for costumes, apparel, accessories, home decorating), and Creative Craft and Floral Ribbons (for decorations and crafts).

"Catalog. Great wholesale ribbons." ed.

Roth Import Co. 212-840-1945
13 West 38th St. (5-6th) NYC 10018
Hours: 9-5:30 Mon-Fri
"Metallic braids and cords, beaded fringe, etc." ed.

Royale Draperies Inc. 212-431-0170
289 Grand St. (Eldridge) NYC 10002
Hours: 9-5:30 Mon-Fri/ 9-5 Sun
"Good variety trims and braids, cable cord, remnants; inexpensive."

Martin Schorr Co. 212-719-4870
216 West 38th St. (7-8th) NYC 10018
Hours: 8:20-5 Mon-Fri
"Washable ribbons, velvet, grosgrain, satin, jaquard; woven labels."

Smith & Yates 212-666-4191
782 West End Ave. (98th) NYC 10025
Hours: By appt.
"Fine quality trims; order from sample books." ed.

So-Good 212-398-0236
28 West 38th St. (5-6th) NYC 10018
Hours: 9-5 Mon-Fri
"Ribbons, braid, piping." ed.

Textile Ribbon Co. 212-391-6923
63 West 38th St. (5-6th) NYC 10018
Hours: 9-4:30 Mon-Fri
"All types; some trims." ed.

L. P. Thur 212-243-4913
126 West 23rd St. (6-7th) NYC 10011
Hours: 9-6 Mon-Fri
"Trims, antique buttons." ed.

Tinsel Trading 212-730-1030
47 West 38th St. (5-6th) NYC 10018
Hours: 10:30-5 Mon-Fri/ 12-5 Sat
"Metallic trims and tassels; antique trims." ed.

TRIMMINGS: UPHOLSTERY & DRAPERY

See also TRIMMINGS: RIBBONS, BRAID, CORD, etc.

BAER FABRICS 502-583-5521
515 East Market, Louisville, KY 40202
Hours: 9-5:30 Mon-Sat
Distributor of full line of 'Conso' trims and supplies. (See display ad page 127.)
"Shipment within 24 hours for in-stock items." ed.

S. Beckenstein 212-475-4525
130 Orchard St. (near Delancey) NYC 10002
Hours: 9-5:30 Sun-Fri
"Drapery and some upholstery trims; lots of fabrics." ed.

Brunschwig & Fils Inc. 212-838-7878
979 Third Ave. (58-59th) NYC 10022
Hours: 9-5 Mon-Fri
"Decorator house; traditional American and European trims, fabric, wallpaper; expensive." ed.

Conso 212-556-6316
104 West 40th St. (B'way-6th) NYC 10018
Hours: 9-5 Mon-Fri
"Wholesale drapery and upholstery trims and supplies." ed.

Greentex Upholstery Supplies 212-206-8585
236 West 26th St. (7-8th) NYC 10001
Hours: 8-4 Mon-Thurs/ 8-2 Fri
"Upholstery supply house; simple selection." ed.

Kago Upholsterers Supply Co. 718-441-0600
124-16 101st Ave., Richmond Hill, NY 11419
Hours: 8:30-5 Mon-Fri/ 8:30-1 Sat
"Reasonably priced upholstery braids and trims." ed.

Standard Trimming Corp. 212-755-3034
1114 First Ave. 5th Fl. (61st) NYC 10021
Hours: 9-5 Mon-Fri
"Custom trims and tassels; stock of very old and elaborate trims; see Ed Goodman." ed.

Van Wyck Drapery Hardware Supply Corp. 212-925-1300
39 Eldridge St. (Canal) NYC 10002
Hours: 8-5 Mon-Thurs/ 8-4 Fri/ 9-4 Sun
"Tassels, tiebacks, cord." ed.

TROPHIES & AWARDS

Alpha Engraving Co. 212-247-5266
888 Eighth Ave. (52nd-53rd) NYC 10019
Hours: 9-5:30 Mon-Fri
"Engraved trophies, awards; metal and plastic engraved signs; name tags." ed.

Gordon Novelty Co. Inc. 212-254-8616
933 Broadway (21-22nd) NYC 10010
Hours: 9-4:30 Mon-Fri
"Prize ribbons, wholesale novelties, magic tricks, jokes, Halloween items; catalog." ed.

J. Loria & Sons Inc. 212-925-0300
178 Bowery (Kenmare) NYC 10012
Hours: 10-6 Mon-Fri/ 10-4 Sat
"All types of trophies, plaques, engraving, ribbons, etc." ed.

Malcolm & Hayes Silversmiths 212-682-1316
694 Third Ave. (44th) NYC 10017
Hours: 8:30-6 Mon-Fri
"Awards, trophies, certificates, ribbons, silver cups; printing and engraving." ed.

Murray Rackoff Inc. 212-869-5093
25 West 39th St. (Madison-5th) NYC 10018
Hours: 9-5:30 Mon-Fri
"Large selection trophies; engraving; catalog." ed.

TROPICAL FISH

See also PET SUPPLIES

AQUARIUM DESIGN 212-308-5224
979 Third Ave. (58-59th) NYC 10022 718-225-6815
Hours: By appt. (24 hour emergency service)

Manufacturers & Custom Designers of Aquariums & Ecological Life Support Systems. Installation & Maintenance. Hand caught marine fish. Rare corals & shells. 24 hour emergency service. Film credits on request.

aquarium design®

"Provide stabilized environment (clear water) for location work." ed.

Broadway Aquarium & Pet Shop 212-724-0536
648 Amsterdam Ave. (91-92nd) NYC 10025
Hours: 9:30-6 Mon-Fri/ 9:30-5:30 Sat
"Basic neighborhood pet supply store." ed.

Crystal Aquarium 212-534-9003
1659 Third Ave. (93rd) NYC 10128
Hours: 10-7 Mon-Sat/ 12-5 Sun (closed Sun in Summer)
"Aquariums, fish specialists; pet store for fish lovers." ed.

Exotic Aquatics

8 Cornelia St. NYC 10014 212-675-6355
Hours: 11-7 Mon-Fri/ 11-6 Sat/ 12-5 Sun

271½ Amsterdam Ave. (72-73rd) NYC 10023 212-873-8655
Hours: 10-9 Mon-Fri/ 10-7 Sat/ 11-6 Sun

"Unique, exotic fish, birds, reptiles." ed.

Fish & Pet Town 212-752-9508
241 East 59th St. (2-3rd) NYC 10022
Hours: 11-7:30 Mon-Fri/ 10:30-6 Sat/ 12-5 Sun
"Large selection fish, dog and cat supplies." ed.

Fish Town USA 212-889-3296
513 Third Ave. (34th) NYC 10016
Hours: 12:30-6:30 Mon-Fri/ 10:30-7 Sat/ 10:30-6 Sun
"Rare and exotic fish, aquariums." ed.

Petland Discounts

132 Nassau St. (Ann-Beekman) NYC 10038 212-964-1821
Hours: 9-7 Mon-Fri/ 10-6 Sat/ 11-5 Sun

7 East 14th St. (5th) NYC 10003 212-675-4102
Hours: 9-8 Mon-Fri/ 10-6:30 Sat/ 11-5 Sun

304 East 86th St. (2nd) NYC 10028 212-472-1655
Hours: 10-9 Mon-Fri/ 10-6 Sat/ 11-5 Sun

"Good selection of pet supplies; birds, fish, small animals." ed.

TWINES & CORDAGE

See also PACKING MATERIALS

Amalgamated Cordage 516-484-5470
34 Harvor Park Dr., Ft. Washington, NY 11050
Hours: 9-5 Mon-Fri (office) / 7-4 Mon-Fri (warehouse)
"Wholesale cotton jute, sisal twine and cord." ed.

American Cord & Webbing Co. Inc. 212-695-7340
505 Eighth Ave. (35th) NYC 10018
Hours: 9-5:30 Mon-Fri
"Wholesale cotton, jute, webbing, tape, binding, elastic cord and webbing." ed.

Independent Cordage Co. 212-925-4240
38 Laight St. (Hudson-Varick) NYC 10013
Hours: 9-5 Mon-Fri
"Natural and synthetic cords and ropes." ed.

Norman Librett Inc. 914-636-1500
64 Main St., New Rochelle, NY 10801
Hours: 9-5 Mon-Fri
"Wholesale rope and cordage." ed.

Seaboard Twine & Cordage Co. Inc. 212-732-6658
49 Murray St. (Church-B'way) NYC 10007
Hours: 8:30-4:30 Mon-Fri
"Twines of all description; natural and synthetic fibres." ed.

William Usdan & Sons 212-226-6177
52 Thompson St. (Broome) NYC 10012
Hours: 8-4:30 Mon-Fri
"Poly cordage." ed.

TYPEWRITERS see BUSINESS MACHINES & TYPEWRITERS

UPHOLSTERERS

See also PROP & SCENIC CRAFTSPEOPLE

City Upholstery 718-449-5242
3000 Ocean Pkwy. (23rd) Bklyn 11235
Hours: 8-4:30 Mon-Fri
"Upholstery work only." ed.

Eclectic Properties Inc. 212-799-8963
204 West 84th St. (B'way-Amsterdam) NYC 10024
Hours: 9-5 Mon-Fri or by appt.
"Ask for Suri." ed.

McHUGH/ROLLINS ASSOCIATES INC. 718-643-0990
79 Bridge St. (York-Front) Bklyn 11201
Hours: 9-6 Mon-Fri
24 hour turnaround available on rush orders. Complete refinishing and strengthening for entertainment needs. See Leslie. (See display ad page 300.)
"Full service prop shop." ed.

Carl Olmstead Upholstery 212-206-1488
122 West 26th St. (6-7th) NYC 10001
Hours: 8-5 Mon-Fri
"Upholstery, slip covers and draperies." ed.

Pretty Decorating 212-674-1310
29 Avenue A (2nd) NYC 10009
Hours: 9-5 Sun-Fri
"Fast service, upholstery, slip covers, drapes." ed.

Harold Rudin Decorators Inc. 212-265-4716
753 Ninth Ave. (50-51st) NYC 10019 212-757-5639
Hours: 9-5 Mon-Fri
"Quick service, reasonable prices; best to be explicit with your order." ed.

Twentieth Century Draperies Inc. 212-925-7707
70 Wooster St. (Spring-Broome) NYC 10012
Hours: 9-5 Mon-Fri
"Custom draperies, curtains, bedspreads, tablecloths, upholstery; see Ken Sandberg; your fabric or theirs." ed.

I. Weiss and Sons 212-246-8444
2-07 Borden Ave. L.I.C. 11101
Hours: 8:30-4:30 Mon-Fri
"Drapery, rigging, scrims, soft goods; very helpful." ed.

UPHOLSTERY TOOLS & SUPPLIES

See also DOWN, BATTING & FIBERFILL
See also FABRICS: DRAPERY, SLIP COVER, UPHOLSTERY
See also FOAM SHEETING & SHAPES
See also TRIMMINGS: UPHOLSTERY & DRAPERY
For caning supplies, see RATTAN, REED & RAFFIA

American Cord & Webbing Co. Inc. 212-695-7340
505 Eighth Ave. (35th) NYC 10018
Hours: 9-5:30 Mon-Fri
"Webbing, binding, cotton, jute, elastic webbing; wholesale." ed.

BAER FABRICS 502-583-5521
515 East Market, Louisville, KY 40202
Hours: 9-5:30 Mon-Sat
Full selection of upholstery tools and supplies. Supplier of full line to the upholstery trade. (See dislay ad page 127.)
"Shipment within 24 hours for in-stock items." ed.

BZI Distributors 212-966-6690
105 Eldridge St. (Grand-Broome) NYC 10002
Hours: 9-5:30 Mon-Fri/ 9-5 Sun
"Major upholstery supply house." ed.

Greentex Upholstery Supplies 212-206-8585
236 West 26th St. (7-8th) NYC 10001
Hours: 8-4 Mon-Thurs/ 8-2 Fri
"Upholstery needles, tacks, staples, snap tape, velcro, trims, webbing."

Inner Space Foam & Upholstery Center 212-533-9590
34 Avenue A (2nd) NYC 10009 212-982-5382
Hours: 10:30-6 Mon-Sat
"Foam rubber, polyester fibers, pillow forms." ed.

Kago Upholsterers Supply Co. 718-441-0600
124-16 101st Ave., Richmond Hill, NY 11419
Hours: 8:30-5 Mon-Fri/ 8:30-1 Sat
"Small shop, reasonable prices; upholstery braids and trims, supplies." ed.

Kirsch Drapery Hardware 212-966-6690
105 Eldridge St. (Grand-Broome) NYC 10002
Hours: 9-5:30 Mon-Fri/ 9-5 Sun
"Fair selection of drapery trims; good drapery hardware." ed.

K. P. Williams Co. 212-683-8162
295 Madison Ave. (41st) NYC 10017
Hours: 9-5 Mon-Fri
"Tools, staples, foam." ed.

VACUUMFORMING & VACUUMFORMED PANELS

Brooklyn Model Works 718-834-1944
60 Washington Ave. (Park-Flushing) Bklyn 11205
Hours: 9-5 Mon-Fri
"Special props, casting and reproduction, vacuuforming, mechanization." ed.

CHRISTO VAC/COSTUME ARMOUR INC. 914-534-9120
PO Box 325, Shore Road, Cornwall-on-Hudson, NY 12520 212-585-1199
Hours: 9-4 Mon-Fri
Wood paneling, library, bricks, etc. Unpainted/painted. Catalogue & custom work, props, masks. Up to 4' x 12'. (See display ad page 299.)
"Also stock and custom armor and weaponry." ed.

E & T Plastic Mfg. Co. Inc. 718-729-6226
45-33 37th St. (off Queens Blvd) L.I.C. 11101
Hours: 9-5 Mon-Fri
"Vacuumforming, plexi, acrylic, acetate, lexan, teflon; call Elliot." ed.

Electra Displays 516-585-5659
90 Remington Blvd., Ronkonkoma, NY 11779 212-420-1327
Hours: 9-5 Mon-Fri
"Vacuumformed panels: brick, etc." ed.

THE GREAT AMERICAN MARKET 213-461-0200
826 N. Cole Ave., Hollywood, CA 90038
Hours: 8-5 Mon-Fri/ Sat by appt. only
(See display ad on the divider page.)
"Instaset vacuumformed scenery, tin ceilings, architectural elements, book backs. Catalog." ed.

Honatech Inc. 914-965-7677
185 Riverdale Ave., Yonkers, NY 10705
Hours: 8-5 Mon-Fri
"Small scale plastic fabrication machines; vacuumform, injection mold, blow mold, etc." ed.

McHUGH/ROLLINS ASSOCIATES INC. 718-643-0990
79 Bridge St. (York-Front) Bklyn 11201
Hours: 9-6 Mon-Fri
Custom vacuforming. Our molds or yours. See Leslie or Jim. (See display ad page 300.)
"Full service prop shop." ed.

Provost Displays 212-279-5770
618 West 28th St. (11-12th) NYC 10001
Hours: 9-4:30 Mon-Fri
"Vacuumform shapes and custom vacuumforming up to 4'x12'." ed.

THE SET SHOP 212-929-4845
3 West 20th St. (5th) NYC 10011
Hours: 9-6 Mon-Fri/ 10-4 Sat
Stock bricks, tile, columns, shake shingle, fieldstone. (See display ad page 316.)
"Full scene shop; non-union." ed.

VARIETY STORES

Lamston's

39 Broadway (Exchange Alley) NYC 10006 212-425-3060
Hours: 8-6 Mon-Fri

346 Sixth Ave. (W. 4th) NYC 10011 212-982-2337
Hours: 9:30-7:30 Mon-Sat/ 12-5 Sun

275 Third Ave. (22nd) NYC 10010 212-777-4840
Hours: 9-6:15 Mon-Sat (Thurs, Fri til 7)

273 West 23rd St. (8th) NYC 10011 212-929-8567
Hours: 9-6:20 every day (Thurs, Fri til 7:45)

4 Park Ave. (34th) NYC 10016 212-683-3150
Hours: 8-6 Mon-Fri (Thurs til 7)/ 9-6 Sat

270 Madison Ave. (39th) NYC 10016 212-689-8118
Hours: 8-6 Mon-Fri/ 10-5 Sat (closed Sat in Jul, Aug)

1251 Sixth Ave. (50th) NYC 10020 212-757-3430
Hours: 8-6 Mon-Fri

477 Madison Ave. (51st) NYC 10022 212-688-0232
Hours: 8-6 Mon-Fri/ 10-5:30 Sat

1381 Sixth Ave. (56th) NYC 10019 212-581-3656
Hours: 8-6:30 Mon-Fri/ 9:30-6 Sat/ 12-5 Sun

1082 Second Ave. (57th) NYC 10022 212-421-7355
Hours: 9-6:30 Mon-Fri (Thurs til 7)/ 9:30-6 Sat/ 12-5 Sun

773 Lexington Ave. (61st) NYC 10021 212-751-0885
Hours: 8-6:30 M-F (Mon, Thurs til 8)/ 10-6:30 Sat/ 12-5 Sun

(continues next page)

1279 Third Ave. (74th) NYC 10021 — 212-861-1150
Hours: 9:30-6:30 Mon-Fri/ 9:30-6 Sat

1251 Lexington Ave. (84th) NYC 10028 — 212-535-3499
Hours: 9:30-6 Mon-Sat (Thurs, Fri til 6:45)/ 12-5 Sun

"Alternative selection to Woolworths." ed.

Victory 5 & 10 — 212-246-1930
360 West 55th St. (9th) NYC 10019
Hours: 9-6 Mon-Sat
"A bit of everything; green vinyl window shades; helpful." ed.

Woolworth's

120 West 34th St. (6-7th) NYC 10001 — 212-563-3523
Hours: 9:55-7:45 M,Th,F/ 9:55-5:45 Tu,W,Sat/ 11-4:45 Sun
"Main store; check here first." ed.

761 Broadway (8-9th) NYC 10003 — 212-475-7440
Hours: 8:35-5:45 Mon-Fri/ 10-5:45 Sat

12 East 14th St. (5th-B'way) NYC 10003 — 212-691-6290
Hours: 9:30-5:45 Mon-Sat (Thurs, Fri til 6:15)/ 12-4 Sun

46 East 23rd St. (Park-Madison) NYC 10010 — 212-254-8541
Hours: 7:30-5:30 Mon-Fri/ 10-4:30 Sat

170 East 42nd St. (Lexington-3rd) NYC 10017 — 212-687-0676
Hours: 8-6 Mon-Fri/ 10-4:45 Sat

755 Seventh Ave. (50th) NYC 10019 — 212-246-5069
Hours: 8:15-7:30 Mon-Fri/ 9-7:30 Sat

983 Eighth Ave. (57th) NYC 10019 — 212-265-4686
Hours: 9:05-5:40 Mon-Sat

976 Third Ave. (59th) NYC 10022 — 212-755-8634
Hours: 9-7:30 M,Th/ 9-6:30 T,W,F/ 12-5 Sat,Sun

1133 Third Ave. (66th) NYC 10021 — 212-861-6455
Hours: 9-6:30 Mon-Fri/ 9:30-6 Sat

1504 Second Ave. (78-79th) NYC 10021 — 212-861-6500
Hours: 9:30-6:50 Mon-Fri/ 9-6 Sat

Broadway & 79th St. NYC 10024 — 212-362-7088
Hours: 9:35-6:15 Mon-Sat/ 12-5 Sun

"A bit of everything; main store has largest selection." ed.

WALLCOVERINGS
See also CORK
See also VACUUMFORMING & VACUUMFORMED PANELS
See also HOME DECORATING & IMPROVEMENT CENTERS

Bradbury & Bradbury Wallpaper 707-746-1900
PO Box 155, Benicia, CA 94510
Hours: 9-5 Mon-Fri
"Manufacturer of handprinted wallpapers of 19th century designs." ed.

Brunschwig & Fils Inc. 212-838-7878
979 Third Ave. (58-59th) NYC 10022
Hours: 9-5 Mon-Fri
"Decorator house, expensive; traditional American and European styles." ed.

Clarence House 212-752-2890
40 East 57th St. (Madison-Park) NYC 10022
Hours: 9-5:30 Mon-Fri
"Wallpaper to the trade; repros of traditional and historical patterns." ed.

Connaissance Fabrics Inc. 212-752-6365
979 Third Ave. (58-59th) NYC 10022
Hours: 9-5 Mon-Fri
"Wallpapers, to the trade." ed.

Design Gallery 212-532-3610
443 Third Ave. (30-31st) NYC 10016
Hours: 10-6 Mon-Sat (Thurs til 8)
"Wallpapers, plus complete design service; linens, etc." ed.

Donghia Textiles
485 Broadway (Broome) NYC 10013 (office) 212-477-9877
Hours: 9-5 Mon-Fri
979 Third Ave. (60th) NYC 10022 (showroom) 212-935-3713
Hours: 9:30-5 Mon-Fri
"Contemporary "California Drop Cloth," traditionals, floral, paisley."

M. Epstein and Sons 212-265-3960
809 Ninth Ave. (53rd-54th) NYC 10019
Hours: 8-5:15 Mon-Fri/ 8:30-3 Sat (except summer months)
"General theatrical paint store; wallpaper and supplies." ed.

Philip Graf Wallpapers Inc. 212-755-1448
979 Third Ave. (58-59th) NYC 10022
Hours: 9:30-5 Mon-Fri
"Wallpaper, to the trade; large selection of styles." ed.

Janovic Plaza

213 Seventh Ave. (21-22nd) NYC 10011 212-243-2186
Hours: 7:30-6:30 Mon-Fri/ 9-6 Sat

1150 Third Ave. (67th) NYC 10021 212-772-1400
Hours: 7:30-6:30 Mon-Fri/ 8-5:45 Sat

159 West 72nd St. NYC 10023 212-595-2500
Hours: 7:30-6:30 Mon-Fri (Tues til 8)/ 9-6 Sat/ 11-5 Sun

"Home decorating center; wallpaper, paint and supplies." ed.

Katzenbach & Warren Inc. 212-759-5410
979 Third Ave. (57th) NYC 10022
Hours: 9-5 Mon-Fri
"Repros of the papers of Colonial Williamsburg; wholesale." ed.

Kirk-Brummel 212-477-8590
979 Third Ave. (58-59th) NYC 10022
Hours: 9-5 Mon-Fri
"To the trade; general selection." ed.

Laura Ashley Inc. 212-371-0606
714 Madison Ave. (63rd) NYC 10021
Hours: 10-6 Mon-Sat (Thurs til 7)
"Fabrics and wallcoverings in coordinating patterns." ed.

Andre Matenciot Co. Inc. 212-486-9064
979 Third Ave. (58-59th) NYC 10022
Hours: 9-5 Mon-Fri
"Custom wallpaper and fabrics; to the trade." ed.

Schumacher 212-644-5900
939 Third Ave. (56th) NYC 10022 (showroom)
Hours: 9-4:45 Mon-Fri
"Large collection Victorian wallpapers and matching fabrics; to the trade." ed.

Wallpaper East Inc. 212-861-9420
1190 Third Ave. (69th) NYC 10021
Hours: 10-5 Mon-Fri
"Retail, large variety." ed.

Wallpaper Mart 212-889-4900
187 Lexington Ave. (29-30th) NYC 10016
Hours: 10-6:30 Mon-Fri (Thurs til 7)/ 10-5 Sat
"Geometrics, art deco, traditional, scenics and contemporary in stock."

Wolf Paints 212-245-7777
771 Ninth Ave. (51-52nd) NYC 10019
Hours: 7:30-5:30 Mon-Fri/ 8-5 Sat
"Large selection of wallpapers, upstairs; also paints and supplies."

WEAVING SUPPLIES

Bell Yarn Co. 212-674-1030
75 Essex St. (Delancey) NYC 10002
Hours: 8:30-5:45 Sun-Fri
"Fox and Wonoco yarns." ed.

Contessa Yarns 203-423-3479
PO Box 37, Lebanon, CT 06249
Hours: 8-4 Mon-Fri (closed 12-1)/ 9-4 Sat/ 1-4 Sun
"Wool, silk, linen, cotton, rayon, novelty yarns." ed.

Coulter Studios Inc. 212-421-8083
118 East 59th St. 2nd Fl. (Lexington-Park) NYC 10022
Hours: 10-6 Mon-Sat
"Yarn, looms, needlepoint, weaving supplies." ed.

Fiber Works 212-286-9116
313 East 45th St. (1-2nd) NYC 10017
Hours: 11-6:30 Mon-Sat
"Wonderful yarns; expensive." ed.

Fibre Yarn Co. Inc. 212-719-5820
48 West 38th St. (5-6th) NYC 10018
Hours: 8:30-4:30 Mon-Fri
"Many types of yarn, incl. chenille, silk, embroidery thread." ed.

Glimakra Looms & Yarns Inc. 216-333-7595
19285 Detroit Road, Rocky River, OH 44116
Hours: 9-5:30 Mon-Sat
"Wide selection wool, linen, cotton, hemp yarns." ed.

M. E. Yarn & Trimmings 212-260-2060
177 East Houston St. (1st) NYC 10002
Hours: 8:30-5 Mon-Fri
"Yarn, also trims, buttons, lace." ed.

School Productions 212-679-3516
1201 Broadway 3rd Fl. (28-29th) NYC 10001
Hours: 9-5 Mon-Fri
"Yarn, looms." ed.

Sunray Yarn Co. 212-475-0062
349 Grand St. (Essex-Ludlow) NYC 10002
Hours: 9:30-5 Sun-Fri
"Yarn, big selection embroidery threads." ed.

John Wilde & Bro. Inc. 215-482-8800
3705 Main St., Philadelphia, PA 19127
Hours: 10-5:30 Mon-Fri/ 10-5 Sat
"Wool yarns and carded wools." ed.

The Yarn Center 212-921-9293
61 West 37th St. (5-6th) NYC 10008
Hours: 10-6 Mon-Fri (Thurs til 7)/ 10-5 Sat
"Wide selection of yarns." ed.

WELDERS & SPOT WELDERS

ABC Spring Co. 212-675-1629
16 West 22nd St. (5-6th) NYC 10010
Hours: 9:30-5 Mon-Fri
"Spring steel wire, rod; custom fabrication." ed.

Bournonville Welders 212-246-7558
237 West 60th St. (Amsterdam-West End) NYC 10023
Hours: 8-4:30 Mon-Fri
"Spot welders, sometimes while you wait; any size item, also cutting."

McHUGH/ROLLINS ASSOCIATES INC. 718-643-0990
79 Bridge St. (York-Front) Bklyn 11201
Hours: 9-6 Mon-Fri
Custom metal fabrication in aluminum, steel & brass. See Jim.
(See display ad page 300.)
"Full service prop shop." ed.

Wire Frame Shop 212-586-4239
622 West 47th St. (11-12th) NYC 10036
Hours: By appt.
"Iron and spot welding; wire frames for novelty hats and headpieces."

WELDING SUPPLIES

Allcraft Tool & Supply Co. 212-246-4740
64 West 48th St. (5-6th) NYC 10036
Hours: 9-4:30-Mon-Fri
"Welding, soldering, metal casting equipment and supplies; propane in 20 lb. tanks." ed.

T. W. Smith Welding Supply 212-247-6323
545 West 59th St. (10-11th) NYC 10019
Hours: 7:30-4 Mon-Fri
"Soldering and welding supplies; propane tanks and regulators; will buy back empties." ed.

WICKER ITEMS

See also BASKETS

Azuma

387 Sixth Ave. (Waverly) NYC 10012 212-989-8690
Hours: 10-9 Mon-Sat/ 11-7:30 Sun

25 East 8th St. (University-5th) NYC 10003 212-673-2900
Hours: 10-9 Mon-Sat/ 11-7:30 Sun

666 Lexington Ave. (55th) NYC 10022 212-752-0599
Hours: 10-7:30 Mon-Fri/ 10-6:30 Sat/ 12-5:45 Sun

251 East 86th St. (2nd) NYC 10128 212-369-4928
Hours: 10-8 Mon-Sat/ 11-7 Sun

"Baskets, bamboo shades, mats; furniture, housewares, personality posters." ed.

Deutsch Inc. 212-532-5780
196 Lexington Ave. (32nd) NYC 10016
Hours: 9-6 Mon-Fri (flexible Sat. hours Spring/Summer)
"Wicker furniture and trunks; good prices; catalog." ed.

The Gazebo 212-832-7077
660 Madison Ave. (61st) NYC 10021
Hours: 9-6:30 Mon-Sat/ 1:30-6 Sun
"Expensive wicker furniture (limited selection), quilts, rag rugs." ed.

Natural Furniture Warehouse 718-857-5959
604 Pacific St. (Flatbush-4th Ave.) Bklyn 11217 718-857-5967
Hours: 10-7:30 Mon-Sat/ 12-6 Sun
"Importer of wicker furniture and wicker items; cheap." ed.

Walter's Wicker Wonderland 212-758-0472
991 Second Ave. (52nd-53rd) NYC 10022
Hours: 9:30-5:30 Mon-Fri
"Wicker furniture and furnishings; will rent." ed.

The Wicker Garden 212-348-1166
1318 Madison Ave. (93-94th) NYC 10028
Hours: 10-5:30 Mon-Sat
"Antique wicker furniture, linens; pricey." ed.

The Wickery 212-889-3669
342 Third Ave. (25th) NYC 10010
Hours: 10:30-6:30 Mon-Fri/ 10:30-6 Sat
"Wicker baskets, hampers, trunks, shelf units, mats, some furniture."

WINEMAKING SUPPLIES

Milan Home Brewing Lab 212-226-4780
57 Spring St. (Lafayette-Mulberry) NYC 10012
Hours: 9-4:45 Mon-Fri/ 9-2:30 Sat
"Good selection wine bottles, jugs, corks, vats, caps and cappers, etc; brochure." ed.

Piper Histick no phone
PO Box 683, Clinton, CT 06413
Hours: mail order only
"Beer and cordial supplies; catalog available." ed.

NOTES

THE
GREAT
AMERICAN
MARKET

COMPANIES

All companies listed alphabetically with address, phone(s) and page references to the Product and Services section.

This section can be used like the "White Pages" to quickly find a company's address or phone. It can also be used to look up a company's product information in the Products and Services section.

*A Company name in CAPS indicates an advertiser.

A & B Beacon Business Machines
36 West 33rd St.
New York, NY 10001
212-736-1440 212-564-7855
(p. 47)

A & B Leather & Findings Co.
500 West 52nd St.
New York, NY 10019
212-265-8124
(p. 200, App-1)

A & N Fabrics
268 West 39th St.
New York, NY 10018
212-719-1773
(p. 125)

A & S Bias Binding Co. Inc.
159 Varick St.
New York, NY 10013
212-924-7040
(p. 242)

A & S Book Co.
274 West 43rd St.
New York, NY 10036
212-695-4897
(p. 216)

A & S Button Co.
131 Essex St.
New York, NY 10002
212-674-0669
(p. 244)

A & S Novelty Packaging & Display Corp.
2179 83rd St.
North Bergen, NJ 07047
201-861-4226
(p. 161)

A & S Ribbon Supply Co.
108 West 27th St.
New York, NY 10001
212-255-0280
(p. 158, App-1)

A-1 Advance Sewing Machine Co. Inc.
521 Broadway
New York, NY 10012
212-226-5621
(p. 321)

A-1 Astoria Foundry
51-25 35th St.
L.I.C., NY 11101
718-392-2340
(p. 48)

A-Flushing Woodworking
196-15 Northern Blvd.
Flushing, NY 11358
718-357-4373 718-357-4244
(p. 171)

A. D. M. Tronics Inc.
153 Ludlow Ave.
North Vale, NJ 07647
201-767-6040
(p. 218)

A.P.A. Studios
230 West 10th St.
New York, NY 10014
212-929-9436 212-675-4894
(p. 332)

AA Abbingdon Ceiling Co.
2149 Utica Ave.
Brooklyn, NY 11234
718-236-3251 718-258-8333
(p. 14)

AA Armato & Son
1701 Second Ave.
New York, NY 10028
212-737-1742
(p. 189)

AA Feather Co./ Gettinger Feather Corp.
16 West 36th St.
New York, NY 10018
212-695-9470 212-695-9477
(p. 364)

AAA American Flag Decorating Co Inc
40 West 37th St. 3rd Fl.
New York, NY 10018
212-279-4644
(p. 153)

AAA Appliance Rentals & Sales Co.
40 West 29th St.
New York, NY 10001
212-686-8884
(p. 355)

AAA Restaurant Equipment
284 Bowery
New York, NY 10012
212-966-1891
(p. 172, 195)

AAAA Metropolitan Co.
165 West 23rd St.
New York, NY 10011
212-741-3385
(p. 323)

AAB AMERICAN TRADING CORP.
599 Sixth Ave.
New York, NY 10011
212-691-3666
(p. 321)

Aasbo Lumber & Cabinet Makers
1834 Second Ave.
New York, NY 10128
212-222-6200
(p. 212)

Abacrome Inc.
151 West 26th St. 6th Fl.
New York, NY 10001
212-989-1190
(p. 153)

Abbey Locksmiths
1617 Second Ave.
New York, NY 10028
212-535-2289
(p. 192)

Abbey Materials Corp.
575 Underhill Blvd.
Syosset, NY 11791
212-772-0380
(p. 190)

Abbey Rent-All
203-16 Northern Blvd.
Bayside, NY 11361
718-428-0400
301 S. Broadway,
Hicksville, NY 11801
516-681-1323
(p. 355)

ABC Carpet Co. Inc.
881 Broadway
New York, NY 10003
212-677-6970
(p. 156)

ABC Foam Rubber Center Inc.
77 Allen St.
New York, NY 10002
212-431-9485
(p. 161)

ABC Spring Co.
16 West 22nd St.
New York, NY 10010
212-675-1629
(p. 341, 381)

ABCO Signs
212 West 79th St.
New York, NY 10024
212-496-8284
(p. 326)

ABET RENT-A-FUR
307 Seventh Ave. Rm. 1203
New York, NY 10001
212-989-5757
(p. 76)

Abetter Cork Co.
262 Mott St.
New York, NY 10012
212-925-7755
(p. 85)

Abie's Baby Inc.
524 West 23rd St.
New York, NY 10011
212-741-1920
(p. 171)

Able Elevator & Door Repair Co.
37 Cooper Square
New York, NY 10003
212-674-7607
(p. 116)

Abraham's Magazine Service
56 East 13th St.
New York, NY 10003
212-777-4700
(p. 216)

Academy Clothes Inc.
1703 Broadway
New York, NY 10019
212-765-1440
(p. 82)

ACADIA SCENIC INC.
100 Newark Ave.
Jersey City, NJ 07303
201-332-1327
(p. 313, 325)

Accountants for the Public Interest
36 West 44th St. Rm. 1201
New York, NY 10036
212-575-1828 212-575-1816
(p. App-9)

ACCU-COSTUMES
84 East 7th St.
New York, NY 10003
212-260-1496 212-228-4389
(p. 95)

Accurate Plastics
18 Morris Place,
Yonkers, NY 10705
914-476-0700
(p. 274, 275)

Ace Audio Visual
118 East 28th St. #508
New York, NY 10016
212-683-2850
(p. 24)

ACE BANNER & FLAG CO.
107 West 27th St.
New York, NY 10001
212-620-9111
(p. 153)

Ace Display Fixture
2 West 31st St.
New York, NY 10001
212-279-5927
(p. 219)

Ace Galleries
91 University
New York, NY 10003
212-260-2720
(p. 6)

Ace High Ladder
611 Jackson Ave.
Bronx, NY 10455
212-665-9700
(p. 197)

Acme Carpet Cleaning
241 West 17th St.
New York, NY 10011
212-279-1448
(p. 57)

Acme Emblem
122 West 26th St.
New York, NY 10001
212-255-7880
(p. 117)

Acme Foam
900 Dean St.
Brooklyn, NY 11238
718-622-5600
(p. 161)

Acme Marble Works Inc.
160 17th St.
Brooklyn, NY 11215
718-788-0527 718-965-3560
(p. 221)

Actors' Equity Association
165 West 46th St.
New York, NY 10036
212-869-8530
(p. App-9)

Actors' Equity Association
Audition Center
165 West 46th St.
New York, NY 10036
212-869-8548
(p. App-31)

Actors Factory Theatre
149 West 29th St.
New York, NY 10001
212-594-1494
(p. App-23)

Actor's Heritage
262 West 44th St.
New York, NY 10036
212-944-7490
(p. 226)

Actor's Outlet
120 West 28th St.
New York, NY 10001
212-807-1590
(p. App-23)

Actors Playhouse
100 Seventh Ave. S.
New York, NY 10014
212-691-6226 212-741-1215
(p. App-19)

AD-MART INC.
200 Park Ave. South
New York, NY 10003
212-777-4141 800-354-2102
(p. 106)

Adco Signs
122 West 29th St.
New York, NY 10001
212-564-8773
(p. 326, 329)

Added Treasures
577 Second Ave.
New York, NY 10016
212-889-1776
(p. 6, 68, 225)

Adelphia Container Corp.
206 North 10th St.
Brooklyn, NY 11211
718-388-5202
(p. 29)

Adequate Rubber Stamp Co. Inc.
141 West 41st St.
New York, NY 10036
212-840-1588
(p. 312)

Adhesive Products Corp.
1660 Boone Ave.
Bronx, NY 10460
718-542-4600
(p. 1)

Adhesive Products Corp.
1660 Boone Ave.
Bronx, NY 10460
718-542-4600
(p. 51)

Adirondack Rents
219 East 42nd St. 5th Fl.
New York, NY 10017
212-972-1700
(p. 167)

ADIRONDACK SCENIC
20 Elm, Glens Falls,
NY 12801
518-798-8321
(p. 313, 351)

Adler Kurt S.
1107 Broadway
New York, NY 10010
212-924-0900
(p. 106)

Adler Rug Cleaning
644 Whittier St.
Bronx, NY 10474
718-328-4433
(p. 57)

Aegean Imports
PO Box 1061
Belmont, CA 94002
415-593-8300
(p. 64, 121)

Aetna Felt Corp.
1075 Lousons Rd.
Union, NJ 07083
201-688-0760
(p. 137)

AFRICAN FABRIC PRINTS
303 Fifth Ave. Rm. 813
New York, NY 10016
212-725-1199
(p. 119)

African Trader
138 West 72nd St.
New York, NY 10023
212-724-3114
(p. 119)

AGH Distributors Inc.
225 West 39th St.
New York, NY 10018
212-221-3440
(p. 239)

Aid Auto Stores
45 Avenue A
New York, NY 10009
212-777-0030
645 Eleventh Ave.
New York, NY 10036
212-757-6969
1365 First Ave.
New York, NY 10021
212-535-3470
1740 First Ave.
New York, NY 10028
212-722-2688
(p. 27)

Ain Plastics Inc.
300 Park Ave. South
New York, NY 10010
212-473-2100 212-823-4200
(p. 273, 274, 275)

Air Systems Courier
122 East 42nd St.
New York, NY 10017
212-687-6240 800-223-6795
(p. 323)

Ajax Typewriter Corp.
230 East 59th St.
New York, NY 10022
212-832-9650
(p. 47)

Alberts Hosiery
2113A Broadway (main store)
New York, NY 10023
212-595-5860
20 West 43rd St.
New York, NY 10036
212-719-5729
600 Madison Ave.
New York, NY 10022
212-755-6483 (continues)

Alberts Hosiery (continued)
611 Madison Ave.
New York, NY 10022
212-753-7141
925 Lexington Ave.
New York, NY 10021
212-988-1195
658 West 181st St.
New York, NY 10033
212-568-8600
(p. 77)

Albino William Antiques
56 East 11th St.
New York, NY 10003
212-677-8820
(p. 6)

Alcone Company Inc./
Paramount Theatrical
5-49 49th Ave.
L.I.C., NY 11101
718-361-8373
(p. 218, 51, 55, 99, 141, 351, 259)

Alessandro Danny Ltd.
1156 Second Ave.
New York, NY 10021
212-421-1928 212-759-8210
(p. 152)

Alexander Butcher Block & Supply
176 Bowery
New York, NY 10013
212-226-4021
(p. 47, 172)

Alexander Oriental Rug & Carpet Co.
8 Crambrook Rd.
New City, NY 10956
914-634-3070
(p. 156)

Alexander's Department Store
731 Lexington Ave.
New York, NY 10022
212-593-0880
4 World Trade Center
New York, NY 10048
212-466-1414
(p. 104)

Alexanders Hardware
60 Reade St.
New York, NY 10007
212-267-0336
(p. 166, 181)

Alfred Mfg. Corp.
350 Warren,
Jersey City, NJ 07302
201-332-9100
(p. 367)

Alice Tully Hall
1941 Broadway
New York, NY 10023
212-362-1911 212-362-1900
(p. App-27)

Alice's Antiques
552 Columbus Ave.
New York, NY 10025
212-874-3400
(p. 6)

Alice's Underground
380 Columbus Ave.
New York, NY 10024
212-724-6682
(p. 68)

ALJO MFG. CO. INC.
450 Greenwich St.
New York, NY 10013
212-966-4046
(p. 254)

All-Tame Animals
37 West 57th St.
New York, NY 10019
212-752-5885
(p. 4)

Allan Uniform Rental
738 Broadway
New York, NY 10003
212-242-3338
(p. 82)

Allcraft Tool & Supply Co.
64 West 48th St.
New York, NY 10036
212-246-4740
(p. 191, 355, 381)

Allen Office Furniture
165 West 23rd St.
New York, NY 10011
212-929-8228
(p. 171)

Allen Richard Center Theater
36 West 62nd St.
New York, NY 10023
212-489-1940
(p. App-23)

Alliance of Resident Theatres
(ART)/New York
325 Spring St. Rm. 315
New York, NY 10013
212-989-5257
(p. App-9)
Allied Insulation Corp.
319 Oak St.
Perth Amboy, NJ 08861
201-324-0040
(p. 48)
Allied Reproductions
11 Stone St. 5th Fl.
New York, NY 10004
212-943-9067
(p. 282)
Allracks Industry Inc.
325 West 38th St.
New York, NY 10018
212-244-1069
(p. 323)
Almac Plastics Inc.
47-42 37th St.
L.I.C., NY 11101
718-937-1300
(p. 275)
Almy C. M. & Son Inc.
37 Purchase St.
Rye, NY 10580
914-967-6040
(p. 73)
Alpha Business Machines
300 Fifth Ave.
New York, NY 10001
212-682-6666
(p. 47)
Alpha Engraving Co.
888 Eighth Ave.
New York, NY 10019
212-247-5266
(p. 326, 370)
Alpha-Pavia Bookbinding Co. Inc.
55 West 21st St.
New York, NY 10010
212-929-5430
(p. 36, 37)
Alps Paper Parnes Co.
225 Division Ave. #10-F,
Brooklyn, NY 11211
212-279-3219
(p. 251)
Alter Bath & Kitchen
317 Lexington Ave.
New York, NY 10016
212-683-1682 212-683-6012
(p. 192)
ALTMAN LUGGAGE
135 Orchard St.
New York, NY 10002
212-254-7275
(p. 211)
Altman Stage Lighting
57 Alexander,
Yonkers, NY 10701
914-476-7987
(p. 201)
Altman's B.
361 Fifth Ave.
New York, NY 10016
212-679-7800
(p. 104)
Alufoil Products Co. Inc.
135 Oser Ave.
Hauppauge, NY 11787
718-789-3069
(p. 228)
Alyn Trading Corp.
1141 Broadway
New York, NY 10001
212-689-7060
(p. 44, 268)
Amalgamated Cordage
34 Harvor Park Dr.
Ft. Washington, NY 11050
516-484-5470
(p. 372)
AMAS Repertory Theatre
1 East 104th St. 3rd Fl.
New York, NY 10029
212-369-8000
(p. App-23)
Amato Opera
319 Bowery
New York, NY 10003
212-228-8200
(p. App-27)
Ambassador Arts
122 West 27th St. 8th Fl.
New York, NY 10001
212-243-4290
(p. 329)

Ambassador Theatre
219 West 49th St.
New York, NY 10019
212-245-9570 212-239-6200
(p. App-17)

AMCAN Feather Co./Sil-Ko Mfg.
26-32 Skillman Ave.
New York, NY 11101
718-729-1552
(p. 364)

America Hurrah Antiques
766 Madison Ave.
New York, NY 10021
212-535-1930
(p. 6, 307)

American Cord & Webbing Co. Inc.
505 Eighth Ave.
New York, NY 10018
212-695-7340
(p. 247, 372, 374)

American Costume Jewelry Novelty
104 West 29th St.
New York, NY 10001
212-239-1222
(p. 62)

American Council for the Arts
570 Seventh Ave.
New York, NY 10018
212-354-6655
(p. App-9)

American Craft Council
401 Park Ave. South,
New York, NY 10016
212-696-0710
(p. App-9)

American Crayon Co. The
1706 Hayes Ave., PO Box 2358
Sandusky, OH 44870
419-625-9121
(p. 254)

American Design Components
62 Joseph St.
Moonachie, NJ 07074
201-939-2710
(p. 232)

American Fabrics Co.
29 West 36th St.
New York, NY 10018
212-868-0100
(p. 366)

American Felt & Filter Co.
34 John St.
Newburg, NY 12550
914-561-3560
(p. 137)

American Fencer's Supply Co.
1180 Folsom St.
San Francisco, CA 94103
415-863-7911
(p. 150)

American Finish and Chemical Co.
1012 Broadway, Chelsea
MA 02150
617-884-6060
(p. 156)

AMERICAN HANGER & FIXTURE INC.
520 West 27th St.
New York, NY 10001
212-279-5280
(p. 94, 220)

American Heritage Publishing Co.
Library
10 Rockefeller Plaza
New York, NY 10020
212-399-8930
(p. App-4)

American International Medical
Equipment Sales
780 East 138th St.
Bronx, NY 10454
718-993-4400
(p. 224)

American Kennels
55 West 8th St.
New York, NY 10011
212-260-6230
786 Lexington Ave.
New York, NY 10021
212-838-8460
(p. 267)

American Machine & Motor Co.
22 Howard St.
New York, NY 10013
212-226-4577
(p. 355)

American Museum of Natural History
Library
79th & Central Park West
New York, NY 10024
212-873-1300
(p. App-4)

American National Bag & Burlap
528 Bergen St.
Brooklyn, NY 11217
718-857-8050
(p. 46)

American Notion Co. Inc.
336 West 37th St.
New York, NY 10018
212-563-0480
(p. 239)

American Optical Co.
14 Mechanic St.
South Bridge, MA 01550
617-765-9711
(p. 110)

American Place Theatre
111 West 46th St.
New York, NY 10036
212-247-0393 212-246-3730
(p. App-19)

American Silk Label
1 Linden Place
Great Neck, NY 11022
516-829-8300
(p. 197)

American Stage Lighting
1331 North Ave.
New Rochelle, NY 10804
914-636-5538 212-584-5600
(p. 201)

American Star Cork Co. Inc.
175 N. 9th St.
Brooklyn, NY 11211
718-388-7126
(p. 85)

American Surplus Trading
62 Joseph St.
Moonachie, NJ 07074
201-939-2710
(p. 115)

American Theatre of Actors
314 West 54th St.
New York, NY 10019
212-581-3044
(p. App-23)

American Uniform Headwear
36 Anderson Ave.
Fairview, NJ 07022
201-943-0143
(p. 64)

American Wood Column Corp.
913 Grand St.
Brooklyn, NY 11211
718-782-3163
(p. 14, 166)

America's Hobby Center (Modad's)
146 West 22nd St.
New York, NY 10011
212-675-8922
(p. 185)

Amerlite Aluminum Co.
211 West 28th St.
New York, NY 10001 (showroom)
212-986-9559
(p. 14)

AMES JOYCE
335 East 65th St.
New York, NY 10021
212-535-3047
(p. 101, 210)

Ames Ronald E.
712 Washington St. #GA
New York, NY 10014
212-242-4956
(p. 86)

Ames Stapling and Nailing Systems
1261 Broadway 9th Fl.
New York, NY 10001
212-684-4667
(p. 355)

Amity Arts Center
22 West 15th St.
New York, NY 10011
212-924-5295
(p. App-31)

Amity Notions
315 West 36th St.
New York, NY 10018
212-279-3129
(p. 241)

Ampex Copy World
135 Madison Ave.
New York, NY 10016
212-889-1400
(p. 282)

Amtec International
PO Box 527
E. Setauket, NY 11733
516-751-8282
(p. 49)

Anand India Shop
30 Rockefeller Plaza, Shop 11
New York, NY 10112
212-247-2054
(p. 120)
Anania Brothers
46 West 46th St.
New York, NY 10036
212-869-5336
(p. 324)
Anatomical Chart Co.
7124 N. Clark St.
Chicago, IL 60626
312-764-7171 800-621-7500
(p. 196)
Anchor Label & Tag Co.
10 West 33rd St. Rm. 1222
New York, NY 10001
212-244-4363
(p. 197)
Anchor Tool & Supply Co.
PO Box 265, Chatham
NJ 07928
201-635-2094
(p. 24)
Anderson Aileen Corset Shops Inc.
977 Sixth Ave.
New York, NY 10018
212-736-2338
(p. 78)
Anderson Judith Theatre
442 West 42nd St.
New York, NY 10036
212-279-4200
(p. App-19)
Andrews Susan D.
c/o Center Stage
700 N. Calvert St.
Baltimore, MD 21202
301-685-3200
(p. 286)
Andros Imported Shirting Inc.
39 West 32nd St.
New York, NY 10001
212-279-7313
(p. 125)
Andy's Chee-Pees
14 St. Marks Place
New York, NY 10003
212-674-9248 (continues)

Andy's Chee-Pees (continued)
16 West 8th St.
New York, NY 10011
212-460-8488
(p. 68)
Anello & Davide Ltd. Theatrical Footwear
30-35 Drury Lane, WC2
London, England
01-836-6744
(p. 60)
Angelo's Bicycle Service
140 West 83rd St.
New York, NY 10024
212-362-1122
(p. 33)
Anichini Gallery
7 East 20th St.
New York, NY 10003
212-982-7274
(p. 68, 210)
Animal Actors International
RD 3 Box 221
Washington, NJ 07882
201-689-7539
(p. 4)
Animal Hair Mfg.
175 Beard St.
Brooklyn, NY 11231
718-852-3592
(p. 178)
Animal Outfits for People Co.
252 West 46th St.
New York, NY 10036
212-840-6219
(p. 95)
Animal World
219 East 26th St.
New York, NY 10010
212-685-0027
(p. 267)
Ann-Morris Antiques
239 East 60th St.
New York, NY 10022
212-755-3308
(p. 7)
Annex The
552 West 53rd St.
New York, NY 10019
212-246-1050
(p. App-23)

Anthology Film Archives Library
491 Broadway
New York, NY 10013
212-226-0100
(p. App-4)

Antique Amusements
1420 80th St.
Brooklyn, NY 11228
718-837-0405
(p. 4)

Antique Auto Props
307 Patterson Ave.
East Rutherford, NJ 07073
201-933-0542
(p. 26)

ANTIQUE BICYCLE PROP SERVICE
113 Woodland
Mont Vale, NJ 07645
201-391-8780 914-735-9769
(p. 34)

Antique Shoes & Things Inc.
18 First Ave.
New York, NY 10009
212-673-4532
(p. 60, 68)

Antiques Plus
744 Coney Island Ave.
Brooklyn, NY 11218
718-941-8805
(p. 7)

APF Inc.
783 Madison Ave.
New York, NY 10021
212-988-1090
(p. 164)

APPLAUSE THEATRE BOOKS
211 West 71st St. (main store)
New York, NY 10023
212-496-7511
100 West 67th St. (sale/used books)
New York, NY 10023
(p. 37)

Apple Corps Theatre
336 West 20th St.
New York, NY 10011
212-929-2955
(p. App-23)

APPLE FOAM & PLASTIC INC.
180 Miller Place
Hicksville, NY 11801
516-433-2151 718-529-5991
(p. 263)

Aqua Baths Inc.
351 West Broadway
New York, NY 10013
212-431-4840
(p. 192)

AQUARIUM DESIGN
979 Third Ave.
New York, NY 10022
212-308-5224 718-225-6815
(p. 371)

Arbee Men's Wear Inc.
1598 Second Ave.
New York, NY 10028
212-737-4661
(p. 81)

Archer Surgical Supplies Inc.
544 West 27th St.
New York, NY 10001
212-695-5553
(p. 224)

Architectural Antique Exchange
715 N. Second St.
Philadelphia, PA 19123
215-922-3669
(p. 7, 14)

Arciero Pam
RFD #1, PO Box 210
Ashford, CT 06278
203-429-0786 212-580-7257
(p. 301)

Arden's
1014 Sixth Ave.
New York, NY 10018
212-391-6968
(p. 64)

Argo Taximeter Shop
21-46 44th Dr.
L.I.C., NY 11101
718-937-4600
(p. 346)

Argosy Book Stores Inc.
116 East 59th St.
New York, NY 10022
212-753-4455
(p. 37, 220, 279)

Arista Flag Corp.
575 Eighth Ave. 4th Fl.
New York, NY 10018
212-947-8887
(p. 153)

Arista Surgical Supply Co.
67 Lexington Ave.
New York, NY 10010
212-679-3694
(p. 103, 224)

Ark Theatre The
131 Spring St.
New York, NY 10012
212-431-6285
(p. App-23)

Arlene Novelty Corp.
263 West 38th St.
New York, NY 10018
212-921-5711
(p. 244)

Armo Co., Div. of Crown Textiles
1412 Broadway
New York, NY 10018
212-391-5880
(p. 140)

Army & Navy Supply Stores
1938 Third Ave.
New York, NY 10029
212-534-1600
(p. 82)

Arnold Bias Products & Trimming Co.
591 Broadway
New York, NY 10012
212-966-3017
(p. 242)

Arnold Tobacco Shop
323 Madison Ave.
New York, NY 10017
212-697-1477
(p. 330)

Arnold Wood Turning Co.
38 Nardozzi Pl.
New Rochelle, NY 10801
914-235-0822
(p. 166)

Aronson Samuel & Son
135 West 17th St.
New York, NY 10011
212-243-4993
(p. 156)

Arrow Graphics
514 West 24th St.
New York, NY 10011
212-807-0816
(p. 332)

Arrow Stationers Inc.
9 East 46th St.
New York, NY 10017
212-986-5659
(p. 342)

Art Cut Glass Studio
RD# 1, Box 10
Fawn Drive, Matawan, NJ 07747
201-583-7648
(p. 178)

Art Flag Co. Inc.
6 West 18th St.
New York, NY 10011
212-473-8282 212-929-3035
(p. 153)

Art For Industry
521 Fifth Ave. 17th Fl.
New York, NY 10036
212-757-3638
(p. 17)

Art Handicrafts Leather Co.
3512 Flatlands Ave.
Brooklyn, NY 11234
718-252-6622
(p. 198)

Art Outlet Inc.
200 East 59th St.
New York, NY 10022
212-751-5443
(p. 165)

Art-Max Fabrics
250 West 40th St.
New York, NY 10018
212-398-0755 212-398-0756
(p. 125)

Artbench
254 East 89th St.
New York, NY 10128
212-427-3770
(p. 174)

Arte Primitivo Inc.
3 East 65th St.
New York, NY 10021
212-570-0393
(p. 37, 120)

ARTHUR FRISCH CO. INC.
1816 Boston Rd.
Bronx, NY 10460
212-589-4100
(p. 276)

Arthur Richards Ltd.
91 Fifth Ave. 2nd Fl.
New York, NY 10003
212-247-2300
(p. 76)

Artistic Frame Co.
390 McGuinness Blvd.
Brooklyn, NY 11222
212-289-2100
(p. 170)

Artistic Ribbon and Novelty Co.
22 West 21st St.
New York, NY 10010
212-255-4224
(p. 367)

ArtKraft Strauss Sign Corp.
830 Twelfth Ave.
New York, NY 10019
212-265-5155
(p. 326)

Arts and Crafters Inc.
175 Johnson St.
Brooklyn, NY 11201
718-875-8151
(p. 298)

ASAP Photo Lab
40 East 49th St.
New York, NY 10017
212-832-1223
(p. 271)

Ash Sam Music Stores
160 West 48th St.
New York, NY 10036
212-245-4778
(p. 236)

Ashil Fabrics
101 West 34th St./1313 Broadway
New York, NY 10006
212-560-9049
(p. 125)

Asian House
888 Seventh Ave.
New York, NY 10019
212-581-2294
(p. 121)

ASSOCIATED DRAPERY & EQUIPMENT CO.
40 Sea Cliff Ave.
Glen Cove, NY 11542
718-895-8668 516-671-5245
(p. 99, 141, 154)

Associated Fabrics Corp.
104 East 25th St.
New York, NY 10010
212-689-7186
(p. 364)

Associated Manufacturers Tubular Pipings Inc.
252 West 37th St.
New York, NY 10018
212-736-3458
(p. 243)

Association of Theatrical Artists and Craftspeople
1742 Second Ave. #102
New York, NY 10128
718-596-0501 212-586-1925
(p. App-9)

Astor Lace and Trimmings
132 West 36th St.
New York, NY 10018
212-736-0475
(p. 366)

Astor Place Theatre
434 Lafayette
New York, NY 10003
212-254-4370
(p. App-19)

Astro Minerals
155 East 34th St.
New York, NY 10016
212-889-9000
(p. 312)

Astrology Bookshop
789 Lexington Ave. 2nd Fl.
New York, NY 10021
212-832-8958
(p. 37)

Asty (Div. of A & T Importers)
150 Green St.
Brooklyn, NY 11222
718-383-8100
(p. 158)

Atkinson Brooks Theatre
256 West 47th St.
New York, NY 10036
212-974-9424 212-245-3430
(p. App-17)

Atlantic Blue Print Co. Inc.
575 Madison Ave.
New York, NY 10022
212-755-3388
(p. 282)

Atlantic Powdered Metals Inc.
225 Broadway
New York, NY 10007
212-267-4900
(p. 252)

Atlantic Research Labs Corp.
29-05 40th Rd.
L.I.C., NY 11101
718-784-8825
(p. 154)

Atlantis 2 Total Scuba
498 Sixth Ave.
New York, NY 10011
212-924-7556
(p. 338)

ATLAS CLEANING CLOTH CORP.
10 Greene St.
New York, NY 10013
212-226-1042 212-925-6661
(p. 133)

Atlas Leather Co.
155 West 29th St.
New York, NY 10001
212-736-7044
(p. 198)

Atlas Scenic Studios Ltd.
46 Brookfield Ave.
Bridgeport, CT 06610
203-334-2130
(p. 313)

Atwater Inc.
627 West Main St., PO Box 247
Plymouth, PA 18651
717-779-9568
(p. 249)

Audi E. J.
317 East 34th St.
New York, NY 10016
212-679-7580
(p. 167)

Audio Exchange
57 Park Place
New York, NY 10007
212-964-4570
28 West 8th St.
New York, NY 10011
212-982-7191
(p. 24)

AUDIO VISUAL RENTALS INC.
75 Ninth Ave.
New York, NY 10011
212-807-1563
(p. 201)

Audio-Visual Promotion Aids Inc.
611 Broadway
New York, NY 10012
212-477-5540
(p. 201)

Augliera Anthony
34 Hamilton St.
West Haven, CT 06516
203-933-3994
(p. 234)

Augustine Reggie
100 West 72nd St. #4C
New York, NY 10023
212-787-4176
(p. 86)

Austen Display Corp.
139 West 19th St.
New York, NY 10011
212-924-6261
(p. 106)

Austin Ltd.
140 East 55th St.
New York, NY 10022
212-752-7903
(p. 78)

Automatic Steam Products Corp.
43-20 34th St.
L.I.C., NY 11101
718-937-4500
(p. 190)

Avery Fisher Hall
Broadway at 65th
New York, NY 10023
212-874-2424 212-580-8700
(p. App-27)

Axelrod S. Co. Inc.
7 West 30th St.
New York, NY 10001
212-594-3022
(p. 110)

Ayers Percussion
415 West 48th St.
New York, NY 10036
212-582-8410
(p. 236)

Azuma
387 Sixth Ave.
New York, NY 10012
212-989-8690
25 East 8th St.
New York, NY 10003
212-673-2900
666 Lexington Ave.
New York, NY 10022
212-752-0599
251 East 86th St.
New York, NY 10028
212-369-4928
(p. 30, 122, 382)

- B -

B & B Electric Motor & Control
39-40 Crescent
L.I.C., NY 11101
718-784-1313
(p. 232)

B & H Foto & Electronics Corp.
119 West 17th St.
New York, NY 10011
212-206-1010 212-807-7474
(p. 269)

B & J Fabrics
263 West 40th St.
New York, NY 10018
212-354-8150 212-354-8212
(p. 125)

B & M Sales & Service
29 Seventh Ave. South
New York, NY 10014
212-929-8170
(p. 346)

B & Z Steel
78 Greene St.
New York, NY 10012
212-966-5855
(p. 323)

B. C. Theatre
337 East 8th St.
New York, NY 10011
212-254-4698
(p. App-23)

B. L. Dental Co. Inc.
135-24 Hillside Ave.
Richmond Hills, NY 11418
718-658-5440
(p. 103)

Baccarat Inc.
55 East 57th St.
New York, NY 10022
212-826-4100
(p. 55)

Bachmeier & Co. Inc.
31 Rizzolo Rd., PO Box 400
Kearny, NJ 07032
201-997-0606
(p. 254)

Bacig Mfg. Co.
3611 14th Ave.
Brooklyn, NY 11218
718-871-6106
(p. 94)

BACK 40 THE
75 Ninth Ave.
New York, NY 10011
212-807-1563
(p. App-31)

Back Date Magazines
228 West 23rd St.
New York, NY 10011
212-243-9349
(p. 216)

Back Pages Antiques
125 Greene St.
New York, NY 10012
212-460-5998
(p. 4)

Baehm Paper Co.
53 Murray St.
New York, NY 10007
212-267-1892
(p. 251, 263)

BAER FABRICS
515 East Market
Louisville, KY 40202
502-583-5521
(p. 1, 94, 112, 113, 120, 125, 133, 135, 137, 139, 140, 141, 145, 147, 148, 149, 161, 190, 241, 243, 244, 247, 248, 249, 250, 321, 361, 364, 366, 367, 369, 374)

Bakit Bath & Construction Corp.
32 East 30th St.
New York, NY 10016
212-683-6093
(p. 192)

Bal-Toggery Knits Inc.
43-10 23rd St.
L.I.C., NY 11101
718-937-2400
(p. 72)

Balloon Creations
12 West 37th St. Suite 904
New York, NY 10018
212-719-5083
(p. 29)

Balooms Ltd.
147 Sullivan St.
New York, NY 10012
212-473-3523 212-673-4007
(p. 29)

Balter Sales
209 Bowery
New York, NY 10002
212-674-2960
(p. 55)

Bamboo and Rattan Works
470 Oberlin Ave. S.
Lakewood, NJ 08701
201-370-0220
(p. 308)

Banks G. Theatrical & Custom Footwear
320 West 48th St.
New York, NY 10036
212-586-6476
(p. 60)

BARBIZON ELECTRIC CO. INC.
426 West 55th St.
New York, NY 10019
212-586-1620
(p. 115, 201, 254, 257)

Barclay Church Supply Inc.
26 Warren St. 2nd Fl.
New York, NY 10007
212-267-9432
(p. 310)

Barclay-Rex Pipe Shop
7 Maiden Lane
New York, NY 10038
212-962-3355
(p. 330)

Barewood Furniture Stripping
106 Ferris St.
Brooklyn, NY 11231
718-875-9037
141 Atlantic Ave.
Brooklyn, NY 11201
718-875-3833
(p. 174)

Bargain Spot
64 Third Ave.
New York, NY 10003
212-674-1188
(p. 236, 269, 348, 355)

Bari Restaurant Equipment
240 Bowery
New York, NY 10012
212-925-3786
(p. 195)

Barnes & Noble Bookstore Inc.
199 Chambers St.
New York, NY 10007
212-608-1023
105 Fifth Ave.
New York, NY 10003
212-807-0099
600 Fifth Ave.
New York, NY 10020
212-765-0590
(p. 37, 40)

Barney's New York
106 Seventh Ave.
New York, NY 10011
212-929-9000
(p. 78)

Baron Art and Antique Movers
143 First Ave.
New York, NY 10003
212-475-3791
(p. 234)

Barr Specialty Corp.
236 West 26th St.
New York, NY 10001
212-243-4562
(p. 137)

Barrett Hill Inc.
133 West 25th St. 3rd Fl.
New York, NY 10010
212-242-4745
(p. 106)

Barry Supply Co.
36 West 17th St.
New York, NY 10011
212-242-5200
(p. 183)

Barrymore Ethel Theatre
243 West 47th St.
New York, NY 10036
212-974-9534 212-239-6200
(p. App-17)

BASH THEATRICAL LIGHTING INC.
3401 Dell Ave.
North Bergen, NJ 07047
212-279-9265 201-863-3300
(p. 203)

Baskin Engravers
21 West 47th St.
New York, NY 10036
212-869-5048
(p. 119)

Bass & Bass
265 Park Ave. South
New York, NY 10010
212-228-5120
(p. 195)

Bass Rudolph
175 Lafayette St.
New York, NY 10013
212-226-4000
(p. 356)

Bauer Samuel & Sons Inc.
145 West 29th St.
New York, NY 10001
212-868-4190
(p. 200)

Bay Fastening Systems Inc.
7204 20th Ave.
Brooklyn, NY 11204
212-259-0801
(p. 1)

Bay Ridge Lumber
6303 5th Ave.
Brooklyn, NY 11220
212-492-3300
East Second & Hobart Ave.
Bayonne, NJ 07002
212-745-7311
(p. 212)

Bayridge Flameproofing
8321 Third Ave.
Brooklyn, NY 11209
718-748-5216
(p. 154)

Beacon Chemical
125 MacQuesten Parkway South
Mt. Vernon, NY 10550
914-699-3400
(p. 229)

Beacon Theatre
2124 Broadway
New York, NY 10023
212-874-9323 212-874-1717
212-874-1768
(p. App-20)

Beal Charley
203 Bleecker St. #7
New York, NY 10012
212-260-2912
(p. 286)

Beam Supply Inc.
45-40 21st St.
L.I.C., NY 11101
212-475-5253
(p. 338)

Beardslee Transmission Equip. Co.
27-22 Jackson Ave.
L.I.C., NY 11101
718-784-4100
290 East Jericho Turnpike
Mineola, NY 11501
516-747-5557
(p. 232)

Beatty-Page Inc.
360 Furman St.
Brooklyn, NY 11201
718-522-6400
(p. 229)

Beaujard Jean Paul
209 East 76th St.
New York, NY 10021
212-249-3790 (p. 7)

Beaumont Vivian Theatre
150 West 65th St.
New York, NY 10023
212-874-9257 212-787-6868
(p. App-17)

Beck Martin Theatre
302 West 45th St.
New York, NY 10036
212-245-9770 212-246-6363
(p. App-17)

Beckenstein S.
130 Orchard St.
New York, NY 10002
212-475-4525
(p. 101, 125, 135)

Beckenstein S.
130 Orchard St.
New York, NY 10002
212-475-4525
(p. 370)

Beckerich Joanne
400 Madison St.
Hoboken, NJ 07030
201-963-8575
(p. 286)

Beckett Samuel Theatre
412 West 42nd St.
New York, NY 10036
212-594-2826
(p. App-20)

Beckmann Felt Co.
120 Baxter St.
New York, NY 10013
212-226-8400
(p. 137)

Beckmann Theatre
314 West 54th St.
New York, NY 10019
212-581-3044
(p. App-23)

Beck's Photography Studio
37-44 82nd St.
Jackson Heights, NY 11372
718-424-8751
(p. 3)

Beer-Stern Co.
50 West 34th St.
New York, NY 10001
212-279-4380
(p. 367)

Beethoven Pianos
1645 First Ave.
New York, NY 10028
212-288-2099
(p. 236)

Behar Helen World of Bargains
195 Seventh Ave.
New York, NY 10011
212-924-3588
(p. 191, 361)

Belasco Theatre
111 West 44th St.
New York, NY 10036
212-730-9344 212-239-6200
(p. App-17)

Belden-Stark
386 Park Ave. South
New York, NY 10016
212-686-3939
(p. 354)

Bell Medical Supply
40 East 65th St.
New York, NY 10021
212-744-4059
(p. 224)

Bell Moving
43-47 162nd St.
Flushing, NY 11358
718-461-8870
(p. 234)

Bell Yarn Co.
75 Essex St.
New York, NY 10002
212-674-1030
(p. 380)

Bella & Co.
200 Michael Dr.
Syosset, NY 11791
516-921-6868
(p. 137)

Belmont Takara
17 West 56th St.
New York, NY 10019
212-541-6660
(p. 33)

Bendheim S. A. Co. Inc.
122 Hudson St.
New York, NY 10013
212-226-6370
(p. 175)

Bendix Carvings Inc.
17 Gazza Blvd.
Farmingdale, NY 11735
516-249-9191
(p. 310)

Bendix Moldings
235 Pegasus Ave.
Northvale, NJ 07647
212-597-6666
(p. 231)

Ben's Babyland
87 Avenue A
New York, NY 10009
212-674-1353
(p. 169)

Bentley & Simon
450 Seventh Ave.
New York, NY 10123
212-695-0554
(p. 73)

Ber-Sel Handbags
79 Orchard St.
New York, NY 10002
212-966-5517
(p. 64)

Berg & Brown Inc.
1368 Lexington Ave.
New York, NY 10128
212-369-5800
(p. 13)

Berg Winfred
499 Ocean Ave.
East Rockaway, NY 11518
516-599-5010
(p. 232)

Bergdorf Goodman
754 Fifth Ave.
New York, NY 10019
212-753-7300
(p. 105)

Berkey K & L Custom Services
222 East 44th St.
New York, NY 10017
212-661-5600
(p. 271)

Berkley Furniture Gallery of London
899 First Ave.
New York, NY 10022
212-355-4050
(p. 7)

Berloni William Theatrical Animals
314 West 52nd St., Box 37 (mail only)
New York, NY 10019
212-974-0922
(p. 4)

Bernie's Discount Center
821 Sixth Ave.
New York, NY 10001
212-564-8582
(p. 13)

Bernstein & Sons
30 West 29th St.
New York, NY 10001
212-683-2260
(p. 220)

Berton Plastics Inc.
170 Wesley St.
So. Hackensack, NJ 07606
201-488-6700 212-695-8135
(p. 51)

Best Emblem & Insignia Co.
636 Broadway
New York, NY 10012
212-677-4332
(p. 278)

Best Hardware & Mill Supply Inc.
1513 Jericho Turnpike
New Hyde Park, NY 11040
516-354-0529
(p. 356)

Best Little Stage In Town
8 West 19th St.
New York, NY 10011
212-924-7467
(p. App-29)

Best of Everything Ltd. The
307 East 77th St.
New York, NY 10021
212-734-2492
(p. 68)

BESTEK THEATRICAL PRODUCTIONS LTD.
386 East Meadow Ave. (rental shop)
East Meadow, NY 11554
516-794-3953
218 W. Hoffman Ave. (prod'n shop)
Lindenhurst, NY 11757
516-225-0707
(p. 203, 313, 349)

Beta Custom Furniture
18 West 23rd St.
New York, NY 10011
212-243-3695
228 East 51st St.
New York, NY 10022
212-355-1029
1519 Third Ave.
New York, NY 10028
212-794-9222
(p. 173)

Better Times Antiques
500 Amsterdam Ave.
New York, NY 10024
212-496-9001 212-724-2286
(p. 7)

Better-Pak Container Co.
555 West 25th St.
New York, NY 10001
212-675-7330
(p. 251)

Bettinger's Luggage
80 Rivington St.
New York, NY 10002
212-674-9411
(p. 211)

Bettmann Archives
136 East 57th St.
New York, NY 10022
212-758-0362
(p. App-4)

Beu-Tex
25 West 39th St. #700
New York, NY 10018
212-398-1681
(p. 139)

BFO Plus Inc.
149 Fifth Ave. 2nd Fl.
New York, NY 10010
212-673-9026
(p. 79)

Bi-Rite Photo Electric Inc.
15 East 30th St.
New York, NY 10016
212-685-2130
(p. 269)

Biagiotti L.
259 Seventh Ave.
New York, NY 10001
212-924-5088
(p. 14, 45, 49, 344)

Big Apple Lights
533 Canal St.
New York, NY 10013
212-226-0925
(p. 203)

Big Four Pile Fabrics
452 Broadway
New York, NY 10013
212-966-2466
(p. 139)

Bigelow Joseph
RR 4, PO Box 291A
Greenwood Lake, NY 10925
914-477-3864 212-586-0260
(p. 86)

Bijan Royal Inc.
60 East 11th St.
New York, NY 10003
212-228-3757 212-533-6390
(p. 7)

Biltmore Theatre
261 West 47th St.
New York, NY 10036
212-974-9350 212-582-5340
(p. App-17)

Bird Jungle
401 Bleecker St.
New York, NY 10014
212-242-1757
(p. 267)

Black Ox Metal Finishing
34-11 10th St.
L.I.C., NY 11106
718-274-2104
(p. 276)

Blade
212 West 15th St.
New York, NY 10011
212-620-0114
(p. 150)

Blader Henry
1020 N. Central Ave.
Woodmere, NY 11598
212-327-8632
(p. 321)

Blake-Harrison Paper Corp.
2179 83rd St.
N. Bergen, NJ 07047
201-868-4200 212-868-2360
(p. 263)

Blalock Cheryl
308 West 78th St.
New York, NY 10024
212-799-5424 212-580-2800
(p. 301)
Blan Electronics
56 Warren St.
New York, NY 10007
212-233-6288
(p. 115)
Bland's
1554 California
Denver, CO 80202
303-573-6255
(p. 65)
Blatt Bowling & Billiard Corp.
809 Broadway
New York, NY 10003
212-674-8855
(p. 338)
Bloch Susan Theatre
206 West 26th
New York, NY 10011
212-420-1360
(p. App-20)
Bloom & Krup
206 First Ave.
New York, NY 10009
212-673-2760
(p. 13)
Bloom Abe & Sons Inc.
144 West 19th St.
New York, NY 10011
212-924-2560
(p. 241)
Bloom Shoe Store
311 Sixth Ave.
New York, NY 10014
212-243-8749
(p. 60)
Bloomfield Plastic Co.
28 Montgomery
Bloomfield, NJ 07003
201-743-6900
(p. 275)
Bloomingdales
1000 Third Ave.
New York, NY 10022
212-355-5900
(p. 105)
Blue & White Men's Shop Inc.
50 East 58th St.
New York, NY 10022
212-421-8424
(p. 79)
Blue Bell Lumber & Moulding Co.
501 East 164th St.
Bronx, NY 10456
212-923-0200
2360 Amsterdam Ave.
New York, NY 10033
212-923-0200
(p. 212)
Blumenthal Leather Corp.
1123 Broadway
New York, NY 10010
212-242-3650
(p. 198)
Bob Michael's Surplus Metals
321 Canal St.
New York, NY 10013
212-226-6467
(p. 228)
Bogies Antique Furs & Clothing
201 East 10th St.
New York, NY 10003
212-260-1199
(p. 68)
Bok Lei Tat Inc.
213 Canal St.
New York, NY 10013
212-226-1703
(p. 122)
Boken Inc.
513 West 54th St.
New York, NY 10019
212-581-5507
(p. App-29)
Boken II
111 Leroy St.
New York, NY 10014
212-924-0438
(p. App-29)
Bollman George & Co.
350 Fifth Ave.
New York, NY 10118
212-564-6480
110 East Main
Adamstown, PA 19501
215-484-4361
(p. 65)

Bon-Marche
55 West 13th St.
New York, NY 10011
212-620-5550
1060 Third Ave.
New York, NY 10021
212-620-5592
(p. 167, 168, 206)

Bond Button Co.
203 West 38th St. 3rd Fl.
New York, NY 10018
212-719-2100
(p. 244)

Bond Clothes
1290 Broadway
New York, NY 10001
212-564-8310
(p. 79)

Bond Parade Float Co.
551 Main Ave.
Wallington, NJ 07057
201-778-3333
(p. 106)

Bond Street Suspender & Belt Corp.
34-01 38th Ave.
L.I.C., NY 11101
718-361-8070
(p. 59)

Bonded Locksmiths
2414 Broadway
New York, NY 10024
212-586-6886
(p. 192)

Bonnie Enterprises Inc.
22 Jackson Dr.
Cranford, NJ 07016
201-272-9300
(p. 244)

Bonsai Dynasty Co.
851 Sixth Ave.
New York, NY 10001
212-695-2973
(p. 159)

Bonwit Teller
4 East 57th St.
New York, NY 10022
212-593-3333
(p. 105)

Books of Wonder
464 Hudson St.
New York, NY 10014
212-989-3270 (p. 40)

Booth Theatre
222 West 45th St.
New York, NY 10036
212-239-6200
(p. App-17)

Borg Textiles
1450 Broadway
New York, NY 10018
212-221-0570
(p. 139)

Boro Blue Print Co. Inc.
52 Court St.
Brooklyn, NY 11201
718-625-3227
(p. 282)

Bournonville Welders
237 West 60th St.
New York, NY 10023
212-246-7558
(p. 381)

Boutross Imports
260 Fifth Ave. 7th Fl.
New York, NY 10001
212-685-5860
(p. 210)

Bowery Lane Theatre/
Jean Cocteau Rep.
330 Bowery
New York, NY 10012
212-677-0060
(p. App-23)

Bowery Lighting Corp.
132 Bowery
New York, NY 10013
212-966-4034
144 Second Ave.
New York, NY 10022
212-832-0990
275 Columbus Ave.
New York, NY 10023
212-877-7014
(p. 207)

Bowl & Board
9 Saint Marks Place
New York, NY 10003
212-673-1724
(p. 194)

Boxer Abraham
34 West 27th St. 6th Fl.
New York, NY 10001
212-689-3210
(p. 59)

Boyle John & Co.
3 Westchester Plaza
Elmsford, NY 10523
914-347-3170
(p. 133)

Bradbury & Bradbury Wallpaper
PO Box 155
Benicia, CA 94510
707-746-1900
(p. 378)

Bradford Consultants
16 East Homestead Ave.
Collingswood, NJ 08108
609-854-1404
(p. 203)

Bramlett Thomas Assoc. Inc.
219 Grand St.
Hoboken, NJ 07030
201-659-3565 212-255-7018
(p. 298, 313, 325)

Brancusi of N.Y. City Inc.
938 First Ave.
New York, NY 10022
212-688-7980
(p. 168)

Brascomb & Schwab
148 Second Ave.
New York, NY 10003
212-777-5363
247 East 10th St.
New York, NY 10003
212-254-3168
(p. 70)

The Brass Loft
20 Greene St.
NYC 10013
212-226-5467
(p. 44)

Brauner J & D
298 Bowery
New York, NY 10012
212-477-2830
(p. 47)

Braunstein Sharon
c/o Alliance Theatre
1280 Peachtree St. N.E.
Atlanta, GA 30309
404-898-1133
(p. 286)

Bridge Kitchenware
214 East 52nd St.
New York, NY 10022
212-688-4220
(p. 194, 195)

Bridge Refrigeration Inc.
65 Second Ave.
New York, NY 10003
212-674-0840
(p. 13)

Brief Essentials
1407 Broadway
New York, NY 10018
212-921-8344
(p. 78)

Brigandi Coin Co.
60 West 44th St.
New York, NY 10036
212-869-5350
(p. 84)

Brins Telecommunications
126 West 26th St.
New York, NY 10001
212-807-6000
(p. 347)

Brite Electric Sales Corp.
221 East 38th St.
New York, NY 10016
212-687-1313
(p. 115)

Broadhurst Theatre
235 West 44th St.
New York, NY 10036
212-730-9035 212-239-6200
(p. App-17)

Broadway Aquarium & Pet Shop
648 Amsterdam Ave.
New York, NY 10025
212-724-0536
(p. 371)

Broadway Bazaar
2025 Broadway
New York, NY 10023
212-873-9153
(p. 167, 193)

Broadway Button & Buckle Co.
35-37 West 38th St.
New York, NY 10018
212-575-0520
(p. 244)

BROADWAY CLOTHING
39 West 14th St. #502
New York, NY 10011
212-675-6019
(p. 95)

Broadway Dance Center
1733 Broadway 4th Fl.
New York, NY 10019
212-582-9304
(p. App-31)

Broadway Electric
862 Broadway New York, NY
10003
212-673-3906
(p. 115)

Broadway Panhandler
520 Broadway
New York, NY 10012
212-966-3434
(p. 194)

Broadway Party Service
868 Kent Ave.
Brooklyn, NY 11205
718-783-2700
(p. 266)

Broadway Theatre
1681 Broadway
New York, NY 10019
212-664-9587 212-239-6200
(p. App-17)

Broderson Charles Inc.
873 Broadway, Studio 612
New York, NY 10003
212-925-9392
(p. 27)

Brooklyn Academy of Music,
Opera House
300 Layfayette Ave.
Brooklyn, NY 11238
718-636-4128
(p. App-27)

Brooklyn Model Masters
1307 Gravesend Neck Rd.
Brooklyn, NY 11229
718-339-9250
(p. 185)

Brooklyn Model Works
60 Washington Ave.
Brooklyn, NY 11205
718-834-1944
(p. 45, 298, 317, 332, 375)

Brooklyn Museum,
Art Reference Library
200 Eastern Parkway
Brooklyn, NY 11238
718-638-5000 x 308
(p. App-4)

Brooklyn Paint Fair
1010 Coney Island Ave.
Brooklyn, NY 11230
718-434-8000
(p. 257, 259)

Brooks Brothers
346 Madison
New York, NY 10017
212-682-8800
(p. 79)

Brooks Robert L.
235 East 53rd St.
New York, NY 10022
212-486-9829
(p. 15)

BROUWER GARY
100 West 23rd St. 2nd Fl.
New York, NY 10011
212-645-1615
(p. 86)

Brown & Silver Inc.
813 Westchester Ave.
Bronx, NY 10455
212-589-7200
(p. 183)

Brown Arthur and Brothers Inc.
2 West 46th St.
New York, NY 10036
212-575-5555
(p. 20, 51, 165)

Brown Iris
253 East 57th St.
New York, NY 10022
212-593-2882
(p. 111)

Brown Jerry Imported Fabrics
37 West 57th St.
New York, NY 10019
212-753-3626
(p. 128)

BRUCE & BRUCE SCENERY
155 Attorney St.
New York, NY 10002
212-460-5050
(p. 317)

Brunschwig & Fils Inc.
979 Third Ave.
New York, NY 10022
212-838-7878
(p. 370, 378)

Brusca Ice & Wood
2148 2nd Ave.
New York, NY 10029
212-744-6986
(p. 189)

Buchholz Fred
202 West 88th St.
New York, NY 10024
212-874-7700
(p. 335)

Buffalo Batt and Felt Corp.
3307 Walden Ave.
Depew, NY 14043
716-683-4100
(p. 112)

Building Block
33 West 21st. St.
New York, NY 10010
212-929-3347
(p. 47)

Business Committee for the Arts
1775 Broadway
New York, NY 10019
212-664-0600
(p. App-10)

Butler Lumber
220 West 14th St.
New York, NY 10011
212-243-2612
2311 Third Ave.
New York, NY 10035
212-369-9012
(p. 212)

Buttonhole Fashions Inc.
580 Eighth Ave. 5th Fl.
New York, NY 10018
212-354-1420
(p. 117)

Byrke Decks
22 Freeman St.
New Brunswick, NJ 08901
201-249-3863 609-924-7446
(p. 103)

BZI Distributors
105 Eldridge St.
New York, NY 10002
212-966-6690
(p. 101, 341, 374)

- C -

C & C Metal Products
48 West 37th St.
New York, NY 10018
212-695-1679
(p. 244, 361)

C & F Liberty Fabrics
250 West 39th St.
New York, NY 10018
212-354-9360
(p. 128)

C K & L Surplus
307 Canal St.
New York, NY 10013
212-966-1745
(p. 356)

C-Thru Ruler Co.
6 Britton Drive, PO Box 356
Bloomfield, CT 06002
203-243-0303
(p. 94)

Cadillac Plastic & Chemical Co.
35-21 Vernon Blvd.
L.I.C., NY 11106
718-721-8484
(p. 275)

Cahn M. J. Co. Inc.
15 East 22nd St.
New York, NY 10010
212-477-3570
(p. 149)

Cake Masters
120 West 72nd St.
New York, NY 10023
212-787-1414
23 University Pl.
New York, NY 10003
212-477-3370
236 Ninth Ave.
New York, NY 10011
212-924-1818 (continues)

Cake Masters (continued)
1394 Sixth Ave.
New York, NY 10019
212-581-3090
1111 Third Ave.
New York, NY 10021
212-759-7212
1353A Third Ave.
New York, NY 10021
212-879-1414
2345 Broadway
New York, NY 10024
212-787-0998
2631 Broadway
New York, NY 10025
212-749-3340
(p. 28)

Calico Corners
1040 Mamaroneck Ave.
Mamaroneck, NY 10543
914-698-9141
(p. 135)

Camera Barn Inc. The
1272 Broadway
New York, NY 10001
212-947-3510
(p. 270)

Camera Mart
460 West 54th St.
New York, NY 10019
212-757-6977
Stage 1 West
212-757-3715,6
Stage 2 West
212-757-3525,6
Stage 54 West
429 West 54th St.
New York, NY 10019
212-757-0407,8
(p. App-29)

Canal Army & Navy
334 Canal St.
New York, NY 10013
212-334-9680
(p. 82)

Canal Hardware
305 Canal St.
New York, NY 10013
212-226-0825
(p. 183)

Canal Jean Co. Inc.
304 Canal St.
New York, NY 10013
212-431-8439
504 Broadway
New York, NY 10013
212-226-1130
(p. 82)

Canal Luggage Inc.
378 Canal St.
New York, NY 10013
212-925-9750
(p. 180)

Canal Lumber
18 Wooster St.
New York, NY 10013
212-226-5987
(p. 212)

Canal Plastic Center
345 Canal St.
New York, NY 10013
212-925-1032 212-925-1164
(p. 275)

Canal Rubber Supply Co.
329 Canal St.
New York, NY 10013
212-226-7339
(p. 112, 162, 272)

Canal Surplus
363 Canal St.
New York, NY 10013
212-966-3275
(p. 228)

Cancer Care Thrift Shop
1480 Third Ave.
New York, NY 10028
212-879-9868
(p. 352)

Candle Shop
118 Christopher St.
New York, NY 10014
212-989-0148
(p. 48)

Canick's Floor Covering
611 Ninth Ave.
New York, NY 10036
212-582-4759
(p. 156)

Canvas Specialty Co.
8000 Cooper Ave.
Glendale, NY 11385
718-326-1900
(p. 133)

Capezio Dance-Theatre Shop
755 Seventh Ave.
New York, NY 10019
212-245-2130
(p. 72)

Capezio East
136 East 61st St.
New York, NY 10021
212-758-8833
(p. 72)

Capezio in the Village
177 MacDougal St.
New York, NY 10011
212-477-5634
(p. 73)

Capezio Wholesale Shoes
717 Fifth Ave.
New York, NY 10022
212-751-2828
(p. 73)

Capitol Fishing Tackle
218 West 23rd St.
New York, NY 10011
212-929-6132
(p. 152)

Capo Michael Antiques
831 Broadway
New York, NY 10003
212-982-3356
(p. 7)

Captain Haggerty's Theatrical Dogs
1748 1st Ave.
New York, NY 10128
212-410-7400
(p. 4)

Capt. Hook Marine Antiques & Shells
South Street Seaport
New York, NY 10038
212-344-2262
(p. 221, 320)

Carborundum Corp./ Insulation Div.
PO Box 808
Niagara Falls, NY 14302
716-278-6221 716-278-2000
(p. 24)

Carcanagues Jacques Inc.
119 Spring St.
New York, NY 10012
212-431-3116
(p. 121)

Cardel Ltd.
615 Madison Ave.
New York, NY 10022
212-753-8880
(p. 55)

Carelli Costumes
594 Ninth Ave. 2nd Fl.
New York, NY 10036
212-765-6166
(p. 95)

Carlyle Rubber Co. Inc.
40 Worth St. Rm. 700
New York, NY 10006
212-349-3810
(p. 273)

Carnegie Hall
161 West 56th St.
New York, NY 10019
212-974-9841 212-247-7800
212-903-9600
(p. App-27)

Carolina Biological Supply
2700 York Rd.
Burlington, NC 27215
919-584-0381
(p. 196)

Carpet Loft
161 Sixth Ave
New York, NY 10013
212-924-2400
903 Broadway
New York, NY 10010
212-505-0770
(p. 157)

Carroll Musical Instrument Service
351 West 41st St.
New York, NY 10036
212-868-4120
(p. 236)

Carroll Sound Inc.
88 Executive Ave.
Edison, NJ 08817
212-533-6230
(p. 236)

Carroll Studios
351 West 41st St.
New York, NY 10036
212-868-4120
(p. App-31)

Cars of Yesterday Rentals
State Hwy No. 9W
Alpine, NJ 07620
201-784-0030
(p. 26)

Carter, Milchman & Frank
28-10 37th Ave.
L.I.C., NY 11101
718-361-2300
(p. 356)

Caruso Josie
327 East 89th St. #4W
New York, NY 10128
212-876-8551
(p. 286)

Casa Moneo Imports
210 West 14th St.
New York, NY 10011
212-929-1644
(p. 120, 124)

Casamassima & Sons
407 East 50th St.
New York, NY 10022
212-355-3734
(p. 189)

Casey J. C.
55 Seventh Ave. South
New York, NY 10014
212-243-0357
(p. 312)

Cast of Thousands
50 West St.
New York, NY 10006
212-425-1631
(p. 49)

Castile Unpainted Furniture
2737 Broadway
New York, NY 10025
212-662-1474
(p. 173)

Caswell-Massey Co. Ltd.
518 Lexington Ave.
New York, NY 10017
212-755-2254
(p. 7)

Catholic Book Shop of New York
150 West 32nd St.
New York, NY 10001
212-594-8431
(p. 310)

Causarano Ralph
31-57 Vernon Blvd.
L.I.C., NY 11106
718-728-2116
(p. 35)

Cementex Co. Inc.
480 Canal St.
New York, NY 10013
212-226-5832
(p. 51)

Center for Arts Information
625 Broadway
New York, NY 10012
212-677-7548
(p. App-10)

Center for Musical Antiquities
544 East 86th St.
New York, NY 10028
212-744-8168
(p. 236)

Center for Occupational Hazards
5 Beekman St.
New York, NY 10038
212-227-6220
(p. App-14)

Central Carpet Cleaning
301 Norman Ave.
Brooklyn, NY 11222
212-567-9200
(p. 57)

Central Carpet
426 Columbus Ave.
New York, NY 10024
212-787-8813
(p. 157)

Central Movers
358 Classon Ave.
Brooklyn, NY 11238
718-622-2660
(p. 234)

Central Opera Service
c/o The Metropolitan Opera
Lincoln Center
New York, NY 10023
212-799-3467 212-957-9871
(p. App-10)

Central Shippee
46 Star Lake Rd.
Bloomingdale, NJ 07403
201-838-1100
(p. 137)

Centre Firearms
10 West 37th St.
New York, NY 10018
212-244-4040
(p. 16)

Century Elevator
4 Court Sq.
L.I.C., NY 11101
718-937-6200
(p. 117)

Ceramic Supply of NY & NJ Inc.
534 La Guardia Pl.
New York, NY 10012
212-475-7236
(p. 281)

Ceramica Gift Gallery
1009 Sixth Ave.
New York, NY 10018
212-354-9216
(p. 56)

Ceramica Mia
405 East 51st St.
New York, NY 10022
212-759-2339
(p. 354)

Cerney D/L
13 East 7th St.
New York, NY 10003
212-673-7033
(p. 70)

Cerulean Blue Ltd.
119 Blanchard, PO Box 21168
Seattle, WA 98111
206-625-9647
(p. 254)

Chairs Caned
133 West 72nd St. 7th Fl.
New York, NY 10023
212-724-4408
(p. 174)

Chandler Collar Replacement
87 Nassau St.
New York, NY 10038
212-962-7570
(p. 62)

Channel Home Center
101 Terhune Ave.
Lodi, NJ 07644
201-473-4950
23 West Glen Ave.
Paramus, NJ 07652
201-447-0444
(p. 188)

Chapman Diane
117 West 69th St. #1B
New York, NY 10023
212-719-5604 212-246-8484
(p. 88)

Charbert Fabrics Corp.
90 Park Ave.
New York, NY 10016
212-986-8081
(p. 148)

Charles Miniatures
246 Lafayette St.
New York, NY 10012
212-966-1580
(p. 185)

Charlotte Ford Trunk Ltd.
PO Box 536
Spearman, TX 79081
806-659-3027
(p. 181)

Charlsen Nadine
364 Union St. #2
Brooklyn, NY 11231
718-625-0262
(p. 288)

Charrette Drafting Supply Corp.
5 West 45th St.
New York, NY 10036
212-921-1122
215 Lexington Ave.
New York, NY 10016
212-683-8822
(p. 20, 36, 185, 356)

Charrot L. J. Co. Inc.
149 West 24th St.
New York, NY 10011
212-242-1933
(p. 106)

Chateau Theatrical Animals
608 West 48th St.
New York, NY 10036
212-246-0520
(p. 5)

CHEAP JACK'S VINTAGE CLOTHING
167 First Ave.
New York, NY 10003
212-473-9599
841 Broadway
New York, NY 10003
212-777-9564
(p. 70)

Chef Restaurant Supplies
294-296 Bowery
New York, NY 10012
212-254-6644
(p. 56, 195)

Cheffo Nick Signs
2317 East 21st St.
Brooklyn, NY 11229
718-769-0034
(p. 326)

Chekhov Michael Studio Inc.
19 West 36th St. 8th Fl.
New York, NY 10018
212-736-1544
(p. App-31)

Chelsea Decorative Metal Co.
6115 Cheena
Houston, TX 77096
713-721-9200
(p. 14)

Chelsea Desk Co.
360 Lexington Ave.
New York, NY 10017
212-682-6050
(p. 171)

Chemco (Resin Crafts)
6475 Sierra Lane
Dublin, CA 94568
415-829-5000
(p. 51)

Chemical Waste Disposal Co.
42-14 19th Ave.
Astoria, NY 11105
718-274-3339
(p. App-14)

Chenko Studio
167 West 46th St.
New York, NY 10036
212-944-0215
(p. 95)

Cherry Lane Theatre
38 Commerce
New York, NY 10014
212-989-2020
(p. App-20)

Chess Shop
230 Thompson St.
New York, NY 10012
212-475-9580
(p. 175)

Cheung Fat Co.
61 Mott St.
New York, NY 10013
212-349-0727
(p. 122)

Chicago Hair Goods Co.
428 S. Wabash Ave.
Chicago, IL 60605
312-427-8600
(p. 178)

Chicago Latex Products
1030 Morse Ave.
Shaumburg, IL 60193
312-893-2880
(p. 51)

Childcraft Center
155 East 23rd St.
New York, NY 10010
212-674-4754
150 East 58th St.
New York, NY 10155
212-753-3196
(p. 170, 359)

China Books & Periodicals
125 Fifth Ave.
New York, NY 10003
212-677-2650
(p. 40, 122)

China Seas
979 Third Ave.
New York, NY 10022
212-752-5555
(p. 122)

Chinatown 10 Cent Store
25 Elizabeth St.
New York, NY 10013
212-966-4778
(p. 122)

Chingos & Sons Inc.
818 Sixth Ave.
New York, NY 10001
212-689-0476 212-684-6938
(p. 158, App-1)

Chips Men's Store
14 East 44th St.
New York, NY 10017
212-687-0850
(p. 79)

Christie Edward G.
208 West 88th St.
New York, NY 10024
212-799-0216
(p. 301)

Christine Fye
147 West 22nd St.
New York, NY 10011
212-243-8703
(p. 290)

CHRISTO VAC/COSTUME ARMOUR INC.
PO Box 325, Shore Road
Cornwall-on-Hudson, NY 12520
914-534-9120 212-585-1199
(p. 375)

Cibu Lighting
1482 Third Ave.
New York, NY 10028
212-535-9529
(p. 207)

Cinderella Flower and Feather Co.
57 West 38th St.
New York, NY 10018
212-840-0644
(p. 364)

Cine 60
630 Ninth Ave.
New York, NY 10036
212-586-8782
(p. 203)

Cine Studio
241 West 54th St.
New York, NY 10019
212-581-1916
(p. App-29)

Cinema Galleries Ltd.
515 West 26th St.
New York, NY 10001
212-244-2243
(p. 296)

CINEMABILIA
10 West 13th St.
New York, NY 10011
212-989-8519
(p. 40, 226)

Circa 1890
265 East 78th St.
New York, NY 10021
212-734-7388
(p. 7)

Circle Blue Print Co.
225 West 57th St.
New York, NY 10019
212-265-3674
(p. 282)

Circle Braid Co.
247 West 37th St.
New York, NY 10018
212-730-8171
(p. 367)

Circle Elevator
272 Lafayette St.
New York, NY 10012
212-431-1319 212-254-4086
(p. 117)

Circle Fabrics
263 West 38th St.
New York, NY 10018
212-247-2260 212-719-5153
(p. 137)

Circle Ice & Cube Co.
491 Tenth Ave.
New York, NY 10018
212-535-8864 212-873-7469
(p. 189)

Circle Repertory Company
99 Seventh Ave. S.
New York, NY 10014
212-924-9358 212-924-7100
(p. App-20)

Circle-In-The-Square Theatre
1633 Broadway
New York, NY 10019
212-997-9513 212-581-0720
(p. App-17)

Circle-In-The-Square, Downtown
159 Bleecker
New York, NY 10014
212-254-6330 212-473-9784
(p. App-20)

City Barrel
421 Meeker Ave.
Brooklyn, NY 11222
718-388-9227
(p. 29)

City Center
131 West 55th St.
New York, NY 10019
212-974-9833 212-246-8989
(p. App-17)

City Chemical
132 West 22nd St.
New York, NY 10011
212-929-2723
(p. 51)

City Electric Supply Co.
510 West 34th St.
New York, NY 10001
212-564-5454
(p. 115)

City Emblem Mfg. Co.
6031 Myrtle Ave.
Brooklyn, NY 11385
718-366-2040
(p. 117)

City Knickerbocker Inc.
781 Eighth Ave.
New York, NY 10036
212-586-3939
(p. 207)

City Stage Co. (CSC Rep.)
136 East 13th St.
New York, NY 10003
212-677-4210
(p. App-23)

City Upholstery
3000 Ocean Pkwy.
Brooklyn, NY 11235
718-449-5242
(p. 373)

Clairmont-Nichols Inc.
1016 First Ave.
New York, NY 10022
212-758-2346
(p. 348)

Claremont Riding Academy
175 West 89th St.
New York, NY 10024
212-724-5100
(p. 5, 185)

Clarence House
40 East 57th St.
New York, NY 10022
212-752-2890
(p. 378)

Clark Transfer
121 New York Ave.
Trenton, NJ 08638
212-580-4075 609-396-1100
(p. 234)

Clay Pot The
162 Seventh Ave.
Brooklyn, NY 11215
718-788-6564
(p. 281)

Clifton Plastics Inc.
557 E. Baltimore Ave.
Clifton Heights, PA 19018
215-622-3900
(p. 275)

Clock Hutt
1050 Second Ave.
New York, NY 10022
212-759-2395
(p. 58)

Clurman Harold Theatre
412 West 42nd St.
New York, NY 10036
212-594-2370 212-594-2828
(p. App-20)

Coca-Cola Bottling Co.
977 East 149th St.
Bronx, NY 10455
212-292-2424
(p. 225)

Coca-Cola Co./Public Relations
11969 Ventura Blvd. Suite 107
Studio City, CA 91604
213-877-0607
(p. 225)

Cockpit The
627 Broadway 7th Fl.
New York, NY 10012
212-420-1600
(p. 82)

Coco-Nut The
4529 Woodhaven Ave.
Marietta, GA 30067
404-564-0244
(p. 225)

Coe Sidney Inc.
65 West 37th St.
New York, NY 10018
212-391-6960
(p. 361)

Cohen Ezra Corp.
307 Grand St.
New York, NY 10002
212-925-7800
(p. 210)

Coin Machine Distributors Inc.
425 Fairview Park Dr.
Elmsford, NY 10523
914-347-3777
(p. 4)

Coliseum Books Inc.
1771 Broadway
New York, NY 10019
212-757-8381
(p. 40)

Collector's Armoury Inc.
800 Slaters Lane, PO Box 1061
Alexandria, VA 22313
703-684-6111 800-336-4572
(p. 16)

Collector's Cabinet
153 East 57th St.
New York, NY 10022
212-355-2033
(p. 320)

Colling Brenda
592 Manhattan Ave. #3L
Brooklyn, NY 11222
718-383-3839
(p. 88)

Collyer-Sparks Construction Corp.
30 East 33rd St.
New York, NY 10016
212-684-0900
(p. 175)

Colonial Decorative Displays
160 11th Ave.
New York, NY 10011
212-255-9620
(p. 107)

Colonial Gloves and Garments
54 Penataquet Ave.
Bayshore, NY 11706
516-968-8888
(p. 63)

Colonnades Theatre
428 Lafayette
New York, NY 10003
212-673-2222
(p. App-20)

Colony Records
1691 Broadway
New York, NY 10019
212-265-2050
(p. 237, 309, App-1)

Color Wheel Inc.
227 East 45th St.
New York, NY 10017
212-697-2434
(p. 271)

Colorcraft Ltd.
PO Box 936
Avon, CT 06001
800-243-2712 203-282-0020
(p. 254)

Colson Casters
Meecham Ave.
Elmont, NY 11003
516-354-1540
(p. 349)

Colt Firearms
545 New Park Ave.
West Hartford, CT 06110
PO Box 186 (mail)
Hartford, CT 06102
203-236-6311
(p. 16)

Columbia Blue & Photoprint Co. Inc.
14 East 39th St.
New York, NY 10016
212-532-9425
(p. 282)

Columbia Lighting and Silversmiths
499 Third Ave.
New York, NY 10016
212-725-5250
(p. 276)

Columbia University, Avery Architectural & Fine Arts Library
Avery Hall, Columbia University
New York, NY 10027
212-280-3501
(p. App-4)

Columbus Avenue Bazaar
540 Columbus Ave.
New York, NY 10024
212-362-7335
(p. 167, 193)

Comet Fibers Inc.
845 Meeker Ave.
Brooklyn, NY 11222
718-388-1887
(p. 112)

Comfort Industries
39-35 21st St.
L.I.C., NY 11101
718-392-5300
(p. 113, 162)

COMMERCIAL DRAPES CO. INC.
9209 Flatlands Ave.
Brooklyn, NY 11236
718-649-8080
(p. 99, 349)

Commercial Plastics
98-31 Jamaica Ave.
Richmond Hill, NY 11418
718-849-8100
(p. 1, 276)

Commonwealth Felt
160 Fifth Ave. Rm. 714
New York, NY 10010
212-243-7779
(p. 138)

Compleat Strategist The
11 East 33rd St.
New York, NY 10016
212-685-3880
(p. 175, 185)

Conde Nast Publications Library
350 Madison Ave.
New York, NY 10017
212-880-8244
(p. App-4)

Conklin T. E. Brass & Copper Inc.
345 Hudson
New York, NY 10014
212-691-5100
(p. 228)

Connaissance Fabrics Inc.
979 Third Ave.
New York, NY 10022
212-752-6365
(p. 378)

Connoisseur Pipe Shop
51 West 46th St.
New York, NY 10036
212-247-6054
(p. 331)

Connor Eileen
PO Box 154 Radio City Sta.
New York, NY 10101
212-246-6346
(p. 88, 288)

Conran's
160 East 54th St.
New York, NY 10022
212-371-2225
2-8 Astor Place
New York, NY 10003
212-505-1515
(p. 168, 207)

Conso
104 West 40th St.
New York, NY 10018
212-556-6316
(p. 370)

Consolidated Canvas Co.
89 Seventh Ave.
New York, NY 10011
212-929-4880
(p. 133)

CONSOLIDATED DISPLAY CO. INC.
4501 W. Cortez St.
Chicago, IL 60651
312-486-3040
(p. 86, 99, 107)

Consolidated Productions
PO Box 277
Duarte, CA 91010
213-469-5000
(p. 234)

Constantine Albert & Sons
2050 Eastchester Rd.
Bronx, NY 10461
212-792-1600
(p. 184, 231, 356)

Conte R.
1841 Park Ave.
New York, NY 10035
212-534-1416
(p. 48)

Contessa Yarns
PO Box 37
Lebanon, CT 06249
203-423-3479
(p. 380)

Continental Arms Corp.
697 Fifth Ave. 4th Fl.
New York, NY 10022
212-753-8331
(p. 16)

Continental Felt
22 West 15th St.
New York, NY 10011
212-929-5262
(p. 138)

Continental Sewing Supply Co.
104 West 25th St.
New York, NY 10001
212-255-8837
(p. 321)

Cool Runnin'
73 Second Ave.
New York, NY 10003
212-473-6311
(p. 119)

Cooper Classics
132 Perry St.
New York, NY 10014
212-929-0094
(p. 26)

Cooper Hewitt Museum of Design Library
2 East 91st St.
New York, NY 10028
212-860-6868
(p. App-5)

Cooper Union for the Advancement of Science and Art Library
Cooper Square
New York, NY 10003
212-254-6300 x 323
(p. App-5)

Cooper-Wiss
33 Littleton Ave.
Newark, NJ 07107
201-622-4670
(p. 319)

Corham
300 Central Ave.
White Plains, NY 10606
914-946-7373 (p. 18)

Corinne Offset
737 Broadway
New York, NY 10003
212-777-8083
(p. 282)

Cork Products Co. Inc.
19 West 21st St.
New York, NY 10011
212-691-0960
(p. 86)

Corn Joseph & Son Inc.
141 West 28th St.
New York, NY 10001
212-695-1635
(p. 76)

Corset Accessories
611 Broadway Rm. 626
New York, NY 10012
212-677-0223
(p. 245)

Cort Theatre
138 West 48th St.
New York, NY 10036
212-997-9776 212-239-6200
(p. App-17)

Cosby Gerry & Co. Inc.
3 Penn Plaza
New York, NY 10001
212-563-6464
(p. 65, 339)

Cosmo Hosiery Shops
425 Fifth Ave.
New York, NY 10016
212-532-3111
(p. 78)

Costello Charles
31 West 38th St.
New York, NY 10018
212-391-8355
(p. 33)

COSTUME ARMOUR INC.
PO Box 325, Shore Road
Cornwall-on-Hudson, NY 12520
212-585-1199 914-534-9120
(p. 16, 298)

Costume Collection The
1501 Broadway
New York, NY 10036
212-221-0885 (continues)

Costume Collection (continued)
601 West 26th St.
New York, NY 10001
212-989-5855
(p. 96, 325)

Costume Society of America
15 Littlejohn Rd., PO Box 761
Englishtown, NJ 07726
201-536-6216
(p. App-5)

Costumer Service Co.
1695 North Pointe #301
San Francisco, CA 94123
415-931-7349
(p. 94)

Cotto Valentin
117 West 96th St.
New York, NY 10025
212-663-0334
(p. 234)

Cougar Sports Inc.
590 Central Park Ave.
Scarsdale, NY 10583
914-723-2266
(p. 339)

Coulter Studios Inc.
118 East 59th St. 2nd Fl.
New York, NY 10022
212-421-8083
(p. 380)

Country Floors
300 East 61st St.
New York, NY 10021
212-758-7414
(p. 354)

Cowhey J. & Sons Inc.
Marine Equipment
440 Van Brunt St.
Brooklyn, NY 11231
718-625-5587
(p. 221, 349)

Craft Caravan Inc.
127 Spring St.
New York, NY 10012
212-966-1338
(p. 120)

Craft Clerical Clothes
247 West 37th St. 17th Fl.
New York, NY 10018
212-764-6122
(p. 73)

Craig Paul Ltd.
14-15 D'Arblay St.
London, England W1V3SP
01-437-5467
(p. 229)

Crane Susan Inc.
8107 Cancellor Row
Dallas, TX 75247
214-631-6490 212-260-0580
(p. 107)

CRAWFORD & FIELD INC.
111 Water St.
Brooklyn, NY 11201
718-855-4431
(p. 317)

Crazy Eddie
405 Sixth Ave.
New York, NY 10011
212-242-1126
212 East 57th St.
New York, NY 10022
212-980-5134
(p. 25)

Creative Cakes
400 East 74th St.
New York, NY 10021
212-794-9811
(p. 28)

Crouch & Fitzgerald
400 Madison Ave.
New York, NY 10017
212-753-1808 212-755-5888
(p. 211)

Crown River
50-25 34th St.
L.I.C., NY 11101
718-706-0420
(p. 107)

Crown Sewing Maching Service
2792 Broadway
New York, NY 10025
212-663-8968
(p. 321)

Crozier Fine Arts
630 West 26th St.
New York, NY 10003
212-741-2024
(p. 235)

Crystal Aquarium
1659 Third Ave.
New York, NY 10128
212-534-9003
(p. 371)

Crystal Factory Outlet
55 Delancey St.
New York, NY 10002
212-925-8783
(p. 56)

Crystal Resources Inc.
130 East 65th St.
New York, NY 10021
212-744-1171
(p. 312)

Cuckoo Clock Mfg. Co.
32 West 25th St.
New York, NY 10010
212-255-5133
(p. 59)

Cultural Assistance Center
330 West 42nd St. Rm. 1701
New York, NY 10036
212-947-6340
(p. App-10)

Cultural Council Foundation
625 Broadway
New York, NY 10012
212-473-5660
(p. App-10)

Cultured Design Ltd.
548 West 28th St.
New York, NY 10001
212-594-8690
(p. 18, 107)

CULVER PICTURES
150 West 22nd St. #300
New York, NY 10011
212-645-1672
(p. 226, 227)

Cushing W. & Co.
PO Box 351
Kennebunkport, ME 04046
207-967-3711
(p. 254)

Cutawl Co.
Route 6
Bethel, CT 06801
203-792-8622
(p. 356)

- D -

D & C Textile Corp.
124 West 36th St.
New York, NY 10018
212-564-6200
(p. 128)

D & R Embroidery Co.
29 East 31st St.
New York, NY 10010
212-686-6920
(p. 117)

D & R Auslander Hardware
123 Chambers St.
New York, NY 10007
212-267-3520
(p. 341)

D.H.A. Lighting Ltd.
533 Canal St.
New York, NY 10013
212-219-2218
(p. 203)

Daley Kevin
59-42 57 Rd.
Maspeth, NY 11378
718-326-1130
(p. 288)

Dallek
269 Madison Ave.
New York, NY 10017
212-684-4848
(p. 171)

Dalton B. Booksellers
170 Broadway
New York, NY 10038
212-349-3560
396 Sixth Ave.
New York, NY 10012
212-674-8780
666 Fifth Ave.
New York, NY 10103
212-247-1740
(p. 40)

Dance Notation Bureau
33 West 21st St. 3rd Fl.
New York, NY 10010
212-807-7899
(p. App-10)

Dance Notation Bureau (Studios)
33 West 21st St. 3rd Fl.
New York, NY 10010
212-807-7899 (p. App-31)

Dance Theatre Workshop
219 West 19th St.
New York, NY 10011
212-691-6500
(p. App-10, App-27, App-31)

Dance- June Lewis & Company
48 West 21st St. 7th Fl.
New York, NY 10014
212-741-3044
(p. App-31)

Dancing Waters
250 West 57th St.
New York, NY 10019
212-247-1348
(p. 335)

Daniels Carpet Service
3322 Ave. K
Brooklyn, NY 11210
718-377-2387
(p. 157)

Danskin Inc.
350 Fifth Ave.
New York, NY 10118
212-736-1006
(p. 73)

Darcel Jacques Inc.
50 West 57th St.
New York, NY 10019
212-753-7576
(p. 178)

Daroma Restaurant Equipment Corp.
196 Bowery
New York, NY 10012
212-226-6774
(p. 196)

Darrow's Chick Fun Antiques
1174 Second Ave.
New York, NY 10021
212-838-0730
(p. 8, 359)

Datel Stores of NY
1211 Sixth Ave.
New York, NY 10036
212-921-0110
(p. 85)

David's Outfitters Inc.
36 West 20th St.
New York, NY 10011
212-691-7388
(p. 74, 82)

Davis David
346 Lafayette
New York, NY 10002
212-982-7100
(p. 21)

Davis Michael Shipping Corp.
29 East 61st St.
New York, NY 10021
212-832-3655
(p. 235)

Dawn Animal Agency
160 West 46th St.
New York, NY 10036
212-575-9396
(p. 5)

Day-Glo Color Corp.
303 Wilson Ave.
Newark, NJ 07105
212-986-1120
(p. 262)

Dayton Tool Grinding
59 Carmine St.
New York, NY 10014
212-675-1071
(p. 35)

Daytona Trimmings Co.
251 West 39th St.
New York, NY 10018
212-354-1713 212-354-1716
(p. 367)

DAZIAN INC.
423 West 55th St.
New York, NY 10019
212-307-7800
(p. 107, 133, 138, 141)

De La Concha
1390 Sixth Ave.
New York, NY 10019
212-757-3167
(p. 331)

De-Sign Letters
15 East 18th St.
New York, NY 10003
212-673-6211
(p. 326)

Dean & Deluca
121 Prince St.
New York, NY 10012
212-254-7774
(p. 194)

DeCamp June
120 Haven Ave. #22
New York, NY 10032
212-568-9331
(p. 88, 288)

De'Cor Embroideries Co. Inc.
250 West 40th St.
New York, NY 10018
212-354-8668
(p. 117)

Decorators Hardware Co.
155 East 52nd St.
New York, NY 10022
212-755-2168 212-755-0895
(p. 166, 182, 183)

Decorator's Walk
979 Third Ave. 18th Fl.
New York, NY 10022
212-355-5300 212-688-4300
(p. 101, 135)

Decorator's Warehouse
665 Eleventh Ave.
New York, NY 10019
212-489-7575
(p. 168)

Defender Industries
255 Main St.
New Rochelle, NY 10801
914-632-3001
(p. 52, 221)

Defiance Button Machine
456 Nordhoff Pl.
Engelwood, NJ 07631
212-594-0330
(p. 245)

DeFillipo Dom Studio Inc.
215 East 37th St.
New York, NY 10016
212-986-5444 212-867-4220
(p. 335, App-29)

Dekor Flocking
183 Wisner Ave.
Middleton, NY 10940
914-342-1432
(p. 156)

Delancey Live Poultry
205 Delancey St.
New York, NY 10002
212-475-9875
(p. 5)

Delbon & Co.
121 West 30th St.
New York, NY 10001
212-244-2297
(p. 320)

DelSemme's Artists' Materials Inc.
27 West 14th St.
New York, NY 10011
212-675-2742
(p. 21)

Delvoye Janet
7 Suydam Ave. #2
Edison, NJ 08817
201-985-7381
(p. 88, 301)

Demarest Charles Inc.
PO Box 238
Bloomingdale, NJ 07043
201-492-1414
(p. 308)

Deming Thomas A. Co. Inc.
470 Westside Ave.
Jersey City, NJ 07304
201-333-8609 212-732-2659
(p. 103, 168)

Denaro Sal
174 Degraw St.
Brooklyn, NY 11232
718-875-1711
(p. 288, 303)

Denney Michael
23 East 74th St. #14B
New York, NY 10021
212-861-7303
(p. 288)

Dependable Delivery Inc.
360 West 52nd St.
New York, NY 10019
212-586-5552
(p. 238)

Depression Modern
137 Sullivan St.
New York, NY 10012
212-982-5699
(p. 8)

Dept. H.E.W., Region 2
26 Federal Plaza
New York, NY 10007
212-264-2485
(p. App-14)

Der-Dav Custom Riding Boots & Shoes
783 Coney Island Ave.
Brooklyn, NY 11218
718-856-6913
(p. 60)

Design Associates
76 S. Union St.
Lambertville, NJ 08530
609-397-1588
(p. 250, 317)

Design Craft Fabric Corp.
7227 Oak Park
Niles, IL 60648
312-647-0888
(p. 138, 250)

DESIGN ETC. INC.
155 West 68th St. #825
New York, NY 10023
212-874-3814
(p. 107)

Design Furniture Warehouse
902 Broadway
New York, NY 10011
212-673-8900
(p. 168)

Design Gallery
443 Third Ave.
New York, NY 10016
212-532-3610
(p. 378)

Detail Associates
PO Box 197
Santa Monica, CA 93454
805-934-1868
(p. 185)

Deutsch Inc.
196 Lexington Ave.
New York, NY 10016
212-532-5780
(p. 382)

Devon Shops
111 East 27th St.
New York, NY 10016
212-686-1760
(p. 170)

Dharma Trading Co.
PO Box 916
San Rafael, CA 94915
415-456-1211
(p. 254)

DHL Worldwide Courier Express
2 World Trade Center
New York, NY 10048
718-917-8000
(p. 323)

Diamond Discount Fabric Center
165 First Ave.
New York, NY 10009
212-228-8189 212-674-9612
(p. 128)

Diamond Ice Cube Co. Inc.
216 West 23rd St.
New York, NY 10011
212-675-4115
(p. 189)

Diamond Needle
159 West 25th St.
New York, NY 10001
212-929-2277
(p. 248, 321)

Diane Button Co.
225 West 37th St.
New York, NY 10018
212-921-8383
(p. 245)

Diaz Oliverio
866 Broadway
New York, NY 10003
212-475-7080
(p. 331)

Dieu Donne Press & Paper
3 Crosby St.
New York, NY 10013
212-226-0573
(p. 21)

Direct Fastening Service Corp.
132 West Houston St.
New York, NY 10012
212-533-4260
(p. 356)

Direct Safety Co.
7815 S. 46th St., PO Box 8018
Phoenix, AZ 85040
800-528-7405
(p. App-15)

Disc-O-Mat
474 Seventh Ave.
New York, NY 10001
212-736-1150 (continues)

Disc-O-Mat (continued)
1518 Broadway
New York, NY 10036
212-575-0686
716 Lexington Ave.
New York, NY 10022
212-759-3777
(p. 309)

Discount Fabrics of Burlington NJ
202 West 40th St.
New York, NY 10018
212-354-9275
(p. 128)

Discoveries Inc.
120 East 23rd St. Rm. 305
New York, NY 10010
212-254-8591
(p. 107)

Dixie Foam Co.
20 East 20th St.
New York, NY 10003
212-777-3626
(p. 162)

Dixie Gun Works
Highway 51 Bypass
Union City, TN 38261
901-885-0561
(p. 16)

Dixon's Bicycle Shop
792 Union St.
Brooklyn, NY 11215
718-636-0067
(p. 34)

Dobbs Hats
1290 Sixth Ave. #1449
New York, NY 10019
212-582-8650
(p. 65)

Dollsandreams
1421 Lexington Ave.
New York, NY 100128
212-876-2434
(p. 111)

Dollspart Supply Co. Inc.
5-15 49th Ave.
L.I.C., NY 11101
718-361-0888
(p. 110, 111)

Donghia Textiles
485 Broadway
New York, NY 10013 (office)
212-477-9877
979 Third Ave.
New York, NY 10022 (showroom)
212-935-3713
(p. 378)

Donjer Products Co.
55 Alder St.
West Babylon, NY 11704
516-293-5822
(p. 156)

Donna Motor Sales
15 Roosevelt Ave.
Belleville, NJ 07109
201-759-7838
(p. 26)

Door Store The
1 Park Ave.
New York, NY 10022
212-679-9700
210 East 51st St.
New York, NY 10022
212-753-2280
(p. 168)

Dory Duplicates
PO Box W, Salem
NY 12865
518-854-7613
(p. 84)

Doubleday Book Shop
673 Fifth Ave.
New York, NY 10022
212-953-4805
724 Fifth Ave.
New York, NY 10019
212-397-0550
(p. 41)

Douglas & Sturges
730 Bryant St.
San Francisco, CA 94107
415-421-4456
(p. 52)

Dover Publications Inc.
180 Varick St.
New York, NY 10014
212-255-3755
31 East 2nd St.
Mineola, NY 11501
516-294-7000 (p. 41, App-5)

Down East Enterprises Inc.
240 Lafayette St.
New York, NY 10012
212-925-2632
(p. 113)

Doyle William Galleries
175 East 87th St.
New York, NY 10128
212-427-2730
(p. 8)

DRAMA BOOKSHOP
723 Seventh Ave. 2nd Fl.
New York, NY 10036
212-944-0595
(p. 41)

Dream Wheels
295 Mercer St.
New York, NY 10012
212-677-0005
(p. 339)

Dremel Service Center
PO Box 1468
Racine, WI 53401
414-554-1390
(p. 185)

Dritz-Scovill
PO Box 5028
Spartanburg, SC 29304
803-576-5050
(p. 241)

Drucker Max Fabrics Inc.
469 Seventh Ave.
New York, NY 10018
212-244-5015
(p. 145)

Duffy & Quinn Inc.
366 Fifth Ave.
New York, NY 10001
212-688-2885
(p. 74)

Duggal Color Projects Inc.
9 West 20th St.
New York, NY 10011
212-242-7000
(p. 268, 271)

DuKane Fabrics
453 Broadway
New York, NY 10013
212-964-1554 212-925-8400
(p. 139)

Dulchin B. Inc.
170 Seventh Ave.
New York, NY 10011
212-243-6741
(p. 183, 356)

Dulken & Derrick Inc.
12 West 21st St. 6th Fl.
New York, NY 10010
212-929-3614
(p. 364)

Dumont Camera Corp.
893 Broadway
New York, NY 10003
212-475-1700
(p. 270, 271)

Dunhill Alfred of London
620 Fifth Ave.
New York, NY 10020
212-481-6950
(p. 331)

DUO-FAST CORP.
31-07 20th Rd.
L.I.C., NY 11105
718-726-2400
(p. 1, 345, 357)

Duplex Novelty
575 Eighth Ave.
New York, NY 10018
212-564-1352
(p. 245, 361)

Dura-Foam Products Inc.
63-02 59th Ave.
Maspeth, NY 11378
718-894-2488
(p. 52, 162)

Dworkin & Daughter
1214 Lexington Ave.
New York, NY 10028
212-988-3584
(p. 62)

Dyersburg & Morgan Inc.
240 Madison Ave.
New York, NY 10016
212-679-7733
(p. 139)

Dykes Lumber
348 West 44th St.
New York, NY 10036
212-246-6480 (continues)

Dykes Lumber (continued)
26-16 Jackson Ave.
L.I.C., NY 11101
718-534-1640
(p. 213, 231)

- E -

E & J Repair Service
245 Eighth Ave.
New York, NY 10011
212-691-7171
(p. 321)

E & T Plastic Mfg. Co. Inc.
45-33 37th St.
L.I.C., NY 11101
718-729-6226
(p. 276, 375)

E.U.E./Screen Gems Ltd.
222 East 44th St.
New York, NY 10017
212-867-4030
(p. App-29)

Eagle Buckram Co. Inc.
8 Washington Place
New York, NY 10003
212-477-5529
(p. 229)

Eagle Ceramics
12266 Wilkins Ave.
Rockville, MD 20852
301-881-2253
(p. 24)

Eagle Supply Co.
327 West 42nd St.
New York, NY 10036
212-246-6180
(p. 21, 261, 329)

Eagles Antiques
1097 Madison Ave.
New York, NY 10028
212-772-3266
(p. 8)

EARLY HALLOWEEN
10 West 19th St.
New York, NY 10011
212-691-2933 212-243-1499
(p. 70, 296)

Earthworks & Artisans
251 West 85th St.
New York, NY 10024
212-873-5220
(p. 281)

East Coast Film Cars
749-57 Hicks St.
Brooklyn, NY 11231
718-624-6050 718-624-6881
(p. 26)

East Side Antiques
55 East 11th St.
New York, NY 10003
212-677-8820
(p. 8)

East Side Copy Center
15 East 13th St.
New York, NY 10003
212-807-0465
(p. 282)

East-East
230 East 80th St.
New York, NY 10021
212-861-3692
(p. 122)

Eastern Artists & Drafting Materials
352 Park Ave. South 11th Fl.
New York, NY 10010
212-725-5555
(p. 21)

Eastern Chain Works Inc.
144 West 18th St.
New York, NY 10011
212-242-2500
(p. 183)

Eastern Doll Corp.
37 Greene St.
New York, NY 10013
212-226-1535
(p. 110)

Eastern Findings Corp.
19 West 34 St. 12th Fl.
New York, NY 10001
212-695-6640
(p. 191)

Eastern Model Aircraft
365 40th St.
Brooklyn, NY 11232
718-768-7960
(p. 185)

Eastern Mountain Sports
611 Broadway
New York, NY 10012
212-505-9860
20 West 61st St.
New York, NY 10023
212-397-4860
(p. 339)

Eastern Safety Equipment Co. Inc.
5920 56th Ave.
Maspeth, NY 11378
718-894-7900
(p. App-15)

Eaves-Brooks Costume Co.
21-07 41st Ave.
L.I.C., NY 11101
718-729-1010
(p. 96)

ECCENTRICITIES
41 Union Square West
New York, NY 10003
212-924-9411
(p. 96, 108)

Echo Antiques
451 Third Ave.
New York, NY 10016
212-689-4241
(p. 8)

Eck & Krebs Scientific Lab
Glass Apparatus Inc.
27-09 40th Ave.
L.I.C., NY 11101
718-786-6077
(p. 196)

Eclectic Furniture Center
35 Main St.
Southampton, NY 11968
516-283-8850
(p. 168)

Eclectic Properties Inc.
204 West 84th St.
New York, NY 10024
212-799-8963
(p. 8, 84, 101, 296, 325, 373)

Eclectic Properties, Inc.
204 West 84th St.
New York, NY 10024
212-799-8963
(p. 238)

Economy Foam Center/AAA Foam Center
173 East Houston
New York, NY 10002
212-473-4462
(p. 138, 162)

Economy Optical Co./Optical City
135 West 14th St.
New York, NY 10011
212-243-4884
(p. 63)

Edelstein Stephen
771 West End Ave. #4C
New York, NY 10025
212-666-9198
(p. 288)

Edge Grinding Shop
388 Fairview Ave.
Fairview, NJ 07022
201-943-4109
(p. 35)

Edison Theatre
240 West 47th St.
New York, NY 10036
212-997-9473 212-757-7164
(p. App-17)

Edith's Nostalgia
469 Amsterdam Ave.
New York, NY 10024
212-362-8713
(p. 8, 207)

Edmund Scientific Co.
101 East Gloucester Pike
Barrington, NJ 08007
609-547-3488 800-257-6173
(p. 196, 232)

EFEX Specialists
35-39 37th St.
L.I.C., NY 11101
718-937-2417
(p. 335)

Eigen Supply Co.
236 West 17th St.
New York, NY 10011
212-255-1200
1751 First Ave.
New York, NY 10128
212-255-1200
317 Atlantic Ave.
Brooklyn, NY 11201
212-255-1200 (p. 277)

890 STUDIOS
890 Broadway
New York, NY 10003
212-475-2870
(p. App-31)

80 Papers
80 Thompson St.
New York, NY 10012
212-966-1491
(p. 21)

Eis J. & Sons Appliances
105 First Ave.
New York, NY 10003
212-475-2325
(p. 13)

Eisen Brothers Inc.
239 West 39th St. 3rd Fl.
New York, NY 10018
212-398-0263
(p. 245)

Eising M. & Co.
1036 Lexington Ave.
New York, NY 10021
212-744-1270
(p. 63)

Eisner Brothers
76 Orchard St.
New York, NY 10002
212-475-6868
(p. 81)

Eisner Shade
29 Norman Ave.
Brooklyn, NY 11222
718-389-5850
(p. 101)

Elder Craftsmen The
846 Lexington Ave.
New York, NY 10021
212-861-5260
(p. 181)

Eldridge Textile Co.
277 Grand St.
New York, NY 10002
212-925-1523
(p. 210)

Electra Displays
90 Remington Blvd.
Ronkonkoma, NY 11779
516-585-5659 212-420-1327
(p. 108, 203, 328, 375)

Electric Appliance Rental & Sales
40 West 29th St. 2nd Fl.
New York, NY 10001
212-686-8884
(p. 13)

Elegant John of Lex
812 Lexington Ave.
New York, NY 10021
212-935-5800
(p. 32)

Eliot Karen Beth
1469 Lexington Ave. #71
New York, NY 10128
212-410-4106
(p. 288)

Ellen O'Neill's
242 East 77th St.
New York, NY 10021
212-879-7330
(p. 62)

Ellertson David
400 West 43rd St. #23R
New York, NY 10036
212-736-8730
(p. 288)

Ellington Galleries Ltd.
93 University Place
New York, NY 10003
212-982-1522 212-982-1523
(p. 8)

Ellis Import Co. Inc.
44 West 37th St.
New York, NY 10018
212-947-6666
(p. 361)

Elter G.
740 Madison Ave.
New York, NY 10021
212-734-4680
(p. 165)

Elvee Pearl Co.
40 West 37th St.
New York, NY 10018
212-947-3930
(p. 361)

Emery Worldwide
184-54 149th Ave.
Jamaica, NY 11413
212-995-6400
(p. 323, App-1)

Empire Artists Materials
851 Lexington Ave.
New York, NY 10021
212-737-5002
(p. 21)
Empire Dyestuffs Corp.
206 Spring St.
New York, NY 10012
212-925-8737
(p. 255)
Empire Hair Processing Corp.
4514 Eleventh Ave.
Brooklyn, NY 11219
718-438-5777
(p. 178)
Empire Stages of New York
50-20 25th St.
L.I.C., NY 11101
212-392-4747
(p. App-29)
Empire State Chair Co. Inc.
305 East 63rd St.
New York, NY 10021
212-421-9470
(p. 172)
Empress Gala
260 West 39th St. 14th Fl.
New York, NY 10018
212-719-1315
(p. 128)
emptybirdcage studios
9235 Foster Ave.
Brooklyn, NY 11236
718-272-5281
(p. 108, 298)
Enchantments Inc.
341 East 9th St.
New York, NY 10003
212-228-4394
(p. 251)
Encore Studio
410 West 47th St.
New York, NY 10036
212-246-5237
(p. 296)
Encyclopedia & Reference
Book Center
175 Fifth Ave.
New York, NY 10010
212-677-2160
(p. 41)
Engineering Model Associates
570 Grove Rd.
Thorofare, NJ 08086
609-848-7700
PO Box 63258
Los Angeles, CA 90063
213-261-8171
(p. 186)
Enkay Trading Co. Inc.
600 Atkins Ave.
Brooklyn, NY 11208
718-272-5570
(p. 357)
Ensemble Studio Theatre
549 West 52nd St.
New York, NY 10019
212-247-3405 212-247-4982
(p. App-23)
Entermedia Theatre
189 Second Ave.
New York, NY 10003
212-777-6230
(p. App-20)
Epstein M. and Sons
809 Ninth Ave.
New York, NY 10019
212-265-3960
(p. 102, 157, 252, 258,
259, 261, 378)
Equity Library Theatre
310 Riverside Dr.
New York, NY 10025
212-663-2028 212-663-2880
(p. App-20)
Erlanger N., Blumgart & Co.
1450 Broadway
New York, NY 10018
212-221-7100
(p. 128)
ERSKINE-SHAPIRO THEATRE TECHNOLOGY
37 West 20th St.
New York, NY 10011
212-929-5380
(p. 332)
Eschem Specialty Chemical Corp.
139 Allings Crossing Rd.
West Haven, CT 06516
212-966-231 203-934-8661
(p. 1)

Esro Products Inc.
900 Broadway
New York, NY 10011
212-777-6010
(p. 135, 144)

Essex Umbrella Corp.
101 Essex St.
New York, NY 10002
212-674-3394
(p. 67)

Esteban A. & Co.
8-10 West 19th St.
New York, NY 10011
212-989-7000
(p. 283)

Ethical Dental Supplies
3217 Quenten Rd.
Brooklyn, NY 11234
718-376-2025
(p. 104)

Eton's Luggage Shop
1124 Sixth Ave.
New York, NY 10036
212-921-1212
(p. 211)

Eugene Doll & Novelty Co.
4012 Second Ave.
Brooklyn, NY 11232
718-788-1313 718-965-2958
200 Fifth Ave.
New York, NY 10010
212-675-8020
(p. 111)

European Woolens Inc.
177 Orchard St.
New York, NY 10002
212-254-1520
(p. 149)

Evans-Friedland Steel Productions
155 East 29th St.
New York, NY 10016
212-532-1011
(p. 323)

Ever Ready Blue Print
200 Park Ave. South
New York, NY 10003
212-228-3131
(p. 283)

Everybody's Thrift Shop
261 Park Ave. South
New York, NY 10010
212-355-9263 (p. 352)

The Eye Shop
50 West 8th St.
NYC 10011
212-673-9450
(p. 63)

Exchange Photo Offset Corp.
111 Broadway
New York, NY 10006
212-962-4040
(p. 283)

Executive Photo & Supply Corp.
120 West 31st St.
New York, NY 10001
212-947-5290
(p. 270)

Exotic Aquatics
8 Cornelia St.
New York, NY 10014
212-675-6355
271½ Amsterdam Ave.
New York, NY 10023
212-873-8655
(p. 371)

- F -

F & J Police Equipment
904 Melrose Ave.
Bronx, NY 10451
212-665-4535
(p. 278)

F & R Fabric Shop Inc.
239 West 39th St.
New York, NY 10018
212-391-9083 212-391-9084
(p. 128)

Fabdec
3553 Old Post Road
San Angelo, TX 76904
915-944-1031
(p. 255)

Fabric Library The
63 West 38th St. Rm 500
New York, NY 10018
212-302-0925
(p. App-5)

Fabric Warehouse
406 Broadway
New York, NY 10013
212-431-9510
(p. 128)

Fabrications
1740 Massachusetts Ave.
Cambridge, MA 02138
617-661-6276
(p. 129)

Facsimile Book Shop Inc.
16 West 55th St.
New York, NY 10019
212-581-2672
(p. 41, 124)

Fairbanks Douglas Theatre
432 West 42nd St.
New York, NY 10036
212-239-4321
(p. App-21)

Fairfield County Estate Liquidators
66 Fort Point Rd.
E. Norwalk, CT 06855
203-838-6541
(p. 168)

Falcon Safety Products
1065 Bristol Rd.
Mountainside, NJ 07092
201-233-5000
(p. 248)

Falcon Supply Co.
468 Newfield Ave. Raritan Ctr.
Edison, NJ 08837
201-225-5050
(p. 251)

Falk Surgical Corp.
259 East 72nd St.
New York, NY 10021
212-744-8082
(p. 224)

FANTASY FACTORY OF MANHATTAN INC.
1500 Hudson St., PO Box 1405
Hoboken, NJ 07030
201-656-3160
(p. 303)

FAO Schwarz
745 Fifth Ave.
New York, NY 10151
212-644-9400
(p. 360)

Far Eastern Fabrics, Ltd.
171 Madison Ave.
New York, NY 10016
212-683-2623
(p. 147)

Farbman Robin
225 West 80th St.
New York, NY 10024
212-580-1291
(p. 289)

Farkas Films
385 Third Ave.
New York, NY 10016
212-679-8212
(p. App-29)

Farm & Garden Nursery
2 Sixth Ave.
New York, NY 10013
212-431-3577
(p. 159)

Faroy Inc.
225 Fifth Ave.
New York, NY 10010
212-679-5193
(p. 48)

Fashion Institute of Technology,
Library/Media Service
227 West 27th St.
New York, NY 10001
212-760-7780
(p. App-5)

Fastex, Div. of Illinois Tool Works
195 Algonquin Rd.
Des Plaines, IL 60016
312-299-2222
(p. 245)

Fe-Ro Fabrics
147 West 57th St.
New York, NY 10019
212-581-0240
(p. 129)

Feartek Productions/ Canthus Inc.
15 West 20th St.
New York, NY 10011
212-741-5190
(p. 108)

Federal Express
560 West 42nd St.
New York, NY 10036
212-777-6500
(p. 323)

Fedyszyn Marjorie
360 Union St. #D1
Brooklyn, NY 11231
718-596-4655
(p. 289)

Feiden Margo Galleries
51 East 10th St.
New York, NY 10003
212-677-5330
(p. 279, 310)

Feldman Lumber
2 Woodward Ave.
Ridgewood, NY 11385
718-495-5000
63 Third Ave.
Bayshore, NY 11706
516-665-3800
692 Hopkins Ave.
Brooklyn, NY 11212
718-498-8200
(p. 213)

FELLER PRECISION INC.
1290 Oak Point Ave.
Bronx, NY 10474
212-589-9600
(p. 317)

Felsen Fabric Corp.
264 West 40th St.
New York, NY 10018
212-398-9010
(p. 129)

Feng James
425 14th St. #A2
Brooklyn, NY 11215
212-499-1601
(p. 88, 289)

Fiber Works
313 East 45th St.
New York, NY 10017
212-286-9116
(p. 380)

Fibre Case and Novelty Co. Inc.
708 Broadway 7th Fl.
New York, NY 10003
212-254-6060
(p. 151)

Fibre Yarn Co. Inc.
48 West 38th St.
New York, NY 10018
212-719-5820
(p. 380)

Fibre-Metal Products Co.
Baltimore Pike
Concordville, PA 19331
215-459-5300
(p. 65, App-15)

Fifth Ave. Rug Exchange
665 Fifth Ave.
New York, NY 10022
212-688-2088
(p. 157)

FIFTH SEASON INC. THE
180 Miller Pl.
Hicksville, NY 11801
516-933-6250
(p. 329)

57th St. Copy Center
151 West 57th St.
New York, NY 10019
212-581-8046
(p. 283)

Film Fleet
218 West 61st St.
New York, NY 10023
212-245-8396
(p. 27)

Film Video Arts
819 Broadway 2nd Fl.
New York, NY 10011
212-673-9361
(p. App-10)

Fina Michael C. Co.
580 Fifth Ave.
New York, NY 10036
212-869-5050
(p. 330)

Finale Inc.
15 West 37 St.
New York, NY 10018
212-840-6255
(p. 64)

Financial Management Center
36 West 44th St. Rm. 1208
New York, NY 10036
212-575-1816 212-575-1828
(p. App-10)

Fine Art Finishing
315 East 91st St. 6th Fl.
New York, NY 10028
212-831-6128
(p. 174)

Fine Arts Materials Inc.
346 Lafayette St.
New York, NY 10012
212-982-7100
(p. 255)

Fine Murry M. Lumber
175 Varick Ave.
Brooklyn, NY 11237
718-381-5200
(p. 32, 213)

Fiore Joseph
66 Hayes St.
Freeport, NY 11520
516-867-1812
(p. 289)

Fireside Theatre Book Club
Dept. ER-658
Garden City, NY 11530
mail only
(p. App-5)

Fireworks by Grucci
Association Rd.
Belleport, NY 11713
516-286-0088 800-227-0088
(p. 335)

First Avenue Bazaar
1453 First Ave.
New York, NY 10021
212-737-2003
(p. 167, 193)

First Nighter Formals
5 West 22nd St.
New York, NY 10010
212-675-5550
(p. 74)

First Stop Housewares
1025 Second Ave.
New York, NY 10022
212-838-0007
(p. 194)

FISCHER DISPLAY LIGHTING INC.
PO Box 140 Westchester Station
Bronx, NY 10461
212-597-7576
836 Logan St.
Brooklyn, NY 11208
718-498-5236
(p. 203, 205)

Fischer Elizabeth
72A Fourth Ave.
Brooklyn, NY 11217
718-643-3949
(p. 289)

Fish & Pet Town
241 East 59th St.
New York, NY 10022
212-752-9508
(p. 267, 372)

Fish Town USA
513 Third Ave.
New York, NY 10016
212-889-3296
(p. 372)

Fisher & Gentile, Ltd.
1412 Broadway
New York, NY 10018
212-221-1800
(p. 129)

Fisher Scientific Co.
52 Fadem Rd.
Springfield, NJ 07081
201-379-1400
(p. 273)

Five Eggs
436 W. Broadway
New York, NY 10012
212-226-1606
(p. 122)

Flameproof Chemical Co.
635 West 23rd St.
New York, NY 10011
212-242-2265
(p. 154)

Flanagan Robert
124 Hall St.
Brooklyn, NY 11205
718-636-6280
(p. 222, 289, 303)

Flax Sam Art Supplies
15 Park Row
New York, NY 10038
212-620-3030
111 Eighth Ave.
New York, NY 10011
212-620-3000 212-620-3010
12 West 20th St.
New York, NY 10011
212-620-3038 (continues)

Flax Sam Art Supplies (continued)
25 East 28th St.
New York, NY 10016
212-620-3060
747 Third Ave.
New York, NY 10017
212-620-3050
55 East 55th St.
New York, NY 10022
212-620-3060
(p. 21, 22, 52)

Fleischer Frames
32 West 39th St.
New York, NY 10018
212-840-2248
(p. 165)

Fleischer Tube Distributing Corp.
71 Saxon Ave.
Bayshore, NY 11706
516-968-8822
(p. 273)

Flesch Bruce Leather Artisan
72 East 7th St.
New York, NY 10003
212-673-7129
(p. 88)

Flex Molding
16 East Lafayette St.
Hackensack, NJ 07601
201-487-8080
(p. 231)

Flex Products
West 34540 Rd. Q
Okauchee, WI 53069
414-367-3331
(p. 52)

Flexitoon Ltd.-Craig and Olga Marin
46 West 73rd St. Rm. 3A
New York, NY 1
212-877-2757
(p. 303)

Florenco Foliage Systems Worldwide
920 East 149th St.
Bronx, NY 10455
212-402-0500
(p. 18, 108)

Florentine Craftsmen Inc.
46-24 28th St.
L.I.C., NY 11101
212-532-3926 718-937-7632
(p. 171, 344)

Flowers Thom
13A Newel St.
Brooklyn, NY 11222
718-398-8574
(p. 289)

FLYING ROBERT THEATRICAL CRAFTS
101 Wooster St.
New York, NY 10012
212-334-9130
(p. 88, 289)

Flynn Stationers
46 East 59th St.
New York, NY 10022
212-758-2080
(p. 342)

Foam Tex
51 East 21st St.
New York, NY 10010
212-674-8440
(p. 162)

Folklorica Imports Inc.
89 Fifth Ave.
New York, NY 10003
212-255-2525
(p. 30, 120)

Folkus Dan
465 Haddon Ave.
Collingswood, NJ 08108
609-858-9736 212-929-7988
(p. 289)

Fonda Boutique
209 East 60th St.
New York, NY 10022
212-759-3260
(p. 70)

Fone Booth The
12 East 53rd St.
New York, NY 10022
212-751-8310
(p. 347)

Forbidden Planet
821 Broadway
New York, NY 10003
212-473-1576
(p. 41, 216)

Force Machinery Co.
2271 US Hwy 22
Union, NJ 07083
201-688-8270
(p. 357)

Ford Piano Supply Co.
4898 Broadway
New York, NY 10034
212-569-9200
(p. 341)

Foremost Lumber
60 North 1st St.
Brooklyn, NY 11211
718-388-7777
(p. 213)

FOREPLAY STUDIOS
33 Greene St.
New York, NY 10013
212-226-0188
(p. 317)

Forman's
82 Orchard St.
New York, NY 10002
212-228-2500
(p. 76)

40th St. Trimmings Inc.
252 West 40th St.
New York, NY 10018
212-354-4729
(p. 241, 366, 367)

47th St. Photo Inc.
35 East 18th St.
New York, NY 10003
212-260-4410 800-221-7774
116 Nassau St.
New York, NY 10038
212-608-6934
115 West 45th St.
New York, NY 10036
212-260-4410
67 West 47th St.
New York, NY 10036
212-260-4410
(p. 270, 347)

46th Street Theatre
226 West 46th St.
New York, NY 10036
212-245-9455 212-221-1211
(p. App-17)

Fortunoff
681 Fifth Ave.
New York, NY 10022
212-758-6660
(p. 330)

Foundation Center
79 Fifth Ave. 8th Fl.
New York, NY 10003
212-620-4230
(p. App-11)

Foundation for the Extension & Development of the American Professional Theatre (FEDAPT)
165 West 46th St.
New York, NY 10036
212-869-9690
(p. App-11)

Four Colors Photo Lab
10 East 39th St.
New York, NY 10016
212-889-3399
(p. 271)

Four Star Stage Lighting
585 Girard Ave.
Bronx, NY 10451
212-993-0471
(p. 205)

Fourth Wall The
3010 Ave. J
Brooklyn, NY 11210
718-258-7953
(p. 317)

Fox Sewing Machines Inc.
307 West 38th St.
New York, NY 10018
212-594-2438
(p. 113, 322)

Foxworthy Michael
430 West 49th St. #14
New York, NY 10019
212-397-1119
(p. 290)

FOY INVENTERPRISES INC.
PO Box 60141
Las Vegas, NV 89160
702-732-3396 702-732-4077
(p. 161)

Frames By You Inc.
136 West 72nd St.
New York, NY 10023
212-874-2337
(p. 165)

Frank Wally Ltd.
344 Madison Ave.
New York, NY 10017
212-687-9222 (p. 331)

Frankel Fred & Sons Inc.
19 West 38th St.
New York, NY 10018
212-840-0810
(p. 361)

Franklin Fibre-Lamitex Corp.
2040 Jericho Turnpike, PO Box 1146
New Hyde Park, NY 11040
718-347-2120 516-437-7791
(p. 276)

Fran's Basket House
295 Route 10
Succasunna, NJ 07876
201-584-2230
(p. 30)

Fredericks K. L.
203 West 20th St.
New York, NY 10011
212-255-4539
(p. 88)

Fredrick Nomi
409 East 90th St.
New York, NY 10128
212-348-8944
(p. 290, 303)

Freed Edwin Inc.
151 West 46th St.
New York, NY 10036
212-391-2170
(p. 191)

Freed of London Ltd.
108 West 57th St.
New York, NY 10019
212-489-1055
(p. 60)

Freelance Photographers' Guild Library
251 Park Ave. South
New York, NY 10010
212-777-4210
(p. App-6)

French & Spanish Book Corp. The
115 Fifth Ave.
New York, NY 10003
212-673-7400
610 Fifth Ave.
New York, NY 10020
212-581-8810
(p. 41, 124)

French Samuel Inc.
45 West 25th St.
New York, NY 10010
212-206-8990
(p. 41)

Frick Art Reference Library
10 East 71st St.
New York, NY 10021
212-288-8700
(p. App-6)

Friedman & Distillator (Owl Mills)
88 W. Broadway 5th Fl.
New York, NY 10007
212-233-6394
(p. 146, 229, 243, 245, 367)

Friedman H. & Sons
225 Secaucus Rd.
Secaucus, NJ 07094
201-348-3555
(p. 196)

Frielich Bros./Deutsch Bros.
670 Broadway
New York, NY 10012
212-777-3051
(p. 229)

Frielich Robert S. Inc.
396 Broome St.
New York, NY 10013
212-254-3045
211 East 21st St.
New York, NY 10010
212-777-4477
(p. 278)

Frisbee Frank
712 Washington St. #GA
New York, NY 10014
212-242-4956
(p. 89)

Frontier Fabrics
144 Chambers
New York, NY 10007
212-925-3000
(p. 135)

Funny Business Comics
666 Amsterdam
New York, NY 10025
212-799-9477
(p. 216)

Funny Store Inc.
1481 Broadway
New York, NY 10036
212-730-9582
(p. 217)

Fuss William
218 East 53rd St.
New York, NY 10022
212-688-0350
(p. 18)

- G -

Gailor John
137 Varick St. 7th Fl.
New York, NY 10014
212-243-5662
(p. 36)

Gampel Supply Corp.
39 West 37th St.
New York, NY 10018
212-398-9222
(p. 110, 229, 368)

Garbo Fred
PO Box 129
Norway, ME 04268
207-743-2860
(p. 303)

Garden State Tanning
215 Lexington Ave.
New York, NY 10016
212-679-8910
(p. 199)

Garment Center Sewing Machine Inc.
555 Eighth Ave.
New York, NY 10018
212-279-8774
(p. 113, 322)

Garnett Brown Prop Rentals
119 West 23rd St. #509
New York, NY 10011
212-691-5250
(p. 8)

Garrett Wade Co. Inc. The
161 Sixth Ave.
New York, NY 10013
212-807-1155
(p. 357)

Gateway Hobbies Inc.
60 West 38th St. 3rd Fl.
New York, NY 10018
212-221-0855
(p. 16)

Gazebo The
660 Madison Ave.
New York, NY 10021
212-832-7077
(p. 307, 382)

Geffman Nat Co.
237 West 35th St.
New York, NY 10001
212-947-3864 212-947-3865
(p. 250)

Gelberg Braid Co. Inc.
243 West 39th St.
New York, NY 10018
212-730-1121
(p. 368)

Gem Glass Co.
790 Eleventh Ave
New York, NY 10019
212-247-7145
(p. 175)

Gem Monogram & Cut Glass Corp.
623 Broadway
New York, NY 10012
212-674-8960
(p. 207)

Gem Sporting Goods
29 West 14th St.
New York, NY 10011
212-255-5830
(p. 339)

Gemco Dental Lab Inc.
1010 McDonald Ave.
Brooklyn, NY 11230
718-438-3270 718-871-3900
(p. 104, App-1)

General Drapery Services
635 West 23rd St.
New York, NY 10011
212-924-7200
(p. 57, 102, 154)

General Reproduction Products
401 Kinderkamack Rd.
Oradell, NJ 07649
201-261-6666
(p. 36)

Gene's 79th St. Discount Bicycles
242 East 79th St.
New York, NY 10021
212-288-0739 212-249-9218
(p. 34)
Gerardo John R. Inc.
30 West 31st St.
New York, NY 10001
212-695-6955
(p. 180)
GERRIETS INTERNATIONAL
RR #1, 950 Hutchinson Rd.
Allentown, NJ 08501
609-758-9121
(p. 99, 103, 144, 205, 349)
Gershwin Theatre (Uris)
1633 Broadway
New York, NY 10019
212-664-8473 212-586-6510
(p. App-17)
Gewirtz-Egert (aka World Associates)
160 West 28th St.
New York, NY 10001
212-563-2420
(p. 200)
Giant Photo Inc.
200 Park Ave. South 5th Fl.
New York, NY 10003
212-982-3840
(p. 268)
Giardinelli Band Instrument Co.
151 West 46th St.
New York, NY 10036
212-575-5959
(p. 237)
GILSHIRE CORP. SCENERY STUDIO PROD.
11-20 46th Rd.
L.I.C., NY 11101
718-786-1381
(p. 263)
Gilsoul B. & Partners
247 West 29th St.
New York, NY 10001
212-868-8414
(p. 178)
Gimbels Department Store
1275 Broadway
New York, NY 10001
212-736-5100 (continues)

Gimbel's Department Store (cont.)
125 East 86th St.
New York, NY 10028
212-348-2300
(p. 105)
Ginsburg Moe
162 Fifth Ave.
New York, NY 10010
212-242-3482
(p. 79)
GIRARD DESIGNS/JANET GIRARD
300 Morgan Ave.
Brooklyn, NY 11211
212-782-6430
(p. 89)
Gitlin Harry Inc.
121 West 19th St.
New York, NY 10011
212-243-1080
(p. 205)
Giurdanella Brothers
4 Bond St.
New York, NY 10012
212-674-2097 212-674-2176
(p. 354)
Gladson Herbert
45 West 45th St.
New York, NY 10036
212-730-0602
(p. 129)
GLADSTONE FABRICS
16 West 56th St. 2nd Fl.
New York, NY 10019
212-765-0760
(p. 129, 133, 139, 144, 146, 147, 148, 149, 230. 250)
Glamour Glove Corp.
902 Broadway
New York, NY 10010
212-777-4633
(p. 64)
Glantz N. & Son
218 57th St.
Brooklyn, NY 11220
718-439-7707
(p. 261)
Glass Henry and Co.
1071 Sixth Ave.
New York, NY 10018
212-840-8200
(p. 129)

Glassmasters Guild
27 West 23rd St. 4th Fl.
New York, NY 10010
212-929-7978
(p. 177, 257)

Glazier Hardware Supply
25-07 36th Ave.,
L.I.C., NY 11106
718-361-0556
(p. 183)

Glick & Blitz
246 West 37th St.
New York, NY 10018
212-594-2267
(p. 245)

Glimakra Looms & Yarns Inc.
19285 Detroit Road
Rocky River, OH 44116
216-333-7595
(p. 380)

Global Imports
160 Fifth Ave.
New York, NY 10010
212-741-0700
(p. 175)

Glori Bead Shoppe
172 West 4th St.
New York, NY 10014
212-924-3587
(p. 361)

Go Fly A Kite
153 East 53rd St.
New York, NY 10022
212-308-1666
1201 Lexington Ave.
New York, NY 10028
212-472-2623
(p. 360)

Godmother's League
1457 Third Ave.
New York, NY 10028
212-988-2858
(p. 352)

Goel India Co.
17 West 29th St.
New York, NY 10001
212-683-0290
(p. 120)

Gold Leaf & Metallic Powders Inc.
2 Barclay St.
New York, NY 10007
212-267-4900
(p. 252)

Gold Rose Fabrics
209 West 37th St.
New York, NY 10018
212-869-2590
(p. 140)

Gold Seal Rubber Co.
47 West 34th St. Rm. 725
New York, NY 10001
212-564-3128
(p. 60)

Goldberg's Marine
12 West 37th St.
New York, NY 10018
212-840-8280
(p. 221)

Golden Fleece The
204 West 20th St.
New York, NY 10011
212-691-6105
(p. App-27)

Golden John Theatre
252 West 45th St.
New York, NY 10036
212-764-0199 212-239-6200
(p. App-18)

Golden Typewriter & Stationery Corp.
2525 Broadway
New York, NY 10025
212-749-3100
(p. 22, 342)

Goldman Jack Embroidery
250 West 40th St.
New York, NY 10018
212-391-0816
(p. 117)

Goldsmith Mannequins
10-09 43rd Ave.
L.I.C., NY 11101
718-937-8476
(p. 179)

Goodall Elizabeth
175 Bleecker St. #4
New York, NY 10012
212-477-6437
(p. 89, 290)

Goodwill Industries of Greater NY
402 Third Ave.
New York, NY 10016
212-679-0786
(p. 352)
Goody Sam
666 Third Ave.
New York, NY 10017
212-986-8480
51 West 51st St.
New York, NY 10019
212-246-8730
(p. 309)
Gootnick Jane
204 West 88th St.
New York, NY 10024
212-724-2056
(p. 222, 303)
Gordon Books
12 East 55th St.
New York, NY 10022
212-759-7443
(p. 41)
Gordon Button Co. Inc.
142 West 38th St.
New York, NY 10018
212-921-1684
(p. 245)
GORDON NOVELTY CO. INC.
933 Broadway
New York, NY 10010
212-254-8616
(p. 217, 370)
Gordon Rodney
39 West 14th St. Rm. 501
New York, NY 10001
212-620-9018 718-522-7081
(p. 89, 222)
Gotham Galleries
80 Fourth Ave.
New York, NY 10003
212-677-3303
(p. 9, 169, 174)
Gotham Wardrobe Rental
581 Sixth Ave.
New York, NY 10011
212-691-9200
(p. 77, 79)
Gothic Cabinet Craft
168 Fifth Ave.
New York, NY 10010
212-242-1897
1655 Second Ave.
New York, NY 10028
212-288-2999
2543 Broadway
New York, NY 10025
212-749-2020
(p. 173)
Gothic Color Co.
727 Washington St.
New York, NY 10014
212-929-7493
(p. 1, 154, 253, 259)
Grace Costumes
250 West 54th St. #502
New York, NY 10019
212-586-0260
(p. 96)
Gracious Home
1220 Third Ave.
New York, NY 10021
212-535-2033
(p. 32, 182, 183, 194)
Graf Philip Wallpapers Inc.
979 Third Ave.
New York, NY 10022
212-755-1448
(p. 378)
Grainger
58-45 Grand Ave.
Maspeth, NY 11378
718-326-1598
1 Park Dr.
Melville, NY 11747
516-391-3030
(p. 232, 357)
Granada TV Rentals
416 Third Ave.
New York, NY 10016
212-679-9600
1410 Sixth Ave.
New York, NY 10019
212-308-0900
1069 Third Ave.
New York, NY 10021
212-935-4410
(p. 25)

Grand Brass Lamp Parts
221 Grand St.
New York, NY 10013
212-226-2567
(p. 207)

Grand Silk House
357 Grand St.
New York, NY 10002
212-475-0114
(p. 147)

Grandmont E. de Inc.
43 Broadway #1941
New York, NY 10004
212-943-2740
(p. 148)

Grass Roots Press
6 Murray St.
New York, NY 10007
212-732-0557
(p. 283)

GREAT AMERICAN MARKET THE
826 N. Cole Ave.
Hollywood, CA 90038
213-461-0200
(p. 37, 205, 375)

GREAT AMERICAN SALVAGE CO./
Architectural Antiques
34 Cooper Square
New York, NY 10003
212-505-0070
(p. 14)

Great Atlantic Paper Packaging Corp.
281-289 Butler St.
Brooklyn, NY 11217
718-858-3636
(p. 345)

Green Joanne
39 Charles St. #3
New York, NY 10014
212-989-1664 212-794-2400
(p. 89, 303)

GREENBERG & HAMMER INC.
24 West 57th St.
New York, NY 10019
212-246-2835
(p. 241, 243)

Greene Elliot & Co. Inc.
37 West 37th St.
New York, NY 10018
212-391-9075
(p. 362)

Greenhouse Garden Center
115 Flatbush Ave.
Brooklyn, NY 11217
718-636-0020
(p. 159)

Greentex Upholstery Supplies
236 West 26th St.
New York, NY 10001
212-206-8585
(p. 370, 374)

Greenwich House Thrift Shop
548 LaGuardia Place
New York, NY 10012
212-473-3065
(p. 352)

Greenwich Nursery
506 Ninth Ave.
New York, NY 10018
212-947-1170
(p. 159)

Greenwich Village Plumbers Supply
35 Bond St.
New York, NY 10012
212-254-9450
(p. 277)

Greif Brothers
24 West Lake Ave.
Rahway, NJ 07065
212-285-9844
(p. 30)

Grey Owl Indian Crafts
113-15 Springfield Blvd.
Queens Village, NY 11429
718-464-9300
(p. 65, 121, 362, 364)

Greyhound Package Service
Port Authority Bus Terminal
Ninth Ave. & 41st St.
New York, NY 10036
212-971-6405 (gen. info.)
(p. 324, App-1)

Grillion Corp.
191 First St.
Brooklyn, NY 11215
718-875-8545
(p. 213)

Gringer & Sons
29 First Ave.
New York, NY 10003
212-475-0600
(p. 13)

Grolan Stationers Inc.
1800 Broadway
New York, NY 10019
212-247-2676 212-247-1684
(p. 342)

Grucci Fireworks by
Association Rd.
Belleport, NY 11713
516-286-0088 800-227-0088
(p. 335)

Grumbacher M. Inc.
460 West 34th St.
New York, NY 10001
212-279-6400
(p. 22)

Guardian Rivet & Fastener
70 Air Park Dr.
Ronkonkoma, NY 11779
516-585-4400
(p. 245)

Gudebrod Inc.
262 King St., PO Box 357
Pottstown, PA 19464
215-327-4050
(p. 153)

Guerin P. E.
23 Jane St.
New York, NY 10014
212-243-5270
(p. 182, 192)

Gum Jerry
399 4th St.
Brooklyn, NY 11215
718-788-2599
(p. 89)

Gurian's
276 Fifth Ave.
New York, NY 10001
212-689-9696
(p. 135)

- H -

H & R Corporation
401 East Erie Ave.
Philadelphia, PA 19134
215-426-1708
(p. 232, 345)

H Bar C Ranchwear
101 West 21st St.
New York, NY 10011
212-924-5180
(p. 81)

H-Y Photo Service
16 East 52nd St.
New York, NY 10022
212-986-0390
(p. 268)

H. T. Sales
718 Tenth Ave.
New York, NY 10019
212-265-0747
(p. 357)

Haar & Knobel Uniform Corp.
49 Orchard St.
New York, NY 10002
212-226-1812
(p. 79, 82)

Hacker Art Books
54 West 57th St.
New York, NY 10019
212-757-1450
(p. 42)

Hadco Aluminum and Metal Corp.
104-20 Merrick Blvd.
Jamaica, NY 11433
718-291-8060
(p. 228)

Haft Theatre (Fashion Inst. of Tech.)
227 West 27th St.
New York, NY 10001
(p. App-23)

Hahn Brother
571 Riverside Dr.
New York, NY 10031
212-926-1505
(p. 235)

Hale David
6762 Elmen St.
Philadelphia, PA 19119
215-848-2448
(p. 161)

Halstan II
2056 Broadway
New York, NY 10023
212-496-8571
(p. 79)

Hamberger David
410 Hicks St.
Brooklyn, NY 11201
718-582-7101
120 East 23rd St. #509 (showroom)
New York, NY 10010
212-852-7101
(p. 55, 108, 263)

Hamburger Woolen Co. Inc.
440 Lafayette St.
New York, NY 10011
212-505-7500
(p. 149)

Hamilton Copy Center
967 Lexington Ave.
New York, NY 10021
212-535-2456
2933 Broadway
New York, NY 10025
212-666-3179
(p. 283)

Hammacher-Schlemmer
147 East 57th St.
New York, NY 10022
212-421-9000
(p. 105)

Hammond Map Store Inc.
57 West 43rd St.
New York, NY 10036
212-398-1222
(p. 220)

Hampton Sales
750 Stewart Ave.
Garden City, NY 11530
718-895-1335
(p. 13, 25)

Hansen Joseph C.
423 West 43rd St.
New York, NY 10036
212-246-8055
(p. 100)

Hansen Ken Photographic Co.
920 Broadway
New York, NY 10010
212-777-5900
(p. 270)

Happy Hoosier Trucking Co.
342 West 56th St.
New York, NY 10019
212-765-7868
(p. 235)

Hardman Paul Machinery Co.
621 South Columbus Ave.
Mt. Vernon, NY 10553
914-664-6220
(p. 189)

Hardy James G.
11 East 26th St.
New York, NY 10010
212-689-6680
(p. 210)

Harlequin Studios
203 West 46th St.
New York, NY 10036
212-819-0120
(p. App-32)

Harman Importing Corp.
16 West 37th St.
New York, NY 10018
212-947-1440
(p. 362)

Harmony Hobby
196-30 Northern Blvd.
Bayside, NY 11358
718-224-6666
(p. 16, 186)

Harold Trimming Co.
315 West 36th St.
New York, NY 10018
212-695-4098
(p. 368)

HARPER JANET STUDIO
279 Church St.
New York, NY 10013
212-966-1886
(p. 89, 222)

Harris Hardware
17 West 18th St.
New York, NY 10011
212-243-0468
(p. App-15)

Hart Joseph M. & Sons
365 Central Ave.
Bohemia, NY 11716
516-567-7722
(p. 200, 246)

Hart Multi-Copy Inc.
152 West 42nd St.
New York, NY 10036
212-730-0277
(p. 283)

Hartley House Theatre
413 West 46th St.
New York, NY 10036
212-787-1073
(p. App-23)

Harvest Printing
250 West 54th St.
New York, NY 10019
212-246-8635
(p. 239, 283)

Harvey Electronics
2 West 45th St.
New York, NY 10036
212-575-5000
(p. 25)

Harvey Joel Distributors Inc.
783 East 42nd St.
Brooklyn, NY 11210
718-859-9103
(p. 158)

Haskins Shamrock Irish Store
205 East 75th St.
New York, NY 10021
212-288-3918
(p. 124)

Hastings Tile & Il Bagno Collection
201 East 57th St.
New York, NY 10022
212-755-2710
(p. 354)

Hat/Cap Exchange
Fourth & Main Sts., PO Box 266
Betterton, MD 21610
301-348-2244
(p. 65)

HATCRAFTERS
20 North Springfield Rd.
Clifton Heights, PA 19018
215-623-2620
(p. 65)

HAUSSMANN A. INTERNATIONAL CORP.
118 West 22nd St. 9th Fl.
New York, NY 10011
212-255-5661
(p. 52, 253, 255, 257, 259)

Hayes Helen Theatre
240 West 44th St.
New York, NY 10036
212-730-9197 212-944-9450
(p. App-18)

Hays Earl Press
10707 Sherman Way
Sun Valley, CA 91352
818-765-0700
(p. 239)

Headlines
200 West 48th St.
New York, NY 10036
212-246-5762
(p. 239)

Hecht Sewing Machine & Motor Co.
304 West 38th St.
New York, NY 10018
212-563-5950
(p. 322)

Heckscher Theater
1230 Fifth Ave.
New York, NY 10025
212-534-2804
(p. App-21)

Heller A. J.
21-21 51st Ave.
L.I.C., NY 11101
718-729-5210
(p. 157, 354)

Hellinger Mark Theatre
237 West 51st St.
New York, NY 10019
212-974-9506 212-757-7064
(p. App-18)

Hendler Hyman & Sons
67 West 38th St.
New York, NY 10018
212-840-8393
(p. 368)

Henry Street Settlement
466 Grand St.
New York, NY 10002
212-598-0400
(p. App-23)

Henschel Victor
1061 Second Ave.
New York, NY 10022
212-688-1732
(p. 157)

Herbert Dancewear Co.
902 Broadway 18th Fl.
New York, NY 10010
212-677-7606
(p. 73)

Herbert Gladson
45 West 45th St.
New York, NY 10036
212-730-0602
(p. 129)
Herlin J. N. Inc.
68 Thompson St.
New York, NY 10012
212-431-8732
(p. 42)
Herman I. J.
15 West 38th St.
New York, NY 10018
212-221-8981
(p. 230)
Herman's Formal Wear
1190 Sixth Ave.
New York, NY 10036
212-245-2277
(p. 74)
Herman's World of Sporting Goods
110 Nassau St.
New York, NY 10038
212-233-0733
39 West 34th St.
New York, NY 10001
212-279-8900
135 West 42nd St.
New York, NY 10036
212-730-7400
845 Third Ave.
New York, NY 10022
212-688-4603
(p. 339)
Hersh Joseph
1000 Sixth Ave.
New York, NY 10018
212-391-6615
(p. 241)
Herzberg-Robbins Inc.
209 West 38th St.
New York, NY 10018
212-354-6030
(p. 179, 220)
HEUSTON COPY
11 Waverly Place
New York, NY 10003
212-222-2180
2372 Broadway
New York, NY 10024
212-222-2149 (continues)

HEUSTON COPY (continued)
2879 Broadway
New York, NY 10025
212-222-2149
(p. 283, 284)
Heveatex
106 Ferry St., PO Box 2573
Fall River, MA 02722
617-675-0181
(p. 53)
Hildan Crown Containers
15th & Bloomfield, PO Box 371
Hoboken, NJ 07030
212-947-0130
(p. 251)
Hill C. R. Co.
2734 West 11 Mile Rd.
Berkley, MI 48072
313-543-1555
(p. 191)
Hippen Lynn
411 West 50th St. #2-B
New York, NY 10019
212-757-2058
(p. 303)
Hippodrome Hardware
23 West 45th St.
New York, NY 10036
212-840-2791
(p. 183, 357)
Hirsh Jane
PO Box 204
Eastford, CT 06242
203-974-2145
(p. 304)
Historic Newspaper Archives
1582 Hart St.
Rahway, NJ 07065
201-381-2332 800-526-7843
(p. 239, App-1)
Hittner M. A. & Sons Inc.
39 East 4th St.
New York, NY 10003
212-477-6500
(p. 235)
Hoboken Bolt & Screw
1700 Willow Ave.
Hoboken, NJ 07030
201-792-0450
(p. 349)

Hodges L. Costume/Fashion Books
Old Church St.
London, England
01-352-1176
(p. 42)

Hoelzer Hiream Inc.
1411 Third Ave. 16th Fl.
New York, NY 10021
212-288-3211
(p. 310)

Hoffman S. Sewing Center
5507 13th Ave.
Brooklyn, NY 11219
718-851-1776
(p. 322)

Hoffritz
515 West 24th St.
New York, NY 10011
212-924-7300
Penn Station Terminal
New York, NY 10001
212-736-2443
Grand Central Terminal
New York, NY 10017
212-682-7808
331 Madison Ave.
New York, NY 10017
212-697-7344
30 Rockefeller Plaza
New York, NY 10112
212-757-3497
203 West 57th St.
New York, NY 10019
212-757-3431
(p. 320)

Holgate & Reynolds
1000 Central Ave.
Wilmette, IL 60091
312-251-2455
(p. 186)

Holland Cut Rate Stationery
325 Canal St.
New York, NY 10013
212-226-0118
(p. 342)

Hollywood Shoe Service
78 West 36th St.
New York, NY 10018
212-239-8625
(p. 324)

Holmes Medical & Ambulance
510 Flatbush Ave.
Brooklyn, NY 11225
718-287-5858
(p. 224)

Holy Land Art Co. Inc.
160 Chambers St.
New York, NY 10007
212-962-2130
(p. 74, 310)

Honatech Inc.
185 Riverdale Ave.
Yonkers, NY 10705
914-965-7677
(p. 375)

Hooker Howe Costume Company
46-52 South Main
Haverhill, MA 01830
617-373-3731
(p. 96)

Hoover Richard
240 West 98th St.
New York, NY 10025
212-662-5455
(p. 290)

Horikoshi Inc.
55 West 39th St.
New York, NY 10018
212-354-0133
(p. 147)

HORIZON SCENIC STUDIOS INC.
161 Abington Ave.
Newark, NJ 07107
201-481-6070
(p. 317, 325)

Horne Nat Theatre The
440 West 42nd St.
New York, NY 10036
212-736-7185
(p. App-24)

Horseman V Antiques
348 Third Ave.
New York, NY 10010
212-683-2041
(p. 9, 45)

Horseman VI Antiques
995 Second Ave.
New York, NY 10022
212-751-6222
(p. 9, 45)

Horvath & Assoc.
95 Charles St.
New York, NY 10014
212-741-0300
(p. App-29)

Hosmer Dorrance Corp.
PO Box 37
Campbell, CA 95009
408-379-5151
(p. 218)

Hotaling News Agency
142 West 42nd St.
New York, NY 10036
212-840-1868
(p. 216, 239)

House of Oldies
35 Carmine St.
New York, NY 10014
212-243-0500
(p. 309)

House of Pile Fabric Inc.
27 Mercer St.
New York, NY 10013
212-226-1568
(p. 140)

Housewares & Gifts
184 Orchard St.
New York, NY 10002
212-473-8011
(p. 56)

Housner Co.
240 West 35th St.
New York, NY 10001
212-244-1655
(p. 94)

Howard Notion and Trimming Co.
149 Essex St.
New York, NY 10002
212-674-4550 212-674-1321
(p. 241)

Hub Floral
155 West 23rd St.
New York, NY 10011
212-255-2447
(p. 18)

Hudson Chromium Co. Inc.
20-20 Steinway St.
L.I.C., NY 84119
718-226-7046
(p. 276)

Hudson Dental Supplies
153 Amsterdam Ave.
New York, NY 10023
212-362-5488
(p. 104)

Hudson Envelope Corp.
West 17th St.
New York, NY 10011
212-691-3333
(p. 343)

Hudson Guild Theatre
441 West 26th St.
New York, NY 10012
212-760-9816 212-760-9810
212-760-9836
(p. App-21)

HUDSON SCENIC STUDIO
125 Bruckner Blvd.
Bronx, NY 10454
212-585-6704
(p. 318)

Hudson Vagabond Puppets
Van Wyck Ave.
Blauvelt, NY 10913
914-359-1144 914-735-5732
(p. 304)

Hudson's
105 Third Ave.
New York, NY 10003
212-473-7320 212-473-0981
(p. 83, 339)

Hughes Evan G. Inc.
522 Third Ave.
New York, NY 10016
212-683-2441
(p. 9)

Hunrath William
153 East 57th St.
New York, NY 10022
212-758-0780
(p. 182)

Huntington Dental Supply
29 West 35th St.
New York, NY 10001
212-563-0818
(p. 104)

Huntley Paul Productions Inc.
10 West 19th St.
New York, NY 10011
212-243-4475
(p. 179)

HYDRO/AIR INC.
PO Box 131 Ryder Station
Brooklyn, NY 11234
718-338-5068 212-267-4524
(p. 189)

Hymo Textile Corp.
444 Broadway
New York, NY 10013
212-226-3583
(p. 140)

- I -

Ian's Boutique Inc.
5 St. Marks Place
New York, NY 10003
212-420-1857
1151 Second Ave.
New York, NY 10021
212-838-3969
(p. 70)

IATSE Local 1
1775 Broadway
New York, NY 10019
212-489-7710
(p. App-11)

IATSE Local 52
326 West 48th St.
New York, NY 10036
212-399-0980
(p. App-11)

IATSE Local 798
1790 Broadway
New York, NY 10019
212-757-9120
(p. App-11)

Ideal Cord and Trimming
317 St. Paul's Ave.
Jersey City, NJ 07306
201-656-2414
(p. 363)

Ideal Thread Co.
915 Broadway
New York, NY 10010
212-677-0118
(p. 249)

Ideal Wig Co.
37-11 35th Ave.
Astoria, NY 11101
718-361-8601
(p. 179)

Idesco Corp.
25 West 26th St.
New York, NY 10010
212-889-2530
(p. 198)

Ikelheiner-Ernst Inc.
601 West 26th
New York, NY 10001
212-675-5820
(p. 151)

Image Bound
220 East 23rd St.
New York, NY 10010
212-686-0773
(p. 284)

Images
9 East 37th St. 8th Fl.
New York, NY 10016
212-889-8510
(p. 284, App-2)

Immerman David
40 Calton Lane
New Rochelle, NY 10804
914-632-6463
(p. 311)

Imperial Feather Co.
6209 Fifth Ave.
Brooklyn, NY 11220
718-748-1700
(p. 364)

Imperial Theatre
249 West 45th St.
New York, NY 10036
212-245-9374 212-239-6200
(p. App-18)

Imperial Wear Men's Clothing
48 West 48th St.
New York, NY 10036
212-719-2590
(p. 79)

Independent Cordage Co.
38 Laight St.
New York, NY 10013
212-925-4240
(p. 372)

Independent Printing Co.
215 East 42nd St. (pickups)
New York, NY 10017
212-661-3222
141 East 25th St. (plant)
New York, NY 10010
212-689-5100
(p. 284)

Industrial Plastics
309 Canal St.
New York, NY 10013
212-226-2010
(p. 1, 53, 162, 273, 276, 344)

Industrial Supply Co. of Long Island
47-30 Vernon Blvd.
L.I.C., NY 11101
718-784-1291
(p. 357)

Inner Space Foam & Upholstery Center
34 Avenue A
New York, NY 10009
212-533-9590 212-982-5382
(p. 162, 374)

Institute of Professional Puppetry
Eugene O'Neill Theatre Center
305 Great Neck Road
Waterford, CT 06385
203-443-5378
(p. App-11)

INTAR
420 West 42nd St.
New York, NY 10036
212-695-6134
(p. App-24)

Inter-Coastal Textile Corp.
480 Broadway
New York, NY 10013
212-925-9235 212-925-9236
(p. 135)

Inter-Mares Trading Co. Inc.
1064 Rt. 109
Lindenhurst, NY 11757
516-957-3467
(p. 308)

Interart Theatre
549 West 52nd St.
New York, NY 10019
212-246-1050
(p. App-24)

International Alliance of Theatrical Stage Employees (IATSE)
1515 Broadway
New York, NY 10036
212-730-1770
(p. App-11)

International Home
440 Park Ave. South
New York, NY 10016
212-684-4414
(p. 169)

International Honeycomb Corp.
456 Sacket Point Rd.
North Haven, CT 06473
203-288-7722
(p. 263)

INTERNATIONAL PAPER COMPANY
Taylorsville Road Highway 90
Statesville, NC 28677
704-872-8974 800-438-1701
(p. 27, 108, 165, 263, 269, 328-329)

International University Booksellers
30 Irving Place
New York, NY 10003
212-254-4100
(p. 216)

IPF International
11-13 Maryland Ave.
Paterson, NJ 07503
201-345-7440
(p. 170)

Irreplaceable Artifacts
14 Second Ave. (warehouse)
New York, NY 10003
212-777-2900
1046 Third Ave.
New York, NY 10021
212-223-4411
(p. 15, 152)

Irving's Food Center Inc.
48-01 Metropolitan Ave.
Ridgewood, NY 11385
212-220-0800
(p. 109)

Irvington House Thrift Shop
1534 Second Ave.
New York, NY 10021
212-879-4555
(p. 352)

Isabella
24-24 Steinway St.
Astoria, NY 11103
718-278-7272
(p. 14, 192)

Italian Tile Import Corp.
410 Market St.
Elmwood Park, NJ 07407
201-796-0722 212-736-0383
(p. 354)

Ivy Crafts Import Co.
5410 Annapolis Rd.
Bladensburg, MD 20710
301-779-7079
(p. 255)

IZQUIERDO MARTIN STUDIO LTD.
118 West 22nd St. 9th Fl.
New York, NY 10011
212-807-9757
(p. 89, 146, 222, 290)

- J -

J & L Mfg. Co.
21 Castle Ave.
Fairfield, CT 06430
203-368-1609
(p. 230)

J & R Music World
33 Park Row
New York, NY 10038
212-349-0062 212-349-8400
23 Park Row
New York, NY 10038
212-732-8600
27 Park Row
New York, NY 10038
212-227-4777
25 Park Row
New York, NY 10038
212-513-1858
(p. 25, 309, 347)

J. J. Hat Center
1276 Broadway
New York, NY 10001
212-244-8860
(p. 66)

J. Levine Co.
58 Eldridge St.
New York, NY 10002
212-966-4460
(p. 74)

Jack & Co.
128 East 86th St.
New York, NY 10028
212-722-4455 212-722-4609
(p. 74)

Jackson William H. Co.
3 East 47th St.
New York, NY 10017
212-753-9400
(p. 152)

Jacobs Joseph Leather Corp.
10 East 33rd St. 9th Fl.
New York, NY 10001
212-683-7460 212-683-7985
(p. 199)

Jad Luggage Shop
1420 Sixth Ave.
New York, NY 10019
212-752-8251
(p. 212)

JAF Industries
248 West 35th St.
New York, NY 10001
212-868-2350 212-563-3831
(p. 94)

James & Sons Costumiers
1230 Arch
Philadelphia, PA 19107
215-922-7409
(p. 65)

Jameson Larry
390 Union St.
Brooklyn, NY 11231
718-834-1714 212-794-2400
(p. 304, 335)

Jamie Canvas Co.
496 La Guardia Pl.
New York, NY 10012
212-505-1256
(p. 22)

Janovic Plaza
159 West 72nd St.
New York, NY 10023
212-595-2500 (continues)

Janovic Plaza (continued)
213 Seventh Ave.
New York, NY 10011
212-243-2186
1150 Third Ave
New York, NY 10021
212-772-1400
(p. 32, 102, 258, 379)

Jasco Fabrics Inc.
450 Seventh Ave.
New York, NY 10123
212-563-2960
(p. 129)

Jauchem & Meeh
79 Bridge St.
Brooklyn, NY 11201
718-875-0140 212-382-3535
33555 Rose Ave.
Venice, CA 90291
213-396-2803
(p. 335)

Jay Bee Magazine Stores Inc.
134 West 26th St. Basement
New York, NY 10001
212-675-1600
(p. 216)

Jay Bee Photo Suppliers
133 Fifth Ave.
New York, NY 10003
212-420-9797
(p. 270)

Jay Lord Hatters
30 West 39th St.
New York, NY 10018
212-221-8941
(p. 66)

Jay Notions & Novelties Inc.
22 West 38th St.
New York, NY 10018
212-921-0440
(p. 368)

JBJ Discount Pet Shop
151 East Houston St.
New York, NY 10002
212-982-5310
(p. 267)

Jean's Silversmiths
16 West 45th St.
New York, NY 10036
212-575-0723
(p. 330)

Jellybean Photographics
99 Madison Ave.
New York, NY 10016
212-679-4888
(p. 272)

Jems Sound Ltd.
785 Lexington Ave.
New York, NY 10021
212-838-4716
(p. 25)

Jensen Tools Inc.
7815 S. 46th St.
Phoenix, AZ 85040
602-968-6231
(p. 115)

Jensen-Lewis Co. Inc.
89 Seventh Ave.
New York, NY 10011
212-929-4880
(p. 134, 171)

Jerryco Co. Inc.
601 Linden Place
Evanston, IL 60202
312-475-8440
(p. 233, 345)

Joel & Aronoff Inc.
425 Victoria Terrace
Ridgefield, NJ 07657
212-695-0855 201-945-8686
(p. 117)

Joel Associates - On Stage
PO Box 434
Madison, NJ 07940
201-377-6466
(p. 60)

Joffrey Ballet Foundation
130 West 56th St.
New York, NY 10019
212-265-7300
(p. App-32)

Johnke Peter
400 West 43rd St.
New York, NY 10036
212-868-7567
(p. 215, 335)

Johnny Jupiter
884 Madison Ave.
New York, NY 10021
212-744-0818
(p. 9, 360)

Johns-Cronk Inc.
39 West 19th St. 11th Fl.
New York, NY 10011
212-741-8161 212-741-8162
(p. 90, 96)

Johnson Susan
1469 Lexington Ave. #33
New York, NY 10128
212-369-9594
(p. 290)

Joia Interiors Inc.
149 East 60th St.
New York, NY 10022
212-759-1224
(p. 9)

Jonas Brothers Taxidermy
1901 S. Bannock
Denver, CO 80223
303-777-3377
(p. 347)

Jones Robert W.
329 East 92nd St. #3B
New York, NY 10128
212-410-4341
(p. 222, 290)

Joong WHA Industrial of NY Inc.
55 West 39th St.
New York, NY 10018
212-840-1570
(p. 147)

Jorgenson Warren
309 East 92nd St. #2A
New York, NY 10128
212-369-1642
(p. 290)

Joyce Theatre The
175 Eighth Ave.
New York, NY 10011
212-242-0800 212-691-9740
(p. App-27)

Juilliard School The
Broadway at 66th
New York, NY 10023
212-799-5000
(p. App-27)

Just Above Midtown Theater
503 Broadway
New York, NY 10012
212-228-3125
(p. App-24)

Just Shades
21 Spring St.
New York, NY 10012
212-966-2757
(p. 207)

- K -

K & D Export-Import
101 West 28th St.
New York, NY 10001
212-736-0556
(p. 18)

K & W Fashions
40 West 37th St. 10th Fl.
New York, NY 10018
212-947-9380
(p. 64)

Kabat Textile Corp.
215 West 40th St.
New York, NY 10018
212-398-0011
(p. 129)

Kabram & Sons Inc.
257 Bowery
New York, NY 10002
212-477-1480
(p. 196)

Kago Upholsterers Supply Co.
124-16 101st Ave.
Richmond Hill, NY 11419
718-441-0600
(p. 370, 374)

Kahaner Inc.
228 West 38th St.
New York, NY 10018
212-840-3030
(p. 362)

Kalfarans D. & Sons Inc.
475 Atlantic Ave.
Brooklyn, NY 11217
718-875-2222
(p. 157)

Kalmo Textiles Inc.
125 West 45th St.
New York, NY 10036
212-221-1033
(p. 130)

KAMAR PRODUCTS INC.
PO Box 227
Irvington-on-Hudson, NY 10533
914-591-8700
(p. 177)

Kaminstein Brothers
29 Third Ave.
New York, NY 10003
212-777-7170
(p. 184, 357)

Kamkin Victor Inc.
149 Fifth Ave.
New York, NY 10010
212-673-0776
(p. 42, 125, 239)

Kamvakis Diamond
165 West 29th St.
New York, NY 10001
212-736-1924
(p. 199)

Kaplan Howard French Country Store
35 East 10th St.
New York, NY 10003
212-674-1000
(p. 9, 32)

Karp Jules J.
372 Seventh Ave.
New York, NY 10001
212-279-1024
(p. 84)

Karp Robert Container Corp.
618 West 52nd St.
New York, NY 10019
212-586-4474
(p. 252)

Karpen Ben Brass Corp.
212 East 51st St.
New York, NY 10022
212-755-3450
(p. 45, 152)

Kasbah
85 Second Ave.
New York, NY 10003
212-982-8077
(p. 74)

Kastendieck Jan
40 Harrison St. #14B
New York, NY 10013
212-962-1042
(p. 90)

Katagiri & Co. Inc.
224 East 59th St.
New York, NY 10022
212-755-3566
(p. 123)

Katen K. & Co. Inc.
244 Fifth Ave. 4th Floor
New York, NY 10001
212-683-5257
(p. 210)

Katzenbach & Warren Inc.
979 Third Ave.
New York, NY 10022
212-759-5410
(p. 379)

Kauffman H. & Sons Saddlery
139 East 24th St.
New York, NY 10010
212-684-6060
(p. 311)

KAUFMAN SURPLUS INC, ARMY & NAVY
319 West 42nd St.
New York, NY 10036
212-757-5670
(p. 83)

Kaufman-Astoria Studios
34-31 35th St.
Astoria, NY 11106
212-692-5600
(p. App-29)

KAVENAGH CLAUDIA
220 West 98th St.
New York, NY 10025
212-666-5682
(p. 291)

Kawahara Lighting
1288 Third Ave.
New York, NY 10021
212-249-0007
1461 Third Ave.
New York, NY 10028
212-772-9777
(p. 208)

Kay Leather Goods Repair Service
10 West 32nd St.
New York, NY 10001
212-564-1769
(p. 181)

Kay's Home Decorating
Rt. 17 North
Lodi, NJ 07644
201-843-4400
(p. 188)
Kaysam Co.
27 Kentucky Ave.
Paterson, NJ 07503
201-684-5700
(p. 29)
Kee Klamps
PO Box 207
Buffalo, NY 14225
716-685-1250
(p. 349)
Keefe & Keefe Ambulance
429 East 75th St.
New York, NY 10021
212-988-8800
(p. 224)
Kelly Bob Wig Creations Inc.
151 West 46th St.
New York, NY 10036
212-819-0030
(p. 179, 218)
Kelter-Malce
361 Bleecker St.
New York, NY 10014
212-989-6760
(p. 307)
Kempler George J. Co. Inc.
160 Fifth Ave. 3rd Fl.
New York, NY 10010
212-989-1180
(p. 169)
Kenmore Leasing Corp.
352 Park Ave. South
New York, NY 10010
212-683-1888
(p. 296)
Kentshire Galleries
37 East 12th St.
New York, NY 10003
212-673-6644
(p. 9)
Kern & Son
250 West Broadway
New York, NY 10013
212-431-6273
(p. 265)
Kervar Inc.
119 West 28th St.
New York, NY 10001
212-564-2525
(p. 19, 158, App-2)
Keystone Uniform Cap
428 North 13th St.
Philadelphia, PA 19123
215-922-5493
(p. 66)
Kiesling-Hess Finishing Co.
525 West 24th St.
New York, NY 10011
212-206-7177 215-457-0906
(p. 154)
Kirk-Brummel
979 Third Ave.
New York, NY 10022
212-477-8590
(p. 379)
Kirsch Drapery Hardware
105 Eldridge St.
New York, NY 10002
212-966-6690
(p. 375)
Kitchen The
59 Wooster St.
New York, NY 10012
212-255-5793
(p. App-27)
Kite Vikki
105 Bergen St. #4
Brooklyn, NY 11201
718-852-7791
(p. 291)
Klein Joseph M. Tall Men's Stores
118 Stanton St.
New York, NY 10002
212-228-1166
(p. 80)
Kliegl Brothers
32-32 48th Ave.
L.I.C., NY 11101
718-786-7474
(p. 205)
Knechtel Janet
41 Florence St.
London, England N1
01-431-1835
(p. 90, 291, 304)

Knomark Corp.
132-20 Merrick Blvd.
Jamaica, NY 11434
718-276-3400
(p. 255)

Knoud M. J.
716 Madison Ave.
New York, NY 10021
212-838-1434
(p. 311)

Koch Auditorium
245 Lexington Ave.
New York, NY 10016
212-679-2201
(p. App-24)

Kochendorfer
413 West Broadway
New York, NY 10013
212-925-1435
(p. 35, 358)

Kolb Andrew & Son Ltd.
112 Madison Ave.
New York, NY 10016
212-684-2980
(p. 17, 279)

Kollman Bryan
30 East 20th St.
New York, NY 10003
212-505-1524
(p. 90)

Koniak William Inc.
191 Bowery
New York, NY 10002
212-475-9877
(p. 173)

Koppel Pleating Inc.
240 West 37th St. 10th Fl.
New York, NY 10018
212-736-9494
(p. 118)

Kordol Fabrics
194 Orchard St.
New York, NY 10002
212-254-8319
(p. 130)

Kovacs George Lighting Inc.
831 Madison Ave.
New York, NY 10021
212-861-9500 212-861-9848
(p. 208)

Kover King
120 West 44th St.
New York, NY 10036
212-575-7744
(p. 226)

Kraft Hardware Inc.
306 East 61st St.
New York, NY 10021
212-838-2214
(p. 182)

Kraus & Sons Inc.
245 Seventh Ave.
New York, NY 10001
212-620-0408
(p. 118, 153)

Krieger Top Hats
410 Sunrise Highway
Lynbrook, NY 11563
516-599-3188
(p. 66)

Kroll Stationers
145 East 54th St.
New York, NY 10022
212-541-5000
(p. 343)

Kroupa's Kreatures (Jim Kroupa)
429 West 24th St. #43
New York, NY 10011
212-691-0699
(p. 304)

Ktenas Pete
166 West 50th St.
New York, NY 10019
212-247-4850
(p. 324)

Kuehn Valerie
525 Monroe St.
Hoboken, NJ 07030
201-798-0537
(p. 291)

Kulyk Theatrical Footwear
72 East 7th St.
New York, NY 10003
212-674-0414
(p. 61)

Kunz Peter Co. Inc.
RD 1 Creek Rd., PO Box 223
High Falls, NY 12440
914-687-0400
(p. 335)

Kushnick Beth
400 West 25th St. #1F
New York, NY 10001
212-924-0729
(p. 291)

Kusten Robin S.
246 Vanderbilt Ave.
Brooklyn, NY 11205
718-789-1737
(p. 90, 291)

KUTTNER ANTIQUES
56 West 22nd St. 5th Fl.
New York, NY 10010
212-242-7969
(p. 9, 297)

- L -

L. I. Beef
565 West St.
New York, NY 10014
212-243-8967
(p. 5, App-2)

La Belle Epoch
211 East 60th St.
New York, NY 10022
212-319-7870
(p. 62)

La Bern Novelty Co. Inc.
1011 Sixth Ave.
New York, NY 10018
212-719-2131
(p. 246)

La Cuisiniere
968 Lexington Ave.
New York, NY 10021
212-861-4475
(p. 194)

La Delice Bakery
372 Third Ave.
New York, NY 10016
212-532-4409
(p. 28)

La Lame Inc.
250 West 39th St. 5th Fl.
New York, NY 10018
212-921-9770
(p. 150, 249, 368)

La Mama, E.T.C.
74A East 4th St.
New York, NY 10003
212-475-7710
(p. App-24)

La Mode Hat Block Co.
64 West 36th St.
New York, NY 10018
212-947-0638
(p. 230)

LaBiche T. C.
159 Carroll St. #1L
Brooklyn, NY 11231
718-802-9484
(p. 291)

Lady Madonna Maternity Boutique
793 Madison Ave.
New York, NY 10021
212-988-7173
(p. 77)

Lafayette Button Co.
237 West 37th St.
New York, NY 10018
212-354-3020
(p. 248)

Lafitte Inc.
151 West 40th St. 19th Fl.
New York, NY 10018
212-354-6780
(p. 150)

Lamb's Theatre
130 West 44th St.
New York, NY 10036
212-997-1780 212-221-1031
212-575-0300
(p. App-21, App-32)

Laminex-Craft
892 Second Ave.
New York, NY 10017
212-751-6143
(p. 198)

Lamston's
39 Broadway
New York, NY 10006
212-425-3060
346 Sixth Ave.
New York, NY 10011
212-982-2337
275 Third Ave.
New York, NY 10010
212-777-4840 (continues)

Lamston's (continued)
273 West 23rd St.
New York, NY 10011
212-929-8567
4 Park Ave.
New York, NY 10016
212-683-3150
270 Madison Ave.
New York, NY 10016
212-689-8118
1251 Sixth Ave.
New York, NY 10020
212-757-3430
477 Madison
New York, NY 10022
212-688-0232
1381 Sixth Ave.
New York, NY 10019
212-581-3656
1082 Second Ave.
New York, NY 10022
212-421-7355
773 Lexington Ave.
New York, NY 10021
212-751-0885
1279 Third Ave.
New York, NY 10021
212-861-1150
1251 Lexington Ave.
New York, NY 10028
212-535-3499
(p. 376-377)

Langenberg Hat
Box 38
Vienna, MO 65582
314-422-3377
(p. 66)

Larry & Jeff's 85th St. Bicycles
204 East 85th St.
New York, NY 10028
212-794-2201
(p. 34)

Larson Color Corp.
123 Fifth Ave.
New York, NY 10003
212-674-0610
(p. 272)

Larue
14 West 39th St. Rm. 501
New York, NY 10001
212-620-9018 212-477-3529 (p. 90)

Last Wound-up The
290 Columbus Ave.
New York, NY 10023
212-787-3388
(p. 360)

Latin Quarter Theatre
Broadway at 48th St.
New York, NY 10036
212-586-3903 212-977-7222
(p. App-18)

Laub A. Glass
1873 Second Ave.
New York, NY 10029
212-734-4270
(p. 177, 311)

Laufer L. & Co.
39 West 28th St.
New York, NY 10001
212-685-2181
(p. 148, 243)

Laura Ashley Inc.
714 Madison Ave.
New York, NY 10021
212-371-0606
(p. 130, 136, 379)

Lawrence Jack Theatre
359 West 48th St.
New York, NY 10036
212-245-9202 212-307-5452
212-307-5547 212-308-5933
(p. App-21)

LAWRENCE TEXTILES INC.
1412 Broadway
New York, NY 10018
212-730-7750
(p. 130, 134, 138, 140, 146, 147, 149, 150)

Lazar Cathy Inc.
155 East 23rd St.
New York, NY 10010
212-473-0363
(p. 90, 291)

League of American Theatres & Producers
226 West 47th St.
New York, NY 10036
212-764-1122
(p. App-11)

League of Off Broadway Producers & Theatre Owners
1540 Broadway Rm. 711
New York, NY 10036
212-869-8282
(p. App-11)

Leathercraft Process Corp.
62 West 37th St.
New York, NY 10018
212-586-3737 212-564-8980
(p. 58)

Leathersales (aka Minerva Leather)
78 Spring St.
New York, NY 10012
212-925-6270
(p. 199)

Lee Art Shop
220 West 57th St.
New York, NY 10019
212-247-0110
(p. 22, 165, 253)

Lee Fordin Sales
19 West 44th St.
New York, NY 10036
212-840-7799
(p. 151)

Lee Lee Coins
32 West 47th St.
New York, NY 10036
212-586-7782
(p. 85)

Lee Ralph
463 West St. #D405
New York, NY 10014
212-929-4777
(p. 223)

Lee Spring Co.
1462 62nd St.
Brooklyn, NY 11219
718-236-2222
(p. 341)

Lee's Mardi Gras Enterprises Inc.
565 Tenth Ave. 2nd Fl.
New York, NY 10036
212-947-7773
(p. 61, 80, 179)

Lee's Studio Gallery
211 West 57th St.
New York, NY 10019
212-265-5670
(p. 208, 279)

Leesam Plumbing
124 Seventh Ave.
New York, NY 10011
212-243-6482
(p. 192, 277)

Leith Herbert Design
250 Walnut St.
Englewood, NJ 07631
201-871-9532
(p. 90, 291, 304)

Leitner Uniforms Inc.
26 Bowery
New York, NY 10013
212-267-8740 212-267-8765
(p. 83)

Lending Trimming Co. Inc.
179 Christopher St.
New York, NY 10014
212-242-7502
(p. 363)

LeNoble Lumber Co. Inc.
500 West 52nd St.
New York, NY 10019
212-246-0150
(p. 164, 213, 265)

Leo's Antiques
2190 Broadway
New York, NY 10024
212-799-6080
(p. 10)

Let There Be Neon
38 White St.
New York, NY 10013
212-226-4883
(p. 328)

Letter Craft Inc.
1128 Madison Ave.
Patterson, NJ 07503
212-582-7799 201-684-1130
(p. 328)

Lettering Directions Inc.
29 West 38th St. 6th Fl.
New York, NY 10018
212-869-3130
(p. 284)

Levin Sam Metal Products Corp.
1002 Grand St.
Brooklyn, NY 11211
718-782-6885
(p. 191, 200, 246, 366)

Levine J. Co.
58 Eldridge St.
New York, NY 10002
212-966-4460
(p. 74)

Lew Novick Inc.
45 West 38th St.
New York, NY 10018
212-221-8960 212-354-5046
(p. 146, 366)

Lewis Adele Inc.
101 West 28th St.
New York, NY 10001
212-594-5075
(p. 30, 281)

Lewis of London New York, NY Inc.
215 East 51st St.
New York, NY 10022
212-688-3669
(p. 170)

Lexington Avenue Bazaar
1037 Lexington Ave.
New York, NY 10021
212-734-8119
(p. 167, 193)

Lexington Equipment Co.
35 East 19th St.
New York, NY 10003
212-533-7840
(p. 33)

Lexington Luggage Ltd.
793 Lexington Ave.
New York, NY 10021
212-223-0698
(p. 181)

Liberty Cap & Hat Mfg. Co. Inc.
56 Bogart
Brooklyn, NY 11206
718-456-6644
(p. 66)

Liberty Die and Button Mold Corp.
264 West 35th St. Rm. 1200
New York, NY 10001
212-564-3860
(p. 246)

Liberty of London Shops Inc.
229 East 60th St.
New York, NY 10022
212-888-1057
(p. 136)

Librett Norman Inc.
64 Main St.
New Rochelle, NY 10801
914-636-1500
(p. 372)

Life-Like Products Inc.
1600 Union Ave.
Baltimore, MD 21211
301-889-1023
(p. 186)

Light Inc.
1162 Second Ave.
New York, NY 10021
212-838-1130
(p. 208)

Lillian Costumes
226 Jericho Turnpike
Mineola, NY 11501
516-746-6060
(p. 218)

Lincoln Lite
761 Tenth Ave.
New York, NY 10019
212-581-7610
(p. 208)

Lincoln Piano Service
1459 Third Ave.
New York, NY 10028
212-734-6385
(p. 237)

Lincoln Scenic Studios
560 West 34th St.
New York, NY 10001
212-244-2700
(p. 28, 318)

Lincoln Terrace Cleaners
149 Amsterdam Ave.
New York, NY 10023
212-874-3066
(p. 114)

Link Bernard Theatrical
104 West 17th St.
New York, NY 10011
212-929-6786
(p. 318)

Lion Theatre
422 West 42nd St.
New York, NY 10036
212-736-7930
(p. App-21)

Listokin & Sons Fabrics Inc.
87 Hester St.
New York, NY 10002
212-226-6111
(p. 130, 364)

Little House, Astoria The
11-44 31st St.
Astoria, NY 11106
212-726-3231
(p. App-29)

Livingston Celeste
57 Thompson St. #2C
New York, NY 10012
212-226-4182
(p. 90)

Lobel's Prime Meats
1096 Madison Ave.
New York, NY 10028
212-737-1372
(p. 5)

Loctite Corp.
705 N. Mountain Rd.
Newington, CT 06111
203-278-1280
(p. 2)

London Gene
106 East 19th St. 9th Fl.
New York, NY 10003
212-533-4105
(p. 70)

London Majesty Inc.
1211 Sixth Ave.
New York, NY 10036
212-221-1860
(p. 80)

Longacre Hardware Supply Co.
801 Eighth Ave.
New York, NY 10019
212-246-0855
(p. 350)

Longacre Theatre
220 West 48th St.
New York, NY 10036
212-974-9462 212-239-6200
(p. App-18)

Looking Too
211 West 72nd St.
New York, NY 10023
212-874-0400
(p. 78)

Lopresto Charles
330 West 38th St.
New York, NY 10018
212-947-7281
(p. 179)

Lord & Taylor
424 Fifth Ave.
New York, NY 10018
212-391-3344
(p. 105)

Lord John Bootery
428 Third Ave.
New York, NY 10016
212-532-2579
(p. 61)

Loria J. & Sons Inc.
178 Bowery
New York, NY 10012
212-925-0300
(p. 371)

Lortel Lucille Theatre
121 Christopher St.
New York, NY 10014
212-924-8782
(p. App-21)

Louis Kipnis & Sons Inc.
252 Broome St.
New York, NY 10002
212-674-7210 212-674-0397
(p. 62)

Loutzker Harry & Sons
312 East 22nd St.
New York, NY 10010
212-473-1880
(p. 208)

Love Diane Inc.
851 Madison Ave.
New York, NY 10021
212-879-6997
(p. 19)

Love Harriet
412 West Broadway
New York, NY 10012
212-966-2280
(p. 70)

Love Saves the Day
119 Second Ave.
New York, NY 10003
212-228-3802
(p. 71)

Lovelia Enterprises Inc.
356 East 41st St.
New York, NY 10017
212-490-0930
(p. 268)

Low N. S. & Co. Inc.
220 East 23rd St. 3rd Fl.
New York, NY 10010
212-532-4120
(p. 225)

Lubin Charles Co.
131 Saw Mill River Rd.
Yonkers, NY 10701
914-968-5700
(p. 19, 158)

Lucas Daphne
28 Addison Way
London, NW, England 116AP
01-455-3110
(p. 42)

Lucas Phyllis Gallery
981 Second Ave.
New York, NY 10022
212-755-1516 212-753-1441
(p. 17, 279)

Lucchesi Eugene Inc.
859 Lexington Ave.
New York, NY 10021
212-744-6773
(p. 344)

Lucidity Inc.
775 Madison Ave.
New York, NY 10021
212-861-7000
(p. 273)

Lumberland
409 Third Ave.
New York, NY 10016
212-696-0022
(p. 213)

Luna Tech Inc.
PO Box 2495
Huntsville, AL 35804
205-533-1487
(p. 336)

Lunt/Fontanne Theatre
205 West 46th St.
New York, NY 10036
212-997-8816 212-575-9200
(p. App-18)

Lupari Displays Ltd.
225 Port Richmond Ave.
Staten Island, NY 10302
718-727-4986
(p. 109, 265)

Lyceum Theatre
149 West 45th St.
New York, NY 10036
212-997-9472 212-239-6200
(p. App-18)

Lynch Kenneth & Sons
78 Danbury Rd.
Wilton, CT 06897
203-762-8363
(p. 15, 231, 344)

Lynne J. M.
59 Gilpin Ave.
Haupaug, NY 11788
516-582-4300
(p. 250)

- M -

M & J Trimmings
1008 Sixth Ave.
New York, NY 10018
212-391-9072
(p. 246)

M & J Trimmings
1008 Sixth Ave.
New York, NY 10018
212-391-9072
(p. 362, 365, 368)

M. E. Yarn & Trimmings
177 East Houston St.
New York, NY 10002
212-260-2060
(p. 246, 366, 368, 380)

M. H. Industries
PO Box 322
New Cumberland, PA 17070
717-774-7096
(p. 186)

Mac Leather Co. Inc.
428 Broome St.
New York, NY 10013
212-964-0850 212-431-9440
(p. 199)

Macy's Department Store
151 West 34th St.
New York, NY 10001
212-971-6000
(p. 105, 268)

Mad Monk
500 Sixth Ave.
New York, NY 10011
212-242-6678
(p. 281)

Madison Avenue Bazaar
1186 Madison Ave.
New York, NY 10028
212-348-3786
(p. 167, 193)

Madison Men's Shop
26 Eleventh Ave.
New York, NY 10011
212-741-9777
(p. 83)

Magid Corp. (Magix)
4 Allwood Ave.
Central Islip, NY 11722
516-234-1660
(p. 200)

Maginsen Phillis
c/o Museum of the City of NY
Fifth Ave. & 103rd St.
New York, NY 10029
212-534-1672
(p. 311)

Magnet Wire Inc.
112-01 Northern Blvd.
Corona, NY 11368
718-651-0900
(p. 115, 341, 350)

Mail Order Plastics Inc.
302 Canal St.
New York, NY 10013
212-226-7308
(p. 328)

Majestic Embroideries & Stitching
325 West 38th St. 6th Fl.
New York, NY 10018
212-244-5450
(p. 118)

Majestic Reproductions Co. Inc.
979 Third Ave.
New York, NY 10022
212-753-1883 212-753-1850
(p. 45)

Majestic Theatre
247 West 44th St.
New York, NY 10036
212-764-1750 212-239-6200
(p. App-18)

Make-Up Center Ltd. The
150 West 55th St.
New York, NY 10019
212-977-9494
(p. 218)

Malabar Ltd.
14 McCaul St.
Toronto, Ontario, CAN M5T-1V6
416-598-2581
(p. 96)

Malcolm & Hayes Silversmiths
694 Third Ave.
New York, NY 10017
212-682-1316
(p. 198, 330, 371)

Malli Dale & Co. Inc.
35-30 38th St.
L.I.C., NY 11101
718-706-1233
(p. 336)

Manhattan Ad Hoc Housewares
842 Lexington Ave.
New York, NY 10021
212-752-5488
(p. 194)

Manhattan Center Stage
704 Broadway
New York, NY 10003
212-477-0800
(p. App-32)

Manhattan Doll Hospital & Disc Toys
176 Ninth Ave.
New York, NY 10011
212-989-5220
(p. 111)

Manhattan Ladder Co. Inc.
31-24 14th St.
L.I.C., NY 11106
718-721-3352
(p. 197)

Manhattan Laminates Ltd.
520 West 36th St.
New York, NY 10018
212-239-8588
(p. 164)

Manhattan Marine & Electric Co. Inc.
116 Chambers St.
New York, NY 10007
212-267-8756
(p. 222)

Manhattan Neon Signs Corp.
335 West 38th St.
New York, NY 10018
212-714-0430
(p. 328)

Manhattan Shade & Glass Co.
1297 Third Ave.
New York, NY 10021
212-288-5616
(p. 177)

Manhattan Supply Co.
151 Sunnyside Blvd.
Plainview, NY 11803
718-895-1474
(p. 215)

Manhattan Theatre Club
321 East 73rd St.
New York, NY 10021
212-472-0600 212-288-2500
(p. App-21, App-32)

Manhertz Bernard
44 Greene St.
New York, NY 10013
212-925-8586
(p. 215)

Maniatis Michael
48 West 22nd St.
New York, NY 10010
212-620-0398
(p. 336)

Manny's Millinery Supply Co.
63 West 38th St.
New York, NY 10018
212-840-2235
(p. 230, 365)

Marble Textures Ltd.
140 East 59th St.
New York, NY 10022
212-755-5891
(p. 221)

Marburger Surgical
34 Irving Place
New York, NY 10003
212-420-1166
(p. 225)

Marco Co.
187 Lafayette St.
New York, NY 10013
212-966-6025
(p. 278)

Margola Import Corp.
48 West 37th St.
New York, NY 10018
212-695-1115
(p. 362)

Margon Corp.
2195 Elizabeth Ave.
Rahway, NJ 07065
212-943-2797 201-382-7700
(p. 110)

Marimekko Store
7 West 56th St.
New York, NY 10019
212-581-9616
(p. 136, 211)

Marion & Co.
315 West 39th St. 16th Fl.
New York, NY 10018
212-868-9155
(p. 175)

Mark's Antiques
595 Coney Island Ave.
Brooklyn, NY 11218
718-284-4591
(p. 10)

Marquee Theatre
183 Second Ave.
New York, NY 10003
212-777-6230
(p. App-24)

Marta Marleen
25 Grove St.
New York, NY 10014
212-989-4684
(p. 90, 223, 292)

Martin Audio
423 West 55th St.
New York, NY 10019
212-541-5900
(p. 205)

Martin Deborah Alix
580 Tenth St.
Brooklyn, NY 11215
718-499-4649
(p. 292)

Martin Paint
73 Christopher St.
New York, NY 10014
212-929-8223
387 Park Ave. South
10016
212-684-8119
588 Ninth Ave.
New York, NY 10036
212-664-9875
1489 Third Ave.
New York, NY 10028
212-650-9563
308 West 125th St.
New York, NY 10027
212-864-9712
(p. 188)

Marymount Manhattan Theatre
221 East 71st St.
New York, NY 10021
212-737-9611
(p. App-27)

MASQUE SOUND & RECORDING CORP.
331 West 51st St.
New York, NY 10019
212-245-4623
(p. 332)

Master Dyeing Co.
24-47 44th St.
L.I.C., NY 11103
718-726-1001
(p. 114)

Matenciot Andre Co. Inc.
979 Third Ave.
New York, NY 10022
212-486-9064
(p. 379)

Matera Barbara
890 Broadway 5th Fl.
New York, NY 10003
212-475-5006
(p. 96)

Matera Canvas Products
5 Lispenard St.
New York, NY 10013
212-966-9783 (p. 134)

Mathieson
153 West 27th St. Rm. 803
New York, NY 10001
212-675-5081
(p. 215)

Matrix Video
727 Eleventh Ave.
New York, NY 10019
212-265-8500
(p. App-29)

Mattia Louis
980 Second Ave.
New York, NY 10022
212-753-2176
(p. 208)

Max Millinery Center
13 West 38th St.
New York, NY 10018
212-221-8896
(p. 66, 230)

Maxilla Mandidle Ltd.
78 West 82nd St.
New York, NY 10024
212-724-6173
(p. 197)

Maxine Fabrics Co.
62 West 39th St.
New York, NY 10018
212-391-2282
(p. 130, 149)

Maxwell Lumber
211 West 18th St.
New York, NY 10011
212-929-6088
25-30 Borden Ave.
L.I.C., NY 11101
212-929-6088
(p. 214, 231)

Mayer Import Co. Inc.
25 West 37th St.
New York, NY 10018
212-391-3830
(p. 362)

Mayer Joseph Co. Inc.
22 West 8th St.
New York, NY 10011
212-674-8100
(p. 22)

Mayhew
509 Park Ave.
New York, NY 10022
212-759-8120
(p. 56, 171)

May's Department Store
44 East 14th St.
New York, NY 10003
212-677-4000
(p. 105)

McClain-Moore Susan/MCL Designs Inc.
31 West 21st St. 7th Fl.
New York, NY 10010
212-206-7500
(p. 223, 292, 304)

McCreedy & Schreiber Boots & Shoes
37 West 46th St.
New York, NY 10036
212-719-1552
213 East 59th St.
10022
212-759-9241
(p. 61)

McDUFFEE KAREN
72A Fourth Ave.
Brooklyn, NY 11217
718-643-1655
(p. 91, 292)

McGraw-Hill Bookstore
1221 Sixth Ave.
New York, NY 10036
212-512-2000
(p. 42)

McGuire Francie Anne
23 Old Bergen Rd.
Jersey City, NJ 07305
201-332-6003
(p. 292)

McHugh James P.
110 West 94th St. #2A
New York, NY 10025
212-222-3509 718-643-0990
(p. 292)

McHUGH/ROLLINS ASSOCIATES INC.
79 Bridge St.
Brooklyn, NY 11201
718-643-0990
(p. 19, 46, 298, 325, 336, 373, 376, 381)

McKearnan Betsy
616 Second St.
Brooklyn, NY 11215
718-788-1942 212-902-2286
(p. 292)

McKilligan Supply
435 Main St.
Johnson City, NY 13790
607-798-9335
(p. 358)

McLamb Perry
461 West 49th St. #2A
New York, NY 10019
212-265-1378
(p. 91)

McMorran Sherry
31 Hampton Ave.
Toronto, Ontario, Canada M4K2Y5
416-465-9752
(p. 91, 304)

McNamara Maria R.
677 Oakdale Ave.
St. Paul, MN 55107
612-224-7267
(p. 91, 223, 292, 304)

McPherson Jim
413 Washington St. #1
Hoboken, NJ 07030
201-795-0697
(p. 305)

Mearl Corp.
41 East 42nd St. Rm. 708
New York, NY 10017
212-573-8500
(p. 262)

Meat & Potatoes Theatre
306 West 38th St. 4th Fl.
New York, NY 10018
212-564-3293
(p. App-24)

Mechanical Felt & Textiles Co.
1075 Lousons Rd.
Union, NJ 07083
201-688-0690
(p. 138)

Meckley's Ernie New Hat Shop
Mountain Home Road
Sinking Spring, PA 19608
215-678-0160
(p. 66)

Medicraft Shops Inc.
1313 York Ave.
New York, NY 10021
212-288-7128
(p. 83)

Mehron Inc.
45E Route 303
Valley Cottage, NY 10989
212-997-1011 914-268-4106
(p. 218)

Mel's Lexington Formal Wear
129 East 45th St.
New York, NY 10017
212-867-4420
(p. 74)

Memorial Sloan-Kettering Thrift Shop
1410 Third Ave.
New York, NY 10028
212-535-1250
(p. 352)

Memory Shop
68 Thompson St.
New York, NY 10012
212-431-8732
(p. 227)

Menash Inc.
2305 Broadway
New York, NY 10024
212-877-2060
462 Seventh Ave.
New York, NY 10018
212-695-4900
(p. 22, 343)

Mendez Ray-Props, Models, Creatures
220 West 98th St. #12-B
New York, NY 10025
212-864-4689
(p. 336)

Mercer Glassworks Inc.
55 Washington St.
Brooklyn, NY 11201
718-625-4555
(p. 197)

Mercury Neon Signs (Friedman Signs)
69 East 116th St.
New York, NY 10029
212-369-0220
(p. 328)

Merkin Concert Hall
129 West 67th St.
New York, NY 10023
212-362-8060
(p. App-32)

Mernsmart
75 Church St.
New York, NY 10007
212-227-5471
525 Madison Ave.
New York, NY 10022
212-371-9175
(p. 80)

Merrow Sales Corp.
364 Elwood Ave., PO Box 98
Hawthorne, NY 10532
914-769-4909
(p. 322)

Messmore & Damon
530 West 28th St.
New York, NY 10001
212-594-8070
(p. 318)

Metro Bicycle Store
332 East 14th St.
New York, NY 10003
212-228-4344
546 Sixth Ave.
New York, NY 10011
212-255-5100
1311 Lexington Ave.
New York, NY 10028
212-427-4450
(p. 34)

Metro Giant Photo
200 Park Ave. South Rm. 501
New York, NY 10003
212-477-1792
(p. 269)

Metro Scenery Studios Inc.
215-31 99th Ave.
Queens Village, NY 11429
718-464-6328
(p. 318)

Metro Sewing Machines
148 East 20th St.
New York, NY 10016
212-725-4770
(p. 322)

Metropolitan Impex Inc.
966 Sixth Ave.
New York, NY 10018
212-564-0398 212-244-8558
(p. 365)

Metropolitan Lumber & Hardware
175 Spring St.
New York, NY 10012
212-246-9090
617 11th Ave.
New York, NY 10036
212-246-9090
(p. 214, 277)

Metropolitan Museum of Art,
Irene Lewisohn Costume Ref. Library
Fifth Ave. and 82nd St.
New York, NY 10028
212-879-5500 x 628
(p. App-6)

Metropolitan Museum of Art,
Photograph and Slide Library
Fifth Ave. and 82nd St.
New York, NY 10028
212-879-5500 x 3261
(p. App-6)

Metropolitan Opera The
Broadway at 65th St.
New York, NY 10023
212-362-6000 212-799-3100
(p. App-27)

Metropolitan-Keller Co.
270 West 38th St.
New York, NY 10018
212-563-2591
(p. 118, 246)

Mexican Folk Art
108 West Houston
New York, NY 10012
212-673-1910
(p. 121)

Meyers A. & Sons Corp.
325 West 38th St.
New York, NY 10018
212-279-6632
(p. 242)

Meyrowitz E. B. Inc.
40 Broad St.
New York, NY 10038
212-267-3221 (continues)

Meyrowitz E. B. Inc. (continued)
520 Fifth Ave.
New York, NY 10036
212-840-3880
520 Madison Ave.
New York, NY 10022
212-753-7536
839 Madison Ave.
New York, NY 10021
212-628-9202
1171 Madison Ave.
New York, NY 10028
212-744-6565
(p. 63)

Michael-Jon Costumes Inc.
39 West 19th St.
New York, NY 10011
212-741-3440
(p. 96)

Micro-Mo Electronics Inc.
742 Second Ave. S.
St. Petersburg, FL 33701
813-822-2529
(p. 233)

Microflame Inc.
3724 Oregon Ave. South
Minneapolis, MN 55426
612-935-3777
(p. 358)

Mid-Century Textile Corp.
212 West 35th St.
New York, NY 10018
212-239-4411
(p. 130)

Midtown Antique Shop
814 Broadway
10003
212-759-5450 212-982-2150
(p. 10)

Midtown Bicycles
360 West 47th St.
New York, NY 10036
212-581-4500
(p. 34)

Midtown Neon Sign Corp.
550 West 30th St.
New York, NY 10001
212-736-3838
(p. 328)

Midtown Truckers
3rd Ave. & 32nd St.
New York, NY 10016
212-683-5838
(p. 235)

Midtown Typewriter
124 West 23rd St.
New York, NY 10011
212-255-4752
(p. 47)

Mike's Carpenter Shop
254 West 88th St.
New York, NY 10024
212-595-8884
(p. 214)

Milan Home Brewing Lab
57 Spring St.
New York, NY 10012
212-226-4780
(p. 383)

Miligi Raymond Pleating Co.
660 Newbridge Rd.
East Meadow, NY 11554
516-783-1713
(p. 118)

Millar George and Co.
161 Sixth Ave.
New York, NY 10013
212-741-6100
(p. 252)

Miller Harness Co. Inc.
123 East 24th St.
New York, NY 10010
212-673-1400
(p. 312)

Miller Tube Corp. of America
133-05 32nd Ave.
Flushing, NY 11354
718-939-3000
(p. 208)

Milliken & Co.
1045 Sixth Ave.
New York, NY 10018
212-819-4200
(p. 149)

Millions of Fabrics Inc.
584 Eighth Ave.
New York, NY 10018
212-719-2113
(p. 130)

Millner Brothers
472 Broome St.
New York, NY 10013
212-966-1810
(p. 284)

Milne Judith & James Inc.
524 East 73rd St.
New York, NY 10021
212-472-0107
(p. 307)

Milton's Store
255 West 17th St.
New York, NY 10011
212-741-3400
(p. 10)

Mine Safety Appliances Co.
600 Penn Center Blvd.
Pittsburg, PA 15235
412-273-5000
(p. App-15)

Minetta Lane Theatre
18 Minetta Lane
New York, NY 10012
212-420-8000
(p. App-21)

Minskoff Rehearsal Studios
1515 Broadway 3rd Fl.
New York, NY 10036
212-575-0725
(p. App-32)

Minskoff Theatre
200 West 45th St.
New York, NY 10036
212-840-9797 212-869-0550
(p. App-18)

Miron Lumber Co.
268 Johnson Ave.
Brooklyn, NY 11206
718-497-1111
(p. 214)

Mirrex Corp.
7 Evans Terminal
Hillside, NJ 07205
201-353-3370
(p. 177)

Mirror Theatre
at St. Peters Church
619 Lexington Ave.
New York, NY 10022
212-223-6440
(p. App-21)

Mitten Letters
85 Fifth Ave.
New York, NY 10003
212-741-1000
(p. 328)

Mixing Times Ltd.
2403 Broadway
New York, NY 10024
212-595-1505
(p. 56)

Mixon, Aris & Co.
381 Amsterdam Ave.
New York, NY 10024
212-724-6904
(p. 56)

Model Masterpieces
PO Box 1634
Englewood, CO 80150
303-789-4898
(p. 186)

Model Shipways Co. Inc.
39 W. Ft. Lee Rd., PO Box 85
Bogota, NJ 07603
201-342-7920
(p. 186)

Modell's
200 Broadway
New York, NY 10038
212-962-6200
111 East 42nd St.
New York, NY 10017
212-962-6200
243 West 42nd St.
New York, NY 10036
212-279-7143 212-962-6200
(p. 340)

Modern Artificial Flowers & Display
517 West 46th St.
New York, NY 10036
212-265-0414
(p. 19, 109)

Modern International Wire
35-11 9th St., PO Box 6072
L.I.C., NY 11106
718-728-1475
(p. 342)

Modern Miltex Corp.
280 East 134th St.
Bronx, NY 10454
800-323-5106 212-585-6000
(p. 2, 162)

Modern Woolens
129 Orchard St.
New York, NY 10002
212-473-6780
(p. 150)

Modlin Fabrics
240 West 40th St.
New York, NY 10018
212-391-4130
(p. 130)

Monsanto, Plastics and Resins Div.
800-325-4330
(p. 53)

MONTANA LEATHERWORKS LTD.
47 Greene St.
New York, NY 10013
212-431-4015
(p. 61)

Moormends Luggage Shop
1228 Madison Ave.
New York, NY 10128
212-289-3978
(p. 212)

Morse Stacey
42 Berkley Place
Brooklyn, NY 11217
718-783-4375
(p. 91)

Morsette Zoe
11-14 46th Ave. #2-I
L.I.C., NY 11101
718-784-8894
(p. 91, 292)

Morton Interior Design Bookshop
989 Third Ave.
New York, NY 10022
212-421-9025
(p. 42)

Mosse Lyndon
160 West End Ave.
New York, NY 10023
212-724-5413
(p. 292)

Mothers Sound Stage
210 East Fifth St.
New York, NY 10003
212-260-2050
Stage A: 212-260-3060
Stage B: 212-260-4510
(p. App-29)

Movers Supply House Inc.
1476 East 122nd St.
Bronx, NY 10469
212-671-1200
(p. 252)
Movie Star News
134 West 18th St.
New York, NY 10011
212-620-8160
(p. 227)
Mr. Lucky Dog Training School
27 Crescent St.
Brooklyn, NY 11208
718-827-2792
(p. 5)
Mud, Sweat & Tears
654 Tenth Ave.
New York, NY 10036
212-974-9121
(p. 281)
MULDER/GOODWIN INC.
1200 Broadway #2C
New York, NY 10001
212-689-9037
(p. 91, 97, 305)
Murphy Christopher
3605 Sedgwick Ave. #B12
Bronx, NY 10463
212-543-5902
(p. 293)
Museum Books Inc.
6 West 37th St. 4th Fl.
New York, NY 10018
212-563-2770
(p. 42)
Museum of Modern Art Library
11 West 53rd St.
New York, NY 10019
212-708-9433
(p. App-6)
Museum of the City of New York
Fifth Ave. at 103rd St.
New York, NY 10029
212-534-1672
(p. App-6)
Music Box Theatre
239 West 45th St.
New York, NY 10036
212-245-9850 212-239-6200
(p. App-18)
Music Exchange
151 West 46th St. 10th Fl.
New York, NY 10036
212-354-5858
(p. 237)
Music Inn
169 West 4th St.
New York, NY 10011
212-243-5715
(p. 237)
Music Store at Carl Fisher
62 Cooper Square
New York, NY 10003
212-677-0821
(p. 237)
Music Theatre International
49 East 52nd St.
New York, NY 10022
212-975-6897
(p. App-6)
Musical Theatre Works Inc.
133 Second Ave.
New York, NY 10003
212-677-0040
(p. App-32)
Mutual Hardware
5-45 49th Ave.
L.I.C., NY 11101
718-361-2480
(p. 55, 94, 163, 180, 259, 350, 358)
Myers Jimmy
250 West 35th St.
New York, NY 10001
212-947-8115
(p. 97)
Mythology Unlimited Inc.
370 Columbus Ave.
New York, NY 10024
212-874-0774
(p. 312, 360)

- N -

N K Industries Inc.
43 West 28th St.
New York, NY 10001
212-725-5546
(p. 158)

Nasco Life Form Models
901 Janesville Ave.
Fort Atkinson, WI 53538
414-563-2446
(p. 19, 197)

Nasti Displays Inc.
93-13 Liberty Ave.
Ozone Park, NY 11417
718-835-2271
(p. 109)

Nat Horne Studios
440 West 42nd St.
New York, NY 10036
212-736-7128
(p. App-32)

Nathan A. E. Co.
11 East 36th St.
New York, NY 10018
212-354-8160
(p. 131)

Nathan Charles S. Clearance Center
711 Third Ave.
New York, NY 10017
212-683-8990
(p. 172)

Nathan's Boning Co.
302 West 37th St. 4th Fl.
New York, NY 10018
212-244-4781
(p. 244)

Nathin Louis Inc.
47 Bayard St.
New York, NY 10013
212-962-4851
(p. 83)

National Association of Broadcasting Employees & Technicians (NABET) Local 15
1776 Broadway #1900
New York, NY 10019
212-265-3500
(p. App-11)

National Association of Display Industries (NADI)
120 East 23rd St. 3rd Fl.
New York, NY 10010
212-982-6571
(p. App-12)

National Flag & Display
43 West 21st St.
New York, NY 10011
212-675-5230
(p. 154)

National Hatters Supply Co. Inc.
670 Broadway
New York, NY 10012
212-777-0232
(p. 230)

National Leather & Shoe Findings Co.
313 Bowery
New York, NY 10003
212-982-6227
(p. 200)

National Reprographics Inc.
110 West 32nd St.
New York, NY 10001
212-736-5674
666 Third Ave.
New York, NY 10017
212-736-5674
(p. 284)

National Sponge Corp.
231 Norman Ave.
Brooklyn, NY 11222
718-383-5055
(p. 338)

National Theatre of Puppet Arts
58 Rose Ave.
Great Neck, NY 1
516-487-3684
(p. 305)

National Video Center
460 West 42nd St.
New York, NY 10036
212-279-2000
(p. App-30)

Natural Fiber Fabric Club
PO Box 1115
Mountainside, NJ 07092
mail only
(p. App-7)

Natural Furniture Warehouse
604 Pacific St.
Brooklyn, NY 11217
718-857-5959 718-857-5967
(p. 30, 382)

Naversen, Ronald
c/o Theatre Dept., Univ. of Florida
Gainesville, FL 32611
no phone
(p. 293)

Nederlander Theatre
208 West 41st St.
New York, NY 10036
212-221-9770 212-921-8000
(p. App-18)

Nedra Antiques Oak Furniture Co.
1566 Second Ave.
New York, NY 10028
212-737-8747
(p. 10)

Needle-Needle Co.
11 East 31st St.
New York, NY 10016
212-684-0226
(p. 248)

Neighborhood Cleaners Association
116 East 27th St.
New York, NY 10016
212-684-0945
(p. 114)

Neighborhood Group Theatre
420 West 42nd St.
New York, NY 10036
212-279-4200
(p. App-24)

Nelson's Folly Antiques
152 East 79th St.
New York, NY 10021
212-755-0485
(p. 222)

Neon Eddy
PO Box 753
Healdsburg, CA 95448
707-433-1400
(p. 328)

Ness Andrew
23-17 38th St. #1R
Astoria, NY 11105
718-204-0287
(p. 293)

Nevada Meat Market
2012 Broadway
New York, NY 10023
212-362-0443
(p. 5)

New Apollo Theatre
234 West 43rd St.
New York, NY 10036
212-997-9059 212-921-8558
(p. App-18)

New Dramatists
242 West 44th St.
NYC 10036
212-757-6960
(p. App-24)

New Era Hardware & Supply
832 Ninth Ave.
NYC 10019
212-265-4183
(p. 184, 342, 350, 358)

New Federal Theater
466 Grand St.
New York, NY 10002
212-598-0400
(p. App-24)

New Theatre
62 East 4th St.
New York, NY 10012
212-673-0691
(p. App-24)

New Vic Theatre
219 Second Ave.
New York, NY 10003
718-793-5563
(p. App-24)

NY Bias Binding Corp.
370 West 35th St.
New York, NY 10001
212-564-0680
(p. 243)

New York Bound Bookshop/
Urban Graphics
43 West 54th St. 4th Fl.
New York, NY 10019
212-245-8503
(p. 42)

NY Builders
99 Jane St.
New York, NY 10013
212-255-7752
(p. 354)

NY Central Supply Co.
62 Third Ave.
New York, NY 10003
212-473-7705
(p. 22, 253)

NY City Archives Municipal Dept.
31 Chambers St.
New York, NY 10007
212-566-5292
(p. App-7)

NY City Dept. of Cultural Affairs
2 Columbus Circle
New York, NY 10019
212-974-1150
(p. App-12)

NY City Dept. of General Services, Warehouse
11 Water St.
Brooklyn, NY 11201
718-643-4677
(p. 345)

NY City Dept. of Parks, Forestry Division
Henry Hudson Pkwy & 148th St.
New York, NY 10031
no phone
(p. 32)

NY City Health Deptartment/ Environmental Health
26 Federal Plaza
New York, NY 10007
212-246-5131
(p. App-14)

New York Conservatory of Dance
226 West 56th St. 3rd Fl.
New York, NY 10019
212-664-9144 212-581-1908
(p. App-32)

NY Doll Hospital
787 Lexington Ave.
New York, NY 10021
212-838-7527
(p. 112)

NY Exchange for Women's Work
660 Madison Ave.
New York, NY 10021
212-753-2330
(p. 181)

NEW YORK FLAMEPROOFING CO. INC.
635 West 23rd St.
New York, NY 10011
212-924-7200
(p. 155)

New York Florists Supply Co.
103 West 28th St.
New York, NY 10001
212-564-6086
(p. 158, App-2)

New York Frame and Picture Co.
29 John St. 2nd Fl.
New York, NY 10038
212-233-3205
(p. 165)

New York Gardener Ltd.
501 West 23rd St.
New York, NY 10011
212-929-2477
(p. 159)

New York Marble Works Inc.
1399 Park Ave.
New York, NY 10029
212-534-2242
(p. 221)

New York Nautical
140 West Broadway
New York, NY 10013
212-962-4522
(p. 220)

New York Prop Rental
Pier 62-North River
New York, NY 10011
212-924-5111
(p. 297)

New York Public Library & Museum of the Performing Arts at Lincoln Center
111 Amsterdam Ave.
New York, NY 10023
212-870-1630
(p. App-7)

New York Public Library, Donnell Library Center, Art Library
20 West 53rd St.
New York, NY 10019
212-621-0618
(p. App-7)

New York Public Library, Picture Collection, Mid-Manhattan Library 3rd Fl.
8 East 40th St.
New York, NY 10016
212-340-0877
(p. App-7)

New York Public Library, Schomburg Center for Research in Black Culture
515 Lenox Ave.
New York, NY 10025
212-862-4000
(p. App-7)

NY Replacement Parts
1464 Lexington Ave.
New York, NY 10128
212-534-0818
(p. 277)

New York Shakespeare Festival/ Public Theatre
425 Lafayette St.
New York, NY 10003
212-598-7150 212-598-7100
Anspacher Theatre: 212-473-9499
Delacorte Theatre: 212-535-5630
Main Green Room:
212-475-9156 212-475-9553
Newman Theatre: 212-674-9695
(p. 297, App-21)

New York State Theatre
62nd & Columbus Ave.
New York, NY 10023
212-877-470 212-870-5570
(p. App-18, App-27)

New York Times Pictures The
229 West 43rd St.
New York, NY 10036
212-556-1243
(p. App-7)

Newark Electronics
25 Rte. 22 E.
Springfield, NJ 07081
212-349-7087 201-376-9500
(p. 116)

Newel Art Gallery
425 East 53rd St.
New York, NY 10022
212-758-1970
(p. 10, 15, 297)

Newhouse Mitzi E.
150 West 65th St.
New York, NY 10023
212-787-6868
(p. App-18)

NICCOLINI ANTIQUES-PROP RENTALS
114 East 25th St.
New York, NY 10010
212-254-2900
(p. 10, 59, 297)

Niedermaier
435 Hudson
New York, NY 10014
212-675-1106
(p. 109)

Night Owl Musical Supply
251 West 30th St.
New York, NY 10001
212-563-6410
(p. 237)

NIHDA FREDERICK STUDIO
279 Church St.
New York, NY 10013
212-966-1886
(p. 91, 223, 293)

95th Street Studio
206 East 95th St.
New York, NY 10028
212-831-1946
(p. App-30)

NIOSH / Department H.E.W., Region 2
26 Federal Plaza
New York, NY 10007
212-264-2485
(p. App-14)

No Smoking Playhouse
354 West 45th St.
New York, NY 10036
212-582-7862
(p. App-24)

Noble Plants
106 West 28th St.
New York, NY 10001
212-206-1164
(p. 160)

Nolan Scenery Studio
1163 Atlantic Ave.
Brooklyn, NY 11216
718-783-6910
(p. 318)

North River Studios
Pier 62 North River
New York, NY 10011
212-807-0735
(p. App-30)

Northeastern Scale Models Inc.
Box 425, Methuen
MA 01844
617-688-6019
(p. 186)

Northern Hydraulics Inc.
801 East Cliff Rd.
Burnsville, MN 55337
612-894-8310
(p. 189, 233)

Northern Leather
166 Flatbush Ave.
Brooklyn, NY 11217
718-875-7720 718-783-7755
(p. 200)

Northsouth Trading Inc.
28 Elizabeth St.
New York, NY 10013
212-964-4459
(p. 123)

Northwest Fibre-Glass Inc.
3055 Columbia Ave. NE
Minneapolis, MN 55418
612-781-3494
(p. 53)

Norton Drapery Services
151 West 19th St.
New York, NY 10011
212-575-8266
(p. 114)

Norton Safety Products
2000 Plainfield Pike
Cranston, RI 02920
401-943-4400
(p. App-15)

Nostalgia Alley
547 West 27th St. 3rd Fl.
New York, NY 10001
212-695-6578
(p. 10, 297)

Nostalgia Decorating Co.
PO Box 1312
Kingston, PA 18704
717-288-1795
(p. 226, 279)

Nourafchan V. A. (Tori)
514 East 5th St. #8
New York, NY 10009
212-673-0642
(p. 293)

NOVEL PINBALL & JUKEBOX CO.
595 Tenth Ave.
New York, NY 10036
212-736-3868
(p. 4)

NOVELLINO NINO/COSTUME ARMOUR INC.
PO Box 325, Shore Road
Cornwall-on-Hudson, NY 12520
914-534-9120 212-585-1199
(p. 293)

NOVELTY SCENIC
40 Sea Cliff Ave.
Glen Cove, NY 11542
516-671-5245 718-895-8668
(p. 350)

Novik Lew Inc.
45 West 38th St.
New York, NY 10018
212-221-8960 212-354-5046
(p. 146, 366)

Nye Ben Makeup Inc.
11571 Santa Monica Blvd.
W. Los Angeles, CA 90025
213-477-0443
(p. 219)

- O -

O. K. Uniform Co. Inc.
512 Broadway
New York, NY 10012
212-966-1984 212-966-4733
(p. 83, App-15)

Oaksmith Antiques
1321 Second Ave
New York, NY 10021
212-535-1451
(p. 10)

Oasis/ Stage Werks
263 Rio Grande
Salt Lake City, UT 84101
801-363-0364
(p. 103)

Obsolete Fleet
45 Christopher St.
New York, NY 10014
212-255-6068
(p. 27)

Ocean Caskets
17 Thames St.
Brooklyn, NY 11206
718-497-0770
(p. 48)

Oestreicher's Prints
43 West 46th St.
New York, NY 10036
212-719-1212
(p. 279)

Off-Broadway Boutique
139 West 72nd St.
New York, NY 10023
212-724-6713
(p. 76)

OFFRAY C. M. & SONS INC.
Route 24, PO Box 601
Chester, NJ 07930
201-879-4700
(p. 368)

Ohio Theatre
64 Wooster St.
New York, NY 10012
212-279-4200 212-868-3592
(p. App-24)

Ohio Traveling Bag
811 Prospect Ave.
Cleveland, OH 44115
216-621-5963
(p. 200)

Ohlinger's J. Movie Material Store
120 West 3rd St.
New York, NY 10012
212-674-8474
(p. 227)

Ohrbach's
5 West 34th St.
New York, NY 10001
212-695-4000
(p. 105)

Okin Irvin K. (Abby)
244 West 102nd St. #1B
New York, NY 10025
212-663-0483
(p. 293)

Old Brassware
797 Coney Island Ave.
Brooklyn, NY 11218
718-469-5644 718-646-6847
(p. 45)

Old-Fashioned Milk Paint Co.
PO Box 222
Groton, MA 01450
617-448-6336
(p. 262)

Olden Camera
1265 Broadway
New York, NY 10001
212-725-1234
(p. 270)

Oldies, Goldies & Moldies Ltd.
1609 Second Ave.
New York, NY 10028
212-737-3935
(p. 11)

Oliphant Studio
38 Cooper Sq.
New York, NY 10003
212-741-1233
(p. 28)

Olmstead Carl Upholstery
122 West 26th St.
New York, NY 10001
212-206-1488
(p. 373)

Olympic Unpainted Furniture
141 Fifth Ave.
New York, NY 10010
212-982-8504 212-533-0843
(p. 173)

Omicron Production Service/
Don Marks
333 West 52nd St. Suite 410
New York, NY 10019
212-245-2570
(p. 227)

Omicron Production Service/
George Fenmore
254 West 54th St.
New York, NY 10019
212-977-4140
(p. 227)

One Hour Framing Shop
1169 Sixth Ave.
New York, NY 10036
212-944-9429
(p. 165)

110 West Antiques
110 West Houston St.
New York, NY 10012
212-505-0508 (p. 71)

O'Neill Eugene Theatre
230 West 49th St.
New York, NY 10019
212-245-9442 212-246-0220
(p. App-18)

O'Neill's Ellen
242 East 77th St.
New York, NY 10021
212-879-7330
(p. 71)

Orberg John
32 Leroy St.
New York, NY 10014
212-741-2392
(p. 305)

Orienhouse Enterprises Inc.
424-426 Broadway
New York, NY 10013
212-431-8060
(p. 123, 211)

Oriental Dress Co. The
38 Mott St.
New York, NY 10013
212-349-0818
(p. 123)

Oriental Rattan Co.
1154 Flushing Ave.
Brooklyn, NY 11237
718-386-8200
(p. 308)

Orpheum Theatre
126 Second Ave.
New York, NY 10003
212-477-2477 212-460-0990
(p. App-21)

Osborne C. S. Tools
125 Jersey St.
Harrison, NJ 07029
201-483-3232
(p. 191, 201)

OSHA / U.S. Department of Labor
90 Church St. Rm. 1407
New York, NY 10007
212-264-9840
(App-14)

Otto Gerdau Co. The
82 Wall St.
New York, NY 10005
212-709-9647
(p. 308)

Ottomanelli Bros.
1549 York Ave.
New York, NY 10028
212-772-7900
(p. 6)

Ottomanelli's Meat Market
281 Bleecker St.
New York, NY 10014
212-675-4217
(p. 6)

Our Studios
147 West 24th St.
New York, NY 10011
212-807-8464
(p. App-32)

Our Studios Theatre
147 West 24th St.
New York, NY 10011
212-695-5342
(p. App-24)

Outwater Plastics
PO Drawer 403
Wood Ridge, NJ 07075
201-340-1040 800-631-8375
(p. 273)

Ouzts Randall
1390 Second Ave. #5B
New York, NY 10021
212-288-1637
(p. 91)

Overland Stage Co. %1-3
511 West 54th St.
New York, NY 10019
212-581-4460 212-581-4469
212-736-1776
(p. App-30)

Overseas Moving Specialists Inc.
112 North 12th St.
Brooklyn, NY 11211
718-963-4200 718-388-1000
(p. 235)

Oxford Fibre Cases
762 Wythe Ave.
Brooklyn, NY 11211
718-858-0009 212-226-6561
(p. 151)

- P -

P & G New and Used Plumbing Supply
155 Harrison Ave.
Brooklyn, NY 11206
718-384-6310
(p. 193, 278)

P & S Trading Co.
159 Varick St.
New York, NY 10013
212-924-7040
(p. 158)

P C Computer Rental
1 Penn Plaza #4532
New York, NY 10001
212-532-2555
(p. 85)

P. K. Supply Co. Inc.
2291 Nostrand Ave.
Brooklyn, NY 11210
718-377-6444
(p. 23, 330)

PA-KO Cutlery & Scales
104 South St.
New York, NY 10038
212-962-8641
(p. 153, App-2)

PACKAGE PUBLICITY SERVICE
27 West 24th St. #402
New York, NY 10010
212-255-2872
(p. 227)

Padded Wagon The
120 West 107th St.
New York, NY 10025
212-222-4880
(p. 235)

Padob Fabrics Inc.
251 West 39th St. 3rd Fl.
New York, NY 10018
212-221-7808
(p. 150)

Pageant Book & Print Shop
109 East 9th St.
New York, NY 10003
212-674-5296
(p. 42, 280)

Pahl William Equipment Corp.
232 West 58th St.
New York, NY 10019
212-265-6083
(p. 33)

Palace Theatre
1564 Broadway
New York, NY 10036
212-245-9751 212-757-2626
(p. App-18)

Palo Imports
184 Greenwood Ave.
Bethel, CT 06801
203-792-2411
(p. 112)

Pan American Textiles Inc.
37-12 74th St.
Jackson Hts., NY 11372
718-478-4636
(p. 120)

Panache Antique Clothing
525 Hudson St.
New York, NY 10014
212-242-5115
(p. 71)

Pandemonium Puppet Co.
58 Spring St.
Williamantic, CT 06226
203-423-5882
(p. 305)

Paper East
866 Lexington Ave.
New York, NY 10021
212-249-0129
(p. 266)

Paper House
18 Greenwich Ave.
New York, NY 10011
212-741-1569
300 Columbus Ave.
New York, NY 10023
212-799-2076
1370 Third Ave.
New York, NY 10021
212-879-2937
2235 Broadway
New York, NY 10024
212-595-5656
(p. 266)

Paperback Booksmith
393 Fifth Ave.
New York, NY 10016
212-889-7707
(p. 43)

Paradise Bootery
1586 Broadway
New York, NY 10036
212-974-9855
(p. 61)

Paradise Design
800 Sixth Ave.
New York, NY 10001
212-684-3397
(p. 160)

Paradise Palms Inc.
810 Sixth Ave.
New York, NY 10001
212-689-4968
(p. 160)

Paragon Book Gallery Ltd.
2130 Broadway
New York, NY 10023
212-496-2378
(p. 43, 123)

Paragon Restaurant World
250 Bowery
New York, NY 10012
212-226-0954
(p. 196)

Paragon Sporting Goods Co.
867 Broadway
New York, NY 10003
212-255-8036
(p. 340)

Paramount Beauty
251 West 50th St.
New York, NY 10019
212-757-6996
(p. 33)

Paramount Buttonhole & Eyelet Co.
580 Eighth Ave. 5th Fl.
New York, NY 10018
212-279-3908
(p. 118)

Paramount Thread
151 West 26th St. 4th Fl.
New York, NY 10001
212-255-0470
(p. 249)

Paramount Wire Inc.
1523 63rd St.
Brooklyn, NY 11219
718-256-2112
(p. 159, 342)

Paris Lighting Fixture Co. Inc.
136 Bowery
New York, NY 10013
212-226-7420
(p. 208)

Park East Sewing Center
1358 Third Ave.
New York, NY 10021
212-737-1220 212-737-9189
(p. 322)

Park Slope Typing & Copy Center
90 Seventh Ave.
Brooklyn, NY 11217
718-783-0268
(p. 284)

Paron Fabrics
60 West 57th St.
New York, NY 10019
212-247-6451
37 West 57th St.
New York, NY 10019
212-980-0052
(p. 131)

Parsons Art Supply
70 Fifth Ave.
New York, NY 10011
212-675-6406
(p. 23)

PARSONS-MEARES LTD.
142 West 14th St. 5th Fl.
New York, NY 10011
212-242-3378
(p. 97)

Party Bazaar
390 Fifth Ave.
New York, NY 10018
212-695-6820
(p. 265, 266)

Parviz Nemati
790 Madison Ave. 2nd Fl.
New York, NY 10021
212-861-6700
(p. 58)

PASTERNACK H. G. INC.
151 West 19th St.
New York, NY 10011
212-460-5233
(p. 2, 346)

Patelson Joseph Music House
160 West 56th St.
New York, NY 10019
212-582-5840
(p. 237)

Paterson Silks
36 East 14th St.
New York, NY 10003
212-929-7861
(p. 102, 113, 131, 136)

Patriarche & Bell Inc.
94 Parkhurst
Newark, NJ 07114
201-824-8297 212-242-4400
(p. 244)

Patron Transmission Co. Inc.
129 Grand St.
New York, NY 10013
212-226-1140
(p. 233)

Patterson J. Scenic Studios
4312 Liberty Ave.
North Bergen, NJ 07047
201-866-0316 212-864-5499
(p. 318)

Paul's Veil & Net Corp.
66 West 38th St.
New York, NY 10018
212-391-3822 212-221-9083
(p. 64, 365, 366)

Paver Dennis
41 Union Sq. West #206
New York, NY 10003
212-924-9411
(p. 92, 293)

Payne Robin Lu
159 Milton St. #2W
Brooklyn, NY 11222
718-383-5329
(p. 293)

Pearl Art & Craft Supply Inc.
Rt.1 & Gills Ln.
Woodbridge, NJ 07095
201-634-9400
(p. 23)

Pearl Paint Co. Inc.
308 Canal St.
New York, NY 10013
212-431-7932
2411 Hempstead Turnpike
East Meadow, NY 11554
516-731-3700
(p. 23, 166, 187, 253, 257, 258, 261)

Pearl River Chinese Products Emporium
13-15 Elizabeth St.
New York, NY 10013
212-966-1010
(p. 123)

Pearl Showroom
42 Lispenard
New York, NY 10013
212-431-7932
(p. 23, 172)

Peerless Rattan and Reed Mfg. Co.
222 Lake Ave., PO Box 636
Yonkers, NY 10701
914-968-4046
(p. 308)

Peerless Umbrella
6 West 32nd St.
New York, NY 10001
212-239-0021
(p. 67)

Pellon Corp.
119 West 40th St.
New York, NY 10018
212-391-6300
(p. 141)

Penny Copy Center
2643 Broadway
New York, NY 10025
212-222-6047
(p. 285)

Pentimenti
126 Prince St.
New York, NY 10012
212-226-4354
(p. 71)

People's Flowers Corp.
786 Sixth Ave.
New York, NY 10001
212-686-6291
(p. 19, 159, 160)

Peoples J. J. Ethan Allen Galleries
71 Fifth Ave.
New York, NY 10003
212-989-1700
(p. 169)

Perfection Blue Print Co. Inc.
6 West 48th St
New York, NY 10020
212-541-9060
(p. 285)

Performing Garage The
33 Wooster
New York, NY 10013
212-966-3651 212-966-9796
(p. App-24)

Peridance Center
33 East 18th St. 5th Fl.
New York, NY 10003
212-505-0886
(p. App-32)

Perkins H. H. Inc.
10 South Bradley Rd.
Woodbridge, CT 06525
203-389-9501
(p. 308)

Perma Plant Inc.
123 Leverington Ave.
Philadelphia, PA 19127
215-482-2100
(p. 19)

Perosi Ceramic Studio
166 Morningstar Rd.
Staten Island, NY 10303
718-981-9686
(p. 281)

Perry Street Theatre
31 Perry St.
New York, NY 10014
212-255-9186 212-255-7190
(p. App-25)

Personal Computer Service
322 Eighth Ave.
New York, NY 10001
212-206-1480
(p. 85)

Personality Posters
653 Eleventh Ave.
New York, NY 10036
212-977-3210
(p. 280)

Petcar Textile Dyers
34 South 1st
Brooklyn, NY 11211
718-782-0424
(p. 114)

Petland Discounts
132 Nassau St.
New York, NY 10038
212-964-1821
7 East 14th St.
New York, NY 10003
212-675-4102
304 East 86th St.
New York, NY 10028
212-472-1655
(p. 267, 372)

Petrella Gabriel
196 Fourth Ave.
Brooklyn, NY 11217
718-852-1656
(p. 49)

Pfeifer Frederich
53 Warren St.
New York, NY 10007
212-964-5230
(p. 350)

Phoenix Poultry Market
159 Grand St.
New York, NY 10013
212-226-5455
(p. 6)

Phoenix Studios Inc.
537 West 59th St.
New York, NY 10019
212-581-7721 212-581-7670
(p. App-30)

Phone Boutique
828 Lexington Ave.
New York, NY 10021
212-319-9650
(p. 347)

Phone City Inc.
1152 Sixth Ave.
New York, NY 10036
212-869-9898
126 East 57th St.
New York, NY 10022
212-644-6300
(p. 348)

Phoneco
Route 2
Galesville, WI 54630
608-582-4124
(p. 348)

Photo Exchange
1 West 20th St.
New York, NY 10011
212-675-6582
(p. 270)

Phylmor Furrier Supply Inc.
149 West 28th St.
New York, NY 10001
212-563-5410
(p. 134, 199)

Pic Designs
PO Box 1004, Benson Rd.
Middlebury, CT 06762
203-758-8272
(p. 233)

Picheny & Konner
270 West 39th St.
New York, NY 10018
212-944-8877
(p. 131)

Pierre Deux Fabrics
381 Bleecker St.
New York, NY 10014
212-675-4054
(p. 131)

Pierre Deux
369 Bleecker St.
New York, NY 10014
212-243-7740
(p. 11)

Piller Lawrence
1930 47th St.
Brooklyn, NY 11204
718-633-3555
(p. 252)

Pincover Industrial Supply Co. Inc.
4730 Broadway
New York, NY 10040
212-926-1019
(p. 95)

Pineider Inc.
725 Fifth Ave.
New York, NY 10022
212-688-5554 212-688-5613
(p. 343)

Pink Pussycat Boutique
161 West 4th St.
New York, NY 10012
212-243-0077
(p. 119, App-2)

Pintchik Paints
478 Bergen St.
Brooklyn, NY 11217
718-783-3333
278 Third Ave.
New York, NY 10010
212-982-6600
1555 Third Ave.
New York, NY 10028
212-289-6300
8419 5th Ave.
Brooklyn, NY 11209
718-238-5333
4209 Avenue U
Brooklyn, NY 11234
718-951-9300
31-48 Steinway St.
Astoria, NY 11103
718-721-5321
(p. 102, 188, 258)

Pioneer Piano Corp.
934 Eighth Ave.
New York, NY 10019
212-586-3718
(p. 237)

Piper Histick
PO Box 683
Clinton, CT 06413
no phone
(p. 383)

Pipeworks
400 Madison Ave.
New York, NY 10019
212-755-1118
(p. 331)

Piston Hyman E. Antiques
1050 Second Ave.
New York, NY 10022
212-753-8322
(p. 45, 268)

Place Off Second Avenue For Antiques
993 Second Ave.
New York, NY 10022
212-308-4066
(p. 11)

Planned Parenthood Thrift Shop
324 East 59th St.
New York, NY 10022
212-371-1580
(p. 352)
Plastic Fabricators
1804 Plaza Ave.
New Hyde Park, NY 11040
718-468-2233
(p. 274)
Plastic Works
2107 Broadway
New York, NY 10023
212-362-1000
1407 Third Ave.
New York, NY 10021
212-535-6486
(p. 274)
Platters & Props Inc.
160 First Ave.
New York, NY 10009
212-473-4299
(p. 11)
Players Theatre
115 MacDougal St.
New York, NY 10011
212-674-9281 212-254-5076
212-254-8138 212-598-4337
(p. App-21)
Playhouse 91
316 East 91st St.
New York, NY 10128
212-831-2000 212-831-2001
(p. App-22)
Playwrights Horizons
416 West 42nd St.
New York, NY 10036
212-279-4200 212-564-1235
(p. App-22)
Pleasure Chest
156 Seventh Ave. South
New York, NY 10014
212-242-2158
302 East 52nd St.
New York, NY 10022
212-371-4465
(p. 119)
Plested Enrique
126 Riverside Dr. #6A
New York, NY 10024
212-799-2950 (p. 92, 294)
Plitt, Segall & Sons Inc.
137 West 37th St.
New York, NY 10018
212-921-4040
(p. 131)
Plume Trading Co.
PO Box 585, Rt. 208
Monroe, NY 10950
914-782-8594
(p. 66, 121, 362, 365)
Plumer Derald G. Ltd.
153 West 27th St. #502
New York, NY 10001
212-243-2089
(p. 294)
Plymouth Theatre
236 West 45th St.
New York, NY 10036
212-391-8878 212-239-6200
(p. App-19)
Pocker J. & Son Inc.
824 Lexington Ave.
New York, NY 10021
212-838-5488
(p. 17, 166, 280)
Poison Control Center of New York
455 First Ave.
New York, NY 10016
212-764-7667 212-340-4494
(p. App-14)
Poko Puppets Inc.- Larry Engler
12 Everit St.
Brooklyn, NY 11201
718-522-0225 212-575-0488
(p. 305)
Poli Fabrics
132 West 57th St.
New York, NY 10019
212-245-7589
(p. 131)
Polk's Model Craft Hobbies Inc.
314 Fifth Ave.
New York, NY 10001
212-279-9034
(p. 187, 233)
Pollyanna Corp.
535 Eighth Ave. 19th Fl.
New York, NY 10018
212-563-5340
(p. 246)

Polycoat Systems Inc.
5 Depot St.
Hudson Falls, NY 12839
518-747-0654
(p. 53)
Polyform Products
9420 W. Byron St.
Schiller Park, IL 60176
312-678-4836
(p. 187)
Polytek Development Corp.
PO Box 384
Lebanon, NJ 08833
201-236-2990
(p. 53)
Pomponio S.
6 Varick St.
New York, NY 10013
212-925-9453
(p. 215, 274)
Pony Circus Antiques Ltd.
381 Second Ave.
New York, NY 10010
212-679-9637
(p. 11)
Ponzo Rosemary
14-21 30th Dr.
Astoria, NY 11102
718-932-1161
(p. 92)
POOK DIEMONT & OHL INC.
135 Fifth Ave.
New York, NY 10010
212-982-7583
(p. 161, 350)
Portuguese Fur Felt Hat Co.
84 Pryor St. SW
Atlanta, GA 30303
404-688-6719
PO Box 517
Adamstown, PA 19501
215-484-4361
(p. 230)
Poseidon Bakery
629 Ninth Ave.
New York, NY 10036
212-757-6173
(p. 29, 121)
Poster America/Yesterday
138 West 18th St.
New York, NY 10011
212-206-0499
(p. 280)
Poster Mat
37 West 8th St.
New York, NY 10011
212-228-4027
(p. 280)
Posters Originals Ltd. Art Posters
924 Madison Ave.
New York, NY 10021
212-861-0422
(p. 280)
Pottery Barn
231 Tenth Ave.
New York, NY 10011
31212-741-9120
49 Greenwich Ave.
New York, NY 10014
212-741-9140
250 West 57th St.
New York, NY 10107
212-741-9145
117 East 59th St.
New York, NY 10022
212-741-9132
2109 Broadway
New York, NY 10023
212-741-9123
1451 Second Ave.
New York, NY 10021
212-741-9142
1292 Lexington Ave.
New York, NY 10128
212-741-9134
(p. 31, 57)
Pottery World
807 Sixth Ave.
New York, NY 10001
212-242-2903
(p. 31, 281)
Practicals Catalog
PO Box 3118
San Luis Obispo, CA 93403
805-544-3650
(p. 209)

Precision Projection Systems Inc.
11563 Radley St.
Artesia, CA 90701
213-865-2534
(p. 205)

Preferred Typographics
2209 Coney Island Ave.
Brooklyn, NY 11223
718-339-3800
(p. 285)

Premier Doll Accessories Inc.
168 7th St.
Brooklyn, NY 11215
718-788-8051
(p. 111)

Premier Plastics/Premier Plexiglass
220 East 60th St.
New York, NY 10022
212-288-9300
(p. 276)

Preston Edward
26 Cornelia St.
New York, NY 10014
212-989-7945
(p. 71)

Pretty Decorating
29 Avenue A
New York, NY 10009
212-674-1310
(p. 373)

Price Louis Paper Co. Inc.
350 West 31st St.
New York, NY 10001
212-564-3810
(p. 95)

Primary Stages Company Inc.
584-6 Ninth Ave.
New York, NY 10036
212-333-7471
(p. App-32)

Primrose Trimming Co.
333 West 39th St.
New York, NY 10018
212-736-8214
(p. 242)

Prince Lacquer & Chemical Corp.
413 Kent Ave.
Brooklyn, NY 11211
718-387-8313
(p. 262)

Prince Lumber Co. Inc.
406 West 15th St.
New York, NY 10011
212-777-1150
(p. 214)

Princely Co. Inc.
1201 Broadway
New York, NY 10001
212-685-5295
(p. 16)

Princeton Antique Bookservice
2915-17-31 Atlantic Ave.
Atlantic City, NJ 08401
609-344-1943
(p. App-8)

Pro Am Music Resources Inc.
63 Prospect St.
White Plains, NY 10606
914-761-6667
(p. App-8)

PRO CHEMICAL & DYE INC.
PO Box 14
Somerset, MA 02726
617-676-3838
(p. 255, App-2)

Pro Piano
85 Jane St.
New York, NY 10014
212-206-8794
(p. 237)

Pro Print Copy Center
134 Fifth Ave.
New York, NY 10011
212-807-1900
236 Park Ave. South
New York, NY 10003
212-677-7691
51 East 19th St.
New York, NY 10003
212-473-3200
41 East 28th St.
New York, NY 10016
212-685-4990
51 West 43rd St.
New York, NY 10036
212-302-0446
(p. 285)

PRO-MIX INC.
50 Webster Ave.
New Rochelle, NY 10801
914-633-3233 (p. 332)

Pro-Tape and Supply Inc.
832 Eighth Ave.
New York, NY 10019
212-586-8873
(p. 346)

Production Arts Lighting Inc.
636 Eleventh Ave.
New York, NY 10036
212-489-0312
(p. 163, 206)

Progressive Fibre Products Inc.
826 Broadway
New York, NY 10003
212-777-0487
(p. 151)

Promenade Theatre
2162 Broadway
New York, NY 10024
212-580-1313 212-580-3777
(p. App-22)

Prop House Inc. The
653 Eleventh Ave. 4th Fl.
New York, NY 10036
212-713-0760
(p. 297)

Prophecies Antiques
483 Atlantic Ave.
Brooklyn, NY 11217
718-855-4285
(p. 11)

Props for Today
15 West 20th St. 7/8th Fl.
New York, NY 10011
212-206-0330
(p. 297)

Props, Displays & Interiors Inc.
132 West 18th St.
New York, NY 10011
212-620-3840
(p. 297)

Provincetown Playhouse
133 MacDougal St.
New York, NY 10011
212-777-2571 212-777-1827
(p. App-22)

Provost Displays
618 West 28th St.
New York, NY 10001
212-279-5770
(p. 109, 376)

Prym Newey Canada Inc.
1854 Beaulac
St. Laurent, Quebec, H4R 2E7
514-336-5874
(p. 248)

Prym William Inc.
Main St.
Dayville, CT 06241
203-774-9671 800-243-1832
(p. 242)

Pucci Manikins
578 Broadway
New York, NY 10012
212-219-0142
(p. 179, 220)

Puerto Rican Traveling Theatre
276 West 43rd St.
New York, NY 10036
212-354-1293
(p. App-25)

Puppet Loft The
180 Duane St.
New York, NY 10013
212-431-7627
(p. 305, App-33)

Puppet People The
c/o Mallory Factor Inc.
275 Seventh Ave.
New York, NY 10001
212-869-1600
(p. 305)

Puppet Works- Nicholas Coppola
287 3rd Ave.
Brooklyn, NY 11215
718-638-5217
(p. 306)

Puppeteers of America Inc.
5 Cricklewood Path
Pasadena, CA 91107
213-797-5748
(p. App-12)

Puppetry Guild of Greater New York
PO Box 244
New York, NY 10116
212-929-1568
(p. App-12)

Pusilo Robert Studio
255 West 18th St.
New York, NY 10011
212-675-2179
(p. 71)

Putnam Rolling Ladder Co. Inc.
32 Howard St.
New York, NY 10013
212-226-5147
(p. 198)

PVC Supply Co.
304 Spring St.
New York, NY 10013
212-741-0900
(p. 273)

- Q -

Quaigh Theatre
108 West 43rd St.
New York, NY 10036
212-221-9088
(p. App-25, App-33)

Quarry The (Quarry Enterprises Inc.)
183 Lexington Ave.
New York, NY 10016
212-679-2559
(p. 354)

QUARTET THEATRICAL DRAPERIES CORP.
1163 Atlantic Ave.
Bklyn, 11216
718-857-2841
(p. 100, 134, 144, 155)

- R -

R & D Latex Corp.
5901 Telegraph Rd.
Commerce, CA 90040
213-724-6161
(p. 53)

R & S Cleaners Inc.
188 Second Ave.
New York, NY 10003
212-475-9412
(p. 58)

R. C. I. Radio Clinic Inc.
2290 Broadway
New York, NY 10024
212-877-5151 (continues)

R. C. I. Radio Clinic Inc. (cont.)
2599 Broadway
New York, NY 10025
212-864-6000 212-663-7700
(p. 25)

Racenstein J. Co.
611 Broadway
New York, NY 10012
212-477-3383 212-477-2353
(p. 338)

Rachman Bag Co.
126 Front St.
Brooklyn, NY 11201
718-625-1511
(p. 46)

Rackoff Murray Inc.
25 West 39th St.
New York, NY 10018
212-869-5093
(p. 371)

Radiac Research
261 Kent
Brooklyn, NY 11211
718-963-2233
(p. App-14)

Radio City Music Hall
1260 Sixth Ave.
New York, NY 10019
212-246-4600 212-246-4600
(p. App-19)

Radix Group Int'l/Friedman & Slater
Cargo Bldg. 80
Room 215, Jamaica, NY 11430
718-656-5912
(p. 324)

Rainbow Trading Co. Inc.
5-05 48th Ave.
L.I.C., NY 11101
718-784-3700
(p. 308)

RAINTREE ASSOCIATES
8 Woodsend Rd. South
Dix Hills, NY 11746
516-643-3835
(p. 19, 160)

Ralbovsky John A.
1469 Lexington Ave. #71
New York, NY 10128
212-410-4106
(p. 294)

Rambusch
40 West 13th St.
New York, NY 10011
212-675-0400
(p. 177, 311)

Rand McNally & Co.
10 East 53rd St.
New York, NY 10022
212-751-6300
(p. 220)

Raven Screen
124 East 124th St.
New York, NY 10035
212-534-8408
(p. 206)

Ray Beauty Supply Co. Inc.
721 Eighth Ave.
New York, NY 10036
212-757-0175
(p. 33, 179)

Raydon Gallery
1091 Madison Ave.
New York, NY 10028
212-288-3555
(p. 18)

Raymond Ben Co.
623 Broadway
New York, NY 10012
212-777-7350
(p. 146)

Rayne David Ltd.
130 Montague St.
Brooklyn, NY 11201
718-852-7866
(p. 80)

RB Studios
235 Park Ave. South
New York, NY 10003
212-505-7474
(p. 274)

Red Caboose The
16 West 45th St. 4th Fl.
New York, NY 10036
212-575-0155
(p. 187)

Ree Charles Co. Inc.
381 Fifth Ave.
New York, NY 10016
212-685-9077 212-532-3552
(p. 166)

Reeves Brothers
1271 Sixth Ave.
New York, NY 10020
212-315-2323
(p. 144)

Reeves J. Matthew
105 Bergen St.
Brooklyn, NY 11201
718-596-4293
(p. 92)

Reeves Teletape
304 East 44th St.
New York, NY 10017
212-573-8888
Ed Sullivan Theatre
53rd & Broadway
New York, NY 10019
212-307-4881
RT 3
841 Ninth Ave.
New York, NY 10019
212-307-4885
(p. App-30)

Regal Plating Co. Inc.
85 South St.
Providence, RI 02903
401-421-2704
(p. 277)

Regan Furniture Corp.
711 Third Ave.
New York, NY 10017
212-683-8990
(p. 172)

Reid John Costumes Inc.
49 West 24th St. 7th Fl.
New York, NY 10010
212-242-6059
(p. 97)

Reisman S. Sons Inc.
244 West 39th St.
New York, NY 10018
212-947-3121 212-947-3122
(p. 242)

Reiter Brothers
473 Broadway
New York, NY 10013
212-226-4062
(p. 59)

REJOICE LTD./G. ZELLER, J. SPECTOR
40 West 39 St.
New York, NY 10018
212-869-8636
(p. 2, 17, 46, 53, 55, 104, 152, 155, 163, 219, 336, App-15)

RELIABLE & FRANK'S NAVAL UNIFORMS
106 Flushing Ave.
Brooklyn, NY 11205
718-858-6033
(p. 83)

Remco Press Inc.
54 West 21st St.
New York, NY 10010
212-242-4647
(p. 285)

Reminiscence Inc.
74 Fifth Ave.
New York, NY 10011
212-243-2292
(p. 71)

Rempac Foam Corp.
84-182 Dayton Ave. Bldg. 1F
Passaic, NJ 07055
201-773-8880
(p. 162)

Renar Leather Co.
68 Spring St.
New York, NY 10012
212-349-2075
(p. 199)

Rensay Inc.
49 East 58th St.
New York, NY 10022
212-688-0195
(p. 348)

Repeat Performance Thrift Shop
220 East 23rd St.
New York, NY 10010
212-684-5344
(p. 353)

Research Council of Make-Up Artists
52 New Spaulding St.
Lowell, MA 01851
617-459-9864
(p. 219)

Ressler Importers Inc.
80 West 3rd St.
New York, NY 10012
212-674-4477 212-533-5750
(p. 170)

REYNOLDS DRAPERY SERVICE INC.
7440 Main St.
Newport, NY 13416
315-845-8632
(p. 58, 100, 118, 155, 350)

Rialto Florist
707 Lexington Ave.
New York, NY 10022
212-688-3234
(p. 160, App-2)

RICHARD THE THREAD/ROY COOPER
1433 N. Orange Grove
Hollywood, CA 90046
800-621-0849(x226) 213-874-1116
(p. 242, 246, 266)

Richards Aqua Lung & Sporting Goods
233 West 42nd St.
New York, NY 10036
212-947-5018
(p. 340)

Richter Ben Co.
85 Fifth Ave.
New York, NY 10003
212-255-5373
(p. 267)

Rickels
1520 Forest Ave.
Staten Island, NY 10302
718-448-3434
(p. 188)

Ridiculous Theatrical Co.
1 Sheridan Square
New York, NY 10014
212-691-2271
(p. App-22)

Ritz Theatre
225 West 48th St.
New York, NY 10036
212-664-9154 212-582-4022
(p. App-19)

Riverside Church
120th St. at Claremont
New York, NY 10027
212-864-2929
(p. App-27)

Riverside Shakespeare Co.
165 West 86th St.
New York, NY 10024
212-877-6810
(p. App-25)

Riverwest Theatre
155 Bank St.
New York, NY 10014
212-243-0259
(p. App-25, App-33)

Rivoli Merchandise Co.
54 Howard St.
New York, NY 10013
212-966-5035
(p. 255)

Rizzoli International Bookstore
31 West 57th St.
New York, NY 10019
212-759-2424
(p. 43)

Robbins D. & Co. Inc.
70 Washington St.
Brooklyn, NY 11201
718-625-1804
(p. 217)

Robelan Displays Inc.
150 Fulton Ave.
Garden City, NJ 11040
516-747-5300
(p. 109)

Robinson Martin P.
46 Gold St.
New York, NY 10038
212-406-9760
(p. 306)

Robinson Robbie Textile Corp.
270 West 39th St. 4th Fl.
New York, NY 10018
212-921-1164
(p. 134, 141, 146)

Rochelle Millinery
700 Madison Ave.
New York, NY 10021
212-593-3232
(p. 66)

Rodgers & Hammerstein Theatre Library
598 Madison Ave.
New York, NY 10022
212-486-0643
(p. App-8)

Roe Jerry Enterprises Inc.
432 Austin Place
Bronx, NY 10455
212-993-7766
(p. 220)

Rogers Charles P.
149 West 24th St.
New York, NY 10011
212-807-1989
(p. 45)

Rogers Foam Corp.
3580 Main St.
Hartford, CT 06120
203-246-7234
(p. 163)

Roland Willie
4017 15th Ave.
Brooklyn, NY 11218
718-854-3325
(p. 113, 322)

Rollins Leslie
110 West 94th St. #2A
New York, NY 10025
212-222-3509 718-643-0990
(p. 294)

Romano Trading Inc.
628 West 45th St.
New York, NY 10036
212-581-4248
(p. 345)

Romeo John Workshop Inc.
44 Wells Ave.
Yonkers, NY 10701
914-965-3994
(p. 318)

Rooke Harmer
3 East 57th St.
New York, NY 10022
212-751-1900
(p. 85)

ROSCO LABORATORIES INC.
36 Bush Ave.
Port Chester, NY 10573
914-937-1300 800-431-2338
(p. 46, 53, 100, 103, 144, 163, 253, 256, 257, 259, 261, 262, 269)

Rosco Research Center
118 West 22nd St. 9th Fl.
New York, NY 10011
212-929-1300
(p. 256)

ROSE BRAND TEXTILE FABRICS
517 West 35th St.
New York, NY 10001
212-594-7424 800-223-1624
(p. 100, 134, 145, 346)

Rose Stationery
79 Fifth Ave.
New York, NY 10003
212-255-6340
(p. 343)

Rosen & Chadick
246 West 40th St.
New York, NY 10018
212-869-0136
(p. 131)

Rosen-Paramount Glass
45 East 20th St.
New York, NY 10003
212-532-0820
(p. 177)

Rosenthal Jan
126 St. Marks Place #18
New York, NY 10009
212-254-4991
(p. 306)

Rosenzweig Lumber Corp.
801 East 135th St.
Bronx, NY 10454
212-585-8050
(p. 184, 214)

Rosetta Electrical Co. Inc.
73 Murray St.
New York, NY 10007
212-233-9088
21 West 46th St.
New York, NY 10036
212-719-4381
(p. 116, 209)

Ross Sales Co.
58 Third Ave.
New York, NY 10003
212-475-8470
(p. 35, 179, 320)

Rossiter Deed
130 Sickletown Rd.
West Nyack, NY 10994
914-358-7474
(p. 336)

Roth Import Co.
13 West 38th St.
New York, NY 10018
212-840-1945
(p. 67, 362, 365, 369)

Roundabout Rehearsal Space
71 Eighth Ave. 3rd Fl.
New York, NY 10014
212-420-1360 212-929-9703
(p. App-33)

Roundabout Stage One
100 East 17th St.
New York, NY 10003
212-420-1883 212-420-1360
(p. App-22)

Royal Court Rep
301 West 55th St.
New York, NY 10019
212-977-2582
(p. App-25)

Royal Oaksmith Ltd.
982 Second Ave.
New York, NY 10022
212-751-3376
(p. 11)

Royal Wear Hosiery
23 Orchard St.
New York, NY 10002
212-226-2450
(p. 256)

Royale Draperies Inc.
289 Grand St.
New York, NY 10002
212-431-0170
(p. 369)

Royale Theatre
242 West 45th St.
New York, NY 10036
212-391-8879 212-239-6200
(p. App-19)

Rubber Stamps Inc.
16 West 22nd St.
New York, NY 10011
212-675-1180
(p. 313)

Ruben Bead Importing Co. Inc.
45 West 37th St.
New York, NY 10018
212-840-0500
(p. 362)

Rubicon Boutique Inc.
849 Madison Ave.
New York, NY 10021
212-861-3000
(p. 77)

Ruby's Book Sale
119 Chambers St.
New York, NY 10007
212-732-8676
(p. 43)

Rudin Harold Decorators Inc.
753 Ninth Ave.
New York, NY 10019
212-265-4716 212-757-5639
(p. 102, 373)

Rug Warehouse
2222 Broadway
New York, NY 10024
212-787-6665
(p. 157)

Rule Jim
9 North C St. #D
Lake Worth, FL 33460
305-586-7842
(p. 294)

RUPERT, GIBBON & SPIDER INC.
718 College St.
Healdsburg, CA 95448
707-433-9577
(p. 256)

Russell Uniform Co.
44 East 20th St.
New York, NY 10003
212-674-1400
(p. 83)

- S -

S & L Dress Suit Rental Co.
145 West 42nd St.
New York, NY 10036
212-582-4983 212-582-3858
(p. 76)

S & L Jack Electronics
28-14 Steinway St.
Astoria, NY 11103
718-545-8843
(p. 116)

S & S Hosiery
156 West 50th St.
New York, NY 10019
212-586-3288
(p. 73)

S M P Graphic Service Center
26 East 22nd St.
New York, NY 10010
212-254-2282
(p. 269, 285)

Sacred Feather
417 State
Madison, WI 53703
608-255-2071
(p. 67)

Safari Archery
86-15 Lefferts Blvd.
Richmond Hill, NY 11418
718-441-8883
(p. 340)

Saffer Al
106 West 28th St.
New York, NY 10001
212-675-2249
(p. 31, 159)

Saint James Gourmet Importers
565 West St.
New York, NY 10014
212-243-1120
(p. App-2)

Saint Laurie Ltd.
897 Broadway
New York, NY 10003
212-473-0100
(p. 77, 80)

Saks Fifth Ave.
611 Fifth Ave.
New York, NY 10022
212-753-4000
(p. 106)

Salvage Barn Antiques
525 Hudson St.
New York, NY 10014
212-929-5787
(p. 11)

Salvation Army Store
536 West 46th St.
New York, NY 10036
212-757-2311
40 Avenue B
New York, NY 10009
212-473-9492
180 First Ave.
New York, NY 10009
212-475-9560 (continues)

Salvation Army Store (continued)
208 Eighth Ave.
New York, NY 10011
212-929-9719
268 West 96th St.
New York, NY 10025
212-864-8609
26 East 125th St.
New York, NY 10035
212-289-9617
34-06 Steinway
L.I.C., NY 11101
718-784-9880
(p. 353)

Salwen Paper Co.
PO Box 4008
Edison, NJ 08816
201-225-4000
(p. 265)

Sand & Siman Inc.
34 West 32nd St.
New York, NY 10001
212-564-4484
(p. 64)

Sanders D. F. & Co.
386 W. Broadway
New York, NY 10012
212-925-9040
952 Madison Ave.
New York, NY 10021
212-879-616571
(p. 57, 194, 195)

Sanders Dave and Co.
111 Bowery
107 Bowery (mailing address)
New York, NY 10002
212-334-9898
(p. 182, 358)

Sanelle Wood Products Corp.
315 East 86th St.
New York, NY 10028
212-348-1500
(p. 209)

SANTELLI GEORGE INC.
465 S. Dean St.
Englewood, NJ 07631
201-871-3105
(p. 17, 151)

Santelli Salle D'Armes
40 West 27th St.
New York, NY 10001
212-683-2823
(p. 151)

Sara Glove Co.
16 Cherry Ave. PO Box 4069
Waterbury, CT 60704
203-574-4090
(p. App-15)

Saraco Glass Corp.
3710 13th Ave.
Brooklyn, NY 11218
718-438-7757
(p. 177)

Sargenti A. Co. Inc.
453 West 17th St.
New York, NY 10011
212-989-5555
(p. 344)

Sarsaparilla - Deco Designs
5711 Washington St.
West New York, NJ 07093
201-863-8002
(p. 209, 226)

Sava Industries Inc.
70 Riverdale Ave.
Riverdale, NJ 07454
201-835-0882
(p. 233)

Saxon Textile Corp.
744 Broadway
New York, NY 10003
212-677-3680
(p. 134)

Say It In Neon
434 Hudson St.
New York, NY 10014
212-691-7977
(p. 329)

Scafati & Co.
225 Fifth Ave. Rm. 812
New York, NY 10010
212-686-8784
(p. 20)

Scalamandre Silks Inc.
950 Third Ave.
New York, NY 10022
212-980-3888
(p. 136)

Scandinavian Ski Shop
40 West 57th St.
New York, NY 10019
212-757-8524
(p. 340)

Scarlet Leather The
96 Christopher St.
New York, NY 10014
212-255-1155
(p. 77, 80)

Schachters Babyland
81 Avenue A
New York, NY 10009
212-777-1660
(p. 170)

Schacter J. Corp.
115 Allen St.
New York, NY 10002
212-533-1150
(p. 211)

Schaper Maya Cheese & Antiques
152 East 70th St.
New York, NY 10021
212-734-9427
(p. 11)

Scher Fabrics Inc.
5 Penn Plaza
New York, NY 10001
212-736-0240
(p. 131)

Schirmer Music
40 West 62nd St.
New York, NY 10023
212-541-6236
(p. 238)

Schlesinger B. & Sons Inc.
249 West 18th St.
New York, NY 10011
212-206-8022
(p. 84, 278)

Schmeeler Bill Wellington Enterprises
55 Railroad Ave. Bldg 10, PO Box 315
Garnerville, NY 10923
914-429-3377
(p. 337)

Schmitt Catherine
744 Undercliff Ave.
Edgewater, NJ 07020
201-224-6272
(p. 294)

Schneider's
20 Avenue A
New York, NY 10009
212-228-3540
(p. 170)

Schoepfer Studios
138 West 31st St.
New York, NY 10001
212-736-6939
(p. 347)

Schoffner Jody
20-59 36th St.
Astoria, NY 11105
718-726-1476
(p. 92, 306)

School of Visual Arts Library
209 East 23rd St.
New York, NY 10010
212-679-7350 (x67)
(p. App-8)

School Productions
1201 Broadway 3rd Fl.
New York, NY 10001
212-679-3516
(p. 380)

Schorr Martin Co.
216 West 38th St.
New York, NY 10018
212-719-4870
(p. 369)

Schultz Linda C.
125 West 96th St. #6J
New York, NY 10025
212-222-0477
(p. 92, 294)

Schumacher
939 Third Ave.
New York, NY 10022
212-644-5900
(p. 136, 379)

Schwartz M. & Sons Feathers Corp.
45 Hoffman Ave.
Haupaug, NY 11787
516-234-7722
(p. 365)

Scott Angela
341 East 78th St.
New York, NY 10021
212-535-1839
(p. 36)

Scott Aviation (Div. of ATO Inc.)
25 Erie St.
Lancaster, NY 14086
716-683-5100
(p. App-15)

Scott Hatters Inc.
620 Eighth Ave.
New York, NY 10018 (main store)
212-840-2130
201 West 42nd St.
New York, NY 10036
212-947-3455
(p. 67)

Scottie's Gallery & Antiques
624 Coney Island Ave.
Brooklyn, NY 11218
718-851-8325
(p. 11)

Scottish Products Inc.
133 East 55th St.
New York, NY 10022
212-755-9656
(p. 124, 150)

Screamers
423 West 55th St.
New York, NY 10019
212-245-3237
(p. 109)

Screaming Mimi
100 West 83rd St.
New York, NY 10024
212-362-3158
(p. 71)

Screw and Supply
71 Box St.
Brooklyn, NY 11222
718-383-8710
(p. 184)

Sculptor's Supplies Ltd.
99 East 19th St.
New York, NY 10003
212-673-3500
(p. 54)

Sculpture Associates Ltd.
40 East 19th St.
New York, NY 10003
212-777-2400
(p. 54)

Sculpture House Casting
38 East 30th St.
New York, NY 10016
212-684-3445
(p. 344)

Sculpture House Inc.
38 East 30th St.
New York, NY 10016
212-679-7474
(p. 54, 338)

Seaboard Twine & Cordage Co. Inc.
49 Murray St.
New York, NY 10007
212-732-6658
(p. 372)

Seal Reinforced Fiberglass
23 Bethpage Rd.
Copiague, NY 11726
516-842-2230
(p. 49)

Search N' Save Thrift Shop
1465 Third Ave.
New York, NY 10028
212-988-1320
(p. 353)

Sears Roebuck & Co. (catalog sales)
137-61 Northern Blvd.
Flushing, NY 11354
212-445-9050 212-445-5500
169-21 Hillside Ave.
Jamaica, NY 11432
212-291-6666 212-739-5225
2307 Beverly Rd.
Brooklyn, NY 11226
212-469-8888 212-469-8000
400 E. Fordham Rd.
Bronx, NY 10458
212-933-1200 212-295-3200
(p. App-16)

Seashell Boutique
208A Columbus Ave.
New York, NY 10023
212-595-3024
(p. 320)

Seashells Unlimited Inc.
590 Third Ave.
New York, NY 10016
212-532-8690
(p. 320)

Sebro Thread Corp.
145 Ave. & Hook Creek Blvd.
Valley Stream, NY 11581
516-872-6125 212-525-1004
(p. 249)

Second Avenue Bazaar
501 Second Ave.
New York, NY 10016
212-683-2293
(p. 167, 193)

Second Coming Ltd. The
72 Greene St.
New York, NY 10012
212-431-4424
(p. 71)

Second Stage Theatre
2162 Broadway
New York, NY 10024
212-787-8302
(p. App-22, App-33)

Second Storey Theatre
189 Second Ave.
New York, NY 10003
212-777-6230
(p. App-25)

Second Time Around Thrift Shop
220 East 23rd St.
New York, NY 10010
212-685-2170
(p. 353)

Secondhand Rose
573 Hudson St.
New York, NY 10014
212-989-9776
(p. 12)

Security Office Furniture Co. Inc.
140 West 23rd St.
New York, NY 10011
212-924-1485
(p. 172)

Segal Brothers
205 Nassau St.
Brooklyn, NY 11201
718-383-2995
(p. 233, 351, 358)

Segal Fabric Center Inc.
159 Orchard St.
New York, NY 10002
212-673-3430
(p. 132)

Segrin Danny
56 Warren St.
New York, NY 10007
212-227-5986
(p. 306)

Seguin Jamie Paul
355 West 85th St. #8
New York, NY 10024
212-580-8275
(p. 92)

Seguin Mirror & Brass Inc.
202 East 70th St.
New York, NY 10021
212-628-1460
(p. 177)

Selby Furniture Hardware Co.
17 East 22nd St.
New York, NY 10010
212-673-4097
(p. 182)

Seminole Furniture Shops Inc.
115 East 23rd St.
New York, NY 10010
212-505-7211
(p. 169)

Senz Ira
13 East 47th St.
New York, NY 10017
212-752-6800
(p. 180)

Sequins International Corp.
110 West 40th St.
New York, NY 10018
212-221-3121
(p. 363)

Service Party-Rental Co.
521 East 72nd St.
New York, NY 10021
212-288-7384 212-288-7361
(p. 266, 330)

Service Trimmings
142 West 38th St.
New York, NY 10018
212-921-1680
(p. 246)

SET SHOP THE
3 West 20th St.
New York, NY 10011
212-929-4845
(p. 20, 28, 163, 164, 258, 261, 265, 274, 301, 346, 376, 319, 325, 336)

Seven Continents Enterprises Inc.
133 West 25th St. 9th Fl.
New York, NY 10001
212-691-1195
(p. 109)

Seven Corners Ace Hardware
216 West 7th St.
St. Paul, MN 55102
800-328-0457
(p. 358)

Shackman B. & Co. Inc.
85 Fifth Ave.
New York, NY 10003
212-989-5162
(p. 112, 360)

Shadey Business
163 West 10th St.
New York, NY 10014
212-255-1480
(p. 209)

Shadovitz Brothers Dist. Inc.
1565 Bergen St.
Brooklyn, NY 11213
718-774-9100
(p. 178)

Shaftel Lisa
332 East 74th St. #4B
New York, NY 10021
212-249-2581
(p. 223. 294, 306)

Shakespeare and Co. Booksellers
2259 Broadway
New York, NY 10024
212-580-7800
(p. 43)

Shalit Willa
340 Riverside Dr.
New York, NY 10025
212-316-3470
(p. 223)

Shamash & Sons Inc.
42 West 39th St.
New York, NY 10018
212-840-3111
(p. 148)

Shantz Associates Inc.
15 East 40th St.
New York, NY 10016
212-889-1770
(p. 246)

Sheffy Nina A.
838 West End Ave.
New York, NY 10025
212-662-0709
(p. 294)

Shell Sponge & Chamois Co.
384 Broadway
New York, NY 10013
212-966-3250
(p. 338)

Shellcraft, Div. of Cresthill Ind.
519 Eighth Ave.
New York, NY 10018
212-947-1960
(p. 363)

Shelter West Co.
217 Second Ave.
New York, NY 10003
212-673-6341
(p. App-25)

Shep R. L.
PO Box C-20
Lopez Island, WA 98261
206-468-2023
(p. 43)

Sher Plastics
450 Seventh Ave.
New York, NY 10123
212-760-9660
(p. 247)

Sherman Nat
711 Fifth Ave.
New York, NY 10022
212-751-9100
(p. 331)

Sherov Machine Corp.
149 Allen Blvd.
East Farmingdale, NY 11735
516-454-8899
(p. 215)

Sheru
49 West 38th St.
New York, NY 10018
212-730-0766
(p. 363)

Shoe Repair Supply Corp.
1250 4th St. NE
Washington, DC 20002
202-842-0505
(p. 201)

Show Tech
15 Chapel St.
Norwalk, CT 06850
203-854-9336
(p. 319)

Showroom Display Hangers
155 West 29th St.
New York, NY 10001
212-695-5167
(p. 95)

Showroom Outlet
625-35 West 55th St.
New York, NY 10019
212-581-0470
(p. 18, 298)

Shriver Christopher
144 Franklin St.
New York, NY 10013
212-925-0933
(p. 294)

Shubert Theatre
225 West 44th St.
New York, NY 10036
212-764-0184 212-239-6200
(p. App-19)

Shui Hing Inc.
46-48 Bowery, Arcade 26
New York, NY 10013
212-964-0548
(p. 123)

Sideshow
184 Ninth Ave.
New York, NY 10011
212-675-2212
(p. 12)

Sid's Hardware
345 Jay St.
Brooklyn, NY 11201
718-875-2259
(p. 184)

Siegel Paul Antiques
808 Broadway
New York, NY 10003
212-533-5566
(p. 12)

Siff Brothers
251 West 39th St.
New York, NY 10018
212-730-1045
(p. 247)

Sigma Leather Inc.
68 Spring St.
New York, NY 10013
212-679-8000
(p. 199)

Sil-Ko Mfg. Co. Inc./AMCAN Feather
1385 Broadway Rm. 1006
New York, NY 10018
212-729-1552
(p. 365)

Silk Surplus
223 East 58th St.
New York, NY 10022
212-753-6511
1147 Madison Ave.
New York, NY 10028
212-794-9373
(p. 136, 148)

SILVER & SONS HARDWARE
711 Eighth Ave.
New York, NY 10036
212-247-6969
(p. 351)

SILVER JACK
1780 Broadway Rm. 303
New York, NY 10019
212-582-3298 212-582-3389
(p. 72, 76, 80)

Silver Screen
35 East 28th St.
New York, NY 10016
212-679-8130
(p. 227)

Silvercup Studios
42-25 21st St.
L.I.C., NY 11101
718-784-3390
(p. App-30)

Silverii Katherine
41 Union Square W.
New York, NY 10003
212-924-9411
(p. 92)

Silver's W. H. Hardware
832 Eighth Ave.
New York, NY 10019
212-247-4406 212-247-4425
(p. 24, 180, 351, 358)

Simmons Fastener Corp.
1750 Broadway
Albany, NY 12204
518-463-4234
(p. 351)

Simon Hardware
421 Third Ave.
New York, NY 10016
212-532-9220
(p. 193)

Simon Neil Theatre (Alvin)
250 West 52nd St.
New York, NY 10019
212-974-9445 212-757-8646
(p. App-19)

Simon's Hardware
421 Third Ave.
New York, NY 10016
212-532-9220
(p. 182)

Simpson C. J.
401 West 24th St. #16
New York, NY 10011
212-924-3272
(p. 295)

Singer Buttonhole & Eyeleting Co.
302 West 37th St.
New York, NY 10018
212-736-1943
(p. 118)

Singer D. Textile Co.
55 Delancey St.
New York, NY 10002
212-925-4818
(p. 132)

Sino-American Commodities Center
27-33 West 23rd St.
New York, NY 10010
212-741-8833
(p. 123)

Sir George Ltd.
2884 Broadway
New York, NY 10025
212-866-2700
(p. 80)

Siska George C.
8 Rosol Lane
Saddlebrook, NJ 07662
201-794-1124
(p. 247)

Skil Corp.
75 Varick St.
New York, NY 10013
212-226-7630
(p. 358)

Slide Shop Inc.
220 East 23rd St. 4th Fl.
New York, NY 10010
212-725-5200
(p. 272)

Slomon's Labs Inc.
9-11 Linden St.
Newark, NJ 07102
201-623-0909
(p. 2)

Small Parts Inc.
6901 NE 3rd Ave., PO Box 381736
Miami, FL 33238
305-751-0856
(p. 228, 233)

Smith & Grey Corp.
44 East 20th St.
New York, NY 10003
212-674-1400
(p. 278)

Smith & Warren Co.
154 Grand St.
New York, NY 10013
212-966-1917
(p. 279)

Smith & Watson Inc.
305 East 63rd St.
New York, NY 10021
212-355-5615
(p. 12)

Smith & Yates
782 West End Ave.
New York, NY 10025
212-666-4191
(p. 367, 369)

Smith David
127 West 85th St. #3B
New York, NY 10024
212-595-8626 212-730-1188
(p. 295)

Smith T. W. Welding Supply
545 West 59th St.
New York, NY 10019
212-247-6323
(p. 29, 191, 381)

Smolka Co. Inc.
182 Madison Ave.
New York, NY 10016
212-679-2700
(p. 193)

Smooth-On-Corp.
1000 Valley Rd.
Gillette, NJ 07933
201-647-5800
(p. 2, 54)

SMP Graphic Service Center
26 East 22nd St.
New York, NY 10011
212-254-2282
(p. 285, App-2)

Snow Craft Co. Inc.
112 South 6th St.
New Hyde Park, NY 11040
718-347-4473
(p. 163)

Snyder Harry
70 Hester St.
New York, NY 10002
212-925-0855
(p. 132)

So-Good
28 West 38th St.
New York, NY 10018
212-398-0236
(p. 369)

Soccer Sport Supply Co.
1745 First Ave.
New York, NY 10128
212-427-6050
(p. 340)

Soho Repertory Theatre
80 Varick St.
New York, NY 10013
212-925-2588
(p. App-25)

Sol Tool Co.
164 Lafayette
New York, NY 10013
212-925-0923
(p. 215)

Solco Plumbing Supply Co.
209 West 18th St.
New York, NY 10011
212-243-2569
(p. 278)

Soltex Thread and Yarn Co.
30 West 24th St.
New York, NY 10001
212-243-2000
(p. 249)

Some's Uniforms
65 Rt. 17
Paramus, NJ 07652
201-843-1199 212-564-6274
(p. 279)

Sonoco Products Co.
PO Box 582
Montville, NJ 07045
201-263-1400
(p. 265)

Sound Associates Inc.
424 West 45th St.
New York, NY 10036
212-757-5679
(p. 332)

Sound of Music
PO Box 221
Stillwater, NJ 07875
201-383-7267
(p. 26)

SOUTH AFRICAN FEATHERS
325 N. 13th St.
Philadelphia, PA 19107
215-925-5219
(p. 365)

South Street Seaport Museum: Store
207 Front St.
New York, NY 10038
212-669-9400
(p. 221)

South Street Theatre
406 West 42nd St.
New York, NY 10036
212-279-4200 212-564-0660
(p. App-22, App-25)

Southern Manufacturing Corp.
PO Box 32427
Charlotte, NC 28232
704-372-2880
(p. 24)

Space at City Center The
133 West 55th St.
New York, NY 10019
212-246-8989
(p. App-22)

Space Surplus Metals Inc.
325 Church St.
New York, NY 10013
212-966-4358
(p. 228)

Spaeth Design Inc.
423 West 55th St.
New York, NY 10019
212-489-0770
(p. 110)

Speakeasy Antiques
799 Broadway
New York, NY 10003
212-533-2440
(p. 12, 226)

Special Effects Unlimited
18 Euclid Ave.
Yonkers, NY 10705
914-965-5625
(p. 46, 337)

Special Products
1437 W. Morris St.
Indianapolis, IN 46221
317-632-5321
(p. 256)

Special Shapes Co. Inc.
1354 Napierville, PO Box 487R
Romeoville, IL 60441
312-586-8517
(p. 187)

SPECIALTY SIGNS CO. INC.
6 West 18th St.
New York, NY 10011
212-243-8521
(p. 329)

Spectra Dynamics Products
415 Marble Ave. NW
Albuquerque, NM 87102
505-843-7202
(p. 2)

Speed-Graphics
150 East 58th St.
New York, NY 10155
212-486-0209
(p. 285)

Spence-Chapin Thrift Shop
1424 Third Ave.
New York, NY 10028
212-737-8448
(p. 353)

Spencer William
Creek Road
Mount Laurel, NJ 08060
609-235-3764
(p. 169, 209)

Sperling Beauty Supplies
13639 Vanowen
Van Nuys, CA 91405
818-781-6300
(p. 219)

Spiegels
105 Nassau St.
New York, NY 10038
212-227-8400
(p. 340)

Spirit of America Antiques
269 West 4th St.
New York, NY 10014
212-255-3255
(p. 307)

Spitz Sol Co.
50 Commerce Dr.
Hauppauque, NY 11788
516-231-0010
(p. 111)

Sportiva-Sporthaus Inc.
1627 Second Ave.
New York, NY 10028
212-734-7677
(p. 340)

Sprott Eoin Studio Ltd.
Astoria Studio, 37-11 35th Ave.
Astoria, NY 11106
718-784-1407 718-784-1629
(p. 301, 337)

Sprotzer Tools & Hardware Co. Inc,
7 Harrison St.
New York, NY 10013
212-966-2220
(p. 2)

St. Clement's
423 West 46th St.
New York, NY 10036
212-265-4375 212-246-7277
(p. App-22)

St. James Gourmet Importers
565 West St.
New York, NY 10014
212-243-1120
(p. 6)

St. James Theatre
246 West 44th St.
New York, NY 10036
212-730-9506 212-398-0280
(p. App-19)
St. Mark's Church in the Bowery
234 East 11th St.
New York, NY 100
212-674-8112
(p. App-27)
St. Marks Place Sewing Machines
78 East 1st St.
New York, NY 10009
212-254-3480
(p. 322)
Staflex Co.
7 West 36th St.
New York, NY 10018
212-279-3000
(p. 141)
Stage Lighting Distributors
346 West 44th St.
New York, NY 10036
212-489-1370
1653 N. Argyle Ave.
Hollywood, CA 90028
213-466-8324 800-228-0222
(p. 164)
Stage Managers' Association
PO Box 539, Old Chelsea Station
New York, NY 10113
212-691-5633
(p. App-12)
Stage Step
PO Box 328
Philadelphia, PA 19105
212-567-666 800-523-0961
(p. 103))
Stagelight Cosmetics Ltd.
630 Ninth Ave.
New York, NY 10036
212-757-4851
(p. 219)
Staging Techniques
342 West 40th St.
New York, NY 10018
212-736-5727
(p. 206)
Stamford Housewrecking
1 Barry Place
Stamford, CT 06902
203-324-9537
(p. 15)
Standard Felt Co.
13636 S. Western Ave.
Blue Island, IL 60406
312-597-9870
Box 871 (115 S. Palm Ave.)
Alhambra, CA 91802
818-282-3165
(p. 138)
Standard Plating Corp.
71 Spring St.
New York, NY 10012
212-925-5313
(p. 277)
Standard Tile
214-70 Jamaica Ave.
Queens Village, NY 11428
718-465-8282
(p. 355)
Standard Trimming Corp.
1114 First Ave. 5th Fl.
New York, NY 10021
212-755-3034
(p. 363, 370)
Star Buttonhole & Button Works Co.
242 West 36th St.
New York, NY 10018
212-736-4960
(p. 118)
Star Magic
743 Broadway
New York, NY 10003
212-228-7770
(p. 43, 280, 312, 348, 360)
Starbuck Studios
162 West 21st St.
New York, NY 10011
212-807-7299
(p. 275)
Starr Jana
236 East 80th St.
New York, NY 10021
212-861-8256
(p. 72)

Stat Store
148 Fifth Ave.
New York, NY 10011
212-929-0566
(p. 286)

State Office Supply & Printing Co.
150 Fifth Ave.
New York, NY 10011
212-243-8025
(p. 343)

State Supply Equipment Co. Inc.
210 Eleventh Ave.
New York, NY 10001
212-645-1431
(p. 180, 298, 348)

Statue of Liberty Gallery Shop
519 Hudson St.
New York, NY 10014
212-929-4180
(p. 226)

Staylastic-Smith Inc.
90 Hatch St., PO Box C-903
New Bedford, MA 02741
617-999-6431
(p. 248)

Stefanie Ceramics
973 Broadway
Bayonne, NJ 07002
201-436-3161
(p. 281)

Stein Edward Woolen Co.
184-08 Jamaica Ave.
Hollis, NY 11423
718-454-7475
(p. 150)

STEINLAUF & STOLLER INC.
239 West 39th St.
New York, NY 10018
212-869-0321 800-637-1637
(p. 242)

STEIN'S COSMETIC CO.
430 Broome St.
New York, NY 10013
212-226-2430
(p. 219)

Steinway & Sons
109 West 57th St.
New York, NY 10019
212-246-1100 718-721-2600
(p. 238)

Stepan Chemical Co. (Urethane Dept.)
22 West Frontage Rd.
Northfield, IL 60093
312-446-7500
(p. 54)

Steps Dance Studio
2121 Broadway
New York, NY 10023
212-874-2410
(p. App-33)

Sterling Net & Twine Co. Inc.
18 Label St.
Montclair, NJ 07042
201-783-9800
(p. 145)

Stern & Stern Textiles Inc.
315 Park Ave. South
New York, NY 10022
212-460-1980
(p. 146)

Stetson Hat Co.
1775 Universal
Kansas City, MO 64120
816-483-8889
(p. 67)

Stevdan Stationers
474 Sixth Ave.
New York, NY 10011
212-243-4222
(p. 343)

Stevens-Pascucci Daphne
146 West 73rd St. #2B
New York, NY 10023
212-724-9898
(p. 92, 295)

Stewart Color Labs Inc.
563 Eleventh Ave.
New York, NY 10036
212-868-1440
(p. 269)

Sticht Henry Co.
27 Park Place
New York, NY 10007
212-732-8163
(p. 116)

Stick-A-Seal Tape (United Mineral)
129 Hudson St.
New York, NY 10013
212-966-4330
(p. 346)

Stieglbauer Assoc. Inc.
29 Front St.
Brooklyn, NY 11201
718-624-0835
(p. 319)

Stimpson Edwin B. & Co. Inc.
900 Sylvan Ave.
Bayport, NY 11705
516-472-2000
(p. 247)

Stock Drive Products
55 South Denton Ave.
New Hyde Park, NY 11040
516-328-0200 516-328-3300
(p. 233)

Stoddard Richard Performing Arts
90 East 10th St.
New York, NY 10003
212-982-0440
(p. 43)

Stokes Cap & Regalia
475 Ellsmere, Scarborough
Ontario, Canada M1R4E5
416-444-1188
(p. 67)

Strand Book Store Inc.
828 Broadway
New York, NY 10003
212-473-1452
159 John St.
New York, NY 10038
212-809-0875
(p. 44)

Straw Into Gold
3006 San Pablo Ave.
Berkeley, CA 94702
415-548-5241
(p. 256)

Stribbons Ltd.
11 East 26th St. 12th Fl.
New York, NY 10010
212-532-3000
(p. 248)

Stroblite Co. Inc.
430 West 14th St. Rm. 507
New York, NY 10014
212-929-3778
(p. 256, 262)

Stroheim & Romann Inc.
155 East 56th St.
New York, NY 10022
212-691-0700
(p. 136)

Stuart Paul
Madison Ave. at 45th
New York, NY 10017
212-682-0320
(p. 81)

STUDIO
250 West 14th St.
New York, NY 10011
212-924-4736
(p. 97)

Studio 84
245 East 84th St.
New York, NY 10028
212-988-0500
(p. App-30)

Studio 39
144 East 39th St.
New York, NY 10016
212-685-1771 212-889-9616
212-889-0910
(p. App-30)

Studio 305 Inc.
305 Amsterdam Ave.
New York, NY 10023
212-724-8758
(p. 286)

Studio and Forum of Stage Design
727 Washington St.
New York, NY 10014
212-924-5035
(p. App-12)

Studio Instrument Rentals
310 West 52nd St.
New York, NY 10019
212-975-0920
(p. 238)

Stupell Carole Ltd.
61 East 57th St.
New York, NY 10022
212-260-3100
(p. 57)

Stuyvesant Bicycle
349 West 14th St.
New York, NY 10014
212-254-5200
(p. 34)

Stuyvesant Bicycle East
326 Second Ave.
New York, NY 10003
212-254-9200
(p. 35)

Stuyvesant Town Ice & Cube
325 East 21st St.
New York, NY 10010
212-473-6784
(p. 190)

Stylecrest Fabrics, Ltd.
214 West 39th St.
New York, NY 10018
212-354-0123
(p. 132)

Styro Sales Co. Inc.
25-34 50th Ave.
L.I.C., NY 11101
718-786-1791
(p. 163)

Success Binding Corp.
636 Broadway
New York, NY 10012
212-226-6161
(p. 243)

Sullivan Street Playhouse
181 Sullivan St.
New York, NY 10012
212-674-3838
(p. App-22)

Sunray Yarn Co.
349 Grand St.
New York, NY 10002
212-475-0062
(p. 380)

Super Glue Corp.
184-08 Jamaica
Hollis, NY 11423
718-454-4747
(p. 3)

Super Textile Co. Inc.
108 West 39th St. 5th Fl.
New York, NY 10018
212-354-5725
(p. 148)

Superior Fashion Menswear
85 Orchard St.
New York, NY 10002
212-431-8505
(p. 81)

Superior Lamp & Electrical Supply Co.
394 Broadway
New York, NY 10010
212-677-9191
(p. 209)

Superior Model Forms Co.
545 Eighth Ave.
New York, NY 10018
212-947-3633
(p. 114)

Superior Specialties Inc.
5925 Broadway
Bronx, NY 10463
212-543-1767
(p. 20, 138)

Superior Steam Iron Co. Inc.
111-31 44th Ave.
Corona, NY 11368
718-699-6464
(p. 190)

Supermud Pottery
2875 Broadway
New York, NY 10025
212-865-9190
(p. 282)

Supersnipe Comic Book Art Emporium
PO Box 1102, Gracie Station
New York, NY 10028
212-879-9628
(p. 216)

Supply Store NYFD
250 Livingston
Brooklyn, NY 11201
718-403-1635
(p. 84)

Supreme Felt & Abrasives Co.
4425 T-James Place
Melrose Park, IL 60160
312-344-0134
(p. 139)

Supreme Label Corp.
109 West 27th St.
New York, NY 10001
212-255-2090
(p. 197)

Supreme Steam Appliance Corp.
157 West 26th St.
New York, NY 10001
212-929-7349
(p. 190)

Sure-Snap Corp.
241 West 37th St.
New York, NY 10018
212-921-5515
(p. 247)

Surplus Metals
321 Canal St.
New York, NY 10013
212-226-6467
(p. 228)

Sussel Electronics, Howard Sussel
411 East 53rd St.
New York, NY 10022
212-935-0632
(p. 337)

Sussman Ruth
340 West 57th St.
New York, NY 10019
212-757-8968
(p. 228)

Sutter Textile Co.
257 West 39th St.
New York, NY 10018
212-398-0248
(p. 132)

Sutton Clock Shop
139 East 61st St.
New York, NY 10021
212-758-2260
(p. 59)

Swift Adhesives
Allings Crossing Rd.
West Haven, CT 06516
212-966-2318 203-934-8661
(p. 3)

Switches Unlimited
34-11 56th St.
Woodside, NY 11377
718-478-5000
(p. 116)

Symphony Space
2537 Broadway
New York, NY 10025
212-864-1414
(p. App-27)

Syms Clothing
45 Park Place
New York, NY 10007
212-791-1199
(p. 81)

System Lumber Co.
517 West 42nd St.
New York, NY 10036
212-695-0380
(p. 214)

- T -

Taffy's Dancewear
1776 Broadway 2nd Fl.
New York, NY 10019
212-586-5140
(p. 73)

Tall Size Shoes
3 West 35th St.
New York, NY 10001
212-736-2060
(p. 61)

Talon Zippers
1350 Broadway Rm. 1815
New York, NY 10018
212-564-6300
(p. 250)

Tamary Dora
264 West 40th St.
New York, NY 10018
212-944-0272 212-992-9031
(p. 146)

Tandy Leather Co.
330 Fifth Ave.
New York, NY 10001
212-947-2533
(p. 199)

Tannen Louis Inc.
6 West 32nd St. 4th Fl.
New York, NY 10001
212-239-8383
(p. 217)

TAUTKUS RICHARD
100 West 23rd St.
New York, NY 10011
212-691-8253
(p. 93, 295)

Tay Art Supplies Co.
27 Third Ave.
New York, NY 10003
212-475-7365
(p. 23)

Taymor Julie
718 Broadway #10C
New York, NY 10003
212-475-4829
(p. 223, 306)

Techni-Tool
Apollo Road
Plymouth Meeting, PA 19462
215-825-4990
(p. 116)

Technical Assistance Project of the American Dance Festival (TAP)
1860 Broadway Rm. 1110
New York, NY 10023
212-586-1925
(p. App-12)

Technical Library Services Inc.
213 West 35th St.
New York, NY 10001
212-736-7744
(p. 3, 36)

Teddy's Lamp & Lighting Fixture Parts
182 Grand St.
New York, NY 10013
212-925-5067
(p. 209)

Television Rental Co.
118 East 28th St. #508
New York, NY 10016
212-685-3344
(p. 26)

Tempia Norman
409 East 90th St. #1B
New York, NY 10128
212-348-8944
(p. 49, 223, 306, 337)

Tender Buttons
143 East 62nd St.
New York, NY 10021
212-758-7004
(p. 247)

Tent & Trails
21 Park Place
New York, NY 10007
212-227-1760
(p. 341)

Tepee Town Inc.
Port Authority Bus Terminal
New York, NY 10036
212-563-6430 (p. 81)

Terilyn Costumes
210 West 70th St. #311
New York, NY 10023
212-496-1639
(p. 97)

Terminal Music
166 West 48th St.
New York, NY 10036
212-869-5270
(p. 238)

Termine Richard
434 East 89th St. #A
New York, NY 10128
212-289-4057
(p. 306)

Testfabrics Inc.
200 Blackford Ave.
Middlesex, NJ 08846
201-469-6446
(p. 132)

Textile Resources
PO Box 90245
Long Beach, CA 90809
213-431-9611
(p. 256)

Textile Ribbon Co.
63 West 38th St.
New York, NY 10018
212-391-6923
(p. 369)

Theatre 22
54 West 22nd St.
New York, NY 10010
212-243-2805
(p. App-33)

THEATRE ARTS BOOKSHOP
405 West 42nd St.
New York, NY 10036
212-564-0402 212-564-0403
(p. 44)

Theatre Communications Group (TCG)
355 Lexington Ave.
New York, NY 10017
212-697-5230
(p. App-13)

Theatre Development Fund
1501 Broadway
New York, NY 10036
212-221-0885
(p. App-13)

Theatre for the New City
162 Second Ave.
New York, NY 10003
212-254-1109
(p. App-25)

Theatre Four/Negro Ensemble Co.
424 West 55th St.
New York, NY 10019
212-246-8545
165 West 46th St.
New York, NY 10036
212-575-586
(p. App-22)

Theatre Guinevere
15 West 28th St.
New York, NY 10001
212-279-4200
(p. App-25)

THEATRE MACHINE
20 River Road
Bogota, NJ 07603
201-488-5270
(p. 319)

THEATRE MAGIC
6099 Godown Rd.
Columbus, OH 43220
614-459-3222
(p. 17, 46, 54, 164, 206, 217, 337)

Theatre of Magic
771 West End Ave.
New York, NY 10025
212-663-5380
(p. App-25)

Theatre of the Open Eye
316 East 88th St.
New York, NY 10128
212-534-6909 212-534-6363
(p. App-25)

Theatre Off Park
28 East 35th St.
New York, NY 10016
212-679-5684
(p. App-25)

Theatre Opera Music Institute Inc.
23 West 73rd St.
New York, NY 10023
212-787-3980
(p. App-28, App-33)

Theatre Production Services
133 West 19th St.
New York, NY 10011
212-206-7555
(p. 351)

Theatre Projects
155 West 72nd St. #503
New York, NY 10023
212-873-7211
(p. App-8)

Theatre Techniques Associates Inc.
PO Box 335
Cornwall-on-Hudson, NY 12520
212-585-1070
(p. 319)

Theatrebooks Inc.
1576 Broadway 3rd Fl.
New York, NY 10036
212-757-2834
(p. 44)

Theatreffects, Lewis Gluck
152 West 25th St.
New York, NY 10001
212-242-6754
(p. 337)

Theatrical Wardrobe Attendants Union
Local 764
1501 Broadway
New York, NY 10036
212-221-1717
(p. App-13)

Things Antique
483 Amsterdam Ave.
New York, NY 10024
212-873-4655
(p. 12)

Think Big
390 Broadway
New York, NY 10012
212-925-7300
(p. 217)

Third Avenue Bazaar
1145 Third Ave.
New York, NY 10021
212-988-7600
1362 Third Ave.
New York, NY 10021
212-861-5999
(p. 167, 193)

Thompson Art Mirror Co. Inc.
50 Dey St.
Jersey City, NJ 07306
212-929-3085
(p. 178)

Thonet Industries
305 East 63rd St. 14th Fl.
New York, NY 10021
212-421-3520
(p. 173)

Three Lives & Company Ltd.
154 West 10th St.
New York, NY 10014
212-741-2069
(p. 44)

3-G Stage Corp.
236 West 61st St.
New York, NY 10023
212-247-3130
(p. App-30)
Stage I 212-247-3147
Stage II 212-247-3148
(p. App-3)

3M Adhesives
15 Henderson Dr.
West Caldwell, NJ 07006
212-285-9600
(p. 3)

3M Company
3M Center
St. Paul, MN 55144
612-733-1110 612-733-5454
(p. App-16)

380 Services
380 Bleecker St.
New York, NY 10014
212-255-6652
(p. 286)

Thrift Shop East
1430 Third Ave.
New York, NY 10028
212-744-5429
(p. 353)

Thru the Lens Foto Co.
1296 First Ave.
New York, NY 10021
212-734-0245
(p. 272)

Thunder and Light
171 Bowery
New York, NY 10002
212-219-0180
(p. 209)

Thur L. P.
126 West 23rd St.
New York, NY 10011
212-243-4913
(p. 247, 369)

Tianguis Folk Art
284 Columbus Ave.
New York, NY 10023
212-799-7343
(p. 121)

Tic Tock Clock Co.
763 Ninth Ave.
New York, NY 10019
212-247-1470
(p. 59)

Tiffany & Co.
727 Fifth Ave.
New York, NY 10022
212-755-8000
(p. 57)

Tigers Only
PO Box 1025
Freehold, NJ 07728
201-928-4440
(p. 5)

Tile Distributors
7 King's Highway
New Rochelle, NY 10801
914-633-7200
(p. 355)

Times Square Shoppers World Ltd.
201 West 49th St.
New York, NY 10019
212-765-8342
(p. 218)

Times Square Stage Lighting
318 West 47th St.
New York, NY 10036
212-245-4155
(p. 164, 206)

Tinsel Trading
47 West 38th St.
New York, NY 10018
212-730-1030
(p. 147, 369)

Tiny Doll House
231 East 53rd St.
New York, NY 10022
212-752-3082
(p. 112)

Tip Top/Lebensfeld Top Equipment
222 Bowery
New York, NY 10012
212-925-1998 212-925-1999
(p. 173)

Tischler Marvin
74 West 47th St.
New York, NY 10036
212-719-1647
(p. 119)

Toffler Herbert L. & Sons Inc.
902 Broadway
New York, NY 10010
212-982-5700
(p. 149)

Tokyo Bookstore
521 Fifth Ave.
New York, NY 10175
212-697-0840
115 West 57th St.
New York, NY 10019
212-582-4622
(p. 44, 123)

Tool Warehouse
9 Willow Park Center
Farmingdale, NY 11735
516-420-1420
(p. 359)

Tower Chemist Inc.
1257 Second Ave.
New York, NY 10021
212-838-1490
(p. 225)

Tower Optical
PO Box 251
South Norwalk, CT 06856
203-866-4535
(p. 348)

Tower Records
692 Broadway
New York, NY 10012
212-505-1500
1961 Broadway
New York, NY 10023
212-799-2500
(p. 310)

Town Hall
123 West 43rd St.
New York, NY 10036
212-840-2824
(p. App-28)

Toy Balloon Corp.
204 East 38th St.
New York, NY 10016
212-682-3803
(p. 29)

Toy Park
112 East 86th St.
New York, NY 10028
212-427-6611
(p. 360)

Tracy Frank (Bearing Industry Corp.)
14 Wooster St.
New York, NY 10013
212-226-3500
(p. 234)

Trader The
385 Canal St.
New York, NY 10013
212-925-6610 212-925-6634
(p. 84)

Train Shop The
23 West 45th St.
New York, NY 10036
212-730-0409
(p. 187)

Trash & Vaudeville Inc.
4 Saint Marks Place
New York, NY 10003
212-982-3590
(p. 72)

Travers Tool Co.
25-26 50th St.
Woodside, NY 11377
718-932-9400
(p. 359)

Trebor Textiles Inc.
275 West 39th St.
New York, NY 10018
212-221-1818
(p. 132)

Tree Mark Shoe Co. Inc.
27 West 35th St.
New York, NY 10001
212-594-0720
(p. 61)

Tremont Nail Co.
PO Box 111
Wareham, MA 02517
617-295-0038
(p. 182)

Tremont Pleating Ltd.
306 West 37th St.
New York, NY 10018
212-279-2232 212-279-4266
(p. 118)

Trenk Morris
90 Orchard St.
New York, NY 10002
212-674-3498
(p. 78)

Treo Label Co. Inc.
16 West 22nd St.
New York, NY 10010
212-243-6561
(p. 197)

Tri-Ess Sciences Inc.
622 West Colorado St.
Glendale, CA 91204
818-247-6910
(p. 337)

Tricon Colors Inc.
16 Leliarts Lane
Elmwood Park, NJ 07407
201-794-3800
(p. 256, 261)

Trieste Export Corp.
568 Twelfth Ave.
New York, NY 10036
212-246-1548
(p. 345)

Trim Corporation of America
459 West 15th St.
New York, NY 10011
212-989-1616
(p. 110)

Trinity Theatre
164 West 100th St.
New York, NY 10025
212-496-8923
(p. App-25)

Tripler F. R. & Co.
366 Madison Ave.
New York, NY 10017
212-922-1090
(p. 62, 81)

TRITON GALLERIES INC.
323 West 45th St.
New York, NY 10036
212-765-2472
(p. 280)

Triumph Belt Inc.
555 Eighth Ave. 24th Fl.
New York, NY 10018
212-564-5700
(p. 59)

Truck & Warehouse Theatre
79 East 4th St.
New York, NY 10003
212-254-5060
(p. App-26)

Tudor Electrical Supply Co. Inc.
226 East 46th St.
New York, NY 10017
212-867-7550
(p. 116)

Tunnel Barrel & Drum Co.
85 Triangle Blvd.
Carlstadt, NJ 07072
212-925-8190
(p. 30)

Tunnel Machinery Exchange
353 Canal St.
New York, NY 10013
212-226-0727
(p. 228, 234)

Tunnel Stationery
301 Canal St.
New York, NY 10013
212-431-6330
(p. 343)

Twentieth Century Draperies Inc.
70 Wooster St.
New York, NY 10012
212-925-7707
(p. 102, 373)

Twentieth Century Plastics
3628 Crenshaw Blvd.
Los Angeles, CA 90016
213-731-0900
(p. 271)

20-20 Colorists
20 West 20th St.
New York, NY 10011
212-255-6579
(p. 115)

Twigs Inc.
399 Bleecker
New York, NY 10014
212-620-8188
(p. 160)

- U -

U-Haul Moving & Storage
562 West 23rd St.
New York, NY 10011
212-562-3800
(p. 235, App-3)

U.S. Balloon Mfg. Co.
1613 Oriental Blvd.
Brooklyn, NY 11235
718-646-1110
(p. 29, 210)

U.S. Egg
1 Worth St.
New York, NY 10013
212-925-1713
(p. 265)

U.S. Games Systems Inc.
38 East 32 St.
New York, NY 10016
212-685-4300
(p. 175)

Ullman Jeffrey
145 West 27th St. #4E
New York, NY 10001
212-929-5614
(p. 93)

Umanov Matt Guitars
273 Bleecker St.
New York, NY 10014
212-675-2157
(p. 238)

Umla Walter E. Inc.
180 6th St.
Brooklyn, NY 11215
718-624-3350
(p. 214)

Uncle Sam Umbrella Shop
7 East 46th St.
New York, NY 10017
212-687-4780 (continues)

Uncle Sam Umbrella Shop (continued)
161 West 57th St.
New York, NY 10019
212-247-7163 212-582-1976
(p. 68)

Uncle Steve's
343 Canal St.
New York, NY 10013
212-226-4010
(p. 26)

Uniform World
Oswald Place
Staten Island, NY 10309
718-981-4000
(p. 84)

Union Pin Co.
Box 427
New Hartford, CT 06057
203-379-3397
(p. 248)

Unique Clothing Warehouse The
718 Broadway
New York, NY 10003
212-674-1767
(p. 81)

United Beauty Supply
49 West 46th St.
New York, NY 10036
212-719-2324
(p. 33)

United City Ice Cube Co.
44th St. & Tenth Ave.
New York, NY 10019
212-563-0819
(p. 190, App-3)

United Corrugated Shipping Supplies
84 Ferris
Brooklyn, NY 11231
718-855-7755
(p. 252)

United House Wrecking
328 Selleck St.
Stamford, CT 06902
203-348-5371
(p. 15)

United Parcel Service
601 West 43rd St.
New York, NY 10036
212-695-7500
(p. 324)

United Resin Products Inc.
100 Sutton St.
Brooklyn, NY 11222
212-384-3000
(p. 3)

United Scenic Artists (USA)
Local 829
575 Eighth Ave. 3rd Fl.
New York, NY 10018
212-736-4498
(p. App-13)

United States Bronze Powders
PO Box 31, Route 202
Flemington, NJ 08822
201-782-5454
(p. 253)

United States Gypsum
Kor Center East A
Interstate Industrial Park
Bellmawr, NJ 08031
609-933-2171
(p. 54)

United States Institute of Theatre Technology (USITT)
330 West 42nd St.
New York, NY 10036
212-563-5551
(p. App-13)

Universal Musical Instrument Co.
732 Broadway
New York, NY 10003
212-254-6917
(p. 238)

Universal Rehearsal & Recording
17 West 20th St.
New York, NY 10011
212-929-3277
(p. App-33)

University Dental Supply Co.
220 East 23rd St.
New York, NY 10010
212-889-0232
(p. 104)

Unpainted Furniture by Knosos
538 Sixth Ave.
New York, NY 10011
212-242-0966
(p. 174)

Unsloppy Copy Shop
5 West 8th St.
New York, NY 10011
212-254-7336
(p. 286)

UPI Photo Library
48 East 21st St. 11th Fl.
New York, NY 10010
212-777-6200
(p. App-8)

Urban Archeology
135 Spring St.
New York, NY 10012
212-431-6969
(p. 15)

Urethane Products Co. Inc.
Plaza Ave.
New Hyde Park, NY 11040
718-343-3400 516-488-3600
(p. 54)

Urmson Kathy
252 Carlton Ave.
Brooklyn, NY 11205
718-522-0368
(p. 295)

US Dept. of Labor
90 Church St. Rm. 1407
New York, NY 10007
212-264-9840
(p. App-14)

US Fur Cleaners Inc.
208 West 29th St.
New York, NY 10001
212-736-4777
(p. 58)

US General Hardware
700 Mid-Island Shopping Plaza
Hicksville, NY 11801
516-433-2562
(p. 359)

Usdan William & Sons
52 Thompson St.
New York, NY 10012
212-226-6177
(p. 373)

Utilla Richard
112 Christopher St.
New York, NY 10014
212-929-7059 (continues)

Utilla Richard (continued)
244 East 60th St.
New York, NY 10022
212-737-6673
(p. 72)

Utrecht Art & Drafting Supplies
111 Fourth Ave.
New York, NY 10003
212-777-5353
(p. 23)

- V -

Vadar Industries Ltd.
750 Tenth Ave.
NY 10019
212-307-6556 800-221-9511
(p. 145, 351)

Van Doren Rubber Co. Inc.
2220 Orangewood
Anaheim, CA 92806
714-772-8270
(p. 62)

Van Dyke Jill
154 East 7th St. #RW
New York, NY 10009
212-533-4192
(p. 93)

Van Gogh Movers
126 Wooster St.
New York, NY 10012
212-226-0500 212-431-5450
(p. 235)

Van Wyck Drapery Hardware Supply
39 Eldridge St.
New York, NY 10002
212-925-1300
(p. 370)

Van-Man Adhesives Corp.
100 S. 4th St.
Brooklyn, NY 11211
718-384-6110
(p. 3)

VANCO STAGE LIGHTING INC.
R1 Box 477A Rt. 210
Stony Point, NY 10980
914-942-0075 800-55VANCO
(p. 206)

Vandam Theatre
15 Vandam St.
New York, NY 10013
212-242-251
(p. App-22)

VanDyke Hatters
90 Greenwich Ave.
New York, NY 10011
212-929-5696
(p. 67)

Variety Scenic Studios
25-19 Borden Ave.
L.I.C., NY 11101
718-392-4747
(p. 28, 100, 319)

Vee's Fashions
5 Pell St.
New York, NY 10013
212-962-3063
(p. 124)

Velasquez David
523 Hudson St. #5RS
New York, NY 10014
212-929-1724
(p. 307)

Velcro USA
406 Browne Ave., PO Box 4806
Manchester, NH 03108
603-669-4892
220 Little Falls Rd.
Cedargrove, NJ 07009
201-661-0714
(p. 250)

Velvets Inc.
PO Box 165, Short Hills
NJ 07078
201-379-4272
(p. 132)

Venaglia Mark Victor
244 West 21st St.
New York, NY 10011
212-691-1141
(p. 295)

Veritas
527 West 45tn St.
New York, NY 10036
212-581-2050
(p. App-30)

Vertipile Co.
261 Fifth Ave. #503
New York, NY 10016
212-679-6390 800-225-6315
(p. 156)

Veteran Caning Shop
550 West 35th St.
New York, NY 10001
212-868-3244
(p. 174, 309)

Veteran Leather Co.
204 25th St.
Brooklyn, NY 11232
718-768-0300
(p. 201)

Victor Machinery Exchange
251 Centre St.
New York, NY 10013
212-226-3494
(p. 215)

Victoria Falls
451 W. Broadway
New York, NY 10012
212-254-2433
(p. 72)

Victory 5 & 10
360 West 55th St.
New York, NY 10019
212-246-1930
(p. 377)

Vidachrome Inc.
1260 West 35th St. Rm. 503
New York, NY 10018
212-391-8124
(p. 272)

Vigdor Linda
53 East 97th St. #1B
New York, NY 10029
212-289-1218
(p. 93, 295)

Viking-Criterion Paper Co.
55-30 46th St.
Maspeth, NY 11378
718-392-7400
(p. 3)

Village Corset Shop The
49 East 8th St.
New York, NY 10003
212-473-1820
(p. 78)

Village Flute & Sax Shop
35 Carmine St.
New York, NY 10014
212-243-1276
(p. 238)

Village Gate
160 Bleecker St.
New York, NY 10012
212-475-5120
(p. App-22)

Village Oak
456 Hudson St.
New York, NY 10014
212-924-7651
(p. 12)

Village Oaksmith Antiques
1321 Second Ave.
New York, NY 10021
212-535-1451
(p. 12)

Vincent's
136 West 21st St. 6th Fl.
New York, NY 10011
212-741-3423
(p. 97)

Vineyard Theatre
309 East 26th St.
New York, NY 10010
212-696-4103
(p. App-28)

Vintage Wood Works
513 S. Adams
Fredericksburg, TX 78624
512-997-9513
(p. 15)

Virginia Theatre
245 West 52nd St.
New York, NY 10019
212-974-9853 212-977-9370
(p. App-19)

Vogue Hat Block & Die Corp.
129 West 20th St.
New York, NY 10011
212-243-6400
(p. 230)

Volunteer Lawyers for the Arts
1560 Broadway #711
New York, NY 10036
212-575-1150
(p. App-13)

Von Rosentiel Helene Inc.
382 11th St.
Brooklyn, NY 11215
718-788-7909
(p. 58, 311)

Vortex Theatre
164 Eleventh Ave.
New York, NY 10011
212-206-1764
(p. App-26)

- W -

Wagner Sherle International Inc.
60 East 57th St.
New York, NY 10022
212-758-3300
(p. 193)

Walbead Inc.
29-76 Northam Blvd.
L.I.C., NY 11101
718-392-7616
(p. 111, 363)

Wall St. Camera Exchange Inc.
82 Wall St.
New York, NY 10005
212-344-0011
(p. 271)

Wallpaper East Inc.
1190 Third Ave.
New York, NY 10021
212-861-9420
(p. 379)

Wallpaper Mart
187 Lexington Ave.
New York, NY 10016
212-889-4900
(p. 379)

Walter's Wicker Wonderland
991 Second Ave.
New York, NY 10022
212-758-0472
(p. 382)

Walton Hauling & Warehouse Corp.
609 West 46th St.
New York, NY 10036
212-246-8685
(p. 236)

Ward Jack Color
220 East 23rd St. 4th Fl.
New York, NY 10010
212-725-5200
(p. 272)

Warlock Shop/ Magical Childe
35 West 19th St.
New York, NY 10011
212-242-7182
(p. 251)

Washington Millinery Supply
8501 Atlas Dr.
Gathersburg, MD 20760
301-963-4444
(p. 231)

WAVES
32 East 13th St.
New York, NY 10003
212-989-9284
(p. 12, 26)

Weinstock Brothers Inc.
384 Third Ave.
New York, NY 10016
212-532-8057
(p. 184)

Weiser Samuel Inc.
132 East 24th St.
New York, NY 10010
212-777-6363
(p. 44, 251)

Weiss & Katz
187 Orchard St.
New York, NY 10002
212-477-1130
(p. 132)

Weiss & Mahoney
142 Fifth Ave.
New York, NY 10011
212-675-1915 212-675-1367
(p. 84, 341)

WEISS I. & SONS INC.
2-07 Borden Ave.
L.I.C., NY 11101
212-246-8444
(p. 101, 145, 155, 374)

WEISS PETER DESIGNS
32 Union Square East
New York, NY 10003
212-477-2659
(p. 301, 337)

Welcome Home Antiques
556 Columbus Ave.
New York, NY 10024
212-362-4293
(p. 12)

Weller Fabrics Inc.
54 West 57th St.
New York, NY 10019
212-247-3790
(p. 132)

Weller Soldering Equipment
Box 728
Apex, NC 27502
919-362-7510
(p. 191)

West Side Bicycle
231 West 96th St.
New York, NY 10025
212-663-7531
(p. 35)

West Side Comics
107 West 86th St.
New York, NY 10024
212-724-0432
(p. 217)

West Third Street Bazaar
125 West 3rd St.
New York, NY 10012
212-673-4138
(p. 167, 194)

Westbeth Theatre Center
151 Bank St.
New York, NY 10014
212-691-2272
(p. App-26, App-33)

Westchester Fiberglass
55 Purdy Ave.
Port Chester, NY 10573
914-939-5543
(p. 49)

Westchester Hobby
102 East Post Rd.
White Plains, NY 10601
914-949-7943
(p. 187)

Westchester Scenic
578 Nepperhan Ave.
Yonkers, NY 10701
914-423-0407
(p. 319)

Westchester Taxidermy Quality Mounts
2814 Hickory St.
Yorktown Heights, NY 10598
914-245-1728
(p. 347)

Western Costume Co.
5335 Melrose Ave.
Hollywood, CA 90038
213-469-1451
(p. 97)

Westmore Shoe Repair
331 West 57th St.
New York, NY 10019
212-245-7487
(p. 324)

Westside Arts Theatre
407 West 43rd St.
New York, NY 10036
212-541-8394 212-246-6351
(p. App-22)

Whiting and Davis
10 West 33rd St.
New York, NY 10001
212-736-5810
(p. 229)

Whittman Lawrence Co.
1395 Morkoni Blvd.
Copiague, NY 11726
516-842-4770
(p. 49)

Wicker Garden The
1318 Madison Ave.
New York, NY 10028
212-348-1166
(p. 382)

Wicker's Randy Uplift Inc.
506 Hudson St.
New York, NY 10014
212-929-3632
(p. 210)

Wickery The
342 Third Ave.
New York, NY 10010
212-889-3669
(p. 31, 382)

Wifemistress
1044 Lexington Ave.
New York, NY 10021
212-570-9529
(p. 78)

Wig City
2895 Third Ave.
Bronx, NY 10455
212-585-3300
(p. 180)

Wild H. L.
510 East 11th St.
New York, NY 10009
212-228-2345
(p. 184)

Wilde John & Bro. Inc.
3705 Main St.
Philadelphia, PA 19127
215-482-8800
(p. 381)

Wilke Pipe Shop
400 Madison Ave.
New York, NY 10017
212-755-1118
(p. 331)

Williams Brad
214 Riverside Dr. #109
New York, NY 10025
212-865-0088
(p. 224, 295, 307)

Williams K. P. Co.
295 Madison Ave.
New York, NY 10017
212-683-8162
(p. 375)

Willoughby-Peerless Camera Store
110 West 32nd St.
New York, NY 10001
212-564-1600
(p. 271)

Willson Safety Prod/Div WGM Safety
PO Box 622
Reading, PA 19603
215-376-6161
(p. App-16)

Wilton Co.
18th & Franklin St.
Columbia, PA 17512
717-684-9000
(p. 268)

Winik Seymour Inc.
245 West 29th St.
New York, NY 10001
212-563-3622
(p. 199)

Winsor and Newton Inc.
555 Winsor Dr.
Secaucus, NJ 07094
201-864-9100
(p. 23)

Winston's Contemporaneous Hardware
91 Greenwich Ave.
New York, NY 10014
212-242-1681
(p. 195)

WINTER CO. INC. THE
323 Sixth St. Top Fl.
Brooklyn, NY 11215
718-499-2206
(p. 93, 295, 326)

Winter Garden Theatre
1634 Broadway
New York, NY 10019
212-664-9608 212-239-6200
(p. App-19)

Winzer Ernest
1828 Cedar Ave.
Bronx, NY 10453
212-294-2400
(p. 114, App-3)

Wire Frame Shop
622 West 47th St.
New York, NY 10036
212-586-4239
(p. 381)

Witkin Harriet Assoc.
210 Eleventh Ave. 4th Fl.
New York, NY 10001
212-691-1286
(p. 110)

Wittenberg A. Surgical Appliance
1400 Madison Ave.
New York, NY 10029
212-876-7023
(p. 225)

Wolf Forms
39 West 19th St. 8th Fl.
New York, NY 10011
212-255-4508
(p. 114)

Wolf Paints
771 Ninth Ave.
New York, NY 10019
212-245-7777
(p. 253, 258, 261, 379)

Wolf Paper and Twine Co.
680 Sixth Ave.
New York, NY 10010
212-675-4870
(p. 252)

Wolf-Gordon Wallcovering Inc.
132 West 21st St.
New York, NY 10011
212-255-3300
(p. 86)

Wolff Computer
1841 Broadway
New York, NY 10023
212-307-6545
(p. 85)

Wolff Harold C. Inc. Hardware
127 Fulton St. 3rd Fl.
New York, NY 10038
212-227-2128
(p. 359)

Wolff Office Equipment
1860 Broadway
New York, NY 10023
212-246-7890
(p. 172)

Wolfman-Gold & Good
484 Broome St.
New York, NY 10016
212-431-1888
(p. 31, 195, 211)

Women's Inter-Art Center
549 West 52nd St.
New York, NY 10019
212-246-1050
(p. 326)

Women's Occupational Health Resource Center
60 Haven Ave. Rm. B-106
New York, NY 10032
212-781-5719
(p. App-14)

Wood Audrey Theatre
359 West 48th St.
New York, NY 10036
212-307-5452 212-307-5547
212-308-5933
(p. App-22)

Woodard T. American Antiques/Quilts
835 Madison Ave.
New York, NY 10021
212-988-2906 (p. 308)

Wooden Indian Antiques
60 West 15th St.
New York, NY 10011
212-243-8590
(p. 57)

Woolworth's
120 West 34th St.
New York, NY 10001
212-563-3523
761 Broadway
New York, NY 10003
212-475-7440
12 East 14th St.
New York, NY 10003
212-691-6290
46 East 23rd St.
New York, NY 10010
212-254-8541
170 East 42nd St.
New York, NY 10017
212-687-0676
755 Seventh Ave.
New York, NY 10019
212-246-5069
983 Eighth Ave.
New York, NY 10019
212-265-4686
976 Third Ave.
New York, NY 10022
212-755-8634
1133 Third Ave.
New York, NY 10021
212-861-6455
1504 Second Ave.
New York, NY 10021
212-861-6500
Broadway & 79th St.
New York, NY 10024
212-362-7088
(p. 377)

Workbench
470 Park Ave. South
New York, NY 10016
212-481-5454
2091 Broadway
New York, NY 10023
212-724-3670
1320 Third Ave.
New York, NY 10021
212-753-1173
(p. 169)

World of Guns
33 Gazza
Farmingdale, NY 11735
516-249-1832
(p. 17)
Worth Auto Supply
31 Cooper Square
New York, NY 10003
212-777-5920
(p. 27)
WPA Theatre
138 Fifth Ave.
New York, NY 10011
212-691-2274 212-206-0523
(p. App-26)
Writers' Theatre
133 Second Ave.
New York, NY 10003
212-777-7005
(p. App-26)

- X -

X-Acto Corp.
45-35 Van Dam St.
L.I.C., NY 11101
718-392-3333
(p. 187)

- Y -

Yale Picture Frame and Molding Co.
770 Fifth Ave.
Brooklyn, NY 11232
718-788-6200
(p. 232)
Yankee Peddler
639 Hudson St.
New York, NY 10003
212-243-2005
(p. 13)
Yardstick Fabric Store The
54 West 14th St.
New York, NY 10011
212-924-7131
(p. 133)
Yarn Center The
61 West 37th St.
New York, NY 10008
212-921-9293
(p. 381)
Yates Vernon
782 West End Ave.
New York, NY 10025
212-666-4191
(p. 93)
Yomiuri Press/ Yomiuri Shimbun
41 East 42nd St.
New York, NY 10017
212-661-5977
(p. 124, 239)
York End Antiques
1388 Lexington Ave.
New York, NY 10128
212-534-0777
(p. 174)
York Feather & Down Corp.
10 Evergreen Ave.
Brooklyn, NY 11206
718-497-4120
(p. 113)
York Floral
804 Sixth Ave.
New York, NY 10001
212-686-2070
(p. 20, 160)
York Novelty Imports Inc.
10 West 37th St.
New York, NY 10018
212-594-7040
(p. 363)
Young Louise Gartlemann
243 West 21st St. #1D
New York, NY 10011
212-675-7497
(p. 93, 296, 307)
Young Steve
243 West 21st St. #1D
New York, NY 10011
212-675-7497
(p. 307)
Yuille Scott
59 Strong Place
Brooklyn, NY 11231
718-858-4161
(p. 296)

Yurkiw Mark Ltd.
568 Broadway
New York, NY 10012
212-226-6338
(p. 338)

- Z -

Zabar's Mezzanine
2245 Broadway
NY 10024
212-787-2000
(p. 195)
Zanfini Canvas/ Zanfini Brothers
57 Front St.
Brooklyn, NY 11201
718-625-6630
(p. 134, App-3)
Zanki Donna E.
1923 Oswego St.
Aurora, CO 80010
303-364-5299
(p. 93, 224)
Zarin Harry Co.
72 Allen St. 2nd Fl.
New York, NY 10002
212-226-3492
(p. 102, 136)
Zauder Brothers
10 Henry St.
Freeport, NY 11520
516-379-2600
(p. 180, 219)
Zeeman Corp.
575 Eighth Ave.
New York, NY 10018
212-947-3558
(p. 231)
Zimmet Dr. M. Optometrist
805 Eighth Ave.
New York, NY 10019
212-246-5556
(p. 63)
Zipper Service
11 West 32nd St.
New York, NY 10001
212-947-7770
(p. 181)
Zotta Alice
2 West 45th St.
New York, NY 10036
212-840-7657
(p. 311)
Zucker Products Corp.
236 West 18th St.
New York, NY 10003
212-741-3400
(p. 366)
ZYGAROWICZ ANNETTE
9235 Foster Ave.
Brooklyn, NY 11236
718-272-5281
(p. 296)

APPENDIXES

AFTER HOURS

Services available after 1am or before 7am

A & B Leather & Findings Co. 212-265-8124
500 West 52nd St. (10-11) NYC 10019
Hours: 6am- 3pm Mon-Fri
"Barge, Magix, Fiebings, rawhide lacings, glovers and lacing needles."

A & S Ribbon Supply Co. 212-255-0280
108 West 27th St. (6-7th) NYC 10001
Hours: 5am- 2pm Mon-Fri
"Wholesale satin and grosgrain ribbon." ed.

Chingos and Sons Inc. 212-689-0476
818 Sixth Ave. (28-29th) NYC 10001 212-684-6938
Hours: 4am- 3pm Mon-Fri
"Wholesale floral supplies and flowers." ed.

Colony Records 212-265-2050
1691 Broadway (49th) NYC 10019
Hours: 9:30am-2:30am Mon-Fri/ 10am-3am Sat
"Large selection of popular and classical records, sheet music; will ship anywhere." ed.

Emery Worldwide 212-995-6400
184-54 149th Ave. Jamaica, NY 11413
Hours: 24 hours at airport office
"Fast service by air." ed.

Gemco Dental Supplies 718-438-3270
1010 McDonald Ave., Bklyn, 11230 718-871-3900
Hours: 6:30-6 Mon-Fri
"Dental tools, teeth, lab equipment; see Leo Weiss." ed.

Greyhound Package Service (gen. info.) 212-971-6405
Port Authority Bus Terminal (priority svc.) 212-971-6331
9th Ave. & 41st NYC 10036 (arrival info.) 212-6311
Hours: 24 hours every day (pickup & delivery) 212-971-6407
"Package shipping by bus." ed. (pickup & delivery) 212-971-0483

Historic Newspaper Archives 201-381-2332
1582 Hart St., Rahway, NJ 07065 800-526-7843
Hours: Orders taken 24 hours
"Back date newspapers, originals 1880-1974, of major US cities; catalog available." ed.

Images 212-889-8510
9 East 37th St. 8th Fl. (5th) NYC 10016
Hours: 24 hours
"Typesetting; expensive, very good and reliable: see Steve Mahler."

Kervar Inc. 212-564-2525
119 West 28th St. (6-7th) NYC 10001
Hours: 6:30am- 3pm Mon-Fri
"Floral supplies, silk flowers, artificial greenery, fruits, vegetables; wholesale only." ed.

L. I. Beef 212-243-8967
565 West St. (Gansevoort-W. 12th) NYC 10014
Hours: 5am-2pm Mon-Fri
"Pheasant, quail, game with feathers; also beef." ed.

New York Florists Supply Co. 212-564-6086
103 West 28th St. (6th) NYC 10001
Hours: 5am-2:30pm Mon-Fri/ 5am-12 noon Sat
"Floral supplies; wholesale only." ed.

Pa-Ko Cutlery & Scales 212-962-8641
104 South St. (near Fulton) NYC 10038
Hours: 2am- 10am Mon-Fri
"Scales, knives, gloves, hooks, scalers, brushes; see Jimmy." ed.

Pink Pussycat Boutique 212-243-0077
161 West 4th St. (6th Ave.) NYC 10012
Hours: 11am-2am Sun-Thurs/ 11am-3am Fri, Sat
"Leather, studs, lingerie, inflatable dolls, handcuffs, drug paraphernalia, sex toys." ed.

PRO Chemical & Dye Co. 617-676-3838
PO Box 14, Somerset, MA 02726
Hours: 24 hour phone service
"Cold water dyes, wide variety of colors." ed.

Rialto Florist 212-688-3234
707 Lexington Ave. (57th) NYC 10022
Hours: 24 hours every day
"Good stock fresh flowers and plants." ed.

Saint James Gourmet Importers 212-243-1120
565 West St. (Gansevoort) NYC 10014
Hours: 4am- 3pm Mon-Fri
"Restaurant supplier of game (with feathers); nice guy, very helpful."

SMP Graphic Service Center 212-254-2282
26 East 22nd St. (B'way-Park Ave. S.) NYC 10011
Hours: 24 hours Mon-Fri/ 11-6 Sat,Sun
"Dry mounting, blow-ups to 4' x 8', many other services." ed.

U-Haul Moving & Storage 212-562-3800
562 West 23rd St. (10-11th) NYC 10011
Hours: 24 hour rental arrangements
"Packing blankets, rent or buy; boxes, dollies." ed.

United City Ice Cube Co. 212-563-0819
44th St. & 10th Ave., NYC 10019
Hours: 24 hour delivery service
"Block, cube, dry ice; purchases at truck 44th St. and 10th Ave."

Ernest Winzer 212-294-2400
1828 Cedar Ave. (179-Major Deegan) Bronx 10453
Hours: 6:30am- 5 pm Mon-Fri
"Drycleaning; pick-up and delivery service." ed.

Zanfini Canvas/ Zanfini Brothers 718-625-6630
57 Front St. Bklyn 11201
Hours: 5am- 3pm Mon-Fri/ or by appt.
"Canvas specialties, custom bags, tarps; see Tony." ed.

DESIGN RESOURCES

American Heritage Publishing Co. Library 212-399-8930
10 Rockefeller Plaza (49th btwn 5-6th) NYC 10020
Hours: 9:30-5:30 Mon-Fri (appt. required)
"Art and history, primarily American; 17,000 volumes; 250,000 pictures; B & W and color." ed.

American Museum of Natural History Library 212-873-1300
79th & Central Park West, NYC 10024
Hours: 11-4 Mon-Fri
"Photographic collection: 500,000 black and white; 60,000 slides." ed.

Anthology Film Archives Library 212-226-0100
491 Broadway (Broome) NYC 10013
Hours: 10-5 Mon-Fri (appt. required)
"Films, stills, posters." ed.

Bettmann Archives 212-758-0362
136 East 57th St. (3rd-Lexington) NYC 10022
Hours: 9-5 Mon-Fri (preferably by appt.)
"Special collections include resources of the BBC Hulton Picture Library (Great Britain's largest picture agency); research fee minimum of $35."

The Brooklyn Museum: 718-638-5000 x 308
Art Reference Library
200 Eastern Parkway (Washington Ave.) Bklyn 11238
Hours: 1-5 Mon-Fri
"Art and ethnology relating to American painting and sculpture, decorative arts, costumes and textiles. Fashion sketches: 1900-1950, leading American designers." ed.

Columbia University: 212-280-3501
Avery Architectural & Fine Arts Library
Avery Hall, Columbia University (B'way & 116th) NYC 10027
Hours: 9-11 Mon-Thurs/ 9-9 Fri/ 10-7 Sat/ 12-10 Sun
"Architecture, archeology, city planning, housing, painting, sculpture, decorative arts, graphic arts. ID and letter of reference required for non-Columbia students." ed.

Conde Nast Publications Inc. Library 212-880-8244
350 Madison Ave. (44th) NYC 10017
Hours: 1-4 Mon-Fri (by appt. only)
"Fashions, houses and gardens, including all art work for Conde Nast magazines." ed.

Cooper Hewitt Museum of Design Library 212-860-6868
2 East 91st St. (5th) NYC 10028
Hours: 9-5:30 Mon-Fri (appt. & ID required)
"Decorative arts and design books on textiles, early natural history, architecture and interiors. The picture collection of 1,500,000 items is filed by category." ed.

Cooper Union for the Advancement of Science and Art Library 212-254-6300 x 323
Cooper Square (3rd Ave. & 8th St.) NYC 10003
Hours: 9-5 Mon-Fri (appt. & ID required)
"Art, architecture." ed.

Costume Society of America 201-536-6216
15 Littlejohn Rd., PO Box 761, Englishtown, NJ 07726
Hours: Initial request by letter for consultation & information.
"Various publications, newsletter and journal; annual membership fee. See Kay Boyer; consultation service for the indentification and conservation of costumes." ed.

Dover Publications 212-255-3755
180 Varick St. 9th Fl. (Houston) NYC 10014
Hours: 9-4 Mon-Fri
"Mail order catalogs with a thorough collection of paperback books on fine arts and crafts with many facsimile reproductions and excellent pictorial archives." ed.

The Fabric Library 212-302-0925
63 West 38th St. Rm 500 (6th) NYC 10018
Hours: 9-5:30 Mon-Fri
"Comprehensive catalog of domestic fabric manufacturers, for reference only." ed.

Fashion Institute of Technology, Library/Media Service 212-760-7780
227 West 27th St. (7th) NYC 10001
Hours: 9-10 Mon-Fri/ 12-5 Sat,Sun
"Fashion, textile and interior design; extensive collection of costumes and textile swatches. Research fee, letter of reference, appointment necessary for special collections." ed.

Fireside Theatre Book Club mail only
Dept. ER-658, Garden City, NY 11530
Hours: mail order only
"Subscription service for original scripts and plays." ed.

Freelance Photographers' Guild Library 212-777-4210
251 Park Ave. South (20th) NYC 10010
Hours: 9-5:30 Mon-Fri
"2-3 million color transparencies and B & W photos, contemporary and historical collection; large format scenic transparencies. Agents in 30 key cities worldwide; charge for reproduction. Not for individual use, company authorization required." ed.

Frick Art Reference Library 212-288-8700
10 East 71st St. (5th) NYC 10021
Hours: 10-4 Mon-Fri/ 10-12 noon Sat (closed Sat: June, July) (not open in August)
"Paintings, drawings, sculpture and illuminated MSS of Western Europe and the US from the 4th century AD to c. 1860. Over 400,000 classified study photographs. ID required." ed.

The Metropolitan Museum of Art: 212-879-5500 x 628
Irene Lewisohn Costume Reference Library
Fifth Ave. and 82nd St., NYC 10028
Hours: 10-1 & 2-4:30 Tues-Fri (appt. required)
"Fashion sketches (originals), photographs, patterns, prints (fashion plates) from late 18th through second half of 20th century. Excellent collection of costumes from 17th-20th centuries." ed.

The Metropolitan Museum of Art: 212-879-5500 x 3261
Photograph and Slide Library
Fifth Ave. and 82nd St., NYC 10028
Hours: 10-4:30 Tues-Fri
"Extensive color and B & W slide and photograph collection covering history of art; 2 week rental policy; fee differs for profit and non-profit; current ID required." ed.

Museum of the City of New York 212-534-1672
Fifth Ave. at 103rd St., NYC 10029
Hours: 10-5 Tues-Sat/ 1-5 Sun
"Extensive 18th-20th century costumes and accessories, collection either made or purchased by New Yorkers." ed.

The Museum of Modern Art Library 212-708-9433
11 West 53rd St. (5th) NYC 10019
Hours: 1-5 Mon-Fri
"Painting, sculpture, graphic arts, drawing, architecture, design, photography, film." ed.

Music Theatre International 212-975-6897
49 East 52nd St. (Madison-Park) NYC 10022
Hours: 9-6 Mon-Fri
"Mail order catalog of musical scores." ed.

Natural Fiber Fabric Club — mail only
PO Box 1115, Mountainside, NJ 07092
Hours: mail order only
"Mail order fabric company that supply quarterly fabric swatches of imported and domestic natural fabrics. $10 subscription per year."

New York City Archives Municipal Dept. — 212-566-5292
31 Chambers St. (Centre) NYC 10007
Hours: 9-4:30 Mon-Fri
"History of the five boroughs. Universal pictures of New York City dating back to the 19th century; also court dockets. Photocopy service available. Good for pictures of specific neighborhoods." ed.

New York Public Library: — 212-621-0618
Donnell Library Center, Art Library
20 West 53rd St. (5th) NYC 10019
Hours: 9:30-7:45 Mon/ 9:30-5:15 Tues-Fri/ 12:30-5:15 Sat
"Books on visual and graphic arts, costume, textile design." ed.

New York Public Library & Museum — 212-870-1630
of the Performing Arts at Lincoln Center
111 Amsterdam Ave. (65th) NYC 10023
Hours: 10-8 Mon, Thurs/ 10-6 Tues, Sat/ 12-6 Wed, Fri
"The most thorough selection of music books and scores, records, drama, dance reference and circulating collections; also non-book materials including videotape archives and specialized research collections, clippings, sketches, etc.; photocopying service."

New York Public Library Picture Collection — 212-340-0877
Mid-Manhattan Library 3rd Fl.
8 East 40th St. (5th) NYC 10016
Hours: 12-5:45 Mon,Wed,Fri/ 12-7:45 Tues/ 10-5:45 Thurs
"2 1/4 million clippings from books and magazines covering pictorial subjects of all areas and periods: free consultation." ed.

New York Public Library Schomburg Center — 212-862-4000
for Research in Black Culture
515 Lenox Ave. (135th) NYC 10025
Hours: 12-5 Mon,Tues,Wed/ 10-6 Thurs,Fri,Sat
"Rare books, records, tapes, photographic and film archives and picture file." ed.

The New York Times Pictures — 212-556-1243
229 West 43rd St. (7-8th) NYC 10036
Hours: 9-5 Mon-Fri
"Over 4 million photos from date of 1st publication: requests for specific photos must be phoned in with date information, fees vary. If research is required add $25 fee." ed.

Princeton Antique Bookservice 609-344-1943
2915-17-31 Atlantic Ave., Atlantic City, NJ 08401
Hours: 9-5 Mon-Fri
"Book ordering service, will find out-of-print books." ed.

Pro Am Music Resources Inc. 914-761-6667
63 Prospect St., White Plains, NY 10606
Hours: 9-5 Mon-Fri
"Mail order catalog of books on theatre, music, costume." ed.

Rodgers & Hammerstein Theatre Library 212-486-0643
598 Madison Ave. (57-58th) NYC 10022
Hours: 9:30-5:30 Mon-Fri
"Mail order catalog of musicals." ed.

School of Visual Arts Library 212-679-7350 x 67
209 East 23rd St. (2-3rd) NYC 10010
Hours: 9-7:30 Mon-Thurs/ 9-5 Fri
"Fine arts, art history, photography, film, graphic design: 30,000 pictures, 30,000 slides. ID and letter of reference required for non-students." ed.

Theatre Projects 212-873-7211
155 West 72nd St. #503 (B'way-Columbus) NYC 10023
Hours: 9-5:30 Mon-Fri
"Advisory service for designing new and renovated buildings for performances." ed.

UPI Photo Library 212-777-6200
48 East 21st St. 11th Fl. (Park Ave. S.-B'way) NYC 10010
Hours: 24 hours Mon-Fri/ 11-7 Sat,Sun
"B & W and color photos; appointment needed, research fee." ed.

ORGANIZATIONS, UNIONS, & SUPPORT SERVICES

Accountants for the Public Interest Inc. 212-575-1828
36 West 44th St. Rm. 1201 NYC 10036 212-575-1816
"Provide ongoing seminar programs to teach basic accounting and bookkeeping procedures to New York based not-for-profit organizations." ed.

Actors' Equity Association 212-869-8530
165 West 46th St. (6th-7th) NYC 10036
"Union for actors and stage managers in legitimate theatre." ed.

Alliance of Resident Theatres (ART)/New York 212-989-5257
325 Spring St. Rm. 315 NYC 10013
"ART/New York serves over 80 of New York City's not-for-profit professional theatres. Through discussion groups, consultations and publications, the Alliance provides its members with services, skills and information to help them survive and flourish. ART/New York also functions as an information center for other artists, related professionals, students, the press, funding sources and the general public. Publishes 'Theatre Times' and a list of Off-Off Broadway Theatres. Jane Moss, executive director." ed.

American Council for the Arts 212-354-6655
570 Seventh Ave. NYC 10018
"Addresses significant issues in the arts through its publication program, information and clearing house services, and the promotion of advocacy on behalf of all the arts." ed.

American Craft Council 212-696-0710
401 Park Ave. South, NYC 10016
"National not-for-profit organization devoted exclusively to the support and encouragement of crafts through a variety of educational programs that stimulate public interest in modern handcrafted objects of high quality design and workmanship. Resources include a museum, reference library, slides, films, and publications for sale." ed.

Association of Theatrical Artists and Craftspeople (office) 718-596-0501
1742 Second Ave. #102 NYC 10128 (job referral service) 212-586-1925
"A not-for-profit professional trade association for craftspeople working in the production fields of entertainment, performance, and presentational media industries. ATAC edits THE NEW YORK THEATRICAL SOURCEBOOK, publishes a quarterly newsletter, sponsors craft related seminars and workshops, provides group health insurance for members and provides health and safety equipment for members at cost. ATAC's job referral service provides potential employers with a valuable resource of unique and talented craftspeople." ed.

Business Committee for the Arts Inc. 212-664-0600
1775 Broadway NYC 10019
"National not-for-profit organization of business leaders committed to supporting the arts." ed.

Center for Arts Information 212-677-7548
625 Broadway NYC 10012
"Cross disciplinary clearinghouse for information and services in arts management on subjects concerning: fundraising, public relations, group health insurance, arts funding. A number of publications available. Research center for grants, loans, fellowships, money for artists." ed.

Central Opera Service 212-799-3467
c/o Metropolitan Opera, Lincoln Center NYC 10023 212-957-9871
"Maintains a library of books and periodicals, and the most comprehensive operatic archives in the United States. COS draws on this unique resource to supply information to its members. Research areas include: repertory, performances, musical materials, translations, scenery, costumes, props (rental, sale or exchange opportunities), company statistics, annual opera statistics USA." ed.

Cultural Assistance Center 212-947-6340
330 West 42nd St. Rm. 1701 NYC 10036
"Publishes 'Space Search', a guide to performing, rehearsal, exhibition and audio visual spaces in the five boroughs." ed.

Cultural Council Foundation 212-473-5660
625 Broadway NYC 10012
"Fiscal management for non-profit arts groups and city agencies. Ian Kramer, director." ed.

Dance Notation Bureau 212-807-7899
33 West 21st St. 3rd Fl. NYC 10010
"A non-profit service organization for dance. Referral of certified dance notators, notation teachers and dance reconstructors. Library, school, bookstore and dance studio." ed.

Dance Theatre Workshop 212-691-6500
219 West 19th St. NYC 10011
"Publishes the 'Poor Dancer's Almanac', a survival manual for choreographers, dancers and management personnel." ed.

Film Video Arts 212-673-9361
819 Broadway 2nd Fl. NYC 10011
"Formerly 'Young Filmmakers'. Rental to non-profit groups or artists at very reasonable rates." ed.

Financial Management Center 212-575-1816
36 West 44th St. Rm. 1208 NYC 10036 212-575-1828
"Provides ongoing accounting services to not-for-profit organizations and small businesses at a reduced fee." ed.

Foundation Center 212-620-4230
79 Fifth Ave. 8th Fl. NYC 10003
"Clearinghouse for private funding information for non-profit groups and individuals. Reference library available." ed.

Foundation for the Extension & Development of the American Professional Theatre (FEDAPT) 212-869-9690
165 West 46th St. NYC 10036
"Service and education organization for developing theatres and producers. Several excellent publications on arts management and seminars." ed.

Institute of Professional Puppetry & Arts 203-443-5378
Eugene O'Neill Theatre Center
305 Great Neck Road, Waterford, CT 06385
"Programs for students, professionals and the general public." ed.

International Alliance of Theatrical Stage Employees (IATSE) 212-730-1770
1515 Broadway NYC 10036
"National office for union representing stagehands and motion picture operators." ed.

IATSE Local 1 212-489-7710
1775 Broadway NYC 10019
"Union representing stagehands and motion picture operators. Local 1's jurisdiction is Manhattan." ed.

IATSE Local 52 212-399-0980
326 West 48th St. NYC 10036
"Film local for New York City." ed.

IATSE Local 798 212-757-9120
1790 Broadway NYC 10019
"Union representing hair and make-up artists for TV and film." ed.

League of American Theatres and Producers 212-764-1122
226 West 47th St. NYC 10036
"Formerly the League of New York Theatres and Producers; an association of Broadway and regional promoters, producers and theatre owners. Research and statistics on the professional theatre and a data bank of technical specs on road houses." ed.

League of Off Broadway Producers and Theatre Owners 212-869-8282
1540 Broadway Rm. 711 NYC 10036
"The association for Off Broadway producers and theatre owners."

National Association of Broadcasting Employees & Technicians (NABET) Local 15 212-265-3500
1776 Broadway #1900 NYC 10019
"Union servicing the film and video industries with production crews."

National Association of Display Industries (NADI) 212-982-6571
120 East 23rd St. 3rd Fl. NYC 10010
"A trade association comprised of manufacturers of visual merchandising materials: store fixtures, mannequins, and other decorative materials. N.A.D.I. sponsors two major trade shows in NYC each year, in June and December. Admission to the showrooms is free; call for exact dates and registration information." ed.

New York City Dept. of Cultural Affairs 212-974-1150
2 Columbus Circle NYC 10019
"Support of cultural institutions and activities through a variety of programs: materials for the arts, an arts apprenticeship program, a city gallery for group art shows, and a public works project providing personnel assistance for cultural institutions." ed.

Puppeteers of America Inc. 213-797-5748
5 Cricklewood Path, Pasadena, CA 91107
"National non-profit corporation for professionals and amateurs. Sponsors festivals, workshops and seminars. Maintains publications, advisory and educational services and an endowment fund. Their audio-visual library is a resource center with archives of recorded history; selections available for borrowing. Contact Gayle Schulter."

Puppetry Guild of Greater New York 212-929-1568
PO Box 244 NYC 10116
"Independent non-profit corporation chartered by Puppeteers of America. Serves as a public awareness and support organization for amateurs, professionals and educators in the New York area. Contact Rod Young." ed.

Stage Managers' Association 212-691-5633
PO Box 539, Old Chelsea Station, NYC 10113
"An association for professional union and non-union stage managers. Information and skill seminars given. Newsletter published with list of job openings. Projects include 'Operation Observation', in which stage managers observe their peers working backstage." ed.

Studio and Forum of Stage Design Inc. 212-924-5035
727 Washington St. NYC 10014
"A professional program in theatre design taught by professionals, including: scene painting, costuming, lighting, sound, crafts, drawing, drafting and more. Lester Polakov, founder, teaches the best scene painting courses in the country." ed.

Technical Assistance Project of the 212-586-1925
American Dance Festival (TAP)
1860 Broadway Rm. 1110 NYC 10023
"Provides job referrals for production personnel and craftspeople, consultation services, information resources including technical specifications on over 500 theatres around the world, and "The Dance Floor Anthology". Call for free schedules and further information." ed.

Theatre Development Fund 212-221-0885
1501 Broadway NYC 10036
"An audience developement organization supporting theatre, music and dance. Administers the Costume Collection, TKTS booths, 'Theatre Access Project' for disabled individuals. Discount tickets available by mail for qualifying individuals and groups (send stamped, self-addressed envelope for information and application. Their 'National Service Program' is an audience developement consultation service."

Theatre Communications Group (TCG) 212-697-5230
355 Lexington Ave. NYC 10017
"National organization for not-for-profit professional theatres. Provides nearly 30 centralized programs and services for theatre institutions and individuals. Publishes 'American Theatre' Magazine and list of member theatres." ed.

Theatrical Wardrobe Attendants Union Local 764 212-221-1717
1501 Broadway NYC 10036
"Freda Briant, business agent." ed.

United Scenic Artists (USA) Local 829 212-736-4498
575 Eighth Ave. 3rd Fl. NYC 10018
"Union representing scenic artists, set, costume and lighting designers, craftspeople, mural artists, diorama, model and display makers." ed.

United States Institute of Theatre Technology (USITT) 212-563-5551
330 West 42nd St. NYC 10036
"Provides an active forum for the development and exchange of practical and theoretical information through its quarterly journal, regular newsletters, annual national conference, and frequent regional meetings." ed.

Volunteer Lawyers for the Arts 212-575-1150
1560 Broadway #711 NYC 10036
"Provides free legal assistance and information to individual artists and not-for-profit arts organizations with arts related legal problems." ed.

HEALTH & SAFETY SERVICES

Center for Occupational Hazards 212-227-6220
5 Beekman St. (Park Row) NYC 10038
"Information, research and resources on art hazards. Speak to Monona Rossol or Dr. Michael McCann. Very helpful." ed.

Chemical Waste Disposal Co. 718-274-3339
42-14 19th Ave. (42nd) Astoria, NY 11105
Hours: 8-5 Mon-Fri
"Chemical waste disposal: see Morris Levy." ed.

Dept. H.E.W., Region 2 212-264-2485
26 Federal Plaza (Duane-Reade) NYC 10007
"Very helpful with NIOSH information. Speak to Dr. Messite." ed.

NYC Health Dept./Environmental Health 212-246-5131
26 Federal Plaza (Duane-Reade) NYC 10007
Hours: 9-4:30 Mon-Fri
"Information on dumping of waste chemicals: speak to Paul Ingrisano." ed.

Poison Control Center of NYC 212-764-7667
455 First Ave. (26-27th) NYC 10016 212-340-4494
"Very helpful with poison control information." ed.

Radiac Research 718-963-2233
261 Kent (Grant) Bklyn 11211
Hours: 7:30-5 Mon-Fri
"Waste chemical disposal pick-up." ed.

US Dept. of Labor 212-264-9840
90 Church St. Rm. 1407 (across from WTC) NYC 10007
"OSHA information and regulations." ed.

Women's Occupational Health Resource Center 212-781-5719
60 Haven Ave. Rm. B-106, NYC 10032
"Information. Will look for women's sizes in occupational clothing."

PERSONAL PROTECTIVE EQUIPMENT

Direct Safety Co. 800-528-7405
7815 S. 46th St., PO Box 8018, Phoenix, AZ 85040
"Bulk or individual safety gear. Rubber gloves, barrier skin creams, face masks and filters. Catalog available." ed.

Eastern Safety Equipment Co. Inc. 718-894-7900
5920 56th Ave. (59-60th) Maspeth, NY 11378
"NIOSH approved respirators for organic vapors, paint spray and dust."

Fibre-Metal Products 215-459-5300
Baltimore Pike, Concordville, PA 19331
"Safety equipment, hard hats." ed.

Harris Hardware 212-243-0468
17 West 18th St. (5-6th) NYC 10011
Hours: 8-5 Mon-Fri/ 8-2:30 Sat
"NIOSH approved respirators for organic vapors, paint spray and dust."

Mine Safety Appliances Co. 412-273-5000
600 Penn Center Blvd., Pittsburg, PA 15235
"NIOSH approved respirators." ed.

Norton Safety Products 401-943-4400
2000 Plainfield Pike, Cranston, RI 02920
"NIOSH approved respirators, sizes for men and women." ed.

O. K. Uniform Co. Inc. 212-966-1984
512 Broadway (Spring-Broome) NYC 10012 212-966-4733
Hours: 9:15-5:30 Mon-Thurs/ 9:30-4 Fri/ 11-4 Sun
"Disposable paper suits and all types of work clothes." ed.

REJOICE LTD./GARY ZELLER, JOYCE SPECTOR 212-869-8636
40 West 39 St. (5-6th) NYC 10018
Hours: By appt. or leave message
Derma-Guard: the water based liquid invisible glove. (See display ad page 333.)
"Special effects consultation and services." ed.

Sara Glove Co. 203-574-4090
16 Cherry Ave., PO Box 4069, Waterbury, CT 60704
Hours: 9-5 Mon-Fri
"Many types and sizes of latex and neoprene gloves." ed.

Scott Aviation (Div. of ATO Inc.) 716-683-5100
25 Erie St., Lancaster, NY 14086
"NIOSH approved respirators." ed.

Sears Roebuck & Co. (catalog sales) 212-445-9050
137-61 Northern Blvd., Flushing, NY 11354 212-445-5500

Sears Roebuck (catalog Sales) 212-933-1200
400 E. Fordham Rd. Bronx 10458 212-295-3200

Sears Roebuck (catalog Sales) 212-291-6666
169-21 Hillside Ave., Jamaica, NY 11432 212-739-5225

Sears Roebuck (catalog Sales) 212-469-8888
2307 Beverly Rd. Bklyn 11226 212-469-8000
"NIOSH and MESA approved respirators for organic vapors." ed.

3M Company 612-733-1110
3M Center, St. Paul, MN 55144 (product info) 612-733-5454
Hours: 7:45-4:30 Mon-Fri
"NIOSH approved respirators. Best line of paper masks available. Catalog on request." ed.

Willson Safety Prod/Div WGM Safety 215-376-6161
PO Box 622, Reading, PA 19603
Hours: 8-5 Mon-Fri
"NIOSH approved respirators." ed.

BROADWAY THEATRES

Ambassador Theatre (backstage) 212-245-9570
219 West 49th St. (B'way-8th) NYC 10019 (b.o.) 212-239-6200

Brooks Atkinson Theatre (backstage) 212-974-9424
256 West 47th St. (B'way-8th) NYC 10036 (b.o.) 212-245-3430

Ethel Barrymore Theatre (backstage) 212-974-9534
243 West 47th St. (B'way-8th) NYC 10036 (b.o.) 212-239-6200

Vivian Beaumont Theatre (backstage) 212-874-9257
150 West 65th St. (Lincoln Center) NYC 10023 (b.o.) 212-787-6868

Martin Beck Theatre (backstage) 212-245-9770
302 West 45th St. (8-9th) NYC 10036 (b.o.) 212-246-6363

Belasco Theatre (backstage) 212-730-9344
111 West 44th St. (6-7th) NYC 10036 (b.o.) 212-239-6200

Biltmore Theatre (backstage) 212-974-9350
261 West 47th St. (B'way-8th) NYC 10036 (b.o.) 212-582-5340

Booth Theatre (b.o.) 212-239-6200
222 West 45th St. (B'way-8th) NYC 10036

Broadhurst Theatre (backstage) 212-730-9035
235 West 44th St. (B'way-8th) NYC 10036 (b.o.) 212-239-6200

Broadway Theatre (backstage) 212-664-9587
1681 Broadway (53rd) NYC 10019 (b.o.) 212-239-6200

Circle In The Square Theatre (backstage) 212-997-9513
1633 Broadway (50th) NYC 10019 (b.o.) 212-581-0720

City Center (backstage) 212-974-9833
131 West 55th St. (6-7th) NYC 10019 (b.o.) 212-246-8989

Cort Theatre (backstage) 212-997-9776
138 West 48th St. (6-7th) NYC 10036 (b.o.) 212-239-6200

Edison Theatre (backstage) 212-997-9473
240 West 47th St. (B'way-8th) NYC 10036 (b.o.) 212-757-7164

46th Street Theatre (backstage) 212-245-9455
226 West 46th St. (B'way-8th) NYC 10036 (b.o.) 212-221-1211

Gershwin Theatre (Uris) (backstage) 212-664-8473
1633 Broadway (51st) NYC 10019 (b.o.) 212-586-6510

John Golden Theatre (backstage) 212-764-0199
252 West 45th St. (B'way-8th) NYC 10036 (b.o.) 212-239-6200

Mark Hellinger Theatre (backstage) 212-974-9506
237 West 51st St. (B'way-8th) NYC 10019 (b.o.) 212-757-7064

Imperial Theatre (backstage) 212-245-9374
249 West 45th St. (B'way-8th) NYC 10036 (b.o.) 212-239-6200

Helen Hayes Theatre (backstage) 212-730-9197
240 West 44th St. (B'way-8th) NYC 10036 (b.o.) 212-944-9450

Latin Quarter Theatre (backstage) 212-586-3903
Broadway at 48th St. (B'way-7th) NYC 10036 (b.o.) 212-977-7222

Longacre Theatre (backstage) 212-974-9462
220 West 48th St. (B'way-8th) NYC 10036 (b.o.) 212-239-6200

Lunt/Fontanne Theatre (backstage) 212-997-8816
205 West 46th St. (B'way-8th) NYC 10036 (b.o.) 212-575-9200

Lyceum Theatre (backstage) 212-997-9472
149 West 45th St. (B'way-6th) NYC 10036 (b.o.) 212-239-6200

Majestic Theatre (backstage) 212-764-1750
247 West 44th St. (B'way-8th) NYC 10036 (b.o.) 212-239-6200

Minskoff Theatre (backstage) 212-840-9797
200 West 45th St. (B'way-8th) NYC 10036 (b.o.) 212-869-0550

Music Box Theatre (backstage) 212-245-9850
239 West 45th St. (B'way-8th) NYC 10036 (b.o.) 212-239-6200

Nederlander Theatre (backstage) 212-221-9770
208 West 41st St. (B'way-8th) NYC 10036 (b.o.) 212-921-8000

New Apollo Theatre (backstage) 212-997-9059
234 West 43rd St. (B'way-8th) NYC 10036 (b.o.) 212-921-8558

New York State Theatre (backstage) 212-877-4700
62nd & Columbus Ave. (Lincoln Center) NYC 10023 (b.o.) 212-870-5570

Mitzi E. Newhouse 212-787-6868
150 West 65th St. (Lincoln Center) NYC 10023

Eugene O'Neill (backstage) 212-245-9442
230 West 49th St. (B'way-8th) NYC 10019 (b.o.) 212-246-0220

Palace Theatre (backstage) 212-245-9751
1564 Broadway (46-47th) NYC 10036 (b.o.) 212-757-2626

Plymouth Theatre (backstage) 212-391-8878
236 West 45th St. (B'way-8th) NYC 10036 (b.o.) 212-239-6200

Radio City Music Hall (backstage) 212-246-4600
1260 Sixth Ave. (50th) NYC 10019 (b.o.) 212-246-4600

Ritz Theatre (backstage) 212-664-9154
225 West 48th St. (B'way-8th) NYC 10036 (b.o.) 212-582-4022

Royale Theatre (backstage) 212-391-8879
242 West 45th St. (B'way-8th) NYC 10036 (b.o.) 212-239-6200

St. James Theatre (backstage) 212-730-9506
246 West 44th St. (B'way-8th) NYC 10036 (b.o.) 212-398-0280

Shubert Theatre (backstage) 212-764-0184
225 West 44th St. (B'way-8th) NYC 10036 (b.o.) 212-239-6200

Neil Simon Theatre (Alvin) (backstage) 212-974-9445
250 West 52nd St. (B'way-8th) NYC 10019 (b.o.) 212-757-8646

Virginia Theatre (backstage) 212-974-9853
245 West 52nd St. (B'way-8th) NYC 10019 (b.o.) 212-977-9370

Winter Garden Theatre (backstage) 212-664-9608
1634 Broadway (50-51st) NYC 10019 (b.o.) 212-239-6200

OFF BROADWAY THEATRES

*Note: most Off Broadway theatres do not have permanent backstage phones. Check with the theatre, at the number listed, for a current backstage phone, if there is one.

Actors Playhouse 100 Seventh Ave. S. (Bleecker-Grove) NYC 10014	(b.o) 212-691-6226 (admin. off.) 212-741-1215
American Place Theatre 111 West 46th St. (6-7th) NYC 10036	(b.o.) 212-247-0393 (admin. off.) 212-246-3730
Judith Anderson Theatre 442 West 42nd St. (9-10th) NYC 10036	212-279-4200
Astor Place Theatre 434 Lafayette (Astor Pl.-W. 4th) NYC 10003	212-254-4370
Beacon Theatre 2124 Broadway (74th) NYC 10023	(backstage) 212-874-9323 (b.o.) 212-874-1717 (admin. off.) 212-874-1768
Samuel Beckett Theatre 412 West 42nd St. (9-10th) NYC 10036	(b.o.) 212-594-2826
Susan Bloch Theatre (former Roundabout) 206 West 26th (8th) NYC 10011	(bookings) 212-420-1360
Cherry Lane Theatre 38 Commerce (Bedford-Barrow) NYC 10014	212-989-2020
Circle-In-The-Square, Downtown 159 Bleecker (Thompson-Sullivan) NYC 10014	(b.o.) 212-254-6330 (reh'l studio) 212-473-9784
Circle Repertory Company 99 Seventh Ave. S. (W. 4th) NYC 10014	(backstage) 212-924-9358 212-924-7100
Harold Clurman Theatre 412 West 42nd St. (9-10th) NYC 10036	(b.o.) 212-594-2370 (admin. off.) 212-594-2828
Colonnades Theatre 428 Lafayette (Astor Pl.- W. 4th) NYC 10003	212-673-2222
Entermedia Theatre 189 Second Ave. (12th) NYC 10003	(bookings) 212-777-6230
Equity Library Theatre 310 Riverside Dr. (at 103rd) NYC 10025	(b.o.) 212-663-2028 (prod. off.) 212-663-2880

Douglas Fairbanks Theatre 432 West 42nd St. (9-10th) NYC 10036	212-239-4321
Heckscher Theater 1230 Fifth Ave. (104th) NYC 10025	212-534-2804
Hudson Guild Theatre 441 West 26th St. (9-10th) NYC 10001	(backstage) 212-760-9816 (b.o.) 212-760-9810 (admin. off.) 212-760-9836
Lambs Theatre 130 West 44th St. (B'way-6th) NYC 10036	(b.o.) 212-997-1780 (admin. off.) 212-221-1031 (bookings) 212-575-0300
Jack Lawrence Theatre 359 West 48th St. (8-9th) NYC 10036	(backstage) 212-245-9202 (b.o.) 212-307-5452 (prod. off.) 212-307-5547 (bookings) 212-308-5933
Lion Theatre 422 West 42nd St. (9-10th) NYC 10036	212-736-7930
Lucille Lortel Theatre 121 Christopher St. (Bleecker-Hudson) NYC 10014	212-924-8782
Manhattan Theatre Club 321 East 73rd St. (1-2nd) NYC 10021 (moving- check for new address and phone)	(b.o.) 212-472-0600 (admin. off.) 212-288-2500
Minetta Lane Theatre 18 Minetta Lane (6th-MacDougal) NYC 10012	212-420-8000
Mirror Theatre St. Peters Church, 619 Lexington (53-54th) NYC 10022	212-223-6440
New York Shakespeare Festival/ Public Theatre 425 Lafayette St. (Astor Pl.-W.4th) NYC 10003 Anspacher Theatre, pay phone Newman Theatre, pay phone Main Green Room Delacorte Theatre (81st-Central Park)	(b.o.) 212-598-7150 (admin. off.) 212-598-7100 212-473-9499 212-674-9695 212-475-9156 212-475-9553 212-535-5630
Orpheum Theatre 126 Second Ave. (7-8th) NYC 10003	(b.o.) 212-477-2477 (admin. off.) 212-460-0990
Players Theatre 115 MacDougal St. (W. 3rd) NYC 10011	(backstage) 212-674-9281 (b.o.) 212-254-5076 (admin. off.) 212-254-8138 (prod. off.) 212-598-4337

Playhouse 91 (b.o.) 212-831-2000
316 East 91st St. (1-2nd) NYC 10128 (admin. off.) 212-831-2001

Playwrights Horizons (b.o.) 212-279-4200
416 West 42nd St. (9-10th) NYC 10036 (admin. off.) 212-564-1235

Promenade Theatre (b.o.) 212-580-1313
2162 Broadway (76th) NYC 10024 (admin. off.) 212-580-3777

Provincetown Playhouse (b.o.) 212-777-2571
133 MacDougal St. (6th-MacDougal) NYC 10011 (admin. off.) 212-777-1827

Ridiculous Theatrical Co. 212-691-2271
1 Sheridan Square (Christopher-7th Ave. S.) NYC 10014

Roundabout Stage One (b.o.) 212-420-1883
100 East 17th St. (Park Ave. S.) NYC 10003 (admin. off.) 212-420-1360

St. Clement's (b.o.) 212-265-4375
423 West 46th St. (9-10th) NYC 10036 (church off.) 212-246-7277

Second Stage 212-787-8302
2162 Broadway (76-77th) NYC 10024

South Street Theatre (b.o.) 212-279-4200
424 West 42nd St. (9-10th) NYC 10036 (admin. off.) 212-564-0660

The Space at City Center 212-246-8989
133 West 55th St. (6-7th) NYC 10019

Sullivan Street Playhouse 212-674-3838
181 Sullivan St. (Bleecker-W. Houston) NYC 10012

Theatre Four/Negro Ensemble Co. (b.o.) 212-246-8545
424 West 55th St. (9-10th) NYC 10019
(admin. off.) 165 West 46th St. (6-7th) NYC 10036 212-575-5860

Vandam Theatre 212-242-2519
15 Vandam St. (6-7th) NYC 10013

Village Gate 212-475-5120
160 Bleecker St. (Thompson-Sullivan) NYC 10012

Westside Arts Theatre (b.o.) 212-541-8394
407 West 43rd St. (9-10th) NYC 10036 (admin. off.) 212-246-6351

Audrey Wood Theatre (b.o.) 212-307-5452
359 West 48th St. (8-9th) NYC 10036 (prod. off.) 212-307-5547
(bookings) 212-308-5933

OFF-OFF BROADWAY THEATRES

Actors Factory Theatre — 212-594-1494
149 West 29th St. (6-7th) NYC 10001

Actor's Outlet — 212-807-1590
120 West 28th St. (6-7th) NYC 10001

Richard Allen Center Theater — 212-489-1940
36 West 62nd St. (B'way-C.P.W.) NYC 10023

AMAS Repertory Theatre — 212-369-8000
1 East 104th St. 3rd Fl. (5th) NYC 10029

American Theatre of Actors — 212-581-3044
314 West 54th St. (8-9th) NYC 10019

The Annex — 212-246-1050
552 West 53rd St. (10-11th) NYC 10019

Apple Corps Theatre — 212-929-2955
336 West 20th St. (8-9th) NYC 10011

The Ark Theatre — 212-431-6285
131 Spring St. (Wooster-Greene) NYC 10012

B. C. Theatre — 212-254-4698
337 East 8th St. (1-2nd) NYC 10011

Beckmann Theatre — 212-581-3044
314 West 54th St. (8-9th) NYC 10019

Bowery Lane Theatre/Jean Cocteau Rep. — 212-677-0060
330 Bowery (2-3rd) NYC 10012

City Stage Co. (CSC Rep.) — 212-677-4210
136 East 13th St. (3-4th) NYC 10003

Ensemble Studio Theatre — (b.o.) 212-247-3405
549 West 52nd St. (10-11th) NYC 10019 — (admin. off.) 212-247-4982

Haft Theatre (Fashion Inst. Tech)
227 West 27th St. (7-8th) NYC 10001

Hartley House Theatre — 212-787-1073
413 West 46th St. (9-10th) NYC 10036

Henry Street Settlement — 212-598-0400
466 Grand St. (Pitt-Willet) NYC 10002

The Nat Horne Theatre 212-736-7185
440 West 42nd St. (9-10th) NYC 10036

INTAR 212-695-6134
420 West 42nd St. (9-10th) NYC 10036

Interart Theatre 212-246-1050
549 West 52nd St. (10-11th) NYC 10019

Just Above Midtown Theater 212-228-3125
503 Broadway (Broome-Grand) NYC 10012

Koch Auditorium 212-679-2201
245 Lexington Ave. (34-35th) NYC 10016

La Mama, E.T.C. 212-475-7710
74A East 4th St. (2-3rd) NYC 10003

Marquee Theatre (bookings) 212-777-6230
189 Second Ave. (12th) NYC 10003

Meat & Potatoes Theatre 212-564-3293
306 West 38th St. 4th Fl. (8-9th) NYC 10018

Neighborhood Group Theatre 212-279-4200
420 West 42nd St. (9-10th) NYC 10036

New Dramatists 212-757-6960
242 West 44th St. (B'way-8th) NYC 10036

New Federal Theater 212-598-0400
466 Grand St. (Pitt-Willet) NYC 10002

New Theatre 212-673-0691
62 East 4th St. NYC 10012

New Vic Theatre 718-793-5563
219 Second Ave. (13-14th) NYC 10003

No Smoking Playhouse 212-582-7862
354 West 45th St. (8-9th) NYC 10036

Ohio Theatre 212-279-4200
64 Wooster St. (Greene) NYC 10012 212-868-3592

Our Studios Theatre 212-695-5342
147 West 24th St. (6-7th) NYC 10011

The Performing Garage (b.o.) 212-966-3651
33 Wooster (Grand-Broome) NYC 10013 (admin. off.) 212-966-9796

Perry Street Theatre (b.o.) 212-255-9186
31 Perry St. (Waverly-W. 4th) NYC 10014 (admin. off.) 212-255-7190

Puerto Rican Traveling Theatre 212-354-1293
276 West 43rd St. (B'way-8th) NYC 10036

Quaigh Theatre 212-221-9088
108 West 43rd St. (B'way-6th) NYC 10036

Riverside Shakespeare Co. 212-877-6810
165 West 86th St. (Columbus-Amsterdam) NYC 10024

Riverwest Theatre 212-243-0259
155 Bank St. (Washington) NYC 10014

Royal Court Rep 212-977-2582
301 West 55th St. (8-9th) NYC 10019

Second Storey Theatre (bookings) 212-777-6230
189 Second Ave. (12th) NYC 10003

Shelter West Co. 212-673-6341
217 Second Ave. (13th) NYC 10003

Soho Repertory Theatre 212-925-2588
80 Varick St. (Grand-Watts) NYC 10013

South Street Theatre 212-279-4200
406 West 42nd St. (9-10th) NYC 10036

Theatre Guinevere 212-279-4200
15 West 28th St. (B'way-6th) NYC 10001

Theatre for the New City 212-254-1109
162 Second Ave. (10-11th) NYC 10003

Theatre Off Park 212-679-5684
28 East 35th St. (Park-Madison) NYC 10016

Theatre of Magic 212-663-5380
771 West End Ave. (97th) NYC 10025

Theatre of the Open Eye (b.o.) 212-534-6909
316 East 88th St. (1-2nd) NYC 10128 (adm. off.) 212-534-6363

Theatre 22 212-243-2805
54 West 22nd St. (5-6th) NYC 10010

Trinity Theatre 212-496-8923
164 West 100th St. (Columbus-Amsterdam) NYC 10025

Truck & Warehouse Theatre — 212-254-5060
79 East 4th St. (Bowery-2nd) NYC 10003

Vortex Theatre — 212-206-1764
164 Eleventh Ave. (23rd) NYC 10011

Westbeth Theatre Center — 212-691-2272
151 Bank St. (Washington) NYC 10014

WPA Theatre — 212-691-2274
138 Fifth Ave. (20-21st) NYC 10011 — 212-206-0523

Writers' Theatre — 212-777-7005
133 Second Ave. (St. Mark's-9th) NYC 10003

DANCE, MUSIC & OPERA HOUSES

Alice Tully Hall — (b.o.) 212-362-1911
1941 Broadway (Lincoln Center) NYC 10023 — (admin. off.) 212-362-1900

Amato Opera — 212-228-8200
319 Bowery NYC 10003

Avery Fisher Hall — (b.o.) 212-874-2424
Broadway at 65th (Lincoln Center) NYC 10023 — (admin. off.) 212-580-8700

Brooklyn Academy of Music, Opera House — 718-636-4128
300 Layfayette Ave Bklyn 11238

Carnegie Hall — (backstage) 212-974-9841
161 West 56th St. (6-7th) NYC 10019 — (b.o.) 212-247-7800
(admin. off.) 212-903-9600

Dance Theatre Workshop — 212-691-6500
219 West 19th St. (7-8th) NYC 10011

The Golden Fleece — 212-691-6105
204 West 20th St. (7-8th) NYC 10011

The Joyce Theatre — (b.o.) 212-242-0800
175 Eighth Ave. (19th) NYC 10011 — (admin. off.) 212-691-9740

The Juilliard School — 212-799-5000
Broadway at 66th (Lincoln Center) NYC 10023

The Kitchen — 212-255-5793
59 Wooster St. NYC 10012

The Marymount Manhattan Theatre — 212-737-9611
221 East 71st St. (2-3rd) NYC 10021

The Metropolitan Opera — (b.o.) 212-362-6000
Broadway at 65th St. (Lincoln Center) NYC 10023 — (admin. off.) 212-799-3100

New York State Theatre — (b.o.) 212-870-5570
62nd & Columbus Ave. (Lincoln Center) NYC 10023 — (admin. off.) 212-877-4700

Riverside Church — 212-864-2929
120th St. at Claremont NYC 10027

St. Mark's Church in the Bowery — 212-674-8112
234 East 11th St. (2-3rd) NYC 100

Symphony Space — 212-864-1414
2537 Broadway (95th) NYC 10025

T.O.M.I. at Park Royal Theatre 212-787-3980
23 West 73rd St. (C.P.W.-Columbus) NYC 10023

Town Hall 212-840-2824
123 West 43rd St. (B'way-6th) NYC 10036

Vineyard Theatre 212-696-4103
309 East 26th St. (8-9th) NYC 10010

SOUND STAGES

Best Little Stage In Town — 212-924-7467
8 West 19th St. (5th) NYC 10011

Boken Inc. — 212-581-5507
513 West 54th St. (10-11th) NYC 10019

Boken II — 212-924-0438
111 Leroy St. (Greenwich St.-Hudson) NYC 10014

Camera Mart
460 West 54th St. (9-10th) NYC 10019 — 212-757-6977
Stage 1 West — 212-757-3715,6
Stage 2 West — 212-757-3525,6
Stage 54 West-429 West 54th St. (9-10th) NYC 10019 — 212-757-0407,8

Cine Studio — 212-581-1916
241 West 54th St. (B'way) NYC 10019

DeFilippo Studio — 212-986-5444
215 East 37th St. (2-3rd) NYC 10016

Empire Stages of New York — 212-392-4747
50-20 25th St. L.I.C. 11101

E.U.E./Screen Gems Ltd. — 212-867-4030
222 East 44th St. (2-3rd) NYC 10017

Farkas Films — 212-679-8212
385 Third Ave. (27-28th) NYC 10016

Horvath & Assoc. — 212-741-0300
95 Charles St. (Bleecker-Hudson) NYC 10014

Kaufman-Astoria Studios — 212-692-5600
34-31 35th St., Astoria, NY 11106

The Little House, Astoria — 212-726-3231
11-44 31st St., Astoria, NY 11106

Matrix Video — 212-265-8500
727 Eleventh Ave. (53rd) NYC 10019

Mothers Sound Stage — 212-260-2050
210 East Fifth St. (2-3rd) NYC 10003
Stage A — 212-260-3060
Stage B — 212-260-4510

National Video Center 460 West 42nd St. (9-10th) NYC 10036	212-279-2000
95th Street Studio 206 East 95th St. (2-3rd) NYC 10028	212-831-1946
North River Studios Pier 62 North River (West Side Hwy-23rd St.) NYC 10011	212-807-0735
Overland Stage Co. 511 West 54th St. (10-11th) NYC 10019	212-581-4460 212-581-4469 212-736-1776
Phoenix Studios Inc. 537 West 59th St. (Amsterdam-W.E.A.) NYC 10019	(office) 212-581-7721 (stage) 212-581-7670
Reeves Teletape	
304 East 44th St. (1-2nd) NYC 10017	212-573-8888
Ed Sullivan, 53rd & Broadway NYC 10019	212-307-4881
RT3, 841 Ninth Ave. (55th) NYC 10019	212-307-4885
Silvercup Studios 42-25 21st St. L.I.C. 11101	718-784-3390
Studio 84 245 East 84th St. (2-3rd) NYC 10028	212-988-0500
Studio 39 144 East 39th St. (B'way) NYC 10016	212-685-1771 212-889-9616 212-889-0910
3-G Stage Corp.	
236 West 61st St. (Amsterdam-W.E.A.) NYC 10023	212-247-3130
Stage I	212-247-3147
Stage II	212-247-3148
Veritas 527 West 45th St. (10-11th) NYC 10036	212-581-2050

REHEARSAL STUDIOS & SPACES

*Note: Some theatres in the "THEATRES" Appendix may also be available for rehearsal and performance rentals.

Actors' Equity Association Audition Center 212-869-8548
165 West 46th St. (B'way-6th) NYC 10036
Hours: office 9:30-5:30 Mon-Fri/ audition days 8-6 Mon-Fri

Amity Arts Center 212-924-5295
22 West 15th St. (5-6th) NYC 10011
Hours: 9:30-9 Mon-Thurs/ 9:30-4 Fri/ available eves., Sat

THE BACK 40 212-807-1563
75 Ninth Ave. (15-16th) NYC 10011
Hours: 9-5 Mon-Fri or by appt.

New, extremely large (60' x 40' x 27' high) rehearsal space with no pillars. 10' x 45' projection screen for large format programming and viewing. Finished blond wood floor for dance, skit and fashion rehearsals. Large freight elevator. Plenty of electrical power. Call for quote.

Broadway Dance Center 212-582-9304
1733 Broadway 4th Fl. (55-56th) NYC 10019
Hours: 9:30-7:30 Mon-Fri/ 10-3:30 Sat/ 11-3 Sun/ & by appt.

Carroll Studios 212-868-4120
351 West 41st St. (8-9th) NYC 10036
Hours: office 8-5 Mon-Fri/ available Sat, Sun

Michael Chekhov Studio Inc. 212-736-1544
19 West 36th St. 8th Fl. (5-6th) NYC 10018
Hours: office 10-4 Mon-Fri

Dance- June Lewis & Company 212-741-3044
48 West 21st St. 7th Fl. (5-6th) NYC 10014
Hours: office 10-10 Mon-Fri/ weekend bookings available

Dance Notation Bureau (Studios) 212-807-7899
33 West 21st St. 3rd Fl. (5-6th) NYC 10010
Hours: office 9:30- 5:30 Mon-Fri/ studio 8-6 Mon-Fri

Dance Theatre Workshop 212-691-6500
219 West 19th St. (7-8th) NYC 10011
Hours: office 10-6 Mon-Fri/ available Sat

890 STUDIOS 212-475-2870
890 Broadway (19th) NYC 10003
Hours: 9:30-7 Mon-Sat

Harlequin Studios 212-819-0120
203 West 46th St. (B'way-8th) NYC 10036
Hours: 9-11 Mon-Fri/ 9-8 Sat,Sun

Nat Horne Studios 212-736-7128
440 West 42nd St. (9-10th) NYC 10036
Hours: office 9:30-9 Mon-Thurs/ 9:30-2 Fri/ avialable eves., weekend

Foundation for the Joffrey Ballet 212-265-7300
130 West 56th St. (6-7th) NYC 10019
Hours: office 9:30-5:30 Mon-Fri/ subject to availability

Lamb's Theatre 212-575-0300
130 West 44th St. (6th-B'way) NYC 10036
Hours: 9-5 Mon-Fri/ weekends available

Manhattan Center Stage 212-477-0800
704 Broadway (Waverly-4th) NYC 10003
Hours: office 9-6 Mon-Fri/ available weekends

Manhattan Theatre Club 212-288-2500
321 East 73rd St. (1-2nd) NYC 10021
Hours: 10-6 Mon-Fri (Moving, check address & availability)

Merkin Concert Hall 212-362-8060
129 West 67th St. (B'way-Amsterdam) NYC 10023
Hours: office 9-7:30 Mon-Fri/ available eves., no weekends

Minskoff Rehearsal Studios 212-575-0725
1515 Broadway 3rd Fl. (44-45th) NYC 10036
Hours: 10-6 Mon-Sat/ available eves., Sun

Musical Theatre Works Inc. 212-677-0040
133 Second Ave. (8th) NYC 10003
Hours: office 10-6 Mon-Fri/ available 10-10 every day

New York Conservatory of Dance 212-664-9144
226 West 56th St. 3rd Fl. (B'way) NYC 10019 212-581-1908
Hours: office 10-7:30 Mon-Fri/ available weekends

Our Studios 212-807-8464
147 West 24th St. (6-7th) NYC 10011
Hours: available 24 hours every day

Peridance Center 212-505-0886
33 East 18th St. 5th Fl. (B'way-Park) NYC 10003
Hours: office 9:45-9 Mon-Fri/ available eves., weekends

Primary Stages Company Inc. 212-333-7471
584-6 Ninth Ave. (42-43rd) NYC 10036
Hours: office 10-6 Mon-Fri/ available 9-10 every day

Puppet Loft 212-431-7627
180 Duane St. (Greenwich St.-Hudson) NYC 10013
Hours: By appt.

Quaigh Theatre 212-221-9088
108 West 43rd St. (Diplomat Hotel) NYC 10036
Hours: By appt.

Riverwest Theatre 212-243-0259
155 Bank St. (West-Washington) NYC 10014
Hours: office 12-11 every day

Roundabout Rehearsal Space (bookings) 212-420-1360
71 Eighth Ave. 3rd Fl. (13-14th) NYC 10014 (studio) 212-929-9703
Hours: office 10-7 Mon-Fri/ available eves., weekends

Second Stage Theatre 212-787-8302
2162 Broadway (76th) NYC 10024
Hours: office 10-6 Mon-Fri/ subject to availability

Steps Dance Studio 212-874-2410
2121 Broadway (74th) NYC 10023
Hours: office 10:30-6 Mon-Fri/ available weekends

Theatre 22 212-243-2805
54 West 22nd St. (5-6th) NYC 10010
Hours: By appt.

Theatre Opera Music Institute Inc. (TOMI) 212-787-3980
23 West 73rd St. (Central Park West-Columbus) NYC 10023
Hours: office 10-5 Mon-Sat/ available til 11 & weekends

Universal Rehearsal & Recording 212-929-3277
17 West 20th St. (5-6th) NYC 10011
Hours: 9 am - 11 pm every day

Westbeth Theatre Center 212-691-2272
151 Bank St. (Washington-West) NYC 10014
Hours: office 9-5 Mon-Fri/ available eves., weekends

INDEX

Specific items and category headings found in the Products and Services section.

- A -

- D -

- H -

- I -

- J -

- K -

- L -

- Q -

- R -

- U -

- V -

- W -

- X -

- Y -

- Z -

NOTES

NOTES

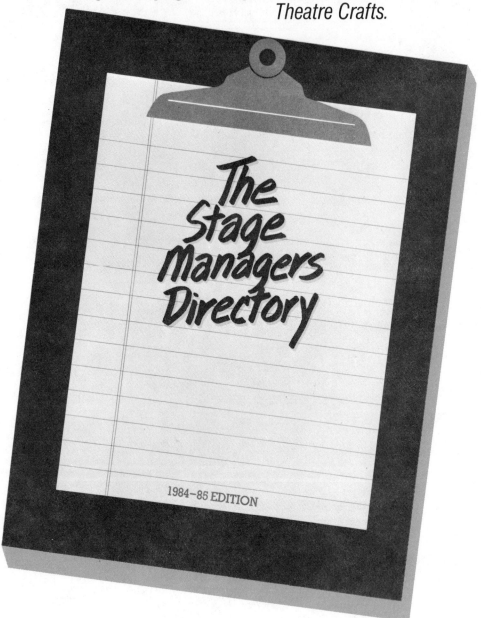

THE NEW YORK THEATRICAL SOURCEBOOK

*FREE DISCOUNTS

Send us new sources or corrections and we will send you a discount coupon good on the next edition of THE NEW YORK THEATRICAL SOURCEBOOK.

YOUR NAME

Address

City/State/Zip

Occupation/Company

NEW SOURCE

Company Name

Address (w/x-streets)

City/State/Zip

Phone

Product or Service

Why you recommend this company?

CORRECTIONS/TYPOS/COMMENTS

(Companies that have moved or gone out-of-business, ideas for new appendixes, comments on the SOURCEBOOK.)

*All sources and corrections are subject to verification by the editors.

Please fold in half and staple or seal here. We'll pay postage. Thanks.

NO POSTAGE
NECESSARY
IF MAILED
IN THE
UNITED STATES

BUSINESS REPLY MAIL
FIRST CLASS PERMIT NO. 5456 NEW YORK, NY

POSTAGE WILL BE PAID BY ADDRESSEE

Broadway Press
350 West 85th St.
New York, NY 10024-9990

Free Discount
for New Sources
(see reverse side)